CW01401826

Eros and Revolution

Studies in Critical Social Sciences

Eros and Revolution

The Critical Philosophy of Herbert Marcuse

By

Javier Sethness Castro

BRILL

LEIDEN | BOSTON

Cover illustration: "The Course of Empire: Desolation" by Thomas Cole (oil on canvas, 1836).

Library of Congress Cataloging-in-Publication Data

Names: Sethness-Castro, Javier, author.
Title: Eros and revolution : the critical philosophy of Herbert Marcuse / by
    Javier Sethness Castro.
Description: Leiden ; Boston : Brill, [2016] | Series: Studies in critical
    social sciences ; 86 | Includes bibliographical references and index.
Identifiers: LCCN 2016011372 (print) | LCCN 2016018302 (ebook) | ISBN
    9789004308695 (hardback : alk. paper) | ISBN 9789004308701 (E-book)
Subjects: LCSH: Marcuse, Herbert, 1898-1979. | Critical theory.
Classification: LCC B945.M2984 S48 2016 (print) | LCC B945.M2984 (ebook) |
    DDC 191--dc23
LC record available at https://lccn.loc.gov/2016011372

Want or need Open Access? Brill Open offers you the choice to make your research freely accessible online
in exchange for a publication charge. Review your various options on brill.com/brill-open.

Typeface for the Latin, Greek, and Cyrillic scripts: "Brill." See and download: brill.com/brill-typeface.

ISSN 1573-4234
ISBN 978-90-04-30869-5 (hardback)
ISBN 978-90-04-30870-1 (e-book)

Printed by Printforce, United Kingdom

I dedicate this book to my mother, who first introduced me to Marcuse;
to the Palestinian people;
to the 43 students from the Raúl Isidro Burgos Rural Teachers' College
of Ayotzinapa, forcibly disappeared on 26 September 2014 in Iguala,
Guerrero state, Mexico;
and to the 33 socialist and anarchist youth killed by an Islamic
State suicide bomber in Suruç, located on the Turkish border with Syria,
20 July 2015.

∴

Contents

PART 2
Reflections on Marcuse

PART 3
Conclusion

Acknowledgements

I wish to thank Glenn Parton, Alexander Reid Ross, Chuck Morse, and Paul Murufas for their assistance in reviewing parts of the manuscript—or, in Glenn's case, the entirety of it—and providing insightful comments as well as suggestions for improvement. I also wish to acknowledge Douglas Kellner for his help in finding citations and biographical data that I required. Many thanks as well to Peter Marcuse, who graciously provided me with a review copy of the sixth volume of his father's *Collected Papers*, thus greatly facilitating the completion of this project.

CHAPTER 1

Introduction: Marcuse, the Utopian

The radical philosopher Herbert H. Marcuse (1898–1979) is perhaps best-known for the influence and guidance he provided to various oppositional and anti-systemic political movements that emerged toward the end of the course of his life, particularly as led by the youth of the world in the mid- to late 1960s and the 1970s. It was due to this *mutual affinity* between Marcuse and the militant youth that the mature thinker was hailed in the main as the "father of the New Left," despite Marcuse's distaste for such a patriarchal title. In a 1969 interview, the public intellectual clearly expresses his position on the epithet he had been donned: "[T]here is one thing the Left does not need, and that's another father image, another daddy. And I certainly don't want to be one." As the association Marcuse makes here to the father-figure suggests, his was a libertarian or "feminist socialism" that resembles anarchism, as the name of this latter formulation implies (Marcuse 2004: 122, 165–172).

In parallel to the critical social theory advanced by the various members of the Frankfurt School, or Institute for Social Research (*Institut für Zosialforschrung*), with which he was affiliated for much of the third decade of his life (1932–1942), Marcuse concerned himself principally with exposing and analyzing the various social-psychological and material obstacles which he believed lay before the coming of liberatory social change and anti-authoritarian revolution, especially in *Soviet Marxism* (1958) and *One-Dimensional Man* (1964). The critical theorist held both the Soviet Union and Western capitalism in contempt, developing in these "twin" volumes a libertarian-socialist critique of both societies. It is in this sense telling that the Hungarian Marxist György Lukács would write from behind the Iron Curtain in 1969 that Marcuse and his colleague Ernst Bloch are "objectively our allies, and, in my opinion, one cannot deny that they are authentic enemies of imperialism" (Lukács 1969).

In the period after World War II, as he became increasingly better-known, Marcuse expressed his anti-imperialist proclivities practically through public criticism of U.S. aggression against Cuba, Vietnam, and much of the rest of Southeast Asia—with these being commitments that would first see him fired from his first professorship at Brandeis University, and that would subsequently escalate to outright death-threats from the KKK and other reactionary groupings and individuals during his tenure at the University of California in San Diego (UCSD). Previously, as the Second World War intensified and Marcuse grew closer with fellow Frankfurter Franz Neumann,

Marcuse left the Institute to join Neumann and Otto Kirchheimer, who worked with the U.S. Office of Strategic Services (OSS). These three intellectuals saw this commitment as a practical anti-fascist means of undermining the cancer of Nazism that had colonized their native Germany. The trio would draw up plans for a radical de-Nazification plan after the German defeat in May 1945, though these were entirely ignored by post-war U.S. occupation authorities, and even radically contradicted in spirit and fact.[1] Though some observers would find in Marcuse's years of work at the OSS and State Department (1942–1951) reason to question or dismiss the contributions he has made to critical social theory and the prospects for anti-authoritarian societal transformation, Marcuse himself remained proud of his work at the OSS to oppose Hitlerism until life's end, as he declares in an interview on his political autobiography that was published in the 1972 volume containing his debate with Sir Karl Popper, *Revolution or Reform?* (Marcuse and Popper 1976: 59). In addition, it should be noted that Marcuse left government service before the genocidal Korean War was launched by the U.S., in anticipation of the homologous atrocities it would later unleash in Vietnam. Marcuse's practical expressions of solidarity with humanity in struggle—further manifested in his embrace of militant feminism and sexual diversity, as well as in his humanistic call for a just settlement in historical Palestine, besides his activism in terms of Cuba, Vietnam, and a world entire to be illuminated by reason and freedom—simultaneously reflect and informed the philosopher's own esteemed contributions in life to redirecting Marxism and anti-systemic thought and action into thoroughly anti-authoritarian directions.

In his introduction to an edited collection of Marcuse's works from the time the thinker spent studying with Martin Heidegger during Germany's short-lived Weimar Republic—a book duly entitled *Heideggerian Marxism*—Richard Wolin claims that Marcuse's youthful ideological attraction was not to Leninism and the Bolshevik example, but instead more to the autonomist currents represented by the thought of Rosa Luxemburg and the practice of the Spartacus League during the German Revolution (Marcuse 2005: xi–xiv.). Such libertarian affinities clearly underpin *Soviet Marxism*, as well as the early Romantic and existentialist studies Marcuse engaged in during Weimar's length of duration after the First World War, in addition to the radical political and philosophical investigations he would undertake during his time as a member of the Frankfurt School, in exile in New York from Nazi Germany. Indeed, Marcuse's

---

1 Instead of implementing radical de-Nazification policies, the U.S. reinstated many fascist criminals in Germany, and called on others to directly aid them (as in the CIA). Notoriously few Nazi leaders were either prosecuted or punished for their atrocities.

concern for the fate of autonomy in thought and action form the very basis for the philosopher's most well-known book, *One-Dimensional Man*, which provides a profound yet almost desperate denunciation of the mechanized and mobilized mirror-image of Soviet society Marcuse saw in the monopoly-capitalist USA of the early 1960s. Beyond his writings and scholarly investigations, furthermore, Marcuse's libertarianism was expressed corporeally in the philosopher-activist's political commitments, starting with his participation as a young man in the German Revolution, taking up arms to defend the Alexanderplatz against right-wing paramilitaries, and representing the Reinickerndorf district of Berlin as an elected delegate of the soldiers' councils that arose during the transient existence of the Revolution.

Nonetheless, after the German Social Democratic Party (SPD) crushed the popular rising at the close of World War I, Marcuse formally resigned his membership, having previously signed on out of disgust at the mindless brutality and absurdity of the raging conflict. Marcuse was never again to join another political party. The philosopher's break with the SPD, philosophical and practical at once, marks a turning point which differentiates his life-course from that of Lukács significantly, given that the latter in 1918 joined the Soviet-aligned German Communist Party (KPD) and would thereafter serve as an apologist for Leninism and even Stalinism. In resisting the path that led Lukács evermore to rationalize authoritarian socialism with the passage of time, Marcuse maintained his autonomy and integrity. For this reason, he is a luminous representative of the alternative position taken by the "homeless left" in the twentieth century—that is, by those who took a consistently critical view that refused to support the established reformist and bureaucratic-totalitarian currents of opposition to capitalism alike.[2] With regard to the impact the German Revolution had on Marcuse, his biographer Barry Kātz notes there to be a fundamental continuity between the critical theorist's radical politics during WWI and the presentation of the estranged artist in the dissertation he completed at the end of his post-war studies in Freiburg on *The German Artist-Novel* (1922): the artist's alienation symbolizes that of the revolutionary, frustrated by the restoration of bourgeois-military power after the great challenge which had just surged against it (Kātz 1982: 53–54). Marcuse's early autonomous political orientation can be said to be echoed as well in his later conceptualization of the *Great Refusal*, which can be defined as a standpoint of

---

2 Incidentally, this dynamic shaped the fate of the Mexican anarchist movement after the "victorious" revolution of 1910–1920, as the *ácratas* either joined the "revolutionary" State apparatus or maintained a more independent path, if they were not assassinated, imprisoned, or assassinated *in* prison (Hodges 1995: 3).

intransigent political and *even physiological* resistance to domination and reification—the basic Weberian tendency of the capital-State system to progress "against the will and the intentions of individuals" (Marcuse 1968: xix).

In terms of political philosophy, Marcuse's categories principally revolve around the concepts of Logos (reason) and Eros. As Morton Schoolman writes, for Marcuse, "philosophy *is* reason, reflection on its every principle and on every assumption of social life" (Schoolman 1980: 33; emphasis added). The theorist develops the former term perhaps most intricately in *Reason and Revolution* (1941), wherein he examines George Wilhelm Friedrich Hegel's contributions to the history of thought, particularly as regards the place of the dialectic in clearing the obstacles which lie before the possibility of the realization of reason and freedom for humanity. Marcuse sublimates these Hegelian concepts into his material and political exploration of Freud's late instinct theory in *Eros and Civilization* (1955): Eros, or the life-giving forces, as against Thanatos, or the death-compulsion. In a 1972 encyclopedic entry on the history of dialectics, Marcuse relays Aristotle's belief that dialectical thought originated with the pre-Socratic philosopher Zeno of Elea (495–430 BCE), while Freud in turn lifted the putative conflict between these two instinctual forces from Zeno's contemporary Empedocles (490–430 BCE) (Marcuse 2014: 312; Freud 1937: 245–246).

Though one may perhaps be tempted to disassociate reason from Eros in one's mind, considering the prevalence of repressive Western notions of the rational and the erotic, Marcuse did not think that Eros contradicted Logos—the exercise of mind, autonomy, and resistance. Instead, as he believed, the two can very much reinforce one other, once their practitioners overcome the indelible connection often made between the concept of reason and instrumental thinking. For Marcuse, as the title of his 1941 work makes clear, reason must not be reduced to instrumental rationality. Instead, it critically can and must open the field to the subversive and erotic reordering of hegemonic irrationality, or Thanatos. The joy, liberation, and life-affirmation both sought and advanced jointly by Logos and Eros is well-illustrated in a declaration made by Hegel, reflecting on the period of the French Revolution in *The Philosophy of History*:

> Never since the sun had stood in the firmament and the planets revolved around it had it been perceived that [humanity's] existence centers in [its] head, i.e. in Thought, inspired by which [it] builds up the world of reality. Anaxagoras had been the first to say that *nous* [mind] governs the world; but not until now had [humanity] advanced to the recognition of the principle that Thought ought to govern spiritual reality. This was

accordingly a glorious mental dawn. All thinking beings shared in the ju-
bilation of this epoch.

HEGEL 1900: 447

While Hegel's statement here may well betray exaggeration as well as Eurocen-
trism in claiming the French Revolution to mark the very *first* appearance of
this principle of reason and revolution in human history, its utopian meaning
is readily perceived—as it is in Bloch's formulation:

> And what of resistance to oppression? In the freshness of the revolu-
> tion and its goals, the Fourteenth of July always infuses a new life and a
> human face, even after and without the Bastille. *This light of 1789 persists
> everywhere.* Like the Ninth Symphony [of Beethoven], which is so close to
> the citizen, it cannot be taken back.
>
> BLOCH 1986b: 65; emphasis added

The case is similar with Marcuse, whose social theory is driven by a veritable
utopianism, in the sense of a deep hope for and commitment to revolutionary social transformation. Crucially, though, in this sense of reflecting on hope
alongside reason and revolution, Marcuse's observation from the second of his
1971 "Jerusalem Lectures" should be here borne in mind, for use of the term
utopia often serves to mislead and mystify: as he claims in this intervention,
"we can accept the term *utopian* only if we believe that the established societies are in themselves eternal" (Marcuse 2004: 157; emphasis added). The
dialectical-historical liberation that would "institute" utopia is at hand and
readily accessible, on Marcuse's account, as he develops it in *Eros and Civilization* and thereafter in "The End of Utopia" (1967)—rather than be illusory
and literally of "no place," as in the word's very definition. Alongside Hegel and
Marx, Marcuse's philosophy was highly influenced by French utopian socialism and German Romanticism, as we shall see. All these sources formed a confluence within Marcuse's mind which yielded the critical theorist's sense that
to negatively illuminate the authoritarianism and atrocities for which capital is
responsible could well turn out to improve the chances against its reign: as he
argues in "Humanism and Humanity" (1962), the "recognition and denunciation of the bad is today more than ever the precondition for overcoming the
bad" (Marcuse 2014: 110). The critical theorist's alternatives are set forth in the
1968 foreword to his collection of writings from the 1930's, *Negations:* "thought
in contradiction must become *more negative and more utopian in opposition
to the status quo*" (Marcuse 1968: xx; emphasis added). Like the twins of reason and Eros, utopia and negativity are similarly conjoined in Marcuse's works

as subversive frameworks. In the estimation of Richard Bernstein, in point of fact, this latter category of negativity is "the deepest, most persistent, and most pervasive theme" in Marcuse's *oeuvre*; for Bernstein, Marcusean negativity forms a principal current within the Critical Theory of the Frankfurt School which seeks practically to "foste[r] the destruction of a repressive, alienating and dominating social reality in order to further the struggle and realization for *genuine* freedom and happiness" (Bernstein 1988: 13–15; emphasis added).

Hence, when considering the Frankfurt School theorists, it is important to acknowledge the importance *critical negativism* had to many of them, especially Marcuse. The fruit of the Frankfurters' reflection on German Ideal-ism and materialism, as well as their lived experienced of historical trauma, this philosophical position holds any given social order that allows for excess human suffering—that is to say, as assessed in accordance with the available means of ameliorating said suffering—to be radically wrong and unaccept-able (Alford 1985: 15–16). As fellow Frankfurter Theodor W. Adorno writes in *Minima Moralia* (1951), referencing the thought of his deceased comrade Walter Benjamin, "So long as there is still a single beggar, [...] there is still myth; only with the last beggar's disappearance would myth be appeased" (Adorno 2005: 199). In the world of Marcuse and his colleagues, critique and negativ-ity come to represent basic forms of practice and protest against prevailing modes that mediate such existing realities as capital, patriarchy, white su-premacy, imperialism, and catastrophic environmental damage in "positive" ways—that is to say, by seeking to integrate the various profound negativi-ties presented and imposed by reality through normalization, when they are not outright ignored. Like his comrades from the Frankfurt School, Marcuse directed considerable critique at positivism and empiricism—these beings ontological frameworks which he considered apologist and reactionary, given quite simply that they "mutilate and abandon the concept of potentiality" in history and society, as Bernstein puts it (Bernstein 1988: 24). Marcuse would importantly wield Hegelian and Heideggerian notions of dialectical develop-ment, reason, and authenticity as liberatory alternatives to the positivism that was then hegemonic in the Western social sciences, as it still is.

Appearing as a chapter of *A Critique of Pure Tolerance* in 1965, Marcuse's essay on "Repressive Tolerance" would present a philosophical justification for insur-rection and the active suppression of fascism and militarism from below. Such a call echoes the historical practice of Gracchus Babeuf and the Conspiracy of Equals, who attempted to organize an uprising against the bourgeois Directory that had taken control of the revolutionary process in France during the Ther-midorian Reaction of 1793, as it does the praxis of the anarchist Ricardo Flores Magón and his comrades in the Mexican Liberal Party (PLM), who organized combative journalism and armed revolts to depose Porfirio Díaz in the run-up to the Mexican Revolution, as well as during its course, in addition to his follower Rubén Jaramillo, who coordinated a *campesino* insurrection through-out much of southern Mexico in 1953 against the State that had appropriated itself of the Revolution, and the Zapatista Army of National Liberation (EZLN), which rose up in arms in Chiapas on 1 January 1994 to defy the entry into law of the North American Free Trade Agreement (NAFTA), seeking to provoke a nation-wide collective insurrection (Hodges 1995: 39, 59–60, 199–200). Like these historical figures, Marcuse would, from the time of his very first public essay on Heidegger and historical materialism in 1928 until his death over half a century later, militantly advocate and agitate for social revolution.

One speculative hypothesis regarding the factors which impelled the libertarian revolutionism—the essential anarchism—of the members of the Frankfurt School is that the negations experienced by Marcuse and the other Frankfurtians in the face of the Nazi takeover of their native Germany and the attendant necessity of their flight and exile accentuated the highly critical views they already had held of social democracy, liberalism, and bourgeois society. Practically all of the Frankfurters felt these three factors to have collaborated in giving birth to outright fascism, as Marcuse argues in his bold 1928 essay on "The Struggle against Liberalism in the Totalitarian View of the State." None-theless, in accordance with Martin Jay's observation on the matter, Marcuse's anarchistic views have also been associated with his existentialist studies and writings, which predate the Nazi takeover and the subsequent exile in New York, such that his libertarianism can be considered a clear and long-standing continuity within his social theory (Jay 1971: 253–254). The critical theorist can furthermore be called a revolutionary humanist, as one can see reflected in his appreciation for the young Marx of the 1844 *Economic-Philosophical Manu-scripts*, his talk on "Humanism and Humanity" before the Berlin B'nai B'rith congress in 1962, and his intervention for the 1964 international symposium on socialist humanism, as collected in a volume edited by the former Institute social psychologist Erich Fromm. Marcuse's enduring radical political activism attests to the dialectical negation of hegemonic negation proceeding not just idealistically in the realm of the mind but also physically and materially, as an expression of one's *Dasein* ("being-in-the-world") and the human *Mitsein* ("being-together").

For these reasons, then, Alain Martineau, author of *Herbert Marcuse's Utopia* (1986), is correct to raise the rarely made comparison between Marcuse and Mikhail Bakunin. These two revolutionaries' analysis converges in their respective anarchical interpretations of Hegelian negativity—a concept Bakunin took to demand "the absolute need for humanity to promote its

future through the total destruction of the status quo"—and in their similarly
libertarian view of power and domination, which were to be outright destroyed rather than appropriated for putatively progressive ends, as on the
orthodox-Marxist, Lenino-Stalinist, and Maoist accounts (Martineau 1986: 44–
45, 103–104). In short, then, Marcuse's political position is that the system must
be overthrown—as Adorno and Benjamin would similarly advocate during
the National-Socialist period and World War II, when Benjamin tragically lost
his life following the failure of a daring flight across the Pyrenees Mountains
from Nazi-occupied France into Franco's Spain, en route to Lisbon, where he
was to board a trans-Atlantic ocean liner and be reunited with his comrade-
refugees in New York. For reasons that will be considered more closely below, it
was Marcuse who stayed truer to Benjamin's revolutionism, as compared with
Adorno, considering the deep disagreements that would develop between the
two philosophers near the time of Adorno's death in 1969 regarding the questions of U.S. imperialism, the New Left, the international student movements,
and the place of activism and praxis under conditions of late capitalism. It was
Marcuse's militant *Dasein* that led him to become a prominent public critic of
the Vietnam War, just as it drove his embrace of the revolutionary toppling of
Fulgencio Batista and the transnational mafia in Cuba as well as the traditional
landowners and *Guomindang* in China which took place after World War II.
Ironically, however, the thinker's enthusiasm for the Cuban and Chinese Revolutions may help explain the relative lack of critical regard in which Marcuse
held the Communist leadership of both countries, at least well into the 1970s—
while the question of Marcuse's take on the People's Republic of China (PRC)
arguably was informed to a degree by his second wife Inge Werner's Maoist
sympathies. Yet thanks to a handful of late interviews reproduced in the most
recent volume of Marcuse's Collected Papers, *Marxism, Revolution, and Utopia*
(2014), it becomes evident that the critical theorist brought his view of these
regimes into accord with his life-long anti-authoritarianism, as he clearly
acknowledges the repressive-technocratic nature of both the PRC and Fidel
Castro's Cuba by life's end.

   Dialectically, then, Marcuse's radical politics of the Great Refusal, in calling
for a total rejection of the death-system of capital, represents a positive manifestation of Eros and hope for Logos and historical progress. Though observers more accommodating to the system often claim—whether in good faith
or not—that Marcuse's intellectual dwelling on the assessment of the various
barriers to liberation runs the risk of overwhelming the subject and advancing
a quiescent politics of pessimism, the very opposite should be seen to be the
case. As in Benjamin's case, revolution and negativity are not contradictory for
Marcuse. Instead, the critical theorist believes that it is the myriad brutalities

and abuses performed by those in power which demands social revolution as a corrective counter-measure. In a parallel to Jean-Paul Sartre in terms of the Algerian and Vietnam Wars, Marcuse accepted and affirmed Adorno's formulation in *Negative Dialectics* of the new categorical imperative imposed by Hitler on "unfree humanity": that it reorient its thoughts and actions so that "Auschwitz will not repeat itself, so that nothing similar will happen" (Adorno 1973: 365). He cites this new categorical imperative explicitly in one of his very last public talks, this on "Ecology and the Critique of Modern Society," which was presented to a youth wilderness class in California in 1979. Marcuse here notes that the ultimate goal of radical social change is the creation of individuals who would be incapable of prosecuting genocide of any kind.

In this way, we see that the dialectic of life-negation and life-affirmation receives due consideration in Marcuse's life-work. Even if it could be said that Marcuse overall concerns himself more with negation than liberation—a claim that would not at first self-evidently be clear—the critical theorist does not seem ever to have fallen into a prolonged period of despair, however desperate and depressing are the analyses he presents at times. In a 1969 interview, Marcuse simply declares that he is "not a defeatist, ever," while in a different interview from July 1968, he claims the *rational* basis for pessimism to be lacking: likely with the recent May 1968 events in Paris in mind, Marcuse observes that "one cannot become defeatist and say there are no visible agents of change" (Marcuse 2014: 199, 180).

Idealism, Materialism, Romanticism, and Judaism

While a more detailed exploration of the various influences and directions of Marcuse's philosophical system will be left to the subsequent chapters of this volume, which examine the theorist's life-work, some initial comments on this question are in order. The philosophical tradition of German Idealism—the contribution its theorists made to social critique and revolutionary struggle—is central to Marcuse's thought, its imprint undeniable—as is the materialist Marxian legacy which emerged historically as a concrete response to the seemingly ethereal nature of Idealism. Moreover, German Romanticism, itself also a "child" of Idealism, would prove critical to Marcuse, particularly as an affirmation of pre- and anti-capitalist social alternatives. From the time of *The German Artist-Novel* (1922), Friedrich Schiller and Charles Fourier would influence Marcuse's revolutionary conception of aesthetics, together with his libertarian-emancipatory vision for social life, labor, pleasure, and leisure. As a matter of fact, at a 1968 UNESCO conference held in Paris to mark 150 years since the birth of Karl Marx, where he presented his "Re-Examination of the Concept of Revolution," Marcuse responded to the question of whether, after presenting his radical re-evaluation of Marx, he would subscribe to anarchism or nihilism, admitting that, if he "had to acknowledge a master," it would most likely *"be Fourier"* (Martineau 1986: 43). From Immanuel Kant, whose *Critique of Judgment* spurred Schiller on to write *On the Aesthetic Education of Man*, Marcuse integrates the transcendental possibilities of art—its embodied resistance to hegemonic one-dimensionality—as in the Kantian concept of beauty as the symbol of morality (Kant 2000: 248–252). This concern for the revolutionary potential of art will consistently resurface throughout Marcuse's career, from the dissertation on German *Kultur* to his final work on *The Aesthetic Dimension* (1978).

One especially Marcusean concept that clearly expresses Idealist-Romantic notions is that of the "new sensibility" which is to develop among members of the socio-political opposition in resistance to hegemonic conformity and authoritarianism. This concept is set forth in *An Essay on Liberation* (1969), though it can be anticipated in the discussion of aesthetics in *Eros and Civiliza-tion.* In fact, in the 1966 "Political Preface" to this latter volume, Marcuse defines the new sensibility as "the determinate negation of Nietzsche's superman":

> [humanity] intelligent enough and healthy enough to dispense with all heros and heroic virtues, [humanity] without the impulse to live dan-gerously, to meet the challenge; [humanity] with the good conscience to make life an end-in-itself, to live in joy a life without fear.
>
> MARCUSE 1966a: xiv

The question of the new sensibility would remain crucial to Marcuse for the remainder of his life, being an integral part of his view of the possibil-ity of transitioning beyond capital—for Marcuse mirrors Antonio Gramsci's view that cultural and instinctual changes must progress to some degree before political revolution takes place, if said upheaval is to be capable of attaining its most humane and far-reaching ends. In a late discussion on "The-ory and Politics" with Jürgen Habermas and company from 1978, Marcuse in fact questions what the value would be of social transformation, if not for the possibility of yielding a "new human being"; he says this new humanity was the very "goal of revolution" according to Marx (Marcuse et al. 1978/9: 133). Marcuse notes during his summer 1967 lectures in Berlin that this "new humanity" could be gleaned in "at least some" of the guerrilla-warfare campaigns being waged against imperialism at that time, as in the policies instituted by formerly colonized peoples within the decolonization process

(Marcuse 1970a: 82). For Marcuse, the libertarian element of revolutionism is essential, both as taken from Marx, but also beyond him; in summer 1968, in an interview conducted on the French Riviera, Marcuse brashly declares that all attempts at revolution are worthless if they do not "contain an element of adventurism": "All the rest is organization, labor unions, social democracy, the establishment. Adventure is always beyond..." (2004: 116).

While Marx had as important an influence on Marcuse as any other historical or philosophical figure, and though the critical theorist describes his own politics in life as Marxist—while "Romantic libertarian-communist" might be a more precise formulation—Marcuse in his life-work was very far from being a Marxist ideologue. In this sense, the theorist's treatment of the father of dialectical materialism is not dissimilar to the treatment he grants Hegel: sympathetic and deeply appreciative, yet not reflexively adorational. Granted, Marcuse integrates a great deal of Marxian thought into his own approach. The negative assessment made in *One-Dimensional Man* of the potential for revolutionary politics among the contemporary U.S. working classes comes from Marx himself, who, as the critical theorist is fond of noting, believed the working class to become "the historic subject of the revolution [only] because it represents the absolute negation of the existing order"—the implication thus being that, if the workers do not represent this *absolute negation*, they are "no longer qualitatively different from any other class and hence no longer capable of creating a qualitatively different society" (Marcuse 2014: 178–179). In a letter to Friedrich Engels, indeed, Marx writes that the proletariat "*is revolutionary or it is nothing* [*at all*]" (Marx 1865; emphasis added). In this sense, ironically, Marcuse is being faithful to Marx in his empirical concern for the integration of U.S. workers under conditions of late capitalism—a "pessimistic" line that would draw endless opprobrium from leftist critics, both during his lifetime and since.

For a self-described Marxist, Marcuse was far from being enthralled to Marx. In *Eros and Civilization*, which Bernstein describes as Marcuse's "most perverse, wild, phantasmal and surrealistic book," Marx is not explicitly mentioned at all (Bernstein 1988: 17). Moreover, in the "Re-Examination of the Concept of Revolution," presented in Paris in May 1968, Marcuse criticizes the mechanical, positivistic faith Marx and many of his followers evince in terms of the mythical inevitability of communist revolution. He counterposes this approach with Rosa Luxemburg's identification of the choice between socialism and barbarism. Thus does he provide a more autonomous account of the possibilities for social change—which is to be engendered consciously, in accordance with the stress on human freedom made by the existentialists, particularly Sartre. Beyond Luxemburg and Sartre, one of Marcuse's primary sources—perhaps more fundamental than even Marx himself—is Fourier, as the philosopher notes in the aforementioned comment on a "master" at the question-and-answer period following his presentation at the UNESCO conference. In *One-Dimensional Man*, Marcuse hails Fourier's recognition that the "total commercialism" of bourgeois society stemmed from positivism, and he mentions the reactionary "positivist denunciation" of Fourier's categories as an expression of the threat sensed by these apologists with regard to Fourier's highly non-conformist attitudes (Marcuse 1964: 172n1). Marcuse is in this sense most candid in "The End of Utopia," where he announces the superiority of Fourier's sensuous utopian socialism over Marx's industrial-productivist prejudices (1970a: 68).

Michael Löwy has a point, then, in describing Marcuse's and Benjamin's socio-political system as amounting to a *revolutionary Romanticism* marked by "nostalgia for precapitalist *Kultur*" (Löwy 1999: 211). Of course, reflection on such historical realities—as in the case of classical Greece and its philosophies, particularly those advanced by the Stoics in terms of natural law—did not imply any sort of affirmation for previously constituted powers on Marcuse's part, whether clerical, monarchical, or feudal. From the discussion of rebellious artists, renegades, and itinerant dissident bands in *The German Artist-Novel*, it is clear with which "side" Marcuse sympathizes. The critical theorist's revolutionary Romanticism is inseparable as well from his progressively more sensible ecological views and his ultimately revolutionary philosophy of nature. In an interview published in *Psychology Today* in 1971, Marcuse announces there to be "absolutely nothing wrong with establishing a libidinal relationship with nature," adding that this may well be an integral part of human liberation (2011: 197). Such nature-oriented libidinality—a crucial facet of Eros—can be traced in Marcuse's own life to his youthful participation in the *Wandervogel* ("wandering birds") hiking group, to be discussed in the next chapter. The development of Marcuse's thought about the environment and non-human life, and the implications these thoughts have today amidst the centrality of prevailing ecological catastrophe, is the specific focus of "Nature and Revolution," Chapter 6 below. Suffice it to say here that Marcuse's well-known affinity for hippopotami can be taken as representative of his love for nature—*biophilia*—and his revolutionary Romanticism as a whole: the walls of the critical theorist's office at UCSD were "lined with pictures of hippopotami," and Marcuse is said to have kept at least a couple dozen hippo models there as well. "They are my favorite animals, in addition to giraffes and elephants [...]. They are passive, non-violent creatures, only violently aroused when they are attacked or threatened" (Juutilainen 1996; Marcuse 2014: 422).

An additional factor to consider in reflecting on the sources that gave rise to Marcuse's system of critical inquiry is the role played in this sense by the Jewish faith—for it was Marcuse's Judaism together with his openly radical-left views that would compel him to flee Germany with his wife Sophie and son Peter just before the Nazis seized power in January 1933. Like many other members of the Frankfurt School circle, Marcuse belonged to the assimilated Jewish high bourgeoisie of imperial Germany, and for this reason did not identify as much with the religion as Benjamin or Fromm did—with the latter having been raised in a more orthodox-Jewish milieu than most of the other Frankfurters (Jay 1973: 33, 88–89). When asked in a posthumously published interview if he denied any link between his revolutionary political views and the "Messianic optimism of Judaism," Marcuse responded that he would, "[a]bsolutely" (2007: 233). Despite this conscious denial, Habermas has argued that great similarities exist between components of the Jewish cultural tradition and German Idealism, such that an ideological predisposition to dialectical thought may have been found in the Judaism of the leading figures of Critical Theory, while Jay hypothesizes that the "strong ethical tone" of the Frankfurt School's political approach reflected the "values to be espoused in a close-knit Jewish home" (Jay 1973: 34–35). Significantly, Peter Marcuse and Erica Sherover, Herbert's third and last wife, present a moving description of Marcuse's relationship to Judaism in a letter to the editors of the *New York Review of Books*, published just a couple months after the philosopher's death in 1979. They write that, while Herbert "was not religious, it was important to him (and it is to us) that he was Jewish," for the "aspect of the Jewish tradition with which Herbert most strongly identified is *the importance it places on the struggle for justice in this life*, in this world: *its insistence on the ongoing effort 'to use life to help bring about a better life'*" (Marcuse and Sherover 1979; emphasis added).

Marcuse's Importance for Radical Politics Today

Intuitively, considering what has been said so far, it is to be imagined that Marcuse's political and philosophical contributions retain a great deal of relevance in the contemporary world. Though this matter is the specific focus of the present work's concluding chapter, "Marcusean Politics in the Twenty-First Century" (Chapter 8), some initial comments on the matter will serve to close this introductory section itself, and make way for the biography proper.

Both as political philosopher and public intellectual, Marcuse affirms anti-authoritarianism and libertarian or *utopian* socialism. In his steadfast

personal and existential resistance to capitalism, social-democratic reformism, and authoritarian-bureaucratic Communism, Marcuse demonstrated
his authenticity as an intellectual. Through his insistent stress on negativity,
Marcuse illuminated the serious limitations of monopoly capital, social democracy, orthodox Marxism, and Leninism. In a sense, Marcuse may be likened to the mythological figure of Cassandra, in light of the profound worry he
expressed for the direction world-history was taking, subjected to the direction
of capital. Martineau emphasizes that all who read Marcuse must understand
the depth of his "apocalyptic message"—an "*urgent warning*" to present and
future generations regarding the threats of fascism, cataclysmic war, and environmental destruction (Martineau 1986: 86–87; emphasis added).

However consistently Marcuse argued *for* revolution over the course of his
life, near life's end he would seem to have come to believe that the prospect
for liberatory social transformation was more of a question for the long term.
In the very last lines to *Counterrevolution and Revolt* (1972), the critical theorist asserts that the "next revolution will be the concern of generations, and
the 'final crisis of capitalism' may take all but a century" (Marcuse 1972: 134).
Nevertheless, the doubt Marcuse betrays here is contradicted by the militant
perspectives he shares throughout much of the rest of the same text, in addition to a number of public addresses he gave around the same time, which
highlight increased trends in u.s. society toward absenteeism, sabotage, and
autogestion at the workplace—in parallel to a generalized societal destabilization of the bourgeois cultural hegemony that had previously gone more or less
unchallenged, as in the thesis on one-dimensionality. In *Counterrevolution and
Revolt* itself, in point of fact, Marcuse offers a new societal diagnosis for the
advanced-industrial core of the world-system, whereby capital calls up desires
and needs that inexorably demand its transcendence, and which may therefore guide desire, consciousness, and action against it.

In a 1972 speech entitled "A Revolution in Values," Marcuse plainly identifies the dominant trends of hegemonic power. Precisely due to the very real
challenge which developing anti-systemic sensibilities and social movements
present, the system

> answers with intensified, legal and extra-legal repression, with the
> organization of the *preventive counter-revolution,* preventive because no
> successful revolution has preceded it in the advanced industrial coun-
> tries. Under these circumstances, the prospects are *not very exhilarating.*
> The initiative today is with the forces of repression. There is no histori-
> cal law according to which capitalism will inevitably be followed by
> socialism. The socialist tradition has always recognized and retained the

alternative: either a free and human society, socialism, or a long period of
civilized barbarism, a society entirely in the hands of an omnipresent and
all-powerful administration and management—*some kind of neofascism.*

MARCUSE 2001: 201; emphasis added

However threatening the specter of a fascist resurgence was then, it unfortunately remains real today, amidst the resurgence of xenophobia and chauvinism in much of Europe and the U.S., especially as reflected in the ascendancy
of Donald Trump; the rise of Islamic State, fueled greatly by Saudi Arabia's
fanatical proselytism of Wahhabism; the 2014 electoral victory of the Hindu-
supremacist Bharatiya Janata Party (BJP) in India; the direct governance by
feudalistic drug-cartels in Mexico and Colombia; the massive crimes of the
Jewish State against the Palestinians; the profound horrors of the Syrian Civil
War; the ascendancy of General Fattah al-Sisi's dictatorship over the revolutionary process in Egypt; and the moral and material support provided by the
U.S. government to these and a myriad of other fascistic realities. Still, while
this specter lives on, and may even be more entrenched now than it was late
in Marcuse's lifetime, the dialectic of reason and liberation continues to progress as well. We see it manifested throughout the world these days, evermore
frequently expressed in profoundly antagonistic manners—the struggle of
humanity against the State and capital. In his 1970 study on Marcuse, André
Nicolas declares that we

are at the confluence of irrepressible forces that envelop the erotic, the
aesthetic, and the ethical within a conscience in revolt against all forms
of repression, or what Marcuse calls *ethical-sexual* or *aesthetic-erotic
rebellion.*

NICOLAS 1970: 163

In "A Revolution in Values," Marcuse discloses that he "believe[s] that it is not
too late", that "barbarism, neofascist barbarism, can still be fought" (Marcuse
2001: 201). It is to be hoped that the prognoses provided by these two—critical
theorist and sympathetic observer alike—remian true today, and that we can
act on them accordingly.

PART 1

Marcuse's Life, 1898–1979

∴

Early Years: Childhood and Youth, War and Revolution, Romanticism, Utopian Socialism, Hegel, Marx, and Heidegger

> What is alive is never merely at hand; it always lives toward a purpose.
> MARCUSE 1932: 145

> Spirit is indeed never at rest but always engaged in moving forward.
> HEGEL 1977 [1807]: 6

Childhood and Youth, War and Revolution

Herbert Hermann Marcuse was born on 19 July 1898 in the Charlottenburg suburb of the German capital of Berlin to his parents Carl and Gertrud, being their first child. Herbert's birth would be followed by that of his sister Else less than four years later and of his brother Erich nearly nine years later. The three Marcuse siblings were born to a family of assimilated, bourgeois Jews: Gertrud was daughter to a wealthy German industrialist, and Carl himself had managed a textile factory for some time before transferring his investments into real estate following Erich's birth in 1907 (Harold Marcuse 2003). The family Carl and Gertrud raised serves as a prominent example of the "ascending industrial-commercial bourgeoisie of the late [German] empire," in the words of Marcuse's biographer Barry Kätz, such that the Marcuses were "comfortably assimilated into the German upper middle class" (Kätz 1982: 16–17). Though Jewish—with the last name Marcuse in fact being etymologically related to that of Karl Marx—the Marcuse family's identification was with Germany and bourgeois society before Judaism, leading Carl and Gertrud to observe only the religious High Holidays with their children, however much this approach saddened Herbert's more observant grandparents (Mackey 2001: 315) Thus, like several other intellectual radicals of his generation—Kätz mentions Max Horkheimer and György Lukács, and to this list can be added contemporaries like Walter Benjamin, Theodor W. Adorno, and Ernesto "Che" Guevara as well as predecessors such as Vladimir Lenin, Marx, and Engels themselves, in addition to the anarcho-aristocrats Alexander Herzen, Mikhail Bakunin,

Peter Kropotkin, Lev Tolstoy, and Práxedis G. Guerrero—Marcuse's childhood
and youth were spent within conditions of considerable class privilege and
material comfort (Kātz 1982: 16). Like most of the rest of the members of the
Frankfurt School circle with whom he would come to be affiliated fleeing Nazi
Germany, Marcuse could rightfully be termed an *Edelkommunist*, or an "aristocratic communist"; it is telling, indeed, that Marshall Berman likens Marcuse
in his most popular decade—the 1960s—to a Count Egmont of sorts (Jay 1973:
9; Kellner 1984: 3). The barbarous end met by many members of Marcuse's
extended family under Hitler notwithstanding, Herbert's youthful experience
as Jew, and that of his family at this time, presented few inhibitions owing
to anti-Jewish prejudice. It is significant, indeed, that many of the Frankfurt
School theorists underplayed Jew-hatred in their account of Nazism, relying
more on materialist, economic explanations.

When Herbert was nine years of age, his father enrolled him in Berlin's
Mommsen Gymnasium, a private school that traditionally had catered to children of the imperial ruling class. Carl presumably felt it important to provide
his children with exceptional educational opportunities such as these, especially because he had never attended university himself (Kātz 1982: 18; Mackey
2001: 315). It is thus highly dialectical that the early interest Herbert took in art,
philosophy, and history—and hence, arguably, the origins of the entire trajectory of his life's work—were cultivated by his classical, humanistic education,
which took place within an academic setting that conventionally had aimed
at grooming youth into "careers of power, status, and influence." As another
reflection of the privileges enjoyed by the Marcuses, in 1911 Carl directed the
move of his family and household staff into a ten-room apartment which Kātz
describes as "luxurious." Some years later indeed, in 1928, Carl and the rest
of the family forsook the former apartment for a "palatial modern mansion"
in Berlin's Dahlem suburb, which came featured with "five reception rooms,
an elegant English fireplace, and accommodation for a household staff of
two housemaids, a cook, a pair of laundry maids, and the driver of the family
Packard." Kātz details that among Carl's favorite pastimes in Herbert's youth
was his membership at a horseriding club, where he associated with business
contacts (Kātz 1982: 18–20, 58–59). For this reason, as the biographer explains,
Marcuse's

> was, then, a secure and comfortable Berlin childhood, sheltered by a close-
> knit nuclear family, money, spacious homes, servants, European holidays,
> and summer excursions to the country, but also exposed to the tradition-
> al monuments of the European cultural inheritance and to modernist

experimentation. Freedom from pressing material concerns helped to
distance the young Marcuse from the practical, social and political issues
created by the expanding [German] empire, and rather opened up for
him the transcendental realm of art and ideas (1982: 22).

Perhaps it was the separation from ordinary people Marcuse experienced by
means of his class privilege which led him at sixteen years old to regard the
coming of the First World War as all amounting to little more than "a damned
nuisance" (Kātz 1982: 21). Marcuse as a teen does not intuitively seem to have
sympathized with internationalist-socialist critics who regarded the war as
an absurd imperialist slaughter. It is unclear whether Adorno's later diagnosis
of "bourgeois coldness" should be applied to the young Herbert's initial reaction to WWI—for Marcuse does not seem to have conceived of the descent
into war as a devastating catastrophe, one that might be more appropriately
met with an approach similar to that of John Holloway's "Scream," which
this autonomous-Marxist considers the very fundament of resistance to the
system: "Faced with the mutilation of human lives by capitalism," we respond
viscerally with "a scream of sadness, a scream of horror, a scream of anger, a
scream of refusal" (Holloway 2010: 1).

One other note about Herbert's pre-war life can fruitfully be made here:
during his teenage years, Marcuse participated in a youth hiking club called
the *Wandervogel* ("wanderers" or "wandering birds"), a commitment that
presumably infused him with orientations differing from those hegemonic
within bourgeois imperial-German culture, as represented most palpably
by his own father. As Kātz notes, in the male youth hiking groups of the
Wandervogel, "'Nature,' 'eros,' [and] 'the *Volk*' were celebrated as the basis of
genuine community" (1982: 19). Such adolescent experiences of the beauty
of nature, coupled with Herbert's immersion in the study of classical thought
and history, reflect a sense of existential alternative that further asserts itself
during his experiences over the course of WWI, particularly at war's end, in
light of the future philosopher's participation in the German Revolution of
1918–1919.

Two years after the outbreak of war—upon turning eighteen—Marcuse
was drafted and ordered to basic military training in Darmstadt, near Frankfurt, but subsequent to his training he was exempt from being sent to the war-
front due to poor eyesight. Transferred thereafter to the Zeppelin Reserves sta-
tioned in Potsdam, Marcuse avoided direct combat and thus was separated
from the highly traumatic experiences of the millions barbarized by imperial
capitalism at the Eastern and Western fronts. Malcolm Miles explains that,

regardless of his own good fortune, Marcuse "became radicalised by the point-less violence of the war" and the worsening authoritarianism following the German military's outright seizure of power in 1916 (Miles 2012: 29–31). It was within this context that Marcuse formally joined the German Social Democrat Party (SPD) the following year—a short-lived and formative experience that would prove to be Marcuse's first and last formal affiliation with any political party, other than for the article he would publish a decade later in the social-democrat journal *Die Gesellschaft*.[1] Marcuse's student Douglas Kellner notes that the privileged youth's decision to join the SPD was "not the result of any well thought-out political theory"—given, indeed, that it was the SPD which chauvinistically had first hailed the coming of war in 1914—but it does amount to a form of protest from a previously apolitical teen (Kellner 1984: 36, 15). Importantly, it was during this short time of SPD membership that Marcuse first came to encounter the writings of Marx (Kātz 1982: 28). An insurrectional popular and socialist opposition flowered in Germany with the coming of the November 1918 revolution, as soldiers and workers themselves mutinied, went on strike, and dispersed power by forming *soviets* similar to those developed by their Russian comrades in the latter's revolution the previous year, thus giving birth to the *Räterepublik* ("council-republic"). As revolutionary turmoil gripped Berlin, Marcuse was elected to represent the soldiers' council of Reinickendorf, a proletarian district of the city (Miles 2012: 31). It was in this charge that he was sent to defend the Alexanderplatz, Berlin's main public square, by return-ing fire against snipers affiliated with right-wing gangs who were targeting pro-testors involved with the revolutionary movement!

Despite the militancy he embodied at the beginning of the German Revolution, Marcuse did not initially embrace the libertarian-communist perspectives advanced by Rosa Luxemburg and Karl Liebknecht in the *Spartakusbund* (Spartacus League), for, as he would later explain, he felt their "intransigent revolutionary aspirations" to be "still remote from the reality of German working-class consciousness" (Kātz 1982: 23, 30). More than the Sparta-cists, Marcuse found the artistic-intellectual model advanced by Kurt Eisner and Gustav Landauer more appealing: though their ethical and aesthetic attempt to transform politics met the common fate of the attempted insurrection—that is, "murder, prison, and ridicule"—Marcuse considered this tendency to have been among the most progressive of the German Revolution (Miles 2012: 31; Kātz 1982: 30–31). He seems to have particularly admired the declaration by

---

1 The definition of *Gesellschaft* is "society," though counterposed to the concept of *Gemein-schaft,* which connotes a "real" or "authentic" community, such that the name of the social-democrat journal suggests a critical stance toward bourgeois or "mechanical" society.

Eisner's sympathizers of an autonomous Socialist Republic in Munich in April 1919—even if it survived only a week of confrontation with the reactionary onslaught (Miles 2012: 31). However, Marcuse definitively renounced his SPD affiliation when the *Freikorps* paramilitaries, acting in the interests of the new Social Democrat authorities who had replaced Kaiser Wilhelm II at war's end, abducted and murdered Luxemburg and Liebknecht in January 1919, amidst generalized repression of the popular insurgency—including the final and desperate uprising two months later, which would see some 1,200 shot down by the SPD and its military affiliates (Kātz 1982: 32). Speaking retrospectively several decades later, Marcuse notes that he was greatly alienated by the SPD's effective alliance with bourgeois power and militarism, as he was by the decisions made by several soldiers' councils to elect former army officers into positions of power during the Revolution (Kellner 1984: 16–17; Marcuse 2014: 428).

Upon resigning from the SPD following his military discharge in December 1918, Marcuse did not join the German Communist Party (KPD), as did Lukács and Karl Korsch—with the latter having later embraced council communism. Kellner argues that it was "no doubt difficult for a young man of Marcuse's class and background to identify himself with the working-class politics of the KPD" (1984: 17). Nonetheless, it is known that Marcuse declared himself to be an "existentialist" at age 20 in 1919, around the same time he met and befriended Lukács and Walter Benjamin (Kātz 1982: 32–33). It is to be imagined that this interest in existentialism influenced and reflected the critical manner in which Marcuse processed the horrors of the war, in addition to his reaction of disgust to its similarly brutal end through the suppression of social revolution. Next to Marxism, then, existentialism became an important philosophical reference-point for Marcuse.

As Miles argues, Marcuse's entire life-long investigations into social and political philosophy after WWI are "suffused" with a desire to "redress the balance of failure in 1919"; in this way, it can be said that the highly traumatizing historical events of WWI and the abortive revolution in Germany rival that of the Nazis' subsequent termination of the Weimar Republic fourteen years later as regards the profundity they would have on the development of Marcuse's practical and philosophical commitments in life (Miles 2012: 27).

Post-War Investigations: Aesthetics, German Romanticism, and Hegel

Following the November 1918 armistice and the suppression of the Spartacus League and the German Revolution which followed, Marcuse returned to the sphere of formal academic inquiry at Humboldt University in Berlin, where he researched classics and German arts and humanities (*Germanistik*). As Kellner writes, Marcuse "gravitated naturally towards his former interests" instead of pursuing the life of a professional revolutionary, given his youth and lack of experience (1984: 18). It was during this earliest period of Marcuse's post-war study in Berlin that he first met Benjamin and Lukács in person (Mackey 2001: 315). In 1920, though, when the rector of the Humboldt University pub-licly welcomed the return of military power, Marcuse transferred his course of study to the University of Freiburg, located in the German countryside at the edge of the Black Forest (Miles 2012: 38). Now in Freiburg, Marcuse met and befriended Max Horkheimer, with whom he would often go see lectures given by Edmund Husserl, the "founder" of phenomenology. Marcuse also there became acquainted with the mathematician Sophie Wertheim, as they both attended lectures presented by Heidegger (Mackey 2001: 316). Kātz remarks that during both this initial post-war period and the later course of study with Heidegger, Marcuse's commitments demonstrate little to no continuity with the militancy of his radical experiences during the war, particularly those that took place at its end, while Habermas similarly concludes that Marcuse's scholarly beginnings point to "rather conservative theoretical posi-tions" (Kātz 1982: 37; Habermas 2000: 230). Yet both such criticisms are rather off the mark—while it may be true that some of Marcuse's early work presents its social critique in veiled fashion, especially as compared to the philosopher's better-known later writings of the 1960s, much of the thinker's radicalism is present as a constant through this early period of philosophical investigation. Indeed, the Marcusean affirmation of revolution is openly declared beginning with the essays from the posited "Heideggerian Marxist" period (1928–1932)—particularly in "Contributions to a Phenomenology of Historical Materialism," Marcuse's first published essay. Given the radicality Marcuse presents in his formulations from the "Heideggerian" phase, then, it may not be an exaggera-tion to endorse Schoolman's view that this early period of Marcuse's writing and research—principally conducted, that is, during the span of the Weimar Republic which followed WWI and predated Nazism—was the single most important of his life (1980: 3). The basis of investigation undertaken by Mar-cuse in his second and third decades on aesthetics and Hegel, and later Marx, would prove foundational for the entirety of the remainder of his life's works. Moreover, they clearly reflect his underlying *Dasein* (being, or "being-in-the-world") well, as his wartime experiences already had.

Marcuse's very first major work, the 1922 dissertation on *Der Deutsche Kün-stlerroman* ("The German Artist-Novel"), can be considered a spring from which would develop many of the directions Marcuse's thought and research would take later in life, for one can see direct lines between this first work and *One-Dimensional Man* (1964) and *The Aesthetic Dimension* (1978; see Chapters 5 and 6, respectively). This dissertation, for which Marcuse was awarded a *magna cum laude* doctorate, represents an early and significant testament to the philosopher's concern for an emancipated society, as against the prevailing oppressive one (Martineau 1986: 10). In Marcuse's own words, the "presupposition of the *Künstlerroman*" is "the dissolution and tearing asunder of a unitary life-form, the opposition of art and life, the separation of the artist from the surrounding world," and "its problem" that of "the suffering and longing of the artist, [her] *struggle for a new community*" (Kātz 1982: 41). Marcuse's text seeks to explore the dynamic relationship between the *Künstlertum* ("artistic experience") and *Menschentum* ("fully human experience"), investigating the artist's alienation from society, amidst the reality that the given world is ordered according to maxims which greatly contradict aesthetic concerns. Dialectically, the *Künstlerroman* also examines the manners in which aesthetic imagination and the artist's refusal to assimilate to dominant society foreshadow a future, non-alienated set of social relations. The young scholar draws heavily in this sense from the *Aesthetics* written by G.W.F. Hegel, especially in terms of this Idealist's discussion of "epic poetry" and the promise of a "poetically ordered world" (Kātz 1982: 41–42, 48). In this way, argues Michael Löwy, Marcuse identifies the "burning aspiration of many romantics or neoromantics for a radical change of life," a transformation that would shatter the "narrow limits of bourgeois-philistine materialism"; in the *Künstlerroman*, in point of fact, Marcuse compares Romantic German artists with utopian socialists such as Charles Fourier (1999: 202).

In distinction to the case in ancient Greece or the world of the Norse sagas—examples of past societies Marcuse considers to have "appeared as the embodiment of art," with "the artistic mode of life merg[ing] undistinguished into the collective life of the people"—the fallen society of medieval Europe, dominated by religious oppression, feudalism, and nascent urban capitalism, presents a world that is "utterly devalued, impoverished, brutal, and hostile, offering no fulfilment" (Marcuse 1978a: 12). As Kātz observes, Marcuse is examining a socio-historical situation that corresponds to "an environment continuous with our own"—hence, no mere philosophical abstraction (1982: 42). Such stifling imperant realities notwithstanding, Marcuse considers the dialectical emergence of a pre-modern European counter-culture made up a "traveling community of musicians and mimes [...] whose assault shatters the stability of the established and ecclesiastical restrictions." Being "total outcasts" who can find "no place" for themselves "in the life-forms of the surrounding world," the excluded itinerant artists represent a negation of hegemonic medieval society, as seen in their repudiation of ecclesiastical and monarchical authority in favor of the reign of the "dignity of the free spirit" within the collective conscious-ness, and their affirmation of "rebellious images of eroticism and play" in place of dominant repressiveness (Marcuse 1978a: 13; Kātz 1982: 42–43). Much of the text of the *German Artist-Novel* is dedicated to extended discussions of the pas-sions, negative and positive, communicated by Johann Wolfgang van Goethe's artists and Thomas Mann's novelas, in addition to the literary relationship between Romanticism and Enlightenment reason (Kātz 1982: 44; Miles 2012: 33, 37). As Miles notes, Marcuse sees in Mann's *Death in Venice* the shatter-ing potential of beauty, which had importantly been identified in antiquity by the Greeks—interrupting the reigning, stifling sense of being, beauty and the erotic lead Mann's bourgeois protagonist Gustav von Aschenbach to descend into madness and ultimate death (2012: 38). Similarly in this text, Marcuse hails the hedonism and life-affirmation exhibited by Gottfried Keller in "Green Henry," or *Der Grüne Heinrich* (Kellner 1984: 24).

As in the artistic vision Albert Camus would formulate some three decades later in *The Rebel,* Marcuse's general point in the *Künstlerroman* is to suggest that

> Romantic activities undoubtedly imply a rejection of reality. But this rejection is not a mere escapist flight, and might be interpreted as the retreat of the soul which, according to Hegel, creates for itself, in its dis-appointment, a fictitious world in which ethics reigns alone.
> CAMUS 1961: 260

In an important way, the dynamic and conflictive interplay between hegemony and opposition which Marcuse identifies in the *Künstlerroman* represents his first written elucidation of Hegelian dialectics, an approach that considers the prospects for the possibility of attaining a "fully human life" (*Menschentum*) even amidst the reality of a social context marked by overwhelming suffering and deprivation. This sort of dialectical vision will be central to Marcuse throughout life, as we shall see. Critically, the author of the *Künstlerroman* has with his first substantive intellectual project invoked the principle of *Künstler-tum,* or artistic-aesthetic experience, and shown it to be totally at odds with the pre-existing, instituted society (Kātz 1982: 43, 52–53). This conflict is reflected well in Marcuse's comments on the July Revolution of 1830, which was itself on his account greatly influenced by Romanticism:

> The French upheaval was the decisive experience for the young German artistic generation: the first great attempt was made there radically to

transform the forms-of-life. There arose an incandescent longing of the oppressed youth to carry through this transformation in practice, directly on the grounds of the current reality; yes, to fight with weapons in their hands [...]. [A]rt was placed in the service of life, submitted to the tendencies of the day; the artist became a [person] of practice, a political and social fighter.

> MARCUSE 1978A: 180–181

Dialectically, of course, the July Revolution which overthrew the Bourbon Charles X made way for bourgeois control of French society, leading to the unprecedented injection of capitalist hegemony into popular culture and, thus, "absolute disenchantment" (Marcuse 1978a: 248). Still, the anticipatory roles played by the Romantics and utopian socialists in the lead-up to the 1830 and 1848 Revolutions were translated into new-found bonds of solidarity forged between artists and people in struggle, such that, while these revolutions themselves were ultimately defeated, an emancipatory popular inter-connectedness survived their suppression, promising future upsurges that would seek to overcome the chasm between present reality and liberatory potentiality. In this way, Marcuse melds a solid abstract principle for emancipation with its various concrete political manifestations as a means of resisting the status quo—with this being yet another example of a coupling of abstract principles and praxis that Marcuse would uphold against the system. Thus is seen the essential revolutionary Romanticism which dominates even Marcuse's earliest work: reflecting on the *German Artist-Novel*, Löwy points out Marcuse's affinities with precapitalist *Kultur* and the theorist's development of "this nostalgia for the past into a radical negation of the present order and into a 'desperate hope' for a radically new future society" (1999: 211).

After Marcuse finished his dissertation on the *Künstlerroman*, his father helped him buy a partnership in the S. Martin Fraenkel antiquarian bookstore in Berlin, where he would serve as catalog researcher, publisher, and bookseller for five years. In 1924, Marcuse and Sophie married, and in their Charlottenburg apartment they founded a "revolutionary *salon*" of sorts which was to host events catering to artistic, activist, and intellectual pursuits; the evidence suggests that discussions of Heidegger's *magnum opus Being and Time* raged at the Marcuse household once the work was published in 1927 (Kātz 1982: 56). During this extended stay in Berlin, Marcuse served as co-editor for the radical arts journal *Das Dreieck* ("The Triangle"), which published seven monthly issues in 1924–1925 dedicated to the avant-garde exploration of philosophy, literature, and politics (Miles 2012: 41; Mackey 2001: 316). Moreover, Sophie and Herbert had their first child, Peter, in 1928.

Friedrich Schiller and Charles Fourier: Utopian Socialism

Marcuse's major personal project from this period was to compile the first bibliography of the poetry and writings of the German Romantic Idealist and aesthetician Friedrich Schiller (1759–1805). The annotation of Schiller's complete works, including previously unknown art-works, was published in 1925, totaling 137 pages in length. Considering the close readings of Schiller with which Marcuse supplemented his expanding knowledge of Marx and Marxist philosophy at this time, it is clear that the writings of this German Romantic bore a significant imprint on Marcuse's thought. In a parallel to the liberatory meaning Marcuse would see in Goethe's affirmation of the "feeling for nature" and the "experience of love" in *Sturm und Drang* ("Storm and Stress"), a spirit which may well have influenced the development of Marcuse's approach to nature and Eros can be seen in the following lines by Schiller, which welcome birds and the arrival of spring (Marcuse 1978a: 42):

> Thou'rt welcome, lovely stripling!
> Thou Nature's fond delight!
> With thy basket fill'd with flowers,
> Thou'rt welcome to my sight!
>
> Huzza! Once more we greet thee!
> How fair and sweet thou art!
> To usher in thy presence
> We haste with joyful heart!
>
> SCHILLER 1882: 31–32

Schiller's hopeful musings on human happiness and progress will also resonate throughout Marcuse's work, particularly as a reflection of the critical theorist's commitment to the ideals of the French Revolution, the radical Enlightenment, and the chance for the dialectical overcoming of capitalism through libertarian socialism:

> Of better and brighter days to come
> [Humanity] is talking and dreaming ever [....]
>
> 'Tis no vain flattering vision of youth,
> On the fool's dull brain descending;
> To the heart it ever proclaims this glad truth:
> Tow'rd a happier life we are tending [...].
>
> SCHILLER 1882: 232

Perhaps most notably, Schiller is the author of the world-historical "Ode to Joy," the text of which Ludwig van Beethoven famously set to the choral finale of his last symphony, No. 9. Indeed, while originally writing the highly utopian piece to celebrate humanity, Schiller had initially titled the piece his "Ode to Freedom." Arguably for this reason, it can be considered a prescient Internationale of sorts:

> Joy, beautiful spark of the divinity,
> daughter of Elysium,
> We enter, burning with fervour,
> heavenly being, thy sanctuary.
> Thy magic powers reunite
> what custom's sword has divided.
> Beggars become princes' brothers
> where thy gentle wings abide.
>
> Whoever has had the great fortune
> to become a friend to a friend,
> Whoever has found a beloved [partner],
> let [her] join our songs of praise!
> Yes, and anyone who can call one soul
> [her] own on this Earth! [...]
>
> Every creature drinks in joy
> at nature's breast;
> All, Just and Unjust,
> follow her rose-petalled path.
> She gives us kisses and wine,
> a true friend, even in death [...]
>
> Endure courageously, you millions!
> endure for the better world! [...]
>
> Be embraced, you millions!
> this kiss is for the entire world!
>> SCHILLER 1785; translation modified

Marcuse must have been greatly impressed by such a revolutionary and humanist spirit as Schiller's. Many of the major texts Marcuse would conceive of over the course of his life bear the strong imprint of Schiller's *Letters on the Aesthetic Education of Man* (1794), which the poet wrote in a series of twenty-seven missives to the Danish Prince Friedrich Christian under the influence of the disillusionment he felt with the rise of the Jacobin Terror in France, as against his previous enthusiasm for the meaning and example of the Revolution (Schiller 1954: 4).

In the very first few letters Schiller writes on aesthetic education, he self-consciously raises the question of why one should concern oneself with aesthetic inquiry at all, in light of his activist belief that the "the most perfect of all works of art" is the "building up of true political freedom." Like Marcuse and Heidegger over a century later, Schiller identifies the deadening socio-political reality of the day: "today Necessity is master, and bends a degraded humanity beneath its tyrannous yoke. *Utility* is the great idol of the age, to which all powers must do service and all talents swear allegiance." Such an alienating context leads the "spiritual service of Art" proverbially to flee the scene—yet art retains a critical political importance, for "it is through Beauty that we arrive at Freedom," claims Schiller. As translator Reginald Snell notes, this opening assertion on Schiller's part sums up the argument of the *Aesthetic Education* well: that is, that humanity must first "pass through the aesthetic condition, from the merely physical, in order to reach the rational or moral." For Schiller to make such a claim, of course, is to place him squarely within the bounds of Idealist and elitist philosophy—as against the praxis of the *sans-culottes* and Jacobins of France—in light of his view that humanity is not yet ready for liberation. Indeed, at the beginning of his fifth letter, Schiller notes that "[i]t is true that deference to authority has declined" since the Revolution, and that humans have "awoken from their long lethargy and self-deception, and by an impressive majority they are demanding the restitution of their inalienable rights"—and not only demanding them, but also "bestirring themselves to seize by force what has [...] been wrongfully withheld from them." Considering the shattering opening provided by 1789, Schiller notes there now to exist the "*physical* possibility of [...] honouring Man [*sic*] at last as an end in himself and making true freedom the basis of political association." Yet he abruptly breaks off with this discussion on the struggle for liberation and the realization of Immanuel Kant's categorical imperative, whereby humanity is to exist as an end in itself, by arbitrarily declaring humanity's moral sentiments to be insufficiently developed for the attainment of generalized freedom. Contradicting his previous point, Schiller goes on to observe that the laboring masses are too exhausted by toil and enthralled to ministers and priests to rally for a "new and sterner struggle with error" (1954: 12, 25–27, 34–35, 49).

In suggesting, then, that art can work to restore the human essence by inverting hegemonic historical trends and thus allow humankind to enjoy socio-political freedom, Schiller strongly rejects the idea that concerned

persons look to the feudal-monarchical State to establish a "better humanity," for Schiller's conception of a reasonable State—one which bears radically
little resemblance to any previously constituted State—is instead itself to be
founded by this improved humanity. Hence, on Schiller's account, all attempts
at reform are to be considered "inopportune" until such time as humanity's
internal divisions have been overcome, and its ideal nature expressed
externally—this by means of engagement with aesthetics and creativity. Thus,
though Schiller feels contemporary humanity to have "lost its dignity," he holds
art dialectically to have "rescued and preserved it in significant stone": in a
veritably Marcusean formulation, he declares that "Truth lives on in the midst
of deception, and from the copy the original will once again be restored." It
is in this sense that Schiller famously declares "Beauty" to be a "a necessary
condition of humanity"; as he announces, insofar as "a humanity shall exist,
[…] *there shall be a Beauty*" (emphasis added). In parallel to his discussion
on the sublime, Schiller claims there to exist two basic human impulses: the
sensuous, which originates in humanity's physical existence and concerns
itself with "*life* in the widest of the sense of the word," and the formal, which,
proceeding from humanity's reason, concerns itself with the freedom and
liberation of the organism, thus aiming at "truth and right." He claims both
impulses to be combined ideally in the expression of the *play impulse*, which
he takes from Kant: the practice of play is to liberate humans from mere necessity and toil in favor of the union of reality and form in beauty, as demanded
by reason—such that Schiller will declare that humankind is "wholly [human]
only when [it] is playing." This notion of the play impulse will be taken up
centrally by Marcuse in his *Eros and Civilization* (1955), and Schiller's emphasis
on the intimate connection between art, beauty, and human happiness will
reverberate in all of Marcuse's other works—particularly his final one, *The
Aesthetic Dimension* (1978).[2] In fact, Marcuse finds in Schiller's development
of the concept of the "noble soul" a reflection of his own insurrectional political views: "A noble spirit is not satisfied with being itself free; *it must set free
everything around it, even what is lifeless*" (emphasis added). Furthermore, the
transcendental hope which Schiller holds for the human imagination will be
similarly preserved and developed within Marcuse's philosophy: "On the wings
of imagination [humanity] leaves the narrow bounds of the present, in which
mere animality is enclosed [*sic*], in order to strive forward to an unbounded
future." Lastly, like Marcuse, Schiller declares that a "*total revolution* is needed
in the whole mode of perception": lacking this, humanity would "not find

---

2   See Chapters 4 and 6 below.

[itself] even on the right road towards the ideal" (Schiller 1954: 7, 31, 45–46, 52, 60, 64–66, 74–77, 80, 111, 115–116, 132).

In the final pages of his twenty-seventh and final letter, Schiller makes a few fragmentary comments on the nature of the future aesthetic State which he hopes to be born from humanity's engagement with the educational recommendations he has made in his letters. He observes:

> In the midst of the awful realm of powers, and of the sacred realm of laws, the aesthetic creative impulse is building unawares a third joyous realm of play and of appearance, in which it releases [humankind] from all the shackles of circumstance and frees [it] from everything that may be called constraint, whether physical or moral.
>
> SCHILLER 1954: 137

As against previously established historical regimes that have confronted humanity with terror, force, and necessity, restricting its activity and "fetter[ing]" its will, the governing principle of the aesthetic state would be nothing more than "[t]o grant freedom by means of freedom." This is self-evidently a rather egalitarian vision, and while Schiller does not explicitly endorse the dissolution of class society, he does humanistically promise equal rights for all in the aesthetic State. Regarding the motivating desire which might impel progress toward such a state, Schiller declares this to exist as a desire "in every finely tuned soul" and in actuality "in [those] few select circles where it is not the spiritless imitation of foreign manners but *people's own lovely nature* that governs conduct" (emphasis added). In Schiller's ideal future society, no one would have need "to encroach upon another's freedom in order to assert [her] own," and his view of the most appropriate constitution for a given State reflects Kant's influence: "I can recognise only as such, the one that enables/Each to think what is right" (Schiller 1954: 137, 140; Schiller 1882: 277.)

Besides Schiller and his predecessor Kant, whose work Marcuse will focus on during his time with the Frankfurt School (see next chapter), the philosophical school known as "utopian socialism," represented by the life and work of Richard Owen, Henri de Saint-Simon, and Charles Fourier, will also indelibly mark the development of Marcuse's thought over time. Of these three, it is Fourier (1772–1837) who will influence Marcuse most profoundly, as the critical theorist links his account of libertarian communism with the liberatory perspectives found in Fourier's thought, following Schiller's postulated union of freedom and beauty—for these represent alternative images to the more authoritarian intepretations of socialism with which all twentieth-century revolutionists were confronted. Next to Hegel and the Romantics, Fourier's passionate ideas will constitute another of Marcuse's pre-Marxian inspirations. His study of Fourier served to expand his investigations into reason, sensuousness, and rationality.

Regarded by many as a madman, Fourier in life presented a visionary image of an alternative society based on free associative labor that would supersede capitalism in favor of a historical movement toward the reality he termed Harmony. Perhaps as an indication of the power of his Romantic imagination (or madness), Fourier stipulated that the course of human history would include a total of thirty-six periods, claiming capitalism (or "Civilisation") to correspond only to the fifth, and Harmony the eighth (Fourier 1971: 50–54, 67). Given Fourier's firm belief in the inevitability of a progressive transition away from repressive civilization, it is no surprise that Fredric Jameson claims him to represent the "French equivalent of Hegel and Wordsworth" (2005: 240). Within a context in which the State had already withered away, Fourier foresees social transformation being propelled by the mass-adoption of forms of social organization based on federations of *phalanstères* (from the ancient Greek *phalanx,* for the military formation), which were to be large communal living-spaces housing exactly 1,620 individuals each—one male and female dyad to correspond to each of the 810 human character types Fourier claimed to have identified—and instituting a communal culture wherein wage labor had been superseded by attractive labor, or *travail attractif* (Jameson 2005: 249; Fourier 1971: 163–170). Important factors that would contribute to the birth of this new society, claimed Fourier, included the emancipation of the passions and the cultivation of sensuousness, as against the rationalism previously advanced by the French *philosophes*. Fourier's vision of the future society placed sexual liberation front and center: the *phalanstères* were to host "planned orgies," and the often-neglected sexual needs of elders were to be attended to by "young and beautiful 'saints' whose philanthropic prostitution is a matter of public celebration" (Jameson 2005: 252). Similarly celebrated and respected in Fourier's view are diverse sexual preferences, or the "polymorphous-perverse" sexuality Marcuse would hail in *Eros and Civilization* (1955), including lesbianism, gayness, and fetishism, among others (Kreis 2000). Besides aiding in the free expression of desire and "natural" behaviors which the history of civilization had largely suppressed, sexual liberation for Fourier serves the end of transforming "life into sheer play," as against the drudgery experienced throughout much of human history, particularly in capitalist Civilization. As with Marcuse's case, Fourier's social criticism did not spare the bourgeois-patriarchal family, which was to be utterly dissolved in the shift to life in *phalanstères* (Jameson 2005: 252). Thus residing in a new social environment marked by the transcendence of the family and the emancipation of erotic life, humans might come to represent a microcosm of Fourier's understanding of the planets of the solar system, which he believed to be bisexual entities actively copulating with one another (Fourier 1971: back cover).

In terms of his overall influence, Fourier has proven highly important to the Western revolutionary tradition, this despite the influential dismissal which Marx and Engels pronounced on his work, as in the latter's "Socialism, Utopian and Scientific": Abraham Maslow, Kropotkin, André Breton, and David Harvey alike cite Fourier as major influences. The Romantic novelist Nathaniel Hawthorne was involved in the founding of Brook Farm in Massachusetts, a social experiment aimed at helping along the coming of Harmony—being a type of practice that was echoed by other Fourierist groups that formed communes in the u.s. and Europe, such as in Utopia, Ohio, and the New Red Phalanx, New Jersey (Fourier 1971: 4, 7, 42). Critically, as well, Fourier's explicit feminism is a noteworthy development within the nascent socialist tradition, dominated as it would later become by Marxism, which in practice often sidelined anti-patriarchal struggles in favor of the theorized primacy of class struggle. It may then be that the enthusiasm Marcuse expressed later in life for the emerging women's liberation movements was sensitized by his early readings of Fourier, who was after all the first writer to use the term feminism—this in a piece written in his final year of life, 1837. In "Of the Condition of Women," Fourier would declare "the extension of privileges to women" to be "the general principle of all social progress" (Fourier 1971: 76–81). Moreover, Fourier's anti-industrial proclivities present a critical, alternative view of human progress opposed to the Prometheanism on offer within much of the Marxist tradition, and this former vision will influence Marcuse and Benjamin alike in their dreams for a "reconciliation with nature" against the contemporary exploitation and destruction of the environment and life-world. Already the affinities between Marcuse's revolutionary (neo)Romanticism and Fourier's view of socialism have been identified; as with Benjamin, the work of recalling the Romantic, pre-capitalist past can serve subversive ends, in Marcuse's view (Löwy 1999: 201, 211).

However similar many of Fourier's orientations may be when compared with those developed later by Marcuse, the two diverge widely on religion, with Fourier conceiving of his views of human progress as emanating from God—though not a Christian God—and Marcuse strongly repudiating theism in favor of human reason. Furthermore, the two would seem to disagree as well on the rights of non-human animals, given Fourier's view of non-human animals as objects to be managed for the benefit of human interests, as opposed to Marcuse's admittedly dynamic yet ultimately respectful position, which would seem at least tentatively to affirm animal liberation (Fourier

1971: 203–204).[3] In addition, unfortunately, Fourier's vision for the future oddly enough remained tied to the perpetuation of social inequality, as the utopian writer promised the poor and all peoples a comfortable guaranteed minimum at the least, but generally opted to retain property, inheritance, and class stratification in society as a whole (Fourier 1971: 23, 26–28, 30). In point of fact, Fourier stipulated that the distribution of resources within *phalanstères* was to be organized with discrimination according to one's social class. What is more, in 1831, Fourier tellingly observes that he feels the Saint-Simonian call for the "abolition of property and heredity" to be a "monstrosity" that had to be utterly rejected (1971: 147, 23). Marcuse's position on class society, in contrast, is explicitly Marxian, desiring the total destruction of classes as arbitrary and absurd historical residues.

Marcuse's Torturous Relationship with Heidegger

After his years working in the antiquarian Berlin bookstore and editing *Das Dreieck,* Marcuse returned to the University of Freiburg to study personally with Martin Heidegger, whose *Being and Time* (1927) had greatly impressed Marcuse and his radical intellectual friends (Miles 2012: 41). Marcuse and company considered Heidegger's *magnum opus* importantly to grapple with existential questions largely ignored by the mainstream Marxist, neo-Kantian, and neo-Hegelian philosophical currents on hand at that time (Kātz 1982: 56; Marcuse et al. 1978/9: 126); in a 1977 interview, Marcuse recalled that his generation would initially hail the work as representing a "new beginning, the first radical attempt to put philosophy on really concrete foundations— philosophy concerned with human existence, the human condition, and not merely abstract ideas and principles" (Marcuse 2005: 166). Though Marcuse had befriended Lukács and read his *History and Class Consciousness* (1923) years before the publication of Heidegger's *Being and Time*, it turned out that Marcuse developed the philosophical basis of his shattering critique of capitalist reification and domination principally through his engagement with Heidegger (Kātz 1982: 63–64). Marcuse seemingly thus was more taken by Heidegger's analysis of "fallenness" and everyday *Das Man* (the "they") than he was by Lukács' groundbreaking treatment of commodity fetishism and the latter's identification of the putatively integrated working class in Western societies— however sympathetic Marcuse would otherwise be to these findings of Lukács during his lifetime.

---

3   See Chapter 7, "Nature and Revolution," below.

According to Richard Wolin, author of *Heidegger's Children: Hannah Arendt, Karl Löwith, Hans Jonas, and Herbert Marcuse* and *The Heidegger Controversy,* Marcuse was at no point in his studies with Heidegger a "convinced Heideggerian." Instead, Wolin claims that Marcuse thought that "Heidegger's existentialism [...] might be serviceable for Marxist ends, [but] rarely the other way around," and that Marcuse's thought remained true to the end of Marxian revolution during his time in Freiburg with Heidegger. In point of fact, it was precisely Marcuse's commitment to Marxist thought which contributed to the emergence of one of the most significant disagreements he had with his phenomenological mentor: that is, that Heidegger's existentialist lamentations on social alienation, though provocative, ultimately serve to mystify and thus perpetuate capitalism by presenting "fallenness" as an irrevocable constant of the human condition (Wolin 2001: 135–136, 148). In this sense, Marcuse holds that Heidegger's treatment of human Being (*Dasein*) "remains remote from [actual] human beings (*Daseiende*)" (Kātz 1982: 73). *Ex post facto*—and particularly in light of Heidegger's adulatory endorsement of Hitler months following his accession to power in 1933, a move that came as a shattering practical shock to his humanely-oriented students and admirers—Marcuse identified misgivings he had had about Heidegger's claims in *Being and Time* regarding the putative orientation of *Dasein* as Being-toward-death. In light of Heidegger's view that one's attitude toward human finitude (or death) largely determined whether one had an authentic or inauthentic character—with inauthenticity, or *Das Man,* serving systematically to repress reflection on mortality—Marcuse felt the Heideggerian obsession with death to be reminiscent of Italian Futurism as well as the explicit political movement most consonant with this philosophy: that is to say, Fascism (Marcuse 2005: 172; Wolin 2001: 163–164). Not unrelatedly, Marcuse finds disconcerting the elitist implications of Heidegger's overall argument, which claims the "self-overcoming" of hegemonic alienation to be possible only for a small, effectively aristocratic minority of Nietzschean iconoclasts (Wolin 2001: 148).

These differences between mentor and student should not be taken as overlooking their clear commonalities, however. For one, the German Romantic tradition deeply influenced both philosophers (Wolin 2001: 171). Moreover, Marcuse importantly integrated the Heideggerian concept of authenticity and its degradation into all his major life's work; as Kātz observes, "existential ontology thus provided for [Marcuse] an explosive, revolutionary category which presupposes the radical transformation of society," for the normative call to "abolish inauthenticity" really amounts to a call for the abolition of the very conditions which give rise to inauthenticity (Kātz 1982: 73). Wolin even sees Marcuse's *One-Dimensional Man* as an application of Heideggerian concepts to post-war U.S. society, and claims Marcuse's speculative musings on a "biological basis for socialism" in *An Essay on Liberation* (1969) to be related to Heidegger's claims regarding the ontological (or pre-social) basis for authentic Being-in-the-world (Wolin 2001: 168, 170).[4]

In this way, though dialogue and mutual interchange transpired for a time between Heidegger and his Marxist "child," Marcuse's perspectives on Heidegger were far from unthinking. While Heidegger is acknowledged by name in the introduction to Marcuse's 1932 dissertation on Hegel's ontology, the lengthy treatise is largely an exploration of the thought of this figure from the German Idealist tradition, not that of Heidegger's existential phenomenology—which is neither to claim that *Hegel's Ontology* altogether lacks Heideggerian imprints, for they certainly are present (Jay 1973: 73). Yet, as Schoolman notes, Hegel's philosophy of historicity yields a human subject who is freer than her Heideggerian counterpart—for this reason did Marcuse sense a closer affinity to Hegel than his mentor (Schoolman 1980: 21). What is more, Marcuse's differences with Heidegger were emboldened by the publication in 1932 of Marx's *Economic-Philosophical Manuscripts of 1844,* which readily provided the humanistic, radical ontological orientations Marcuse had been rather fruitlessly searching for in Heidegger (Kātz 1982: 76–77). As Marcuse observes in a 1978 interview with Habermas in *Telos,* the discovery of Marx's 1844 *Manuscripts* constituted a veritable turning point in his life, inspired as he became with this new "practical and theoretical Marxism" which superseded the "petrified" concept for which Communist Parties stood: "After that, Heidegger versus Marx was no longer a problem for me," Marcuse declares (Abromeit 2004: 141). As a consequence, when Marcuse saw it necessary to flee Germany for Switzerland, with the Nazi takeover of January 1933 coming just a month after the publication of *Hegel's Ontology*, he had already distanced himself considerably from Heidegger. Infamously, the University of Freiburg rector would forever mar his claim to be the philosophical heir of Kant and Hegel with his shameless public embrace of Hitler's rule in November 1933: "Let not principles and ideas rule your being," he announced to students everywhere. "Today, and in the future, only the *Führer* himself is German reality and law" (Marcuse 2005: 170).

It should come as little surprise, then, that no further contact was had between student and rector following this disastrous turn of events, and silence would continue to reign between them until after Hitler's fall. In 1946, Marcuse visited Heidegger in person at his home in Todtnauberg, located

---

4   For further discussion of *One-Dimensional Man,* see Chapter 5 below; on the relationships among Eros, *bios,* socialism, and morality, see Chapter 7.

within the Black Forest, where the two had a conversation that was "not exactly very friendly and very positive," as Marcuse recalls (2005: 165). Though no record of their spoken exchange in Todtnauberg exists, there does exist a short-lived written correspondence between the two which followed their personal meeting. In a 28 August 1947 letter to Heidegger, Marcuse openly challenges his former teacher for first siding with the Nazis in 1933, and then for failing openly to denounce the regime, retract his previous endorsement of it, and publicly clarify his disagreements with Nazism after these had developed a year into Hitler's reign, leading Heidegger to resign his rectorship in protest (Marcuse 1998: 263–264). Speaking in the name of his generation, which was so distressed to see the purported philosopher of authenticity side with Nazi power at its genesis, Marcuse tells his former mentor that

> we cannot make the separation between Heidegger the philosopher and Heidegger the man, for it contradicts your own philosophy. A philosopher can be deceived regarding political matters, in which case he will openly acknowledge his error. But he cannot be deceived about a regime that has killed millions of Jews—merely because they were Jews—that made terror into an everyday phenomenon, and that turned everything that pertains to the ideas of spirit, freedom and truth into its bloody opposite [...]. The philosopher of 1933–34 cannot be completely different than the one prior to 1933; all the less so, insofar as you expressed and grounded your enthusiastic justification of the Nazi state in philosophical terms.
>
> MARCUSE 1998: 264

Heidegger's written response, rudely postmarked some four months after Marcuse's original letter, is evasive and rather banal. Ever the German chauvinist, Heidegger equates the Nazi genocide of the European Jews with the Red Army's treatment of the *OstDeutsche* ("Eastern Germans") residing in occupied territories as Soviet forces advanced westward toward Berlin; in fact, Heidegger opens by admitting to his former student that he "expected from National Socialism a spiritual renewal of life in its entirety, a reconciliation of social antagonisms, and a deliverance of western *Dasein* from the dangers of communism." As his own words demonstrate, Heidegger certainly was in this sense already quite close to fascist ideology before Hitler's rule: for him, the "social antagonisms" which exploded during the Weimar Republic had to be allayed or outright repressed. Though Heidegger admits that a "few of the sentences" he expressed in his pro-Nazi lectures may have been "misleading," there is no sense that the phenomenologist shares the concern held by Marcuse and his colleagues regarding his profoundly inauthentic legitimation of Nazism: he tells Marcuse that, were he to have publicly made any "counter-declaration" against Hitler, his family would likely have been killed, and he adds that he saw little point in disavowing National Socialism after the end of the war. Moreover, Heidegger contemptuously dismisses criticisms made by Marcuse and his comrades of National Socialism, complaining that they judge fascism's beginning by its fruits—world war, genocide, and so on. Marcuse focuses his subsequent reply on Heidegger's view of Nazism as "spiritual renewal," noting that the "end" of Nazism could readily be foreseen in its beginning by any philosophically minded person. Furthermore, he accuses Heidegger's equation of the displacement of East Germans by the Red Army with the Nazi extermination of European Jews of being ludicrous: in Heidegger's attempt to equate the two historical moments, writes Marcuse, the phenomenologist "stand[s] outside of the dimension in which a conversation between men [*sic*] *is* even possible"—even, "outside of Logos" altogether (Marcuse 1998: 265-7). Little surprise, then, that Heidegger did not respond to this final letter.

This mutual antagonism does not seem to have abated during the remainder of Heidegger's lifetime. Yet in 1977, a year after Heidegger's death and close to the end of his own life, Marcuse gave an interview with Frederick Olafson on "Heidegger's Politics." Through this conversation, Marcuse presents his precise and systematic interpretation of the connection between Heidegger's expressed existential philosophy and his infamous embrace of Nazism in 1933. He makes the following observation:

> If you look at [Heidegger's] view of human existence, of being-in-the-world, you will find a highly repressive, highly oppressive interpretation. I have just today gone again through [...] *Being and Time,* and had a look at the main categories in which he sees the essential characteristics of existence or *Dasein*. I can just read them to you and you will see what I mean: 'idle talk, curiosity, ambiguity, falling and being-thrown into, concern, being-toward-death, anxiety, dread, boredom,' and so on. Now this gives a picture which plays well on the fears and frustrations of men and women *in a repressive society—a joyless existence, overshadowed by death and anxiety; human material for the authoritarian personality*. It is for example highly characteristic that love is absent from *Being and Time* [...].
>
> MARCUSE 2005 169–170; emphasis added

Much like Emmanuel Lévinas, who famously declared that "[o]ne can forgive many Germans," though "[i]t is difficult to forgive Heidegger," Marcuse in this interview shares with Olafson his belief that Heidegger's mistake in supporting Nazism constitutes "one of the errors a philosopher is not allowed to commit," as it amounts "actually" to "the betrayal of philosophy as such, and of everything philosophy stands for" (Lévinas 1994: 25; Marcuse 2005: 170). Here, he resurrects his observation to Heidegger in the August 1947 letter that many from his own generation refused even to grant Heidegger a legitimate place in Western philosophy after November 1933, for "philosophy and Nazism are irreconcilable" (Marcuse 1998: 263). Subjecting Heidegger's thought to critical scrutiny in this interview with Olafson, Marcuse declares the phenomenologist's work to be bereft of engagement with actually existing material reality— "the struggle between capitalism and socialism, waged almost daily on the streets [in the Weimar Republic], at the work place, with violence and with the intellect, the outburst of a radically rebellious literature and art"; instead, he accuses Heidegger's thought of generally advancing "a very powerful devaluation of life, a derogation of joy, of sensuousness, fulfillment." That such an outlook is largely congruent with the fascist emphasis on sacrifice may explain Heidegger's enthusiasm for its advent in Germany, suggests Marcuse (Marcuse 1998: 170–171, 172). In this interview, Marcuse also contrasts Heidegger with Sartre, a thinker whose development was also inspired by Heideggerian categories: Marcuse declares Sartre's existentialism to be much more alive than that of Heidegger, given the centrality of "[e]rotic relationships, love, hatred, [...and] the body [...] as it is sensuously experienced" in Sartre's *oeuvre* (Marcuse 2005: 173). Moreover, in his 1978 chat with Habermas and company, Marcuse accuses Heidegger of essentially having appropriated Husserl's transcendental categories as his own and redirecting them noxiously into abstractions (Marcuse et al. 1978/9: 125). Similarly, in a 1963 letter to the Czech philosopher Karel Kosik, Marcuse declares Heidegger's early support for Nazism to have reflected the "deeply anti-humane, anti-intellectual, historically reactionary, and life-repudiating tendencies of his philosophy" (Marcuse 2014: 322).

In sum, then, it can be said that Heidegger's existentialism definitely did influence Marcuse's thought and the course of its development to a degree, but this influence was always limited, balanced out in the first place by Marcuse's pre-existing Hegelian-Marxist orientations and then by the manifestations of disgust which overcame Marcuse when he learned of Heidegger's collaboration with Hitler as he undertook exile with his family. An examination of Marcuse's essays from the theorist's time of study with the phenomenologist may help to illuminate these developments more closely.

Heideggerian Marxism

Provisioning the life-space means, necessarily, altering that which is present-at-hand.

MARCUSE 2005: 30

Marcuse's works from his late studies in Freiburg have been compiled by
Wolin and John Abromeit in a posthumous volume they provocatively entitle
Marcuse's *Heideggerian Marxism* (2005). In chronological terms, the 1928 essay
"Contributions to a Phenomenology of Historical Materialism" comes first
within this period of collaboration with Heidegger. With these "Contributions,"
Marcuse attempts to synthesize existentialism and Marxism, these being two
fields of thought he finds particularly attractive due to their common "insistence on concrete analysis of actual human existence, human beings, and
their world," as he declares retrospectively in his 1977 interview with Olafson
(Marcuse 2005: 166–167). The main question Marcuse raises in this work, one
he takes from his phenomenologist counterpart, is the following one: "what is
authentic existence and how is it possible at all?" (2005: 14). Marcuse's answer
here, which contrasts sharply with Heidegger's own vision of an "aristocratic
radicalism," proposes radical social transformation as a means of overcoming the "fallenness" and generalized inauthenticity that permeates the world
of *Being and Time*. Marcuse declares that the historical possibility of authenticity as identified by Heidegger can be realized only through "overthrowing
the factually existing situation" by means of the "resolute," "radical" or "revolutionary act": "a resoluteness toward authentic existence [...] is only possible
as a 'disavowal' of the past" (Marcuse 2005: 5, 16, 18–19). In Marxian terms, he
holds hope out for proletarian intervention within this negative context, as the
chance for an authentic and revolutionary subjectivity on the part of the workers becomes "possible at the moment when existence itself breaks through
reification," as the people come to identify the dominion of social alienation
and labor radically to combat it. Practically speaking, Marcuse outlines two of
the major obstacles he sees lying before the dialectical development of mass-
revolutionary consciousness: first, a lack of recognition of praxis—rather than,
say, contemplation or reflection—as being the "decisive attitude of human
Dasein"—for it is only praxis which "authentically creates reality"—and
second, a lack of recognition of the "historical fallenness" of the prevailing
situation, its utter inhumanity (2005: 32–33). He closes the essay by arguing
uncompromisingly for advancing the cause of a revolutionary breakthrough:

> Human existence can never become real through a mere change of the
> present reality, because in that case it would never move beyond the
> present existence [...]. 'New' existence is only possible as disavowal [...].
> [I]t is revolution alone that can change the *existence* of historical *Dasein*.
> MARCUSE (2005: 33)

Continuing with the openly subversive and activist implications drawn by
his "Contributions," Marcuse begins his reflections "On Concrete Philosophy"

(1929) by asserting that philosophy's meaning corresponds to its *"making visible of truth."* Such "truth" for Marcuse refers not just to any sort of appraisal of objective reality, or knowledge, but crucially also to action which follows from said knowledge: "*Care* [*Sorge*] for human existence and its truth makes philosophy a 'practical science' in the deepest sense," leading the true philosopher "into the *concrete distress* of human existence." The "occupation" of philosophy "with existence [hence] becomes a concern for the thoroughly concrete difficulties of this existence." If they are honest, Marcuse is saying, philosophers immediately confront the human suffering, ideological mystification, and utter destructiveness propagated by the capitalist mode of production, which reduces human beings to "primarily economic subjects" and *Dasein* in all its variety to mere entrepreneurship and productivity (2005: 34–36 42, 47). Under capitalism, "falseness" (or "fallenness") comes to reign over society in a hegemonic position, invalidating authenticity at the individual level: thus, the restoration of *Dasein* under such conditions can only be effected through "transforming society," argues Marcuse, in an echo of his essay from the previous year. If it is to aid *Dasein's* development toward the societal realization of authenticity, philosophy must "take [...] existence upon itself" and correspondingly "fight for truth"; indeed, Marcuse posits that philosophers have both the right and the *duty* to intervene in "the entirely concrete difficulties of existence," because it is only in this way that the "existential meaning of truth" may in his view be brought to bear: that is, through radical political action. Referring vaguely and indirectly to the continuing saga of revolutionary politics as enacted on the contemporary world stage, Marcuse concludes "On Concrete Philosophy" by warning that philosophy's essentially practical and activist responsibilities are particularly important "in situations where contemporaneous existence has actually been shaken to its foundations, [...] where a struggle is actually taking place over new possibilities of meaning"; in the midst of such struggles, Marcuse stresses, philosophy must not continue traditionally to "stand on the sidelines and [...] occupy itself with 'timeless' discussions" (2005: 51–52).

While these two essays from the first half of Marcuse's period of study with Heidegger demonstrate considerable differences between the two thinkers— plainly stated, social revolution was not primary among Heidegger's concerns in life—it is with Marcuse's "New Sources on the Foundations of Historical Materialism" that his definitive break with his mentor is most clearly expressed. Published in the SPD-aligned journal *Die Gesellschaft* in 1932, this essay reviews the new publication of the previously unknown *Economic-Philosophical Manuscripts of 1844* written by the young Marx. In his review, Marcuse discusses Marx's theory of human alienation through objectified labor, elucidating the historical materialist's dialectical method, which holds out the chance for the fulfillment of humanity's "species-being" through the exercise of human freedom and the overcoming of reification. He notes that a Marxian contemplation of the gap between human existence and essence in capitalist society must lead the philosopher inexorably to advance "radical revolution" as a means of allowing for the flowering of human potential. That human essence is marked by "catastrophe" under capitalism for Marcuse shows the inadequacy of "any mere economic or political *reform*" which would seek incremental change; the "actual situation" must instead confront its "cataclysmic sublation [...] through *total revolution*" (Marcuse 2005: 92–103, 106).

Practically speaking, the communist revolution which Marcuse prescribes as a remedy to the profundity of human alienation would also, on Marcuse's reading of the 1844 *Manuscripts*, abolish labor, or at least its repressive, alienated manifestations. Beyond the transformation or abolition of labor, Marcuse identifies two other principal means of overthrowing reification: the material socialization of production, as well as the emergence of thought which impels and preserves these world-historical political and economic changes. One example of the latter means Marcuse gives would include forms of education and media that serve to develop the "knowledge of objectification" in the struggle for "free self-realization." As in "On Concrete Philosophy," Marcuse envisions philosophy advancing social change through the transcendence of its traditional identity as a merely "theoretical" field of inquiry, and its metamorphosis into a practical guide to revolt and revolution (2005: 109–110, 114).

In the 1844 *Manuscripts,* Marcuse also sees a veritable autonomism in terms of Marx's thoughts on class struggle—which themselves in turn largely reflect Hegel's presentation of the dialectic of lordship and bondage in the *Phenomenology of Spirit* (1807). In the autonomous Marxist account, private property and capitalist domination arise through and are upheld precisely by the source of production of capitalist value: alienated labor. It is for this reason that the worker "has [her] fate in [her] own hands at the origin of estrangement [that is, within the everyday routine of capitalism] and not just after liberation" from its oppressive nature through the toppling of bourgeois power. In his review of the *Manuscripts*, Marcuse also examines Marx's critiques of Hegel and the inherited legacy of German Idealism: from Ludwig von Feuerbach, Marx is shown to find the Hegelian vision of the *Geist*'s "negation of negation" lacking, and thus to believe that a more positive vision was needed, as in communism. In addition, Marcuse presents Marx's materialist criticism of Hegel's Idealist positing of "self-consciousness" or "mind" as the end of human essence and historical struggle. In the view of the founder of historical materialism, instead, it is praxis, "free self-realization, always [...] sublating and revolutionizing preestablished 'immediate' facticity," that more authentically serves the insurrectional specter of human emancipation. Marcuse ends his review by noting that the *Manuscripts* of the early Marx demonstrate his youthful humanism not to be a mere "appendage" to his later critique of political economy (*Capital*), but rather that the later scholarly investigations of political economy for which Marx had been so famous up to this historical point themselves constitute "a continuous confrontation with Hegel," one which Marcuse sees in the *Manuscripts* as having been been present from the very beginning of Marx's philosophical investigations (Marcuse 2005: 112–113, 115–116, 120–121).

Hegel's Ontology and the Theory of Historicity (1932)

Marcuse's work on *Hegel's Ontology and the Theory of Historicity*, which was submitted to Heidegger and the University of Freiburg as Marcuse's *Habilitationsschrift* and published in December 1932, would have represented the fulfillment of the requirements the critical philosopher would have had to complete to embark on an academic career in Germany—one that would have been cut short very quickly, as Hitler came to power a month after the volume's release. In general, the text's prose is exceedingly impenetrable: this may have to do with the highly specialized audience Marcuse wrote it for—Heidegger, that is, as well as Husserl and the rest of the department's review board. With this difficulty in mind, and considering that the text surpasses three hundred pages in length, no attempt at a general synthesis of its argumentation will be presented here. Instead, some of Marcuse's more insightful and even revolutionary claims in the work will be highlighted—ones that echo previously developed thoughts, and that foreshadow future developments.

Marcuse begins his investigation of Hegel's ontological and historical philosophies by defining his main task for the volume: to "disclose and to ascertain the fundamental characteristics of historicity," or what "defines" history and so "distinguishes it from 'nature' or from the 'economy.'" Marcuse claims historicity to signify "the meaning of the Being of the historical," and he finds the movement of history to be indelibly associated with two moments: motility, or the "development" or "unfolding" of authentic *Dasein*, and negativity, in the sense of *negation*. Examining Hegel's *Science of Logic* (1812–1817), Marcuse declares the world of philosophy to be "one of total restlessness," this in contrast to the "total appeasement" which reigns in "the 'upright' world"—an image, perhaps, of 'polite' or mainstream bourgeois society. Situated in dialectical and historical terms, "All 'being' is a having become and a becoming of another 'being'" (Marcuse 1987: 1, 11–12, 67, 178, 12; 2005: 177).

> Thus something does not change itself but passes over into another; it "perishes, passes away." Its unity is only provided by this context of movement: the leaf is only a leaf because it withers. The seed is only a seed because it "passes away" into a fruit. The Being of immediate beings constitutes itself first and foremost through a movement which is the complete *perishing* of the individual something [...].
>
> MARCUSE 1987: 54

As Hegel himself writes in the preface to his *Phenomenology of Spirit*:

> The bud disappears in the bursting-forth of the blossom, and one might say that the former is refuted by the latter; similarly, when the fruit appears, the blossom is shown up in its turn as a *false manifestation* of the plant, and the fruit now emerges as the truth of it instead.
>
> HEGEL 1977: 2

Truth, then, develops dialectically, according to Hegel and Marcuse: in the *Ontology,* Marcuse quotes Hegel's declaration from the *Briefe* that "Truth is not what is merely at rest and simply there; truth is what moves itself, what is alive [....] what is in motion, Life itself" (1987: 146).

In Hegel's reflections on the dialectics of finitude, Marcuse locates the first secular-philosophical treatment of the question of death in Western philosophy, as divorced from the previously hegemonic theocratic analyses of the processes of ending and becoming. Quite like his supervisor Heidegger, Marcuse here exclaims that "[t]he question is finitude as the ontological determination of beings in general!" It would seem that he particularly likes Hegel's suggestion from the *Logic,* that "the hour of [one's] birth is the hour of [her] death," for it is rather reminiscent of the line in *Being and Time* (Marcuse 1987: 55). Amidst the myriad of struggles experienced in life, Marcuse holds out Hegel's hope that the revolutionary human essence necessarily will appear: "Precisely this is the content of the Absolute, to manifest itself." Marcuse thus sees Hegel desiring the liberation of being (*Dasein*) as becoming-manifest in the world from the imagination and thought. In utopian and dialectical terms, the motility of being promises development and differentiation: "All that *is* actual is always something *more*, something *other* than what is exactly there, at hand and present" (Marcuse 1987: 91, 93). The mere fact that social relations are constantly in flux, or under contestation—as in class struggle—is made possible "only because the actual can go beyond [contingency] into another possibility." Arguing against the despair which might have been gleaned contemporarily from the widespread suppression of revolutionary movements in Europe and the related specter of National Socialism in Germany, Marcuse asserts that "[a]ppearance therefore is not the highest mode of being," that "[w]hat is there is not pure and complete," given that "being has not fully come out into thereness, into actuality." Existentially, this problematic grips humanity in a manner reminiscent of the threat of annihilation: according to Marcuse, true existence depends on "completeness and authenticity," hence the ever-dialectical dynamic whereby being attempts to overcome the radical gap between is and ought (1987: 99, 104).

In Marcuse's analyses of Hegel, the prospect for human freedom is related to humanity's degree of comprehension, as well as to its autonomous self-determination. Such autonomy, which Marcuse elsewhere describes as purpose, "Notion," or "concept," presents itself as object of desire to and connection among humans, who relate with each other through this relationship of "determination and purpose needing concrete fulfillment." Human existence is thus centrally marked by a Hegelian—and even Heideggerian—struggle to realize its purported essence, or "truth": as Hegel defines it in the *Logic,* objects become true "when they are what they ought to be." The Idea of "true being" impels humankind "beyond particularity toward the unity of the 'species' humanity, from which and in relation to which alone [it] can be what [it] is." However much he idealistically stresses the importance of consciousness and subjectively, though, Marcuse makes clear his view that the movement toward the realization of the Idea or Notion cannot be limited merely to the life of the mind. Instead, it is productively advanced by exercise of the *will,* which aims at "making the world into what it *ought* to be." Marcuse sees the diffusion of the potentially subversive implications of his critical conception of the Idea as dialectical hope for the present, which "always" amounts to "potentially something that is not in actuality." In materialist terms, Marcuse suggests that the development toward true Being in humanity "is first fulfilled and completed in the historical process itself"—that is, through the conscious creation of a free world (1987: 115–116, 132, 146, 151, 169, 178, 193–195).

Turning to considerations of biology and ontology, Marcuse distinguishes between two forms of life as advanced in Hegel's work: *zoe,* or physical life, and *phos,* or "truthful life." Citing Hegel's youthful investigations of theology, Marcuse explains that *phos,* or the manifestation of potential for liberation and emancipation, is an egalitarian potentiality available to all of humanity: "every human being who emerges into the human world" can become a *photi zomenos,* or "being in the light." Symbiotically, *phos* is stipulated as existing in the world itself, only awaiting its recognition and institution by means of a self-conscious humanity, or *photi zomenos.* Speculatively, Marcuse hypothesizes that the division between the two life-forms could be overcome through the exercise of "'reflection' as a mode of Being," which makes possible the "unity and wholeness" promised against reigning alienation. This is the movement of Spirit (*Geist*) or "Mind," through which, in Hegel's analysis, reason comes to emancipate the world—firstly, by asserting itself in consciousness (Marcuse 1987: 206–208, 228). The essence of existence, according to Hegel, thus amounts to

> infinity as the sublation of all distinctions, the pure movement of axial rotation, *peacefulness itself* as the absolute restless infinity, *independence itself*, in which the differences of the movement are resolved [...].
>
> HEGEL 1977: 106

Through autonomy and independence, then, humans can "recognize" each other and "*reciprocally* and consciously set each other free" (Marcuse 1987: 231, 255).

Continuing with his materialist analysis of the revolutionary functions of reason, Marcuse situates the embodiment of Spirit ("rational self-consciousness") as the emergence of *free people:* "Reason is [...] first actualized in truth through a free people" (Hegel 1977: 214). The *Geist,* then, comes to advance the "unity and universality of free self-consciousness." As a result, the world, or "the existent," comes to be shaped by the "work and act of a people," or many peoples; as a "concrete universal," the people correspond to the *universalization* of human self-consciousness and the activity and deeds which follow from this revolutionary beginning (Marcuse 1987: 274, 295–296). Practically, Marcuse's vision here is of an anarchic, popular reconstruction of world history, one that radically inverts the indifference and hostility evinced by hegemonic power to life. In this way, Marcuse is abstractly suggesting an image which corresponds to the very antithesis of centralization of power represented by the historical example of Napoleon Bonaparte, the "universal individual" whom Hegel would hail as the harbinger of political reason in his mature, conservative years.

Toward the end of *Hegel's Ontology*, Marcuse acknowledges that his unconventional interpretations of Hegel remain anticipatory, noting human liberation to be but a hope—something which Kant might term a "regulatory order of reason," or a motivating vision—that has "not yet 'expanded to become existence'" (Marcuse 1987: 276). Channelling the younger rather than the older Hegel, Marcuse makes the following hopeful declaration on the anti-authoritarian realization of reason—a radical historical goal that will inspire him to press on amidst the various political and philosophical difficulties he will soon come to confront:

So long as Spirit still appears in time, through the real distinctions of past, present, and future, it is still *on its way* to reaching its true self and its true end. *It has not yet completely displayed and brought itself forth.* What it has been and what it will become are not yet a fully realized present. So long as it is still in time, it must still 'enrich' itself, for *there is always something more which 'it must realize and manifest,'* and which is 'at first only inward,' and which has not yet been brought forth and displayed.

MARCUSE 1987: 304; emphasis added

Hitler's Accession and Flight of the Marcuse Family and the Frankfurt School

Hegel's Ontology appeared in December 1932, the same month Marcuse fled with Sophie and Peter to Geneva, Switzerland, just days before the outright Nazi takeover of January 1933. In Geneva, Marcuse worked as a new member of the Frankfurt-based *Institut für Sozialforschung,* or Institute for Social Research, whose other affiliates, as radical German intellectuals, were similarly trying to escape Germany (Miles 2012: 43). In 1931, foreseeing the darkness of fascism, Institute Director Max Horkheimer perspicaciously had decided to transfer the Institute's capital endowment abroad and, with the help of Albert Thomas, director of the International Labor Organization (ILO), founded a Geneva satellite branch (Jay 1973: 26, 29). Marcuse had been recommended to the Institute on the word of Husserl, one of his dissertation examiners, and that of Kurt Riezler, the *Kurator* of the University of Freiburg; moreover, Adorno authored a positive review of *Hegel's Ontology* for the first issue of the Institute's *Zeitschrift für Sozialforschung* (*Journal for Social Research*), finding it to represent a decisive departure from Heidegger and the start of what Kātz terms a "decisive and promising revision" of Hegel's thought (Marcuse 1987: x, xxxi; Jay 1973: 28; Kātz 1982: 84). The combination of praise from Husserl, Riezler, and Adorno led Horkheimer to have Institute psychologist Leo Löwenthal interview Marcuse for possible membership. With Löwenthal's recommendation following that meeting, Horkheimer enthusiastically invited Marcuse to become an official affiliate of the Institute (Marcuse 1987: x; Miles 2012: 43). Nevertheless, as can be imagined, the survival of the Institute and its constituent members came to be radically threatened with the coming of Nazism: its offices were searched by the SA in March 1933, and its Frankfurt center officially shuttered that July, on the charge of anti-State activities (Miles 2012: 43).

As Miles and Jay explain, most of the Institute's members had fled the country by the time the Nazi police physically invaded the Institute, an incident which was followed a month later by the passing of the Act for Reform of the Civil Service, which resulted in the purging of thousands of Jewish and left-wing academics from public positions in Germany (Miles 2012: 43, 50). It was in fact by means of this law that Horkheimer was fired from his position as lecturer at the University of Frankfurt in April, along with Paul Tillich, Karl Mannheim, and numerous others (Jay 1973: 29). After spending a year in Geneva, Marcuse moved with Horkheimer in 1934 to New York, where the Institute had been invited to transfer its operations as an affiliate of Columbia University, based in a house located on West 117th Street in Manhattan (Jay 1973: 39; Marcuse et al. 1978/9: 129).[5] According to Mackey and Kellner, upon arrival in New York, Marcuse immediately began the process of becoming a naturalized U.S. citizen, a status he was granted in 1940 (Mackey 2001: 317; Kellner 1984: 95). Adorno for his part remained in Germany until early 1934, when he traveled to Oxford to begin a four-year course of study at Merton College, after which he would cross the Atlantic with his wife Gretel to reach New York (Jay 1973: 29; Adorno and Benjamin 1999: 25–52, 227–231, 239n8). More saddening is the case of Benjamin, who fled to Paris within a year of the Nazi seizure of power, while his comrades in New York worked to organize safe passage for him; by summer 1940, just months before Benjamin's tragic end, they had investigated getting him an entry visa to the Dominican Republic and even arranged for him to be "len[t]" as a guest lecturer to the University of Havana so that he could at least be safe in Cuba (Adorno and Benjamin 1999: 23, 338–339).

During this period of membership with the Frankfurt School, Marcuse engaged in militant-collective investigation of German philosophy, working with Horkheimer to develop Critical Theory and philosophically undermine the Nazi regime. His official association with the Institute for Social Research would span the time of his flight from Germany until 1942, the year in which he began working in the field of "practical anti-fascism" by lending his intellect to the U.S. Office of Strategic Services (OSS), alongside his colleague and friend Franz Neumann.

---

5   The exact address was 429 West 117th St.

CHAPTER 3

Militant Theorizing in Resistance to Fascism, 1933–1945

[The victim of misery] should keep his [*sic*] senses awake for all humiliations inflicted upon him, and should discipline himself until his suffering
sets him no longer on the downward course of sadness but on the upward
path of revolt.

BENJAMIN 1974: 931

[T]here is no longer beauty or consolation except in the gaze falling on
horror, withstanding it, and in unalleviated consciousness of negativity
holding fast to the possibility of what is better.

ADORNO 2005: 25

The owl of Minerva spreads its wings only with the falling of the dusk.

HEGEL 1952 [1820]: 13

The month prior to the Nazi takeover of the country of Goethe, Hegel,
Feuerbach, and Marx, Herbert Marcuse fled with his wife Sophie and son
Peter to Switzerland. He worked in the Frankfurt School's satellite office in
Geneva until 1934, when he and his family emigrated to the United States,
settling initially in the city of New York. Marcuse was there to join most of
the remaining investigators associated with the Institute for Social Research,
for Director Horkheimer had arranged an *ad hoc* institutional affiliation
with Columbia University, which welcomed the newly relocated Frankfurt
School. The intellectual collective comprised of radical German exiles continued publishing the *Journal for Social Research* from New York, though their
decision initially to continue writing in German without translation arguably
limited their audience within their newfound setting, at least until the *Journal* began to be published in English after the start of World War II (Jay 1973:
114). During its years of sponsorship with Columbia University in New York,
the Institute focused its analyses primarily on the matter which was foremost
in the consciousness of its members: that is, the rise of fascism in their native
Germany.

© KONINKLIJKE BRILL NV, LEIDEN, 2016 | DOI 10.1163/9789004308701_004

Within this process, as Kātz remarks, the Institute's various personalities specialized in analyzing different aspects of Nazism: Franz Neumann, Otto Kirchheimer, and Friedrich Pollock investigated its legalistic and economic features, while Adorno, Löwenthal, and Fromm explored its "cultural and psychological" facets, with Marcuse examining fascism's (anti)philosophical basis. As this intellectual division of labor may suggest, it was primarily with Horkheimer and Adorno that Marcuse felt the greatest philosophical affinities, considering all his fellow German Marxist comrades in exile, yet it was with Neumann that Marcuse arguably developed the closest friendship (Kātz 1982: 91, 107). A more militant and committed leftist than many others in the Frankfurt School circle, Neumann had worked as an SPD-affiliated labor lawyer before his arrest by the Nazis and subsequent escape in spring 1933; fleeing to London, he studied and received a doctorate in political science at the London School of Economics (Franz Neumann Project 2006).

Marcuse's commitments over this time-period involved early collaborations in New York with Horkheimer toward the end of developing the bases and concerns of Critical Theory—the product of which would be Marcuse's "Philosophy and Critical Theory" (1937), published in the *Journal for Social Research* as a follow-up to Horkheimer's 1936 "Traditional and Critical Theory"— and his subsequent work with Neumann to directly investigate the politics, psychology, and ideology of the National Socialist regime. This latter commitment was an independent project the two undertook in the early 1940s, when the Institute faced mounting challenges—primarily political and financial— and as Marcuse and Neumann increasingly gravitated toward seeking employment with the U.S. government as a means of assisting more directly in the wartime mobilization against Nazism.

With the exception of Neumann, Löwenthal, and Pollock, this period of exile in the United States proved central in the development of the pessimism, doubt, and critical skepticism with which the Frankfurt School theorists would come to be associated in the main, even to this day. In an ironic turn of events—ironic, that is, because of Fromm's effective expulsion from the Institute circle by 1939 (Jay 1973: 98)—Adorno and Horkheimer believed German proletarians to have been entirely complicit with the rise and maintenance of Nazism, in keeping with Fromm's findings from a major 1931 study into the attitudes of workers in Weimar Germany, which anticipated that three-quarters of laborers would be neither strongly pro-Nazi nor strongly anti-authoritarian, but rather ambivalent or conformist in the event of a Nazi takeover (Fromm and Maccoby 1970: 24–30). The seemingly mass-appeal which National Socialism attracted, taken together with what they saw as the disquieting absence of significant resistance from workers' movements and from within the established German Left, constituted for Horkheimer and Adorno a shocking contradiction of Marx's vision of human emancipation, which was to be realized dialectically through proletarian struggle. Marcuse does not entirely embrace his colleagues' conclusions in this sense, for he still held out hope in his *Negations* essays (1934–1938) for the oppositional potential of the labor movement. Nonetheless, he too in this period increasingly came to regard the mechanistic and deterministic claims of an intrinsic revolutionary consciousness existing among the proletariat as highly flawed. As in the case of Horkheimer and Adorno, then, the traumatizing emergence of Fascism and the concomitant incapacity of workers to resist this horrendous trend would fundamentally influence the course of the remainder of Marcuse's life and work.

Within this negative context, Marcuse, Adorno, and Horkheimer would come to share the view that truth cannot be reduced to the thought and practice of the working classes, as Marxian theory might suggest. To hold fast to such a position as this would imply the death of all truth amidst this deeply reactionary period of history, marked by the suppression of proletarian revolts in Central Europe after WWI, Franco's Falangist attempt at overthrowing the Spanish Republic, Stalin's show-trials in Moscow, and Hitler's overt preparations for imperialist war (Kātz 1982: 96). For this reason, the dominant view among the Frankurt School theorists came to be that theory should be considered a resting-place for truth, until such future time as when political truth could be taken up again by an insurgent proletariat, or an intervening "self-conscious global subject" (Adorno 1989: 85). During and after the war, Marcuse, like Adorno and Horkheimer, would continuously cast doubt on the revolutionary potential of the Western proletariat, given his view of the great similitude shared by German Fascism and the monopoly capitalism which increasingly dominated many other Western settings, especially U.S. society.

In this sense, the Institute refugee-intellectuals' commitment to Marxism came into dialectical conflict with the political realities of their newfound host society; Adorno and Horkheimer themselves first wrote about the "culture industry" as a response to mainstream U.S. society in *Dialectic of Enlightenment* (1944/1947). Seeking not to alienate Columbia University and State authorities, Horkheimer repeatedly rejected Ernst Bloch's overtures to integrate with the Institute—leading Bloch's monumental three-volume *Principle of Hope* to be written in isolation in the libraries of New York, from 1938 to 1947 (with the first volume published in 1954)—and worked with translator Hans Klaus Brill to censor the French translation of Benjamin's "The Work of Art in an Age of Technological Reproduction" (1936) for its publication in the *Journal for Social Research*. The French "translation" of this essay lacks the original German references to Marx, as well as all other political references, such that "all explicit revolutionary language [was] expurgated" (Leslie 2000: 130–131). The militant conclusion Benjamin proffers in this essay—that, amidst an apocalyptic scenario wherein Fascism renders aesthetic humanity's profound self-alienation, leading the species to anticipate its own destruction as aesthetic pleasure, international communism must "respon[d] by politicizing art"—may well have scandalized Horkheimer, and particularly his sponsors at Columbia (Miles 2012: 67; Benjamin 2003). Benjamin, for his part, communicated to Horkheimer that the changes had irrevocably marred the text, in a parallel to the disappointment he expressed to Gershom Scholem after the Institute editors had similarly revised his 1933 essay on the position of the French writer, considering the various disfigurements for which they were responsible: he even sees reflected in the Institute's editorial policies Fascism's advance over Europe. Also for his 1939 piece on Charles Baudelaire, Horkheimer and company deleted the opening section that discusses Marx's interpretation of revolutionary conspiracies, proletarian upheaval on the barricades, and Louis-Auguste Blanqui (Leslie 2000: 131).

In any case, the wartime experiences of the exiles who found refuge in New York diverged greatly from those of Benjamin, who remained in France under precarious conditions, being forcibly transferred to the Nièvre internment camp by the Vichy authorities shortly after the outbreak of war. Yet thanks to the intercession of Adrienne Monnier, a friend of the poet Paul Valéry, Benjamin was released from this internment. He thereafter returned to Paris to compose his famous eighteen theses "On the Concept of History" (Buck-Morss 1977: 162–163). However, as the French defense failed before the onslaught of Hitler's *Wehrmacht* in May 1940 and the Gestapo seized Benjamin's apartment shortly after German forces occupied Paris, the critical theorist fled south to Lourdes with his sister, and two months later was granted an emergency entry visa to the U.S., thanks to Pollock's intervention (Jay 1973: 197–198). Benjamin had less success obtaining an exit visa from France—such that he joined a small group of refugees guided by Resistance activist Lisa Fittko who sought to enter Spain surreptitiously in late September by scaling the mountainous Pyrenees border: the idea was to cross Spain, reach Lisbon, and traverse the Atlantic to rejoin his comrades in New York. Due to a heart condition, though, Benjamin had great difficulties in completing the journey; during the night of their attempted crossing on 25 September, in fact, he remained all alone in a meadow as the others proceeded with their descent, because he could not keep up with them. The travelers regrouped the next morning and proceeded to the Spanish bordertown of Port-Bou, where they were met with hostility by Franco's police, who announced that just the previous day, orders had come from Madrid stipulating that no one could enter Spain without possessing the proper French exit papers (Fittko 1999: 948–949, 953). Terrified by the prospect of being handed over to the Gestapo directly by the Spanish Fascists, Benjamin, then holed up in a Port-Bou hotel, took a lethal overdose of the morphine he had been carrying with him, and died the next morning (Jay 1973: 198). True pathos grips his suicide letter, which he addressed partly to Adorno:

> In a situation presenting no way out, I have no other choice but to make an end of it. It is in a small village in the Pyrenees, where no one knows me, that my life will come to a close. I ask you to transmit my thoughts to my friend Adorno and to explain to him the situation in which I find myself. There is not enough time remaining for me to write all the letters I would like to write.
>
> FITTKO 1999: 946

As Susan Buck-Morss writes, Benjamin's end represented for his shocked Frankfurt colleagues a "tragic allegory of the contradictions inherent in the historical present": "The war, the horrors committed against Jews in Germany, the loneliness of emigration, combined with the dissipation of potential for revolution, were all expressed in Benjamin's gesture of suicide" (1977: 165).

In part as a reaction to Benjamin's death, and in part due to worsening conflicts with Columbia, Horkheimer left New York with Adorno to relocate to the West Coast in early 1941, settling in the Pacific Palisades suburb of Santa Monica, California. Horkheimer explained the move as being necessary for his health, as based on the advice provided by his U.S. doctors after they had diagnosed him with a mild cardiovascular condition, though Marcuse adds that the Institute director also feared the specter of an ascendant fascism in the U.S. would endanger the work of the School, in a repetition of history (Jay 1973: 172; Marcuse et al. 1978/9: 130).

Expressing their political commitments in a way that differed radically from the fate of their comrade Benjamin and that of millions of other fellow European Jews, yet that also commemorated their martyrdom, Horkheimer and Adorno collaborated in California on writing *Dialectic of Enlightenment: Philosophical Fragments,* just as Hitler's fortunes in the war began to reverse. Tellingly, the *Dialectic*'s original publication with the Social Studies Association in 1944 contains several formulations which openly repudiate capitalist society, whereas the work's subsequent reprint in 1947 shows considerable revision of many such claims: for example, mention of the mass-lynchings carried out contemporarily in the U.S. South is removed in the second edition, and the 1947 version often inserts "existing society" or "existing order" for what originally had been named as class society, liberalism, or capitalism (Horkheimer and Adorno 2002: 272–273). Such changes, indeed, are reminiscent of the previous revisions performed in the interests of the Institute's public relations. Whether such inauthentic moves on Adorno and Horkheimer's part reflect pragmatism in terms of adjusting to U.S. society or signal a right-wing shift in their philosophy is a matter of speculation (Miles 2012: 68). Either possibility anticipates the wholesale endorsement Horkheimer would make of Western capitalism and its imperial devastation of Vietnam in the tumultuous 1960s.

Speculation aside, it remains a fact that the Institute began to face worsening financial difficulties in the late 1930s and early 1940s, as Horkheimer dedicated increasingly more of the Institute's funds to providing for German refugees. Significantly, Fromm left the Institute in 1939 to establish his own psychotherapeutic practice, while Adorno worked part-time at Princeton University at the "Radio Research Project" and Kirchheimer joined the Office of Strategic Services (OSS) (Jay 1973: 98–102, 167–169). Fromm's departure from the Institute, though, was not due to purely economic constraints: as Marcuse explains in his 1978 conversation with Habermas, Fromm became increasingly unwelcome in the Institute's circle after his so-called "castration" of Freudian theory, which amounted to his unorthodox rejection of Freud's libido and late instinct theories, as set forth in *Escape from Freedom* (1941) (Marcuse et al. 1978/9: 127). This break with Fromm would reverberate for decades, particularly as manifested in the acrimonious public debate Marcuse initiated against the critical psychologist in *Eros and Civilization* (1955), wherein he falsely accuses Fromm the neo-Freudian "revisionist" of advancing adjustment to bourgeois society. Fromm would prove to be more than capable of defending himself against such charges, though, as we shall see.[1]

While at the Institute in New York, Marcuse composed the magnificent *Reason and Revolution: Hegel and the Rise of Social Theory* (1941), which powerfully demonstrates the vicissitudes of the Hegelian dialectic: its emergence as a continuation of the radical French Enlightenment and Revolution and its subsequent development in Marx's thought on one side, and the reactionary counter-movement which it provoked among apologists for feudalism and aristocratic Restoration on the other. One of Marcuse's main objectives in *Reason and Revolution* is to denounce the ideology promoted by the reformist

---

1   See the next chapter.

intellectuals associated with the Second International that sought to down-play the deep affinities between Marx and Hegel.[2] Yet perhaps an even grander point which Marcuse wishes to make in *Reason and Revolution* is simply to show that Hegel should in no way be considered a philosophical predeces-sor of fascism in Germany—with this being a claim that apparently had held some sway over Marcuse's contemporaries in the Anglo-American world. In this masterful work, Marcuse credits Hegel for inspiring Marx's emancipatory communist vision, and he gives due consideration to Hegel's early political philosophy, focusing especially on its critical, negative, and subversive mean-ing. No uncritical student himself, Marcuse condemns Hegel's inauthentic and conservative mature political philosophy, describing it as a betrayal of his previous radicalism.

Marcuse's major success in having *Reason and Revolution* published con-verged in time with the financial difficulties faced by the Institute, pushing the development of his philosophical system in more autonomous directions. Another practical factor contributing to this dynamic would seem to have been a crucial miscommunication between Marcuse and Horkheimer. After moving to Los Angeles and considerably reducing his responsibilities at the Institute, Horkheimer contemplated writing a new book, and invited Marcuse to join him and Adorno in southern California to assist in this project. Having followed this advice and moved there in 1942, the Marcuse family—now relocated to Santa Monica—met the unexpected result that Horkheimer had chosen Adorno instead of Marcuse for the role of principal writing partner. It was for this reason that it was Adorno rather than Marcuse who co-authored *Dialectic of Enlightenment* with Horkheimer.[3]

The disappointment implied by this turn of events led Marcuse to forge closer ties with Neumann, and the two began increasingly to collaborate together independently from the Institute, producing direct studies of National Socialism and manuscripts on theories of social change. The various issues gripping the Institute at this time also likely contributed to the decision taken by these two to explore the prospect of joining the U.S. government's war effort against Hitler. In this sense, in a serendipitous parallel to Adorno's positive review of Marcuse's study on Hegel's ontology the previous decade, Marcuse's submission of his studies on the "New German Mentality," "Private Morale in Germany," and "The Elimination of German Chauvinism" to U.S.

---

2 One thinks of Eduard Bernstein, particularly the incrementalism he expresses in *The Precon-ditions of Socialism* (1899).

3 One can speculate as how to the work would have been different, had Marcuse been Horkheimer's co-author.

authorities proved crucial in their acceptance of his application for employment with the Office of War Information and his subsequent tenure with the Office of Strategic Services (OSS) (Marcuse 1998: 18; Mackey 2001: 320). Neumann had already been recruited to the U.S. Board of Economic Warfare in 1941, and went on to work as an economist of Intelligence for the U.S. Chief of Staff the subsequent year, and then joined the OSS as deputy chief director for Central Europe in 1943 (Franz Neumann Project 2006).

Critically, Neumann at this time authored *Behemoth*, an expansive study of the *Structure and Practice of National Socialism* (1944), which claimed the new regime to represent the joint efforts of large industrial business interests, the military, and the Nazi Party bureaucracy. Neumann did not want to claim the totality of German society to have been corrupted by Nazism, such that he held a more hopeful dialectical vision of the revolutionary potential of the oppressed German masses, as compared to the assessments Adorno and Horkheimer had made. Besides his work for the U.S. government and his contributions to a Marxist understanding of Nazism, Neumann supervised Raul Hilberg in his doctoral research regarding the *Destruction of the European Jews*, a three-volume work that was published in 1961, some years after Neuman's death. Marcuse, for his part, worked at the OSS mainly in researching the Nazi regime, which he considered little more than a "cheap gangster melodrama," and he analyzed German media and propaganda, in addition to providing frameworks for understanding Nazi ideology (Mackey 2001: 320; Marcuse 2001: 169). Furthermore, his research team examined the morale of German society, as subjected to National Socialism, and it periodically would present recommendations for methods of psychological warfare to be used against the dictatorship. Sophie Marcuse also contributed in a manner similar to Herbert, offering her knowledge of statistics to U.S. Naval Intelligence, in addition to her work at this time in statistics for the Bureaus of Human Nutrition and Home Economics (Mackey 2001: 320).

Against observers who would see in Marcuse and Neumann's work for U.S. intelligence a highly inauthentic move—as Jay writes, "[w]orking with the OSS and the State Department [later] was not precisely what the Frankfurt School had meant when it advocated revolutionary *praxis*," while in 1969, at the height of Marcuse's popularity, an anonymous article in *Progressive Labor* infamously presented the libelous charge that Marcuse had been working continuously as a government spy since his official departure from civil service in 1951—Kellner clarifies that the payroll of the OSS included a rather broad range of intellectuals, some of whom identified as leftists, and that its composition should not be confused with that of the post-war CIA, dominated as that State organ was by reactionary anti-communists and liberals (Jay 1973: 80; Marcuse 1998: 25).

In point of fact, in *Revolution or Reform?* (1972), Marcuse rejects critics' *ex post facto* condemnation of his work with the OSS, noting that they "seem to have forgotten that the war then was a war against fascism," and that "consequently, I haven't the slightest reason for being ashamed of having assisted in it" (Marcuse 1998: 25n40). He also clarifies that the OSS and CIA "fought like enemies" in the short period during which both agencies coexisted (Marcuse et al. 1978/9: 131). To give one example, the OSS cadre sought to support Ho Chi Minh in Vietnam, whereas the Cold Warriors of the CIA did not. Significantly, as well, it is clear that the U.S. foreign-policy establishment paid no heed to Marcuse and Neumann's vision for the application of broad-sweeping de-Nazification policies in Germany after 1945. As Marcuse observes in an interview from 1977, "[S]ome of the people we considered as primary economic and war criminals [in Germany] are today in some of the most powerful international positions" (Marcuse 2014: 430).

Thus we see that Marcuse's life in this tumultuous and desperate period was concerned principally with intervening to undermine the fascist plague and the capitalist superstructure which had given birth to it, both through militant research and public lectures, as well as through his ambiguously controversial anti-fascist work with the U.S. government. Far from being abstract, the realities of fascism were patently evident to Marcuse and the rest of the members of the Frankfurt School circle: from London, Marcuse's brother Erich had only barely succeeded in extracting his wife and parents from Germany, this in March 1939, "at the last possible moment"; the remainder of the members of the Marcuse family were murdered in Theresienstadt (Kātz 1982: 105–106). In parallel, Marcuse's friend Benjamin succumbed to the fascist death-machine during his attempt to reach Lisbon and cross the Atlantic to be reunited with his comrades in New York. It is to the memory of the innumerable victims of Nazism that Marcuse's revolutionary fire spurred on his investigations and interventions at this time.

Negations (1934–1938)

Negations is a collection of the practical-theoretical investigations of radical philosophy and contemporary totalitarianism that Marcuse engaged in during his time with the exiled Frankfurt School. In these essays he wrote for the *Journal for Social Research*, Marcuse seeks to *negate* the fallen present, accomplishing this end by employing critical philosophical inquiry in a manner that is neither pessimistic nor entirely negative, but actually at times positive— a "negation of the negation" represented by Fascism. In the 1968 preface to the republication of these journal articles, Marcuse notes that each one was inspired by the contemporary possibilities for class struggle and the advancement of materialism and Marxism. The critical theorist observes that, at the time of their writing, the *Negations* essays spoke to his hope that the fall of Nazism would "make possible a more human and more rational society" (Marcuse 1968: xi). The hopes which pervade *Negations*—with the uncharacteristic exception of the anomalous 1937 analysis of "The Affirmative Character of Culture"—speak to the resilience and vitality of Marcuse's philosophy, and its unending desire for "happiness and affirmation," in the words of W. Mark Cobb (2004: 178). In opposition to the closing off of the struggles of "freedom, solidarity, and humanity" expressed and ultimately suppressed in the Spanish Civil War, as juxtaposed with the entrenchment of Fascism in Italy and Germany and Stalin's purges in Moscow, the writings of *Negations* communicate Marcuse's commitment to the subversive view, as he explains in the preface, that "thought in contradiction must become more negative and more utopian in opposition to the status quo" (Marcuse 1968: xx).

The essays which make up *Negations* will here be presented in the chronological order by which they appeared in the *Journal for Social Research*, rather than grouped according to subject, which varies among them. On two occasions below will Marcuse's writings from later in the pre-WWII period be used like mortar to help elucidate his argumentation: in his *Negations* essay denouncing liberalism, as in his *Study on Authority*.

Adorned with a notably self-explanatory title, "The Struggle against Liberalism in the Totalitarian View of the State" (1934) presents Marcuse's interpretation of the historical turn to Fascism as being intimately related to the pre-existing domination of society by the bourgeois class. The work provocatively elucidates the commonly held view among the Frankfurt School intellectuals that "totalitarian violence and totalitarian reason came from the structure of existing society" (Marcuse 1968: xi–xii). Against more mainstream accounts of Nazism that claim it to have been an anti-capitalist movement, Marcuse argues that National Socialism represents a regimentation of liberal capitalism: for him, Fascism constitutes an intensification of already existing repressive trends that succeeded in organizing German society entirely in the interests of large industry. Hitler's populist invective casting Germany as a "proletarian nation" combating global "plutocratic" control is thus for Marcuse pure ideology (Marcuse 2001: 166).

Liberal-capitalist thought already contains within it justifications for dictatorship and war, argues Marcuse, with bourgeois philosophers giving their assent to the State's resort to highly authoritarian methods of suppressing proletarian forms of agitation that might threaten the stability of class society. Besides, it should be obvious to any observer that liberalism effectively sides with Fascism against the specter of "Marxian socialism"; what is more, the similarities between the two political philosophies are seen in the fact that the total-authoritarian State organizes its basic social institutions around private property and the entrepreneurial initiative of capitalists. Marcuse here links the fascist emphasis on submission to a *Duce* or *Führer* with the previous liberal celebration of the "gifted economic leader, the 'born' executive." In light of these considerations, Marcuse concludes that the shift "from the liberalist to the total-authoritarian state occurs within the framework of a single social order." On this account, then, the transition from "free" to monopoly capitalism is no deviation or distortion of liberal theory, but instead marks the passing of the market economy to a "more advanced stage," that of the Fascist State. Hence, Marcuse holds, liberalism "'produces' the total-authoritarian state out of itself" (1968: 9–11, 18–19).

In philosophical terms, Marcuse sees the rise of Fascism as aided along principally by liberal and openly irrationalist ideologies—with liberalism itself to be viewed as one such irrational mode of thought. Against the revolutionary promise of critical-materialist philosophy, which holds human beings to be capable of employing reason toward the end of restructuring society and so universally realizing human potential, Fascism mobilizes "mythical-organic" approaches which invariably bind philosophy to the acceptance of the "natural" order of hierarchy and violence. It is here that liberalism serves Fascism most blatantly: its essentially positivist orientation which equates "natural balance" with an "accidental 'harmony'" leaves the "structure and order" of global society to be determined by the existing "irrational forces" (Marcuse 1968: 6, 15, 18). Like Benjamin, who denounces the German Social Democrats in his "Theses on the Concept of History" for conceiving of historical progress as "unending" and "essentially unstoppable," Marcuse criticizes liberal optimists for bearing considerable responsibility for Hitler's ascendancy (Benjamin 2003: 394–395). Thus, in its marshaling of reactionary naturalism against the specter of reason, fascist-capitalism advances a false liberation, one which "sets loose all irrational powers" to do battle against the specter of true freedom. It is in his reflective conclusion regarding this distressing manifestation of total domination by capital that Marcuse first calls into question the "fate of the labor movement," by gloomily noting it to be "clouded with uncertainty" (Marcuse 1968: 23, 42).

A more philosophical and less practical intervention than the "Struggle against Liberalism," Marcuse's 1936 essay on the "Concept of Essence" continues his previous work to develop an existentialist-Hegelian interpretation of Marx. As such, it is reminiscent of Marcuse's earlier period of study with Heidegger. Marcuse begins by describing the arc of philosophical notions of human autonomy, beginning controversially enough with René Descartes, who is well-known for having equated the realization of human essence—to be achieved by the exercise of scientific investigation—with the manipulation and control of nature. Though Marcuse's early treatment of Cartesianism here is highly uncritical and hence unbecoming of his later thoughts on nature and ecology, his subsequent examination of Kant in this piece provides space for him to assert his libertarian conception of the essential bonds which must exist between the exercise of reason and freedom: "since it is from reason that every improvement of which our condition is capable must spring, freedom is its original right 'and may not be restricted.'" In an egalitarian sense, Kantian autonomy is equally available to all reason-bearing humans: similar in a way to Hegel's later concept of the *Geist*, "each [person] has a voice" in the historical exercise of reason—or at least, everyone has the potential to (Marcuse 1968: 47, 53).

Shifting to the contemporary situation, however, Marcuse laments that autonomous thought and *Dasein* have been largely eclipsed by their opposite, heteronomy and *Das Man*, in accordance with the interests of monopoly capital: "the world of 'absolutely real' facts is dominated by powers concerned with the preservation of this form of reality, in the interest of small and powerful economic groups, against the already real possibility of another form of reality." It is this difference to be overcome, "the tension between essence and appearance," which drives corrective left-wing action, or "universal social contradiction"; as in "On Concrete Philosophy," Marcuse posits an activist desire as stemming from consciousness, asserting that "the incongruity of potentiality and actuality incites knowledge to become part of the practice of transformation." Here, Marcuse warns against holding to positivist notions of action when considering the concept of human essence, given the highly disingenuous nature of the practice of equating observed behavior with the full exercise of human potential. As an alternative, he advances a dialectical-materialist understanding of the problem of essence, which would consider this to be a concept that is indelibly associated with historical development, hence a category which can be "transformed in this life by real [persons]." With this claim, Marcuse is assuredly reiterating his dissatisfaction with Heidegger's static notion of *Dasein*. Developing a line of thought he will explore more at length in *Reason and Revolution* (1941), Marcuse here posits the problem of human essence—potentiality, or becoming—as best helped along by philosophical materialism, which defends reason and freedom through its demand for revolutionary social changes that would allow "individuals' fate [to] depen[d] no longer on chance and the blind necessity of uncontrolled economic relationships" (Marcuse 1968: 63, 66, 69, 77). In terms of his outlook

on the fate of revolutionary struggles to realize human essence, Marcuse here
expresses a significant degree of optimism; he declares boldly that "[t]he
immemorially acquired image of essence was formed in [humanity's] historical
experience [...]":

> All historical struggles for a better organization of the impoverished con-
> ditions of existence, as well as all of suffering [humanity's] religious and
> ethical ideal conceptions of a more just order of things, are preserved in
> the dialectical concept of the essence of [humanity], where they have
> become elements of the historical practice linked to dialectical theory.
>
> MARCUSE 1968: 75

Indeed, on Marcuse's account, the dialectical concept of human essence—the
gap between reality and potentiality within the ever-dynamic movement of
historical development—corresponds to the highest dreams of human historical experience, as the dialectic necessarily must illuminate the depths of
contemporary negativity and then pass to the chance for its inversion: "The
content of reality [is] in a 'bad' form; it is possible that its emancipation from
this form and its realization in a new form are still to be accomplished through
[human] social practice" (Marcuse 1968: 83).

Separate from the "Struggle against Liberalism" and "The Concept of
Essence," Marcuse's 1937 essay "Philosophy and Critical Theory" distinguishes itself as a contribution to the ongoing conversations among the members
of the Frankfurt School regarding the very meaning of critical thought and
inquiry. In this sense, as stated above, it is a response to Horkheimer's 1936
address "Traditional and Critical Theory," which essentially delineated the new
director's vision for materialist social research at the Institute.

Marcuse opens his reflections on the Frankfurt School's mission by identifying two reasons why philosophical materialism should be considered "correct
social theory": firstly, due to its "concern" for "human happiness," and secondly
owing to its associated emphasis on the idea that generalized happiness can
be achieved only through social transformation of "the material conditions of
existence." According to Marcuse, materialist propositions regarding the history and destiny of humanity—ones that make central the struggle of reason
to bring about a "rational organization of society"—retain a universal character. In point of fact, he identifies the "progressive impetus" of the principal
materialist assumptions on human nature—that humanity is "a rational being,
that this being requires freedom, and that happiness is [her] highest good"—
as emanating "precisely" due to their universality. Reason, in this sense, does
not serve to legitimize existing social relations, but instead seeks to subvert

them radically; it is for this reason that Marcuse conceives of reason as a "critical tribunal" that can condemn existing society in favor of an emancipated future one. For Marcuse, materialism advocates universal social revolution in its "claim that all, and not merely this or that particular person, should be rational, free, and happy" (Marcuse 1968: 135–136, 152).

In practical terms, Marcuse's philosophical formulations on reason do not lend themselves to the mainstream Communist support for the Soviet Union, as seen throughout much of the rest of Europe at this time—a critical support which Horkheimer would express in his diaries at this time, as recorded in *Dawn & Decline* (1978: 72–73). Though Marcuse does not explicitly clarify the regime he is criticizing with the following quote, his intended target should be obvious: "Without freedom and happiness in the social relations of [humanity], even the greatest increase of production and the abolition of private property in the means of production remain infected with the old injustice." On the other hand, Marcuse's philosophical stance strongly repudiates all types of apologism for capitalism. In "Philosophy and Critical Theory," he denounces positivism as serving a highly obfuscatory role by "equating human potentialities with those that are real within the established order" (Marcuse 1968: 144–147).

Marcuse closes these reflections by contemplating philosophy's role in bridging the gap between prevailing negativity and the future prospect of "general human relations" within a post-capitalist, stateless set of conditions. He asserts forthrightly that "conceptual thought" alone cannot accomplish this goal, and that "phantasy," or imagination, is required, as Aristotle and Kant stressed. It is phantasy, Marcuse writes, that can break the historical weight of the past within the present, thus preventing the future from being reduced to a conception of little more than an endless repetition of existing fallenness. In spite of the praise he has for the revolutionary role of the human imagination, though, Marcuse is wont to assert that neither the intellectual function of reason nor phantasy can change the world by themselves, for the "construction of the new society" is to be the product of the "the free creation of the liberated individuals" (Marcuse 1968: 135, 154–157).

In the exceptionally negative essay on "The Affirmative Character of Culture" (1937)—one that greatly conflicts with much of Marcuse's previous and future commentary on the social functions of art—Marcuse severely denounces bourgeois cultural norms in general, labeling them generally as having an "affirmative character" that facilitated the coming of Fascism. In advancing the Idealist vision of a "universally obligatory, eternally better and more valuable world that must be unconditionally affirmed," capitalist ideology claims that a better life can be attained "without any transformation of the state of fact."

That "so little trouble" was evinced by the German masses marching "in the communal columns of the authoritarian state" speaks to their colonization by ideologies legitimizing totalitarianism, with affirmative culture principal among these, on Marcuse's account (1968: 95, 125).

Analyzing the historical trajectory of affirmative culture, Marcuse commences by disclosing his view of the early bourgeois period as a relatively progressive historical epoch, amidst the struggle of the middle classes against the "divinely instituted eternity of a restrictive order"—despotism, monarchy, and feudalism. However, as is painfully well-known, the class domination exercised by the newly hegemonic bourgeoisie following its victories over medieval Europe profoundly restricted the realization of the Idealist notions of freedom and reason for the majority of humankind. Subversively, Marcuse notes that bourgeois art generally counterposes "suffering and sorrow" to the "luminous colors of this world," thus dialectically offering visions of life beyond capital— ones experienced in the exercise of the imagination and "anticipatory memory." He claims the Idealist tradition to be "more progressive" than the liberal positivism which it provoked as a counter-reaction among dominant circles, for the former held capitalist society not to be "the last word" in the historical process, insisting instead that humanity "must be led beyond it," as through the materialist methods Marx identified in his critical engagement with the Idealist philosophical tradition. Yet the promise of dialectical-materialist methods are in Marcuse's view largely inhibited by the actual function of art within monopoly capitalism: "the beauty of art is compatible with the bad present, despite and within which it can afford happiness." Differently than theory, which "recognizes the misery and lack of happiness" in existing society but "offers no consolation that reconciles one to the present," the happiness produced by contemplation of beauty and art for Marcuse here amounts to a sort of "consolation" within "an interminable chain of misfortune." The critical theorist declares boldly: *"By exhibiting the beautiful as present, art pacifies rebellious desire"* (Marcuse 1968: 98–100, 116, 118, 121; emphasis added).

The stipulated utopian function of art is thus strongly rejected in "The Affirmative Character of Culture" in favor of an anxiety regarding art's putative function as an effective *anesthetic* (Miles 2012: 54). Marcuse claims the affirmativeness of bourgeois art to have been central in the process of disciplining society into "tolerat[ing] the unfreedom of social existence" under capital:

> It took a centuries-long education to help make bearable the daily reproduced shock that arises from the contradiction between the constant sermon of the inalienable freedom, majesty, and dignity of the person, the magnificence and autonomy of reason, the goodness of humanity

and of impartial charity and justice, on the one hand, and the general degradation of the majority of [humankind], the irrationality of the social life process, the victory of the labor market over humanity, and of profit over charity, on the other.

MARCUSE 1968: 121–122

The reign of affirmative culture, like that of bourgeois power, is reminiscent of bodily death, or the negation of mind: subject to its dominion, people generally "can feel themselves happy even without being so at all." Yet now comes the positive movement of the dialectic: the legitimational constellation of delusion notwithstanding, the very real unhappiness and oppression suffered by the world's majorities are not "metaphysical," Marcuse claims, but rather "the product[s] of an irrational social organization," one whose end could be catalyzed by the elimination of affirmative expressions of culture. Implicitly invoking Fourier's spirit, Marcuse imagines a future society wherein "it becomes possible to have real enjoyment without any rationalization and without the least puritanical guilt feeling, when sensuality, in other words, is entirely released by the soul": romantically, then, the lived will to happiness represents the very "first glimmer of a new culture." Materially, Marcuse writes that "[b]eauty will find a new embodiment when it no longer is represented as real illusion but, instead, expresses reality and joy in reality." He mentions "the unassuming display of Greek statues" and "the music of Mozart or late Beethoven" as examples he conceives of as being illustrations of this dialectical vision—thus recalling Schiller. To his critics, and to those who would criticize the general struggle for social emancipation as inevitably leading to a regimented collective mass, Marcuse anticipates that the "abolition" of the irrationalities of capitalism "will not eliminate individuality, but [instead] realize it" (1968: 116–117, 122, 131, 133).

Continuing his investigations into some of the lines examined in "The Affirmative Character of Culture," Marcuse in his study "On Hedonism" (1938) explores this ancient Greek philosophy as a critical trend that resists Hegel's sobering evaluation of the world's political state, made in the *Philosophy of History:* "History is not the stage of happiness. Periods of happiness are blank pages in it." Marcuse here acknowledges the course of the world (*Weltlauf*), the movement of world history, to carry on "against the happiness of individuals," without any sort of regard for their interests—thus, it appears as the "monstrous Calvary of the spirit." In contradiction to such realities, Marcuse identifies a sense of promise in hedonistic philosophies, which call on humanity to "enjoy [its] existence without sinning against [its] essence, without guilt and shame": foreshadowing his later interest in Freud and his writing of *Eros and Civilization*, Marcuse here declares that humanity's "sensual and sensuous potentialities and needs, too, should find satisfaction" (Marcuse 1968: 160, 162; Schoolman 1980: 82).

Marcuse sees hedonism as a protest against philosophical and societal approaches that seek to internalize and privatize considerations of human happiness, or accept as inevitable the "unfreedom" of existing relations altogether. As against class inequalities and the threat of alienated labor, hedonism "advocates happiness equally for all individuals." Indeed, Marcuse contrasts instrumental reason—which prioritizes "the development of the productive forces, the free rational shaping of the conditions of life, the domination of nature, and the critical autonomy of the associated individuals"—with hedonistic philosophies, which instead call for "the comprehensive unfolding and fulfillment of individual wants and needs, emancipation from an inhuman labor process, and liberation of the world for the purposes of enjoyment." In reflecting on the historical origins of hedonism, marred as they were by the slave economies of antiquity, Marcuse notes that this school of thought arose within a social context that conceptually separated the spheres of labor and happiness entirely, holding them to "belong to different modes of existence." In sum, Marcuse finds hedonism to be a philosophy which "rebels often enough" against social orders that uphold "injustice" and "misery"; the critical theorist writes with enthusiasm of the future possibility that hedonism could be taken up by mass social movements, which then would come "scarcely [to] tolerate unfreedom and would be made completely unsuited for heroic domestication" (Marcuse 1968: 162, 166–168, 172). Such a compelling vision of reason, pleasure, and revolutionary social movements will remain central to Marcuse's thought and life, as we shall see.

Despite the general positive regard with which he regards hedonism, Marcuse clarifies that not all of its associated currents carry the same potential for liberation. Some hedonistic tendencies merely take the "wants and interests" of people in general as "simply given" and "as valuable in themselves," argues Marcuse, to the detriment of analyzing the various means by which class society and hierarchy may distort truth from falsity. Such a perspective on the part of some hedonists constitutes a significant lapse for Marcuse, in light of his sense that "unfreedom is already operative in the needs and wants themselves" of people subjected to the capitalist system—a thought he goes on to develop more systematically in *One-Dimensional Man* (1964).[4] Dialectically, and thus delineating a repudiation of his previous thought on "The Affirmative Character of Culture," Marcuse asserts that an overall increase in the pleasure

---

4   See Chapter 5 below.

felt by the individual—a generalized societal application of hedonism—would "immediately" better the chances for her future liberation, as long as such enjoyment not revel in the "false pleasures" of contemporary society, as in "the abasement of another as well as self-abasement under a stronger will," "meaningless sacrifices," or "the heroism of war" (Marcuse 1968: 168, 183, 190).

In anticipation of a marked political tendency that would recur in his future works, as was already seen in "The Affirmative Character of Culture," Marcuse here vacillates greatly between his concern about the standardizing and legitimizing functions of happiness and social adjustment and the utopian and subversive views he would take of art and pleasure. The following declaration may indicate which of the two he holds more closely in the time after "The Affirmative Character of Culture":

> That there is any happiness at all in a society governed by blind laws is a blessing. Through this happiness, the individual in this society can feel secure and protected from ultimate desperation.
>
> MARCUSE 1968: 191; emphasis added

The remarkable utopianism evident in these lines notwithstanding, Marcuse also makes the following claims while thinking of Hitler's rise, in an expansion of the criticism he had previously made of the tendency of some hedonists to be unwilling to subject the expression of desire and interest to critical evaluation—thereby inviting the critiques that have been made of the anti-democratic tendencies of aspects of Marcusean thought:

> It appears that individuals raised to be integrated into the antagonistic labor process cannot be judges of their own happiness. They have been prevented from knowing their true interest. Thus it is possible for them to designate their condition as happy and, without external compulsion, embrace the system that oppresses them. The results of modern plebiscites prove that [people] separated from possible truth can be brought to vote against themselves. As long as individuals see their interest only as getting along with the given order, such plebiscites pose no problems for the authoritarian apparatus. Terror merely supplements the delusions of the governed. Appeal to interest is untrue.
>
> MARCUSE 1968: 191–192

For Marcuse here, it is "in view of the historical possibility of general freedom" that "actual, really perceived happiness" can be designated as untrue, or as perpetuating societal falsity. In a manner reminiscent of Bakunin, Marcuse claims the "true interests of individuals" to be possible "only in conjunction" with freedom for all individuals. Making implicit reference to the Jacobins and Hegel, Marcuse briefly and abstractly discusses the prospect for the future popular self-management of society, or, as he terms it, the "rational self-administration of the whole in which the subject participates actively": the fall of authoritarian power is to allow for the unification of duty and happiness through autonomous action, or freedom. The "true interest[s]" which Marcuse holds will be evinced under conditions of popular self-management will include "militant solidarity," expanding firstly from one's particular social group, outward toward "the conditions of life of the whole" of human society. In this way, the "attainable form of happiness" can only be realized by the emancipation of those groups who will, like a radical cascade, assist in liberating others and thus realizing the "general liberation of humanity." Hence, in this early period of his life, when his revolutionary humanism predominated over the ecological concerns he would later develop, Marcuse comes to equate the "reality of happiness" principally with the "self-determination of liberated humanity" struggling in common against nature (1968: 192–195, 197, 199).

Studies on Authority and Family

Marcuse's contributions to the 1936 *Studies on Authority and Family* constitute an important gift of his to the body of knowledge being developed by the Frankfurt School in exile. Authored collaboratively among Marcuse, Horkheimer, Fromm, Hans Mayer, Karl Wittfogel, and Paul Honigsheim, the "Studies" in many ways anticipate the production by Adorno and company of *The Authoritarian Personality* (1950), the report summarizing the mass-psychological research Adorno and his colleagues would conduct on 2,000 white middle-class subjects in northern California. This later study crucially discusses the developmental and social-psychological factors that would seem to predispose individuals to prejudice, authoritarianism, and Fascism—that is, to name a few such factors, emotional coldness, manipulativeness, identification with power, conventionality, and hierarchical thinking, among others— and the authors counterpose a straightforward societal recommendation, as regards the project of raising new anti-fascist generations: "All that is really essential is that children be genuinely loved and treated as individual humans." Adorno and his colleagues stress, though, that the task of inhibiting the development of fascist character-types is akin to the problem of overcoming neurosis or nationalism, in that these all are "products of the total organization of society and are to be changed only as that society is changed" (Adorno et al. 1950: 975, 976). The authors of the study take solace in that most of their research subjects do not exhibit extreme ethnocentrism, and they conclude that Fascism is largely imposed by dominant power-groups, rather than represent any organic phenomenon. The corrupted form of *Dasein* that succumbs to Fascism is denied insofar as humans employ Logos and Eros.

> People are continuously molded from above because they must be molded if the over-all economic pattern is to be maintained, and the amount of energy that goes into this process bears a direct relation to the amount of potential, residing within the people, for moving in a different direction.
>
> ADORNO et al. 1950: 976

Marcuse's contribution to the collective "Studies," which focuses on the history of philosophy and repressiveness in German sociology, was separately published as *A Study on Authority* in the early 1970s. In practical terms, the *Study on Authority* continues the investigations Marcuse and the rest of his German Marxist colleagues had launched into the social bases of the rise of Nazism in their native home-country. It is to be surmised that Marcuse believed a critical presentation of the concept of authority as conceived by a number of key Western philosophers—Martin Luther and John Calvin, Kant, Hegel, Edmund Burke, Marx, Georges Sorel, and Vilfredo Pareto—could help to illuminate prevailing power relations, toward the end of subverting and ultimately overturning these and so making way for the realization of the liberatory vision of Hegel and Marx. In this way, *A Study on Authority* follows directly in the established vein of Critical Theory, for, as Marcuse writes in the introduction, "[t]he recognition of authority as a basic force of social praxis attacks the very roots of human freedom: it means [...] the surrender of autonomy (of thought, will, action), the tying of the subject's reason and will to pre-established contents [...]." Moreover, Marcuse asserts, interlocking manifestations of domination and authoritarianism reinforce each other noxiously: "Since subjection is actually repugnant to human nature," he writes, repressed humanity becomes "gradually prepared for types of subordination which are harder to bear. This preparation occurs in the manner of a softening, bowing and bending; it is a continual habituation, through which [humanity] becomes accustomed to subjection" (Marcuse 2008: 7, 34). It is the "preparation" for total authoritarianism promoted by the bourgeois family-unit and the capitalist workplace that Marcuse has in mind here.

To begin with, Marcuse's analysis of Kant's views on authority expresses his disillusion with the founder of German Idealism, for whom Marcuse usually shows a great deal of admiration. As the critical theorist details, though, his negativity here may very well be justified. He observes at the outset that Kant's concept of ethics is deeply linked to Lutheran ideas, particularly in terms of the duty of "reverential obedience" to constituted power: monarchical and feudal. This "doctrine of the actual unconditional authority of worldly government," which mimics Luther's condemnations of the 1524–1525 peasant uprisings in central Europe as the "flood of all wickedness," strangely contradicts Kant's own famous conception of human autonomy, as established in the "Reply to the Question: What is Enlightenment" (1784). Since Kant believes the "free autonomy" of humanity to be "the supreme law," it follows that "[t]o think and to act according to an authority is for Kant characteristic of 'immaturity,' a 'self-inflicted immaturity,' for which the person is [herself] to blame." Given, as Marcuse observes, that "[b]ourgeois society has an 'interest' in 'disciplining' [people] by handling them in an authoritarian manner"—for "here its whole survival is at stake"—it is in a sense perplexing to contemplate how Kant himself transitions from the normative emphasis on human freedom to the effective defense of bourgeois society and its rulers, a move which clearly negates freedom. Simply put, it would seem that Kant rationalizes this contradiction by distinguishing between public and private freedom—claiming the former to bear more weight than the latter—and holding that, within the private realm, one must subordinate one's desire for autonomy to the social demands of discipline and stability. Like Luther, then, Kant came to hold that "right [is] immanent in the civil order," and hence that revolt and rebellion would constitute the "overthrow of all right": *There can thus be no legitimate resistance of the people to the legislative head of state; for a state of right is only possible through submission to his universal legislative will.*" It follows, then, that Kant felt any changes to a "defective political constitution" could be enacted "only by the sovereign himself through *reform*, but not by the people, and, consequently, not by *revolution*" (Marcuse 2008: 20, 35–39, 45–46). Ironically, though, Marcuse recognizes Kant's welcoming of the coming of the French Revolution as "one of the great events in the emancipation of [humanity]," to say nothing of his utopian future vision of perpetual peace in international relations (1998: 123). Marcuse juxtaposes Kant's contradictory defense of absolutism and capitalism with the Idealist's foundational belief in the "transcendental freedom" of humanity and the "unconditional autonomy of the rational person": as a bourgeois, Kant does not wish to see such freedom develop into a "practical social force" (Marcuse 2008: 46). The freedom to think thus does not extend to the freedom to act: in identifying this tension, Marcuse stresses the centrality of Kantian thought within the project of capitalist stabilization, however much critical and transcendental potential can be found in a number of Kant's points.

For the youthful Hegel, who followed Kant, bourgeois society represents an "untrue" type of social organization, one that must dialectically be transcended. As Marcuse observes, the Hegel of *The Philosophy of Right* (1821) describes the "general community" of capitalist society as "nothing more than the mutual dependence of 'selfish' individuals, a world of private satisfaction of needs." For the young Hegel, then, the State is little more than a racket established for the protection of property and privilege. "The authority of the state is thus founded at a level quite beyond the reach of the power of the individual; it is based on the development of a 'world spirit' which has progressed on its road through the centuries up to the truth represented by the state." In Hegel's view, the establishment and maintenance of State power is helped along by two crucial social institutions: the family and the corporation. Both institutions greatly influence one's lot in life, or "rank and dignity," with the family specifically providing an especially egotistical orientation, in its forging of bonds among blood relations for the purpose of inheriting accumulated wealth, and its general reproduction of social and political conformism. Indeed, the bourgeois family constitutes the very "ethical root" of the State, on Hegel's account (Marcuse 2008: 51–52, 59, 61–62).

However, against the backdrop of this negative account of inequality and State power, Marcuse explores the dialectic of lordship and bondage from Hegel's *Phenomenology of Spirit* (1807), which describes both feudal and capitalist social relations well: on the one hand there is the master, whose domination is spurred by "'greed' for the 'enjoyment' of things," a process that necessarily excludes the servant, who encounters the imposed necessity of labor instead of the various comforts enjoyed by her antagonist. Dialectically, though—and suggestive of the later development of the school of autonomous Marxism—Marcuse notes that the servant can come to realize that the authority of the master is rooted in the very labor she performs; hence, this domination is, "in the last analysis, dependent on the servant, who believes in it and sustains it." It is for this reason that the chance to supersede such relations of domination becomes a historical possibility through class struggle. Yet despite this affirming possibility, Marcuse closes his treatment of Hegel here on a sobering note, citing the young Hegel's observation that humanity resigns itself to its submission before the State—the protector of social inequality— only as a result of the latter's application of "absolute force" against the populace (2008: 64–67).

Following his treatment of Kant and Hegel, Marcuse turns to tracing the development of counter-revolutionary justifications of authority in the wake of the French Revolution. He summarizes these lines of thought, advanced famously by Edmund Burke and Joseph de Maistre, as "consciously irrationalist and traditionalist theory." These apologists generally seek to deny the place of critical thought and praxis in shaping historical circumstances, instead elevating existing institutions above reproach by claiming them to be effectively natural, divinely sanctioned, or otherwise beyond question. What is more, reactionary postures such as these seek to distract the subordinated masses by channeling their energies into "useful prejudices" like nationalism, and they advance a highly distorted social anthropology which reduces human nature to little more than Hobbesianism, while claiming consciousness and enlightenment to proceed vertically from the sovereign to the people, if at all. On this account, tellingly, the populace "do[es] not actively belong to society at all, but ha[s] to be protected by it." The result, Marcuse summarizes, is a "total defamation of human reason." The critical theorist demonstrates that these irrationalist philosophers openly advocate feudal restoration, and consider the family a foundational institution for the perpetuation of generalized unreason, much like their liberal counterparts (2008: 67, 70, 72–76. 82).

Marcuse transitions to his consideration of Marx's views on authority by contrasting the latter's outlook with that of essentially all his philosophical predecessors, who from Luther to Kant had stressed the inner and personal aspects of freedom and liberation, never their realization in the "external sphere" of social reality. While some of these past thinkers—particularly Hegel—had come to realize that the concept of freedom can become valid only within the "general community," as opposed to being limited to the individual atomistic level, none of them looked into the very particular forms of social organization which this general community must take, if it is in fact to allow for generalized freedom: that is to say, unlike Marx, these philosophers had not called for the dissolution of bourgeois society and its replacement with a higher form. In this way, the "Beyond" which Marx promises in his practical call for the reduction of the working day—at minimum—and the expropriation of the capitalist class—at maximum—transcends the previous theistic understanding of the Beyond as the overcoming of human alienation; in so theorizing, Marx grounds the chance for human happiness and liberation within material praxis (Marcuse 2008: 84, 87, 96).

In his discussion of Marx, Marcuse describes the theory of reification, whereby the State, which advances the interests of the capitalist minority as against the "general interest," becomes "an alien and independent power, separated from the wishes and acts of the individuals [subject to it]." He notes that this "universal reification" is "already present in the authority of the 'management' of labour." In terms of the common desire by State and capital to dominate is seen the intimacy between the two. Marcuse ties consideration of capitalist power relations into an examination of ideology, declaring that the ruling capitalist class must engage in mass-obfuscation to paper over its mate-rial domination of the whole of society and so tie the subordinated into the perpetuation of the status quo (2008: 94–95).

Separately, Marcuse analyzes Engels' invective as directed against Bakunin and his followers within the First International: Engels is shown to regard it as an "absurdity" that "the principle of authority [is] absolutely bad and the principle of autonomy [is] absolutely good," given that "functional authority" is putatively a necessity "in every social organization," including future anti-capitalist ones. Granted, a future Marxian society would do away with capital-ist authority in the workplace and State, claims Marcuse, but such liberatory tendencies are not to be regarded as absolute, in light of the putative contin-ued importance of leadership and subordination in the prosecution of the class war. From his account here, it remains unclear to what degree Marcuse shares Engels' denunciation of the "undialectical rejection of all authority" at this point in his life (2008: 91–92).

Marcuse concludes his *Study on Authority* by briefly examining two diverg-ing philosophical figures from the early twentieth century: the famed syndi-calist Georges Sorel and the reactionary sociologist and economist Vilfredo Pareto. As described by Marcuse, the trajectory of Sorel, author of *Reflections on Violence* (1908), "is a typical example of the transformation of an abstract anti-authoritarian attitude into reinforced authoritarianism." From his early opposition to the centralization of anti-capitalist struggles, as reflected in his demand for a "loosened, federalized world of proletarian institutions and associations" and a socialism freed from an exclusively economic orientation to be embodied in a non-hierarchical social movement, and his endorsement of proletarian violence and the "eschatological general strike," Sorel would lat-er come to endorse the post-revolutionary emergence of new elites dedicated to maintaining order and improving production schemes. In Marcuse's view, Sorel's unfortunate and contradictory welcoming of a disciplinary elite served to influence the historical development of both Leninism and Fascism (2008: 103–105).

Lastly, Marcuse situates the economist Pareto within a "rationalist-positivist" framework which, in declaring a total "freedom from values," dispenses en-tirely with ethical considerations and hence serves to rationalize prevailing power-arrangements. Pareto is shown to divide human society in two parts, the elite and non-elite. In Pareto's view, the main concern of the elite is merely to "get 'on top' and be able to stay 'on top,'" or to assert power "over other people and things." Being positivist, Pareto has nothing to say about the ends toward which elite power is employed: this consideration, coupled with his concept of the "circulation of elites," leads Marcuse to identify the essential liberalism of Pareto's thought.[5] In addition, Marcuse here considers Pareto's studies into methods of stabilizing ruling-class control, a task the positivist economist observed as requiring the "more or less voluntary consent" of the non-elite, who by sheer number clearly and overwhelmingly could threaten elite domination; in this sense, and though he disagrees with Pareto's effectively apologist conclusions, Marcuse hails the economist's insight into the ideological and psychological means of manipulating the masses into accepting administration by the wealthy and powerful. In material and psychological terms, Marcuse identifies Pareto's emphasis on the family and the exercise of "sentiments of inferiors"—such as "subordination, affection, reverence, fear"—within the perpetuation of authoritarian relations (2008: 106–110).

Marcuse's Direct Investigations of Nazism

Confronted with the outright belligerence exhibited by Hitler's invasion of Poland in September 1939, Neumann and Marcuse increasingly gravitated in the early war years toward lending their vast intellects to the U.S. government in the struggle to undermine and ultimately defeat the National Socialist regime from which they had fled. As a precursor to entering the foreign service, these two withdrew their formal affiliations with the Frankfurt School in favor of joint investigations dedicated to intensive research and examination of the Nazi State. The results of such work included Marcuse's 1941 lecture on "State and Individual under National Socialism," his 1942 study of the "New German Mentality," and his essay examining technological rationality under Fascism, in parallel to the eventual publication of Neumann's comprehensive study of the politics and economics of Nazism, *Behemoth* (1944). Moreover, the duo developed a number of manuscripts on theories of social change and critical philosophy during this time of collaboration. In contrast, their former colleagues Horkheimer and Adorno would at this time in Los Angeles simultaneously be coordinating the gloomy analyses which pervade their *Dialectic of Enlightenment*, a volume that was first published 1944, with a revised text subsequently republished to a larger audience three years later. Consideration of the prominent divergence between these two factions of the Institute for Social Research, with Marcuse and Neumann developing what Kellner terms a "practical-political" conception of Critical Theory "as a theory of social change," helps to "mitigat[e]" the seemingly "widespread opinion that the

---

5   Pareto's concept of the "circulation of elites" refers to the tendency whereby historically progressive events such as revolutions merely result in the replacement of one elite by another.

entire [Frankfurt School] group was turning away from social practice and political action in the 1940s," and it "reveal[s] a quite distinct difference in political orientation between Horkheimer and Adorno in contrast to Marcuse and Neumann" (Marcuse 1998: 12–14).

Such divergence in practical commitments notwithstanding, Marcuse and Neumann were of one mind with Horkheimer and Adorno in viewing the rise of the terroristic-totalitarian Nazi regime as intimately related to the nature of the economic and political conditions out of which it had emerged—that is, liberal, imperialist capitalism. As Marcuse declares at the beginning of his 1941 lecture on "Individual and State under National Socialism," it is the same "forces and interests" that have determined German society "at least since the first World War" that "hold sway over the National Socialist State." Marcuse's account here, which shares a great deal with that of Neumann in *Behemoth*, follows from his earlier interpretations of fascism as the culmination of the authoritarian trends of liberal capitalism, as described in the "Struggle against Liberalism in the Totalitarian View of the State"; Hitler's rule thus is seen as an economic venture financed by the "governing imperialist groups" that was taken to "open up new ways for an economy which was frustrated and had reached the limits of its own power." For Marcuse, Nazism enthrones supreme rule by "big industrial combines" and "military machinery." Whereas the liberal State before it had at least in theory been committed to regulating the concentration of power by capitalist interests, fascism works actively to "abolish or correct the mechanisms which might hamper such concentration." Furthermore, Marcuse finds Nazism to operate through the direct imposition of "technical rationality," or an authoritarian sense of reason derived from the operation of technology which is "applied to the ordering of all human relationships": as the very negation of a critical, Hegelian-Marxian view of rationality which might seek to re-order society along the lines of the "human ends and wants of individuals," Nazism's technical rationality functions only to maintain and uphold the totalitarian arrangement on an ever "increasingly efficient scale." For these reasons, Marcuse notes Nazism not to be the "reversal" but instead the very "consummation of competitive individualism" (1998: 8, 70, 74, 76, 78–80, 86).

Analyzing German culture and society as subjected to Nazism, Marcuse identifies a very conscious effort on the part of the Nazi administration to appeal to their Aryan subjects' "social frustration and submissiveness," their "most brutal and selfish instincts" as cultivated by capitalism: "resentment, envy, cruelty." Members of fascist class society are required to conform to the inegalitarian social arrangement by means of internalization of the Nazis' megalomaniacal erection of hierarchies based on race and ability; Aryan workers, then, alienated though they may be by their relative disenfranchisement under Nazism, are to some extent compensated by being raised above other groups that are in turn rendered "infinitely more fettered, helpless and unhappy than they are." That such a labor aristocracy would hold fellow workers in suspicion and hostility is the very hope held by their fascist rulers: thus are they inoculated from joining in solidarity to overcome the egoism and atomism on which the fascist-capitalist order is based. Besides the fomentation of divisions among workers themselves, Nazism also ties its subject populations into perpetuating domination through the mass-manipulation of German culture, according to Marcuse. As highly affirmative, the types of artistic expression advanced by National Socialism seek to "reconcile" humanity with "with the world as it is," precisely by manipulating individuals into "lik[ing] and perpetuat[ing] a world which uses [them] as a means for oppression." Despite the enormity of thoughtlessness and repression promoted by Nazism, Marcuse at the close of this lecture on individual and State reiterates his life-long conviction that the autonomous standards of "beauty, truth, harmony, [and] reason" expressed in authentic art remain "alien and antagonistic" to all institutions of totalitarian administration (1998: 70, 81, 86, 89–90, 91–92).

After "State and Individual under National Socialism," Marcuse provides a more detailed examination of the psychological, ethical, and philosophical implications of the "new German mentality" expressed by the Aryan masses under Nazism in his 1942 investigation, written in Santa Monica. An exercise in radical sociological inquiry, the "New German Mentality" was clearly written with Marcuse's future line of work with the U.S. Office of War Information in mind—this being the institution to which he would submit the treatise some months after completing it. In this essay, the critical theorist claims that the German people have been so culturally manipulated by Nazi rule that their new orientations signify a large deviation from Western civilization in general, and German *Kultur* in particular. Marcuse identifies two layers to this new mentality: its pragmatic and neo-paganist aspects. Breaking radically with past German historical radicalism, from Hegel to Feuerbach and Marx, National Socialism led its subject population to come to evaluate existence above all in terms of "efficiency, success, and expediency," and thus to adjust wholesale to the new regime, with an eye only to the safeguarding of one's private well-being. In terms of the charge of neo-paganism, Marcuse situates the popularity of Nazism within a deeply rooted German revolt against the more defensible products of "Christian civilization," as typified in the Weimar Republic, including "humanism, the Rights of Man, democracy and socialism." In place of such progressive orientations, Nazism has promoted "anti-Semitism, terrorism, social Darwinism, anti-intellectualism, [and] naturalism," all of which express rebellion against the regulatory principles of Western philosophy—liberty, equality, and fraternity—and "the subordination of might to right, [or] the idea of universal ethics." That the Nazi pageants would commemorate the "grandeur of the heroic age of European society" and specifically celebrate the feudalism of the French *ancien régime* is, then, not surprising for Marcuse (1998: 141, 143–144, 156).

Materially, the new German mentality corresponds to the fascist processes of rationalization which serve to advance "imperialist expansion on a continental scale" by displacing "the moral inhibition[s], waste and inefficiency that stand in the way of ruthless economic and political conquest." All universal laws and standards must be canceled in Nazi ideology, writes Marcuse, for only through the breaking of the restraints on political and economic behavior implied by these can totalitarian imperialism proceed effectively. Amidst the brutality of competition among States and capitalists, Nazism suggests that those who would like to "get along in this world" should jettison "all transcendental ideas" in favor of orienting themselves to "the brute matters of fact"; toward this end, the neo-paganistic naturalism it pushes effectively suppresses the human desire to progress beyond the given, in favor of resignation before prevailing reality. Presumably, the argument goes, the German people largely accepted this anti-rational ideology more or less willingly, and in this way replaced the historical German emphasis on dialectics and Romanticism with a "disillusioned matter-of-factness": people "take what is offered to them and make the best of it," according to Marcuse. Nevertheless, while he stresses that these new mentalities appeal to his notion of the "German character," Marcuse closes by emphasizing the economic factors in Germans' acceptance of Nazism: "education to totalitarian imperialism could be successful only on the basis of immediate material compensations" provided by the regime, such as full employment and the redistribution of spoils of war and of seized Jewish assets, at least among Aryans (1998: 145, 151, 157–159, 163).

With his conceptual intervention on "Some Social Implications of Modern Technology" (1941), Marcuse sketches out his dialectical vision of technology (or "technics"), which takes account of the centrality of technology in the repressive processes of capitalism and fascism and holds out a speculative promise of technological alternatives that instead serve humanity and reason. Marcuse states plainly at the beginning of this piece that "[t]echnics by itself can promote authoritarianism as well as liberty, scarcity as well as abundance, the extension as well as the abolition of toil." The philosopher briefly discusses the trajectory of the dialectic of Enlightenment, which begins with the critical potential of reason Marcuse sees as having arisen with the "rise of the individual" in sixteenth and seventeenth century Europe: building on this initial breakthrough, the materialists would show that true individual rationality could be experienced only within a larger social setting that itself has become rational. In light of the capitalist "progression" toward monopolist and

oligarchical control, though, the concept of reason necessarily had to be corrupted in the main to serve to legitimize the patently evident irrationality and
barbarism of capital; thus, under Fascism, "individualistic rationality has been
transformed into technological rationality." Anticipating much of his subsequent work, Marcuse goes on to assert that this degraded sense of reason is
exercised not just in Nazi war-planning sessions or corporate boardrooms but
instead "characterizes the pervasive mode of thought," one that is machinic
and "spread over the whole society" (1998: 41, 42–45). To illustrate, Marcuse
provides an interesting example:

> A man who travels by automobile to a distant place chooses his route
> from the highway maps. Towns, lakes and mountains appear as obstacles
> to be bypassed. The countryside is shaped and organized by the highway:
> what one finds en route is a byproduct or annex of the highway. Numer-
> ous signs and posters tell the traveler what to do and think; they even
> request his attention to the beauties of nature or the hallmarks of history.
> Others have done the thinking for him, and perhaps for the better. Con-
> venient parking spaces have been constructed where the broadest and
> most surprising view is open. Giant advertisements tell him when to stop
> and find the pause that refreshes. And all of this is indeed for his benefit,
> safety, and comfort; he receives what he wants.
>
> MARCUSE 1998: 46

Perhaps the theorist's claims here are somewhat exaggerated, and one can
indeed question how representative this example is in terms of the general
populace in Western societies, but the argumentation is classically Marcusean:
it illuminates his worry that "[g]etting along is identical with adjustment to the apparatus," and hence that "[t]here is no room for autonomy."
Even people's libidos come to be colonized by the "machine process," with
Marcuse dryly noting that the "average" person "hardly cares for any living
being with the intensity and persistence [she] shows for [her] automobile."
Amidst the stipulated material and emotional integration which even subordinated classes experience vis-à-vis the capitalist system, reason comes to be
reduced to positivism—the mere "matter-of-factness" identified in the "New
German Mentality." In accepting the capitalist life-world and its regnant egoism, even the proletariat is guilty, according to Marcuse: harking back to his autonomist studies of the dialectic of class struggle in Hegel and Marx, Marcuse
argues that the monstrous apparatus, though managed by capitalists, is in fact
produced and upheld by the non-capitalist laboring classes. Hence the following declaration: "the categories of critical thought preserve their truth value
only if they direct the full realization of the social potentialities which they

envision, and they lose their vigor if they determine an attitude of fatalistic compliance or competitive assimilation" (1998: 46–48, 51).

Marcuse proceeds to theorize the "modern masses" as being the product of historical developments which that have facilitated "the growth of authoritarian bureaucracy." The liberation of society, a project to be carried out by the associated people, necessarily requires the realization of critical forms of rationality *en masse*, says Marcuse, for only the "autonomous decision and action" of humanity can bring about "the rational form of human association," which is communism. No faith can for be placed in the dominant public institutions which seek the compliance and obedience of those from below— relegating the masses to being mere "attendants and dependents of large scale industry"—in light of the close association between these forces and private bureaucracies, a point that Marcuse notes Max Weber already had made two decades previously. Conceiving of a counter-movement to such negations, Marcuse here calls for a reactivation of the "unrestricted liberty of thought and conscience" promised by early individualist philosophies, and he affirms the dialectical role technics can play in assisting with this project: for the promises of technology are suppressed "only insofar as they are tied to a social apparatus which perpetuates scarcity." Marcuse then counterposes an account of progress which anticipates the application of technology in ways that help to "decrease the time and energy" dedicated to alienated labor, reduce scarcity, and abolish "competitive pursuits," thus affording humanity the chance to "develop from its natural roots"—a fascinating, romantic vision to which the text will later return for a more in-depth examination (Marcuse 1998: 55–57, 63–65).[6]

For now, it may suffice to note that, in spite the horrors symbolized and implemented by fascism and its technological rationality, Marcuse enthusiastically looks forward to the prospect of future relations wherein "everyone could think and act by [her]self, speak [her] own language, have [her] own emotions and follow [her] own passions." While suggestive of anarchism and utopia, such a state of affairs would not be one of "perennial happiness," Marcuse warns: once the specters of "poverty, hunger, and social ostracism" have been overcome, indeed, humans likely will come to experience far deeper senses of sadness, for under such liberated conditions they would be afforded radically improved capacities and opportunities for contemplating the transience of life. Marcuse closes this essay on an optimistic note, quoting Henry James in a repudiation of Hobbesian and otherwise fatalistic interpretations of human nature: "Every appetite and passion of [humanity's] nature is good and beautiful, and destined to be fully enjoyed" (Marcuse 1998: 65).

---

6   See especially Chapters 4, 5, 6, and 7 below.

Early Theories of Social Change

With Neumann, Marcuse worked on a large intellectual project to analyze theories of social change presented within Western philosophy, a commitment that was likely motivated by the dyad's desire to assist with the contemplation of alternatives to contemporary domination and terror. Indeed, the jointly produced manuscripts "A History of the Doctrine of Social Change" and "Theories of Social Change" (1941–1942) were at one point proposed as the basis for a lecture course at Columbia University, but this plan seems never to have materialized. Marcuse and Neumann open these essays by considering ancient Greek philosophy, which they generally hold in favorable regard, given their interpretation of its basic view of social change as being concerned for "the most fruitful existence": "the fulfillment of the highest potentialities" available to humanity, and hence "conditions resulting in well-being and happiness." Broadly speaking, ancient Greek philosophers are to have held social change to be "a process which could for the most part be identified with the progress of human life," with such progress to be measured, as in the philosophical materialism of modernity, "according to the given possibilities of human life." In this sense, the two cite the pre-Platonic Sophists to be the first philosophical radicals of Western history, especially considering their belief that society is to be "subject to the wants of the individuals for whose sake [it] has been established," rather than serve instituted power and reification. The authors mention Plato's negative view of private property, and they dissociate this reasonable opinion from the toxic combination of "Utopian idealism and reactionary totalitarianism" this student of Socrates expresses in his general political theory. Considered by Neumann and Marcuse to be a classical dialectician of sorts, Aristotle is discussed as viewing existence "in terms of movement and movement as the realization of the substantial potentialities of Being"; his view of historical progression is highly novel within Western philosophy, on this account (Marcuse 1998: 94–97).

These German radicals treat philosophical Stoicism particularly favorably, claiming the Stoic innovation of natural law to hold "certain revolutionary implications," and hence to have greatly influenced "oppositional attitudes" from medieval times to the present. Speaking to these implications, Bloch separately explains how the Stoics appealed to the "primitive commune" of the golden age, affirmed the inherent equality of all humans, sought to advance the unification of humanity through the "rational empire of love," and stressed the natural right to peace and the importance of mutual aid in the historical process (Bloch 1986b: 12–16). In a negative turn of events, nonetheless, Stoic natural law is subsumed into apologism for feudalism and clerical domination in the social philosophy of Thomas Aquinas, and legitimate theory reaches a climax with the thought of Niccolò Machiavelli, whose philosophy directs itself solely at serving State and private power, this by investigating methods to better "dominat[e] the masses" and so stabilize and expand the reach of the "absolute sovereign." In this sense, it would seem that the "only thing that matter[s]" to Machiavelli is "the government's ability to control the social dynamic and to secure prosperity and order." Marcuse and Neumann credit the ruthless Italian statesman for having led those mainstream political philosophers who followed him to concern themselves principally with the conflicts between order and disorder, toward the end of upholding the former against the latter (Marcuse 1998: 96–100, 108).

The joint authors hold British rationalist and empiricist thinkers John Locke and David Hume in a reactionary light. Marcuse and Neumann separate philosophers related to these schools into two categories: optimistic ones, exemplified by figures like Benjamin Franklin and Thomas Jefferson, who hold humans to be basically good and hence worthy of developing their potentialities, yet believe that the unfolding of human potential is best advanced by incrementalist methods, and pessimistic theories, such as those of Edmund Burke and de Maistre, who totally reject all steps taken toward changing existing power relations, which they consider to have been divinely ordered. Indeed, following from their stated belief that monarchs and princes represent the will of God, Burke and de Maistre infamously uphold nationalism, prejudice, and irrationality as values to be inculcated among the masses, so as to breathe life into the moribund, corrupt institution of society; in their development of theories of mass-domination, argue Marcuse and Neumann, such reactionary philosophers "foreshadowed" the absurdities and horrors of Nazism (Marcuse 1998: 21–22, 101, 120).

Against such counter-revolutionary traditions, the authors implicitly invoke the proto-materialist critiques made by some of the ancient Greek philosophers, linking these to the "strong non-conformist critical and predominantly materialist trend[s]" emanating as countercurrents to dominant philosophical and political trends expressed throughout European history. Happily, materialist philosophers are shown to have demanded "the complete transformation of society," and to have concentrated their focus on radically altering property arrangements as a means toward this end. Embodied in heretical movements like the Diggers of the English Revolution and the Anabaptists of the Reformation, materialism has at points in early modern history taken on "an openly revolutionary character" in its calls for the millenarian construction of "a new order of freedom and reason." Its progressive development within the French Enlightenment, moreover, gave rise to the well-known revolutionary interventions of 1789, which Marcuse and Neumann proclaim as having "marked the [historical] point at which humanity had reached the threshold of a free and rational society." The exemplary Claude Adrien Helvétius is taken as a representative philosopher of the positively shattering breakthroughs of the Enlightenment period which predated revolutionary France, given his view that the "abolition of absolutism" and the struggle against clerical domination were preconditions for human emancipation. Like Freud—and, indeed, Marcuse himself— Helvétius asserts the desire for pleasure and the avoidance of pain to drive all human behavior, and from this premise he claims that philosophy normatively must assist in the physical suppression of repressive institutions which deny happiness to humanity. In Helvétius' mind, the political and philosophical struggle to expand happiness seeks to restore human sociality and solidarity, such that the happiness of the individual comes to underpin and expand the freedom of others through the utter eradication of social misery (Marcuse 1998: 101, 113–115, 118). Again like his reviewers themselves, Helvétius holds out the exercise of reason as the best means to advance these revolutionary ends.

Less promisingly, advances in science and industry led proto-socialist Henri de Saint-Simon and positivist Auguste de Comte to argue for repressive means of implementing the knowledge yielded through rational investigation, while Herbert Spencer's utilitarianism is similarly shown to be a type of theory that is entirely acceptable to constituted power—hence little more than a philosophy of resignation. Invoking and carrying on the critical-materialist approach, however, Saint-Simon's socialist student Amand Bazard is demonstrated to have rejected his mentor's fetishization of industrialism, claiming the factory-system inevitably to be bound up with human exploitation, and he counterposes against traditional Saint-Simonianism the outright abolition of industry, exploitation, and property. Finally, following their treatment of Kant, Hegel, and Marx at the close of the text—with the account of these latter figures' philosophies being here bracketed, in light of their considerable presence elsewhere in the present work—Marcuse and Neumann favorably mention the twentieth-century sociologist Lester Ward, who asserts happiness to be the principal goal sought by individual and collective human action, and concomitantly denounces hegemonic irrationality as a barrier to the progressive restructuring of social institutions, as based on the demands of human well-being (Marcuse 1998: 124–130, 136–137).

The Progression of Marcuse's Thought on the Functions of Art Under Fascism

Similar ideas about negation and happiness are examined in Marcuse's "Some Remarks on Aragon: Art and Politics in the Totalitarian Era," a brief 1945 essay which analyzes the wartime poetry and fiction by Resistance writers Paul Éluard and Louis Aragon within the frame of the experience of Nazi occupation of France. In this piece, Marcuse continues to expand upon his previous thoughts on the aesthetic dimension, as developed especially in "The Affirmative Character of Culture" and "On Hedonism." Characteristically, he opens his reflections on these artworks by asserting that the "aim[s]" of intellectual and artistic opposition vis-à-vis the prevailing balance of social forces—which he defines as being humanity's "liberation from domination and exploitation"— have failed to be realized; opposition within such a context thus appears "increasingly impotent and ineffective." Generalized powerlessness carries the day, Marcuse posits, because the "revolutionary forces which were to bring about freedom are being assimilated to the all-embracing system of monopolistic controls": even where "[r]evolutionary social and political theory" calls for what Marcuse sees as the correct courses of "social and political action," it remains "academic," either consciously "co-ordinated with the powers that be, or crushed by them without resonance." Anticipating many of his later societal diagnoses, as well as the later Situationists' concern for the *recuperation* (cooptation) of art, Marcuse announces that "[a]ll indictments are easily absorbed by the system which they indict," as "[r]evolutionary art" comes to be "fashionable and classical" (1998: 201). Not even *El Guernica* is spared Marcuse's melancholic denunciation of museums!

The advancing colonization of art by "monopolistic mass culture" presents a conundrum for Marcuse, as for all artists: how might they recover the "alienating force" of art, one that "continue[s] to express the great refusal?" Marcuse argues that, to function effectively, art must express itself in modes that are "strange, antagonistic, [and] transcendent to normalcy." In short, art must present alternative perspectives and so assist in the struggle for liberation (1998: 202). Specifically, writes Marcuse, contemporary works of art should

> expose the ultimate nakedness of man's (and nature's) existence, stripped of all the paraphernalia of monopolistic mass culture, completely and utterly alone, in the abyss of destruction, despair and freedom.
>
> MARCUSE 1998: 203

In dialectically illustrating the deprivation and negation of life under capital and the authoritarian State, revolutionary art can, in Hegelian terms, help to "illuminate the goal" of human existence: the destruction of capitalism and class society, together with the concomitant emergence of the "free individual" (Marcuse 1998: 203).

Passing to consideration of concrete works of art produced by Resistance writers during and after the war, Marcuse focuses in particular on Aragon's

1945 novel *Aurélien*, which has to do in part with a romance between the title character and Bérénice, a young "petty-bourgeois wife" of a pharmacist who in 1922 comes to visit Paris from the French provinces, there to fall in love with Aurélien and subsequently experience the various confusions and passions associated with authentic interpersonal affection, ones which definitively explode all previous senses of bourgeois normalcy. In Marcuse's view, the couple's transgressive union expresses a total incompatibility with "all normal relationships," and as such reflects love's revolutionary-erotic potential. Eighteen years later, following the German occupation of France, the couple is reunited in the country's south, where Bérénice is now working as a Resistance operative accompanying a Spanish Republican refugee; the very same night of their reunion, Bérénice is killed when a German patrol opens fire on the car in which they are traveling. For Marcuse, "the face of the dying Bérénice appears as the face of France," though rather than symbolize just this country, she negatively represents the whole of the "liberated earth on which the 'promesse de bonheur' [promise of joy] finds its fulfillment." In this way are Eros and revolution tied together: "the goal of political action is love's liberation," for both love and revolutionary praxis seek a happy and joyous Earth, one freed from fascist invaders as well as all other oppressors! (1998: 210–212).

Marcuse closes his remarks on *Aurélien* by stating that, while artists cannot directly "present the fascist reality," any work of art—like any human enterprise at all—which does not at least acknowledge the Nazi terror of the time is nothing less than "inhuman, irrelevant, incidental, untrue." Bringing to mind Benjamin without explicitly naming him, Marcuse ends on a hopeful note by stating that art, instead of advancing conformity and conservatism, can serve as a light that reveals the poverty of dominant forms, and in this way aid in estranging its audiences from the world in which they find themselves trapped; hence can it assist in the collective struggle to recall freedom within contexts of thoroughgoing oppression. In practical political terms, such remembrance could serve as an inspiration for practices that might "dissolve" the fallen present (Marcuse 1998: 214).

Reason and Revolution (1941)

All fictions disappear before truth, and all follies fall before reason.[7]
MARCUSE 1999: 7

---

7   Marcuse is quoting the Jacobin leader Maximilien Robespierre here.

As John Abromeit notes, Marcuse's early interest in the philosophy of Hegel—
evident since the *Künstlerroman*—progressed within a context of great disillusionment on Marcuse's part in terms of the failures of reformist social
democracy and thus, in Marcuse's mind, its proponents, such as Eduard
Bernstein (1850–1932). In the first place, the SPD had suppressed the German
Revolution, and then a decade and a half later would it effectively collaborate
in Hitler's seizure of power (Abromeit 2004: 138). For Marcuse, Hegel's political and ontological philosophies provide a stark alternative to this negating
course of events: based fundamentally on the maxims of reason and human
freedom, the Hegelian dialectic through its fearless acknowledgment of generalized societal negativity expresses "the conviction that what exists is not immediately and already rational but must rather be brought to reason" (Marcuse
1968: 136). The critical and subversive meaning of Hegel's dialectic—the very
opposite of his mature declarations that "the Real is the Rational"—is systematically presented in Marcuse's monumental *Reason and Revolution: Hegel and
the Rise of Social Theory*, a work that advances the Hegelian-Marxist perspectives of Lukács and Karl Korsch, particularly in terms of the latter's council-
communist volume, *Marxism and Philosophy* (1923) (Abromeit 2004: 138).
Moreover, as Schoolman notes, *Reason and Revolution* can at least in part be
seen as the fruit of Marcuse's self-critical appraisal of his previous engagement
with Heideggerian philosophy, the very culmination of a "renewed appreciation of the rationalist tradition in Western philosophy" (Schoolman 1980: 143).
Arguably, Marcuse's main objective in *Reason and Revolution* is to show the
breadth and depth of the *negativity* of Hegel's thought—that is to say, the degree to which his early philosophy (1796–1816) stresses the "fallenness" of society and the need radically to overcome such, so as to give way to the flourishing
of freedom and reason.

   Marcuse opens his introduction to Hegel's thought by claiming the large
school to which his philosophy belongs—German Idealism—to have been the
"theory of the French Revolution," in the sense that each of the major Idealists
"wrote their philosophy largely as a response to the challenge from France to
reorganize the state and society on a rational basis"—that is to say, with the
"freedom and interest of the individual" in mind. Critics of the Jacobin Terror
all, the Idealists nevertheless welcomed the historical breakthrough which the
French Revolution represented. For Marcuse, the importance of the Revolution to Hegel lies in its radical demonstration of the human capacity firstly to
judge the existing situation with reference to the concept of reason—that is,
by contrasting the gap between given reality and its various potentialities—
and secondly to dare to act so as to change reality in an attempt to bring it
into congruence with the demands of reason. Hegel's concept of rationality,

in this sense, does not come to "govern reality" until "reality has become rational in itself"; reason, so to say, "exists only through its realization." To a greater
extent than the other animals, humans have the means to engage in reason
and self-determination, for reason demands freedom—the power to act using knowledge within the struggle to change reality—just as freedom presupposes reason, or the consciousness with which to change the world. In his
youthful writings, Hegel's "end-state"—history's "final goal"—is shown to be
attainment of the "reality of freedom" (Marcuse 1999: 3, 6–7, 410). It is from
such premises that in 1796, at the age of 26, Hegel demands that the State-
form be transcended: "For every State is bound to treat free [people] as cogs
in a machine. And this is precisely what it should not do; hence, the State
must perish" (Hegel 1936: 219). In a similar sense, the Idealist would declare
Statist coercion to be a "negation that must itself be negated," one that must
be "renounced" together with force and violence as the "bas[e]s of human
relationships" (Williams 1997: 76).

Situating German Idealism and Hegel's development of it historically,
Marcuse claims these advances in thought to have "rescued philosophy from
the attack of British empiricism," amidst the tendency of this northern European forerunner of positivism to constrain visions of the course of historical development to limited variations within the enshrined "authority of the fact"—
that is to say, feudalism and capitalism—and thus serve to confine humanity
to "the limits of 'the given,' within the existing order of things and events." If
such philosophy were to be accepted on a mass-scale—as it arguably was in
Nazi Germany, according to Marcuse—it would work to suppress the possibility of subversive ideas, principles, and corresponding actions that are not
readily observable within the main; in essence, then, empiricism remains a
philosophy of "conformism," the very "abdication of reason" (Marcuse 1999:
16–20, 27). Against the legitimational implications of empiricism and positivism, Marcuse defends Hegel's dialectical principles as progressive. Taking as an
illustrative example the statement "this man is a slave" to elucidate the basic
idea of Hegel's method, Marcuse writes:

> According to Hegel, it means that a man (the subject) has become
> enslaved (the predicate), but although he [*sic*] is a slave, he still remains
> man, thus essentially free and opposed to his predicament. The judgment
> does not attribute a predicate to a stable subject, but denotes an actual
> process of the subject whereby the latter becomes something other than
> itself.
>
> MARCUSE 1999: 25

Importantly for Hegel, then, "the facts in themselves possess no authority." The given appearance of the world's realities in no way necessarily corresponds to their "true form," which according to the standard of reason accords with their "real potentialities." Thus, according to Hegel, truth can become real only with the "death of the given state of being" and its supersession through the exercise of mind, toward the generalized achievement of human freedom and happiness—or, what is the same, reason (Marcuse 1999: 26–28).

From even Hegel's earliest writings on theology (1790–1800), Marcuse finds important liberatory and critical perspectives. He relates Hegel as associating the historical institution of private property with reification and alienation: the world marred by property corresponds to a "strange world governed by inexorable laws, a 'dead' world in which human life is frustrated." Subjected to the dominion of private property, humans come to inhabit "a world that is adverse and alien to [their] impulses and desires" (Marcuse 1999: 34–35). As John Clark explains, in addition, the youthful Hegel felt that the "true community" would resemble the "communities of love" developed by anarchistic Christians who followed the teachings of the medieval mystic Joachim of Fiore, who looked forward to the coming Age of the Holy Spirit that would be bereft of masters and slaves—in parallel to the Christian communism that the Spiritual Franciscans attempted to implement together with Indigenous communities in Mesoamerica to resist the designs of Spanish colonialism, as well as Tolstoy's Christian anarchism, as set forth in *The Kingdom of God Is Within You* (Clark 2013: 76, 133; Goldner 2010; Tolstoy 1960). In Marcuse's view, it was due to concern for the precipitous loss of freedom seen in the world around him that Hegel shifted from his study of theology to philosophy, coming soon to counterpose reason against regnant social alienation with the demand that the Earth, rather than continue to be subjected to established custom and irrationality, "be transformed into a medium for the freely developing subject." Practically speaking, upon beginning his academic career in 1801, Hegel would call into question the everyday, common-sense view which leads people to mistake the "accidental appearance of things" with their essence, or potentiality, suggesting instead that the "immediate identity" of essence and existence should only be conceived of as a future possible union to be effected through the exercise of reason and struggle (Marcuse 1999: 42, 45–46).

As Marcuse describes, Hegel's early political writings (1800–1802) themselves retain a dialectical character: they continue expressing and developing the critical libertarian positions of his earliest works, but it is during this period that Hegel begins to introduce more conservative principles which anticipate his mature authoritarianism. Defining the rise of individualistic social relations as leading to a "purely negative" state of affairs, Hegel argues that the extant political system must be destroyed and "transformed into a new rational order," one that corresponds to a "true community" in place of the old, "false" one. The State-form found contemporarily in Prussia, claims Hegel, cannot truly represent the common interest, given that its rulers in fact represent property and "antagonistic private interests" in place of the general welfare: "A multitude of human beings can only call itself a State if it is united for the communal defence of the entirety of its property" (Marcuse 1999: 51–54; 2008: 54). Further, as Hegel observes, under conditions of capitalism, an entirely "alien" and arbitrary force determines whether or not the individual's needs will be fulfilled through the value afforded to labor. The critical and negative nature of such proto-Marxian formulations notwithstanding, Marcuse shows Hegel at this time in fact to have romanticized feudalistic, pre-capitalist social relations as an alternative to prevailing ones, in light of his suggestion that the pre-modern social environment corresponded to a "true community." Moreover, and worryingly, Hegel here emphasizes the centrality of sacrifice and submission of the citizenry to the stronger German State he foresees in the future. Marcuse observes with alarm that such fragmentary obscurantism on Hegel's part previews his later, more developed theory of the post-Napoleonic Prussian State as corresponding to the very embodiment of reason—the crucial breakthrough identified in the young Hegel's understanding that the liberal status quo can in no way serve rationality to the side. Already in his university lectures from 1805–1806, Hegel would define government as the "Mind which knows itself as the universal essence and reality," the very "spirit of reality": "whatever appears within the State must conform to it" (Marcuse 1999: 53, 55–56, 58, 60, 88).

Marcuse's explication of Hegel's famous *Phenomenology of Spirit* (1807) begins on a biographical note: the *Phenomenology*, which Hegel finished just as Napoleon Bonaparte's armies defeated the Prussians at the battle of Jena, acknowledges the dialectical negativity of the French Revolution, whereby the radical attempt to advance human freedom resulted instead in the establishment of a "new despotism" in the Jacobin dictatorship. The author of the *Phenomenology* interprets this failed trajectory using his own developing political biases: that is, that the Revolution's degeneration into Terror resulted from the revolutionaries' supposed insistence on prosecuting liberation via "individuals *against* the state," rather than through the State itself—for Hegel by this point holds "the state alone" to be capable of providing reason to humanity. Marcuse sees Hegel's momentous political and philosophical shift expressed in the *Phenomenology*—that reason had finally triumphed through Napoleon's person, with Bonaparte representing to Hegel the "world-spirit on horseback," such that the importance of rebellion had been eclipsed by the need to accommodate this new world-historical reality—as a rather inauthentic move on Hegel's part, yet one he may have advanced out of a desire to avoid "the terrible contingencies of a new upheaval" against the social overhaul which Napoleon's military victories had instituted throughout much of Europe. As a reflection of the transformation experienced by Hegel at this time, Marcuse writes that the idealist author's ultimate view in the *Phenomenology* is to endorse "absolute knowledge" rather than historical struggle. In Hegel's view, Napoleon represented the "one man able to transform the achievements of 1789 into a state order and to connect individual freedom with the universal reason of a stable social system." Within a context which saw the social conflicts of feudalism increasingly eclipsed by the competition of the bourgeoisie, Hegel believed a rising State could bring unity to humanity. Concretely, Hegel welcomed the introduction of Napoleon's Civil Code in the territories occupied (or "liberated") by his armies, considering the types of reforms the Code would stipulate: the abolition of feudalism, the suppression of clerical power, the strengthening of bureaucracies, and the improvement of the tax system (Marcuse 1999: 91–92, 120, 169–170). It is this idealized "improvement" in State function which Hegel at this time tentatively identifies as amounting to "reason," before he would later equate rationality with the Restoration regimes which inherited power after Napoleon's final defeat in 1815.

Following these introductory comments on the *Phenomenology*, Marcuse examines the philosophical points Hegel presents in the work, which themselves contradict the philosopher's authoritarian political shift to a degree. For existence to accord to its truth, humanity must become free—it must overcome the instituted relations surrounding it, first by discovering through the senses and mind that human society is precisely *unfree*, and thus that progress *into* freedom can be brought about only through an active struggle against domination and subordination—as through class struggle. Marcuse writes that Hegel's philosophical vision in the *Phenomenology* is that of a "self-conscious humanity" which exercises its "right to shape the world." The very end sought by philosophy, claims Hegel, becomes the transformation of the world into its "true form, the world as reason." The possibility for the state of truth to emerge thus demands the dissolution of "bondage and irrationality": in Hegel's concept, the struggle against hegemonic "state[s] of 'negativity'" drives the positive dialectic against the "mistaken form or untruth" of the existing world. Reification, in this sense, can be broken and truth located through the human exercise of thought, which seeks to "make the world what it essentially is, namely, the fulfillment of [human] self-consciousness." For Marcuse, claims of these types on Hegel's part represent a strong repudiation of positivist philosophical approaches, which effectively serve to "giv[e] up the real potentialities of humanity for a false and alien world." Identifying a common point we have seen Marcuse stress time and again in his earlier works, Hegel is shown to declare humanity's historical fate "not [to be] exhausted in the given forms and relations in which [it] may actually appear," such that humanity is "more" than the instituted forms in which it may by accident find itself (Marcuse 1999: 97–99, 100–101, 113).

As has been stated, Hegel believes the prospect for reason and freedom to lie with the degree to which human self-consciousness has developed. Now Marcuse explains that the specific form by means of which this self-consciousness arises, according to Hegel in the *Phenomenology*, is through the "life-and-death struggle" between servant and lord—a suggestive foreshadowing of Marx's theorization of struggles between labor and capital. The very existence of the bondsman as such is dominated by her labor, which she performs to create objects "which do not belong to [her] but to another"—the lord, or the capitalist class, which through this relationship shows itself to be dependent on the very labor performed by its servants. Thus, the "thinghood" or alienation experienced by the servant dialectically opens the possibility of a self-consciousness which freely employs reason toward the understanding that the given world is contingent rather than immutable—that is to say, that the life-world is socially produced by specific power-groups, and hence given to dialectical progression beyond its immediate character, as it is experienced at any particular moment within conditions of alienation. The prospect for freedom in thought—and presumably for its material counterpart, as in Hegel's vision of a "living freedom"—becomes the very "process of history itself," its defining feature, as developed collectively through the "associated We" which arises via the struggle against domination by the lord (Marcuse 1999: 114–120).

In his infamously abstract *Science of Logic* (1812–1816), Hegel builds upon his previously established thoughts on negativity and human essence. As Marcuse writes, Hegel in the *Logic* holds "the existence of things" to be "basically negative," precisely because the given manifestations of truth are in fact false, failing as they do to correspond to the potentialities of being. Hence, the gap between existence and essence—or reality and potentiality—establishes an "Ought" which humanity is driven dialectically to overcome by breaking radically with past and present forms; recalling the earliest essays from his Heideggerian period, Marcuse specifies that this task is not one of political incrementalism, for "[t]he new must be the actual negation of the old and not a mere correction or revision [to it]." Humanity's historical struggle to realize its *Notion*—its rational essence as a "free, independent and self-determining Subject"—necessarily demands the "death of the social order" in which it finds itself entrapped. In sum, then, although reason may not be immediately evident in the character of the historical totality, it nonetheless represents the end-goal to be brought to light through human struggle (Marcuse 1999: 123, 128, 141, 148, 156).

Despite the critical perspectives Hegel advances in the *Phenomenology* and the *Logic*, he rather strangely and infamously would resign his philosophical ideals in favor of conformity with the bourgeois Restoration regimes in the years following Napoleon's defeat. This most conservative period of his, corresponding to his final 15 years of life (1816–1831), established him as the "philosophical dictator of Germany," as Marcuse puts it. His most typical work of these years is the *Philosophy of Right* (1820), which Marx would so famously denounce in his youthful investigations of communist alternatives to the hegemony of State and capital. Whereas Hegel's earlier works had associated the domination of private property with ascendant social alienation and fallenness, Hegel in the *Philosophy of Right* suddenly claims private property to be a precondition for human freedom, and moreover enthusiastically endorses the State-form, despite his own admission that the State as institution remains indifferent to human life: subject to State dominion, "individuals come under the category of means," as Hegel acknowledges. For the dialectical thinker and advocate of critical reason *par excellence*, the task of philosophy after the Bourbon Restoration regresses to one of "reconciling [humanity] to the actual," given Hegel's unexpected—and opportunistic—announcement that all the means for achieving reason are now apparently at hand, following the splintering of the German Reich and the introduction of Napoleonic reforms. Nonetheless, Hegel's infamous betrayal of his previously posited philosophies does not signify a complete embrace of positivism, or a worship of the existent; instead, Marcuse sees Hegel as advocating a *particular* type of State, one that would through bureaucratic regulation check the excesses of the bourgeoisie by operating independently from it, in the name of the free individual, and with her "true interests" in mind. In fact, Marcuse situates Hegel's defense of the Restoration regimes as a rejection of sorts of the "pseudo-democratic" opposition which had emerged from the ranks of the petty bourgeoisie after Napoleon's defeat, considering the highly inegalitarian, xenophobic, and racist political demands it made. In a telling formulation, Marcuse claims such authoritarian movements to much more closely approximate fascist ideology than did Hegel's contemporary statism, which the critical theorist stresses as having been founded on legal principles committed at least in theory to liberal notions of equality (1999: 169–171, 175–176, 179–183, 201, 203, 216, 234).

Such mitigating considerations notwithstanding, Marcuse is clear in his judgment of Hegel's "realist" turn: in glorifying the Prussian monarchy, Hegel was "guilty not so much of being servile as of betraying his highest philosophical ideas." If a student were honestly to return to Hegel's "true" conception of the dialectics of reason and freedom, she would readily be familiarized with a philosophy that could serve to break through Hegel's own "authoritarian formula for saving the given social scheme," writes Marcuse, in favor of affirming a better "future social organization" for humanity. In this way, Marcuse very much follows Marx's criticism of the *Philosophy of Right* in questioning Hegel's enthronement of capital as a move that merely legitimizes accident or chance instead of advancing the cause of a free, rational humanity re-directing world history. Moreover, Marcuse clearly repudiates the Hobbesian take on international relations adopted by Hegel, as reflected in the idealist's apologist assertions that individual States cannot be restricted by higher laws—international law, that is to say. The critical theorist counterposes to such authoritarian rationalization Hegel's own concept of the "World Mind" (*Weltgeist*), which develops through the course of world history to act as an effective check on the hegemony of States (Marcuse 1999: 202–203, 205, 218, 221–223). With this brief comment on the *Weltgeist* in *Reason and Revolution*, Marcuse is negatively expressing his advocacy of an anarcho-popular alternative.

Marcuse concludes his chronological consideration of Hegel's *oeuvre* by examining the fate of the dialectic within the lectures on the *Philosophy of History* (1830–1831). Like the legacy of the French Enlightenment which it continues, Hegel's late thought on the historical struggle to achieve reason assumes that this struggle will in fact prove victorious in the end—that the "bad present" will at some point be negated and replaced by a higher state. Though Hegel is sure of this point, he does not deny the considerable negativity which will grip human society in the interim period before reason is achieved; in fact, to reiterate, he felt periods of happiness to be "blank pages" in the history of the world. However, the very negations of history—human distress, frustration, destruction, and defeat—for Hegel constitute the very means by which the World Mind dialectically comes closer to its realization as generalized freedom and reason: "Sooner or later, the free rationality of thought must come into conflict with the rationalizations of the given order of life." In this sense, no force can stop the "march of thought," which ultimately proves fatal for constituted power (Marcuse 1999: 226, 234, 239).

To illustrate such points, Marcuse uses Hegel's example of Socrates as an embodiment of "revolutionary opposition to the Athenian State," in light of the classical philosopher's shattering conception of individual autonomy as a means of discovering truth, and his personal faithful resistance to "all external authority," which of course upholds falsity. In this vein, Marcuse reiterates that it is through the exercise of mind that the free subject emerges, by discovering that "the truth does not lie in the current norms and opinions." It is precisely this fear of subversion which ironically led Hegel to condemn the English Reform Bill in the year of his death: the German Idealist warned that a political opening such as that afforded by the Bill might subsequently progress into a popular revolution which would smash the existing system in its totality (Marcuse 1999: 243–248).

Reason and Revolution, Part 2: The Rise of Social Theory

Marcuse proceeds within the second half of *Reason and Revolution* to analyze the philosophical successors and interpretors of Hegel within modern social theory: principally, the revolutionism of Marxism and the conservatism of positivism. He finds Hegel's critical tendencies to have been furthered in egalitarian fashion by Marx and his followers, who in their development of the Hegelian dialectic effectively championed human freedom, invoking the idealist's practical recognition that the self-conscious subject can transcend the "immediately given forms of being" and change them by means of the use of reason. For Marx, the very existence of the proletariat as the oppressed class within capitalism shows the falseness and unreason of historical development; instead of freedom, there is "universal suffering" and "universal injustice." Thus, only a "*universal* revolution"—one that would overturn the "*totality* of prevailing conditions" and "replace this with a new *universal* order"—could overcome the "universal negativity" of capitalism, dialectically instituting generalized human freedom. Through Marx, Marcuse sees the chance for this revolutionary process as depending critically on the subjective development of an autonomous rationality among the freely associated individuals that feeds the desire to "change the world," as Marx famously declares at the end of his "Theses on Feuerbach." In this way, Marx establishes an "absolutist" conception of truth which aims at the socialization of production, the abolition of alienated labor, and the free development of the associated individuals. According to Marcuse, it is precisely this absolutism which inoculates Marxism and its practical component—international communism—from the obfuscation advanced by positivism and relativism (1999: 252, 255, 261, 275, 288, 316, 319, 321–322).

Before the advent of Marxism in the years following Hegel's death, though, there developed within European thought a counter-revolutionary reaction which, against the "critical and destructive tendencies" of Hegelian dialectics, sought to lead people in general to take a "positive attitude" toward existing society, as through positive philosophy, the immediate predecessor of positivism.

One of the prime advocates of this type of orientation, the Frenchman Auguste de Comte, the "father" of sociology, focused his investigations on consideration of "the facts" rather than the "transcendental illusions" advanced by rationalism. In an attempt to subvert the "anarchic force of purely revolutionary principles," Comte advanced a philosophy of resignation, argues Marcuse, in condemning all standards which "go beyond" the given reality, thus effectively coming to embrace existing power-arrangements. It is unsurprising, then, that Comte's philosophy calls for an undifferentiated tolerance—thus practically siding with the authoritarian dispensation of capital and State—and, not unrelatedly, that his account of historical progress completely excludes the possibility of revolution. Similarly in Germany, where the Restoration had strengthened the pre-existing hegemony of feudalist aristocracy, F.J. Stahl resurrected medieval concepts of the divine right of kings to suppress the threat posed by Hegelian subversion: in denying the place of radical natural law, he would equate human right with positive right, or those rights already existing and observed, and would cynically interpret given social institutions as naturally occurring, instead of being realities to be shaped and transformed through the exercise of reason. Like Burke and de Maistre, Stahl would outright replace the place of reason with obedience, claiming the latter to be the "foundation of all morality" (Marcuse 1999: 325, 327, 341, 345, 350–352, 355–357, 366–368, 372).

Following his examination of the development of philosophy after Hegel, Marcuse finally closes his grand study by explicitly considering the relationship between Hegelianism and the rise of Nazism, performing this task in part as a criticism of those in the Anglo-American world who had erroneously stipulated an affinity between these two widely diverging political philosophies. For one, Marcuse finds an unbridgeable chasm between fascism's call for the annihilation of the individual within an arational mass and Hegel's championing of the subject as bearer of reason and freedom. Furthermore, as against the Hegelian-Marxist view that political society should be shaped so as to maximize the possibilities for free self-development, Marcuse demonstrates that fascism expressly denies the possibility of ever achieving generalized human happiness. Indeed, Ernst Krieck, a prime Nazi propagandist, saw clearly the threat posed to the fascist project by German Idealism, particularly considering the latter's theorization of "a realm of truth that [is] not subject to the authority of the order that is and of the powers that be" (Marcuse 1999: 408, 413–416). As the critical theorist declares in conclusion:

> The ideological roots of authoritarianism have their soil in the 'violent reaction' against Hegel that styled itself the 'positive philosophy.' The

destruction of the principle of reason, the interpretation of society in terms of nature, and the subordination of thought to the inexorable dynamics of the given operated in the romanticist philosophy of the state, in the Historical School, in Comte's sociology (1999: 418).

In positive terms, Marcuse summarizes his admiration for Idealism as an autonomous, subversive philosophical tradition by declaring that

> German idealism protested the wholesale surrender of the individual to ruling social and political forces. Its exaltation of mind and its insistence on the significance of thought implied [...] an essential opposition to any victimization of the individual. Philosophic idealism was part and parcel of idealist culture. And this culture recognized a realm of truth *that was not subject to the authority of the order that is and of the powers that be.* Art, philosophy, and religion envisioned a world that challenged the claims of the given reality. Idealist culture is incompatible with Fascist discipline and control (1999: 416; emphasis added).

Hence, as Marcuse observes in "The Affirmative Character of Culture," "Hegel goes poorly with an authoritarian state," as "he was for the mind," which "cannot escape reality without denying itself" (1968: 126). Perhaps no better evidence of the total incompatibility between Hegel's dialectical rationalism and fascism can be found than in the infamous line uttered by the prime Nazi political theorist Carl Schmitt, who announced that on 20 January 1933—the day of Hitler's ascent to power—"Hegel, so to speak, died" (Marcuse 1999: 419).

CHAPTER 4

State, Freud, and Orphic Marxism: 1945–1960

> [Humanity] must come to associate the bad conscience not with the
> affirmation but with the denial of the life instincts, not with the rebellion
> but with the acceptance of the repressive ideals.
>
> MARCUSE 1966A: 124

With the coming of the Allied victories over Germany and Imperial Japan
in 1945, the OSS, Marcuse and Neumann's wartime employer, faced a swift
decommissioning within the large wave of post-war demobilization in the
U.S. While Neumann responded to Hitler's defeat by traveling to Germany to
apply his legal training as primary chief of research for the Nuremberg War
Crimes Tribunal, Marcuse remained in Washington for the first few months
after the fall of National Socialism, transferring his work to the State Department, where he took the post of director of the Central European Section
within the Office of Intelligence Research. As director, Marcuse worked principally with Kirchheimer and Neumann in the collective preparation of a
Denazification Guide for the new Germany. Marcuse's practical contributions
to the de-Nazification process continued with his 1946 visit to Germany, as
ordered by State, to investigate the degree to which Nazi political ideology
retained hegemony in post-war German culture and society (Mackey 2001:
320). It was during this visit—Marcuse's first direct contact with his home
country since Hitler's accession—that he sought out his former mentor Heidegger, resulting in the disagreeable meeting the two had in the latter's Black
Forest hut—an event which would cause the two to break off the correspondence they had briefly initiated, once Heidegger attempted to liken the Nazi
genocide of the Jews to the Soviet Army's pillaging of German settlements in
its drive toward Berlin near the war's end.[1] Marcuse continued working on
de-Nazification programs until 1947, holding strongly to the view that former
Nazi officials should be excluded from all public office during Germany's
reconstruction phase: that the U.S. military's occupying forces welcomed
the return to power of several such Nazi figures in the spheres of administration of German industry and politics after May 1945 shows the limited
extent to which Marcuse and his fellow left-wing colleagues had influence

---

1 See Chapters 2 and 3 above.

© KONINKLIJKE BRILL NV, LEIDEN, 2016 | DOI 10.1163/9789004308701_005

on governmental policy (Kātz 1982: 117, 130). The frustration Marcuse must have felt with this turn of events likely influenced his ruminations on the tendency of post-war liberalism to meld into a neo-fascism, as expressed in "33 Theses" (1947).

In the wake of the failures of the solid de-Nazification program sought by Marcuse and company in Germany, the critical theorist experienced much of the remainder of his time State—until 1951, that is—as presenting him with the strange juxtaposition of conflictivity with his liberal anti-communist "Cold Warrior" counterparts at the CIA, who desired outright aggression against the USSR, and the simultaneous opportunity he had to research the Soviet regime and develop philosophical critiques of it in intellectual terms. One tangible result of this dynamic was the 1949 publication by Marcuse's scholarly team of "The Potentials of World Communism," an essay which asserts among other things that the continued "major appeal of Communism" on the global stage "stems from the paradoxical situation of the coexistence of immense social wealth, [and] technological mastery of the productive forces" in certain parts of the world, together with the "widespread want, toil, and injustice" evident throughout the rest of the Earth. The evidence suggests that Marcuse and his "few remaining friends" in the Office of Intelligence Research directed their research for the government at this time in a direction which contradicted the dominant imperial trends which demonized the Soviet Union. There are few indications that this analytical countercurrent at State was taken seriously by the higher echelons of the Truman administration, nonetheless, in a parallel to the fate of the profound vision of de-Nazification advocated by Kirchheimer, Neumann, and Marcuse (Kātz 1982: 132–134).

Thus, while Marcuse did remain in governmental service for what may be taken as a surprisingly long time after the end of the war against Hitler, this should not be seen as any sort of expression of fealty on Marcuse's part for the policies of the Truman administration—for indeed, the rise of the Red Scare which began with Senator Joseph McCarthy's February 1950 speech denouncing the presence of Communists within the State Department created an environment that proved highly alienating to Marcuse. Instead, his prolonged tenure at State seems to have been based on consideration for Sophie Marcuse's cancer diagnosis and the subsequent exacerbation of her prognosis, which led Herbert to remain at his post with State—so as to ensure that Sophie would continue having access to healthcare within the privatized U.S. healthcare system (Mackey 2001: 320; Kātz 1982: 135; Marcuse and Popper 1976: 59). When she finally succumbed to the malignancy in 1951, Marcuse broke with the government—and all other governments—forever. By the time Sophie died, in point of fact, the U.S. government had very clearly expressed its fascistic hostility to the USSR, with anti-Communism taking the place of the prior wartime anti-Nazism in foreign policy (Kātz 1982: 143). This posture of militaristic antagonism differed radically from the critical orientation developed by Marcuse through the investigations of communism and Russian studies in which he engaged himself in the early 1950s, both during but especially after his time at State.

While most of the former members of the Institute for Social Research returned to West Germany in the post-war period to assist with the official transfer of the Institute to the University of Frankfurt once again, Marcuse remained in his adopted home-society, the U.S. The Institute reopened in 1951 under the directorship of Pollock, who would be succeeded by Adorno in 1958; by the time the Institute relocated, Bloch had broken with the circle and taken a professorship in Leipzig, then part of the German Democratic Republic (GDR) (Miles 2012: 86; Zuidervaart 2011). For a year at the end of his tenure at State, Marcuse lectured at the Washington School of Psychiatry; during this period would he begin his preliminary work on the volume that would later become *Eros and Civilization* (1955) (Mackey 2001: 320). It is a testament to Marcuse's love for his deceased wife that he would dedicate his major forthcoming book to her memory. Following her death and his departure from government work, Marcuse received Rockefeller grants to study Russian language and politics first at Columbia's Russian Institute in New York (1952–1954) and then at Harvard's Russian Research Center in Cambridge, Massachusetts (1954–1955). The most concrete fruit of these years of study was the publication in 1958 of Marcuse's *Soviet Marxism: A Critical Analysis*, coming three years after *Eros and Civilization*. *Soviet Marxism*, which can be considered to be among the first critical examinations of the tragic course of Russian developments since 1917, clearly communicates the author's repudiation of Stalinist hegemony on a number of grounds, and it moreover presents a hopeful vision for the development of a true Marxian political movement from within Soviet society. According to Mackey, though, Marcuse openly expresses his dissatisfaction with existing Western and Soviet regimes in the work, but arguably holds the USSR to have been more defensible than the imperialist, proto-fascist West (2001: 323). Regardless of the relative affinities Marcuse supposedly held at this time for the USSR—to reiterate, he clearly acknowledges how corrupted and ideological the Soviet concept of Marxism was—his critical approach does seem to have inspired the emergence of the "Leningrad School" in the late 1970s, this being an intellectual current which called for the deposition of the Soviet bureaucracy through a workers' revolution coordinated by critical philosophers (Martineau 1986: 26).

In *Eros and Civilization*, Marcuse applies Hegelian categories and Marxian considerations to a dialectical treatment of Freud's late theory of the human instincts: an affirmation of uncomprising human liberation, Marcuse's argumentation in *Eros and Civilization*, in the estimation of his friend Norman O. Brown, corresponds to

> one of the great romantic visions, clearly formulated by Schiller and Herder as early as 1793, and still vital in the systems of Hegel and Marx, that the history of [humanity] consists in a departure from a condition of undifferentiated primal unity with [it]self and with nature, an intermediate period in which [humanity]'s powers are developed through differentiation and antagonism (alienation) with [it]self and with nature, and a final return to a unity on a higher level or harmony.
>
> BROWN 1985: 86

According to Kellner, it was with *Eros and Civilization* that Marcuse first "achieved the union of philosophy, politics, psychology, and aesthetics" that would constitute the hallmark of his contributions to Critical Theory (1984: 37). A less enthusiastic review of the text comes from Schoolman, who worries that Marcuse's affirmation of Eros and the pleasure principle in the volume in fact "entails an unwitting celebration of the death instinct" because of the purported closeness between Eros and the "Nirvana principle" Freud identifies in *Beyond the Pleasure Principle* (1980: 112):

> The dominating tendency of mental life, and perhaps of nervous life in general, is the effort to reduce, to keep constant or to remove internal tension due to stimuli (the 'Nirvana principle,' to borrow a term from Barbara Low)—a tendency which finds expression in the pleasure principle; and our recognition of that fact is one of our strongest reasons for believing in the existence of the death instinct.
>
> FREUD 1950: 76

Marcuse will resist this putatively indelible association between pleasure and death, as Eros becomes his archetypal instinctual and even political alternative to the hegemonic Thanatos of capital, State, and domination in the years to come. It is around the time of the publication of *Eros and Civilization* that Marcuse would have another major success in receiving his first professorship, this at Brandeis University in Waltham, Massachusetts, where he taught philosophy and political science from 1954 until 1965.

A final key life-event took place at this time for Marcuse: following the death of his comrade Neumann in an automobile accident in 1953, and after three years of widowerhood since Sophie's death, Marcuse and Franz's widow Inge Werner were married. A former translator with the League of Nations and annotator of the bibliography of *European War Crimes Trials* which she published with the Carnegie Endowment for International Peace in 1951, Inge was also mother to the sons she had borne with Franz, Osha and Michael, both of whom developed into notable radicals.[2] As Mackey explains, this new marriage gave rise to an intimate joint collaboration between the couple, who shared common interests in literature, fine arts, and radical politics. Inge read and criticized all of Marcuse's written works, and in this way became a seminal intellectual partner for Herbert; what is more, given her previous translation work and her superior grasp of the English language in comparison with her new partner, Inge contributed crucially in the effort to improve the way Marcuse communicated with the public, thus greatly facilitating the project of making his body of work more accessible to larger audiences (Mackey 2001: 320).

In the immediate post-war period, then, Marcuse continued his search for radical subjects and opportunities for practical-revolutionary political interventions—with both such projects originating in his first adult experiences during WWI and the German Revolution, continuing theoretically from the start of his university studies in Berlin and Freiburg through to his time with the Frankfurt School and his independent collaborations with Neumann. During this period which corresponded to his middle and later adulthood, Marcuse proceeded in his divergent path away from Horkheimer and Adorno, who by this time had largely given up the "therapeutic" impulse in favor of the "diagnostic" one, especially as communicated in *Dialectic of Enlightenment*. Against such trends toward disengagement, Marcuse "never relaxed his search for alternatives and escapes," writes Kātz; in fact, he exercised this tendency increasingly more after leaving State (1982: 160). This divergence among the major surviving Frankfurt School theorists, which was already demonstrable in the discrepancies in orientation expressed by Adorno and Horkheimer on the one hand and Marcuse and Neumann on the other during the Institute's period of exile in New York, would presage the significant conflicts between the more activist approach favored by Marcuse and the largely academic and

---

2   Osha Neumann is a public defender and writer, author of *Up Against the Wall Motherf**ker* (Seven Stories, 2008), and his brother Michael a professor and critical intellectual, author of *The Case Against Israel* (Counterpunch Books, 2005).

STATE, FREUD, AND ORPHIC MARXISM: 1945–1960   101

idealist ones advanced by Horkheimer and Adorno in the tumultuous period
of the late 1960s, notably on the question of the colonial U.S. war in Vietnam—
as shall be explored in Chapter 5 below.

Post-War Studies: "33 Theses," Francis Bacon, Lukács, Goethe, Friedrich Hölderin, and Erasmus

During his years working for the State Department and thereafter studying at
Columbia and Harvard, Marcuse wrote relatively few pieces, limiting himself
mostly to reviews of contemporary books on social thought and philosophical
examinations of war. Two exceptions to this trend are his "33 Theses" (1947)
and article "Recent Literature on Communism" (1953). It would seem safe to
surmise that, following Sophie's death in 1951 and the militant philosopher's
subsequent abandonment of the world of statecraft, Marcuse felt himself
called to return full-time to his previous subversive study of philosophy, history,
and art. The greatest single fruit of this new phase, which Marcuse passed in
Washington, D.C., New York, and Cambridge, Massachusetts, would be *Eros
and Civilization* (1955).

Written for consideration in a postwar issue of the *Journal for Social Research*,
Marcuse's unpublished "33 Theses" (February 1947) critically explore some of
the dilemmas faced by Western Marxists within the context of an increasingly bipolar post-war global order. His former work with the OSS and ongoing
employment with the U.S. State Department notwithstanding, Marcuse outright declares in this essay that, in the wake of the military defeat of Hitler,
the "world is dividing into a neo-fascist and a Soviet camp." Grimly, he predicts that those Western societies which retained their ruling classes through
the course of the war would follow the example of the Weimar Republic and
"become fascistized in the foreseeable future," with the remainder joining the
Soviets. Paradoxically, though the neo-fascist and Soviet blocs are antagonistic
between themselves, they share a common "anti-revolutionary" orientation
that is "hostile to socialist development," wherever it is that might emerge.
Amidst this rather discouraging global political context, Marcuse sees there as
being "only one alternative for revolutionary theory: to ruthlessly and openly
criticize both systems and to uphold without compromise orthodox marxist
theory against both." His introductory comments here acknowledge that such
a posture is largely "powerless, abstract and unpolitical," but he also claims
the adoption of such a position to be the sole means of remaining true to the
revolutionary struggle (Marcuse 1998: 217).

In these thirty-three theses, Marcuse asserts that fascist processes of militarization have largely doomed the "traditional weapons of proletariat class struggle," considering the extreme asymmetry in military technologies available to the State, as compared to the people or multitude, particularly amidst the monopolization of weaponry by the former and the increasing specialization of professionalized warfare. Under such conditions, the historical call for "the arming of the people" is reduced to "a helpless affair" within the Western-capitalist societies; externally, Marcuse traces the turn to totalitarian terrorism and militarism by the bourgeoisie as inevitably distorting the development of the Soviet Union, which for survival must by needs create an "at least equally powerful military and powerful counter-apparatus" to resist capital's imperialist threats. One unfortunate consequence of this dynamic is that the chance for independent, revolutionary action among the working classes of the world is largely negated by organized labor's accommodation with the directives of the Communist Parties that operate on the orders of Moscow. A related adverse effect of this process is that, amidst the USSR's perceived need for defensive militarism and hierarchy, the Soviet alternative does not come to be seen as a "a freer and happier society" than that which is on offer in Western monopoly capitalism, such that Western proletarians reconcile themselves evermore with the status quo. The outcome, then, as Marcuse declares, is that revolutionary struggle becomes "objectively discredited"! Laborers' political and economic identification with the system, he stipulates, is supplemented by their acceptance of bourgeois cultural norms "in all spheres of social and individual life" as well. Hence Marcuse's challenging conclusion, which anticipates *One-Dimensional Man* and even the later *Counterrevolution and Revolt*: "The developing contradictions of capitalism tend toward fascism or anti-revolutionary state socialism—not toward revolution" (Marcuse 1998: 217–218, 221–222).

In these theses, Marcuse presents two contradictory options for attempting to overcome the imbroglio he has identified: firstly, the option of a Leninist party dictatorship, and secondly an anarcho-syndicalist strategy. Early on in the manuscript, Marcuse claims the observed assimilation of the proletariat into bourgeois society to show the necessity of the "dictatorship of the revolutionary 'avant-garde' over the integrated working class." The implication of such a strategy is that the transitional dictatorship would at the outset treat workers as mere objects of "party manipulation and organization," with the vague hope that labor would at a later point become the subject that autonomously carries forward the revolution, after having been tutored in the supposed ways of liberation. Uncritically hailing the Leninist model, Marcuse here claims the strategy of "communist dictatorship over the proletariat" to represent "the first step toward dictatorship of the proletariat" itself (1998: 221).

At odds with these recommendations, though, are Marcuse's calls later in the theses for the devolution of power from party cadres to the workers themselves: as he writes, the "surrender [of] the production apparatus to the proletariat" and the concomitant creation of "council republic[s]" now becomes the first goal of communist strategy, in contradiction to the theorist's previous comments on dictatorship. Against the productivist and fetishistic characteristics so apparent in the Soviet model, Marcuse clarifies his belief that the socialist "negation" of the capitalist world does not mean "the nationalization of the means of production, nor their better development, nor the higher standard of living, but rather the abolition of domination, exploitation and labor." He warns that the mere expropriation of the capitalist productive apparatus does not by itself ensure socialism: this end can be served, Marcuse asserts, only once "the producers themselves directly administer production" and "themselves determine what, how much, and how long objects are produced." Interestingly, Marcuse here theorizes that the transition to integral socialism could well be catalyzed by an apocalyptical coming of "anarchy and disintegration," as national economies are dissolved in the autonomous reason of the workers reasserting control over the means of production. As a result of such cataclysmic revolutionary changes, Marcuse admits, "poverty and affliction" might well appear to resurge *en masse* at least temporarily, and it may even be that the return of such hardship "cannot be avoided" at all. On this account, then, the "leap into socialism" would constitute a "leap" into living standards less comfortable than those seen contemporarily in capitalist societies, yet Marcuse insists that socialism should be evaluated not using standards of technical rationality but rather of those related to human freedom: "The will to abolish domination and exploitation appears as the will to anarchy." Hence, the prospect of anarchism, a philosophy which seeks total human freedom, could be helped along considerably by the workers' employment of the general strike, which Marcuse identifies critically as representing *"perhaps the only weapon [left] against fascistized capital"* (1998: 218, 223–226).

These innovative anarchist reflections aside, Marcuse ends these theses by seemingly abandoning a syndicalist orientation in favor of the Leninist model, in accordance with his earlier comments in the essay. Claiming rather dubiously that "[o]nly in the theories of the communist parties is the memory of the revolutionary tradition alive," he defines the "political task" in the thirty-third thesis as "reconstructing revolutionary theory within the communist parties and working for the praxis appropriate to it" (1998: 227). This latter task related to praxis does not necessarily conflict with the autonomist musings he shares elsewhere in the document, but the former one obviously does. Hence is seen the importance of these reflections in terms of the development of Marcuse's political philosophy, between authoritarian and libertarian socialism.

In a short review of Benjamin Farrington's *Francis Bacon: Philosopher of Industrial Science* he published three years after "33 Theses," Marcuse notes Bacon (1561–1626) to have been the "conscious philosopher of the rising industrial society," given his dialectically infamous advocacy of innovation in methods designed for the "ever more efficient domination, control, and constraint of nature." Marcuse applauds Bacon's humanitarian interest in "contributing to the alleviation of human wants and sufferings," but he implicitly questions Bacon's instrumental view of external nature—thus invoking the spirit of Schiller and utopian socialism, which will feed into Marcuse's developing concerns for ecology.[3] He also applauds Farrington's communication of Bacon's distaste for the Aristotelian philosophy, which the bourgeois apologist considers to have been "deliberately designed to cripple enterprise," in light of its proto-materialist emphasis on mental and bodily satisfaction rather than industry and profit. In fact, Bacon is shown to consider Aristotle's views as threatening the very "loss of dominion over things"! For this reason, Marcuse concludes that Bacon serves as spokesperson for not only the coming hegemony of the capitalism, but also for the Calvinist-Anglican Reformation which did so much to "emancipate" bourgeois power (Marcuse 1950a: 228–229).

In another short review from 1950 of Lukács' *Goethe and his Time* (1947), Marcuse praises his colleague's rejection of previous "irrationalistic-metaphysical" interpretations of classical German literature in favor of the elucidation of a "whole dimension" within such literature "which the traditional interpretation almost unanimously overlooks or distorts": Marcuse mentions Lukács' examination of the evident influence Enlightenment thought bore on the writings of Goethe and of the links between the French Revolution and the "heroic-utopian desperation" of the works of Goethe's contemporary Friedrich Hölderin (1770–1843), who called for a "cult of nature" and considered classical Greece a great inspiration. Additionally, Marcuse observes that the noted failure of a "bourgeois revolution" in Germany—that is, in its place, the perpetuation of feudal-absolutist relations well into the nineteenth century—leads the most "advanced" representatives of the German middle class of this society to adopt one of three following political philosophies: "romanticist obscurantism," as in Schiller's case; the utopianism of Hölderin; or the "realistic accommodation and resignation" of Goethe and Hegel (Marcuse 1950b: 142–144).

In 1951, Marcuse published an article with the *Annals of the American Academy*, reviewing José Chapiro's book *Erasmus and Our Struggle for*

---

3   See especially Chapter 7 below.

Peace, which had come out the previous year. A translation of *Querela Pacis* ("Complaint of Peace") by Erasmus of Rotterdam (1466–1532), Chapiro's book includes a biographical section which details Erasmus' long-standing "struggle for peace and a united world." For Marcuse, the book shows Erasmus to have been a "true humanist at the beginning of the modern era," both in terms of his uncompromising opposition to the prosecution of war and in his "consistent fight for tolerance and individual freedom," as against the authoritarianism of Luther. Though Erasmus' approaches are not without error—Marcuse observes that he importantly overlooks the "institutional causes of war" and naively seeks to effect peace by appealing to the princes of his day—the reviewer shows himself to be pleased and impressed with Erasmus' example and his reading of Chapiro's volume on him (Marcuse 1951a: 168).

Continued Investigations of Historical Progress, Russian Studies, and the Trajectory of Communism and Reason during the Early Cold War

Reviewing John Nef's *War and Human Progress: An Essay on the Rise of Industrial Civilization* in 1951, Marcuse declares this work "in many ways" perhaps to be "the most important book that has been published recently," considering Nef's investigation of the "interconnection between war and industrial and techno-logical progress." Dividing stages of warfare within modernity into three, Nef notes that the "genesis of industrialism" which began with the conquest of the New World was followed by a period of "limited warfare" corresponding to a limited availability of material resources with which to develop technologies of destruction, but the inhibitions against war found a philosophical basis as well in the pre-capitalist cultural emphasis on "beauty and delight" which was later displaced by the technical rationality of the later industrial-capitalist period. Ironically and negatively, as Nef describes, it was the liberatory forces of the Enlightenment and the French Revolution which opened the dual possibilities of total war and bourgeois industrialism. With the synergy of ascendant bour-geois power and the technological developments that followed, Nef observes how the "horror of personal killing" in war declined following the invention of artillery and other methods of killing "by remote control," leading to a puta-tive weakening of the prior cultural protective mechanisms that had partially inhibited militaristic excess (Marcuse 1951b: 97–99).

In resistance to this depressing panorama, particularly with the the geno-cides and mass-death of WWII in mind, Marcuse shows Nef to hold that the causes of total war can theoretically be regulated by the "collective will and

rational effort" of humanity: for this reason, writes Marcuse, little faith should
be placed in "any of the national or international power groups" that exist.
In point of fact, the critical theorist quotes Nef's observation that "[j]ust as
the modern purveyors of news and entertainment make a caricature of the
common human being and provide fare for this caricature, so modern states
represent only caricatures of the public and the public opinion they are supposed to embody in their politics." As an alternative vision, a peaceful future
can be expected to be realized only on the basis of the "growth of a common
community of understanding" developed by the joint turning of the collective
human spirit to values of "the good, the true, and the beautiful," as against the
"immediate, the practical, the national." Though Marcuse notes Nef to be short
and even "evasive" in his treatment of the practical question of the transition
between these two states, the reviewer observes that Nef's "uncompromising
demonstration" of the "failure" and "guilt" of the organized powers to abolish
war "itself contributes to a future solution"—one that could be brought about
by a future international libertarian-socialist movement (Marcuse 1951b: 100).

Intriguingly, Marcuse in 1953 published a review of Richard Hare's *Pioneers
of Russian Social Thought: Studies of Non-Marxian Formation in Nineteenth
Century Russia and of Its Partial Revival in the Soviet Union* (1951). Hare's
volume examines the philosophies of Russian thinkers including Western-
izers like Vissarion Belinksy (1811–1848) and socialist luminaries such as
Alexander Herzen (1812–1870) and Nikolai Chernyshevsky (1828–1889). Relevant to Marcuse in his focused study of the Russian language is his mention of
Hare's presentation of materials which previously had been unknown to English audiences; moreover, for Marcuse the political analyst, Hare tantalizingly
reports briefly on the "revaluations" made of such nineteenth-century philosophers within Soviet society (Marcuse 1953: 134–135).

In his final public book review from this period, Marcuse wrote an article regarding "Recent Literature on Communism" that examines four works
on Soviet developments from the early 1950s, including one by historian
E.H. Carr. Anticipating *Soviet Marxism* (1958), Marcuse discusses Leninist
theory, whereby the Communist Party comes to replace the proletariat as
the "active revolutionary force," as well as the fate of Leninist victory in Russia, a process he considers to have been largely shaped by the failed German
and other Central European revolutions which emerged after 1917. Echoing
Carr, Marcuse notes that the Stalinist policy of "socialism in one country" had
already largely been decided with the Social-Democrat suppression of the German Revolution. In this review essay, Marcuse seeks to distinguish between
communism and its Soviet interpretations: "Communism is more than and
different from what Stalinism has made of it—more and different not only in

theory, but in actuality." In fact, in practical historical terms, Marcuse observes that a "good case" could be made that "Western Communism was stronger before it came under Soviet-Russian control" and moreover "*is* stronger where it is still largely outside Soviet-Russian control" (emphasis added). In sum, an autonomous sense of communism persists, amidst the established hegemony of authoritarian-socialist, fascist, and liberal-Social Democrat regimes. Considering Marcuse's declaration here that "[n]o philosophy can justify the sufferings of the millions who are again being sacrificed, here and there, on the slaughterbench of World History," he is implicitly suggesting that a global libertarian-communist revolution could uproot the dominant institutions which perpetuate unfreedom and unreason (Marcuse 1954: 517–525).

Within this vein, Marcuse returns in 1954 to his *magnum opus* on Hegel, *Reason and Revolution,* writing a supplementary epilogue which ties the work's complex scope to reflection on the world-situation of the mid-1950's. Alarmingly, Marcuse begins this new commentary by declaring that the fall of Hitler and National Socialism in Germany

> has not arrested the trend toward totalitarianism, [given that] [n]either the Hegelian nor the Marxian idea of Reason have come closer to realization [since the end of the war]; neither the development of the Spirit nor that of the Revolution took the form envisaged by dialectical theory.
>
> MARCUSE 1999: 433

Marcuse interprets the failure of the dialectic to realize either such notion of reason as lying mainly with the stipulated compromise of the revolutionary nature of the Western industrial proletariat, which, rather than be comprised of "free individuals" liberated from "the needs and interests of domination and repression" who would embody the "very negation" of capitalism, has largely integrated itself into the system, making itself into "a positive part of the establishment," according to Marcuse. The critical theorist ties this postulated development specifically into the theory of labor aristocracy, whereby the "supra-profits" obtained by the super-exploitation imposed by Western capitalists on non-European peoples and geographies allow for an overcoming of the tendency toward proletarian impoverishment in Europe and the U.S., thus contradicting Marx's predictions regarding the "immiseration thesis." Instead, wages and living standards for workers in the imperial core rise, just as power becomes overwhelmingly concentrated among the wealthiest and most powerful monopolists, who manipulate and coordinate mass-culture in an attempt to further tie the producers into affirming the status quo. What is more, Marcuse reiterates his point from "33 Theses" that the development of technology further entrenches such inequalities, with the asymmetry in the "instruments of destruction" available to State and populace diverging widely to favor control by the former. Amidst thoroughgoing cultural coordination and military repressiveness, "the development of capitalist productivity [has] stopped the development of revolutionary consciousness," concludes Marcuse, such that the desire to transcend the capitalist present becomes "the dangerous prerogative of outsiders"—at least within Western industrial societies (1999: 435–438).

Another important means by which Marcuse sees capitalism as having stabilized itself amidst its numerous contradictions, thus "absorb[ing] its negativity," has to do with the fate of the Bolshevik takeover in Russia. On the critical theorist's account, the Bolsheviks' international isolation in the wake of the failed attempts to revolutionize Central Europe at the end of the First World War led Lenin and Stalin to embark on processes of "terroristic industrialization" which represented no radical alternative to established capitalism, but rather a reproduction of the "repressive and exploitative" aspects of the very system denounced by Marx. Nevertheless, Marcuse sees Western ruling groups fomenting nationalism as a means of further alienating the subordinated classes from autonomously developing a liberatory course away from the present, with Stalinism for its part very similarly casting the Communist struggle against Western power as the defense of its subject populations, the peoples of the USSR. With these two poles in mind, Marcuse observes at the close of his new epilogue that the "pre-conditioning of the individuals, their shaping into objects of administration, seem to be universal phenomena," and thus that "[t]he idea of a different form of Reason and Freedom" is reduced once again to resembling "Utopia," as in no-place (1999: 437–439).

In a characteristically dialectical finish, however—and anticipating the argument of his forthcoming *Eros and Civilization*—Marcuse ends this reflection optimistically, declaring that the fact that the hegemonic powers of international society, capitalist and Soviet, have mobilized themselves so totally against the "ultimate liberation of the individual" in fact "indicates how real is the possibility of this liberation" (1999: 439).

Marcuse continues engaging with these types of matters in his preface to Raya Dunayevskaya's *Marxism and Freedom* (1958), wherein he notes the "reexamination of Marxian theory" which Dunayevskaya advances to be decidedly urgent, particularly given the intercontinental stabilization of capitalist rule that Marx himself did not foresee. He praises Dunayevskaya for stressing the humanism of Marx's thought—particularly its "*deep-rooted anarchistic and libertarian elements*"—and highlighting the two-dimensional analysis it takes from Hegel, between the Marxian judgment of bourgeois society and the "objective-historical potentialities and capabilities" on hand (emphasis added). With regard to anarchism, Marcuse here emphasizes the importance of redefining freedom as "living without toil" or "anxiety," such that the goal of socialist politics should be to maximize the free time available to the individual by abolishing labor through the employment of the "highest degree of mechanization." In this preface, Marcuse also shares his growing pessimism with regard to the consciousness of the Western proletariat, which he claims to increasingly to have become an affirmation rather than negation of the capitalist system; with this comment, taken alongside his explicit disagreement with Dunayevskaya on the relationship between Leninism and Stalinism—for Marcuse would seem to conceive of the two philosophies as more similar than Dunayevskaya would allow—the theorist anticipates the arguments of his *One-Dimensional Man* seven years later (Marcuse 1958a: 10–15).

Relatedly, Marcuse lambasts German positivist Karl R. Popper in a 1959 review of the latter's *The Poverty of Historicism* (1957), a work that seeks to denounce totalitarian violence and counterpose liberal incrementalism as an alternative. Marcuse opens by considering the dedication Popper makes in the volume to the "countless men and women [...] who fell victim to the fascist and communist belief in Inexorable Laws of Historical Destiny," taking the sociologist to task for unjustly linking fascism and communism, given that Marxian theory and the act of socialist revolution aim "precisely [at] the *abolition* of [...] *oppressive* laws" such as those considered natural and rational—inexorable—by liberalism, whereas fascism expresses much more a "denial of history" and an enthronement *of nature* in place of historical progress. In point of fact, Marcuse accuses Popper of arguing in bad faith, given that the "gradualist and pluralist approach" which the latter advocates is in empirical terms hardly exempt from resorting to atrocious displays of a systematic employment of violence: on this question, Marcuse argues, one need only review the historical record since the origins of liberalism in seventeenth-century Europe. Furthermore, Marcuse takes issue with Popper's equating of Marxism with the Stalinist regime in Russia, observing that the Marxian "theoretical discussion was crushed, not consummated, by the Stalinist plan." As he will do throughout his life, particularly in the 1960s, Marcuse here also notes the distinctions between the differing ends sought in the historical employment of various forms of terror—with these being complicating factors that Popper ignores entirely in his blanket condemnation of revolution leading to State-terrorism. On Marcuse's account, terror "has been used for the preservation of the status quo and for its overthrow, for the streamlining of a declining society and for the release of new political and economic forces." Marcuse here points out the differences, for example, between Jacobin and post-Thermidorian terror, though he clarifies that he is no enthusiast of violence, even of counter-violence from below: the critical theorist unequivocally states all forms of terror to constitute crimes against humanity and "instrument[s] of domination and exploitation" (Marcuse 1972a: 193–197).

In addition, Marcuse criticizes Popper's undialectical condemnation of "holism," or totality, which includes totalitarian as well as anti-totalitarian ideologies. According to Marcuse, Popper's critique papers over the important distinctions between conservative and critical notions of "holism," with the former rationalizing prevailing oppression and the latter seeking to overcome them through revolution. Indeed, Marcuse notes that an "anti-dialectical logic" is central to Popper's argumentation in *The Poverty of Historicism*, for Popper seeks to affirm liberalism as an antidote to totalitarianism without reflectively considering whether an actual relationship exists between the two. Implicitly referencing the work he and his Frankfurt School colleagues had been engaged in for nearly three decades by this point, Marcuse declares "liberalistic society" not to be "immune to totalitarian trends and forces," and he rhetorically asks whether the free market has "prevented or promoted the concentration of power and the corrosion of individual liberties." Marcuse's conclusion to the review is a typically activist one: he observes that liberal tendencies toward totalitarian forms of socio-political organization can be arrested by the existence and action of resistance movements, and that the alternative to ever-increasing barbarism remains a change in the basic structure of society. Thus inverting Popper's line of thought, Marcuse declares that liberal barbarism advances "with the irresistible force of nature—*as if* governed by inexorable laws," such that the "'holism' which has become reality must be met by a 'holist' critique of this reality"—as well as a holistic counter-movement against it (Marcuse 1972a: 202–208).

On Sartre's Existentialism

Marcuse appraises the existentialist philosophy of Jean-Paul Sartre in a 1948 article that deals with the prevailing absurdity which Camus, Sartre, and other existentialists focus on in their writings. Marcuse takes a favorable view of existentialist approaches which show the mind and self as having been "thrown into an 'absurd' world in which the brute fact of death and the irretrievable process of Time deny all meaning," a "world void of purpose and hope." Marcuse recognizes the special importance of the existentialist stress on absurdity in the period after WWII, given the utter irrationality of the continued domination by the "old management" in the post-war era. He welcomes Camus' recognition of the various challenges posed by absurdity and the associated struggle for "freedom and happiness in a world where there is no hope, sense, progress and morrow": Camus identifies this life as "nothing but 'consciousness and revolt,'" with defiance "its only truth." Nonetheless, passing to consideration of Sartre himself, Marcuse sees much of Heidegger reflected, especially in terms of the French writer's putative ontologization or naturalization of the experience of "failure and frustration" in human history. It is due to this tendency on Sartre's part that Marcuse accuses the latter's existentialism of idealism and an "illusory" claim to radicality—particularly given Marcuse's misgivings about the Sartrean conception of freedom, whereby humanity is always actually free, regardless of material and historical circumstances. Marcuse derides this conception by likening it to "Luther's comforting message of Christian liberty." Yet despite the criticisms he raises, Marcuse acknowledges Sartre's expressed commitment to communist revolution, and he finds this tendency within existentialism to be authentic and revolutionary—a negation of ideologies which are content with the mere realization of internal freedom (Marcuse 1972a: 159–162).

Examining these two seemingly contradictory facets of Sartre's existentialism, Marcuse presents Sartre's analysis of the task of "being in an absurd world," which requires firstly the recognition of the depth of alienation and negativity that grips the life-world, and secondly the understanding of the notion that humanity is fully and unquestionably responsible for its existence, in light of its absolute freedom—one that "[n]o power in heaven or earth can force [the individual] to abdicate." Marcuse strongly critiques this notion of absolute freedom and responsibility, noting it ultimately to serve as a "handy justification for the persecutors and executioners," in light of the claim that Sartre believes workers, Jews, and other oppressed groups have freely chosen their subjugation, such that they are equally free to accept or reject such domination (Marcuse 1972a: 160, 164–165, 172–173). Marcuse accuses Sartre of idealism over his account of liberty; he cites the existentialist's questionable observation in *L'Être et le Néant* (*Being and Nothingness*) that "the executioner's tools cannot dispense us from being free" (Sartre 1943: 587). Marcuse summarizes the Sartrean concept satirically:

> The slave is literally and actually free to break [her] chains [...]. Everybody can 'transcend' [her] situation, carry out [her] own project: everybody has [her] absolutely free choice. However adverse the conditions, [humanity] must 'take it' and make compulsion [its] self-realization.
>
> MARCUSE 1972A: 172, 174

Marcuse observes that Sartre himself contemplates the worry the critical theorist is presenting in an article for *Les Temps Modernes*, wherein the existentialist writes that "[t]he revolutionary himself [*sic*]...distrusts freedom. And rightly so. There has never been a lack of prophets to proclaim to him that he was free, and each time in order to cheat him." This is a significant philosophical tension which Marcuse feels Sartre does not adequately resolve in *L'Être et le Néant*, however much he welcomes Sartre's explicit endorsement of revolution as the only means of social liberation, an option that is always open to humanity (1972a: 182–183). In Hegelian terms, Marcuse also finds promise in Sartre's dialectical understanding of human existence as dynamic and constituted through action; as he quotes Sartre in *L'Être et le Néant*, "The being which merely is what it is cannot be free. Freedom is actually the void which is in [humanity]'s heart and which forces the human reality to *create itself* rather than to *be*" (Sartre 1943: 516). In a friendly postscript to the article written in 1965, Marcuse hails Sartre's rise to world-class intellectual status as evidence of the existentialist's authentic revolutionism—Marcuse expresses his joy that Sartre developed his philosophy more by means of the critical rather than affirmative aspects of *L'Être et le Neant* in the interim years. Commenting on Sartre's expressed worry that he has through all his fame become an "institution," Marcuse warmly shares his view that any such institution would be a refuge for "conscience and truth" (1972a: 189–190).

Orphic Marxism and the Struggle of Eros against Thanatos

Next to his later *Essay on Liberation* (1969), *Eros and Civilization: A Philosophical Inquiry into Freud* (1955) is arguably the single-most optimistic and speculative work Marcuse wrote in life. As a radical and highly unconventional investigation into psychology and psychoanalysis, *Eros and Civilization* grounds its basis in Marcuse's established desire to explore the reasons why communism and liberation had not yet been realized on the world stage—and particularly to seek metapsychological explanations for the devastation wrought on humanity by fascist militarism in recent memory: the "[c]oncentration camps, mass exterminations, world wars, and atom bombs" (Marcuse 1966a: 4). Continuing with Marcuse's concern for dialectics, the work acknowledges the centrality of human disenchantment within modernity, given the dominance of an established system that corresponds to Max Weber's concept of the "Iron Cage." Beyond this, the text explores autonomous notions of the exercise of mind and social relations as counter-movements against established social domination.

In his search for a "non-repressive civilization" which could deliver humanity to a state liberated from hierarchy altogether, Marcuse considers encouraging trends within human behavior which suggest that humanity's forms of social organization can be radically transformed, and so become other than what prevails under monopoly capitalism. In essence, *Eros and Civilization* presents Marcuse's materialist critique of Freud's psychological and "even metaphysical" theory of human instincts—as Marcuse notes in *Five Lectures* a year later—by means of which the critical theorist suggests that the repression, destructiveness, and domination which Freud studied and observed do not represent inevitable realities of social life, instead corresponding to "specific historical organization[s] of human existence" which could be transcended by means of a shattering world anti-capitalist revolution that advances a vision of emancipation for all (1966a: 4–5; 1970a: 6).

Marcuse opens the first part of the text, "Under the Rule of the Reality Principle," by stating paradoxically that the view of humanity advanced by Freudian theory represents "the most irrefutable indictment of Western civilization—and at the same time the most unshakable defense of this civilization." For Freud, recorded human history, or civilization, corresponds directly to a history of human repression; it is only when "uncontrolled Eros"—or what Marcuse terms "the great unifying force that preserves all life"—is reined in that civilization can begin, on this account. In this way, the primordial *pleasure principle* in which organic life originally arises and evolves comes to be displaced in favor of the *reality principle*, which allows for the human exercise of reason, work, and productivity. Amidst the new-found dominance of the reality principle, the basic, original human desire for pleasure—which Marcuse, like Freud, argues to be natural and inherent—is repressed. This original site of repression, in Marcuse's analysis, constitutes the germ-cell which over the course of thousands of years will yield the "civilized division of labor, progress, and 'law and order.'" In light of the negating course history has taken to date, a major concern of Marcuse's in *Eros and Civilization* will be to explore the function of the unconscious and phantasy (or imagination) as forms of "thought-activity" connected to the pleasure principle that persist within individuals subjected to the reign of the reality principle, and which thus represent potential and actual sites of resistance (Marcuse 1966a: 11–14, 27, 125, 138). Following Freud, Marcuse finds the early childhood stages of development to show clear indications of the natural human propensity toward eroticism and life-affirmation.

Proceeding beyond these introductory notes, Marcuse presents his theory of ontogenesis, or the "origin of the repressed individual," which incorporates Freud's postulation of a seemingly eternal conflict between the two "primary drives" identified by the psychoanalyst in his late investigations after the First

World War: *Eros*, or the life instinct, as against *Thanatos*, or the death instinct. As the rule of the pleasure principle predates that of the reality principle, it is the former that underpins and sustains the emergence of life itself; archetypally, it is Eros which helps to bind together the cells of the developing organism and thus aid in its progression, maturation, flourishing, and enjoyment. In this way, Eros "continuously counteract[s] and delay[s] the 'descent toward death'" which Freud identified human existence as ultimately amounting to, given his late, pessimistic belief in the strength of the death drive. Against Freudian resignation, Marcuse here suggests that the length of the continuous "detour" against death overseen by Eros might instead demonstrate that the point of life is not at all to die but rather to live. Moreover, Marcuse suggests that the historical strength of the death instinct may well be a reflection of the dominion of hostile external conditions, which lead the organism unconsciously to flee "from pain and want" in the desire for death. Thus, in a real sense, it is the historical "*failure of* Eros" which strengthens the dominion of Thanatos (Marcuse 1955: 22, 25–27, 29, 109).

In Freud's theory, the human ego develops from the id so as to prevent the destruction of the self by means of what would otherwise be its unchecked desire for gratification and pleasure. By this means, through the introduction of *basic repression*, the ego displaces the pleasure principle in favor of the internalization of the reality principle, and adjustment of the life of the mind to conform with the demands of such. The reality principle, in turn, emerges within the context of material scarcity, such that life takes place in a world that is "too poor for the satisfaction of human needs without constant restraint, renunciation, and delay." For this reason, the reality principle demands that the organism engage in labor, and during the time in which the organism is laboring, "pleasure is 'suspended' and pain prevails," with the result that the basic instinct of Eros is weakened, leading ultimately to a "repressive regimentation" of the instincts which favors Thanatos and established reality. Nevertheless, Marcuse is quick to point out here that the mere fact of scarcity should not be separated from consideration of the instituted forms of social organization, which largely have been determined by the power groups that have directed the course of progress over the course of civilization through their various forms of imposing the reality principle: as is evident through reflection on the trajectory of recorded human history, far more often than not, the historical organization of scarcity has "not been distributed collectively in accordance with individual needs" but rather in the interests of perpetuating prevailing relations of domination. With such comments out of the way, Marcuse presents his dialectical critique, claiming that the repressive institutions of the reality principle—or the *performance principle*, as it is manifested in industrial-capitalist societies—correspond to "*additional* controls over and above those indispensable for civilized human association": hence his designation of contemporary oppression and repression as representing "surplus repression." He speculates that, were such surplus repression to be overthrown, the life of a "*free* Eros" would contribute profoundly to the creation of "lasting civilized societal relationships," through the rejection of those institutions and realities which perpetuate the stratification of society "according to the competitive economic performances of its members" (Marcuse 1966a: 30–31, 35–37, 43–44).

In Marxian terms—though Marx himself is not explicitly mentioned, neither at this point nor at any other in the text—Marcuse observes that the reign of the performance principle leads the social majorities to survive under conditions of alienation, amidst the socially constructed necessity of toil— individuals must "submit if they want to live," yet in so toiling, they perpetuate "an apparatus which they do not control." Amidst the reproduction of such conditions of reification and alienation, argues Marcuse, normalization sets in, and the individual comes to "liv[e] [her] repression 'freely' as [her] own life" (1966a: 45–46). Even for those who conform to and succeed within hegemonic standards—being rewarded with material comfort, for example—authentic happiness remains illusory: for, as Marcuse writes,

> In one of his most advanced formulations, Freud once defined happiness as the 'subsequent fulfillment of a pre-historic wish. *That is why wealth brings so little happiness: money was not a wish in childhood*' (1966a: 203; emphasis added).

Anticipating arguments he would expand upon later in *One-Dimensional Man*, Marcuse here notes that the very experience of everyday life under capital comes to be regimented, with autonomy negated first during the arduous work-day and subsequently in the few hours of leisure afforded to laborers: leisure-time is taken in the main as a "re-creation of energy for work" rather than as a time for free self-development, and Marcuse sees a conscious design here, considering the very real risk posed by the possibility of the development of a collective human intelligence which might become aware of the "potentialities of liberation from the reality of repression" and thus struggle politically against the imposed reality (1966a: 48).

Similarly, Marcuse argues at the outset of *Eros and Civilization* that the social organization of sexuality under the reality principle radically contradicts its originary nature, which he defines as being "polymorphous-perverse." In developing his thoughts on sexuality, Marcuse claims that its constrained

channeling into monogamic heterosexual manifestations aims solely at pro-
creation, thus perpetuating the existing system, whereas the manifestation
and exercise of alternative "perversions" effectively serve to rebel against the
institutions which uphold the repressive order. Connected with phantasy and
artistic imagination, sexual perversions "place themselves outside the dominion of the performance principle and [so] challenge its very foundation"; as
embodiments of Eros, they represent "what had to be suppressed so that suppression could prevail and organize the ever more efficient domination of
[humanity] and nature" (1966a: 49–50). In Marcuse's view, the non-procreative
expressions of sexual perversion lead the organism to recall its origins in pleasure; in this is seen the subversive potential of sexual liberation, and the danger it could pose to all hegemony. Making such points, Marcuse advances an
emancipatory vision of alliance among queer and straight individuals alike—a
point to which the text shall shortly return.

Passing from considerations of the origin of the repressed individual,
Marcuse comes to examine Freud's concept of phylogenesis, or the origin of
repressive civilization taken as a whole—as from the phylogenetic trees of
biological science, which represent hypothesized evolutionary relationships
among different species. Noting Freud's speculative anthropological account
from *Moses and Monotheism* to be plagued at the very least by the problem
of "scientific verification," Marcuse nonetheless relates it here in his phylogenetic discussion, taking it perhaps as an extended metaphor. Domination,
according to Freud, originated in humanity within the *primal horde* mode of
social organization, beginning with the imposition of despotic rule by a father
who monopolizes the sexually desirable females of the group for his pleasure and reproduction and demands harsh toil from his children, who in turn
are to provide for his life to exist in comfort. Such inequality inevitably leads
to resentment and hatred of the father among his sons, who unite to rebel
against him, killing him and ultimately even physically devouring his body in
the process. With this primordial rebellion, Marcuse observes, comes the possibility of liberation—a destruction of hierarchy for all time, and a return to
the pre-existing dominance of Eros and the pleasure principle—but the sons,
overtaken by guilt—their internalization of the reality principle previously
imposed by the father—effectively re-establish the domination once exercised by the patriarch-despot. Shifting from a power distribution resembling
centralized monarchy to a diffuse sort of feudalism, the sons establish *brother
clans* (1966a: 59–65).

As against such trends, nevertheless, the destruction of the primeval
father allows for matriarchal societies to blossom, at least for a time; within
these matriarchal contexts, the argument goes, there is seen a "low degree of

repressive domination" and a relatively higher exercise of "erotic freedom." Unfortunately, though, patriarchy ultimately succeeds eventually in reasserting itself within this struggle for power, in no small part by resorting to organized religion as a means of suppressing matriarchal alternatives. In this way, the "crime against the reality principle" represented by the murder of the primeval father "is redeemed by the crime against the pleasure principle"—the active suppression of the very real possibilities of Eros, pleasure, and liberation which are at hand. Given the growing hegemony of slave-economies as instituted by the brother clans, the progress of civilization is assured at this point. Still, such "progression" periodically meets with what Freud would term the *return of the repressed*, a social dynamic whereby new generations come to revolt and rebel against the established system in an attempt to bring external reality into accordance with Eros, which is thought to govern the life of children far more than their more adjusted elders. The resurgence of expressions of resistance signifies the "tabooed and subterranean history of civilization" for Marcuse. Against this eternal return, though, hegemonic interests seek to mobilize society toward the annihilation of the "image of liberation" which has "become increasingly realistic": for Marcuse, this authoritarian dynamic is exemplified in the emergence of the "[c]oncentration and labor camps" of modernity, as in the "trials and tribulations of non-conformists" seen previously and throughout recorded history (1966a: 65–66, 68–69, 71).

It is at this point that Marcuse explicitly introduces his concept of the *dialectic of civilization*, whereby, in negative terms, revolts and revolutions from below historically have merely succeeded in streamlining the repressive apparatus, while, more positively, the modern destructiveness of civilization—its "wars, ubiquitous persecution, anti-Semitism, genocide, bigotry, and the enforcement of 'illusions,' toil, sickness, and misery"—could both in theory and in reality be superseded by means of a conscious reorientation of the material base and technologies developed to date by capitalism. In regards to the first part of this dialectic, Marcuse refers to his previous elucidation of the primal rebellion against the patriarch-despot, noting that "the struggle of the oppressed," from "the slave revolts in the ancient world to the socialist revolution," have merely "ended [up] in establishing a new, 'better' system of domination." "Each revolution has been the conscious effort to replace one ruling group by another"; for this reason, "every revolution has also been a betrayed revolution." As civilization develops, authority becomes increasingly rationalized, "impersonal, objective, universal," as in Weber's theorization of the shift from charismatic or traditional to bureaucratic power; coterminous with this turn of events, Marcuse argues, is a generalized "blunt[ing]" of the individual's consciousness of prevailing relations of domination (1966a: 78, 89–91, 102–103).

The individual does not really know what is going on; the overpowering machine of education and entertainment unites [her] with all
the others in a state of anaesthesia from which all detrimental ideas
tend to be excluded. And since knowledge of the whole truth is hardly
conducive to happiness, such general anaesthesia makes individuals
happy (1966a: 104).

Here is seen the return of Marcuse's concerns on the anesthetic function of
affirmative culture, as laid out in his 1937 essay on the subject. While the overwhelming majority of those subjected to conditions of civilization must necessarily suffer in yielding the majority of their time to alienated labor, they
are in the modern Western context to some degree compensated for such
abnegation through unprecedented access to material, commodified comfort,
which serves to "keep them occupied and divert their attention from the real
issue—which is the awareness that they could both work less and determine
their own needs and satisfactions." Despite this generalized lack of revolutionary consciousness which Marcuse posits, he observes dialectically that,
at their very heights, civilization and domination effectively undermine their
very foundations, given that the subordinated could elect to do away with
the surplus repression that upholds the system of alienation and destruction
at any point, amidst the very real prospect of overcoming scarcity and thus
overthrowing the dominion of the death instinct and performance principle.
Workers, previously understood as instruments who serve domination, could
instead become subjects who appropriate the "social wealth" established by
the course of civilization and thus abolish themselves as instruments, becoming ends in themselves. Against this fatal threat must domination mobilize
itself and its subjects: "Civilization has to defend itself against the specter of a
world which could be free." To ward off such a specter, Marcuse argues, ideological repressiveness becomes most acute at this potentially terminal phase
of repressive civilization, for domination cannot allow another "killing of the
father, not even a 'symbolic' killing—because he may not find a successor"
(1966a: 85, 93–94, 100).

In the second half of *Eros and Civilization*, entitled "Beyond the Reality
Principle," Marcuse shifts his focus from analysis of the historical path leading up to the thoroughly alienated present in favor of more speculative and
life-affirming examinations of various means of displacing capitalist domination from the stage of history. Against Freud, who infamously argued that
civilization cannot be other than repressive, Marcuse posits that the hitherto
repressive organization of the two primary human drives—in essence, the
dominance of Thanatos over Eros—relates to contingent, exogenous factors

which can be overcome by means of a rational appropriation and reorientation of the resources built up by civilization (1966a: 132).

In practical terms, Marcuse notes Freud's observation that mental resistance to the reality principle occurs primarily within the unconscious mind, which preserves the "perpetual but repressed ideas of the collective memory, the tabooed images of freedom." Like the Hegelian *Geist*, phantasy, whether conscious or unconscious, aims at "surmounting" the "antagonistic human reality" by reconciling the individual with society and happiness with reason. Taking form, Marcuse explains, phantasy becomes art, a visible manifestation of the return of the repressed which protests eternally against "the organization of life by the logic of domination" and recalls the past "liberation that failed," the "promise that was betrayed." Whether expressed externally in art or abstractly in the mind, phantasy critically "refus[es] to accept as final the limitations imposed upon freedom and happiness by the reality principle" and so "refuses to forget what *can be*." Hence, phantasy and art are intimately connected with the Marcuse an notion of the Great Refusal, or the "protest against unnecessary repression, the struggle for the ultimate form of freedom," which, citing Adorno, the theorist defines as the freedom to "live without anxiety." Implicitly suggesting that the the the transmogrification of phantasy into socio-political practice would "change the human existence in its entirety," Marcuse posits that the realization of a revolutionary, egalitarian synthesis of the pleasure and reality principles would require that all peoples of Earth experience standards of living which are "vastly lower" than those seen contemporarily in industrial-capitalist societies: thus, consumerist excess would need to be abandoned for all to "live a human life." In contrast to the alienated standards which measure happiness in terms set by the performance principle—for example, with reference to statistical growth in the production and consumption of "automobiles, television sets, airplanes, and tractors"—Marcuse counterposes a vision of universally observed basic human needs and "freedom from guilt and fear." With this alternative conception—doubtlessly informed by his love for Romanticism, German *Kultur*, and utopian socialism, and being a vision which incidentally is largely congruent with anarchism—Marcuse points up the similarities between capitalist West and Soviet East, noting the productivist goal of increasing the efficiency of labor to be the "sacrosanct ideal" of both repressive regimes (1966a: 140–141, 143–144, 149–151, 153, 156, 158).

In an attempt to draft a new, higher concept of reason which would integrate rather than shun sensuousness—and thus advance the "integral fulfillment of [humanity] and nature"—Marcuse presents the Greek mythological figures of Orpheus and Narcissus as alternatives to the prototypical Prometheus, stealer of fire from Mt. Olympus, who Marcuse describes as the "archetype-hero" of the performance principle. Known for their association with beauty, art, and nature, Orpheus and Narcissus share with Dionysus and Bacchanalianism a marginal place in the Greek-mythological pantheon presented by the monopoly-capitalist media (1966a: 160–161, 197). The two

> have not become the culture-heroes of the Western world: theirs is the image of joy and fulfillment; the voice which does not command but sings; the gesture which offers and receives; the deed which is peace and ends the labor of conquest; the liberation from time which unites [humanity] with god, [humanity] with nature (1966a: 162).

Marcuse speculates that the values represented by these archetypal alternatives could serve to reconcile the conflicting instincts of Eros and Thanatos in favor of the former, for they "recall the experience of a world that is not to be mastered and controlled but to be liberated." Quoting the French poet Charles Baudelaire (1821–1867), Marcuse associates Orpheus and Narcissus with a vision wherein "all is order and beauty, luxury, calm, and sensuousness." On Marcuse's account, the Eros expressed by Orpheus and Narcissus "awakens and liberates potentialities that are real in things animate and inanimate," showing the *telos* of the beings of nature to be "'just what they are,' 'being-there,' existing" (1966a: 164–165). In negating the performance principle, the images of Orpheus and Narcissus thus serve to unify humanity with nature, such that "the fulfillment of [humanity] is at the same time the fulfillment, without violence, of nature":

> In being spoken to, loved, and cared for, flowers and springs and animals appear as what they are—beautiful, not only for those who address and regard them, but for themselves, 'objectively.' [...] The song of Orpheus pacifies the animal world, reconciles the lion with the lamb and the lion with [humanity] (1966a: 166).

As poet, "*liberator* and *creator*," Orpheus engenders a "higher order in the world—an order without repression." Importantly in this sense, Marcuse favorably discusses Orpheus' stipulated introduction of homosexuality to the classical world, noting this alternative orientation as rejecting the "normal Eros" out of a desire for a "fuller Eros" (1966a: 170–171). In the open admiration Marcuse here declares for sexual diversity amidst the repressive conformity of 1950s U.S. society, he shows himself to be an important trailblazer in favor of LGBTQ liberation, particularly when compard to contemporary and previous Euro-American Marxists. Vincent Geoghegan notes the similarities between Marcuse's defense of homosexuality and the queer-friendly attitudes of fellow leftist Edward Carpenter (1844–1929), who welcomed non-heterosexual orientations, terming them "Uranian," after the seventh planet of the Solar System:

> It is possible that the Uranian spirit may lead to something like a general enthusiasm of humanity, and that the Uranian people may be destined to form the advance guard of that great movement which will one day transform the common life by substituting the bond of personal affection and compassion for the monetary, legal and other external ties which now control and confine society.
>
> GEOGHEGAN 1981: 56; LAURITSEN and THORSTAD 1974: 86

Besides Carpenter's admittedly visionary interpretation, Marcuse's enthusiasm for "polymorphous-perverse" sexual orientations can fruitfully be juxtaposed with those of Huey P. Newton, who in 1970 speculated that queer individuals "could be the most revolutionary" of all (Newton 2009: 253). Beyond considering Orpheus and non-procreative sexuality, Marcuse declares the image of Narcissus to suggest a conception of life as beauty and existence as contemplation. Thus taken together, the two figures negate what Prometheus and the hegemonic consider all order, embodying a revolutionary destructiveness which allows for a "new reality, [...] governed by different principles" (1966a: 171).

Marcuse further expands on his speculative commentary regarding Greek mythology in his discussion of what he terms the "aesthetic dimension." He begins by favorably citing Kant's equation of beauty with the symbol of morality in his *Critique of Judgment* (1790), and he ties these two concepts together with human freedom, which on Kant's account is to be developed autonomously. Marcuse then specifically relates Kant's theory of aesthetics, stressing that it—in a parallel to the potential influence Orpheus might have in the birth of a new, "non-repressive" civilization—calls for aesthetic objects, whatever they may be ("thing or flower, animal or man"), to be depicted and evaluated not in terms of any sort of utility but rather on the basis of their intrinsic being; in this way, the "pure form" of objects, their "being-there" or "existence," thus is a manifestation of their beauty. Marcuse argues that the emancipatory potential within Kant's thought is readily advanced by his student Schiller, as has been discussed—for Schiller would publish his letters *On the Aesthetic Education of Man* largely under the influence of Kant's *Critique*. For Marcuse, Schiller seeks a "remaking of civilization by virtue of the liberating force of the aesthetic function," which demands a new reality principle based in aesthetics. As in Schiller's *Aesthetic Education*, Marcuse stipulates that this new reality principle would unite the human imagination with its need for beauty, replacing labor with play and universally expanding freedom, as is to be self-legislated by the associated individuals of the Earth to come (Marcuse 1966a: 174, 178, 180, 185–1961). In the "aesthetic state," to reiterate, the universal law is "to give freedom by freedom" (Schiller 1954: 137). Given the Kantian and Schillerian eclipse of toil by play—and the broader replacement of coercively determined relations, or heteronomy, with autonomous, self-determined ones—nature and the world entire would come to be experienced neither as objects of domination, as Cartesianism and capitalism demand, nor as sources of fear— as is the case in many traditional and pre-modern settings. Rather, nature would come to be regarded as a source of "contemplation" and inspiration. The undying promise of such revolutionary changes notwithstanding—humanity would come to outright abolish "fear and anxiety," imagine!—Marcuse here stresses Schiller's point that the goal of the aestheticization of the life-world would first demand "a total revolution in the mode of perception and feeling" (1966a: 187, 189). With this claim, Marcuse implicitly declares his affinity with Antonio Gramsci's arguments regarding the importance of counter-hegemonic cultural transformation as predating political revolution in time, and in this way he anticipates the activist and theoretical commitments he would take on in his remaining quarter-century of life.[4]

In closing, Marcuse discusses how a liberated sexuality, rather than necessarily destroying civilization, as Freud believed, could principally aid Eros in instituting a non-repressive civilization. He argues that the abolition of surplus repression and the regional "spread of the libido" would operate hand-in-hand: as the human organism finds itself no longer principally dedicated to alienated labor, it would become resexualized, experiencing a "reactivation of all erotogenic zones" and a resurgence of alternative sexualities in place of the hegemonic "genital supremacy." In this way, the human body as a whole would come to be an "instrument of pleasure," and the personality in general eroticized. Marcuse hypothesizes that this new-found love of self and other would in turn enhance love of "beautiful work and play" and "beautiful knowledge," leading socialistically to a desire to bring into being the "right and true order of the Polis" (1966a: 201, 211). As a specific example of this dynamic, Marcuse cites anthropologist Margaret Mead's insights into the philosophy of the Arapesh, who reside in what is now Papua New Guinea:

> To the Arapesh, the world is a garden that must be tilled, not for one's self, not in pride and boasting, not for hoarding and usury, but that the yams and the dogs and the pigs and most of all the children may grow. From this whole attitude flow many of the other Arapesh traits, the lack

---

4 See Chapters 5 and 6 below.

of conflict between the old and young, the lack of any expectation of jealousy or envy, the emphasis upon co-operation.

MARCUSE 1966a: 216

Here, Marcuse favorably mentions Fourier's "giant socialist utopia," which critically holds out the possibility of "attractive labor" as against the alienated labor of capitalism, as a European source that espouses a life-philosophy similar to the Arapesh. Further, like Fourier, Marcuse predicts that the revolutionary diffusion of Eros throughout society would result in the "disintegration" of the bourgeois nuclear family-form (1966a: 201, 217).

Lastly, Marcuse emphasizes the role of memory in connecting present and future struggle with historical defeat—and the remembrance of "the forces that caused it"—as well as with the more life-affirming aspects of past societies. Here, he cites the importance of remembrance in Freud's work, Hegel's conclusion to the *Phenomenology of Spirit*, and Benjamin's discussion of the "conscious wish to break the continuum of history," as evinced by the revolutionary Parisian masses during the 1830 July Revolution against the Bourbon Restoration. Indelibly included within the emancipatory function of memory is the struggle to overcome the centrality of death in repressive society, claims Marcuse: humankind bears an "unredeemable guilt" for the staggering totality of individuals who have been murdered by civilization. In light of the extent of such horror, the theorist hypothesizes that the "education for consent to death" serves the ends of submission before the powers that be, who themselves express "a deep affinity to death." For individuals under capital, death only rarely takes place before they "must and want to die." Yet the functioning of memory, which (re)connects the organism with its basis in Eros, leads being to desire its happiness, just as joy seeks eternity (Marcuse 1966a: 231–233, 235–237).

According to Marcuse, "the past continues to claim the future: it generates the wish that the paradise be recreated on the basis of the achievements of civilization." In light of the considerable gap between capitalism and utopia, Marcuse declares death to be "a token of unfreedom, of defeat." Yet dialectically, Marcuse allows for the possibility of death representing a "token of freedom," if it is made to be experienced painlessly and at a self-determined moment of time, with the assurance that the dying person will know that "what [she] love[s] is protected from misery and oblivion" (1966a: 18, 236–237). While Marcuse mentions no particular persons in these moving remarks on death, it is likely that he has Sophie, Benjamin, his lost family-members, other European Jews, and all the millions murdered in the two world wars in mind.

Lectures on Freedom and Progress in Freud's Theory of the Instincts

In 1956, for the centenary of Freud's birth, Marcuse gave two addresses on the psychoanalyst's collected works: "Freedom and Freud's Theory of Instincts" and "Progress and Freud's Theory of Instincts." As much of the content of these lectures constitutes a reiteration of Marcuse's general argumentation in *Eros and Civilization*, his addresses will not be presented in detail here. However, aspects of the lectures do expand upon and illuminate his previous assertions regarding Eros and the struggle for a non-repressive reality principle, and hence merit consideration. As a sidenote, it bears mentioning that it was while giving these lectures that Marcuse first met Jürgen Habermas (Martineau 1986: 15).

In his lecture on freedom, Marcuse largely applies Freudian theory to the analysis of the present situation, or "current politics." He forthrightly claims "irrationality" to be the "rational universal" dominating the prevailing state of affairs—this because, at least among the majorities of Northern societies, the historical development of capitalism has made material comfort widely available. Thus, Marcuse observes that, subjected to the capitalist status quo, "society has fallen prey to and become identified with domination." Though the West's "democratic form[s]" differ from outright fascism in rejecting terror as a means of preserving themselves, such relations of domination are similarly organized in a conscious fashion to suppress liberation, and hence they result in neither freedom nor happiness—for, as he quotes Freud as declaring, "[i]ndividual freedom is not a product of civilization." Instead, unfreedom is generalized in late capitalism, and the bourgeois classes utilize technology to prosecute the "rape of nature" and the "deadening of human nature" (Marcuse 1970a: 1–3, 4, 11–12).

All of this, as Marcuse has argued in *Eros and Civilization* and before, is not at all how matters should or must be. The lecturer boldly reasserts his thesis that Eros, which preserves life, is the originator of civilization, tying the polymorphous nature of sexuality into the collective struggle for "more intensive and extensive pleasure," as manifested in the forging of bonds among humans who seek "the production of a libidinous, that is, happy environment." Historically, Marcuse's thesis goes, humanity begins to engage in "the cultivation of nature and of [itself], cooperation, in order to secure and perpetuate the gaining of pleasure." That the human organism has over time been transformed into an instrument for alienated labor in no way proves that it must necessarily continue so to be: the psychological trauma suffered by the organism during the primordial transition from pleasure to subordination and unfreedom does not correspond to "the psychic condition of civilization as such but only of civilization as domination, that is, of a specific form of civilization." The possibility for the psyche and the collective human body to create a "libidinous civilization" remains open (1970a: 19–20, 22). Toward this end, Freud's instinct theory points importantly to the exercise of human freedom, à la Sartre:

> human freedom is the possibility, even the necessity, of going beyond, negating every given situation in existence, because in relation to [humanity's] possibilities every situation itself is negativity, a barrier, 'something other.' Human existence thus seems, to use Sartre's notion, an eternal "project," which never reaches fulfillment, plenitude, rest (1970a: 23).

Thus, for Eros to intervene as an explosive contradiction to the governing reality principle becomes a critical necessity for human existence. Nevertheless, despite his belief in the historical chance for a form of freedom "in which the repression of the instincts would be abolished along with political oppression," Marcuse continues his dialogue with Freud by affirming the latter's gloominess regarding the very dialectical possibilities for which the critical theorist himself is arguing: "Freud reveals the actual negativity of freedom." The founder of psychoanalysis is shown already in *Civilization and its Discontents* (1930) to have warned that humanity's subjugation of nature and inter-group aggressivity threaten its very existence—with such anxiety over the prospect of self-extermination being expressed by Freud, as Marcuse observes, before the advent of the "atom and hydrogen bombs," and "before that total mobilization that began with the period of fascism *and evidently has not yet reached its peak*" (emphasis added). At the very close of the lecture, Marcuse intimates that the increasing fury of capitalist destructiveness dialectically threatens the world with a "catastrophe" which would, in terms reminiscent of Hegel, "pull the archaic forces down with it in its collapse and thus clear the way to a higher stage" (1970a: 24, 26). It remains unclear whether Marcuse considers this possibility for the precipitous decline of hegemonic rule to result from conscious action on the part of the oppressed, the blind internal contradictions of the capitalist system, or some sort of combination of the two.

Opening his second lecture about Freud on progress and Freudian instinct theory, Marcuse distinguishes between two concepts of progress: technical and humanitarian. The former, known well to those subordinated to capitalist rule, refers more or less to the performance principle, which seeks to aggrandize wealth by means of the expansion of productivity through "the universal domination of nature"; differently, the latter concept, which Marcuse associates with the Idealist tradition and the philosophy of Hegel especially, conceives of progress as the expansion of "human freedom," or "morality," such that "slavery, arbitrariness, oppression, and suffering are reduced" in the course of world history. Given the actual dominance of the former concept of progress over the latter in the history of civilization and capital, the conflicting instincts Freud identified come to be repressively mobilized, as the argument goes in *Eros and Civilization*, with the death instinct manipulated so as to support the imperatives of capitalist imperialism—namely, "the annihilation of nature in the form of the domination of nature and the annihilation of socially sanctioned enemies inside and outside the nation." In a vicious cycle, then, the psychological and material mobilization of death and destruction serves to uphold the brutal totality, in light of the negating reality that the subordinated effectively go along with hegemonic designs, rather than uphold and demand a Hegelian-Marxist sense of human progress. Such reflections lead Marcuse crucially to question whether, alongside the socio-historical Thermidor seen to have arisen in most if not all historical revolutions, there might also exist within individuals a "*psychic* Thermidor" that "*internally* negates possible liberation [...] and that supports external forces of denial" (1970a: 28–30, 35, 39).[5]

Responding to this bleak possibility with reference to the theses he sets forth in *Eros and Civilization*, Marcuse once again argues that the relative hegemony of the death instinct reflects the dominant reality principle of late capitalism, and that a revolutionary reorganization of global society could refashion the instincts in a liberatory manner. By employing "more or less total automation" to abolish alienated labor, Marcuse argues, humanity could abandon life as contemporarily experienced—that is, as a "struggle for existence"—in favor of an approach aiming explicitly at life's enjoyment, as in hedonism. If humanity could at some future point realize such hypothetical transformations, freedom would come to "no longer be an eternally failing project," and time itself would rather than linear come to be experienced as cyclical, as in Friedrich Nietzsche's notion of a "perpetuity of pleasure," claims Marcuse (1970a: 40–41).

Against critics who would dismiss his anarchical interpretation of Freud as fantastical daydreaming, Marcuse concludes his lecture by stressing that his depiction of a seeming "utopia" which itself "has a real basis" should likely be taken as a more politically responsible position than a positivist or defeatist skepticism which effectively serves to legitimize prevailing capitalist depravity (1970a: 43).

---

5   Thermidor refers to the month in the revolutionary French calendar during which bourgeois forces overthrew Robespierre and the Committee for Public Safety, thus halting the Jacobin Terror (1794).

Marcuse's Debate with Fromm on Freud, Therapy, and Adjustment

Reflection on Freud pervaded Marcuse's life in the mid-1950s. This period in his life would also see the emergence of a bitter conflict with Erich Fromm regarding the meaning of psychoanalysis, therapy, and adjustment. The origins of this debate can be traced to the epilogue Marcuse provides to *Eros and Civilization*, entitled "The Limits of Freudian Neo-Revisionism," wherein he chides Fromm and other "revisionists" for having abandoned classical Freudian libido theory and Freud's late instinct theory, and groups his erstwhile comrade together with anti-Marxist and reactionary psychoanalysts such as Karen Horney and Harry Stack Sullivan, whom he similarly accuses of deviating from Freud. In part, Marcuse is motivated in this critique by an almost ultra-left disdain for psychoanalytic therapy, which he associates with resignation before the exigencies of capital. No distinction is made here between mainstream psychotherapy and the innovative approaches developed by Fromm since the 1930s; for Marcuse, Fromm's insistence on the need for analysts to aid their patients to experience happiness is tantamount to advancing the delusional notion that happiness can actually be attained under prevailing alienated conditions. Indeed, in a highly disingenuous formulation which in fact can be considered libelous, Marcuse accuses Fromm of defining "health, maturity, [and] achievement [...] as they are defined by the given society," and he quotes Sullivan's equation of radical character structure with psychopathology as being somehow representative of Fromm's views as well (Marcuse 1966a: 244–248, 256–257).

As an alternative, Marcuse proposes that therapists adopt the goal of "'curing' the patient to become a rebel or—what is saying the same thing—a martyr." He repeats his view that Fromm's stress on care, responsibility, love, happiness, and respect for others cannot realistically be practiced by anyone who is to be expected to retain her sanity in contemporary society, and he contrasts Freud's reportedly radical view that freedom and happiness cannot be attained under repressive civilization with the line of the revisionists, who putatively "see no such difficulty" (1966a: 258–259, 268). As Marcuse would later summarize in "Theory and Therapy in Freud" (1957), the claim is that the Freudian neo-revisionists essentially favor "the smooth incorporation of psychoanalysis into the established system of culture" (Marcuse 2011: 106).

Nevertheless, in an essay revisiting the debate between these two figures thirty years after the fact, John Rickert observes rightly that Marcuse's invective against Fromm is starkly uncomradely in the first place, beyond being shockingly unjustified in terms of reasonableness. Marcuse's critique blatantly ignores the significant libertarian-Marxist contributions made by Fromm in the field of psychoanalysis, starting from his tenure with the Institute for

Social Research to the period following his formal abandonment of Freudian instinct and libido theory, which continued through the time that Marcuse was writing his philosophical inquiry into Freud. It would almost seem as though Marcuse is projecting his defensiveness regarding Freud's libido and late instinct theories in his attack on Fromm: against all the evidence, he insipidly holds that Fromm's psychoanalytic approach loses its critical edge after the therapist would publish *Escape from Freedom* in 1941, and that it is in fact marred by idealism and conformity. As Rickert writes, though, Fromm's social psychology remains solidly critical after his abandonment of libido theory; one thing has little to do with the other, in this case. Admittedly, Fromm's "revisionism" does lead the analyst to de-emphasize sexuality and Eros in relation to the importance Marcuse places on these concepts, but there is no justification for the view that Fromm is serving as an apologist after his formal break with the Frankfurt School, given the consistent emphasis his critical social psychology would place on resistance to repression and oppression. Fromm's work would inspire the developing international Marxist-humanist philosophical tendency, and the psychologist himself would engage in radical political activism until his death in 1980, as reflected in his active opposition to the nuclear arms race, his critique of and protests against the Vietnam War, and his sympathies with revolutionary social transformation. It bears mentioning that Fromm was planning to visit Chile on the invitation of Salvador Allende on the eve of the CIA-backed coup against him, and that he founded the Mexican Psychoanalytic Institute, based in Coyoacán, Mexico City, directing it in a socially critical direction. In short, Marcuse's denunciation of Fromm as revisionist can be maintained only on the basis of gross misrepresentations, "major distortions," and "great violence" with regards to Fromm's life-work (Rickert 1986: 351, 361–363, 368–369, 374–375, 385–386).

Fromm himself would reply to Marcuse's criticisms in the Fall 1955 issue of *Dissent*, in an essay entitled "The Human Implications of 'Instinctivistic Radicalism.'" In this article, Fromm responds to Marcuse's two main points: that he is a philosophical idealist who recommends adjustment to prevailing capitalist alienation, and that Freudian theory is radically critical. In fact expressing a line of thought very close to that of Adorno—one that was actually made during a 1946 address that sought to criticize Fromm on much the same grounds that Marcuse does in *Eros and Civilization*—Fromm accuses Freud of being an undialectical apologist for bourgeois society, stressing the medical and "physical-chemical" basis of his form of materialism, which on Fromm's account certainly is inferior as an explanatory social theory in comparison to Marxian historical materialism (Jay 1973: 105; Fromm 1955: 344). Fromm also stresses that Freud limited his "specific criticism of contemporary

society" to sexual Puritanism, having nothing to say about economic production or class relations, and he questions whether the Freudian theory which
demands greater sexual freedom is in fact radical and liberatory, in light of
the highly permissive attitude the Nazis took toward heterosexual libidinality, and considering the similarity that the emphasis on sexual gratification
bears with the dominant capitalist ideology that demands immediate satisfaction of desire. Reflecting on the dystopia depicted by Aldous Huxley in
Brave New World, Fromm worries that the call to overturn sexual repression
will leave individuals without conflicts and thus effectively serve the existing
system; it is for this reason that he terms an orthodox Freudian approach to
sexuality reformist instead of revolutionary. Fromm then proceeds to challenge
Marcuse's agreement with Freud that the unconscious is governed purely by
sexual desire, and he corrects Marcuse's slanderous claim that his own psychoanalytical approach neglects infancy and childhood as the formative periods
of one's character (1955: 345–347).

Coming to his conclusion, Fromm fields Marcuse's most important point:
that the psychologist is peddling Idealism with his revisionism and thus aiding
the powers that be. In response, Fromm claims that Marcuse's theory assumes
that there exists *no "love, integrity, or inner strength as a reality"* for anyone, and
that to even speak in such terms under capitalism serves ideological functions
(emphasis added). He then shows that Marcuse qualifies these statements to
some degree, using formulations suggesting that "optimal [personal] development" is "*essentially* unattainable" for the "*vast majority*," and he describes how
his own concept of the "productive social character" is observed to be very
rare among individuals subjected to capitalist alienation, whereas the "mar-
keting character" instead prevails, and he clarifies that his own concepts of
happiness and love are very far-removed from the meaning such terms take in
mainstream settings. Referring to the systematic opportunistic and authoritarian dismissal of morality and love made by Lenin and Stalin—an approach he
calls nihilistic—Fromm expressly clarifies his utter rejection of Marcuse's view
that such values are entirely absent from contemporary society, that the analysis of such orientations is nothing more than an ideological commitment, and
that their "encouragement" amounts to a philosophy of adjustment. He closes,
in point of fact, by accusing Marcuse of advancing "human nihilism disguised
as radicalism" (1955: 347–349).

Marcuse responds to Fromm's defense in "A Reply to Erich Fromm," published in the following issue of *Dissent*, wherein he continues his assault against
Fromm's putative reformism, as supposedly reflected in the proposals Fromm
makes in *The Sane Society* (1955) for worker participation in production toward
the end of the humanization of labor. Unjustly, Marcuse accuses Fromm's

newly released book of calling for measures that merely promote a "smoother functioning of the established society" rather than a qualitative break from it. He also responds to Fromm's concerns over his own interpretations of Freud and sexuality, observing Freud not to have equated happiness with uninhibited expressions of sexual desire but instead to have favored the sublimation of the libido into "tenderness and affection." He actually expresses agreement with Fromm's criticism regarding Freud's silence in terms of the critique of capital, though he suggests that Freud's true radicalism can in fact be gleaned in the analyst's insistence that all civilization presupposes alienation, and hence that mere reforms will be fundamentally inadequate in addressing this situation. In the end, Marcuse proudly accepts Fromm's charge of "human nihilism" as a constitutive element of the Great Refusal, and he claims his orientation to be far more revolutionary than that of his psychoanalytic counterpart: "much of what he calls alienation is to me the force which overcomes alienation, and what he calls the positive is to me still the negative" (Marcuse 2011: 102–104).

In his "Counter-Rebuttal" published in the same issue of *Dissent*, though, Fromm "leave[s] it to any reader of *The Sane Society* to judge whether [the book] stands for 'more and better industrial psychology and scientific management,'" as Marcuse claims. His focus in this final exchange is not the sociopolitical aspects of the debate between him and Marcuse, but rather the interpretation of Freud: citing *Civilization and its Discontents* (1930) as a work that is more representative of Freud's views on sexuality and happiness than "The Most Prevalent Form of Degradation in Erotic Love" (1912), from which Marcuse quotes in his "Reply," Fromm in fact does show Freud to define happiness as satisfaction of genital erotic desire and to believe humans to be motivated ceaselessly by the wish for libidinal gratification, however much they must repress their sadistic and coprophilic desires, in accordance with the demands of civilization (Marcuse 2011: 104–106).

If one reviews the course of this debate, it should become clear in the first place that Fromm bests Marcuse, in part owing to his superior familiarity with Freud and psychoanalytical categories. Yet while it is Marcuse who was responsible for the vast majority of distortion and misrepresentation in this correspondence, it must be said that Fromm was not innocent of this charge himself, in light of his mistaken view that Marcuse advocates unrestricted libidinal satisfaction and his misunderstanding regarding Marcuse's distinction between basic and surplus repression, not to mention the critical theorist's call for the transformation of sexuality into Eros (Rickert 1986: 373). It nonetheless bears repeating that Marcuse's opportunistic attack on Fromm was hardly befitting of a relationship which previously had been friendly and productive, in Fromm's sense of the word. The hostility expressed by Marcuse

toward Fromm recalls the depressing sectarian infighting that has gripped
left-wing intellectual circles throughout history, even to this day. Besides, as
Habermas acknowledges in a 1978 conversation with the aging critical theorist,
Marcuse's largely baseless argument against Fromm represents a stark denial
of the critical role which Fromm had played in the early years of the Frankfurt
School, and indeed also in Marcuse's own political development:

> Wasn't Fromm the first to introduce the program of a Marxist social
> psychology to the Institute, at the end of twenties? [...] Wasn't it Fromm,
> certainly urged on by Horkheimer, who tried to reconcile Marx and Freud
> in his own fashion, a fashion decisive for Critical Theory? Wasn't it Fromm
> who made it clear that some trivial psychological assumptions cannot
> determine the subjective factor, but that the latter [...] must integrate
> basic conceptualization of psychoanalysis and Marxism? Isn't the image
> of Fromm that you're painting now heavily colored by the later dispute
> with Fromm the revisionist [*sic*], and isn't his contribution to Critical
> Theory's formative period underestimated?
>
>   MARCUSE et al. 1978/9: 127

Marcuse concedes these points "without reservation," and in response to
Habermas' questioning, notes that Fromm's early investigations of Christianity
and essays in the *Journal for Social Research* were "received as radical Marxist
social psychology" by Institute members (1978/9: 127).

   Finally, it should be noted that, the acrimonious disagreements expressed
between Marcuse and Fromm in the 1950s notwithstanding, the pair would go
on to collaborate on a 1965 symposium on socialist humanism, the results of
which were edited by Fromm in an eponymously published volume. Furthermore, Marcuse significantly requested Fromm to review *One-Dimensional Man*
for *The New York Times*, as he felt the dissident psychologist would be one of
the few readers who would intuitively grasp his theses (Rickert 1986: 399n167).
Though the critical analyst politely declined, basic reflection on the respective intellectual and political projects developed in life by Marcuse and Fromm
should demonstrate their great affinities, and thus show their open conflicts
regarding Freud, therapy, and adjustment to be rather inconsequential, however destructive they were in fact at the time. Jay is right to stress the common
enthusiasm shared by Fromm and Marcuse regarding the discovery of Marx's
1844 *Economic and Philosophical Manuscripts*, from which both developed
their theories of alienation, human need, and human essence, while Rickert
is correct to depict Marcuse and Fromm as the two members of the Frankfurt School who were most committed to the union of theory and practice,

as through their advocacy of radical politics and their participation in anti-
systemic movements (Jay 1973: 89; Rickert 1986: 386).

Soviet Marxism: A Critical Analysis (1958)

Marcuse's *Soviet Marxism* presents a critical take on the Soviet regime, both
its practices as well as its ruling philosophy. For Vincent Geoghegan, the work
represents the application of Marcuse's well-established interest in technical rationality to "an analysis of the USSR" (Geoghegan 1981: 67). The product
of years of study at Columbia University's Russian Institute and Harvard's
Russian Research Center during which Marcuse learned Russian and focused
on examining Russian and Soviet history and politics, *Soviet Marxism* presents
Marcuse's rejection of Stalinism, his contradictory takes on Leninism, and
his advocacy and employment of Hegelian-Marxian thought and praxis for
the present, moving forward into the future. It is striking to note how closely
Marcuse's vision here of a Marxian "third option" beyond those on offer in
the West and the USSR resembles the philosophy of anarcho-syndicalism, or
even that of Marx, who in some interpretations himself in fact advanced the
anarchist cause against capital and State alike, as Maximilien Rubel explains
(1973). The similarities between Marcuse's analysis of the Soviet Union and
anarchist philosophy aside, though, it will be shown that the critical theorist's
view of Bolshevism is not entirely critical. His take on Leninism here is not
so negative, for example, as is the text of the telegram sent out to the Soviet
Politburo in Moscow by the Occupation Committee of the People's Free Sorbonne University during May 1968 ten years later, expressing admiration for
the revolutionary struggle of the *Makhnovshchina* and the Kronstadt sailors
against the autocracy headed by Lenin and Trotsky. This lapse on Marcuse's
part may be explained by a lack of engagement with the question of the extent
of repression meted out by the Bolshevik Party even before Stalinization, or
it may reflect the theorist's desire not to unequivocally reject the tactics of
Lenin and Trotsky, which may to his mind have been too intimately related
to the meaning of the Russian Revolution for the left. For his part, Kellner
claims that Marcuse's desire with *Soviet Marxism* was to contribute to a "thaw"
in Cold War tensions toward the end of "peaceful coexistence" between East
and West, and he argues that Marcuse believed the Soviet Union to hold relatively greater hope for socialism than contemporary Western societies—hence
the view imputed to him by Kellner that the USSR should be supported by all
those who genuinely wished for the coming of a post-capitalist future (Kellner
1984: 226). Yet it would seem that Kellner's analysis is to an extent flawed, for

Marcuse in *Soviet Marxism* clearly repudiates Stalinism and bureaucratic communism altogether. What is less clear, as shall be seen, is Marcuse's assessment of the Leninist legacy, which remains highly variable and confused: far from Adorno's late endorsement of Leninism, as made in a 1956 conversation with Horkheimer, Marcuse's critical appraisal of the Soviet regime includes a degree of denunciation of the early Leninist regime, but cannot be said to be consistently libertarian in this sense (Adorno and Horkheimer 2010: 57).

In *Soviet Marxism*, Marcuse first considers the historical context for the emergence of Leninism as a distinct trend within Marxist philosophy, one which corresponds to the germ-cell of the later Soviet State. He situates the rise of Leninist philosophy within the socio-historical dynamic that ties together proletarian reformism and integration with stabilization of the capitalist system; in point of fact, Marcuse claims the Western proletariat's historical failure to revolutionize society to have been "perhaps the most decisive factor in the development of Soviet Marxism." He mentions the turn to nationalism taken by the European Social Democrats in the decades following Marx's death, considered together with the general rise in living standards experienced by European workers in this period: for Marcuse, the reactionary former tendency represents a toxic by-product of the turn to incrementalism advocated by Engels after Marx had passed, and taken up by Bernstein the revisionist. Such nationalism led to its most logical and regressive outcome when the different sections of the social democrat-controlled Socialist International approved war credits for their respective governments to wage World War I in August 1914. In addition, Marcuse laments the active participation of sectors of organized labor in the campaigns led by capitalists and their armies to suppress the Central European revolutions of 1918–1923. The author thus comes to identify what he terms a "long-range trend toward class collaboration rather than class struggle" in industrial-capitalist societies, one he does not take merely to be a "temporary regression [...] after which the revolutionary trend will be resumed," as may be anticipated by orthodox and optimistic notions of Marxism (Marcuse 1958: 18, 35, 70–71, 74).

In a sense, Leninism and Soviet Marxism—both in theoretical terms, as before 1917, in addition to practically, as seen in the Bolshevik regime after October 1917—were at their origins shaped by an overt strategy aimed at revolutionary social change within the feudal-agrarian societies in which capital was less well-established—this being the strategy of "breaking the chain at its weakest link." The adherents of both philosophies came to be greatly traumatized by the yawning abyss which ultimately separated the newborn Soviet State from the remainder of the global proletariat (Marcuse 1958: 29). Introducing the birth and early development of the Soviet Union in this way,

Marcuse would seem to affirm the view of the course of events in Russia that was held at this time by his colleague Horkheimer, who in the aforementioned dialogue with Adorno claimed it to have been "the fault of the West that the Russian Revolution went the way it did" (Adorno and Horkheimer 2010: 41). Nevertheless, Marcuse at no point shares Horkheimer's earlier positive interpretations of the Stalinist regime, as expressed in a 1930 journal entry, wherein the Institute director acknowledges that it is "extremely difficult to say what conditions are like" in the Soviet Union: he observes that, though he does not "claim to know where the country is going," self-styled revolutionaries should in any case view the "events in Russia as the continuing painful attempt to overcome" the "senseless injustice of the imperialist world"—or, at the very least, they should ask "with a throbbing heart whether [this process] is still underway," much in the same way that a cancer patient clings to the hope for a miraculous cure (Horkheimer 1978: 72–73). Parting company with Horkheimer's dated assessment of the Soviet Union through his clear repudiation of Stalinism in *Soviet Marxism*, Marcuse still does not advance a consistent critique of the Bolshevik regime, as social anarchists and historians such as Emma Goldman, Gregorii Maximoff, Paul Avrich, and Noam Chomsky would do (Goldman 1923/4; Maximoff 1940; Avrich 1967; Avrich 1970; Chomsky 2013).

Controversially, Marcuse locates the "original sin" of the Soviet State in the increasing divergence between the "class interests" of the Russian proletariat and peasantry and the decisions taken by the Bolshevik authorities starting in 1923—that is, at the end of Lenin's lifespan, as his health declined and power ceded evermore from him to Stalin. Prior to this time, then—that is, from 1917 to 1923—Marcuse presumably considers to have corresponded to the "heroic period" of the Russian Revolution, a time characterized by unprecedented gains in sexual liberation and a putatively vibrant libertarian political and socio-cultural environment. In light of such a characterization of Lenin and Trotsky's rule, it should come as little surprise that Marcuse makes no mention of the Bolsheviks' egregious crimes in forcibly putting down hundreds of peasant revolts, shooting down and imprisoning numerous striking workers, suppressing the Kronstadt Commune and the *Makhnovshchina*, and sidelining syndicalism for the militarization of labor (Maximoff 1940; Figes 1996). Instead of bringing such negations to light, Marcuse at one point in the text claims the "differences" between the "first years of the Bolshevik Revolution and the fully developed Stalinist state" to be "obvious," with a dramatic intensification of the exercise of dictatorial controls over "the proletariat and the peasantry" of Russia corresponding to the Stalinist eclipse of Leninism (Marcuse 1958: 74–75, 149, 248).

Paradoxically, though, Marcuse observes earlier in the text that it was Lenin himself who initiated the domination of the Soviet working classes by Party and State, this in response to Russia's isolation and the difficulties it faced with encirclement, hostility, and invasion from Western capitalist powers. Later in *Soviet Marxism*, Marcuse comes forthrightly to acknowledge his clear misgivings with Leninist approaches, however much such an assessment contradicts statements made elsewhere in the text: "A straight road seems to lead from Lenin's 'consciousness from without' and his notion of the centralized authoritarian party to Stalin's personal dictatorship." Marcuse in this way associates the development of Soviet class society with rule by Lenin and Trotsky, claiming their regime to exemplify a "reified, hypostatized power" alien to the wishes and control of the peasantry and proletariat. Yet while at this moment his critique approaches anarchism, council communism, and the early opposition presented to the Bolsheviks by groups such as the Left-Socialist Revolutionaries (SRs), Marcuse elsewhere declares "[n]either centralization nor coordination [to] militate by themselves against progress in freedom and humanity," noting that these means "have more than once been effective weapons in the struggle against oppression and reaction." He moreover communicates his belief in the potential of a progressive employment of terror, as in one which would advance the "destruction of repressive institutions" and the "rational utilization of the productive forces" (1958: 74–75, 105, 112, 145, 196). It is to be imagined that Marcuse is thinking of the example of the Jacobins in the French Revolution being a forerunner of the Bolsheviks and the Russian Revolution when he makes such statements.

Thus it becomes clear from reading *Soviet Marxism* that Marcuse's precise views on the theory and historical practice of Leninism are varied, confused, and often contradictory. Equally clear, however, is Marcuse's utter repudiation of Stalinism, an ideology he cleaves entirely from the Marxist tradition: he declares the Soviet State in 1958 not to be socialist, precisely because of its repressive denial of the socialization of production—the "initiative and control 'from below' by the 'immediate producers.'" In fact, Marcuse forthrightly observes that the centralization of power within Soviet society shows it merely to follow "the general trend of late industrial civilization," whereby the multitude is effectively disenfranchised from popular and democratic self-management. Furthermore, in his critical presentation of Soviet notions of ethics, Marcuse discovers a convergence of Soviet Marxism with the Protestant and Puritan traditions, amidst the stress placed by the former on repressive sexual and social regimentation, as well as its total demand for individual subordination before the requirements of the existing authorities, particularly in terms of labor productivity. Through such considerations is seen the USSR's fundamental continuity with Western monopoly-capitalist societies, argues Marcuse—though once again, he here fails explicitly to link Stalinist domination with the dictatorial continuum founded by Lenin and Trotsky as the Winter Palace fell in October 1917. Marcuse further connects the two putatively opposed superpowers through the common emphasis both regimes place on maintaining vast, repressive police and military apparatuses. Still, he does acknowledge, whether rightly or wrongly, that the Stalinist process of primitive accumulation and forced industrialization has "enabled the Soviet economy to 'telescope' several stages of industrial development" in less than twenty years—thus allowing it materially to have been capable of "withstand[ing] the most powerful war machine of an advanced industrial country," namely Hitler's armies in World War II (1958: 75, 81–82, 92, 94, 171, 189, 233, 235, 243, 251). Oddly, no mention is made in this semi-celebratory note of Stalin's previous closeness with Hitler, as in the Molotov-Ribbentrop Pact of August 1939, which stipulated non-aggression between the Nazi and Stalinist regimes, a stance that was maintained until the fascist invasion of June 1941, which proved as disastrous for the new invaders as had Napoleon's previous foolhardy attempt to crush the resistance of the Russian people.

In parallel to essentially all his other works, Marcuse dedicates space in *Soviet Marxism* to contemplating the possibilities for the dialectical negation of the bureaucratic domination exercised by the USSR over its peoples: he examines the potential for a liberatory "third option" beyond Stalinism and monopoly-capitalism as alternatives. As Marcuse discusses, the dialectics of history continue to progress within Russia and the other Soviet Republics, such that it can be imagined that these formerly alienated spaces would yield to contradiction by means of "shattering" movements that advance and ultimately realize the "abolition of the repressive state and its repressive machinery"—a move which Marcuse feels may not have to imply "violent overthrow in civil war." In this way, perhaps, Marcuse foresees dialectical achievements like those resembling *glasnost'* ("openness") and *perestroika* ("reconstruction" or "reorganization") in the 1980s, the progression of punk rock and feminism in Soviet and post-Soviet Russia—or, indeed, the materialization of the previously mentioned Leningrad School near the end of the theorist's life. From below, Marcuse detects subversive, disruptive potential within Soviet culture itself, especially as expressed by the counter-movement to the stifling cultural mandates dictated by the Stalinist State, with one example of this being those trends which resist the "reinstatement of harmony by administrative decree, [or] the banning of dissonance, discord, and atonality" (1958: 134, 141, 189, 267).

Marcuse observes potential for reformist and revolutionary changes alike emanating from the Soviet Union, with the chance for both improving considerably under conditions of revolutionary, international solidarity, particularly as aimed at defusing tensions between the capitalist West and Soviet State, toward the ultimate end of resolving this conflict altogether and so allowing a substantial reduction in political oppression and repression on both sides, and thus on the global stage as well. The chance for a truly Marxian transformation of the Soviet Union remains a real possibility, concludes Marcuse, with this dialectical threat growing the more the Soviet State continues to promulgate and indoctrinate its subject peoples in Marxian theory. In aiding humanity to overcome the bad present that is gripped by the twins of capitalist and Soviet totalitarianism, such philosophical education "may still turn out to be a dangerous weapon" (1958: 189, 265, 267).

The Ideology of Death

"The Ideology of Death" is the title of Marcuse's contribution to the psychologist Herman Feifel's 1959 volume on *The Meaning of Death*, an essay in which the critical theorist associates the existentialist *submission* to death with obedience to "the master over death: the polis, the state, nature, or the god." At the outset of these reflections, Marcuse contrasts the stoical "acceptance of the inevitable," which is sometimes expressed as outright repression of the consideration of death, from the Idealist "glorification of death" as that which gives meaning to life. The critical theorist argues that the latter attitude serves to glorify the hegemonic interests engaged in determining the negative totality. Marcuse argues even that Socrates' suicide affirmed the principle of the power of the polis over the individual, the "insoluble connection between [...] death and domination." In historical terms, Marcuse observes that the affirmation of death reflects the factical fallenness of human life, and he distinguishes between the attitude toward death on hand in Plato's *Republic*—wherein the philosopher-kings do not consider death to be liberatory, as they already exist "in truth" while alive—and in Christianity, a religion that, in announcing the essential freedom and equality of humans, was hailed at its birth as promising to bridge the significant gap between such humanistic ideals and the conditions of prevailing society. On Marcuse's account, Christianity deals with this contradiction by directing all transcendental hope toward the afterlife, thus effectively serving the interests of domination. Hegel would continue in a similar line, in light of his view of death as being the blissful reconciliation of Spirit. This type of affirmative perspective would in turn live on in Heidegger's "ideological exhortation to death," which was announced at a time that coincided with the preparation of the Nazi death-camps (Marcuse 2011: 123, 125–127, 130).

Opposing himself to Socrates, Christianity, Hegel, and Heidegger, Marcuse holds the biological fact of death to be an overwhelmingly "painful, horrible, violent, and unwelcome event," and he speculates that the cause of reducing human anxiety—both as generally understood, as well as specifically related to mortality itself—could best be served if death were consciously to be "depriv[ed] of its horror and incalculable power as well as of its transcendental sanctity." Rejecting stoical, Idealist, and affirmative interpretations of death, Marcuse argues that contemplation of the fact of death could serve as the "stimulus for incessant efforts to extend the limits of life, to strive for a guilt-less existence," and to advance human autonomy. Expressing a thought he also shares toward the end of *Eros and Civilization*, Marcuse remarks that humanity remains unfree as long as death has not been brought under its own autonomous control, and he adds that such autonomy remains truly illusory as long as death is considered a Hegelian "negation of negation," as in a "*redemption from life*" (emphasis added). Noting like Marx that history progresses through its bad side—civilization "advances" through "death on the field of honor, in the mines and on the highways, from unconquered disease and poverty, by the state and its organs"—Marcuse returns to Freud's insight that the stark indifference of history to human life and happiness may in fact reflect the established organization of global society in defense of power and privilege, and quite like Étienne de la Boétie, he suggests that the stability of this negative totality might be threatened by a reversal of the conformism that upholds the existing system. Radically, and in a manner reminiscent of Benjamin, Marcuse closes his ruminations on death and hegemony by declaring that the prevailing weakness of oppositional forces "perpetuates the feared and hated power" (2011: 126–127, 129–131).

CHAPTER 5

Radical Struggle in the 1960s

"[Humanity] and the world carry enough good future; no plan is itself
good without this fundamental belief within it."

BLOCH 1986a: 447

"[T]he affirmative character of Art could be overcome only in the
dialectical negation of Art, that is to say, its realization in an aesthetic
Lebenswelt ['life-world']."

MARCUSE 2001: 148

"La vérité reste donc à instaurer."[1]

NICOLAS 1970: 56

The title of this chapter, which considers Marcuse's life and work in the
1960s—undoubtedly, the decade of his greatest fame—reflects the confluence
and synergy between the critical theorist's radical philosophy and the revolutionary anti-systemic irruptions that surged in these years. As during much of
the rest of his life, Marcuse in this decade varies considerably in terms of the
hope he sees for the successful supersession of capitalist domination—yet, in
an analogy to bipolar disorder, or manic-depression, it is in this decade that
such variability is arguably most pronounced for Marcuse. To get a sense of
this dynamic, one need only consider the despondency which permeates our
philosopher's 1964 study into the ideology of advanced industrial society, *One-
Dimensional Man*, as juxtaposed with the heights of revolutionary optimism
evinced in the 1969 *Essay on Liberation*. Most intriguingly, Marcuse's move
from one pole to the other was marked in the interim by militant investigations into the meaning and implementation of social revolution, as seen in the
praxis of the anarchistic French insurrectionist Gracchus Babeuf (1760–1797)
and the contemporary decolonization and guerrilla warfare struggles waged in
the global South, as well as by Marcuse's own radical activism against the
evermore genocidal Vietnam War—all being commitments which well reflect
the continued vitality of Marcuse's *Dasein* and his fidelity to the authentic
philosophy he had delineated three decades earlier, concerned as it was

---

1 "The truth remains, then, to be instituted."

© KONINKLIJKE BRILL NV, LEIDEN, 2016 | DOI 10.1163/9789004308701_006

with the "*concrete distress* of human existence" (Marcuse 2005: 36; emphasis added).

What is more, the shift in Marcuse's orientation beyond the Adornian pessimism of *One-Dimensional Man* was surely energized by the various revolts, rebellions, and even revolutions which shook the established system in the mid- to late 1960s, from the emergence of the U.S. middle-class counterculture to the civil-rights and Black Power movements, the growing global opposition to the neo-colonial barbarism on display in Vietnam, the rise of the New Left, and especially May 1968 in France. Beyond these considerations, developments in Marcuse's personal life during these years likely further propelled his uncompromising advocacy of revolutionary societal transformation, as when his embodied transgressions of the positivism and "neutrality" expected of professors led to his dismissal from Brandeis University in 1965, and his undying opposition to the Vietnam War led him to be the target of death-threats made by various reactionaries, most notably the Ku Klux Klan (Miles 2012: 87–88). In point of fact, in summer 1968 came the "Night of the Long Guns," when a group of graduate students studying under the philosopher mounted a rapid response amidst an increased wave of death-threats by patrolling the Marcuse household in La Jolla with shotguns (Sethness Castro 2013).

Marcuse began this most critical of decades in his academic position as professor of philosophy and political science at Brandeis in Waltham, Massachusetts, which he had held starting in 1954. Yet tensions between Marcuse and the school's administration began to develop after the critical theorist openly welcomed the coming of the Cuban Revolution in a 1961 address at a student protest organized against President Kennedy's Bay of Pigs operation. Kathleen Aberle, a colleague from the anthropology department, shared Marcuse's sentiment by one day declaring "Viva Fidel! Kennedy to hell!" The president of the university, Abram Sachar, reacted with fear to such statements, concerned that Brandeis would come to be seen as a refuge for Marxist upstarts (Martineau 1986: 16–17). Once Marcuse organized a course on campus to analyze the "Welfare State and the Warfare State" in 1964—a course that, as the name suggests, was designed to present critical perspectives on the militaristic and welfarist Keynesianism engaged in by the U.S. government, and that concluded with romantic speculation regarding the nature of the society to follow the fall of monopoly capital—the administration urged him to "retire" by refusing to renew his contract (Kātz 1982: 165; Miles 2012: 87). Fortunately, however, Marcuse had met Richard Popkin, the new head of the recently founded Philosophy Department at the University of California San

Diego (UCSD), at a symposium held at UC Berkeley on the continued relevance of Marx's thought that same year. Upon hearing of the critical theorist's difficulties at Brandeis, Popkin proudly invited him to join the philosophy faculty at UCSD (Sethness Castro 2013). Accepting this offer in May 1965, then, led Marcuse to relocate to the unlikely town of La Jolla, California, a place Marcuse would later describe as "probably the most reactionary area in the United States," home to a sizeable military base and numerous "retired colonels and admirals" (Marcuse 2003: 114). Kātz reports that more than 80 percent of the manufacturing jobs on hand in San Diego at that time involved the missile and aircraft industries. Moreover, La Jolla is well-known for being a concentration of wealth and privilege; over 80 percent of its residents voted in favor of Barry Goldwater in 1964 (Kātz 1982: 169; Sethness Castro 2013). So it was into this right-wing maelstrom that Marcuse moved in the middle of the 1960s, taking with him a handful of his brightest graduate students from Brandeis, including Erica Sherover and William Leiss. Incidentally, Sherover, or "Ricky," would become the philosopher's third and final wife, following Inge's death in 1972 (Martineau 1986: 21). In addition, after having first befriended him during her undergraduate years at Brandeis, Angela Davis would reconnect with Marcuse at UCSD following her return to the States from her year of philosophical study in Frankfurt (Davis 1974: 133–197).

The end of Marcuse's time at Brandeis coincided with the publication of what is perhaps his best-known work, *One-Dimensional Man*. Whereas Marcuse's *Soviet Marxism* (1958) can be said in large part to have constituted an application of the philosopher's long-standing concern with technical rationality to the Stalinist regime, *One-Dimensional Man* can in turn be considered a sequel of sorts to *Soviet Marxism*, given its analysis of the reification and mobilization of consciousness advanced by monopoly capital in the "affluent society" of the U.S. (Geoghegan 1981: 67). In addition, *One-Dimensional Man* can be seen as an extension of Heideggerian categories to the impact of late capitalism on everyday life in U.S. society: *das Man* (the conformist "everyone"), "idle talk," absurdity, meaninglessness, conservatism, and total nihilism. The very opening line of the text reflects the influence of Marcuse's former mentor: "A comfortable, smooth, reasonable, democratic unfreedom prevails in advanced industrial civilization, *a token of technical progress*" (Marcuse 1964: 1; emphasis added). Even Marcuse's alarm at the hegemony of capitalist technics in this book suggests a resurgent Heideggerianism of sorts.

Generally speaking, Marcuse in *One-Dimensional Man* engages in an extensive analysis of the various means through which monopoly capital suppresses the multi-dimensional experience of history and existence in the life-world that had been on hand in all prior epochs—as in art, philosophy, and even language. In accordance with the interests of dominant power, one-dimensionality essentially shores up the totalitarian perpetuation of degraded or "fallen" experience. Pluralism under such conditions is nothing but a fraud that facilitates totalitarian control, and the working classes of the u.s. have dialectically been integrated into the system on offer, in this way coming to realize Engels' worst fears regarding the prospect of the proletariat's *embourgeoisement* (Geoghegan 1981: 79). As Adorno writes with reference to Gustav Mahler's symphonies, "hope has grown very poor" in Marcuse's text (1992: 163). In fact, the theorist closes the volume by plaintively citing Benjamin's observation, made at the beginning of the Nazi era, that "[i]t is only for the sake of those without hope that hope is given to us" (Marcuse 1964: 257). In this vein, a mere fifth of the book's pages consider "The Chance of the Alternatives" to the reign of one-dimensionality, and truthfully even less focuses on the possible means of actually displacing its dominance.

The sole positive development Marcuse sees in *One-Dimensional Man* is for the possibility that the non-integrated racial, intellectual, artistic, and *lumpen* minorities—the "outcasts and outsiders" of the affluent society—link up with the national-liberation movements outside the imperial core to catalyze a progression beyond the "beginning of the end" he saw advanced in the Civil Rights Movement (Marcuse 1964: 256–257). Indeed, it was for the Black civil-rights activists and the white and Jewish Northerners who accompanied them that Marcuse claims to have written the text; elsewhere, he describes the latter as exemplary humanist intellectuals (Geoghegan 1981: 86; Marcuse, 2014: 179n8). Within Marcuse's admittedly brief examination of sources of resistance to one-dimensionality at the book's close, the theorist continues with his established line of searching out oppositional subjects to hegemonic unreason, as he had first done in *The German Artist-Novel*, via the identification of traveling bands of non-conformist artists who defied feudal-clerical power in medieval Europe. Next to Camus' *The Rebel,* indeed, *One-Dimensional Man* was considered one of the most influential texts for the Parisian students who rose in rebellion against the "commodity-spectacle society" in May 1968, and in terms of success on the market, it became something of an instant classic, selling over 100,000 copies in the u.s. and being translated into sixteen languages within five years of its publication (Kātz 1982: 168).

Marcuse notably would come greatly to reorient his perspectives in the years that followed the book's release, in parallel to the militant political developments which gripped societies throughout the world as the decade came to a close. This reorientation is perhaps best symbolized in the title of an important 1968 intervention he made, "Beyond One-Dimensional Man," though it can be seen also in his presentation to the 1966 Hegel conference in Prague, "The Concept of Negation in the Dialectic." As Marcuse's reevaluations may suggest, Kellner has a point in claiming the argumentation of *One-Dimensional Man* to have exaggerated the stability of the capitalist system, besides failing to anticipate the world-historical revolts which arose just years after its publication. Still, the volume played an important role in illuminating the very machinations of the system against which the radicals of the New Left would come to rebel (Kellner 1984: 270–271, 280).

Following from some of the fragmentary comments he would make in *One-Dimensional Man* regarding the possibility of a liberatory science and technology—a "new science"—Marcuse made a number of interventions in the early to mid-1960s that both examined the ties of prevailing scientific investigation with domination and expanded on the prospects of transitioning beyond positivism in science. Through these endeavors, Marcuse sought to engage students and practitioners of the natural sciences by publishing in the *Bulletin of Atomic Scientists* and directly addressing students at UCLA and the Oceanography Institute at Scripps College. In addition, Marcuse presented a lecture in 1964 on the radical critique of science his former mentor Edmund Husserl had made near the end of his life.

During the remaining years of the 1960s, Marcuse would come openly and fervently to advocate anti-capitalist social revolution, thus harkening back to the radicality of the very first essays he had published in the late 1920s—particularly "Contributions to a Phenomenology of Historical Materialism" and "On Concrete Philosophy." In point of fact, the vague and often implicit anti-capitalism of *Eros and Civilization, Soviet Marxism,* and *One-Dimensional Man* gave way in this time to a full-fledged endorsement of revolutionary libertarian socialism and militant confrontational politics as well as a defense of anti-systemic counter-violence (Marcuse 2004: 16). In this period, Marcuse penned "Repressive Tolerance" (1965), a highly controversial essay which calls on leftists to actively withdraw tolerance from right-wing and mainstream discourses which support and normalize the profound violence and oppression exercised daily by hegemonic power against prisoners, the institutionalized, racial minorities, women and children, anti-imperialist movements in Africa, Asia, and Latin America, as well as non-human animals and nature. Marcuse bases his argument on the assumption that the violent revolt of the oppressed has historically resulted in at least a momentary pause in the oppression previously upheld by constituted power—as in the French, Cuban, and Chinese Revolutions—and that humanity for this reason should opt to carry forward this type of praxis in place of mindlessly "adjusting" to things as they are. Elucidating Marcuse's argument, Kellner envisions "resistance to the war [against Vietnam] and draft, attacks on the military, strikes and boycotts, civil disobedience, marches on Washington, occupation of universities and factories [...]" (Kellner 1984: 283).

A similarly radical analysis comes in "Ethics and Revolution," published the following year, wherein Marcuse locates the justification of revolutionary praxis within the chance for the freedom and happiness of future generations, and especially in the urgent need to overthrow the profound suffering experienced by the "wretched of the earth" under the capitalist mode of production. Expressing his agreement with Frantz Fanon and Sartre, Marcuse in this and other pieces from this period claims violence emanating from the oppressed against the oppressors to be legitimate and even necessary for the overcoming of domination. Later in the decade, he would stress the importance of the New Left expressing its solidarity with decolonization struggles by working to inhibit the imperial-capitalist monster from within. In a lecture given in Paris in 1968, Marcuse would declare that the fate of the global anti-capitalist revolution, which had been spurred on so significantly by the "elemental socialism in action" on display in the national-liberation movements, "may well be decided in the metropoles" (Marcuse 1969a: 82; 1969b: 30).

In this sense, bridging theory and praxis, Marcuse in 1966 participated at a teach-in at the University of California Los Angeles with a speech on the "Inner Logic of American Policy in Vietnam," which he claimed to be motivated—in a parallel to Noam Chomsky's later elucidation of the "Mafia Doctrine"—by a desire to prevent a liberatory, anti-imperial domino effect from taking hold in Southeast Asia, spreading throughout the global South in general, and even coming to energize the struggles of African-Americans and students closer to home. In this way, Marcuse's analysis here recalls the denunciations made by Marx and Engels of the equivalently reactionary part played by the Russian Empire in the geopolitical sphere of mid- to late nineteenth-century Europe, when Tsar Nicholas I invaded Prussia during the 1848 Revolution to forcibly reinstate the Austro-Hungarian Emperor Franz Josef (Chomsky 2010: 55, 116; Anderson 2010: 42–50). Besides supporting the rise of university occupations and Free Universities in the U.S.—Marcuse would in 1967 declare both to be critical to providing space through which to consider realities that the conventional educational system normally excluded from discussion—resisting the brutality of the Vietnam War became central to Marcuse's thought and work in these years (Marcuse 1970a: 61). In 1965, as a matter of fact, Marcuse criticizes the *Partisan Review*'s editors for their "Statement on Vietnam and the Dominican Republic," claiming their stance of opposition to U.S. policy to be "invalidate[d]" by the anti-communist assumptions they advance in their analysis of the conflict in Southeast Asia (1965a: 646). Despite the hate mail and death-threats he would receive for his opposition to the genocidal war, Marcuse felt strongly that the example of the Vietnamese resistance, together with that of the *barbudos* and Cuban masses who took down Fulgencio Batista, demonstrated the ultimate vulnerability of the capitalist beast, and could even be taken as foreshadowing its defeat from below altogether (Marcuse 1969a: 80–82). On the other hand, in a 1966 lecture on "Aggressiveness in Advanced Industrial Society," Marcuse more negatively interprets the Vietnam War as evidence of a thanotic "repetition compulsion" which could in fact speak to the existence of a global tendency toward suicide.

According to Miles, Marcuse's "moment"—the point in time, that is, which propelled him into worldwide fame as radical public intellectual—came in 1967, when the "Summer of Love" coincided first with his visit to the Federal Republic of Germany to address some five-thousand youth affiliated with the Union of German Socialist Students at the Free University of West Berlin and thereafter with his participation at the Congress on the Dialectics of Liberation in London, a fifteen-day meeting organized by prominent anti-psychiatrists R.D. Laing and David Cooper that also counted with the presence of Stokely Carmichael, Paul Goodman, Paul Sweezy, Allen Ginsberg, and Thich Nhat Hanh (Miles 2012: 86, 97; Marcuse 2004: 18–19; 2014: 331). Thus, as Kātz writes, it was at a time when "any scholar might deservedly have retired to his study and a valedictory opus" that Marcuse, nearing seventy years of age, "threw his energies to an astonishing degree behind the tasks the movement had set for itself" (Kātz 1982: 177). Due in no small part to these tireless efforts Marcuse made to assist the struggles of the New Left, in the closing years of the decade he came to be likened in stature to Marx and Mao themselves—an association many rebellious students would make, uttering the slogan "Marx-Mao-Marcuse!" or painting this trio of names together as graffiti (Marcuse 2004: 7; 2014: 332). He was donned variously as the "guru" or even "father" of the nascent New Left, as it came to be known, which was influenced by Maoism, anarchism, and the national-liberation struggles of the global South. The New Left rejected the exclusive emphasis of the Old Left on the industrial working class as revolutionary subject, and it integrated concern for race, gender, sexuality, ecology, and psychology to its critique of the capitalist system, thus presenting a broad vision for societal liberation (Marcuse 2004: 2, 18).

Following from *Eros and Civilization* and other prior critical-speculative works, Marcuse's summer 1967 lectures in West Berlin and London mirrored the multiplicitous orientation presented by the New Left well: before the German students, he affirmed the contemporary superiority of Fourier over Marx, declared the realization of utopia to be at hand, and provided a stirring defense of natural law and the right to resistance, while in London amidst the flower-children, he presented the goal of "society as a work of art," holding this to correspond to the "oldest dreams of all radical theory and practice"—the abolition of labor, the affirmation of the Kantian dream of life as an end in itself, and the total liberation of the human senses (Marcuse 2004: 83; Miles 2012: 100–101).

Marcuse's trajectory as globally renowned prophet of revolution continued apace in the world-historical year of 1968. In September of that year, when the Soviet military forcibly suppressed the Prague Spring, Marcuse signed a statement with other philosophers from Yugoslavia, Hungary, and Czechoslovakia itself unequivocally condemning the invasion that was published within twelve hours of the invasion, and he militated against the repression in a number of interviews which followed (Marcuse 2004: 118–119). Moreover, enthused as he was by the radical praxis demonstrated by students around the world that year—particularly the occupations of UC Berkeley and Columbia in the U.S.—Marcuse was fortunate enough to witness the *événements* of May 1968 in France first-hand, quite by coincidence (2004: 20). After presenting his paper on "The Re-Examination of the Concept of Revolution" at a UNESCO conference organized in Paris for the one-hundred fiftieth anniversary of Marx's birth (5 May 1818), Marcuse escaped from an assembled group of journalists who had swarmed the conference hall, hoping to inquire into his views of student revolt, and was wisked away by car to the hotel where the North Vietnamese peace delegation then engaged in diplomatic talks with the U.S. was staying; an impromptu and dignified meeting between the activist intellectual and representatives of the people whose resistance he had long hailed then followed (Miles 2012: 123). Subsequent to his address and this fortuitous meeting, Marcuse remained in Paris for the first week of the student-worker uprising (6–12 May), and he duly reported his reflections on this new "French Revolution" to scores of students and faculty the very night he returned to San Diego. Arguably, Marcuse's excitement over the upsurge may have led him to exaggerate the part played by the students in the upsurge, for he claimed that it was the students who "showed the workers what could be done," and that the general strike declared by millions of French proletarians followed from the "slogan and the example of the students" (Marcuse 2004: 42). French geographer Henri Lefebvre and others would provide a different interpretation of the *événements*, emphasizing that the true revolutionary potential of May 1968 came with the mass-intervention of workers, and not before (Miles 2012: 123–124).

Whatever the case may have been, Marcuse's embrace of student rebellion and his public lectures in late 1968 evaluating the position and practice of the

New Left were anathema to his former colleagues Horkheimer and Adorno, who looked on haughtily from Germany at their erstwhile comrade. As the radical student wave came to grip Frankfurt, various youth demanded that the elders of Critical Theory publicly align themselves with the movement and denounce the West German government's complicity with the imperial war in Vietnam. In 1967, student militants shouted "*Horkheimer Raus!*" ("Horkheimer out!") to protest the philosopher's appearance at the Romerplatz in Frankfurt in celebration of "German-American Friendship Week," while in early 1969 youth led by Adorno's former student Hans-Jürgen Krahl occupied the Institute's offices to compel the presumed anti-authoritarian *par excellence* to publicly denounce the Vietnam War—though in response, Director Adorno simply called on the police to clear them out (Jay 1973: 352–353n30; Marcuse 2004: 20). Coming from such a well-known critical theorist, this unbecoming course of action provoked a compelling and grave exchange of letters between Marcuse and Adorno that was cut short by the fatal heart attack Adorno suffered while on vacation in Switzerland in August 1969.

The final year of the 1960s brought the publication of *An Essay on Liberation*, an admittedly utopian and optimistic work which distilled Marcuse's exploration of the developing new sensibility as a Gramscian precondition for social revolution and expanded upon the cursory comments the theorist had made at the end of *One-Dimensional Man* on the subverting forces which might succeed in relegating bourgeois society to the dustbin of history. In this year, Marcuse also spoke to the "Relevance of Reality" at a meeting of the American Philosophical Association in Portland, Oregon, arguing that the struggle to materially change the world must continue to be informed by philosophical reflection rather than be subsumed by pure actionism, while in a pair of interventions made at the 1968 Summer School on Marx and Revolution in Korčula, Yugoslavia, on the relationship between the realm of freedom and the realm of necessity and questions of proletarian self-management, Marcuse warned that a new liberatory sensibility must emerge within workers in revolt if proletarian control is to yield qualitative historical change rather than merely self-managed capitalism.

Continuing to teach his introductory and advanced philosophy courses at UCSD, Marcuse in 1969 met a serious wave of academic repression emanating in no small part from the newly elected California Governor Ronald Reagan (1967–1975), who was determined to remove Marcuse from the public eye. Due to Reagan's aggressive machinations, the UC Regents in 1969 imposed the arbitrary rule that all professors older than seventy could not be promised annual renewals of contract—with this being a threshold which Marcuse surpassed in 1969. While such important public intellectuals as

Sartre, Adorno, and Popper wrote letters of support for Marcuse in his bid to be allowed to continue teaching, the newly septuagenarian critical theorist was ultimately forced to give up his official teaching privileges in this year (Marcuse 2004: 26n35). Never to be defeated, however, Marcuse presented an impassioned argument on the historical imperative for human freedom shortly after Adorno's death in the Alps in 1969 in the very same country in which his friend succumbed.

Marcuse on Cuba

While Marcuse was teaching at Brandeis, the Cuban Revolution overthrew Fulgencio Batista's u.s.-aligned dictatorship, which had reduced the island-nation to little more than a playground for transnational capital. As he would subsequently do in the case of Vietnam, Marcuse made his opposition to the Kennedy administration's reactionary orientation to revolutionary Cuba publicly known. This was indeed, as has been mentioned, one of the major precipitating factors for Marcuse's departure from Brandeis. In a May 1961 speech at a protest-action taken at Brandeis to oppose u.s. policy in the wake of the failed Bay of Pigs operation, Marcuse defends the popular Cuban struggle to remake society along egalitarian lines, and he casts Western powers' fight against "Communism" as in fact representing the suppression of popular insurgent movements. Speaking to the charge of repressiveness imposed by the Castro regime, Marcuse remarks that revolution may well demand the suspension of the civil rights and liberties of those opposed to it, and he accuses Kennedy's pretext for intervention against Castro—namely, his violation of civil rights—of being pure ideology, given the intimate contemporary relationships between the u.s. government and such despots as Chiang Kai-Shek, Francisco Franco, António de Oliveira Salazar, and the military regimes throughout Latin America and the Caribbean. Moreover, Marcuse expresses concern for the degradation of democracy that would foreseeably be provoked by increasingly militarized foreign policies within u.s. society itself, and he raises the worst-case scenario that could follow from Kennedy's aggression—one that nearly came to pass in October 1962, during the infamous "Thirteen Days"—as being nuclear war between the u.s. and Soviet Union. As an alternative vision for foreign policy, Marcuse makes the utopian proposal of opening negotiations with Castro, immediately cutting off all support for foreign dictatorial regimes, and declaring "full support" for insurgent revolutionary movements the world over (Marcuse 2014: 153–156).

Continued Engagement with Critical Theorists and
Lecture on Weber

In the early part of this decade, while still living in Massachusetts, Marcuse kept up his engagement with his former Frankfurt School colleagues: he wrote laudatory missives to Adorno and Horkheimer on their sixtieth and seventieth birthdays, respectively (1963 and 1965), and in 1964 presented a lecture before the fifteenth congress of German sociologists on capitalism and rationality in the thought of Max Weber (Martineau 1986: 16).

In his reflections on "The Position of Thinking Today"—the title of his homage to Adorno for the latter's sixtieth birthday—Marcuse employs a style somewhat uncharacteristic of his own, one that resembles Adorno's more closely. Writing, then, in the spirit of the Frankfurt-based musicologist and dialectician, Marcuse opens his encomium by referencing a handful of random and absurd situations which speak to the prevailing strength of social reification: Marxism, for example, is an object of study in government and private universities, while Samuel Beckett's plays are "great box office hit[s]" on Broadway, dockworkers strike as their union announces the work-stoppage will not affect the handling of military matériel, and the "pitifully helpless" and "tiny" peace groups "compete with each other to keep the subversives out of their ranks" so as not to appear too intransigently radical. Marcuse then notes the unsettling reality that late capitalism "speaks the truth about itself," at least to a degree, such that crimes and accounts of torture performed by the State are "not simply concealed but discussed and even criticized"—yet their recurrence is assured, claims Marcuse, for the system effectively "buys off" the majority of the population by "preserv[ing] and improv[ing] the lives of its members, conquer[ing] ever more space, and even promis[ing] that part of humanity will survive atomic war" (Marcuse 2011: 160–161).

Following such admittedly bleak opening remarks, Marcuse discusses the role of philosophy within this negative context, noting the abstraction with which thought distances itself from the given state of affairs, precisely so as to dialectically hold out the possibility of the "not-yet-given" as a normative goal to be attained. Citing Adorno's famous definition of freedom being the ability to "live differently without anxiety" as foremost among the normative ends to be sought by authentic thought, Marcuse first observes that this human duty distinguishes "spirit and body" from mere "instruments of domination"—a claim in keeping with Adorno's thought—and he then raises the possibility of "historical situations" which could lead to an emancipatory reordering of social relations—with this being a possibility that Adorno would fairly definitively deny for contemporary Western civilization. Marcuse presses on by

acknowledging that, with reference to contexts wherein positivism and instrumental rationality are "total," even dialectical thought cannot by itself provide
the rupture ushering in liberatory social change—despite his observation here
that history is the "history of leaps," and that "existence contains the power
that can transform it." Though theory may not readily be capable of identifying
a concrete world-historical subject of change, consideration of the extent to
which both Western and Soviet blocs go to continuously keep their subject-
populations mobilized against enemies, internal and external, may provide
dialectical hope for what is to come. Marcuse ends his essay for Adorno by
mentioning some of the practical means through which he thinks Critical Theory can help to resist total mobilization: "by disclosing the mechanisms which
enable society to control its members, by exploring and disseminating knowledge about current processes, by liberating consciousness, [and] by probing
into the fissures of the order" (2011: 162–164).

In a similar vein to "On the Position of Thinking Today," Marcuse gave
the title "Overcoming Domination" to the short essay he wrote in honor of
Horkheimer's seventieth birthday in February 1965. In his missive, Marcuse
discusses the history of the Frankfurt School and the life and work of its long-
standing director, Horkheimer, the very founder of a "school of thought" which
emerged from the collaborations of a circle of anti-authoritarian intellectuals, researchers, and theorists. Marcuse observes that many of the youth in
the Western and Soviet blocs recognize in Horkheimer's Frankfurt School an
important reference-point for the application of the "critical theory of society,
as this [had] developed since the nineteenth century, to the current stage of the
industrial order." Marcuse raises the dialectical point that, while the Institute
under Horkheimer's direction was in the main considered "merely a cover for
Marxism," its Critical Theory itself criticized established Marxian and Marxist
philosophies. In Hegelian terms, Marcuse associates the Institute's work with
its members' desire to understand the totality of contemporary society, in light
of the catastrophic collapse the Frankfurt theorists had themselves confronted
most acutely: that of the regression from the relative autonomy of liberal society to outright Fascism, and the repressive subjugation of the "entirety of the
human condition" that shift menacingly signified. Marcuse lauds Horkheimer's
writings for their sensitivity to the brute realities of social exclusion, and their
commemoration of the oppressed, à la Victor Hugo (Marcuse 2011: 164–165).

Marcuse closes his encomium to Horkheimer by discussing the marked
absence of optimism the latter's readers detect in the Institute director's works:

> Hope was never permitted an over presence in his writings, nor as the
> core element of his style; it appears in marginal statements, in adjectives

and attributes [...]. Horkheimer's thought is devoid of sentimentality and evangelism; it does not permit positivity as a consolation.

MARCUSE 2011: 165–166

Marcuse demonstrates his gratitude to Horkheimer's negatively dialectical approach, describing it as a philosophy of "critical intelligence and indictment," the product of an "intellect that cannot and will not give up, no matter how painful things are (or more painful they become)" (2011: 165). In closing, he applauds Horkheimer's emphasis on giving voice to the fundamental negativity of capitalist society, and he declares this type of existential commitment to be a precondition to the successful overcoming of domination.

Appearing in *Negations* (1968), Marcuse's 1964 study on "Industrialization and Capitalism in the Work of Max Weber" elucidates the importance of Weberian sociology to the anti-authoritarianism of Critical Theory—this, despite Weber's own highly conservative orientation, as evinced by his invective against the coming of socialism and the German Revolution, and his explicit recommendation that radical leftists should face the "lunatic asylum, the zoo, [or] the revolver shot." Reappropriating Weber's findings, Marcuse arguably follows in the vein of the unconventionality of his work from a decade before, when he radicalized the psychological conclusions of Freud, another political conservative. In his comments, Marcuse contemplates Weber's formulation of the Iron Cage imposed onto history by capitalist modernity: subjected to the commodity-form, the world is dominated by authoritarian bureaucracy, imperialist rivalries, and war. Marcuse adds that Weber's sociological studies foresaw the future development of conservatism among the masses and the "caesaristic tendencies" that would be adopted by hegemonic power. As against Weber's explicit apologism for class society, in light of the sociologist's association of capitalist bureaucratization with "rationalization," Marcuse suggests that Weber's concept of reason can perhaps be considered to be implicitly critical: Does Weber not communicate an "irony that understands but disavows? Does he by any chance mean to say: *And this you call 'reason'?*" (Marcuse 1968: 201, 203, 208–210, 222, 225–226; emphasis added).

Humanism, Feminism, and Revolution

In the early years of this decade, Marcuse would make two important interventions on humanism—"Humanism and Humanity" and "Socialist Humanism?"—and present his first public comments on women's issues in an interview with the *Das Argument* journal, "The Emancipation of Women in a

Repressive Society." "Humanism and Humanity" was presented as an address to the 1962 B'nai B'rith congress, and "Socialist Humanism?" represents Marcuse's contribution to the international symposium on the eponymous question, the results of which were compiled and edited by Fromm for publication in *Socialist Humanism* (1965), a volume that also includes interventions by Bloch, Dunayevskaya, Bertrand Russell, and Lucien Goldmann. Alongside women's emancipation, Marcuse discusses questions of sexual liberation vis-à-vis revolutionary consciousness in the interview with *Das Argument.*

In his comments on "Humanism and Humanity," which he prefaces as being necessarily negative—since "negativity is a precondition of improvement"—Marcuse describes humanism as a subversive theory, and he praises its commitment to egalitarianism and the project of unifying the species into a "critical intellectual unit." Making reference to history, Marcuse links the philosophical tendency to the concept of humanity, contrasting the scholasticism of medieval Europe with the "pagan" and "libertarian undertone" of Renaissance humanism, as in the figures of Goethe and Baruch de Spinoza, who along with the other European humanists sought to return to a study of classical antiquity as a means of illuminating the shackles of the prevailing world. Our philosopher observes humanism's goal of humanity as a "critical intellectual unit" to depend above all on autonomy and intelligence in thought as well as freedom from necessity. As regards prevailing reality, the dialectical struggle for freedom and reason is, far from improving, instead greatly deteriorating, argues Marcuse with reference to Freud, as the interplay of capital and power politics gets "more global, more destructive, more inhuman." Humanism cannot be blamed for this outcome, of course, and the authoritarian-socialist argument that reduces humanism to mere bourgeois ideology is wrong, Marcuse claims. Yet the humanist movement is itself marginal and powerless—increasingly so, posits Marcuse, amidst the marked trends toward hegemonic destructiveness with the passage of time. Beyond this, humanism stands accused of being to a degree complicit with the political course of the world, in terms of its traditional approach directed at education toward an internal or individual sense of freedom, rather than social and collective liberation. It is this latter, relatively undeveloped aspect of humanism that Marcuse stresses most as an end to be developed in his talk: he believes humanism to demand uncompromising critique of existential and geopolitical existence, particularly amidst the starkly dialectical interplay between entrenched threats of human annihilation and the utopian possibilities of history (Marcuse 2014: 106–111).

In the interrogatory intervention entitled "Socialist Humanism?" Marcuse takes a more negative view of humanism and its socialist interpretation. In all likelihood written around the time of the publication of *One-Dimensional*

Man, the essay shares many themes with that book, and indeed reflects much of its pessimism. Marcuse contrasts the potentialities raised by the contemporary trajectory of capitalist development—namely, self-determination toward the Kantian vision of respecting humans as ends in themselves, to be achieved through the "total reconstruction of the technical apparatus" as led by a "fundamental change" in the "direction of technical progress"—with the mobilization and colonization of the populace of the advanced industrial societies at large. With this latter consideration in mind, Marcuse declares Western workers to "no longer [be] those to whom the revolution once appealed," adding that "their initiative is not likely to revive international socialist solidarity," such that the prospects for a "humanistic reconstruction" of global society have become "very poor." Defining the project of socialist humanism as seeking to sever the association between technical development and "progress in domination and exploitation," Marcuse observes that the need for liberation exists as a "universal need," though one which is not at present recognized by u.s. laborers themselves, with the result that the chance for a Western socialism regresses into mere abstraction. Grimly noting the world-historical task of the proletariat to institute communism as "pertain[ing] to a past stage in the development of industrial society," Marcuse suggests in idealistic terms that those who seek the realization of socialism and humanism should work to strengthen and defend the *consciousness* of the need for emancipation and in this way prepare the "precarious ground for the future alternatives" (Marcuse 1965b: 98–100, 102–103, 105).

Naturally, two principal commitments of this emancipatory consciousness would imaginably be feminism and reflection on women's issues. In his earliest known intervention on these questions, "The Emancipation of Women in a Repressive Society" (1962), Marcuse queries the meaning of women's emancipation, amidst trends which seek to contain feminism within the bounds of the existing system. In the first place, as Marcuse points out, for women to commodify themselves by entering the labor market is not terribly liberatory—just as LGBTQ individuals being allowed to serve openly in the military is not. Even if historically oppressed groups do realize "emancipation" on the terms of bourgeois society, this in no way means that liberation has arrived, stresses Marcuse (2014: 163–164). To recall Marcuse's position of critical negativism can help to illustrate his point here: insofar as fundamentally repressive conditions live on in society, the totality of such a milieu cannot be considered free. As Adorno writes in *Minima Moralia,* "No emancipation without that of society" (2005: 173).

Continuing by means of resorting to a questionable—and chauvinist— view of Sartre's from *L'Être et le Neánt* which claims women to experience

happiness in the bestowal of joy to others, rather than in work, Marcuse speculates that the bourgeois "emancipation" of women will have negative consequences for societal joy—yet he also clarifies that his view must not be taken
as being a traditionalist one opposing itself to the liberation of women from
the domestic sphere! He says that this tension illuminates the general problem:
"in a repressive society even that which is good is bad. You cannot condemn
the good because of this, however." Employing a similar analysis of sexuality,
Marcuse wonders whether the weakening of Victorian mores in u.s. society
serves transcendental or affirmative ends. He observes the decline in taboos
limiting sexual relations to the marital context but worries that the decline of
such taboos could reconcile those benefiting from the pleasures yielded by this
process to society as it is, as through a postulated "repressive desublimation."
Citing Freud, Marcuse observes that society's shift toward freer expressions of
love may not in fact increase pleasure, given his view that managed promiscu-
ity in fact serves the status quo (Marcuse 2014: 164–165, 167, 169). Unfortunately,
the theorist does not here speculate on the subversive possibilities of free love.

Critical Reflections on Science and Technology

Continuing to develop his thoughts on technical rationality and the often
mutually reinforcing yet at times conflicting relationship between science and
capital, Marcuse in the mid-1960s presented a number of interventions exploring these matters as a means of directly engaging students and practitioners
of the natural sciences. All three essays and addresses examined below reflect
Marcuse's concern for a non-positivist and liberatory reformulation of science
and techology, as is first advanced in *One-Dimensional Man*.

"World without Logos" is the name of Marcuse's article that was published
in the *Bulletin of Atomic Scientists* at the beginning of 1964. It is clear, writes
Marcuse, that the development of the scientific method under capitalism
has allowed technique methodically to exploit and transform external nature
toward the end of conquering it totally for human control, and in its putatively
value-neutral exploitation of nature, science has had to "disclaim any concern
for the concrete individual, the perceptible 'body.'" This observation may help
to explain the mutual accommodation between capitalism and the practice
of science, with the latter reinforcing the former's mad purposelessness by
means of reifying and instrumentalizing the life-world. Though Marcuse does
not expressly say so, it is clear that he is referencing nuclear weapons in his
observation about the "*terrible energy* the technical world displays in resisting
the will and thought of the individual," a tendency that could well leave behind

"no nature or human reality" to populate the "substantial cosmos" (emphasis added). Dialectically, Marcuse observes that, however overwhelming and maddening the direction of the technical world, its smooth functioning depends upon the labor of discrete individuals who can autonomously opt to institute other sorts of technical forms that are less destructive—and in so doing reintroduce Logos (reason) to the world. Marcuse relates a world *with* Logos as instituting the "internal meaning" he sees in technics: that is, the liberation of humanity from labor and anxiety, and the transformation of the struggle for life into peace (Marcuse 2011: 141–143).

In "On Science and Phenomenology," a 1964 address dedicated to reflection on Edmund Husserl's *The Crisis of European Science and Transcendental Phenomenology* (1936), Marcuse places his former doctoral supervisor within the pantheon of radical nineteenth-century Western critics of the concept of reason that includes Weber and others—and indeed, he claims Husserl perhaps to be "the most radical of these re-examiners" of rationality. Marcuse presents Husserl's attempt to reintegrate philosophy into science, a project reflected in the phenomenologist's definition of the former discipline as seeking a "radical transformation of humanity" and even "liberation," as against the legitimative functions science has largely served to date. Revolutionary social change, suggests Husserl, is necessary because of the factical collapse of the humanism of reason that has followed the cleaving of science from its philosophical origins; practically, Husserl observes that mainstream science has increasingly linked the domination of nature with the domination of humanity. According to Marcuse, Husserl's alternative view of science would allow the dictates of reason to govern scientific investigation and "define and project ideas and modes of Being beyond and against those established by the prevailing reality." To resist the effective legitimation which the positivist nature of science affords the power-groups who determine its course, Husserl recommends *"therapeutic"* interventions aimed at continuing his own life's work of investigating the phenomenology of modern science and thus clarifying its mystifying functions. Implicitly referencing his work "On Concrete Philosophy" from three decades prior, Marcuse ends his comments on Husserl's criticisms of science by suggesting that philosophy and philosophers themselves may bear responsibility for having eminently ignored the basic humanistic purpose of science, and so facilitated ever-grimmer trends of technological domination (Marcuse 1965c: 279, 281–282, 286, 289).

With "The Responsibility of Science," a 1966 lecture given at UCLA, Marcuse develops themes from "World Without Logos" and his discussion of a "new science" in *One-Dimensional Man*. As Kellner notes, the address continues Marcuse's prior "engagement and critique of the scientific establishment." The radical proposition with which Marcuse opens is that science and scientist alike are responsible for the "use society makes of science" and the "social consequences of science." It is for Marcuse entirely insufficient that practitioners of science claim their work to be guided by "value-indifference," given the very real and destructive ends toward which science is directed under prevailing conditions of capitalist domination: "science [...] collaborates in the construction of the most effective machinery of annihilation in history" (Marcuse 2011: 155, 157).

Marcuse praises the advent of science in the modern period, showing it to have been a critical tool in the struggle to progress beyond "medieval dogmatism and superstition" and the "holy alliance between philosophy and irrational authority," yet he dialectically demonstrates its contemporary regression into a force which aids concentrated power-groups in stifling the exercise of human rationality and autonomy. Recommending that scientists themselves found movements to refuse the application of science to the forces of hegemony and Thanatos, Marcuse acknowledges the ever-burgeoning contradiction between the practice of modern science and the *telos* he claims for it: "like all critical thinking [science] originated in the effort to protect and improve human life in its struggle with nature; the inner *telos* of science is nothing other than the protection and amelioration of human existence." Marcuse closes by affirming the great contributions science and its practitioners could make in the popular struggle for freedom and reason, if they were to commit themselves to deriving practical methods of liberating existence "from its union with death and destruction" (2011: 158–159).

Lastly, Marcuse gave a talk to undergraduate and graduate oceanography students at Scripps College in April 1969. In this intervention, Marcuse praises the relative autonomy afforded to individual scientists in determining the course of their research, even amidst the repressive exigencies of capitalism, which Marcuse tells his listeners they are always free to reject. He stresses that what students of science must *not* do is to hold that they "are *just* scientists" and so "have nothing to do with politics." Instead, he emphasizes that, if the scientist is a servant, she is probably the "most important servant" of existing society; for this reason, scientists are "the servants of the masters *without whom the masters could not be masters.*" (2011: 38n93, 217–218; emphasis added).

One-Dimensional Humanity: Diagnosis, Reflections, and Recommendations

One-Dimensional Man: Studies in the Ideologies of Advanced Industrial Society (1964) is without a doubt Marcuse's best-known work. It is a bleak, at times

RADICAL STRUGGLE IN THE 1960S

dry and academic analysis of the various means by which monopoly capital-ism reproduces itself in its subjects, who on Marcuse's account overwhelm-ingly accept the established system precisely because of this very introjection. Reflecting on the book in a letter to his teacher, Marcuse's student Ronald Aronson—later to become author of *Jean-Paul Sartre: Philosophy in the World* (1980) and *Dialectic of Disaster: A Preface to Hope* (1983)—remarks that the "depressing" and near-desperate analysis of *One-Dimensional Man* "conveys a sense of suffocation [and] of totalitarianism at work everywhere," yet he adds that, through its very existence, the work constitutes a "major step" toward "breaking out of that closing universe" (Aronson 1971: 259). In point of fact, the argumentation Marcuse presents in *One-Dimensional Man* will prove criti-cally important as a diagnostic tool for the militant student movements of the West that began to arise in the years after the work's publication. In this sense, Aronson is right, for *One-Dimensional Man* functions both to alienate or estrange *and* to present an alternative, with the latter corresponding for Marcuse to the "Great Refusal," or an uncompromisingly defiant stance of opposition to the rule of domination. Yet it is easily seen that *One-Dimensional Man* focuses far more on the former concern than the latter, with nearly four-fifths of the text dedicated to an examination of one-dimensionality in thought and social relations.

One-Dimensional Man can provisionally be declared the most Adornian of Marcuse's works, even if Marcuse's final work, *The Aesthetic Dimension,* is also highly marked by Adorno's philosophy, though in a rather different—that is, more straightforwardly positive—way. The 1964 text demonstrates its Adornian character in the deep reservations it expresses about proletarian struggle under conditions of monopoly capital, and in the related horror it expresses for the seemingly universal hegemony of bourgeois culture and ideology in U.S. society, which for this reason increasingly comes to resemble "one huge captive audience" (Marcuse 1964: 245). While workers do make appearances in *One-Dimensional Man*—as they had not, for example, in *Eros and Civilization*—Marcuse mentions the working classes only in empirical, observed terms—negatively, and at a distance. In this can be seen the signifi-cant gap which marked the distance between the hopes Marcuse and other members of the Frankfurt School had held for the proletariat of the "New World" upon emigrating as refugees from Nazism and the relative hopeless-ness evident in the appraisal Marcuse makes of class struggle in the U.S. three decades later. Nevertheless, as the course of the 1960s will show, the pessimism Marcuse expresses in this volume is arguably undue, and it will be the subject of revision as the conservative societal structure of the affluent society is progressively called into question and reordered, both from within and without.

Part 1: One-Dimensional Society

In "The Paralysis of Criticism: Society Without Opposition," the introduction to the first edition of *One-Dimensional Man,* Marcuse outright accuses existing capitalist society of having constructed an entirely irrational world: basing his argument in anarcho-Hegelian value principles which claim that human life *"is worth living,* or rather *can be and ought to be made worth living,"* and that given social relations should be judged against their historical alternatives, especially those more life-affirming ones which could offer greater chances of "an optimal development" for humanity and nature, Marcuse asserts the need for political revolution to overthrow prevailing power relations (emphasis added). Nonetheless, the problem is that, within his reflections on the affluent society of the 1960s U.S., Marcuse cannot readily identify the subject who will enact the necessary historical changes—for advanced-industrial capitalist society succeeds in containing the progression of qualitative social change by integrating such seeming opposites as labor and management, technological advance and increased destructiveness, democratic rule and usurpation, and wealth and misery (1964: xlii–xliii, xliv–xlv).

As against these fatal trends, and against unchecked pessimism, Marcuse recognizes that there exist "forces and tendencies" that "may break this containment and explode the society," yet, much like the French insurrectionist Gracchus Babeuf whom Marcuse will consider later in this decade, the critical theorist notes that such possibilities are largely blocked by the conformity and obedience of the masses as regards the irrational and reprehensible commands emanating from on high. Thus does Marcuse judge the U.S. populace and particularly its working classes according to transcendent principles. In so doing, Marcuse once again breaks company with more orthodox Marxists, who believe devoutly in the intrinsically revolutionary nature of the proletariat and so eschew a resort to an empirical evaluation of such a foundational claim. Marcuse also clarifies at the outset of *One-Dimensional Man* that there still exist large geographical areas both within and outside the advanced-capitalist societies wherein his analysis of one-dimensional ideology does not apply. Anticipating his growing concern for ecology, furthermore, Marcuse defines advanced industrial society as a rather nasty outgrowth of the established historical trend of dominating nature (1964: xlv, xlviii, xlix).

At the beginning of *One-Dimensional Man,* Marcuse seeks to take account of the breadth and depth of ideological colonization on hand in advanced industrial society—in this is seen the work's similarity with Heidegger's critique of *das Man.* Marcuse observes with reference to history that the critical liberties gained at the origins of industrial society—principally, freedom of thought, speech, and conscience—have been inverted, for the "achievement cancels the premises." Monopoly capitalism, on Marcuse's account, has built up such a reified and depraved world as to tend toward totalitarianism through its suppression of the emergence of an "effective opposition against the whole." Far from betraying any absolute sense of despair, however, Marcuse observes that such trends *can* be reversed: first, through the displacement of the false needs that have been superimposed onto individual and society as a means of tying both into reproduction of the system, as through the desire for affluence, and, second, via the concomitant development of true needs demanding liberation and revolution. Again resisting any conformism or subjectivism, Marcuse applies the external principle of the happiness of the individual as his justification for the dissolution of inauthentic bourgeois needs. Still, he rejects the hypothetical usurpation of judgment on the distinction between true and false needs by any self-styled tribunal, and this view, juxtaposed with his concern that the people are actively being prevented from becoming autonomous, leads him openly to consider how those who have been "the object of effective and productive domination [can] by themselves create the conditions of freedom?" In contrast to Plato and Rousseau, Marcuse argues that to contemplate the forcible imposition of reason "upon an entire society is a paradoxical and scandalous idea." But Marcuse does not immediately resolve these tensions, noting instead the definite tendencies in established culture and ideology toward integration, commodity fetishism, and the blunting of critique, contradiction, and counter-mobilization. As he writes famously, "The people recognize themselves in their commodities; they find their soul in their automobile, hi-fi set, split-level home, kitchen equipment" (1964: 1, 3, 5–11).

For Marcuse, increasing affluence and the rising standards of living function to stifle the expression of transcendental concepts and action—either this, or if trends toward transcendence and sublation do emerge, they are quickly diluted in the main to appear as though they pertained to the bounds of the established political system. In this is seen capitalism's totalitarian character, as "society and nature, mind and body are kept in a state of permanent mobilization for the defense of this universe." Marcuse observes that these realities and tendencies call for "*radical subversion*," but he sees few promising signs of revolt and rebellion which would tend toward the communist abolition of labor and the anarchistic "pacification" of existence (1964: 2, 12, 16–18; emphasis added).

Marcuse continues by expanding upon his initial comments on the generalized assuaging of social antagonisms seen under monopoly capitalism, remarking the union of the Welfare and Warfare States to have yielded a "new society" in comparison to its predecessors, one marked principally by the oligarchical concentration of power and the coordination of the manipulation of consciousness through mass-media. In the world of party politics, putative rivals adopt policies and visions that increasingly converge, while Marxism has been invariably associated with the Soviet Union or reduced to social-democratic parliamentarism in West Germany, France, and Italy. Indeed, the analyst of one-dimensionality remarks upon the veritable Orwellianism on exhibit in conventional politics, mentioning the absurdity through which a reportedly "Socialist" party "works for the defense and growth of capitalism"—much like the Spanish PSOE (Partido Socialista del Obrero Español) has done since Franco's death in 1975. Marcuse points out similarly affirmative tendencies within labor in Western societies, which he claims to have undergone considerable *embourgeoisement*—this despite its continued subordination and instrumentalization within the production process. Recalling Weber, Marcuse declares prevailing society to be directed heteronomously with regard to the workers and people in general, who are ruled over in true reification by an apparatus over which they have "no control." As a counter-image to such negations, Marcuse here develops his Marxian vision from *Eros and Civilization* of a non-repressive civilization into a speculative account of another world which could be revolutionized by the liberatory employment of automation as a means of reducing labor, thus giving rise to a qualitatively new "dimension" of leisure (1964: 19–20, 23–34, 36–37, 89).

In "The Closing of the Political Universe," the second chapter of *One-Dimensional Man,* Marcuse shares one of his most candid reflections on the recurring problem of resorting to an "educational dictatorship," though he ultimately rejects it even here. Given social conditions wherein those dominated by hierarchy have been socialized to accept such domination, the critical theorist observes with an implicit nod to Lenin that liberation would seemingly need to arise "from without and from above," and he claims that the "terrible risk" which the prospect of educational dictatorship doubtless represents "may not be more terrible than the [various] risk[s] which the great liberal as well as the authoritarian societies are taking now." Marcuse nonetheless refuses seriously to entertain such a strategy, explaining that dialectics insist that the subordinated attain their freedom autonomously, and that the "end must be operative in the means [taken] to attain it" (1964: 40–41).

In addition, Marcuse in this section seeks to comment on the prospects for the "former colonial or semi-colonial" societies becoming a "third force" opposed to Western monopoly capitalism and Soviet authoritarianism: in radical distinction to the designs which liberalism has in store for the world's social majorities, Marcuse envisions a preservation and improvement of Indigenous traditions and customs, focused on "[s]ocial revolution, agrarian reform, and reduction of over-population," coupled with an industrialization process that departs from the trajectories taken previously by Western and Soviet regimes. He adds, however, that the chances for global popular self-determination are constrained by the imperialist politics enacted by the competing power blocs: as in *Reason and Revolution,* only negatively and potentially does Marcuse suggest the existence of trends which could lead to the "abandonment of neo-colonialism in all its forms" here in *One-Dimensional Man.* Furthermore, Marcuse intriguingly proffers the view that foreign policies of containment directed against the Soviet Union and world communism are mere outgrowths of domestic counterparts designed to suppress the specter of liberation (1964: 45–47, 48, 51–52).

In the minor chord, then, Marcuse attempts to resist the objective decline of "freedom and opposition" that follows from the hegemonic application of technological rationality by stressing the dialectical possibilities made available by capitalist development and pointing to the continued condition of the worst-off, that of the "outsiders and the poor, the unemployed and unemployable, the persecuted colored races, the inmates of prisons and mental institutions." Against the dominion of one-dimensionality, Marcuse raises the chance for the historical "demise of the nation state" together with nationalism, "the national interest[, and] national business," and the criminal international alliances which uphold the system. In thus contradicting the hypothesized *closing of the political universe,* Marcuse holds out the image of an anarchistic political struggle that would "dissolve the [very] basis of domination" (1964: 53, 55).

Arguably, Marcuse's third chapter to *One-Dimensional Man,* "The Conquest of the Unhappy Consciousness" as "Repressive Desublimation"—this latter term referring to a recurring, awkward construction of Marcuse's which has been mentioned above in the context of the hypothesized conservative effects of sexual liberation under capital—in many ways mirrors and updates the cultural pessimism expressed twenty years earlier by Adorno and Horkheimer in *Dialectic of Enlightenment.* Yet the analysis is distinctly Marcusean and as such is less desperate than that of his colleagues. Marcuse contrasts the one-dimensional aesthetics which have adorned the capitalist hegemony over nature and humanity with those on hand in pre-industrial Western settings, the most authentic of which had "expressed a conscious, methodical alienation from the entire sphere of business and industry, and from its calculable and profitable order." Marcuse here posits that this "backward" world, though marred by inequality, labor, and misery, represented a historical stage in which humankind "and nature were not yet organized as things and instrumentalities," as they would later be under capitalism and Fascism. In the "high" forms of Western art, especially literature, Marcuse sees historical confirmation of "another dimension" which is "irreconcilably antagonistic to the order of business"; invariably, as in *The German Artist-Novel,* this multi-dimensionality is represented in "such disruptive characters as the artist, the prostitute, the adulteress, the great criminal and outcast, the warrior, the rebel-poet, the devil, the fool—those who don't earn a living, at least not in an orderly and normal way." Theorizing that historical memory continuously produces the *return of the repressed* in the imagination and the contemplation of social alternatives, Marcuse presents his view of art's essence prior to the development of monopoly capitalism: art had then expressed "the *unhappy consciousness* of the divided world, the defeated possibilities, the hopes unful-filled, and the promises betrayed," and it functioned to denounce the "crimes of society" and the "hell" created by the inhumanity and authoritarianism pro-duced by feudalism alongside nascent bourgeois society (emphasis added). In a discussion of musical lyrics, Marcuse cites French poet Paul Valéry's take on the purpose of art: to "make live in us that which does not exist," and thus to begin to move us toward a new world. Reaffirming his positive account of the revolutionary potential of aesthetics from World War II, when he wrote on Aragon and Resistance poetry, Marcuse declares that true art reveals possibili-ties for nature and humanity that are "repressed and repelled in reality," and that authentic portrayals of beauty stand in for the profound desire for human tranquility and joy. At its most authentic, then, art advances *"the rationality of negation,"* the *Great Refusal,* "the protest against that which is" (Marcuse 1964: 58–62, 63, 68, 73; emphasis added).

This utopian meaning of aesthetics to the side, Marcuse argues that capital-ism and the industrial "conquest of nature" have greatly de-eroticized the life-world, including human relations, such that Eros is reduced to genital sexuality and libido made less polymorphous and perverse, thus resulting in a far less pleasurable experience of the lived environment. With regard to the affluent society, Marcuse claims that there arises a generalized *happy consciousness* among the people which helps to rationalize prevailing power relations of domination: in contrast to the critical Hegelian concept of the *unhappy con-sciousness* which confronts the great distance separating the *is* from the *ought,* the happy consciousness conforms to the given society, holding the course and speed of progress on hand to be rational and positive, in this way yielding the human conscience to industrial-capitalist reification. Marcuse emphasizes that guilt is entirely foreign to the happy consciousness, which has no limits— hence its affinity with the world of the Nazi concentration camps and that of RAND nuclear war game simulations (1964: 72–74, 78, 79–83).

For Marcuse, the happy consciousness represses all consideration of the torture and imperial warfare exercised by hegemonic power in defense of prevailing relations of privilege—the crimes take place "[only] at the margin of the civilized world," in an "underdeveloped" society, and besides, "the Community is too well off to care!" With reference to the seeming opposite of mainstream U.S. society, Marcuse notes that the "productive growth" of the Soviet Union necessarily harms the "libertarian communist opposition" arrayed against authoritarian socialism and Western capitalism alike. The author closes the first part of *One-Dimensional Man* negatively, quoting Bloch: "[...] that which is cannot be true" (Galbraith 1956: 96; Marcuse 1964: 84–85, 102; Bloch 1961: 65).

Part 2: One-Dimensional Thought

Marcuse opens the second part of *One-Dimensional Man* by reiterating the same quote by Bloch and noting just how foreign such a formulation is to everyday thought under conditions of late capitalism. In "Negative Thinking: The Defeated Logic of Protest," he develops his account of reason as resistance to one-dimensional thought: arguing that the "world of immediate experience" must be "subverted" and "transformed" for it to come to fulfill its true potential, Marcuse claims reason to be the "negative" and "subversive" power that allows people the means with which they can come to know the nature of such potential. He locates the origins of this revolutionary philosophy in the thought of the ancient Greeks, who held it to correspond to the mental faculty that would allow human beings to distinguish between truth and falsehood, and he presents the optimistic perspective that, if humans were to embrace reason, they would necessarily act "in accordance in truth," against destruction and annihilation. As our critical theorist declares, "Epistemology is in itself ethics, and ethics is epistemology." Marcuse observes that the "discovery" of the chance for a free set of human social relations is the product of the union of reason and Eros; future liberation is for this reason prefigured in "the exigencies of thought and in the madness of love." He adds that, within the history of philosophy, only the materialists were affected by the "afflictions of human existence," and it is materialism that in turn has intimately influenced the development of the concept of reason, which Marcuse defines authentically as a *"mode of thought and action which is geared to reduce ignorance, destruction, brutality, and oppression"* (emphasis added). It is by means of an insurgent proletariat that a "different logic" and a "contradicting truth" could be implemented in and against the rule of capital (1964: 123–125, 127, 135, 142).

In passing to discuss the rise of technological rationality and the ways this has facilitated the reign of monopoly capital, a system that "perpetuates the struggle for existence and extends it to a total international struggle which ruins the lives of those who build and use this apparatus." Marcuse provides a genealogical account of its emergence through the process of rationalization in Weberian terms. Such rationalization depends upon the quantification and domination of nature and thus the disenchantment of the life-world; it cleaves science from ethics. Presenting a somewhat Heideggerian take on the technologies developed through science for monopoly capitalism—and even citing his old mentor explicitly in the discussion—Marcuse posits that the domination of nature upon which the scientific method is based has itself contributed greatly to political and social domination: "The machine is a slave which serves to make other slaves," as Marcuse quotes philosopher Gilbert Simondon as asserting. Nature and humanity come to be instrumentalized and considered fungible with the development of modern technology, claims Marcuse. Much like Heidegger, he argues that *technology itself* has played a central role in the strengthening of processes of reification. In fact, Marcuse here associates the prevalence of positivist thinking with the "degree to which society becomes industrial and technological." Dramatically, Marcuse suggests that the noxious link between the domination of nature and humanity upheld by technology tends toward the very destruction "of this [terrestrial] universe as a whole." Yet in negative and brief form, Marcuse dialectically surpasses Heidegger and positivism both by engaging in speculation regarding the changes that could come to affect the scientific method, if it were to be overhauled, with the fatal trends excised: the "hypotheses" of a new science would "develop in an essentially different experimental context" without losing their rationality, and science could then "arrive at essentially different concepts of nature and establish essentially different facts" (1964: 144–148, 153–154, 158–159, 166–169, 172). In this way would science come to assist in the subversion of prevailing hegemony.

In the final chapter in this section, "The Triumph of Positive Thinking," Marcuse presents a reformulation of his sustained critique of positivism and expands upon his previous engagement with Fromm by reflecting on the meaning of therapy. The former project, which parallels many previous works of Marcuse, defines positivist ideology as seeking to dismiss all thought of "metaphysics, transcendentalisms, and idealisms" and thus functioning to refuse the consideration of alternative social relations. As one-dimensional philosophy, positivism in fact serves mystifying functions through its obscuring of exploitation and hierarchy and its attendant demand for "[m]agic, witchcraft, and ecstatic surrender" at the individual and global levels. In accordance with his more optimistic notions, Marcuse indicates the philosophical dimension—like the aesthetic one—as a potential site of resistance to positivism and established reality, for it contains space for reflection on spectral

"fictions" and "illusions" that could illuminate the depravity of prevailing
unreason. At his most tame here, Marcuse will accuse positivism of restricting
the human imagination and humanity's historical experience, but at his most
incisive, Marcuse will remind his readers that positivism serves domination
and hegemony in its effective justification of the existing world, which remains
*"that of the gas chambers and concentration camps, of Hiroshima and Nagasaki,
of American Cadillacs and German Mercedes, of the Pentagon and the Kremlin,
of the nuclear cities and the Chinese communes, of Cuba, of brainwashing and
massacres"* (1964: 172–173, 180–182, 186, 189–190; emphasis added).

In the comments on therapy with which he closes this section, Marcuse contrasts the tasks of the physician or nurse with those of the philosopher. While
the former bear responsibility for restoring their patients' health, the latter can
in Marcuse's thought more readily raise the existential question of the *"general
sickness"* driving individual pathologies, in accordance with the philosophical commitment to comprehend "what [the world] has done to [humanity],
and what it can still do" to its inhabitants. Furthermore, Marcuse presents his
view that true philosophy would realize itself by taking on therapeutic purposes, and for the success of such therapy he outlines three goals: the "free[ing
of] thought from its enslavement by the established universe of discourse
and behavior," the elucidation of "the negativity of the Establishment," and
the "project[ion of] its alternatives." Finally, he discloses that philosophy as
therapy would manifest itself through radical political struggle (1964: 183, 199).

Part 3: The Chance of the Alternatives

In the final fifth of *One-Dimensional Man*, the section on the "Chance of the
Alternatives," Marcuse provides a more systematic treatment of the socio-
political and aesthetic forms of resistance to reification he considers in passing earlier in the text. With a nod to the French author Stendhal, Marcuse
discusses the *shock value* or "contrast-character" of beauty—the idea that
beauty presents a radical contradiction to the mundaneness of everyday
life and so "opens (for a short moment) another reality." As Stendhal writes,
beauty represents a *"promesse de bonheur,"* or a promise of joy and human
happiness. Much as Adorno would argue in his *Aesthetic Theory,* Marcuse here
claims the experience of beauty to prefigure the enormous bounty of beauty
which awaits humanity in liberation, just as the experience of fragmentary
freedom anticipates the greater freedom to be attained through revolution.
Dynamically, this relationship grows ever more acute, the more prevailing
society follows increasingly irrational trends: as society takes on an evermore

oppressive character, authentic art must take on increasingly oppositional and critical forms. It is in this sense that Marcuse suggests art to reflect the criteria he wants to establish for "objective historical truth," in terms of progress toward human emancipation. In particular, art represents the goal of the "free development of human needs and faculties," or the pacification of existence, which for Marcuse amounts to the very basis for true dialectical reason. Given this value judgment presented by Marcuse near the close of *One-Dimensional Man*, the author asserts the prospect for reason to depend upon the extent to which monopoly capitalism is overcome by the forces developing within it which it in turn strives to suppress. As the hegemonic consciousness—which is, to repeat, not on Marcuse's account limited to the members of the capitalist class—necessarily reflects and perpetuates unfreedom, the chance for a free consciousness striving for the realization of a "higher historical reality" emerges only in resistance to the established society and its "intolerable conditions" (1964: 210, 214, 220–221, 222–223, 239).

In the final chapter of *One-Dimensional Man*, Marcuse presents the specter of liberation as threatening *"catastrophe"* for the established system. Were technology and the means of production to be appropriated and reoriented toward the end of pacification, civilization could progress to a higher stage and come to institute a revolutionary notion of reason, one that would cause science to meld into the "art of living," as in the image of society as a work of art. Marcuse speculates that such world-historical change, which is to be brought about by a corrective "political reversal," would allow for the establishment of a "universe of qualitatively different relations" among humans themselves, as well as between humanity and nature. Within his elucidation of these subversive hopes for social transformation, Marcuse warns strongly against "all technological fetishism," particularly as expressed by many Marxist prometheans. In anarchistic terms, Marcuse suggests that the project of pacifying existence represents the inversion of the power-struggles engaged in by rival hegemonic groups throughout known history: "Peace and power, freedom and power, Eros and power may well be contraries!" Pacification and revolution should most rationally aim at reducing the overdevelopment on hand in the advanced-industrial societies, writes Marcuse, for this end would serve the causes of equality and joy by bringing to a halt the forces reproducing "moronization, the perpetuation of toil, and the promotion of frustration," as well as the preparations for nuclear annihilation, at the most negative extreme (1964: 227–231, 234–235, 242–243).

In closing, Marcuse raises an argument reminiscent of Robespierre—though the point could arguably also be a Babouvist or Bakuninist one—in light of his insistence that the true chance for liberatory alternatives demands the suppression of the heteronomous needs and satisfactions that tie the masses into the status quo: Marcuse specifically anticipates the collapse of the influence of advertising and television on collective subjectivity. For the human imagination to liberate itself, then, much of what prevails must be repressed; the analysis is similar for the organism, and for nature taken as a whole, in light of the evidently vast pollution, waste, and destructiveness on hand. Self-determination, in this sense, would become real if it were practiced by autonomous individuals who have broken definitively with one-dimensional society, and its prospect would be helped along by the development of an idealist-autonomous consciousness during the preparatory phase which is to predate the surge of a corresponding "historical practice." Marcuse here defines this practice, the "only truly revolutionary exigency," as seeking the outright abolition of domination, which can be defined as *Marcuse's Hegelian end.* Presenting a highly unconventional conclusion for a self-identified Marxist, Marcuse sees glimmers of hope in those groups which remain socially excluded from the affluent society, for their embodied life-experiences form a revolutionary contradiction to monopoly capital (1964: 245–246, 250–253, 255–256). As he writes poignantly,

> When they get together and go out into the streets, without arms, without protection, in order to ask for the most primitive civil rights, they know that they face dogs, stones, and bombs, jail, concentration camps, even death. Their force is behind every political demonstration for the victims of law and order. The fact that they start refusing to play the game may be the fact which marks the beginning of the end of a period (1964: 257).

However, despite the radical negation embodied by non-integrated groups vis-à-vis the affluent society, there can be no assurance that such resistance will lead inexorably to a victorious revolution that overturns all the various ills Marcuse describes in *One-Dimensional Man.* Capitalism may indeed live on, and "the second period of barbarism may well be the continued empire of civilization itself." Nevertheless, there remains the chance that humanity's "most exploited force" can unite with the world's "most advanced consciousness" to finally tear down the global capitalist system (1964: 257).

Marcuse on Marx, Louis Napoleon, and Benjamin

Not long after the release of *One-Dimensional Man,* Marcuse inverted the minor chord found in the book which examines concrete resistance to reification

and domination into his primary concern for investigation and public advocacy. This transition is reflected well in two essays from 1965: an epilogue for a
republication of Marx's *Eighteenth Brumaire of Louis Napoleon* (1852), and an
afterword to a collection of Benjamin's writings, *Critique of Force.*

In his comments on Marx and Louis Napoleon, Marcuse returns to the
concerns that had driven his 1934 essay on liberalism and totalitarianism. He
summarizes Marx's tracing of the self-destruction of liberal bourgeois society,
as manifested in the coup led by Louis Napoleon in 1851 which transformed
Bonaparte's nephew into Emperor Napoleon III, while considering the essay's
contemporary relevance. With Marx, Marcuse remarks on the bourgeoisie's
increasingly Caesarist tendency to mobilize not only against socialism but
also even the institutions to which it had itself given rise—civil rights, that
is, and freedom of speech—if and when these should come to threaten the
interests of profit. The authoritarian state is a racket, then, one that depends
on the consent of the subordinated; in this sense, Napoleon III's "plebiscitary
dictatorship" would not have been able to withstand the revolutionary unification of proletariat and peasantry against it, according to Marcuse. Bringing
the analysis to the present, our philosopher implies that the Western workers who "bear and preserve the apparatus of production and domination" are
akin to the small peasants who supported Louis Napoleon. With a nod to the
hegemony of one-dimensionality, or false consciousness, in Western societies,
Marcuse concludes his reflections on the *Eighteenth Brumaire* by stressing that
the Reason of domination, exploitation, and repression—unreason, that is to
say—does not encompass the full meaning of rationality. Instead, *authentic*
reason is associated with freedom and revolution, and resistance to hegemonic
unreason is in fact seen everywhere, especially among the youth and socially
excluded. For these groupings "was the *Eighteenth Brumaire* written; for them
it is not obsolete" (Marcuse 2014: 117–122).

In a similar vein, Marcuse wrote an afterword to a 1965 collection of writings authored by Benjamin, entitled *Critique of Force* (*Kritik der Gewalt*). In
his most sustained treatment of the thought of his martyred comrade, Marcuse here considers questions of revolution, violence, and the transition away
from capital. He clarifies at the outset that Benjamin's critique of violence
is not absolute; rather, it focuses on *Gewalt,* or the violence of domination,
rather than violence as such. In point of fact, Marcuse declares outright that
Benjamin "took the meaning of the word 'peace' too seriously to be a pacifist,"
and he shows that his friend rejected the view which privileges the sacred-
ness of human life over the imperative for social revolution, as reflected in the
Benjaminian concept of "divine violence." To attain a world that could be freed
from *Gewalt* depends on the chance for revolutionary change, which would

likely of necessity involve counter-violence—a "rupture with the continuum" rather than "just eliminating its corruption" (Marcuse 2014: 124–125). For this reason, Marcuse observes, Kant's vision of perpetual peace remains utopian, insofar as it remains indelibly tied to any sort of gradualism or reformism. Not least among Benjamin's critical contributions in this work is the challenge he presents to prevailing notions of progress: the itinerant essayist "reminds us that real progress hinges not on the amelioration of the labor process, but on its supersession; not on the exploitation of nature, but its emancipation; not on the person as such, but the 'just person'" (Marcuse 2014: 125).

Continuing with his analysis of Benjamin's profoundly radical political and philosophical approach, Marcuse hails the suicide's mental image of a "messianic immobilization" of history, identifying this as one of the few authentic evocations of the *truth* of Critical Theory:

> [T]he revolutionary struggle aims at immobilizing that which is happening and has happened—prior to any other positive goals, this negation is the first positive. What humanity has done to humanity and to nature must be stopped, radically stopped—only then can freedom and justice start (2014: 126).

Thoughtlessness and the everyday—*das Man*—must be halted, nature redeemed, and subject and object united. Class struggle and revolution are the means to these ends. Looking both to future and past, the militant opposition maintains alive the hopes for liberation. "[A]s broken ones they break with the latticework of guilt erected by the law-making and law-enforcing order" (2014: 125–127).

Justification of Revolutionary Praxis: "Repressive Tolerance," "Ethics and Revolution," Guerrilla Warfare, "The Question of Revolution," and "Thoughts on the Defense of Gracchus Babeuf"

For about four years—from the time of his dismissal from Brandeis in 1965 to the watershed year of 1968—Marcuse the critical theorist resurrects the express hopes he had communicated with regard to revolution during his period of study in Freiburg with Heidegger, transforming these into a militant endorsement of insurrection and counter-violence against the established system a generation on. In this "stipulation of an enemy" and call to arms "against [...] destructive totalitarianism," Marcuse reflects the trace of the thought of Carl Schmitt, according to Joseph Diaz, however much the content of the respective thinkers diverged (Diaz 2013: 147). In this sense, in the five pieces examined below dating from the mid- to late 1960s, the resurgence of revolutionary, quasi-Schmittian discourse as against the pessimism and quietism advanced by Schmitt's own person is evident.

In "Repressive Tolerance," a major work from 1965 that was published as a chapter in Robert Paul Wolff and Barrington Moore's *A Critique of Pure Tolerance,* Marcuse reaches what could well be considered the apex of his controversy and polemicism. In dismissing what passes contemporarily for tolerance as functioning to "serv[e] the cause of oppression," he calls for a new concept that would utterly repudiate "prevailing policies, attitudes, [and] opinions" in favor of the extension of tolerance to "policies, attitudes, and opinions which are outlawed or suppressed." Though he recognizes that there exists no constituted power which could "translate liberating tolerance into practice," Marcuse states his belief that intellectuals must work to "open the mental space" of society by "recall[ing] and preserv[ing] historical possibilities which seem to have become utopian." Toward this end, he defines the realization of humane social relations as the Hegelian goal of history, and he judges prevailing modes of tolerance harshly in these terms. As dominant powers exercise repression against dissidents at home and abroad and imperil the very future of life on Earth with nuclear weapons, those subjected to such power tend to conform to such imposed realities: "laissez-faire the constituted authorities" becomes the accepted course of action, such that the concept of tolerance comes to betray the end of a tranquil life it had intended to bring about. In this inverted world, "[t]olerance toward that which is radically evil now appears as good because it serves the cohesion of the whole on the road to affluence or more affluence." Given such depths of reification, all sense of progress achieved "in the normal course of events" only serves to shore up the grip of constituted power—hence the need for radical subversion (Marcuse 1965d: 81–83, 93).

Marcuse identifies two sorts of tolerance that are permissible within late capitalism: that of the passive toleration of established ideology, which is allowed to live on "even if [its] damaging effect on [humanity] and nature is evident," and that of the non-partisan tolerance which refuses explicitly to take sides and so effectively serves existing domination. Clearly, neither option is adequate for the task of emancipation. Marcuse counterposes a negative vision wherein the distinction between truth and falsity is collectively determined using human reason, and the numerous factors which obstruct the arrival of liberating conditions jettisoned in the historical process. The process of the realization of universal freedom which for Marcuse constitutes history's *telos* possesses an autonomous truth and sense of right and wrong; its exercise mandates the rejection of a great number of the practices and orientations on hand in existing society. In this is seen the distance between pure tolerance and *repressive tolerance*. With reference to this latter concept, Marcuse holds that reflection on the history of intolerance hailing from absolute monarchies and clerical regimes does not justify passing to an mindlessly indiscriminate tolerance, for the conformist lack of discrimination implied in such a position effectively "impedes liberation and multiplies the victims who are sacrificed to the status quo." Starkly in this sense, Marcuse raises the case of "a newcaster report[ing] the torture and murder of civil rights workers in the same unemotional tone he uses to describe the stockmarket or the weather, or with the same great emotion with which he says his commercials." The bourgeois sense of "objectivity" that allows for the presentation of "gorgeous ads" side by side "with unmitigated horrors [...] *offends against humanity and truth by being calm when one should be enraged,* by refraining from accusation *where accusation is in the facts themselves"* (1965d: 85, 87–88, 97–98; emphasis added).

In contrast to the established pattern of bourgeois-conformist tendencies which perpetuate unreason and destruction, a repressive or discriminating tolerance would actively fight against the hegemonic system run by "politicians, generals, and businessmen" and seek to catalyze the development of a "subversive majority" (1965d: 100, 121). Amidst the established power of the very hegemony that blocks human emancipation, the practice of repressive tolerance admittedly may in the main be seen as taking on undemocratic forms. Concretely, Marcuse envisions

> the withdrawal of toleration of speech and assembly from groups and movements which promote aggressive policies, armament, chauvinism, discrimination on the grounds of race and religion, or which oppose the extension of public services, social security, medical care, etc (1965d: 100).

Besides incorporating such forms of praxis, repressive tolerance on Marcuse's account might also necessitate the suppression of certain educational "teachings and practices" that limit discourse in positivist fashion by "precluding a priori a rational evaluation of the alternatives." A repressive tolerance would thus include "discriminatory tolerance in favor of progressive tendencies," for these hold the true interests of humanity in heart. Generally speaking, Marcuse believes this discriminating tolerance can serve its functions best once it takes on a mass-basis and develops into a counter-movement that could bring about the "reversal of the trend" through total revolution. Social revolution for Marcuse at this time is unlikely to be a non-violent affair; in this essay, he condemns pacifism as reactionary, observing that a distinct difference exists between hegemonic violence—as from State and capital—and the counter-violent force employed by the people to overthrow oppression. Marcuse clearly acknowledges all violence to be "inhuman and evil," but he rejects the notion that all violence is unjustified, as the rebellion of the oppressed against the oppressors demonstrates. One must not equate the the "desperate struggles *for* humanity" with the "great crusades *against* humanity" (1965d: 101–103, 107, 113).

Coming to the question of precisely who will decide between truth and error, or revolution and conservatism, Marcuse claims the only authentic alternative to resorting to the intellectual dictatorship he raises in *Eros and Civilization* and *One-Dimensional Man* to be the establishment of autonomous, self-managed societies. At the individual level, Marcuse delimits the right to a say in politics to those persons who have come to learn "to think rationally and autonomously," though he provides no measurable means by which to assess such a standard (1965d: 106).

In sum, then, repressive tolerance advances intolerance to all reaction, particularly as manifested in the incessant and normalized "clear and present danger" which threatens all humanity in the post-Nazi epoch. For now, the critical theorist places a great deal of emphasis on counter-hegemonic educational efforts aimed at breaking the grip of ideology over the masses: "progress in freedom demands progress in the *consciousness* of freedom" (emphasis added). Art has a critical part to play in this educational struggle, declares Marcuse, for it "stands against history" and "withstands [the] history which has been the history of oppression"—this, by "subject[ing] reality to laws other than the established ones: to the laws of the [Platonic] Form which creates a different reality" (1965d: 89, 109, 112).

In a postscript written to "Repressive Tolerance" in 1968, Marcuse provides some key clarifications and elucidations of the original essay. He notes the "progressive historical force" of tolerance to be located within the concept's potential for the protection of the speech and thought of those who seek radical social change; in a similar sense, the liberatory promise of democracy corresponds to its theoretical "openness to qualitatively different forms [...] of the human existence in general." In existing society, tolerance is extended to the radical critics of society in a merely formal sense, considering the vast inequality between capitalists and revolutionaries in access to means with which to influence public opinion, to say nothing of the juridical assurance that to engage in insurrection—that is, to live out revolutionary theory, rather than merely to discuss it—is to violate the very limits of legality. Given this context, Marcuse recommends the practice of a discriminating tolerance to "restrai[n] the liberty of the Right" as an important line within a larger confluence of intensified struggle for "real democracy"—one whose birth on the world stage would disprove the postulated necessity of an educational dictatorship as a means of moving beyond capitalism (1965d: 85–86, 95, 117, 119, 122). Marcuse ends his post-script on a highly militant note:

> The tolerance which is the life element, the token of a free society, will never be the gift of the powers that be; it can, under the prevailing conditions of tyranny by the majority, only be won in the sustained effort of radical minorities, willing to break this tyranny and to work for the emergence of *a free and sovereign majority*—minorities intolerant, militantly intolerant and disobedient to the rules of behavior which tolerate destruction and suppression (1965d: 123; emphasis added).

Based on the question of whether revolution can be justified ethically, Marcuse's provocative reflections on "Ethics and Revolution," published in *Ethics and Society* in 1966, present the critical theorist's affirmative response to the question he poses. On Marcuse's account, the concepts of revolution and ethics largely converge in holding the "good" and the "right" to consist in the advancement of human freedom and happiness, particularly those of future generations. As against positivism and other forms of apologism for the status quo, revolutionary ethics pose the right of resistance toward the unshackling of human potential and the reduction of "toil, misery, and injustice." Contemplation of the rights to revolution and to resistance leads Marcuse to consider the related question of whether revolutionary violence can be justified in ethical terms. Claiming peaceful revolutions not to "present any problem" to the powers that be, Marcuse mentions Robespierre's distinction between the "despotism of tyranny" and the "despotism of liberty" in a positive light, and he defines revolutionary terror as *counter-violence*, a practice which is legitimate only insofar as it is exercised "in the defense against the oppressors and until they are defeated." Marcuse here warns that revolutionaries, in their impassioned willingness to sacrifice existing "rights and liberties and life itself" for the sake of the joy and freedom of future generations, must not employ "arbitrary violence, cruelty, and indiscriminate terror." He recognizes furthermore that an *absolute* sense of ethics fundamentally would forbid all "suppression and sacrifice" undertaken by revolutionaries in their attempts to secure the life-world for future humanity—if human life is to be considered *ipso facto* sacred, then the distinction Robespierre makes is meaningless. In response to this challenge, Marcuse observes that humanity is in actual fact "confronted with a distinction and a decision," given that daily life under capital exacts significant death and destruction, and "one cannot start becoming moral and ethical at an arbitrary but expedient point of cut off: the point of revolution."

For this reason, Marcuse rejects the pacifist critique, as he values the ethical imperative to overthrow established society over any deontological respect for human life. In Marcuse's view, then, the ends do in fact justify the means, for the advancement of human freedom is the "only legitimate end" of socio-political action, one that outweighs the sacrifices which are necessary to achieve it. As he writes, "[t]he non-violent history is the promise and possibility of a society which is still to be fought for." In Marcuse's view, social revolution invariably involves violence—or counter-violence—on the one hand, while on the other, the struggle to expand the sphere of human freedom cannot justify terror without end, or the imposition of a party dictatorship over the people (1966b: 133–135, 137, 139, 140–141, 144–147).

In a similar vein to "Ethics and Revolution," Marcuse provides a militant defense of guerrilla warfare and anti-systemic upheaval in the Political Preface he added to *Eros and Civilization* in 1966. Employing prose reminiscent of Frantz Fanon—as well as of Sartre's preface to Fanon's 1961 *The Wretched of the Earth*—Marcuse remarks that the measures being taken at that time to uphold the privileges of imperial societies are "transforming the earth into hell," as could be manifestly seen in "Vietnam, the Congo, South Africa, and [...] in Mississippi and Alabama, in Harlem." In the ongoing popular revolts against colonialism, Marcuse observes that the Marxian concept regains its "full validity"—a validation echoed by the radical student movements in Western societies which oppose themselves to war and affluence. Much like Adorno in his 1962 address on the subject, Marcuse here defines progress as the reversal of the dominant historical trajectory: revolution, that is, against the powers that be. He sees in the successful exercise of guerrilla warfare an embodiment of the revolutionary spirit, particularly in the "check" it provides against "the most brutal and destructive machine of all times" (Marcuse 1966a: xiii–xiv, xvi–xvii).

> The spread of guerrilla warfare at the height of the technological century is a symbolic [*sic*] event: the energy of the human body rebels against intolerable repression and throws itself against the engines of repression. Perhaps the rebels know nothing about the ways of organizing a society, of constructing a socialist society; perhaps they are terrorized by their own leaders who know something about it, but the rebels' frightful existence is in total need of liberation, and their freedom is the contradiction to the overdeveloped societies (1966a: xix).

Marcuse expresses his excitement at the prospect that formerly colonized societies could elect to skip over the wasteful, energy-intensive stage of development adopted by the most advanced-industrial capitalist countries and so direct their efforts to addressing "vital individual and collective needs" while keeping production on the human scale. The critical theorist thus sees promise in the contributions of revolutionary armed movements to the inversion of tendencies toward overdevelopment and the "repressive rationalit[ies]" it promotes (1966a: xviii).

In this way, Marcuse declares his unequivocal support for counter-violence, in light of the chance that the "violence which breaks the chain of violence may start a new chain." Critically, he argues that aggressiveness in defense of life can help Eros in its struggle against the hegemonic death-drive. With reference to the world's decolonial movements and the global revolt of youth, Marcuse acknowledges the front lines of the resistance against a civilization that truly threatens to precipitously hasten the end of Freud's "detour to death," just as it blocks the chance for a conscious lengthening of this tour. Beyond the encouraging movements already at hand, he proposes the organized refusal of workers and other collective forms of counter-organization against hegemonic power. Doubtless, the idea here is that the contemporary and ongoing fight for life and the higher possibilities of history can be attained through radical political struggle (1966a: xx–xxi, xxv).

In a 1967 interview on the "Question of Revolution" that consists of just four questions and answers, Marcuse clarifies that guerrilla warfare, though heroic in its unmediated defense of life, cannot by itself pose a "mortal threat" to capitalism, considering that the war-machines of the imperial powers can at any point implement a "Final Solution" to put down all resistance—by "burning and poisoning everything," if need be. This totalitarian setup can only be inhibited by solidarity networks operating inside imperial societies, says Marcuse, with the hopes of international justice to be pursued by a "serious opposition" resting on the resuscitation of global proletarian radicalism. Should this type of intervention fail, warns Marcuse, it is to be imagined that the U.S. empire will simply continue with its militaristic steamroll against international communism, particularly the "*Communism of the poorest*," with all the suffering and loss such a counterrevolutionary outcome would imply. However, on the side of the wretched of the Earth themselves, Marcuse sees transitional potential in national-independence movements within the formerly colonized societies of Africa and Asia, which could cooperate among themselves to resist U.S. capital and thus cause it to retreat, leading subsequently, perhaps, to a critical internal destabilization of the system that would improve the chances of broadly anti-capitalist outcomes the world over (1967a: 4–6).

Also in 1967, Marcuse contributed the concluding essay to the volume *The Defense of Gracchus Babeuf.* This work provides a transcript of the

handwritten defense made 170 years previously by French revolutionary
François-Noël Babeuf—better known as Gracchus Babeuf—before the High
Court of Vendôme of the Directory on the charges of violating a Thermidorian
law prohibiting insurrection, advocacy of a return to the Jacobin Constitution of 1793, and public statements in favor of the redistribution of property
(Scott 1967: 11). Babeuf's defense is a truly brilliant and militant philosophical argument justifying revolutionary direct action to overthrow illegitimate
authority. It illuminates his communist passion for human equality and the
radical struggle he and his comrades from the Conspiracy of Equals undertook
to carry on the legacy of the Great French Revolution, particularly under the
highly reactionary conditions of the reign of the Directory, which had forcibly
cut short the Jacobins' most radical phase of the revolution in 1794 and thereafter installed rule by oligarchical interests which held the people in complete
disregard.

   Among the greatest of the Thermidorian crimes was the Directory's dispatching of General Napoleon Bonaparte to suppress the urban insurrection
of starving Parisians in October 1795, and just months later to shutter the *Club
de Panthéon* at which radical *sans culottes,* dissidents, and ex-Jacobins would
meet to discuss the task of organizing to put an end to the Thermidorian reaction (Scott 1967: 7; Maréchal 1967: 90). Such intensification of repression led
directly to the founding in March 1796 of the Conspiracy of Equals, a grouping
that subsequently planned for an insurrection against the Directory that was
to end with the expropriation of the wealthy by the peasantry and proletariat
in arms. On the eve of its planned uprising, nonetheless, the Conspiracy was
betrayed and sixty-five of its organizers arrested, with several of these tried and
then deported or executed (Scott 1967: 10–11).

   The major written work penned by one of the members of the Conspiracy,
Sylvain Maréchal, was the "Manifesto of the Equals," and though different historical accounts conflict as to the degree to which this Babouvist document
was known to the French public at the time of the Conspiracy's existence and
ultimate suppression, the document provides a communist vision for equality
as based in natural law (Scott 1967: 13; Léger 1949). Addressing the Manifesto in
part to "[m]en of high degree—lawyers, rulers, the rich," Maréchal announces
that "now it is your turn to listen to us. [*Humans*] *are equal. This is a self-evident
truth* [...]. It is our turn to speak. *Listen to our just demands and to the law of
nature which sanctions them*" (emphasis added). Equality for Maréchal and
the Conspiracy is "the first principle of nature, the most elementary need of
[humanity], the prime bond of any decent association among human beings."
Declaring the Conspiracy's goal as the "COMMON GOOD" and its immediate
demand as the the "communal ownership of the earth's resources," Maréchal

presents an anarchistic call for putting an end to the "unnatural division of
society into rich and poor, [...] into *rulers and ruled*" (1967: 91–92). Hence it
becomes clear that the members of the Conspiracy did not necessarily believe,
as Marx and Engels later would, that hierarchy must live on within the revolutionary process of overcoming oligarchical society. Instead, Maréchal declares
the Great French Revolution to be the mere "forerunner of another revolution,
one that will be greater, more solemn, and which will be the last."

Following from this point, Maréchal observes that no "vaster" plan for revolution "has ever been conceived or put into execution," and he closes the Manifesto by heroically heralding the "hour for decisive action," as "the people's
suffering has reached its peak; it darkens the face of the earth. For centuries
chaos has reigned under the name of 'order.' *Now the time has come to mend
matters*" (emphasis added).

> We who love justice and who seek happiness—let us enter the struggle
> for the sake of equality. The time has come to establish THE REPUBLIC
> OF EQUALITY, to prepare an asylum for [humanity]. The time has come
> to set the earth to rights (1967: 94).

Calling on the oppressed of France, the Conspiracy of Equals invites them
to join the egalitarian revolutionary struggle whose realization will allow for
enjoyment of the grand "feast" which nature provides "for all her sons and
daughters." Indeed, in marked distinction to many of the Enlightenment *philosophes* of France, Maréchal includes consideration for happiness and embodied
sensuousness in his call for revolution against hierarchy. Materialistically, he
notes that it is not enough that equality be promised in the Declaration of the
Rights of Man and Citizen, for it must instead exist "in life, in our very midst."
He asserts speculatively that the people will "at last" enjoy the "rapturous happiness [they] ha[ve] sought so long" after moving beyond the inegalitarian
social arrangements they have confronted throughout known history, and his
closing call for the people to recognize the Republic of Equality and work with
the Conspiracy to achieve it is a request for the people to "[o]pen your eyes and
hearts to *full happiness*" (1967: 92, 94–95).

In parallel terms, the struggle for happiness plays a decidedly central role in
Gracchus Babeuf's remarks during the defense he presented to the jurors at the
High Court of Vendôme, which he prepared on his own, having been expressly
denied access to counsel. As the volume's editor John Anthony Scott remarks,
this address "brings to life an extraordinary personality and constitutes the last
utterance of a tragic being who refused to accept human misery and human
injustice, and was ready to die for his beliefs" (1967: 12). Babeuf declares the

very fundament of the philosophy motivating the action he and the rest of the members of the Conspiracy of Equals took to be the advancement of human happiness and freedom; speaking for himself, Babeuf expresses that it was his love for humanity which underpinned his investigations and advocacy of revolutionary change toward an egalitarian set of social relations. Among the numerous radical thinkers and actors Babeuf cites in his defense is included his mention of Saint-Just's famous reflection on the French Revolution—that now, after its advent, "[h]appiness is a new idea in Europe" (Babeuf 1967: 34, 45, 58).

Babeuf's legal defense presents a spirited defense of the right to revolution and a thoroughgoing challenge to the Directory's definition and charge of conspiracy, one that deprives Thermidorian rule of all legitimacy. Addressing himself from the start to his fellow jurors—for, though it refused him the right to counsel, the Directory did not deny him a jury trial—Babeuf claims the entire legal proceedings against him and his co-conspirators to represent a judgment on the very position of advocating thought which inspires subversion and, ultimately, social revolution. Babeuf in no way denies his participation in the Conspiracy of Equals, nor does he disavow his role as editor of the radical journal *Tribune of the People,* which took after Jean-Paul Marat's *Friend of the People.* Instead, he presents a reasoned case justifying the insurrectional deposition of oppressive, illegitimate power. Echoing Maréchal by claiming the legitimacy of any given polity to rest on the degree to which it promotes the happiness of the people who reside within it, Babeuf defends the notion that all citizens have the right to "vigilant[ly]" watch for authoritarian and tyrannical developments which would undermine the principle of popular happiness, to warn others of such eventualities, to "rise up" against "usurpation [and] oppression," and to urge others to do likewise. In point of fact, Babeuf challenges the charge of conspiracy raised against the Babouvists, declaring it to be false, for their conspiracy is against the constituted Directory, not the people—and "a conspiracy not directed against the people cannot be a conspiracy at all" (1967: 20, 22, 28). Moreover, he associates rule by the Directory with *disorder*, in light of the reactionary policies it upheld:

> The accumulation of power and privilege in the hands of a tiny minority already rendered formidable by reason of its wealth alone, and the slavish subjection of practically the entire people to this handful of the mighty— this the prosecution calls *order*. But we call this *disorder. Order* is only thinkable to us when the entire people are free and happy (1967: 34).

Like Marcuse in a way, Babeuf associates positivist philosophies that condemn insurrection with the historical claim of the right of divine kings to rule however they please. Declaring the Directory to be illegitimate, Babeuf counterposes popular sovereignty as the only possible basis for true legitimacy in the ordering of society. He then cites an article of his from the *Tribune of the People* which declares life under the Thermidorians to "not [be] the real Republic. The real Republic is something of which we have not yet made trial." In his defense, Babeuf further defines his communist and egalitarian vision, as based in the suppression of private property, the expropriation of the wealthy, the socialization of work and distributional schemes, and the total abolition of class inequality. In addition, Babeuf raises the revolutionary philosophies of Jean-Jacques Rousseau, Gabriel Bonnot de Mably, and Denis Diderot—though he seems to have confused Diderot for Abbé Morelly, the true author of the *Code of Nature* from which Babeuf draws heavily—as supporting the perspectives and praxis of the Conspiracy: "[t]hese thinkers conceived plans very similar to ours and undertook to make them known." Citing Diderot—or Morelly—from the *Code of Nature*, Babeuf plainly asks, *"Would the rise and fall of empires ever be possible in a world where all property was held in common?"* (1967: 35–36, 42, 46–47, 57, 61, 74; emphasis added). Moreover, developing a precocious materialist critique of Idealism, Babeuf near the close of his comments quotes Armand de la Meuse, a member of the National Convention, from a 1793 speech:

> True happiness for the masses is today only a beautiful dream, not a reality. It cannot be realized without carrying through the revolution in *things* that has already been accomplished in [*people*]'s *minds* (1967: 86).

In his concluding remarks which follow his heroic attempt to philosophically challenge the Directory's case against him and perhaps inspire the jurors to engage in a sort of nullification of the legal proceedings, Babeuf clearly recognizes that the Court will rule against him, override any sympathetic decision from the jury, and cut short his life. In this sense, Babeuf expresses pride at remaining true to his commitment to the people's emancipation; as he declared earlier in his defense, "[t]here is no better way for a [human] to die than to offer [her] life for the sake of justice." However, he foresees in the suppression of the Conspiracy the echo of the murderous fate to which his adopted namesakes were subjected—the Roman reformers Tiberius and Gaius Gracchus, that is to say, who were both assassinated in the second century BCE for attempting to break up the aristocracy's latifundia in the interests of the people—and he despairs over the future to come, as he imagines royalism rising like a leviathan to defeat the Republic. Anticipating Práxedis Guerrero and the Mexican Revolution, though, he announces that it is "better that we should die on our feet rather than live on our knees" and "sacrifice our lives gloriously [...] to save the

lives of others" (1967: 61, 87–88). Movingly addressing his children publicly at
the very close of his defense, Gracchus intimately shares with his family one
of the greatest fears which must grip the *Dasein* of all revolutionaries when
reflecting on their mortality, whether that of themselves, their blood-relatives,
friends, and comrades, or, indeed, humanity in general:

> I have only one thing to make known to you, one bitter regret. I wished
> passionately to do my part in the struggle to bequeath to you freedom,
> the source of all [humanity's] blessings; but I see that slavery will live
> on after me, that at my death I shall leave you in the grip of evil. I have
> nothing, nothing at all to bequeath to you!! I have no wish to pass on to
> you my love of justice, my deep hatred of tyranny, my dedication to the
> cause of equality and freedom, my bright love for the people. These gifts
> would be too deadly: of what use would they be under the royal tyranny
> that is bound to come? I leave you in slavery, and this thought alone will
> torment me at the last. I ought, instead, to advise you how patiently to
> bear your chains. But I cannot! (1967: 88–89).

Turning now from this veritable *pathos* to the sense Marcuse makes of
Babeuf's life and defense before the High Court at Vendôme, the reader can
see a continuation of many of the themes the critical theorist had presented in
One-Dimensional Man and in the essays written since its publication. Marcuse
situates the activity of the Conspiracy of Equals and its plans for insurrection
as being the natural outgrowth of the Babouvists' fondness for Enlightenment
philosophy, "which had prepared the intellectual ground for the democratization of society," and of their compassion for those impoverished by the
reactionary course the French Revolution had taken—the "poor, the down-
trodden, the hungry." Marcuse observes that the participants in the Conspiracy based the justification for their revolutionary program in social-contract
theory, such that, if the original reason for which human society is founded—
that is, the welfare of all—is so radically violated as to have yielded to the vast
social inequalities which marred life under the Directory, the contract is effectively nullified, and the people or their representatives have every right to work
to overturn the status quo. In this way, Babeuf's planned insurrection aimed
at bringing about an admittedly anarchistic sense of order in place of reigning disorder. As Marcuse explains, Babeuf himself grounded his call to arms in
natural law, specifically on the inalienable right of humanity to enjoy a society which would afford each member an equal share of the necessities of life.
That the legitimacy of such arguments had at that time met with criticism "on
the grounds that the existence of such natural law is not demonstrable" was

immaterial to Babeuf, who was not prepared to allow positivist apologism to block progression toward an emancipated future (Marcuse 1967b: 98–100, 103).

Marcuse dedicates exceedingly little of his essay on Babeuf to examining the revolutionist's account of communism or his stress on equality; presumably, Marcuse considered the introductory essay and the transcript of Babeuf's defense which precede his article in *The Defense of Gracchus Babeuf* to present these matters adequately. In what remains of his consideration of the legacy of the Conspiracy, Marcuse emphasizes the lack of popular support the Babouvists are reported to have faced as they planned to launch the insurrection, particularly given the would-be insurgents' despondency over the people's resignation before the power of the Directory as well as their supposed enthrallment to royalism. Marcuse notes such tendencies to correspond to a "[f]amiliar historical situation," one in which the responsibility of the tribune becomes to demonstrate to the people that the established Republic is "not the real Republic," and that the "Revolution is not over." Following this point, Marcuse makes an interjection which arguably may not be in the spirit and keeping of Babeuf's desires, for he describes the course of the planned insurrection as being a revolution undertaken by a "minority" on behalf of the subordinated people who are "deceived, hostile, or apathetic" to the very prospect of such an event: for this reason, then, the expected resort to Terror on the part of the Babouvists following their successful insurrection would not, it is to be imagined, be employed solely against members of the Directory, but also against sections of the people themselves, claims Marcuse. Less controversially, the theorist notes Babeuf's planned revolution to be based on the principle of protecting the people, especially the poor, against their enemies—this by deposing the power of the privileged and prosecuting a radical redistribution of both wealth and power in favor of the popular classes (1967b: 100, 102, 103–104).

Marcuse closes this essay by declaring that Babeuf's agitational form of revolutionary praxis has lived on after his execution by the Directory, particularly in Lenin's Bolshevik model. With this claim, though, Marcuse evinces yet another example of questionable reasoning, for several other historical examples should likely be considered more fitting in terms of advancing the Babouvist message—from the Zapatistas and Magonistas of the Mexican Revolution to the Spanish and Russian anarchist movements. As in *One-Dimensional Man*, Marcuse observes that the tendency of Western capitalism is to reduce the number of poor domestically, such that any return to the Babouvist basing of the revolutionary call to arms on the plight of the poor could be inadvisable within contemporary Western settings. What is more, Marcuse seeks to apply those criticisms of false consciousness he sees in Babeuf's writings to the prevailing reality, as in the critical theorist's declaration that the existence of formal democracy in no way precludes "domination, indoctrination, and manipulation" from reigning hegemonic. Developing Babeuf's argument for the superiority of natural law over established law in his own fashion, Marcuse reminds his readers that the fact elections are held hardly means that the people necessarily constitute the sovereign power in a given State, for "their expressed will is not necessarily their autonomous will," and "their free choice is not necessarily freedom" (1967b: 96, 103–104).

Psychoanalytical Interventions

Beyond his public ruminations calling for a new science and technology, his composition of *One-Dimensional Man,* and his highly militant period which followed, Marcuse in the early to mid-1960s continued to carry forward his insight into social psychology and psychoanalysis, as was reflected in *Eros and Civilization* the previous decade. The fruit of this continued engagement with the intersection of politics, psychology, and sociology was two important lectures: "The Obsolescence of Psychoanalysis" and "Aggressiveness in Advanced-Industrial Society."

Marcuse's 1963 address to the annual meeting of the American Political Science Association, originally entitled "The Obsolescence of Psychoanalysis," appears in printed form in *Five Lectures* as "The Obsolescence of the Freudian Concept of [Humanity]." Marcuse begins this lecture with some general comments on the use of psychotherapy in society, noting as in the epilogue to *Eros and Civilization* that the practitioners of therapy are "faced with a situation in which [their work] seems to help the Establishment rather than the individual," in the sense that psychotherapy in the main serves to aid the individual's adjustment or "submission" to the established society. Nevertheless, Marcuse continues with his argumentation from *Eros and Civilization,* claiming that Freud's positing of an irreconcilable conflict between individual and society is a historically obsolete position, in light of the prospect of doing away with surplus-repression through a radical break with the performance principle of capitalism. In this talk, though, Marcuse focuses his attention more on a distinct factor that shows Freud's conception of humanity to be outdated—namely, the observed decline of the importance of the father and the bourgeois-nuclear family in socializing the children who are raised in late-capitalist society. Under monopoly capital, argues Marcuse, the "nascent ego" of the child is "directly manage[d]" by the media, formal education, and peer groups, in distinction to the past, when the ego and superego were formed by struggling against the father, as Freud had theorized. As Marcuse observes, "the child learns that *not* the father but the playmates, the neighbors, the leader of the gang, the sport, the screen are the authorities on appropriate mental and physical behavior." This results in a false sense of liberation from the father, he stresses, for the historical factors leading to the decline of the father are intimately connected with the increasing *massification* of people in society, whereby the average person, rather than develop autonomously, surrenders her chance of freedom to heteronomous interests. Marcuse likens this negating turn of events to a regression to the Freudian stage of the primal horde, in that society's members allow their own ego-ideals to be replaced by collective ideals fashioned in the interests of domination (Marcuse 1970a: 44, 46–47, 49, 52). As the critical theorist declares:

> The antenna on every house, the transistor on every beach, the jukebox in every bar or restaurant are as many cries of desperation—not to be left alone, by [one]self, not to be separated from the Big Ones, not to be condemned to the emptiness or the hatred or the dreams of oneself. And these cries engulf the others, and even those who still have and want an ego of their own are condemned—a huge captive audience, in which the vast majority enjoys the captor (1970a: 49).

In a parallel to the progressive weakening of Eros amidst the hegemony of Thanatos, Marcuse observes that the capitalist tendency toward massification causes the critical mental faculties to be atrophied, such that the functioning of established bureaucracies is helped along "by the irrational transfer of conscience and by the repression of consciousness." The centrality of the capitalist machine in shaping the collective psyche notwithstanding, Marcuse here refuses to liken prevailing society to an army led by a field marshal, and he instead proposes that it resembles a "society without fathers" (*Vaterlosen Gesellschaft*). Given that this society is not one upheld exclusively by military terror—domestically speaking, at least—Marcuse suggests that its stability is explained with reference to libidinal attachments, many of which are manifested through the sublimation of sexual gratification in the enjoyment of commodities such as automobiles. Besides weakening Eros, then, this type of conformist expression of libidinality facilitates the growth of "instinctual aggression" and "destructive energy" among the masses, and such aggression is in turn diverted by power groups against external enemies who do not affirm the priorities of the established reality principle: Marcuse here mentions "the reds, the commies, the comrades, Castro, Stalin, the Chinese," as well as "pinks, intellectuals, foreigners, [and] Jews." The masses are thus continuously mobilized both "with and against atomic destruction," and Marcuse even goes so far to claim that the Cold War arms race proceeds "with the consent of a large part of the people." The critical theorist admittedly may be exaggerating with this last claim, especially considering that he links it into the development of a confused sociological hypothesis which claims that it is the masses who "determine" the policies advanced by their masters, such that the "formation and mobilization of masses engenders authoritarian rule in democratic form" (1970a: 51, 53, 55, 56, 60).

As he nears the end of his comments, Marcuse speaks to the *repressive desublimation* he identifies on hand in the advanced industrial-capitalist societies of the West. He first examines the question of sexual desublimation—that is, the progressive relaxation of sexual mores seen in the twentieth-century West—and he notes that this does not in fact function to contradict the established society, in contrast to Freud's anarchical view of sexuality, which associates eroticism with "freedom from social control." Instead, under prevailing relations of capitalist hegemony, sexual liberalization takes on the form of a controlled "transgression" which serves to integrate the autonomous pleasure principle into the dominant reality principle, to the detriment of the former. Marcuse observes a similar trend in cultural matters: he argues that art, philosophy, literature, and music under mass conditions lose the critical character these had retained in previous historical epochs, thus further contributing to the strength of the performance principle and the instrumentalization of human life. However, rather than consider such "regressive tendencies" as necessary or foreordained, Marcuse remarks that the "masses" are not the same as the *people* "on whose sovereign rationality the free society [is] to be established," and he suggests that the possibilities for freedom will depend greatly on "the power and unwillingness to oppose mass opinion, to assert unpopular policies, [and] to alter the direction of progress." Practically, he suggests an alternative approach for dissident psychoanalysts to take. As in *One-Dimensional Man,* he calls on such practitioners to help patients develop and strengthen autonomous egos and pursue autonomous ego-ideals—in short, to assist them in "liv[ing] in refusal and opposition to the Establishment" (1970a: 57–58, 60). Incidentally, of course, this radical social-psychological alternative is essentially the same one endorsed by Fromm, with whom Marcuse had had such an acrimonious—and largely overblown—debate nearly a decade prior.

Marcuse's 1966 essay on "Aggressiveness in Advanced Industrial Society" constitutes a revised and updated version of a lecture the critical theorist had given in Chicago before the Psychiatric Society a decade prior. It is truly a moving and challenging intervention, one that reflects the radical despair Marcuse would periodically experience over the course of his life, mirroring his comrades Benjamin and Adorno: the piece evinces a palpable sense of weariness at the overwhelming destruction wrought on Vietnam. In this intervention, Marcuse laments the unleashing of the U.S. military against "one of the poorest, weakest, and most helpless countries of the world." He positively cites an anonymous essay from *Les Temps Modernes* which associates the prosecution of the imperial war with the Puritan tradition in U.S. society: for Marcuse, "the burning of [the enemy's] refuge, defoliation, and the poisoning of [their] foodstuff are not only strategic but also moral operations," as seen from the standpoint of the war's managers (Marcuse 1968: 265). In quoting Senator William Proxmire from Georgia—hardly a radical, being a member of the Armed Services Committee—Marcuse illuminates the general problem:

> I have observed, over a period of almost thirty years in the Senate, that there is something about buying arms with which to kill, to destroy, to wipe out cities, and to obliterate great transportation systems which causes men not to reckon the dollar cost as closely as they do when they think about proper housing and the care of the health of human beings.
> PROXMIRE 1962: 65–66

The critical theorist comes to express his concern regarding the very centrality of aggressivity within advanced-industrial society. He worries that social adjustment demands that, in accordance with the demands of dominant power, "the individual becomes at one and the same time more aggressive and more pliable and submissive," in an imprinting process of sorts. Psychical manipulation of the masses is performed "in the interest of certain businesses, policies, lobbies": philosophically, "the general objective purpose is to reconcile the individual with the mode of existence which his society imposes on [her]." Coming to expressly hail the work of his erstwhile colleague Fromm— particularly the latter's volume on *The Sane Society* (1956)—Marcuse speculates that those who function "normally, adequately, and healthily" within the malaise of capitalism can likely be said to themselves be ill; conversely, he equates "mental health" with the "ability to live as a dissenter, to live a nonadjusted life" (1968: 251, 253, 262). Echoing "Repressive Tolerance," Marcuse dedicates special attention to the role of mass-hegemonic media within this "social mobilization of aggressiveness," noting that these interfaces present the

> killing, burning, and poisoning and torture inflicted upon the victims of neocolonial slaughter [...] in a common-sensible, factual, sometimes humorous style which integrates these horrors with the pranks of juvenile delinquents, football contests, accidents, stock markets reports, and the weatherman (1968: 259).

Such comments recall Hannah Arendt's concept of the banality of evil, one she formulated after reporting in Jerusalem on the trial of the Nazi bureaucrat Adolf Eichmann. Arendt's basic idea is that hierarchical systems of power, which are perpetuated smoothly thanks to unthinking adjustment, allow for the commission of the greatest crimes. Evidently, such considerations can be applied more broadly than the Eichmann case, for mindless conformity also facilitated the genocidal conditions of the Vietnam War, as well as numerous other wars that have been prosecuted since that time, in addition to the more general, grossly inegalitarian socio-economic relations which obtained then, as now—to say nothing of the unchecked destruction of non-human life on Earth. Against the negativity and despair such reflections could yield, Marcuse poses the Hegelian chance for a fundamentally different society, one that would "do away with the market economy" as well as militarism. Naturally, the prospect for such historical change would presuppose that the "power of the dominant interests" be "eliminate[d]." Marcuse here pauses to reflect on his longing for the type of transformative social change that could "reverse the entire prevailing trend"; negatively, he concludes in empirical terms that "[t]here is little evidence for such a development." The question then becomes whether the system can be expected to maintain its stability and growth, and the philosopher's tentative response here is that it will do so precisely by perpetuating the very irrationality which in fact threatens its own existence, as through the specters of nuclear war and ecological catastrophe (1968: 256, 261).

Marcuse closes the essay by referencing Freud's analysis of Thanatos, which the psychoanalyst associated with the "repetition compulsion," or, in Marcuse's definition, the "striving for a state of complete inertia, absence of tension, return to the womb, annihilation"—that is to say, the Nirvana principle. This destructive sort of eternal return will be familiar to those acquainted with Nietzsche's own theory of eternal recurrence. Marcuse concludes with alarm by speculating on the implications Freud's late metapsychological theory hold, when juxtaposed with the barbaric violence unleashed by capital: if the death drive truly does dominate the organism, "then we may indeed speak of a suicidal tendency on a truly social scale, and the national and international play with total destruction may well have found a firm basis in the instinctual structure of individuals" (1968: 267, 268).[2]

---

2 With this pronouncement, Marcuse recalls Benjamin's desperate conclusion in "The Work of Art in the Age of Mechanical Reproduction" (1936): that humanity's "self-alienation has reached the point where it can experience its own annihilation as a supreme aesthetic pleasure" (Benjamin 2003: 270). Marcuse doubtless would agree with Benjamin's claim that the

Activism against the Vietnam War

As the text of "Aggressiveness in Advanced Industrial Society" shows, the brutality of the Vietnam War deeply disturbed Marcuse, for it reminded him of Nazism, and he consistently expressed his public opposition to its prosecution in these years. As has been seen, he hailed the heroic resistance of the Vietnamese people as a critical and inspirational embodiment of the worldwide anti-capitalist struggle while condemning the infernal reduction of their country to the "sacrificial lands of neo-colonialism" (Marcuse 1967a: 4). Marcuse develops these activist perspectives in his "Statement on Vietnam" and his analysis of the "Inner Logic of American Policy in Vietnam."

In a short response to the 1965 *Partisan Review* editorial entitled "Statement on Vietnam and the Dominican Republic," Marcuse takes the periodical's editors to task for castigating critics of the Vietnam War who either claim that Indochina will not "go Communist" if the u.s. withdraws, or who do not care "what happens to the people of Southeast Asia," as long as the war comes to an end. Inverting the editorial line, Marcuse expresses his belief that, the longer the u.s. prolongs its neo-colonial war in Asia, the stronger the communist alternative will become, and he further clarifies that the advent of communism need not contradict the *Partisan Review*'s advocacy of the creation of "free societies" the world over. In fact, Marcuse suggests that communism could be of critical importance in the struggle to advance global freedom, in terms of the project of carrying through the "fundamental social and economic changes which would abolish existing inequality, privilege, and repression," and in a parallel to his 1961 intervention on Cuba, the theorist clarifies that revolution in the Third World may well take on forms that may seem "undemocratic" to Western observers. Lastly, echoing the analysis from *Soviet Marxism,* he observes that communist struggle stimulates the continued growth of capitalism "in competitive coexistence" (Marcuse 1965a: 646–649).

In "The Inner Logic of American Policy in Vietnam," a talk he gave at a teach-in at a student-occupied UCLA in March 1966, Marcuse boldly demystifies the brazen lies promoted by the u.s. government and hegemonic media in their

---

task of communists faced with such madness is to "politiciz[e] art," as against the fascist aestheticization of the very real tendencies toward self-destruction. Marcuse and Benjamin would have concurred that a radical subject must arise to intervene and disrupt this cycle of mindlessness, anomie, absurdity, and death.

attempts to justify the aggressively imperial war against Vietnam. He readily clarifies that the U.S. military's "fight for freedom" in Southeast Asia is actually waged in defense of indigenous power groups whose very existence is based on "exploitation and slavery." The genocidal war targeting the Vietnamese people is directed against a popular war for liberation, one launched by revolutionary groups seeking the institution of thoroughgoing agrarian reforms and the related deposition of traditional rulers, foreign capitalists, and imperialist-friendly governments like those of Ngô Đình Diệm and his various successors. The Vietnamese Communists are threatening to U.S. interests because, if their anti-feudal efforts were to succeed, they conceivably would expropriate foreign capital and block future investment ventures in the country, thus "reducing the capitalist hinterland" in the region to an unacceptable degree (Marcuse 2004: 38–39). Moreover, Marcuse identifies the risk that a Vietnamese Revolution would prove inspirational for other liberation struggles in the colonized world—maybe even domestic ones:

> Seen in this perspective, our [*sic*] Vietnam policy is only one of a policy which extends from West Germany to Indonesia, from Turkey to Japan—a policy which is, perhaps, reflected in Mississippi and Alabama as well (2004: 39).

Furthermore, Marcuse notes the central importance of the gargantuan military budget to U.S. capitalism, and he observes that the Vietnamese resistance provides a convenient Other against whom the "primary aggressiveness" cultivated within the U.S. public can be productively directed. In Vietnam, on Marcuse's account, the U.S. government is merely following its established strategy of supporting the forces of *ancien régimes* as a counter to the emerging dangers posed to both traditional rulers and international capital by disruptive social movements such as that led by the Vietnamese Communists. To inhibit the menace contained within the theory of the "domino effect," then, the U.S. wages war in defense of a reactionary military dictatorship which functions to "sustain or reinstate" the very conditions which perpetuate the misery and dependence of the Vietnamese people—with this goal representing one of the prime ends sought by the U.S. foreign-policy establishment in Marcuse's time, as since. Inverting Hegel's prescient declaration that "America" will be the "land of the future, where [...] the burden of World History shall reveal itself," Marcuse closes his comments here by condemning the United States as having degenerated into the "advance guard of repression and reaction" on the world stage (Marcuse 2004: 39–40; Hegel 1900: 84).

Summer 1967 Lectures before the German SDS and Congress
on the Dialectics of Liberation: On Utopia, Radical Opposition,
and Violence

In summer 1967—the time of the coming of Marcuse's "moment," according
to Miles—Marcuse visited West Germany to give two addresses to the Union
of German Socialist Students (SDS) at the West Berlin Free University, and
he subsequently continued to London to participate in the Congress on the
Dialectics of Liberation, where he spoke on "Liberation from the Affluent
Society." In these three lectures, Marcuse provides characteristically thoughtful
contributions on subjects as varied as utopian and scientific socialism, natural
law, the problem of the transition away from capitalism, violence and counter-
violence, Vietnam, and defeatism.

   The first of these addresses, "The End of Utopia," expresses Marcuse's
insistence on the need for a historical rupture to avert capitalism's expedi-
tious transformation of Earth into hell. In Marcuse's view, such a "break
with the historical continuum" would finally lead beyond the unfree reality
of all previously recorded societies and thus transcend Marx's designation
of humanity's "prehistory." Before the German students, Marcuse argues that
certain aspects of Marx's work must be de-emphasized, particularly in terms
of the stress on the development of the productive forces and on positivist
progressivism: Marcuse instead calls for "difference rather than progress" and
the "negation" of past history "rather than its positive continuation." Inverting Engels' famous critique of pre-Marxian conceptions of socialism, Marcuse
proposes that the realization of socialism in the contemporary world may well
proceed "from science to utopia" rather than the other way around. Marcuse
of course realizes that the practicality of realizing utopia—and thus of abolishing its characterization in the main as being purely speculative, tied to "no
place"—is at present blocked by the conservatism of the "manipulated population," who re-entrench the system by reproducing the "needs" artificially
inculcated by prevailing society (1970a: 62–63, 65). Marcuse then proposes an
alternative vision of the overturning of hegemonic needs through the affirmation of "liberating and gratifying needs" whose institution and observation
could assist in the bringing about of the very end of utopia and the coming of
libertarian socialism. Such transcendental needs would include

   the negation of the need for the struggle for existence [...]; the negation of
   the need to earn one's living; the negation of the performance principle, of
   competition; the negation of the need for wasteful, ruinous productivity,

which is inseparably bound up with destruction; [...] the need for calm, the need to be alone, with oneself or with others whom one has chosen oneself, the need for the beautiful, the need for "undeserved" happiness [...] (1970a: 66, 67).

If expressed externally in the life-world, these new needs could open the possibility for revolutionary social relations and the reordering of the life-world: Marcuse foresees them as catalyzing movement toward existential-political reconstruction and remediation, as in the "abolition of the terrors of capitalist industrialization and commercialization," the "total reconstruction of the cities," and the "restoration of nature." Defining his view of the qualitative difference between established society and the possible "new socialism" of the future, Marcuse sees this distinction as emanating from the "aesthetic-erotic dimension" of *Dasein* and consciousness, and within this context he cites Fourier's ludic emancipatory vision as preferable to Marx's productivist proclivities. He concludes his remarks by calling for an oppositional movement which is to be "free of all illusion but also of all defeatism"—neither possessed of illusion so as not to blindly believe in its inevitable triumph nor of defeatism, which prematurely hands victory to established society. As he states near the beginning of the lecture, any approach which condemns the end of utopia out of hand errs in over-emphasizing the power of "counterforces and counter-tendencies" which themselves can be overthrown within the process of social revolution (1970a: 64, 67–69).

Several interesting points and clarifications are raised in the question-and-answer period with the students in the audience after Marcuse's lecture. In response to a question inquiring into Marcuse's view of the subversive possibilities of pop music, the critical theorist clarifies that he in no way considers the emergence of hippie or beatnik lifestyles a revolutionary development, though he does indicate that they signify "anarchically unorganized, spontaneous tendencies" which prefigure a "total break" with the false needs imposed by capital; hence, he praises these tendencies as advancing aspects of the qualitative change of needs, as in their refusal to participate in the affluent society. Later, Marcuse shares his evaluation of the *lumpenproletarian* and petit-bourgeois elements of society, which he does not consider to be revolutionary either, though he notes the role of the intelligentsia as a possible exception in this sense. When a student complains that his address does not deal with the practical struggle of transitioning toward the end of utopia, Marcuse responds in Gramscian terms by stressing the importance of developing a new sensibility as a precondition for such a transition: he argues that "work on the development of consciousness" should be considered "one of the chief tasks of materialism today, of revolutionary materialism." Though Marcuse stresses the necessity of liberating consciousness, he also acknowledges how "ridiculous and impotent" such consciousness may seem, in light of the tremendously concentrated power to which such an exercise of mind opposes itself. While in the discussion period Marcuse does reiterate his thesis from *One-Dimensional Man* regarding the empirical integration of the working classes into advanced-industrial society, he adds that in Europe the situation is different than in the United States, such that parts of the European proletariat remain consciously in conflict with capitalism. With reference to the Vietnamese resistance to the U.S. war, Marcuse remarks that those groups which remain external to the "blessings" of capitalism more readily express the need to abolish it, and he distinguishes between the spontaneous nature of the emergence of such needs in national-liberation struggles and the voluntarist character of the expression of such needs in industrialized societies. Channeling Schiller—as well as Robespierre, Babeuf, Bakunin, and others—he argues that the present task in the West is to "transform the will itself, so that people no longer want what they now want." While the situation in such a context is markedly different than it is in Vietnam, Marcuse declares that the two efforts can be linked fruitfully (1970a: 69–71, 73–75, 77–78).

Regarding a student's expressed concern that revolutionary processes tend toward the destruction of their own humanistic bases as they come overwhelmingly to be driven by hatred, Marcuse clarifies his view that the "hatred of exploitation and oppression is itself a humane and humanistic element," adding that "[n]othing is more terrible than the sermon, 'Do not hate thy opponent,' *in a world in which hate is thoroughly institutionalized*" (emphasis added). He nonetheless recognizes the legitimacy of the student's worry, observing that the boundary between humanism and terror is "horribly and extraordinarily in flux." For this reason, the critical theorist stresses the need to prevent the regression of one into the other, given that "[o]ne can hit an opponent, one can vanquish an opponent, without cutting off [her] ears, without severing [her] limbs, without torturing [her]."[3] Furthermore, Marcuse accepts the validity of another student's reservations about the idealist underpinning of the lecture, given the reality that, "for new, revolutionary needs to develop, the mechanisms that reproduce the old needs must be abolished," while the destruction of these very mechanisms itself demands pre-existing needs to lead to such abolition. This is the cycle in which Marcuse finds humanity to be trapped, and

---

3   Marcuse's point here bears much affinity to the approach of Práxedis Guerrero, who shortly before his death in the Mexican Revolution wrote that "Hatred is not necessary in the struggle for liberty [...]. Despotism can be annihilated without hatred" (1924: 97).

he concedes that he sees no easy way out of it. Moreover, Marcuse here distinguishes between domination and "rational authority," with the latter exemplified by the hierarchy in knowledge and ability which divides an airplane pilot from her passengers: rational authority, in this sense, corresponds to the "basic repression" of Freudian theory, while domination as exploitation and oppression is the analogue here for the "surplus repression" to be done away with by revolutionary social change (1970a: 79–81).

Two other questions fielded by Marcuse in the discussion after his lecture delve more deeply into his thought on the question of the transition away from capitalism, a problem which he also contemplates in his essay on Gracchus Babeuf this same year. He openly asks whether onlookers should expect the development of a new sensibility as emerging organically from within existing society, or if the need for a radical break might require the institution of a dictatorship or "counteradministration" that would put an end to "the horrors spread by the established administration." As in "Repressive Tolerance," Marcuse announces in his defense that "no one could be more for a democracy than I am," though he clarifies that no true democracy can be said to exist in the contemporary world. Within this political constellation, Marcuse claims that he finds it highly unlikely for the "state of almost total indoctrination and coordination" to "turn into its opposite in an evolutionary way": for this reason, he says, "some intervention must occur in some way," and "the oppressors must be suppressed" (1970a: 76, 80). In light of his word-choice here, then, it is not immediately evident that Marcuse is in fact calling for dictatorial transitional methods, given that the task of suppressing the oppressors does not necessarily require Jacobin- or Bolshevik-style authoritarianism.

The second of Marcuse's July 1967 lectures before the sds at the West Berlin Free University, "The Problem of Violence and the Radical Opposition," presents an exposition of Marcuse's views on contemporary resistance to capitalism as well as pacifism and counter-violence.

Speaking with reference to contemporary oppositional movements among u.s. students, Marcuse claims these to represent a "decisive factor of transformation" that could perhaps in time become a revolutionary force. As in "The End of Utopia," Marcuse once again reiterates his view that student radicals cannot at this point themselves be considered as presenting an anti-systemic challenge to the established society, and he completely rejects the notion attributed by some to him that the hippies are the "heir to the proletariat!" Besides disclosing these clarifications, Marcuse in his comments examines the emergence of a two-fold opposition to the status quo, as seen in the struggles of those confined to the "ghettos," whose "vital needs" advanced capital "cannot and will not gratify," and of the more privileged activists who similarly desire a radically different society and world. These more privileged dissidents, who more or less constitute the "neo-anarchis[t]" U.S. New Left, take as the target of their rage the normal functioning of U.S. society—and thus advance a critique that in no way spares the working classes of this country, as Marcuse acknowledges. On the other hand, opposition from the underprivileged arises among individuals and groups of national and racial minority status who are considered to be marginal to the productive process, while globally the "new proletariat" is for Marcuse to be found among the masses of the neo-colonized societies who are openly battling the designs of imperialism. Focusing particularly on the problem of the Vietnam War in this sense, Marcuse affirms the prior analysis he had made of that conflict in "The Inner Logic of American Policy on Vietnam," claiming it to be based on the U.S. administration's desire to prevent a loss of hegemony in Southeast Asia and, more broadly, the world over. In this vein, Marcuse declares that "the success of the Vietnamese liberation struggle could give the signal for the activation of such liberation movements in other parts of the world much closer to the metropolis where gigantic investments have been made." Optimistically, Marcuse observes that the war in Vietnam may signify "a turning point in the development of the system," and even "perhaps the beginning of the end." He finds "world-historical novelty" in the desperate yet effective counter-movement represented by the Vietnamese people's war against U.S. aggression (Marcuse 2004: 57–59, 60, 64).

As he progresses in his comments, Marcuse comes to the question of whether the opposition to capitalism and domination is to take on the form of "harmless ritual" or of actual resistance, as in civil disobedience. Philosophically, he recognizes the right of resistance to "belon[g] to the oldest and most sanctified elements of Western civilization," and he explains that the existence of this right justifies engaging in a "potentially liberating" sort of counter-violence against the violence of "suppression [...] and aggression" exercised by the Establishment. With such considerations in mind, and recalling "Ethics and Revolution," Marcuse dismisses strict pacifism as an effectively reactionary orientation, for it serves to "reproduc[e] the existing institutionalized violence." However, Marcuse does not greatly develop these positions of his on violence and counter-violence. Instead, he discusses the emphasis among revolutionary people of color on community-building in the U.S., and he reflects a gender essentialism of sorts in observing that women have greater potential for sympathy to radical positions, for they are putatively "more accessible to humane arguments than men are" (2004: 62–63).

In closing, Marcuse stresses that most all contemporary oppositional groupings are working only at the stage of preparing a different sort of future for the world—a necessary stage in terms of the ultimate fall of capitalism and the

State. Only the national-liberation efforts of the day are fully engaged in this type of anticipatory struggle, argues Marcuse. They together with the "ghetto rebellion[s]" represent for Marcuse the "living, human negation of the system." Concretely, Marcuse's prescriptions for immediate action place stress on social efforts to diffuse the liberation of consciousness throughout society, beyond the sphere of small radical political collectives, which can perhaps serve as the "nucle[i] of revolution": everyone must come to realize that prevailing society threatens utter annihilation due to the willingness of hegemonic power groups to employ brute force in defense of the profits they extract from humanity and nature. Implicitly summoning his colleague Günther Anders' call for the "imperiled of all lands" to "unite!" against the threat of nuclear destruction, Marcuse warns that "the life of everyone is [in fact] at stake," and he advocates that the societal project of the liberation of consciousness be lived out practi-cally: "[t]he whole person must demonstrate [her] participation and [her] will to live [...] in a pacified, human world." The responsibility to concretize the Great Refusal is one which prevails even if no discernible progress toward revo-lution can be identified, insists Marcuse; people must "fight on" and "resist" if they "want to live as human beings" (2004: 64–65, 67; Anders 1982: 381).

As with "The End of Utopia," the question-and-answer period which follows Marcuse's second lecture proves productive. Marcuse here clarifies that, while national-liberation movements hold great promise, they cannot overthrow global capitalism alone—hence the need to link anti-colonial developments with the growing opposition in the core of the world system so as to produce a revolutionary "confluence" of the "forces of change." Responding to a student's skepticism regarding the employment of humanitarian arguments as a means of preparing for social transformation—"what does th[e] worker care about the terror in Vietnam?"—Marcuse strongly repudiates the positivism implied in this notion. The critical theorist argues that to rest one's critique of capital-ism on the self-referential basis of reified consciousness necessarily excludes "historically transcendent concepts" which represent negations of the system: "for the system is not humane, and humanitarian ideas belongs to the nega-tion of the system." Against certain opportunistic strains even within Marxism, Marcuse reflects on the past and present specters of fascism, and he asserts that "humanitarian and moral arguments" are not ideological but instead "can and must become central social forces." Responding to the query of another student, and continuing from his argument as presented in the lecture, Marcuse repeats his previously established distinction between "revolutionary terror" and "White terror": whereas the former "implies its own abolition in the process of creating a free society," this dynamic cannot be said to hold analo-gously for reactionary terror (2004: 66–67, 72). Lastly in this sense, Marcuse presents what may well be considered *one of the most impassioned arguments he makes in life*—this in favor of radical natural law and the right of resistance, following the challenge another student makes to this right:

> The doctrine of the right of resistance has always asserted that appealing to the right of resistance is an appeal to a higher law, which has universal validity, that is, which goes beyond the self-defined right and privilege of a particular group [...]. Now you will say that such a universal higher law simply does not exist. I believe that it does exist. Today we no longer call it natural law, but I believe that if we say today that what justifies us in resisting the system is more than the relative interest of a specific group and more than something that we ourselves have defined, we can demonstrate this. *If we appeal to humanity's right to peace, to humanity's right to abolish exploitation and oppression*, we are not talking about self-defined, special, group interests, but rather and in fact *interests demonstrable as universal rights* (2004: 73; emphasis added).

After concluding his lectures to the German SDS youth, Marcuse traveled to London to participate in the Congress on the Dialectics of Liberation. In his address to the conference, "Liberation from the Affluent Society," Marcuse invokes the ludic, joyful spirit of the space—and of the New Left as a whole—by beginning with the remark that he is "very happy to see so many flowers here," for "flowers by themselves have no power whatsoever" and so must be protected against "aggression and destruction" by conscious human beings. Speaking to the place of the dialectic of liberation from the "bad" and "false" system of capitalist patriarchy within the context of the affluent societies of the West, Marcuse continues with his line from "The End of Utopia" in stressing that activists should not shy away from advancing transcendental concepts which prefigure the future emancipated society, even and especially if they appear "as utopian, as idealistic, as metaphysical" and therefore "ridiculous" for "the normal people in all camps"—for these stances, Marcuse says, are the forms which such concepts must take on if they are to represent the "determinate negation" of established society and thus assist in its supersession, in favor of a qualitatively different form of existence (2004: 76, 77–78). As a compelling illustration of this type of thought, Marcuse cites Benjamin's quotation of reports made during the 1871 Paris Commune that

> in all corners of the city of Paris there were people shooting at the clocks on the towers of the churches, palaces, and so on, thereby consciously or half-consciously expressing the need that somehow time has to be

arrested; that at least the prevailing, the established time continuum has to be arrested, and that a new time has to begin [...] (2004: 78).

Invoking Benjamin's concept of *Jetztzeit* ("now-time"), Marcuse turns to discussing the relationship between quantitative and qualitative change, or the analogous tension between reform and revolution: here, he says that quantitative changes do not necessarily negate the chance for revolution—a "change of the very system as a whole"—but instead can help bring about this end. Yet, as in *Eros and Civilization,* Marcuse identifies as a significant obstacle the repressive dialectic of civilization, whereby the arrival in history to material conditions that would allow for universal qualitative change is diverted instead to mere reproduction of the given system, with its "accelerating waste, planned obsolescence, and destruction" on the one hand and "poverty and misery" on the other. Indeed, Marcuse defines this fatal interplay as the "syndrome of late capitalism," the very inseparability of rational and irrational, and he notes that this malaise produces a "mutilated" and "frustrated" human existence, one that will lead the victims of the system to even defend their own oppression. In this sense, while revolutionary social transformation is "objectively necessary" as the sole means of ensuring human freedom, the subjective factor to bring about such revolution is largely lacking under conditions of affluence. As with the German students, Marcuse suggests that, confronted with such a conundrum, leftists should affirm the transition from scientific to utopian socialism in holding out the Kantian image of "life as an end in itself" and the Freudian-Marxist vision of a liberated human sensibility that struggles externally for the reordering of the life-world (2004: 79–82). Like Gramsci and Goldman, Marcuse argues that such qualitatively different features of the future society presuppose a "total trans-valuation of values" and even a "new anthropology," one to be embodied by

> a type of [human] who is biologically incapable of fighting wars and creating suffering [...,] who has a good conscience of joy and pleasure, and who works, collectively and individually, for a social and natural environment in which such an existence becomes possible (2004: 82).

Hence, in addition to the socio-political changes which would come with liberation, qualitative change is also to involve "organic, instinctual, [and] biological changes" which are to assist in the unshackling of the creative imagination and the very creation of an "'aesthetic' reality," or *"society as a work of art"* (emphasis added). It is critical to enliven such aesthetic needs and goals before the transition to the new society, Marcuse stresses, for to suggest that these are to emerge only after the revolution would run the risk of perpetuating much of the repressiveness on hand in capitalist society within post-capitalist settings (2004: 82–83).

In closing, Marcuse considers non-integrated social groups as the possible champions of the dialectic of liberation. With reference to the intelligentsia, the critical theorist remarks that the "fatal prejudice" held historically among many workers against intellectuals has served to weaken forces in opposition to capital, and for the present and foreseeable future, he declares that this group has a "decisive preparatory function" to play in terms of raising awareness of the depravity of prevailing social relations. Contemplating the hippie movement, Marcuse finds much of it to be "masquerade and clownery on the private level," though he recognizes the potential of tendencies such as the Diggers and Provos, who refuse to "play the rules of a rigid game" and advance a vision of a "nonaggressive form of life" for society. Arguing that today "all education is therapy," Marcuse makes the following practical suggestion to his audience: "We must each of us generate in ourselves, and try to generate in others, the instinctual need for a life without fear, without brutality, and without stupidity" (2004: 84–86).

As writers and educators, philosophers can serve only to prefigure a liberated society. Speaking in the year before 1968, Marcuse shares his pessimistic view that no mass movement seeking such ends will be seen "in the near future" (2004: 86). Fortunately, however, he was mistaken in this assessment.

1968: A New Dawn for Humanity?

The various explosive upsurges which met the year 1968 around the globe greatly heartened Marcuse in terms of his Kantian and Hegelian hopes for humanity. He enthusiastically welcomed the occupations which dissident students performed in u.s. universities this year, and the May 1968 events in France demonstrated conclusively that the gloomy theses of *One-Dimensional Man* were far from justified. Marcuse saw the radical movements of 1968 as an important counterpart to the decolonization struggles being waged at the peripheries of empire. It was with great joy that he lent his analytical abilities to reflecting on the various successes and shortcomings of this militant wave, as in "Re-Examination of the Concept of Revolution," "Reflections on the French Revolution," "Beyond One-Dimensional Man," "Peace as Utopia," and "On the New Left."

Marcuse presented his "Re-Examination of the Concept of Revolution" in May 1968 at the UNESCO conference in Paris that was organized for the sesquicentennial of Marx's birth; serendipitously, it was due to his presence at this time in the French capital that he was granted an impromptu meeting with the Vietnamese diplomatic corps engaged in the preliminary Paris peace talks following his intervention at the conference. What is more, of course, the timing of the conference allowed him the unprecedented opportunity to witness the start of the student-worker insurrection against Charles de Gaulle and capitalism itself that shook the city and France as a whole that fateful month.

As in numerous other works from this period, Marcuse in his "Re-Examination" hails the revolutionary potential of the national-liberation movements of the global South, holding them largely to have replaced the proletariat of the advanced-industrial societies as the active radical subject which Marx had hoped for—this, despite the fact that Marxian theory as originally developed focused consciously on developments within the imperial core of capital. He finds great promise in the chance that decolonial movements could provide an embodied alternative to the Western and Soviet blocs by constructing socialism from a "new below" that is "not integrated into the value system of the old societies." Yet Marcuse emphasizes that the true potential of the global decolonization efforts can be realized only through an inhibition of capitalist imperialism, as exercised from within the metropole. With this observation, the critical theorist turns to consider the oppositional groupings of the West, who comprise a rather small minority of the overall population, and indeed face "hostility" and "resentment" from the working-class majority. Marcuse nonetheless still holds that it is the workers who retain the status of the subject of possible social transformation, such that the opposition in the West can become revolutionary only if and when labor comes to endorse it. In this observation of the critical theorist's can be seen the continuity of his thought with the Marxian concept (1969b: 29–31).

Nevertheless, Marcuse's main conclusion in the "Re-Examination" is that the traditional Marxian account of revolutionary social change—which is to be enacted as a majority affair leading to a popular seizure of power in the most advanced-industrial societies and the subsequent establishment of proletarian dictatorships which are to oversee the socialization of production—is outdated, "pertain[ing] to a stage of capitalist productivity and organization which has been overtaken." Moreover, Marx did not sufficiently anticipate the degree to which the ruling classes would resort to genocide and mass-indoctrination to perpetuate their rule. According to Marcuse, another reason for the relative obsolescence of the Marxian view is the founder's own "positivistic prejudice" regarding the "inexorable necessity" of the shift from capitalism to communism, a process the historical materialist felt would prove as solid as a law of science. Marcuse stresses that the alternative Rosa Luxemburg had posed between socialism and barbarism must be incorporated into contemporary accounts of revolution—for it is not beyond the realm of possibility that the "self-propelling" power which carries along "the indoctrinated and integrated" could decide to "*strike the fatal blow*" before the forces of opposition agglutinate sufficiently to resist such an eventuality, as Luxemburg's own personal fate demonstrates (emphasis added). If outright suppression were to become the *dénouement* of contemporary struggle, remarks Marcuse soberly, the very re-examination of revolution in which he is engaged would become merely an abstraction (1969b: 31, 34).

Returning to California after his time in France, Marcuse shared his "Reflections on the French Revolution" before hundreds of UCSD students and faculty on the very night of his arrival. For his audience he describes the *événements* of the beginning of the revolt, precipitated as they were by the dispatching of riot police by the rector of Sorbonne University against protesting students—this being a move which led to mass-spontaneous action on the students' part to construct barricades from automobiles and arm themselves with the "good cobblestones of Paris" to liberate the Latin Quarter from the police. When security forces attacked the barricades that first night and displaced the students using various types of gas grenades, the local population of the Latin Quarter intervened "definitely and decisively" on the side of the students, reports Marcuse, raining down all sorts of projectiles onto the forces of order in the streets below. Critically, Marcuse stresses this popular support for the students as representing "the greatest difference between the events in Paris and here" in the U.S. (2004: 41–42). In world-historical fashion, such popular forms of resistance on the first day and night of the rebellion expeditiously developed into a general strike involving ten million workers within a matter of days.

While his commentary deals only with the first week of the *événements* of this new French Revolution, Marcuse can still be said to depict a misleading narrative of the events, given his view that the student rebellion proved more crucial than the workers in the development of the popular uprising. Though it was the street battles in the Latin Quarter which inspired the mass-intervention of workers, the students' actions cannot be considered more important than the protests and wildcat strikes which followed, as the philosopher suggests. Beyond this, Marcuse speaks to the typically conservative and opportunistic responses taken by the established Communist bureaucracy in France vis-à-vis the revolt, and he continuously emphasizes the spontaneous nature of the various revolutionary developments emerging from the popular spirit of radical counter-power. Identifying the students' embodied opposition as "a refusal to continue to accept and abide by the culture of the established system," he claims it to be fundamentally anti-systemic, "a total protest," one that is socialist yet "rejects from the beginning the repressive construction of socialism." Speculating as to the reasons why Parisian workers would come out *en masse* to support the students' demands, while no similar solidarity is observed among movements in U.S. society, Marcuse offers his San Diego audience a couple of reasons which recall his comments before the German students the previous year: first, that contemporary French society is still very far from the affluence on hand in the U.S., while the historically revolutionary legacy of the workers of France remains very much alive. Marcuse hails the spontaneity instituted in the 1968 French Revolution as a "new element... which surpasses all traditional organization," and he expressly endorses a vision of mass-revolutionary direct action rather than the capture of State organizations as the goal which militants should seek to realize in the wake of the example provided by the radical students and workers of Paris (2004: 43–45).

Influenced greatly by the events in France, Marcuse's late 1968 address "Beyond One-Dimensional Man" indicates how greatly the critical theorist had shifted his perspectives from a marked pessimism in just four years. Reveling in the various explosive social movements which had emerged throughout the world since the publication of *One-Dimensional Man*, Marcuse here theorizes the development of the new sensibility which would in his view accelerate the coming of a future liberated society. In this sense, the qualified repudiation which Marcuse engages in of his most famous book here represents a bridge of sorts between this work and his most optimistic one, *An Essay on Liberation* (1969).

Placing Hegel's infamous apologism on its head in a manner reminiscent of Adorno in *Minima Moralia*—wherein the German aesthetician asserts that "the whole is the false"—Marcuse begins his revision of *One-Dimensional Man* by declaring "the real" to be "absurd" and "the absurd" to be "rational." Taking account of three significant historical developments which militate against capitalist meaninglessness—and, indeed, which to an extent call into question the conclusions he previously had made in his 1964 volume—Marcuse points out the relentless struggle to bring about a "truly libertarian, humanistic construction of socialism," as in revolutionary Cuba and China; the effective "sustained and successful resistance" of the people of Vietnamese against the U.S. superpower; and the increasing militancy of groupings in the belly of the beast itself. With regard to this final development, which for him corresponds to an "opening of the one-dimensional society," Marcuse reiterates that such resistance has developed largely outside of the milieu of the working classes, yet he anticipates that the surge in such radical elements can help "activate [...] the repressed rebellious force among the laboring classes" and so greatly improve the chances for revolutionary social transformation. At stake within this struggle, Marcuse observes, is the emergence of a new consciousness or sensibility, one that would yield a "new rationality" which rejects the irrationalities of capitalism, Stalinism, and the Soviet Union (Adorno 2005: 50; Marcuse 2001: 112–113, 115). Citing Camus' book *The Rebel* by name, Marcuse sketches out a vision of the developing sensibility which is quite commensurate with his prior theorizing of the Great Refusal:

> *L'homme revolté:* that is today he or she [or ze] whose senses can no longer see and hear and taste what is offered to them, whose very instincts militate against oppression, cruelty, ugliness, hypocrisy and exploitation. And who also rebels on these same grounds, against the traditional higher culture of the West—rebel against it because of its affirmative, reconciling, "illusory" features (2001: 115).

Echoing themes from "The Affirmative Character of Culture" and *Eros and Civilization,* Marcuse argues that this emerging revolutionary consciousness would protest the "internalization" of love and the "illusory beautification and mitigation of the horror of reality"; retaining his dialectical analysis of civilization, Marcuse here argues not for the suppression of civilization, but rather for that of its "archaic exploitative aspects"—in a move that would strengthen Eros against the evidently hegemonic power of Thanatos. Providing a vision of a global movement which would break radically with resignation, conformity, and instrumental reason, Marcuse envisions a jettisoning of the "rat race" in place of a redirection of production toward the abolition of poverty, the "elimination" of "spiritual and material garbage," and, indeed, the very construction of a *"a peaceful and beautiful universe"* (emphasis added). Referring to the revolutionary upsurge of May 1968 in Paris, Marcuse expresses his agreement with the playful observation that Marx's fourth volume of *Capital* was written on the walls of Sorbonne University, and to this he adds that these same walls gave birth to Kant's fourth *Critique,* "namely the critique of productive imagination." Closing on a dialectically practical note, Marcuse remarks on the developing new "language" of the global protest movement, which is quite distinct from the language used by the Establishment; he recommends that this evolving language of protest remain comprehensible to society at large, so as to continue with the encouraging signs of social rebellion and revolt (2001: 115–118).

Speaking at his next engagement at the September 1968 Conversation on Humanism in Salzburg, Austria, Marcuse entitled his address "Peace as Utopia." In using this title, the critical theorist clearly links his argument with

Kant's utopian-cosmopolitan hopes for a future world society to be governed
by "Perpetual Peace." In point of fact, as well, the name Marcuse gives to this
talk also recalls Adorno's utopian musings at the close of Part II of *Minima
Moralia,* where the musicologist declares that "[n]one of the abstract concepts
comes closer to the fulfilled utopia than that of eternal peace" (Adorno 2005:
99–100). Expressing his profound differences with the militarist-apologist
Hans Morgenthau, a major contributor to the "realist" school of international
relations theory who also presented at this same conference, Marcuse begins
his address on humanism by citing the well-known graffiti produced at the
Sorbonne in May 1968: "Be realistic; demand the impossible!" Marcuse quickly
dispatches with the "realism" of international relations theory by claiming its
followers to *"confus[e] the established reality with reality itself"* and, in effect, to
naturalize relations of domination, aggressiveness, and inter-group competition as eternal characteristics of the human condition (Marcuse 2011: 166–167).

Focusing his intervention on the prospect of peace defined not as *"the time
span between wars"* but as the very substance of *"social life,"* Marcuse asserts
that enjoyment of this latter end would be possible only through the revolutionary overthrow of the hegemonic powers of the world: private property and
the performance principle in the West, and the bureaucratic authoritarianism and "power politics" on hand in the Soviet sphere. At the individual and
social levels, Marcuse argues that humanity's habits and behavior would need
to be radically overhauled, such that the very instincts of the organism would
rebel against the values of "cruelty" and "barbarism" which uphold the prevailing domination of the world by imperialist-militarist power blocs. In hopeful
terms, Marcuse sees this type of revolutionary change already being advanced
by the *"global revolt of youth,"* particularly that of students, and he hails this
development as being "the single authentic movement for peace" and, as such,
the "genuine hazard" faced by hegemony (emphasis added). Here, Marcuse is
clear not to advocate any sort of pacifism, arguing that the chance for realizing
social peace to be one that "cannot be attained through peaceableness" but
will instead "require a fight"—and perhaps even "war" (2011: 168–170).

> But there are very different kinds of war [...]. There is a war against
> Vietnam and there is a war against the Nazis. There are the wars of the
> dynasties, and there are wars of liberation. There are wars of conquest as
> with Caesar and Pompey, and there are uprisings of slaves. There are wars
> of domination and wars against domination (2011: 170).

Marcuse elucidates some of the constructive ends which could be pursued in a
world freed of war: the abolition of poverty, alienated labor, and the competitive

struggle for existence; the exhaustion of the instinctual reservoirs of aggressive energy; the redirection of primary aggressiveness toward the protection and furtherance of life; and the construction of a world that finally allows the promises of science and technology to be realized. Within such a context, freedom is not to be defined and implemented either by elites or those subjected to them but instead instituted by "emancipated human beings" who, in Kantian terms, conduct their lives as ends in themselves, thus breaking totally with the historical tendency to reduce humanity to an object of manipulation. Marcuse acknowledges in closing that, while it may well be "realistic" to hold the merely possible chance for peace as utopia to be "easily annihilated by the counterpoised possibility of total repression," the development of repressive civilization to date has brought humanity to the very "threshold" of the world-historical changes that could lead such utopian possibilities to become actuality (2011: 171–172).

In December 1968, for the twentieth anniversary of the radical New York-based newspaper *The Guardian*—not to be confused with the British *Guardian*—Marcuse gave a speech "On the New Left," having been introduced at this event by the militant activist Bernadine Dohrn (Marcuse 2004: 27). On the one hand, in this talk Marcuse speaks to the increasingly desperate political and existential realities imposed by the tenacious ability of capitalism to perpetuate itself, declaring that "We cannot wait and we shall not wait" to overthrow it:

> We cannot wait and we shall not wait. I certainly cannot wait. And not only because of my age. I don't think we have to wait. And even I, I don't have any choice. Because I literally couldn't stand it any longer if nothing would change. Even I am suffocating (2004: 122).

On the other hand, though—echoing his pronunciations on the partial obsolescence of *One-Dimensional Man*—Marcuse expresses the thought that, while the workers of the advanced-industrial societies are at present largely assimilated into the system, they will "certainly not [be] integrated for ever," for, in dialectical terms, "[n]othing is for ever in history." While at first glance such a statement may be taken to represent yet more "utopianism" from Marcuse, he explains in his comments that what humanity is facing is a "temporary stabilization" of capitalism, such that the practical task of activists who identify with the New Left should be to "arouse the consciousness and conscience of the others" and militate in favor of a decentralized "disintegration of the system." Marcuse here discourages any return to Leninist tactics and instead endorses the pursuit of a "*libertarian* socialism," hailing the "alleged infantile radicals" of his day for maintaining postures of relative independence from the dominant system—for in Marcuse's view, this autonomy holds great promise in terms of the prospects of working for the "preparation [of] a society without exploitation" (2004: 123, 124–125, 127). Ending on a personal note, Marcuse declares his wish to continue working alongside the radicals of the New Left for as long as he is able to do so.

In an interview held on the French Riviera in summer 1968, published in October for *The New York Times Magazine* as "Marcuse Defines his New Left Line," Marcuse shares several illuminating musings and clarifications of interest vis-à-vis his life and intellectual and political projects of the time. For one, he legitimately objects to the juxtaposition of his name and image with those of Che Guevara and Rudi Dutschke, for example, given that the latter have "truly risked and are still risking their lives in the battle for a more human society," while he has not—with the fact that these words were uttered on the very French Riviera not being least among such considerations. Clearly delineating his disagreements with Horkheimer and Adorno regarding the emergence of the radical student movements, though not mentioning the pair by name, Marcuse surmises that the students' righteous militancy derives in part from their desire to apply their knowledge of the humanities—the principles of natural law, the "inalienable" right of resistance, and so on—to the world in which they find themselves, ruled over as it is by rotten and ossified interests. Likening the militant students to the intellectual forerunners of the French Revolution of 1789, Marcuse claims their roles to be the revelation of reality to the integrated masses and to serve as society's spokespeople. In this conversation, Marcuse also expresses his pessimism for the prospect of social revolution in the u.s., precisely because in this setting the students are so far-removed from the workers—in contradistinction to the case of the radical upsurge seen in Paris just months previously. Furthermore, he reiterates his belief in the distinction between the violence of domination and a counter-violence which resists such, and, as in "Repressive Tolerance," he speculates that an intellectual dictatorship would likely be less oppressive than the prevailing dictatorship of capital. On this point, Marcuse contrasts the cruelty of the thoughtless Eichmann with that imposed and overseen by Robespierre and Saint-Just (2004: 100–101, 106, 108, 114–115).

In Hegelian-Marxian terms, Marcuse in this interview shares a few passing visions of the productive possibilities of a post-capitalist future. With regard to socio-ecological matters, a generalized rising to overturn capitalism could allow for the institution of technologies which would put an end to air pollution altogether. Additionally, besides overcoming poverty and inequality, a society freed from capitalist irrationality would have the ability to overthrow the massively wasteful production regime of the old society, and in place of engineering private automobiles, such a society could vastly improve and humanize public transportation. In these terms, Marcuse welcomes the example of the Cuban Revolution, which he observes as having brought about "tremendous progress" for the people of that country and hope for the world; relatedly, he shares his opinion that many of the "reprehensible" acts seen to take place in Communist countries have to do with the militarized rivalry which such societies are forced to engage in with the Western power bloc—to echo his analysis from *Soviet Marxism.* Lastly in this sense, and perhaps most compellingly—however strange the juxtaposition may be with his reflections on authoritarian socialism—Marcuse in this conversation expresses a particularly warm attitude toward anarchism: he welcomes the "anarchist element" in the New Left and the student movements as a "very powerful and very progressive force," praising the students for having adopted revolutionary spontaneity as a means of expressing their dissatisfaction with the state of the world, amidst their justified perception of the counter-revolutionary nature of "traditional political organizations," the Communist parties included (2004: 102, 104–105, 107, 112). Marcuse thus calls for a new form of militant political organization inspired by anarchism:

> a new, very flexible kind of organization, one that does not impose rigorous principles, one that allows for movement and initiative. An organization without the "bosses" of the old parties or political groups. This point is very important (2004: 102).

However revealing his friendly attitude to anarchism may be here, Marcuse denies that he himself is an anarchist, in response to the interviewer's desire for clarification on the question. The critical theorist rationalizes this denial by invoking an uncharacteristically conventional definition of the term, one that flatly contradicts the sketch of the political philosophy he provided just moments before in the conversation:

> I am not an anarchist because I cannot imagine how one can combat a society which is mobilized and organized in its totality against any revolutionary movement, against any effective opposition; I do not see how one can combat such a society, such a concentrated force [...] without any organization. It won't work (2004: 102).

Marcuse the great heterodox and anti-authoritarian thinker thus succumbs to Old Left nostrums when confronted with the question of whether his political philosophy is anarchist—this, despite the rather evident fact that an overwhelming majority of his work is entirely commensurate with this tradition.

An Essay on Liberation (1969)

In *An Essay on Liberation*—first written before the *événements* of May 1968, thereafter revised, and published in 1969—Marcuse is at his most optimistic and utopian point in life. He is perhaps even more visionary in this work than in *Eros and Civilization.* Starkly repudiating the overarching argument of *One-Dimensional Man*, Marcuse announces that the hegemonic homogeneity of monopoly capital is starting to break up, as evidenced in guerrilla warfare movements at the global periphery and inner-city revolts in the U.S. core. Marcuse sees in the struggles of the peoples of Vietnam, Cuba, and China emancipatory models that aim at both resisting the "affluent monster" and averting the institution of authoritarian socialism, while he observes that even U.S. capitalism "cannot indefinitely deliver its goods," as urban uprisings and student opposition movements speak to the evident limits of the system. In France in May and June 1968, the "libertarian power of the red and black flags" was evident for all the world to see: Marcuse triumphantly declares that this spirit of rebellion will live on and likely intensify, no matter its transient eclipse. Marcuse embraces the essential anarchism of the anti-systemic movements of 1968, for they raise the possibility of a social revolution which would subordinate production to the flowering of solidarity, the abolition of poverty, and the institution of perpetual peace (Marcuse 1969a: viii, ix–x, 7).

Whether the revolts and rebellions of 1968 turn out to be successful in yielding societal transformation or remain an "abortive revolution," Marcuse welcomes these events as being a veritable *turning point* in world history: though he says it would be "irresponsible" to "overrate" the chances of the opposition as regards the task of toppling global capitalism, the militant cognizance and demonstration that life has been reduced to a *"plaything* in the hands of politicians and managers and generals" still represents a hopeful opening, and perhaps the beginning of the end of domination (1969a: viii–x).

Marcuse begins his discussion of liberation by considering revolutionary morality, or ethics. In an illustrative example of his approach, the critical theorist contemplates the concept of obscenity in existing society.

> Obscenity is not the picture of a naked woman who exposes her pubic hair but that of a fully clad general who exposes his medals rewarded in a war of aggression; obscene is not the ritual of the Hippies but the

declaration of a high dignitary of the Church that war is necessary for
peace (1969a: 8).

Marcuse thus calls for morality and ethics to be employed in revolt against
the Establishment. In contrast to more orthodox Marxists, Marcuse declares
morality to be other and more than mere ideology, for it can become a "political weapon" in the midst of a decidedly amoral society. Marcuse links morality and revolution intimately in his comments: indeed, in biological terms, he
hypothesizes that morality is a fundamental "'disposition' of the organism."
It is in this speculative biological sense that Marcuse finds political radicalism to express the "elementary, organic foundation of morality in the human
being." Much like Bakunin and other anarchists, Marcuse here expresses
the thought that the realization of human happiness would depend upon a
mass-expression of solidarity that would abolish humanity's present division
into antagonistic classes and states, thus progressing beyond the prevailing
context in which the happiness of some is based upon the suffering of others.
Anchoring contemporary radical social movements to the historical continuum in which they find themselves, Marcuse mentions the First International
as being the "last attempt to realize the solidarity of the species" through
proletarian struggle, and he hails the Spanish Revolution once again as having raised the image of an "unforgettable, hopeless fight of a tiny minority
against the combined forces of fascist and liberal capitalism." It is clear that
Marcuse sees many parallels between the Spanish Civil War and the ongoing
contemporary upsurges throughout the world, particularly with reference to
the "union of young intellectuals and workers" in the International Brigades
that helped resist the fascist onslaught on the Iberian peninsula (1969a: 8,
10, 14).

   These affirming thoughts notwithstanding, Marcuse continues to insist that
social revolution remains a minority concern in the most "advanced" affluent
societies, given his theory regarding the continued psychological coordination
of the Western working masses and their own seeming acceptance of bourgeois
cultural norms, serving "conservative [and] *even* counterrrevolutionary" ends
(emphasis added). This return of the long-standing hypothesis on integration
complements Marcuse's seemingly new-found interest in biology, for the critical theorist speculates that humans can have a "second nature" introjected
into them which ties them *"libidinally and aggressively* to the commodity
form" (emphasis added). As ever, Marcuse raises the question of how liberation might develop and progress from within such reified settings. His unique,
anti-authoritarian claim is now that the repressed biological orientation of the
organism toward cooperation and socialism could surface and express itself

by means of the development of a new human sensibility reflective of Eros (1969a: 11, 15–19).

In this sense, Marcuse reiterates his highly heterodox and allegorical recommendation that Marx and realism yield to Fourier and surrealism (1969a: 22). During May 1968—the "rebellion for the total transvaluation of values"— graffiti produced by militant students depicting the founder of historical materialism was juxtaposed with portraits of André Breton, the "founder" of surrealism, just as the slogan "all power to the imagination" accompanied the call for "all power to the workers' councils":

> the piano with the jazz player stood well between the barricades; the red flag well fitted the statue of the author of *Les Misérables*; and striking students in Toulouse demanded the revival of the language of the Troubadours, the Albigensians (1969a: 22).

The new sensibility has taken on political form, Marcuse observes enthusiastically. Its realm traverses Western capitalism and Soviet authoritarianism, its spread contagious due precisely to the profound contradictions that mobilize to stifle its birth. In the Soviet East, dissidents continue to accept socialism but desire to do away with its authoritarian-bureaucratic degradation, and in this way they converge with the radical movement in the West, which is increasingly "socialist or anarchist" (1969a: 22, 59).

The erotic new sensibility impels revolution to overturn injustice and abolish misery—in place of the previous burdens of poverty and labor, it anticipates a world infused by calm, playfulness, sensuality, and beauty. It seeks to join with a liberated scientific orientation to produce an *aesthetic ethos* that would conceive of society as an art-work to be created, and in this way separate its adherents from identification and complicity with the hegemonic perpetrators of war, renunciation, and repression. Politically and existentially, this aesthetic sensibility "will not have redeemed the [evident] crimes against humanity," but it can lead those taken by it to "become free to stop them and to prevent their recommencement." The "new sensorium" produced through conscious revolt is reflected ludically in cultural trends of resistance in Russia, as symbolized by "miniskirts against the apparatchiks [and] rock 'n' roll against Soviet Realism." For Marcuse, the revolutionary demands made by the emancipated senses anticipate a future without the market, terror, or exploitation. Metaphorically, this aesthetic morality propels the immunological suppression of malignant capital and all its residues, both material and spiritual— for art represents a cipher of the *kalokagathon* (the "beautiful-virtuous") and stands in for the Idea of historical progress. At once productive and creative, as Kant had envisioned, the new sensorium could help guide regenerative social forces, particularly scientific and technological ones, in the construction of an environment wherein the "nonaggressive, erotic, receptive faculties" of humans join with the "consciousness of freedom" toward the pacification of humanity and nature. Marcuse claims such tendencies to be readily observed in the increasingly manifest desire for the closure of whole urban areas from automobile access, the "decommercialization of nature," and the replacement of highways and parking lots with parks and gardens, among other favored means of remaking society (1969a: 25–31, 42, 45).

Beyond this, Marcuse considers the linguistic rebellion developed within the U.S. counterculture, particularly by people of color, as an important site of resistance to the Orwellian manipulation of language that would endlessly reaffirm a one-dimensional life-world. He sees great promise in the popularity of the slogan "black is beautiful," and indeed he finds in Black musical traditions and innovations a veritable revocation of Beethoven's Ninth Symphony ("To Joy") which speaks to continued unhappiness, oppression, and exclusion. In forcibly removing the veils which obscure reality, art becomes a transitional force, one that helps along the struggle for social revolution as based on self-determination, self-realization, and the observance of goals which would *"enhance, protect, and unite life on earth"* (1969a: 36, 46–48; emphasis added).

In his analysis of subverting forces propelling the transition away from capital, Marcuse adopts an especially anarchist point of view. Against commentators who would mystify the arguments he had previously made, the critical theorist clarifies that, though internal resistance to the affluent society comes principally from the racially oppressed and middle-class youth in revolt, the proletariat in U.S. society has in no way been eclipsed by the *lumpenproletariat*. However actually integrated Marcuse holds the mass of U.S. workers to be, he clarifies that any prospect for radical social change still rests with their volition. Hence his conclusion that the contemporary period is to be a "period of enlightenment prior to material change," one in which socio-political education passes into the realm of praxis: "demonstration, confrontation, rebellion." Similarly to the manner in which the gap between *is* and *ought* drives forward the dialectic in Hegel's formulation, Marcuse theorizes that education and knowledge themselves impel collective organization against the violence, wastefulness, irrationality, and destructiveness of prevailing society. With this in mind, Marcuse clearly states that any commitment to the buttressing of dominant liberalism merely delays the birth of human emancipation, and that legitimate resistance must by needs take on an uncivil, extra-parliamentary, and perhaps even "anti-democratic" character. Observing that the charges of "[g]enocide, war crimes, crimes against humanity are not effective arguments against a government which protects property, trade, and commerce at home while it perpetrates its destructive policy abroad," Marcuse defends revolutionary direct action as a means of resisting domination and democratizing society—and of linking the present struggle with the "historical power of the general strike and the factory occupation, of the red flag and the International" (51–53, 61–62, 65–69).

In the final chapter of the *Essay,* "Solidarity," Marcuse reaffirms agrarian decolonial movements of the global South as representing an "external proletariat" to the capitalist system. Reflecting on the fate of these insurgent movements, particularly in Cuba and Vietnam, Marcuse restates his belief that revolution in the affluent societies is a necessary precondition for the success of upheavals against the imperial monster in the former colonies and neo-colonies, in light of the clear economic and military ties which exist between Western oligarchies and the ossified indigenous ruling classes. Inverting Lenin, then, Marcuse declares that the "chain of exploitation must break at its strongest link." He welcomes people's resistance movements in Cuba and Vietnam together with the Chinese Cultural Revolution as holding out the prospect for a popular and non-repressive implementation of socialism which would avoid the Stalinist specter and the threat of nuclear war altogether. Declaring the "anarchic element" to be an "essential factor" in the present struggle against domination, Marcuse foresees a conscious humanity calling into question the prevailing direction of progress, taking account of the "centuries of misery and hecatombs of victims" produced by capitalism, and concluding that it has been enough. Autonomy and cooperation as libertarian-socialist solidarity would provide the content of the life-commitments of the members of the future free society, stresses Marcuse. In response to the question of how liberated individuals would live under such unfamiliar conditions, Marcuse cites the words of a "young black girl," who plainly states that humans would "be free [now] to think about what we are going to do" (1969a: 80–82, 85, 88, 90–91).

Other Interventions from 1969: On Student Protest, "The Relevance of Reality," Qualitative Change, and Self-Determination

Beyond publishing the *Essay on Liberation,* Marcuse in 1969 engaged in a number of other important public interventions, speaking to the role of student protest, the continued importance of theory vis-à-vis practice, and the need for a Gramscian new sensibility to develop not only among the conscious opponents of the established system but also among the workers themselves at large, if the promise of liberation beyond capital is to be come true.

In a short piece published in the *New York Times* in May 1969, "Student Protest is Nonviolent Next to Society Itself," the critical theorist situates the ongoing student occupations and disruptions of that year within the context of the "general aggressiveness and hypocrisy" of established society—in particular, the continuous massacres in Vietnam and the ongoing oppression of "racial and national minorities." Quite simply put, when compared with the normalized violence of everyday life that is administered by those in power, student protest is non-violent (Marcuse 2004: 46).

"The Relevance of Reality" is the name of Marcuse's address at the March 1969 meeting of the Pacific Division of the American Philosophical Association, held in Portland, Oregon. As a recognition of his status as world-renowned critical theorist, indeed, Marcuse was named the honorary president for this conference. In his address to the assembled philosophers, Marcuse opens with a discussion of the example of Socrates, whose well-known promotion of critical thought ultimately came to be considered a "political offense" by the Athenian authorities, amidst the threat his advocacy of questioning posed to the established concepts regulating the interplay between citizenry and State. Criticizing Socrates in a controversial manner, though, Marcuse argues that his suicide represented a "surrender to the order of the state" which necessarily separated the philosopher's radical, normative critique from a commensurate sort of praxis, one that ideally would demand a consistent stance of opposition to the prevailing order (Marcuse 2011: 172–174). By embodying civil *obedience* in taking his own life, Marcuse argues, Socrates "establish[es] the essential harmlessness of philosophical thought" and "its essential non-commitment":

> [N]on-commitment made into a Principle of Non-Intervention, according to which the philosopher is to continue to *think* about the Beautiful, the Good, and the True while refraining from *doing* something about them in reality, outside his academy (2011: 174).

As he continues with his comments, Marcuse jumps from the chronological "beginning" to the "end" of Western philosophy, coming to consider the move from Hegel to Marx as a shift from political and philosophical accommodation to "radical activism." He then reflects on the overwhelming intrusion of prevailing reality to contemporary philosophical investigation, as in the ethical interruptions represented by "Auschwitz, the Indonesian massacres, and the war in Vietnam." "The weight of reality has become too heavy," Marcuse declares, yet he resists the notion he ascribes to action-oriented militants of the day—that consideration of the relevance of reality should lead radicals to jettison theory as a "superfluous" and indulgent commitment. Instead, the critical theorist argues that reality's burdens demand a "renewed and restructured theoretical effort," for, as he observes, "one's theoretical house is not necessarily a [mere] sanctuary from reality," as it may "also be a workshop for intellectual weapons offered to reality." Far from advancing any sort of Adornian dismissal of worldwide upheaval, Marcuse acknowledges openly that "relevant today is the action, the practice that can get us *out* of a society in which well-being, even *being* is at the price of destruction, waste, and oppression on a global scale." He argues that the prospect of mass-revolutionary praxis itself demands increased knowledge and theoretical commitment, such that activism should not be privileged to the exclusion of philosophy, for "action itself—in order to be able to attain its goal—calls for thought." Closing by considering Marx's famous final thesis on Feuerbach, Marcuse insists that Marx never meant to advance pure actionism, and he argues that today "the world must be interpreted again in order to be changed." His conclusion before the assembled philosophers in Portland thus is a militantly practical one, for he insists that they and he alike still remain highly relevant to the present tasks of fomenting life-affirming societal transformation (176–178, 181–182).

In his "Reconsideration" of "The Realm of Freedom and Realm of Necessity," as delivered at the 1968 Summer School "On Marx and Revolution" in Korčula, Yugoslavia, in the presence of Ernst Bloch, Marcuse continues the spirit of "The End of Utopia" by affirming that the strains within socialist thought tabooed in the main as "utopian" may well represent the very qualifying factors which would differentiate authentic socialism from the established societies in East and West alike. These "repressed aspects and images of socialism" are being being brought to the fore by rebellious students throughout the world, especially in France, argues the critical theorist. In this address, Marcuse uses the term "militant minority" and "*détonateur*" for the first time to qualify the role such student movements can play, for they express "what is still unarticulated and repressed among the vast majority of the population" (Marcuse 1969c: 20–21; 1969d: 328). Implicitly invoking his previous criticisms of Fromm, Marcuse makes clear that the radical students, in seeking to redefine socialism, do not exclude either humanism or "socialist humanism" from critique: in Marcuse's analysis, humanism for these young radicals "is inseparable from the affirmative higher culture of bourgeois society" and from "the repressive idea of the person or personality who can *fulfill* [*her*]*self* without making excessive demands on the world, by practicing the socially required degree of resignation." In this sense, Marcuse argues, what the New Left activists are agitating for is a revision of the traditional Marxian conception of the relationship between the realms of necessity and freedom, or time spent in labor and outside of it. To be specific, they seek to introduce an autonomous sense of self-determination into the realm of necessity, such that the preconditions of socialism would incorporate not only the reduction of the working day and the socialization of production but also the "emergence" of a new humanity liberated from "the aggressive and repressive needs and aspirations and attitudes of class society." Marcuse is thus referencing his work in the *Essay on Liberation* regarding the new sensibility here: he observes that capitalism is perpetuated both in the production process and through culture, as in the very "mind and body" of those subjected to its rule. "[S]ocialism is first of all a new form of human existence," declares Marcuse. It is thus not enough for him that the capitalists be expropriated by the proletariat, if the members of this newly hegemonic class themselves reproduce capitalist values. A "qualitatively different society" can for this reason come about in Marcuse's view only insofar as production is managed by individuals who institute goals different than those on offer in the established repressive order (1969c: 21–25).

In "Revolutionary Subject and Self-Government," the title given to his response to questions raised by his "utopian" musings on the relationship between the realms of freedom and necessity at Korčula, Marcuse first fields a student's inquiry into who or what he considers to be the revolutionary subject of contemporary reality. Marcuse formulates his reply using three criteria: the radical subject must have a "vital need" for abolishing the existing system; it must be capable of both "risking what [it] has and what [it] can get" within the system in favor of effecting radical change; and it must practically have the ability to either initiate or altogether complete the overthrow of the prevailing system. Returning to the analysis of *One-Dimensional Man*, Marcuse observes that the majority of workers in the most advanced-industrial capitalist societies lack such a need for revolution and are in this sense unwilling to risk everything to commit themselves to bringing about system change. In Hegelian-Marxian terms, as the critical theorist notes, the working class is *in itself* or objectively revolutionary due to its proximity to the production system—considering the radical alternatives workers could institute at the point of production—but it is not *subjectively* revolutionary, "for itself." As such, the proletariat is both within the capitalist system and also *of* the capitalist system (1969d: 326–327).

Marcuse closes this intervention by reformulating his previous points, noting that self-government can be liberatory only if a "liberating change in the controlling groups themselves has occurred." Quite like Gramsci, Marcuse stresses that the promise of revolutionary self-management can be realized only *after* the workers have broken instinctually with class society. Marcuse here expresses his concern that, if humanity must await the genesis of proletarian control over the economy before effecting the ideological and cultural break with capitalism, this break may well be indefinitely delayed—or it may come entirely too late. In closing, Marcuse declares that the onset of workers' self-management would itself signify "great progress," but he is clear to conclude that it would not by itself imply the onset of socialism as "a qualitatively different form of life" (1969d: 328–329).

Marcuse's 1969 Debate with Adorno on Theory and Praxis

A most fascinating exchange of letters took place between Marcuse and Adorno in 1969, beginning in the month of February—shortly after Adorno and Habermas had called on the police to clear the Frankfurt offices of the Institute for Social Research, which had been occupied by militant students organized by Adorno's former doctoral student-turned-critic, Hans-Jürgen Krahl—and ending in August, as Adorno lay dying in Switzerland after having suffered a heart attack while on vacation from the confrontational scenes on offer in Frankfurt. Marcuse delays until April to send his response to Adorno's initial letter of 14 February inviting him to speak at a forthcoming event at the Institute's campus. Adorno, who had served as Institute director since 1958, briefly describes the turmoil at the university in this missive. In his reply, Marcuse expresses dismay at his counterpart's resort to police action, and he cites this move as reason for his own reluctance to accept the Institute's invitation to speak in Frankfurt. Identifying his sympathies as lying with Germany's student radicals, Marcuse reminds Adorno that the militancy of the young stems at least in part from the intellectual anti-authoritarianism the Institute's collective members had been famously advancing for decades; he makes the rather obvious point—which may not have been so obvious to Adorno, after all—that the cause of Critical Theory is better served by students in revolt than by the repressive forces of the State (Marcuse and Adorno 1999: 125). To focus on whether or not the students' precise protest tactics are the most well thought-out is to miss the point, argues Marcuse, for it is the desperate struggle of the youth to translate Critical Theory into revolutionary praxis which should meet with the support of the founders of this philosophical school, regardless of how unrealistic it may be to expect that such protests will by themselves be capable of bringing down capitalism. In this sense, Marcuse very much associates the militant students with his notion of the Great Refusal, which in the context of brutal colonial warfare demands an anti-systemic embodiment:

We know (and [the students] know) that the situation is not a revolutionary one, not even a pre-revolutionary one. But this same situation is so terrible, so suffocating and demeaning, that rebellion against it forces a biological, physiological reaction: *one can bear it no longer, one is suffocating and one has to let some air in* (1999: 125; emphasis added).

Rejecting Habermas' infamous denunciation in 1967 of a specter of "Left Fascism" emanating from the radical German youth movements—a nasty charge which Adorno, too, may well have found apt—Marcuse expresses to his colleague that the metaphorical oxygenation produced by the students is "certainly not the air of the establishment." Beyond this, he claims he should likely fall into despair if those fashioning themselves to be critical theorists "appear to be on the side of a world that supports mass murder in Vietnam, or says nothing about it, and which makes a hell of any realms that are outside the reach of its own repressive power" (1999: 125–126).

Adorno's reply to Marcuse a month later recalls the practical conservatism of Horkheimer's directorship of the Institute during its years of exile in New York: the current director remarks that the organization's finances would likely be jeopardized by the "circus" which would accompany a talk by Marcuse at the Institute's campus. Rather strangely for the co-author of the *Authoritarian Personality,* as well, Adorno declares that the police should not on principle be "abstractly demonized," and he expresses no remorse for his decision to call on them to clear the occupation, claiming that "no other course of action" was possible, especially in terms of observing his responsibility to assure the integrity of Benjamin's collected works, which were safeguarded in the Institute's Frankfurt offices. He also shares his dialectical concern that the New Left-inspired students might be transformed into authoritarians, as based on his interpretation of the echoes of "thoughtless violence" he claims to have confronted during the student protests in Frankfurt. Furthermore, Adorno suggests to Marcuse that he should likely protest not only the "horror of the napalm bombs" dropped by the U.S. military but also the "unspeakable Chinese-style tortures" practiced by the Vietcong, if his *angst* over the war in Southeast Asia is to be authentic and not ideological (1999: 127–128).

Marcuse for his part finds these claims greatly lacking. He argues firstly that the occupations and interruptions of lectures as undertaken by students can be justified, while so casually resorting to police action cannot—which is not to say that he categorically rejects calling on them in all situations. He nonetheless outrightly rejects the basis for Adorno's concern that the students would somehow suddenly shift maximally from Left to Right, observing that nothing in their movement "indicates such a change," and he warns that Adorno's reactive call for an equal denunciation of the Pentagon and the Vietcong threatens to "immediately tur[n] into a justification and apology for the aggressor"; in point of fact, Marcuse explicitly considers it "inhuman" to "say that one may not protest against the agony of imperialism, without in the same breath accusing those who desperately fight against this hell by whatever means they can." Implicitly critiquing Horkheimer's decidedly uncritical defense of the U.S. war effort, Marcuse tells Adorno their colleague's worry over the "Chinese on the Rhine" is impossible to countenance when in fact it is the U.S. military which occupies that river valley. With regard to the German students, Marcuse posits that the extra-parliamentary opposition they have carried out serves as an example of the critical principle that contestation becomes possible only through direct action, given the colonization of bourgeois democracy by monopolistic interests which block qualitative change from being effected through traditional political methods. Marcuse clearly presents his defense of the student radicals in this letter: he claims that their potential must be held up and advanced by all critical intellectuals, in light of the suffocating hegemonic reality against which they stand, considering how terrible the system's cost is "in human life" (1969: 129–130).

In his letter in response—his second-to-last before death—Adorno presents to Marcuse an attempt at justifying his negative take on the German student protest movement, declaring it to lack even the "tiniest prospect" of "effecting a social intervention." Morever, Adorno sees it as provoking the "undiminished fascist potential" within German society itself as well as giving rise to "tendencies which [...] directly converge with fascism," as in the students' "blind" prioritization of action over scholarly investigation. Demonstrating his Zionist bias, Adorno then employs an example of students shouting down the Israeli ambassador in Germany as illustration of his worry that the students might precipitously "fli[p] over into fascism." Marcuse fundamentally disagrees with his theoretical counterpart, pointing in his next letter to the cases of France, the U.S., and South America as showing the collective power of militant student groupings, and though he reiterates his view that even consciously anti-systemic students would not comprise a revolutionary subject, he does identify them as the "strongest" and "perhaps the only" factor in the West that could catalyze the "internal collapse of the system of domination today" (1969: 131–133).

Moving beyond consideration of the student radicals, Marcuse dedicates the rest of his final letter to Adorno to arguing that the Institute must adopt a clear position against the U.S. war in Vietnam and in favor of the popular liberation struggle there. He also condemns a recent interview Horkheimer had given in *Spiegel* in which the former Institute director claimed the only alternative to liberal democracy to be dictatorship—with this being a declaration that could greatly undermine the place of anti-capitalist and critical struggle in the contemporary world. Marcuse reminds Adorno of the Institute members' previous theoretical work on Fascism, which emphasized the tendency of liberalism to become ever-more authoritarian, as the bourgeois class attempts to preserve its rule—to exercise a direct "régime of force"—and he clarifies to his counterpart that really existing liberal democracy "carries out, pays for, and arms neo-colonialism and neo-fascism," and in this way "obstructs liberation." He closes by delivering a *coup de grâce* against Horkheimer's bourgeois apologism, stressing the importance of distinguishing between the violence of domination and counter-violence directed against such. With reference to the world-historical struggle being waged at that moment in Southeast Asia, Marcuse argues that "the Vietnamese peasant who shoots his landlord who has tortured and exploited him for decades is not doing the same thing as the landlord who shoots the rebelling slave" (1969: 134–135).

It is unfortunate that these devastating points raised by Marcuse are not discussed more in his correspondence with Adorno. The next time Adorno replies, he is mere days from death, having suffered a myocardial infarction on vacation in the Swiss Alps. Recognizing his condition to be that of a "badly damaged Teddie," Adorno openly expresses alarm in his final letter at the prospect that Horkheimer's *Spiegel* interview would lead to a "*serious* rift" between Marcuse and the former Institute director. Lucidly revising his previous comments on the student radicals, Adorno acknowledges their "merits" from his death-bed, for now he sees clearly that they wish to arrest the "smooth transition to the totally administered world." The moribund philosopher nonetheless retains some of his previous skepticism, considering the intermixing he sees between such progressive aspects of the student movement and the ones that are for him more questionable—a "dram of madness," in the dialectician's words (1969: 135–136).

Revisiting "Repressive Tolerance" and Civil Rights with the ACLU and Fred Schwarz of the Christian Anti-Communist Crusade

In May 1969, during the time that his correspondence with Adorno was ongoing, Marcuse participated in a conference organized by the American Civil Liberties Union (ACLU), at which he spoke on the perspectives he had advocated a few years previously in "Repressive Tolerance." As in his original essay, Marcuse in this address describes civil liberties as originating historically from the struggle "against secular and clerical absolutism," and he claims said liberties not to be ends in themselves but rather means to "assure and extend the freedom and progress of society for *all* its citizens" (emphasis added). He argues that the political assumptions undergirding democratic societies are based on true popular sovereignty and the substantive freedom to form opinion, such that, whenever either of these two principles is factually absent, people's power is effectively illusory, and decision-making powers in fact rests with ruling power-groups. Describing the "military-industrial labor conglomerate" of U.S. society as exemplifying this latter tendency, Marcuse contrasts the conservative majority with the activist radical minorities who would seek to persuade the populace at large of the rationality of their own views. He adds that, owing to the existing oligarchical structure of society, these radicals run the serious risk of remaining a self-perpetuating minority. It is in this sense that he returns to his opening remarks regarding the historically progressive function of civil liberties, which is *de facto* denied. Within such a stifling context, in an implicit echo of Babouvism, Marcuse insists that radicals are right to engage in civil disobedience against the "illegitimate majority" which affirms not popular sovereignty but instead the *"powers over popular sovereignty"* (Marcuse 2014: 290–293).

Marcuse then specifies that right-wing and left-wing movements cannot be "equated with respect to their social position, power, goals, and functions," and that for this reason civil liberties should not be considered absolute but rather be applied in a discriminatory fashion. For Marcuse, there can be no right to advocate imperial war, exploitation, racism, fascism, or genocide. Thus, under the prevailing "fallen" conditions of the capitalist colonization of democracy, the concept of "civil liberty" must emphasize minoritarian direct action and extra-parliamentary praxis toward the end of arousing the awareness of existing injustices among general populace. Mentioning the "practitioners and propagandists of truly murderous and suicidal violence on a global scale," Marcuse calls for the overwhelming "primary violence" of Vietnam, militarism, the inner-cities, and the aggressive conquest of outer space to be eliminated as a means of addressing the "secondary" or *counter-violence* which erupts from below as a Newtonian reaction against the oppression overseen and directed by hegemonic power-groups (2014: 293–297).

A year later, in "The True Nature of Tolerance," published in the *Los Angeles Times,* Marcuse responds to a column written by Pepperdine University's chancellor, William S. Banowsky, regarding a protest the critical theorist had made against the appearance at UCSD of Dr. Fred Schwarz, an affiliate of the Christian Anti-Communist Crusade. Clarifying that his opposition to Schwarz's presence on campus had to do not with the reactionary's right to speak but rather with his qualifications to lecture in an accredited course, Marcuse reiterates his view that freedom of speech has *"objective* limits," and though he acknowledges that his line from "Repressive Tolerance" contains potential risks, he argues that these are "infinitely smaller" than those that are run by continuing to tolerate the brutally irrational prevailing dominant interest-groups. Specifying that he wishes to contribute to the creation of a form of tolerance that would be consonant with the concept's original meaning—that is, to be a "weapon for humanity"—Marcuse concludes by observing it to be "ludicrous" to celebrate "freedom and tolerance" at the same time as "whole areas of the world [are turned over] to fascist and military dictatorships" and entire countries are burned, bombed, and poisoned (2014: 218–221). In sum, then, he accuses the Establishment of intolerance through its very propagation and toleration of inhumanity.

"Marxism and the New Humanity: An Unfinished Revolution"

Marcuse considers the relationship among Marxism, liberalism, and religion in his comments on the "Unfinished Revolution" for a "New Humanity," which he presented at Temple University in Philadelphia in 1969. In this lecture, Marcuse describes Marxism as the child of the French Revolution, as it seeks to implement the "progressive ideas of liberalism" which in bourgeois society exist only as dreams and abstractions: namely, freedom, equality, and solidarity. Marcuse then reviews the basic difference between Marx and liberals, as is reflected in the former's emphasis that only social revolution could realize the Enlightenment's emancipatory ideals, in marked contrast to the conformist gradualism expressed in this regard by the latter. Importantly, the theorist identifies the *"radical libertarian element* in Marxian theory" within the vision Marx had for the realization of humanity's "sensuous species being," and he melds the basic human capability for transforming the world with Marx's claims regarding the human need for freedom, peace, and gratification—thus making an implicit reference to his own take on the relationship between the new sensibility and revolutionary change (emphasis added). In this way, Marcuse points up Marx's erotic side, as against the rationalism and positivism with which the dialectical materialist is often paired, and along these lines, he argues that post-capitalist society should be based on simple living rather than any continuation of bourgeois affluence (Marcuse 2014: 340–344).

Concluding his treatment of Marx here, Marcuse suggests that communism's libertarian radicalism marks a significant break with the Puritanism of liberalism, and so ties it much more closely with the "great radical heretic movements" of European history, such as humanism and the "libertarian trends" within Christianity, such as the Joachimite Brothers of the Free Spirit who had so influenced the young Hegel. The critical theorist closes by claiming contemporary rebel-clerics who have "joined the struggle against fascism in all its forms" to comprise a key part of the global anti-authoritarian movement, alongside the student radicals. In associating the resurgent libertarian political trends with "anarchist, heretic tendencies" that previously had been "long forgotten or reduced," Marcuse remarks that the global anti-systemic movements constitute a political materialization of a repressed insurgent morality (2014: 345).

"Freedom and the Historical Imperative"

This study of Marcuse's thought and work during the critical theorist's "moment" in the 1960s will close by considering an important lecture the now world-famous prophet of revolution would give at the International Encounter in Geneva in 1969: "Freedom and the Historical Imperative." Seeking to base his discussion of the bases of historical imperatives objectively, Marcuse posits here that the point of human existence is "self-preservation *and* growth," with the possibilities for the latter corresponding in Hegelian terms to the historical potentialities on offer, as in the relation between *is* and *ought.* From this definition, Marcuse proceeds to claim the realization of freedom to be the very historical imperative facing humanity—that of a freedom which allows humankind to "determine its own life without depriving others of this ability," thus being one that has never before existed in recorded history. The dialectical progression toward such a state of affairs depends in the first instance on the negation of what exists; only after the hegemonic system has been displaced can positive freedom as self-determination be enacted *en masse.* In a parallel to Sartre, Marcuse posits that the very concept of freedom affords humanity the choice to transcend the given situation: the Subject is free to decide whether the future will be characterized by socialism or barbarism. In its political, intellectual, and moral dimensions, the revolution exists independently of whether or not the Subject observes it and strives to bring it to fruition. The affirming socialist alternative to dominant unreason which Marcuse raises in this lecture is one which advances the "replacement of the [existing] system itself by one of self-determination on the basis of collective control of the means of production" (1972a: 212–218).

Marcuse nonetheless does return to the pessimistic tone of *One-Dimensional Man*, expressing doubt about the chances for the revolutionary institution of the historical imperative for freedom. He observes soberly that the material and intellectual culture which is the mark of the oppression in these [Western] societies may well continue to integrate the population into the capitalist system, and the latter may well be able to reproduce itself on an enlarged scale through neo-colonial exploitation abroad and militarization at home, plus the profitable conquest of outer space, and the collaboration of the Soviet Union (1972a: 219).

Incidentally, this is one of the first times Marcuse mentions the colonization of outer space in any of his writings. In "Freedom and the Historical Imperative," the critical theorist considers the likelihood of the militarization of space as "executed by robots in machines," and he observes capitalist competition as increasingly taking on a machinic character, as the workings of the system are progressively computerized, and the very functioning of the human mind itself comes increasingly to resemble computer operations. In these terms, Marcuse shares his despair regarding the prospect that the capitalist system will just "go on for a very long time, ravaging the people, the land, the sea, and the air, polluting the bodies and the minds [of the people]—with the latter adapting themselves to the situation"; the threat of such a development raises the specter of a "perfect barbarism" for Marcuse, one which synthesizes "freedom and automatism." Marcuse thus acknowledges gravely that the case against liberation "is a very strong one," at least in conformist and positivist terms— yet he advances a convincing foundation for the imposition of the "revolutionary imperative" on the millions of Westerners who may not expressly desire revolution: that is to say, through consideration of the system's victims, the "wretched of the Earth" (1972a: 219–222). Returning in this way to the argument of "Ethics and Revolution," Marcuse asserts that the rights and freedoms of the colonized, formerly colonized, and radically excluded outweigh the liberties of relatively affluent Westerners to continue enjoying themselves at the former's expense—and he is quite correct to do so.

Positively, Marcuse contemplates an image of global qualitative change whereby social reality is totally reconstructed via the abolition of poverty and exploitation and the redesigning of the life-world on a human scale. The probability of such an outcome cannot be assured by any iron law of history, announces Marcuse; its fulfillment rests solely on human choice, and it thus "remains the ultimate imperative of theoretical and practical reason." The likelihood of such reasonable choice intervening is to be assisted in turn by the evolution of mass-radical political consciousness (2014: 222–223).

CHAPTER 6

Marcuse's Final Decade: Continuities, Discontinuities, and Intensification (1970–1979)

> The essential demands of the revolution—abolition of alienated labor, equal opportunities for self-determination, pacification of nature, solidarity—thus have an *erotic basis* in subjectivity [...]. Society, and emancipation as a sociohistorical process, act through Eros itself—in sharp distinction to sexuality and sexual liberation, which can take place just as well within class society. The unfolding of the life instincts, Eros, requires social change, revolution; the revolution requires the instinctual foundation.
>
> MARCUSE 1980a: 42

Herbert Marcuse's final decade of life, which ended with his death in Starnberg, West Germany, in July 1979, was marked principally by continuities with the optimistic-revolutionary hopes of the second half of the 1960s as well as with the liberatory currents of the critical social theory he had been developing for more than half a century. As Marcuse would declare in a 1978 interview, he felt "a little more optimistic" that "things are going to change" after having witnessed the global uprising of 1968 (Marcuse 2014: 378). However, these final years of life also saw the philosopher introduce certain unprecedented and even unexpected methods into his socio-political theorizing. Plainly stated, while he continued to affirm militant goals and orientations at the beginning of the turn of the decade—as in "Cultural Revolution" (1970), an intervention in which Marcuse expressly seeks to shatter the nihilistic reign of *das Man* over the life-world—he to some degree came to revise his previous endorsement of revolutionary perspectives in favor of more incrementalist approaches. In *Counterrevolution and Revolt* (1972), he calls for the militant youth to undertake a "long march through the institutions," and in "The Movement in a New Age of Repression" (1971), he recommends that the oppositional movement adopt a "United Front" strategy that would see it at least temporarily forge ties with liberal elements as a "lesser evil" against the resurging capitalist leviathan, which had managed to hold onto power despite the various threats to its hegemony which arose in the late 1960s. Even in 1977, the critical theorist philosopher would argue that an "alliance with the liberal democratic forces"

© KONINKLIJKE BRILL NV, LEIDEN, 2016 | DOI 10.1163/9789004308701_007

is "indispensable" for the self-styled revolutionary movement in the U.S., in part owing to the marked lack of a mass-base of radicals in that society (2014: 426–427).

Reflecting on such marked discontinuities within his political thought, Marcuse would argue that his turn toward "realism" was justified by an honest appraisal of the prevailing political situation, which had in his view changed since the end of the previous decade. Now in the 1970s, on Marcuse's account, the ruling classes were engaged in a fascistic "preventive counterrevolution" which sought to eliminate all possibilities of a breakthrough toward liberation from below, as had been prefigured by the multitude of disruptive movements from the previous decade. Amidst this significantly more challenging political environment, Marcuse declares that the struggle to overthrow capitalism would likely take far longer than even he had anticipated a few year prior—at the end of *Counterrevolution and Revolt,* in fact, he announces that this process may take a century.

Nevertheless, while Marcuse's views on political strategy can be seen to have "mellowed" in the minor chord in his final decade, it is important to contrast such discontinuities with the far more prominent *continuities* in militant analysis the critical theorist would provide in his twilight years, as seen in *Counterrevolution and Revolt* itself, and especially in his very last work, *The Aesthetic Dimension* (1978). Contemplation of this latter volume should surely dispel any doubts one might hold that Marcuse had retreated from his long-standing advocacy of social revolution at life's end. In this sense, it is crucial to contrast his radical take on politics with the questionable and even reactionary conclusions reached by his former Frankfurt School colleagues Adorno and Horkheimer, who opposed the militant student movements of the 1960s. Rather stunningly, Horkheimer supported the Vietnam War as a check against the spread of Maoism, and he ultimately argued for an accommodation with bourgeois society. Additionally, in terms of historical analysis, it bears mentioning that Adorno and Horkheimer's hesitancy to endorse radical praxis near life's end mirrored the Institute's early prioritization of theory over action, a tendency which had greatly alienated council-communist Karl Korsch and sinologist Karl Wittfogel from contributing to the Frankfurt School's work some four decades prior (Jay 1973: 13–16).

In light of Marcuse's continued militancy to death, then, the stipulated "mellowing" the critical theorist *par excellence* underwent in his final decade must in reality be seen as merely relative and partial. This holds even for the period which followed the eclipse of the philosopher's utopian optimism, with the passionate optimism of "Cultural Revolution" representing something of a hold-over from the revolutionism of the 1960s. In *Counterrevolution and Revolt,* a text in which Marcuse diagnoses hegemonic power's empirical transition toward a more openly barbarous modality of governance, the advocacy of the "long march" comes almost as an afterthought within an extended militant reflection on the position of the "Left Under the Counterrevolution"—a chapter that discusses the importance of decentralization, council democracy, confrontational direct action, and radical education as means of securing the future possibility of the coming world-historical revolution that is to emancipate humanity. The third part of *Counterrevolution and Revolt,* which examines the mutually reinforcing relationship between art and social transformation, is similarly revolutionary in its analysis, as it suggests that authentic artworks help their audiences to imagine and reflect on alternatives to the prevailing miserable reality. In this section, Marcuse even quotes Beethoven in a letter wherein the Romantic composer expresses the hope that his symphonies could aid suffering humanity (Marcuse 1972b: 104). The radical analysis of art in *Counterrevolution and Revolt* in turn foreshadows the argument of *The Aesthetic Dimension.*

In the interim years between these two major works of his, indeed, Marcuse would continue to entertain notions of a political *Rausch* ("intoxication") that could help break with the system of domination, as in the defense of the New Left he presents in a 1975 lecture at the University of California Irvine and the correspondence he maintains with a Chicago-based Surrealist collective. In a debate the critical theorist held in 1972 with positivist champion Karl Popper, furthermore, Marcuse self-evidently presents a defense of revolution as against Popper's liberal apologetics. What is more, with reference to international anti-systemic developments, Marcuse in this final decade would on a number of occasions affirm the example provided by the course of the Chinese Revolution, pointing—whether rightly or wrongly—to its tendencies toward decentralization and a non-authoritarian implementation of socialism. The critiques one could present in hindsight against this potentially legitimative attitude vis-à-vis Maoism notwithstanding, Marcuse fortunately seems to have brought his libertarian-socialist sensibilities into sync with his take on China in his very final years.

Beyond the more negative and pessimistic discontinuities to which Marcuse would in part yield in his final decade, however, he also identifies a number of important new developments in these years that could belie the basis for such negativity. For one, he makes two fundamental revisions to his thesis on one-dimensionality in *Counterrevolution and Revolt:* first, that capitalism, much like the sorcerer's apprentice, now tends to create needs which it cannot meet and that hence demand the transcendence of this very system; and second, that it effectively expands the working class by extending the basis of exploitation to declassed middle-class elements, in a potentially suicidal development. Furthermore, and relatedly, he observes with joy that the stability of capitalism is increasingly coming to be challenged, as more and more people come to recognize the utter depravity of the system. In a 1972 debate with Raymond Aron—as in his interventions *Revolution of Reform?* and "The Failure of the New Left?"—Marcuse points specifically to the breakdown of cultural hegemony over larger segments of the working classes, who at their most militant engage in wildcat strikes and mindful sabotage of the workplace (2014: 356). Moreover, in these final years Marcuse would publicly embrace the emerging women's liberation movement as one of the most promising counter-hegemonic developments on hand in Western societies, and he dedicates some of his work in these years to consideration of the promise of feminism—most importantly in "Marxism and Feminism" (1974), wherein he affirms the radical struggle against male supremacy and the characteristically dominant-aggressive values advanced by patriarchy in conjunction with capital. In this address, presented at Stanford University, he counterposes a speculative vision of a "feminist socialism" as a critical contribution to revolutionary struggle. Lastly, in his very last years, Marcuse would acknowledge the similarly radical potential of the ecology movement, as in "Protosocialism and Late Capitalism" (1978) and the "Children of Prometheus" (1979). Besides framing capitalism as an inherently anti-ecological force, he would in his final interventions specifically mention the nuclear power industry on several occasions in a negative light. A more systematic discussion of Marcuse's views on nature, non-human animals, and environmentalism will be presented in the following chapter, "Nature and Revolution."

Besides these critical interventions, Marcuse in his final decade continued with his concerns regarding the Vietnam War by publishing a disturbing analysis of the reactionary mass-defense of Lieutenant William Calley following his 1971 conviction by a military tribunal for his prosecution of the My Lai massacre of 1968, and he penned a condemnation of Henry Kissinger's authoritarian cynicism in a 1972 commentary on the U.S. Secretary of State's press conference regarding peace talks with the North Vietnamese. Marcuse finds in the popular rush to defend the murderous Calley evidence of a "proto-fascist syndrome" on hand in the U.S., one that belies his more optimistic interpretations of prevailing trends in the imperial center, while in his article on Kissinger, he laments that the people guard "deadly silence," "hav[ing] abdicated" their responsibility to force a cessation of the neo-colonial genocide against the Vietnamese (2014: 334). Additionally, at the end of 1971 and the first few days of 1972, Marcuse traveled with Inge to historical Palestine to present a couple of lectures in West Jerusalem on aesthetics, as well as to engage in a fact-finding mission of sorts

aimed at reducing regional tensions between Israel, the Palestinians, and the
Arab world, toward the ultimate end of effecting a just resolution. Nonetheless,
the humanistic potential of such a trip—symbolized well in Inge's explicitly
anti-Zionist proclivities—was arguably tempered to a degree by Marcuse's
contradictory pro-Israeli sentiments, as expressed in a public debate with
Rudi Dutschke a month after Israel's occupation of the remaining portions of
former Palestine during the Six-Day War of June 1967.

In point of fact, a palpable tension exists between Marcuse's 1970 announcement in *Israel Horizons* that the concept of freedom—if it is not to be repressive or false—must exist for "*all* [peoples], *all* races, *all* civilizations" and the
foundational support he would express for the Jewish State's right to exist
from 1967 through the time of his visit to the region and until death (Marcuse
1970b: 17). This Zionist position aside, and Marcuse's highly peculiar request
for a meeting with Israeli Defense Minister Moshe Dayan during his trip notwithstanding, the philosopher certainly does present a humanist perspective
in his article "Israel is Strong Enough to Concede," published upon the conclusion of his and Inge's visit. The couple's on-the-ground research involved
interviews with Palestinians as well as Israelis; far surpassing the vast swath of
Western commentary on the question at the time, Marcuse acknowledges the
significant suffering imposed on the Indigenous Palestinians by the founding
of Israel, and he calls for the birth of a Palestinian State whose nature would
be determined by a popular vote, in exchange for the Arab countries' recognition of the Jewish State. Later in his final decade, additionally, Marcuse would
analyze and denounce the tactics taken up by the Red Army Faction in West
Germany on both practical and philosophical grounds ("Murder is Not a Political Weapon," 1977), and he also would enthusiastically review the crucial contributions made by East German dissident Rudolf Bahro in his *The Alternative
in Eastern Europe* (1977) as regards a dissection of "actually existing socialism."
The critical theorist would then expand Bahro's analysis of a transition beyond
"protosocialism" to the late-capitalist context in Western societies, in "Protosocialism and Late Capitalism." Yet, in an echo of a perennially recurring problem in Marcuse's *oeuvre,* the critical theorist does not in this essay explicitly
disclose whether he embraces or rejects Bahro's rather authoritarian recommendations for inducing this transition.

In personal terms, Marcuse's experiences during his final decade of life led
him to confront several challenges and negations that would be reflected in his
1974 disclosure to interviewer Bill Moyers that he had "found very great sadness
in living" (2014: 163). For one, Marcuse lost his teaching privileges at UC San
Diego at the turn of the decade after the Regents collaborated with Governor

Reagan to impose an arbitrary, ageist stipulation proclaiming that professors seventy years of age and older could not be promised annual renewals of contract—and though intellectual luminaries from Popper to Sartre wrote to the administration on Marcuse's behalf, this was not enough to protect the critical theorist's position for more than a year (Sethness Castro 2013). In addition, Inge succumbed to cancer in 1972, leading Marcuse into a profound depression; he wrote nothing of substance that year, and canceled all previous speaking engagements (Kātz 1982: 210–211). In a poem he composed after Inge's passing, Marcuse expresses the following thoughts:

> When we say love
> We know
> That death is stronger than love
> That love is sad
> Deathly sad
> And cannot be otherwise.
> For all love seeks eternity
> And that can never be.
>
> MARCUSE 2007: 196–197

However, when Angela Davis, one of his favorite former graduate students, was arrested by the FBI in October 1970 for having owned the firearms used by Jonathan Jackson and company in their attempt to force the authorities to release George Jackson from Soledad Prison by taking over a San Rafael courthouse and holding hostages a few months prior, Marcuse mobilized himself expeditiously in her defense (2011: 199). Despite the real risks to himself, particularly amidst the numerous death-threats he had received from various reactionaries, Marcuse paid a substantial portion of Davis' bail, publicly challenged UCLA's expulsion of the Black militant following her incarceration, submitted legal affidavits to the courts on her behalf, and with Inge visited her on multiple occasions in the San Rafael jail (Kātz 1982: 187).

In a public letter to Davis written a month after her arrest, Marcuse recognizes the vast differences in life-circumstances separating himself from his then-incarcerated ex-student, who had been surrounded from birth by a world of "cruelty, misery, and persecution," and he praises the militant Marxist-feminist's deep concern for the fate of her own people and "the oppressed everywhere." He observes knowingly that Davis could not limit her commitment to Black liberation to the confines of classroom and her study of German Idealism, but instead had somehow to make the Idealists' stress on human freedom concrete (2011: 49–50). As he argues during an appearance on NBC in January 1971, it was "precisely because" Davis was a true intellectual that she "took seriously what she read in the works": "She refused to treat the liberating ideas of Western civilization as mere textbook material [...]—for her, they were alive and had to become reality—here and now, not in some far away days [...]" (2014: 214–215). Beyond this, Marcuse would favorably cite Davis' "Women and Capitalism," which she wrote while incarcerated in Palo Alto, during his public addresses in these years, especially "Marxism and Feminism."

Certainly, another source for Marcuse's anxiety and sadness in his final years stemmed from his philosophical awareness regarding the worsening tendencies toward a retrenched totalitarianism on hand in Western settings, particularly U.S. society. In a number of his interventions from this last decade—"The Movement in a New Age of Repression," *Counterrevolution and Revolt*, "A Revolution in Values," and "The Failure of the New Left?"—Marcuse expressly concludes by considering the evident trends toward total social control. Much as during his youth in the 1930s—and thus signifying yet another critical way in which Marcuse's political theory at life's end underwent an intensification rather than a mellowing—the theorist repeatedly insisted that only a properly well-organized left-wing movement could impede what increasingly seemed to be the inevitable march of capital toward a new Fascism. On that note, Marcuse in his last couple of years movingly spoke more and more of Auschwitz and its victims, as well as all other victims of genocide, particularly ongoing genocides, as well as those which could be expected in the future of the world which he was soon to leave, if capital were not stopped in its tracks. Indeed, Marcuse dedicates an essay to "Lyric Poetry after Auschwitz" (1978), wherein he contemplates his friend Adorno's observation that to write poetry after the Nazi genocide of European Jewry would be barbaric. Disagreeing with Adorno, Marcuse instead recommends that artists must affirm the memory of those murdered by the Nazis and recall the countless multitudes killed and suppressed by prevailing authoritarian-capitalist relations. Indeed, *The Aesthetic Dimension* can in a sense be considered a response to the growing threat of a neo-fascism, in light of its emphasis on the revolutionary contributions to be made by authentic art in the struggle to secure joy and life in the face of suffering, absurdity, and death.

At the end of July 1979, the world lost a world-historical partisan of revolution. The same month he presented the "Children of Prometheus" in Frankfurt, Marcuse was fittingly slated to travel to Madrid to participate in a televised panel to reflect on the film *¡Viva Zapata!* (*El País* 1979). Unfortunately, like Adorno a decade prior, he suffered a heart attack shortly after his talk in Frankfurt and was hospitalized in Starnberg, where he ultimately succumbed to a stroke. A memorial service was then held in the woods of Starnberg, being attended by his son Peter, his stepson Michael, his third wife Erica, and his grandson Harold, in addition to Habermas, Dutschke, and Moishe Postone, among others. While these figures were present in corporeal form to commemorate Marcuse's death, it would not be an exaggeration to say too that the critical theorist's deceased colleagues Adorno, Bloch, and Benjamin were spectrally present in Marcuse's mind during his final years of life, as at his memorial service in the Starnberg forest. In accordance with the wishes of Erica, or "Ricky", who did not want the Germans to incinerate yet another Jew, Marcuse's body was cremated in Austria, and the philosopher's ashes placed in an urn that she took back with her to the U.S. Marcuse was for this reason not given a proper burial until fifteen years after Ricky's death, when in 2003 his ashes were returned to Germany and finally buried in Berlin (Harold Marcuse 2004). Characteristically, the gravestone on his final resting place bears the slogan *Weitermachen!*—meaning "Keep it up!" or "Continue!"

Marcuse's Assessment of the State of the Radical Opposition in the Early 1970s: "Cultural Revolution," "The Movement in a New Age of Repression," and "A Revolution in Values"

In three important interventions from the early years of his last decade of life—"Cultural Revolution," "The Movement in A New Age of Repression," and "A Revolution in Values"—Marcuse evaluates the relative strengths and weaknesses of Western radical oppositional movements and provides recommendations, philosophical and practical, for their future improvement. Of these three works, "Cultural Revolution" is far and away the most optimistic, as Kellner points out, given that it was presented at a time when the various rebellious advances of the 1960s were still fresh in the collective memory (Marcuse 2001: 122). In contrast, Marcuse's argument in "The Movement in a New Age of Repression" is more measured; in fact, it signifies something of a turning point in Marcuse's analytical method, for in this piece the theorist proffers new perspectives—even reformist ones—which he claims to reflect the geopolitical change toward conditions that are substantially more difficult for left formations. The lecture thus foreshadows the relative pessimism of *Counterrevolution and Revolt.*

In the unpublished monograph "Cultural Revolution" (1970), one of Marcuse's single-most expansive and visionary interventions made in life, the critical theorist presents a sweeping analysis of the possibility for a mass-transformation in the human sensibility that could then yield an overturning of capitalist alienation. Continuing with the Gramscian analysis he had advanced in the 1960s, particularly in *An Essay on Liberation,* Marcuse initiates his reflections on cultural revolution by contemplating the historical failure of libertarian social upheaval, a cause that had been advanced in Europe by medieval dissidents, Enlightenment *philosophes*, Charles Fourier, and the young Marx. He suggests that a principal reason for the historical failure of the emancipatory visions favored by these groups and individuals has been the conscious "suppression" and "atrophy" of the "roots of liberation" in the human instincts and sensibility, as overseen by hegemonic social relations. Given this diagnostic line, Marcuse places a critical emphasis on strengthening the human passions as anticipatory Platonic Forms that would prefigure the construction of a "cosmos of *Justice* where satisfaction would be in the free human productivity in creating a good world for everyone." For Marcuse, the "object world" that is opened by the prospect of such an instinctual transition is based on *solidarity:* he reiterates his call for an emancipation of the senses, which would yield novel modes of perception and imagination and, hopefully, a reconfiguration of the relationship between subject and object—with this latter change affecting relationships among humans as well as the relationship between humanity and nature. Marcuse writes that the new sensibility would concretely take on the form of self-management in the workplace—"and beyond," that is, throughout society. Compellingly in this sense, Marcuse notes that exploitation would "not really [be] abolished," "its heritage not really thrown off," until nature came to be considered a sphere of intrinsic value with its own rights to autonomy (2001: 124, 129, 131–132, 145).

Reaffirming his analysis from *Eros and Civilization,* Marcuse notes in this address that the ascendancy of Eros that would accompany revolutionary changes would in no way be limited to the private and sexual sphere, but would instead involve a socialization of all interpersonal relations as well as of the entirety of the "common universe": it would seek to build an entirely new world. Specifically, he speculates that this more erotic instinctual structure would seek gratification in "cooperation, love, friendship; in the pursuit of knowledge, in the creation of a pleasurable environment, in the *kalokaynos:* the beautiful and the good." Dialectically, rather than destroy civilization, the liberated instincts would seek to "destroy [its] destructive basis" and so reshape it in a life-affirming manner. As before, Marcuse clarifies that the new world to be built by Eros would not represent a perfect society in which conflict and pain have been abolished in favor of "universal love and charity," but one that would instead reduce suffering and anxiety to an "attainable minimum." At stake, then, is the very development of a sensuous-rational culture to be guided by the mind, as by art, toward the end of shattering common experience and opening the possibility of the future liberated society. Linking instinctual rebellion with political upheaval, Marcuse says the former leads to the latter only through the materialization of the Great Refusal, a process whereby the "intellect (and the intelligentsia)" utterly reject any "pact with the Establishment" and any chance of being "accessor[ies] to the crimes against humanity." In this sense, liberation begins at the individual level; the myriad inanities and cruelties of capital can be overcome only consciously through the autonomous self-development of peoples working together to construct a different society (2001: 133, 136, 139, 148–149, 151, 158).

Reflecting on the resurgent threat of a new Fascism in closing, Marcuse urgently indicates the need to intensify the struggle against capital: for if it is not, the fight may be indefinitely lost. In terms of such prospects, Marcuse finds hope in the increasing worker militancy on hand in u.s. society, alongside the countercultural resistance. He also points to a historical example from 1953 in France, when a general strike was instituted out of *sadness,* due to the people's perception that "nothing was right." Closely mirroring the closing lines of his friend Franz Neumann's *Behemoth* (1944), wherein the legal theorist writes that capital "can only be overthrown by the conscious political action of the oppressed masses," Marcuse concludes that the increasingly authoritarian and thanotic system can be brought down solely through the action of those who effectively prop it up by reproducing its power through labor, and he stresses that the task of helping to extend this effort is the continued work of the militant left-wing minority (Marcuse 2001: 158, 160–162; Neumann 1944: 476).

Marcuse's February 1971 address at uc Berkeley, "The Movement in a New Age of Repression: An Assessment," continues with many of the points the theorist had been making with regards to the potential of revolution at the end of the 1960s and in "Cultural Revolution," yet it also reflects a few noteworthy concessions to "realism" on the septuagenarian's part. Marcuse begins this public assessment by admitting—as with his 1968 talk "On the New Left"— that he finds it difficult to engage in theoretical analysis when the prevailing situation "seem[s] to cry out for action—no matter what action—so that we don't suffocate, so that we don't bust up." Moreover, he observes that the project of advancing an engaged theory faces acute practical difficulties of diffusion and reception, given the prevalence of "Orwellian language" as the norm of communication imposed by State and capital, as well as among the people themselves. Nevertheless, he proceeds to present the two main theses of his assessment: optimistically, that the remaining years of the twentieth century may well see the advent of the "first world historical revolution," and that, at the opposite pole, the chance for this revolution is being actively inhibited by the reactionary power of the u.s. government, both at home and abroad. Marcuse defines the prospect of the next revolution as being world-historical due to the very real possibilities which exist to redirect the capitalist base toward the total abolition of poverty and exploitation, thus allowing for the realization of "integral socialism" to be feasible "from the [very] beginning," rather than be postponed indefinitely "to a second phase which may never arrive" (Marcuse 2004: 142–144). Marcuse sees particular hope in the example provided by the Chinese Revolution, which for him has advanced a non-authoritarian implementation of socialism that avoids bureaucratization, and he reiterates his emphasis on the demand that the capitalist chain be broken at its "strongest link," within the imperial core:

> Just consider for one moment what a radical change in the imperialist metropole would do on a global scale. It would mean the collapse of the lackey regimes in the Third World and not only in the Third World. It would remove a major obstacle to the development of the European revolutions; it would allow an independent development of the Chinese and Cuban revolutions; and perhaps it would mean a political upheaval in the Soviet Union itself (2004: 143).

Combining transformation in the spheres of economics, politics, and culture, this revolution would "far outdo" its historical predecessors, in Marcuse's view. Passing to discuss the problem of the revolutionary subject within the imperial center of the capitalist world-system, Marcuse speaks to the role of the metropolitan working classes, clarifying that, though the "large majority" of workers have been integrated within these contexts, this negative reality in no way effaces the class struggle, which will exist as long as class society persists. Due to its position as the "human base" of the productive apparatus of capital, the working class retains its potentially revolutionary nature, observes Marcuse, however bourgeois and counter-revolutionary the cultural values many of its constituent members may express at any given moment. Faithfully, Marcuse here declares that it is only through the process of struggle that the revolutionary subject can be expected to emerge. With regard to existing sources of revolt, Marcuse acknowledges conscious resistance to capitalism emanating from the protest of non-conformist youth and "rebellious middle class" elements that reject all identification with the system, and he points out this dialectical dynamic as indicating how consumer society may well turn out to be the very gravedigger of capitalism (2004: 144–148).

Marcuse dedicates the remainder of his comments on "The Movement" to examining contemporary radical strategy. Sketching out the reactive steps taken by hegemonic power to counter the emerging threats to its continued dominance—an argument he develops more fully in *Counterrevolution and Revolt*—he observes that the ruling class knowingly directs its repressive power against militant people of color and student movements rather than organized labor, given the considerably greater threat posed by the former two forces as regards capitalist stability at that time (2004: 148). Defining this new phenomenon from above as a "preventive counterrevolution," Marcuse is clear to note that this negating turn of events does not yet indicate that the U.S. State has become fascist, though he recognizes that some of the "possible preconditions" for such an outcome are already on hand:

> They are well known and I will just give you a list: the courts, used more and more as political tribunals; the reduction of education and welfare in the richest country in the world; antidemocratic legislation, such as preventive detention and the no-knock laws; economic sanctions if you are politically and otherwise suspect; the intimidation and self-censorship of the mass media. These are very frightening signs (2004: 148).

Marcuse declares that history cannot be said to be repeating itself precisely, for it "never repeats itself in the same form." Regarding this question of an emergent Fascism, he observes that, though the radical opposition cannot identify any "charismatic leader" or "any s.s. or s.a." at hand, this may indeed suggest that such measures may no longer be needed. "If necessary, other organizations can perform the job, perhaps even more efficiently. I do not have to tell you which organizations I have in mind" (2004: 148).

In terms of revolutionary strategy, Marcuse makes several suggestions in this talk: that radicals find ways of communicating their ideas to ordinary people toward the end of extending the reach of the oppositional movement, that the resistance adopt a sort of "United Front" among the different dissident factions, that it work to construct counter-institutions against the established ones, that it not confuse personal with social liberation, that it overcome its "widespread anti-intellectualism," and that it advocate for a "radical reconstruction" rather than "destruction" of the university system. In terms of political linguistics, Marcuse argues that the employment of terms like "imperialism, exploitation, and capitalism" should be used among those within the movement, but that they have limited sense for those outside it, such that they should be "translated" into understandable concepts. Intriguingly, Marcuse discloses that this is "one of the very rare cases where I am in favor of ordinary language." In a similar sense—and perhaps reflecting his own rising doubts about revolutionism— Marcuse prefaces his avowal of the United Front strategy with a public apology, declaring that he now believes there to be "such a thing as a lesser evil," and noting that the radical opposition faces such an unfavorable situation in the face of the preventive counterrevolution that "even some temporary alliances and compromises with *certain liberals* seem to be appropriate." Specifically, he argues that aid from liberals may help the left with its material problem of the "total lack of funds" (2004: 149–152).

Marcuse continues similarly in this realist line by announcing that the 1960s are definitively over—that "the heroic period of beautiful spontaneity, of personal anti-authoritarianism, of hippie rock and shock" has passed—and that the radical opposition must acknowledge the shift toward preventive counterrevolution being organized by hegemony. Relatedly, he argues that the movement should adopt "no premature anarchism" in the face "of a deadly powerful enemy." Marcuse here also affirms a strategy of developing radical counter-institutions as a means of breaking the establishment's monopoly on information and of preparing for such time as when the repressive present has been superseded in favor of a free society. Returning to his argument from "The Relevance of Reality," Marcuse once again declares his opposition to the rampant anti-intellectualism he observes within the movement, and he stipulates that Marx's famous concluding thesis on Feuerbach must not be interpreted as favoring pure actionism over theory, considering his view that "never has theory, never has the effort of thinking, of knowing what is going on and what can be done about it, been needed more than it is today." In this sense, the critical theorist holds that, "more than ever before," revolutionary practice cannot be severed from theory as a guide—much as the human brain requires the corpus callosum to coordinate the activity of both cerebral hemispheres for optimal functioning. Expanding on this thought, Marcuse warns that the movement must not undialectically consider the universities mere props of the establishment to be destroyed, but should instead demand an overhaul of the education system, toward the end of distributing knowledge in an egalitarian fashion as a means of helping to cope with prevailing reality as well as the "things that will come [...] very soon" (2004: 151–152).

Marcuse concludes his address on "The Movement" by distinguishing between activism and revolutionary organizing: the latter depends on mass-popular support, which in contemporary U.S. society exists only for the militant racial minorities, not the students. Arguing against the use of offensive violence against the system, Marcuse defends the position which would allow for no more than a limited use of counter-violence, or violent self-defense, as "[t]here have been enough martyrs and enough victims." He recommends his listeners to "preserve your strength as a political force" in order to "become those who prepare the soil, the minds, and the bodies for a new society"—this, "while you are still alive, while you are still young, while you are still capable of thinking, of talking, of loving, of resisting and fighting" (2004: 153).

Marcuse continues to develop the sentiments of "Cultural Revolution" and "The Movement" in his 1972 address "A Revolution in Values," which he presented at a February 1972 conference on Science, Technology, and Values held at the University of South Florida in Tampa. In this intervention, the critical theorist revindicates the contemporary moves toward cultural revolution in Western society as a repudiation of the reigning performance principle and the society it shores up—hence, of the undeniable bourgeois tendency toward "self-propelling destruction and domination." Against these negations, Marcuse sees the potentially anti-systemic movements advancing cultural revolution as a demand for "freedom and solidarity as a quality of the human existence," to be attained through the abolition of the capitalist social relations that instrumentalize and objectify laboring humanity. Concretely, Marcuse counterposes his definition of socialism to reigning capitalist barbarism, stressing the centrality of aesthetic values within this transition, given his Kantian and Schillerian view that these are "inherently non-exploitative [and] non-repressive." For the liberation struggle to stress aesthetic concerns would aid significantly in the battle against the "male aggressiveness of patriarchal civilization," argues Marcuse, who here mentions the world-historical nature potential of the women's liberation movement for the first time in his *oeuvre*. Whether correctly or not, though, he declares that the feminist movement as then constituted did not "seem conscious of its truly subversive radical potential," as seen in the chance for the institution of a "less aggressive Reality Principle" (197–199).

Much like Camus before and Subcomandante Insurgente Marcos/Galeano after him, Marcuse here underscores the importance of joy in the struggle for liberation, as against the "inner-worldly asceticism" that had been previously identified by Max Weber as underpinning the rule of capital. Reiterating the claims of his analyses from the previous decade, the preeminent social critic observes that revolutionary values are currently expressed only among "minorities"—the non-integrated groups of "youth, the women, the black and brown population, the young workers, the intelligentsia." Though he in no way jettisons the continued importance of the working classes in the struggle against the instituted form of society—for indeed, he makes clear that these minority groups cannot themselves "replace [the workers] as the basis of radical social change"—he does claim the radical minorities to be the "sole catalysts of change" at present. Though their numbers be small, they represent the general interest, says Marcuse: their needs "are in reality the needs of the entire underlying population" (2004: 199–200).

While the title of this talk and Marcuse's general argument within it may seem to tend toward pure Idealism—in the sense, that is, that the loci of change and progress would appear to be concentrated within thought and the mind—this charge would not be entirely justified. In Gramscian terms, Marcuse notes that philosophical and cultural change can and often does precede societal upheaval. "The ascendance of new radical values [...] tends to become a material force," and these revolutionary sentiments can "foreshado[w] the internal weakening, perhaps even disintegration of this society." Clearly, Marcuse here is echoing Marx's famous dictum that "theory becomes a material force as soon as it has gripped the masses" (Marx and Engels 1975: 182). Juxtaposing this affirming historical possibility against the capitalist tendency to threaten "the very survival of [humanity] as a human race," Marcuse points out the imperative for social revolution: "today's revolution of values no longer proceeds within the established continuum of quantitative progress, but it tends to break this continuum. It is a *qualitative leap* into the possibilities of an essentially different way of life" (Marcuse 2004: 196–197, 199).

Following the political-sociological trends he had identified in *Eros and Civilization,* as before, Marcuse closes this address by warning that the governing power structure is fully cognizant of the very real threats it faces due to the possibilities of organization and rebellion from below. In light of the historical failure of revolution to date, though, Marcuse flatly remarks that "the prospects are not very exhilarating" at present. As in *One-Dimensional Man* and the "Re-Examination of the Concept of Revolution," Marcuse here repeats his criticism of the blind optimism of scientific socialism and orthodox Marxism, observing in closing that "[t]here is no historical law according to which capitalism will inevitably be followed by socialism." Then raising the intuitive opposition between the choice for socialism or barbarism—the former being "a free and human society," or "a society entirely in the hands of an omnipresent and all-powerful administration and management"—Marcuse optimistically hypothesizes that "it is not too late," that "barbarism, neo-fascist barbarism, can still be fought." Nevertheless, much like his comrade Benjamin, who in *One-Way Street* writes that, "before the spark reaches the dynamite [...], the lighted fuse must be cut," Marcuse warns that all could be lost if the specters of capitalist-fascism are not successfully inhibited in the near term—"it may [then] very well be too late" (Benjamin 1979: 80; Marcuse 2004: 201).

Revolution or Reform? Marcuse's Debate with Popper

Being something of an admittedly surreal encounter, Marcuse's 1972 debate with German positivist philosopher Karl Popper is appropriately entitled *Revolution or Reform?* As in the critical 1959 review Marcuse had made of Popper's

The Poverty of Historicism, the basic conflict between these two philosophical figures can be summarized in the counterposition of the title's two terms,
with Marcuse presenting a revolutionary perspective on prevailing society, as
against Popper's liberal and positivist reformism.

Besides introductory biography, opening comments, and conclusion, the
Marcuse-Popper debate is divided into two main sections, "Critique and Program" and "Theoretical Background." In the former section, in contrast to Popper's vacuous liberal apologism, which is typified in the statement that "[o]ur
western democratic societies [...] are very imperfect and in need of reform, but
they are the best ever," Marcuse discusses revolutionary politics and shares his
shifting view of the U.S. working class—that its integration into capitalism is
breaking down—adding by means of clarification that workers' struggles in
places like France and Italy hold more promise than does the case in the U.S.
He explains this discrepancy with reference to the gap in affluence that sepa-
rates these societies from the U.S. In response to the question of from where
revolution could begin today in the advanced-industrial societies, Marcuse
suggests this as emanating from the "general inhumanity, dehumanization,
and disgust at the waste and excess of the so-called consumer society," pointing out the "very strong objective and social reasons for [experiencing] disgust"
with this society. The critical theorist furthermore endorses the council system as a transitional form for the socialization of production, and he explicitly states his view that all contemporary "radical opposition" must take on an
"extra-parliamentary" character—thus reiterating the view he had expressed
to Adorno in the correspondence the two maintained shortly before the latter's death. In contrast to the anthropological perfection the interviewer dis-
ingenuously projects into Marcuse's thought—"[a] human being who always
does good"—the philosopher clarifies that his theory presumes a "human
being who first of all, and perhaps for the first time in history, really *can* act
in solidarity and do good" (emphasis added). He also observes there to be no
assurance that the toppling of capitalism would necessarily usher in an anti-
authoritarian society: "History is not an insurance agency. One can't expect
guarantees" (Marcuse and Popper 1976: 67, 72–77).

As Marcuse's foil, Popper communicates a number of absurd opinions: for
example, that the violence expressed against the Kennedy brothers, Martin
Luther King, Jr., and even in the Vietnam War "are not a consequence of the
form of government or of the so-called system of domination" on hand in the
U.S. He repeats his established position that violence "always leads to more
violence," and that revolutions inevitably terminate with the destruction of the
revolutionaries and their ideals (1976: 80, 86, 102–103). While Marcuse does not
engage these points—though one could return to his 1959 review of Popper's

book or his "Thoughts on the Defense of Gracchus Babeuf" to imagine what he likely would have said—he leaves his audience with a response to the posed question of what "ultimate moral impulse animates the philosopher Herbert Marcuse in committing himself so much to radical politics":

> Commit? Look, for me this is not some special commitment. It comes quite naturally, quite spontaneously. I simply cannot think today without, as a matter of course, thinking about what is going on around me, about what is happening in the world. And, indeed, not only in my immediate surroundings, but in the ghettos of the United States, in Southeast Asia, Latin America, *everywhere that misery, cruelty, and repression stare one in the face.* Even if one doesn't want to look one feels it, reads of it, knows it. I wouldn't say it is a special commitment for me; it is the natural expression of my existence.
>
> MARCUSE and POPPER 1976: 101; emphasis added

Counterrevolution and Revolt (1972)

> For history indeed repeats itself; it is this repetition of domination and submission that must be halted, and halting it presupposes knowledge of its genesis and of the ways in which it is reproduced: critical thinking.
>
> MARCUSE 1972b: 56

Part 1: The Left under the Counterrevolution

Marcuse commences his 1972 volume *Counterrevolution and Revolt* by depicting a disturbing and honest portrait of the sordid means which capital and the State had been taking up at that time in defense of the established system: repeating the horrors of Nazism, the transnational capitalist class engages in massacres in Vietnam, Indonesia, "the Congo, Nigeria, Pakistan, and the Sudan" to suppress threatening movements and actions taken by those from below. Marcuse laments that much of Latin America has been subjected to Fascist dictatorship, commenting that a "constant flow of arms from the rich countries to the poor [ones] helps to perpetuate the oppression of national and social liberation." He plaintively recalls the hundreds of students murdered in October 1968 at the Plaza de las Tres Culturas in Mexico City, as well as those killed at Jackson State and Kent State universities in 1970, and he acknowledges some of the various Black militants similarly martyred around the turn of the decade: Malcolm X, Martin Luther King, Jr., Fred Hampton, and George Jackson. Marcuse uses all these repressive data points as evidence to suggest that Western capitalism has arrived at a new stage, one which corresponds to a preventive "organization of counterrevolution at home and abroad" that has been imposed to stave off even the remotest chances of the world's peoples engaging in thoroughgoing revolutionary upheaval (1972b: 1–2).

Breaking from his opening contemplation of the various negations of the rule of capital, Marcuse proceeds to consider its inversion. As in "The Movement in a New Age of Repression," Marcuse here describes the looming specter of revolution as holding out the chance of becoming the "most radical of all historical revolutions," for the prospect of a defeat of the U.S. establishment would likely result in the fall of its allied military dictatorships throughout the globe and the concomitant ascendancy of popular movements which would enact "long overdue radical social and economic changes" the world over. Reiterating the utopian goals he had been stressing at least since *Eros and Civilization*, Marcuse envisions a shift in the overdeveloped societies which overturns the Promethean tradition of fetishizing economic growth and industrial expansion, leading instead to the self-directed creation of a life-world that "would no longer perpetuate violence, ugliness, ignorance, and brutality." However, upon turning to an empirical evaluation of the question of whether there exist resistance trends in Western societies that could prefigure or even accelerate the coming of such world-historical changes, Marcuse declares that little such revolutionary potential exists. Nonetheless, he expresses a determinate rejection of the views he had held a decade prior, claiming now that capitalism in fact *extends* the potential "mass base" for revolution—this, by entrenching alienation on the one hand and "generat[ing] needs which threaten to explode the capitalist framework" on the other (1972b: 2–3, 5–6).

In Marcuse's view, the *objective* grounds that call for the self-conscious abolition of capitalism should be plain for all to see—for the system lives on only "through the global destruction of resources, of nature, of human life"—yet the problem is that the *subjective* conditions, or the popular embrace of revolutionary analysis and orientation, are largely lacking in Western settings. Hence Marcuse's declaration that the "most necessary revolution appears as the most unlikely one," at least in the West. On the other hand, this static reality, taken at a cross-section in time, might be belied by the increasing tendency of monopoly capitalism to erode the former independence of the middle classes and so transform members of this class into "direct servants of capital," thus further expanding the "base of exploitation" beyond the traditional mass of blue-collar workers (1972b: 7, 9–10).

Through such considerations is seen the "universal servitude" and degradation of human dignity perpetuated by the ruling counterrevolution—which has by this time cast off "all pretensions of truth and justice" in favor of continuing its brutal operations quite openly. Marcuse observes that the U.S. police evermore resemble the S.S. in appearance and in action, particularly considering their suppression of student activists and "black and brown militants," especially members of the Black Panther Party. While the critical theorist adds to his reflections on police brutality contemplation of the pervasive surveillance methods and the subordination of Congress before the Executive and the military, he does clarify that the prevailing Nixon administration cannot be considered a fascist regime, yet he worries that its contributions to the preventive counterrevolution might in fact make more likely the future coming of Fascism. Marcuse certainly expresses concern over the existence of a "proto-fascist syndrome" among parts of the U.S. populace at large, pointing as evidence to the "almost religious identification" made by many with the murderous Lt. Calley, overseer of the 1968 My Lai massacre, and he cites an interview conducted with the mother of one of the students shot at Kent State, who wholeheartedly embraces the National Guard's use of force against student protestors. Marcuse observes that monopoly capitalism has developed a "frightening reservoir of violence" in everyday U.S. society, given the military's resort to "overkill" and its training for genocide, the "normalization of war crimes," and the brutalization of "vast prison population[s]." Within this disconcerting context, Marcuse claims an "effectively organized radical Left" to be humanity's sole hope, and though he claims that the prospect of a future fascist takeover would itself be incapable of entirely suppressing the coming of revolution for all time, the fear is that it could do so indefinitely—perhaps for an exceedingly long time. The chance for libertarian socialism against looming totalitarianism will in this sense ultimately depend on consciousness, freedom, and will: as Rosa Luxemburg declared amidst the depths of the First World War, the liberatory alternative of socialism remains a choice to be consciously instituted (1972b: 14, 24–29).

Following from his study of and personal engagement with the New Left movements, Marcuse dedicates some of his attention in *Counterrevolution and Revolt* to examining the status of the radical opposition in the advanced-industrial societies of the West—much as he had done with "Cultural Revolution" and "The Movement in a New Age of Repression." Noting the New Left to have advanced the most utopian and radical countervalues and proposals toward the end of impelling qualitative social change in the West, Marcuse situates its relative isolation from the workers and people at large in U.S.

society as following from the very radicality of its demands. For one, the *new sensibility* developed by New Left activists represents a shocking condemnation not only of Establishment culture but also of conventional working-class culture—thus, for the great mass of people, it takes on an alien, "elitarian" character. What is more, this veritable gap between militant minority and people in general reflects the marked lack of societal familiarity with Marxian and anti-authoritarian thought and praxis in the first place; it does not help that the qualitative difference between the status quo and social liberation is obscured within the minds of most people, the encouraging resort to wildcat strikes and factory occupations among an avant-garde of workers notwithstanding. In a manner reminiscent of Marcuse's days with the Frankfurt School in the 1930s and early 1940s, the writer suggests that Marxian theory can represent a *reservoir* of promise, even within a non- or pre-revolutionary setting (1972b: 21, 29–33).

The remainder of the political analysis the critical theorist offers in *Counterrevolution and Revolt* revolves around questions of militant strategy. Marcuse emphasizes the importance of increasing the number of left sympathizers in U.S. society, organizing a broad-based struggle against capital from "all dependent classes," and promoting libertarian cultural transformation through extra-parliamentary radicalization of producers, *lumpens,* and intelligentsia. Quoting Luxemburg, indeed, Marcuse announces that the subordinated population will radicalize itself "by extirpating to the last root its old habits of *obedience and servility*" (emphasis added). In place of the traditionally favored tactic of a seizure of State power, Marcuse endorses decentralizing tendencies which he sees as serving to disrupt production and provoke radical cascades resulting in the "serious dysfunctioning of the whole" altogether. He thus hails the return of the council system as a popular alternative to the previous model of mass-bureaucratic parties and insists that the demand for direct democracy must be central to all leftist politics (1972b: 39–45). Marcuse overall welcomes the trend toward workers' control and the popularity of the slogan "All Power to the People," but he clarifies that the revolutionary potential of both causes depends upon the self-transformation of the people themselves within the process of struggle:

> the majority of the people are *de facto distinct from* and *apart from* their government [...]. [T]his goal [of self-government] *pre*supposes a radical change in the needs and consciousness of the people. The people who have the power to liberate themselves would not be the same people, the same human beings, who today reproduce the status quo—even if they are the same individuals (1972b: 46).

Marcuse here strongly warns against any fragmentation or compartment-
alization of the anti-systemic struggle: in a manner reminiscent of Adorno,
Bakunin, and Simone de Beauvoir alike, he writes that there can be "no revolution without individual liberation, but also no individual liberation without
the liberation of society." Recalling "Repressive Tolerance," Marcuse defends
confrontational "educational" actions like Jonathan Jackson's 1970 armed
takeover of the Marin County courthouse—though he does not name
Jackson by name—in addition to occupations of destructive institutions and
the heckling of individual apologists for imperial war and aggression. Importantly, however, Marcuse here observes that martyrdom has not greatly aided
the cause of political transformation in historical terms, adding that the revolutionary suicide theorized by Huey P. Newton "remains suicide." Nevertheless,
he acknowledges that it would be "self-righteous indifference" to demand that
revolutionaries continue living rather than die for the cause—this would be
"an insult to the Communards of all times." Like Camus in *The Rebel*, then,
Marcuse here reiterates his defense of revolutionary counter-violence, for, as
he writes, the "desperate [violent] act" may "for a brief moment tear the veil
of justice and expose the faces of brutal suppression," and even "arouse the
conscience of the neutrals." On principle, Marcuse declares all pacifistic and
absolute denials of the resort to counter-violence as functioning to "condemn
the victims of the system to the prolonged agony of waiting" and "prolonged
suffering." As a piercing form of resisting the misery and despair imposed on
the people, revolutionary force seeks to overthrow violence altogether, argues
Marcuse, and he suggests that one of the most menacing forms such force
could take in prevailing society would be the *unlimited general strike* (1972b:
48, 52–53).

In general terms, Marcuse recommends a "United Front" strategy to build
up counter-institutions, and he endorses Rudi Dutschke's call for radical youth
to engage in a *long march through the institutions* as a means of extending
the radical base. While the endorsement of such tactics may seem a highly
perplexing position for the critical theorist to take—if one reflects on the militant direction of Marcuse's overall argument in this text—it is worth returning to the clarifications provided by the public intellectual in "The Movement
in a New Era of Repression." In this address, he argues that the call for the
"long march" in no way implies an accommodation with "the deadly game of
parliamentary democracy," but should instead be taken as an affirmation of
the importance of learning how prevailing institutions operate "on the job,"
in preparation for their liberatory reconstruction after the revolution (1972b:
55–56; 2004: 151–152).

Part 3: Art and Revolution and Conclusion

In the third and fourth sections of *Counterrevolution and Revolt,* Marcuse discusses the developments in cultural revolution he believed could make for possible future political revolution. The "radically nonconformist" goals sought by revolutionaries in the contemporary world demand equally dissident forms of communication, or art, by which Marcuse means music and literature. Marcuse here argues that works of art contain the ability to symbolize alternatives to regnant one-dimensional society, at least temporarily and through illusion (*Schein*). For Marcuse, authentic art expresses the desire for *sensuous culture* and the radical emancipation of the senses—it *"strikes at the roots of capitalism* in the individuals themselves" (emphasis added). Defining some of the parameters of the instrumental rationality that have served as the very underpinnings of capitalist society, having systematically "militated against libertarian tendencies, debased sex, discriminated against women, and imposed repression for the sake of God and business," Marcuse identifies bourgeois intellectual culture as advancing ideology based on philosophical Idealism. Yet he declares that the dominance of classical bourgeois culture has by this time in the early 1970s disintegrated to a certain degree, given the turn to "super-Orwellianism as normal communication" and the stipulated historical decline of paternal power within the nuclear family—and as the dialectical inversion of such trends, Marcuse considers the work of a number of artists from bourgeois modernity: Bertolt Brecht, Eugène Delacroix, and Pablo Picasso, for example. Reflecting on ancient Greek and medieval European art, the critical aesthetician here speculates that the timelessness of literature and music reflects the centrality of the place of beauty within the human imagination, and he suggests that tragic art embodies the permanent revolution for "secular liberation" and human happiness, the "promise of liberation" (79–82, 84–89).

Reflecting on the parameters of his mature aesthetic theory, Marcuse acknowledges that these late views of his on art contradict his earlier ones rather significantly, particularly considering the highly negative critique he had made of the "Affirmative Character of Culture" some thirty-five years before. Still, as he observes,

> There is no work of art which does not break its affirmative stance by the 'power of the negative,' which does not, in its very structure, evoke the words, the images, the music of another reality, of another order repelled by the existing one and yet *alive in memory and anticipation,* alive in *what*

happens to men and women, and in *their rebellion against it* (1972b: 92; emphasis added).

Much like Adorno, Marcuse remarks that the strength of the grip of reaction over the present enhances the importance of art as a cipher of the "images and tones" that could "break through the established universe of discourse and preserve the future." Revolutionary art thus can "ope[n] the established reality to another dimension": that of an emancipated world no longer dominated by the "forces of repression." Shakespeare's tragedies in particular communicate to Marcuse the hope for the end of all violence; they demonstrate that truth is to be found "in the beauty, tenderness, and passion of the victims, and not in the rationality of their oppressors." On the individual level, the experience of literary pieces and musical works aids the human being to resist instrumental rationality by facilitating recollection and invoking alternatives to the present: as in the symphonies of Gustav Mahler, art can recall "the voice, beauty, calm of another world here on earth." Commenting on the broadly world-historical meaning of phantasy and creativity, Marcuse posits that, "[i]f art dreams of liberation within the spectrum of history, dream realization through revolution must be possible." The point is for the dreams, sleeping and waking, to take on a radical political character (1972b: 87, 92–95, 100, 102).

Within these reflections on aesthetics, Marcuse also provides insightful comments on his view of the art-works associated with contemporary rebellion. In this sense, he declares that art cannot directly "represent" revolution but can only "invoke it in another medium." With this consideration in mind, Marcuse expresses his distaste for white "rock," which he holds to stand for "performance" and profit-schemes, as rock audiences undergo a group therapy of sorts which "temporarily" removes inhibitions and privatizes liberation. In contrast, he considers folk art, including Black musical traditions, to represent a subversive language alongside the high art of literature and paintings: Beethoven and the blues to "help suffering [humanity]." In addition to Black music, Marcuse claims Black poetry to be similarly radical, for it gives voice to "total rebellion" and speaks to the universal demand of respect for human life. Indeed, Marcuse here asserts that art's fate is "linked to that of the revolution," and that an "internal exigency [...] drives the artist to the street—to fight for the Commune [...and] for all revolutions which have the historical chance of liberation." Revolutionary art will always oppose itself to "affirmative, integrated, blunted" cultural forms—for it symbolizes the *"rupture, the leap"* (1972b: 80, 104, 112–115, 122, 125, 127–128).

In his conclusion to *Counterrevolution and Revolt,* Marcuse criticizes cultural radicals for their tendency undialectically to condemn the concept of reason as being inextricably linked to bourgeois society, though he lauds these radicals' stress on developing means of self-determination and exercises in non-alienated social relations, in addition to their emphasis on the importance of nature in the political struggle. He emphasizes the "vital need for total transformation," amidst the "repulsive unity of opposites" seen in daily life under capital: the symbiosis between "the erotic play of the sea [...] and the booming death industries at its shores, between the flight of the white birds and that of the gray air force jets, between the silence of the night and the vicious farts of the motorcycles..." Marcuse underscores the need to fuse politics and aesthetics, reason and sensibility, toward the end of radical activism, a project which he feels should not shy away from expressing hatred "against all that which is inhuman." Affirming the continued relevance of the analysis from *One-Dimensional Man,* he remarks that the subordinated continue to identify with their leaders, given that the authorities "still deliver the goods" and—as seen in the fate of Che Guevara and the Mexican students at Tlatelolco—periodically massacre "the enemies who threaten the continued delivery of these goods." Invoking Brecht, who famously identified the seeming criminality of merely "talk[ing] about a tree" within bourgeois society, Marcuse observes that it now seems "a crime merely to *talk* about change while one's society is transformed into an institution of violence, terminating in Asia the genocide which began with the liquidation of the American Indians." Echoing his prior analyses of the suffocating reality, Marcuse declares that praxis will be far more effective than discourse in working to topple the powers overseeing such genocidal trends. He closes by suggesting that the fate of this end-goal will depend on the ability of the youth to sustain a resilient and protracted struggle against the Establishment—for the fall of capitalism, he announces, "may take all but a century" (1972b: 129–130, 133–134).

Marcuse's Late Championing of Feminism

Late in life, as the women's liberation movement gained prominence in Western societies, Marcuse came to consider feminism as a novel and increasingly critical and radical source of resistance to domination and capital; notably, he concurs with feminist theorists in their stress on patriarchy as underpinning the capitalist system. Marcuse first expresses his views on feminism in "The Emancipation of Women in a Repressive Society" (1962), as we have seen, while he comes to embrace the women's liberation movement in "A Revolution in Values." Significantly, the critical theorist develops his view of the revolutionary relevance of the movement in *Counterrevolution and Revolt,* and especially in his 1974 address "Marxism and Feminism." As will be readily evident to the reader, Marcuse's interpretation of feminism does contain questionable formulations, as seen in his ambivalent essentialization of gender, yet it is highly radical in its endorsement of androgyny and its tying together of women's liberation with general societal emancipation, as seen in the concept of "feminist socialism."

Beyond "A Revolution in Values," Marcuse provides some fragmentary analysis of his take on the feminist potential at the end of the second part of *Counter-revolution and Revolt,* "Nature and Revolution." He associates the "*destructive* productivity" which capital has imposed on the life-world with a ruling "male principle" and thus suggests—while bordering on gender essentialism—that a liberated society would be a "*female* society" governed by Eros rather than Thanatos. As in his more systematic treatment of these questions in "Marxism and Feminism," Marcuse here declares the women's liberation movement to represent a hopeful development in terms of the project of decisively transforming the instinctual structure of individuals from patriarchal aggressivity to erotic pacification. In essentialist terms, indeed, Marcuse goes so far as to suggest that, between male and female, a *natural* contrast exists, such that it is the woman who "'embodies,' in a literal sense, the promise of peace, of joy, of the end of violence"—though a couple of lines later, he concedes that for observers to locate this image itself in the female sex may have more to do with their own socialization under capital and patriarchal rule than with any truth-claim. Nevertheless, in socio-historical terms, Marcuse finds something of a reservoir of emancipatory potential in women, given his view that, due to their stipulated isolation from the productive sphere—the supposed realm of men—women have been "less brutalized by the Performance Principle" and so may remain "closer to [their] sensibility." Rather strangely, though, Marcuse then suggests that men may be more dehumanized than women, since they "suffer not only the conveyor belt and assembly line but also the standards and 'ethics' of the 'business community'" (1972b: 74–75, 77). Given such a comment, it would seem that the critical theorist had not reflected adequately on de Beauvoir's work, among that of others, before penning such lines. Yet he continues with his identification of women as a promising "counter-force" to the established patriarchal-capitalist system, importantly calling them one of its potential "gravediggers," and he concludes this section of his 1972 volume with an affirming analysis of Delacroix's *Liberty Leading the People* (1830):

> In this sense too, the woman holds the promise of liberation. It is the woman who, in Delacroix's painting, holding the flag of the revolution, leads the people on the barricades. She wears no uniform; her breasts are

bare, and her beautiful face shows no trace of violence. But she has a rifle in her hand—for the end of violence is still to be fought for... (1972b: 78).

"Marxism and Feminism," a lecture Marcuse gave at Stanford University in March 1974, presents the revolutionary promise he sees in the feminist movement as well as his advocacy of *feminist socialism* and the androgynous ideal. Marcuse opens this address by stating that women's liberation may well be "the most important and potentially the most radical political movement that we have" at present. He states his commonality with the feminist movement in holding that a specific movement for women's liberation is "justified" and "necessary" due to the specific and very real repression imposed upon women over the historical course of patriarchal civilization. Against bourgeois feminism, Marcuse argues that the true goals of women's liberation can be achieved only through a revolution that would do away with capitalism and all other forms of class society in favor of a new, emancipatory reality principle that would overturn "the established dichotomy between masculine and feminine." As feminist, the socialist concept which aims at a qualitative change in social relations must represent the very *antithesis* of the "aggressive and repressive needs and values of capitalism as a form of *male-dominated culture*" (emphasis added). In this sense, Marcuse sees great potential for the traditionally understood feminine qualities of "receptivity, sensitivity, non-violence, [and] tenderness" to assist in the struggle against patriarchal-capitalist Thanatos. Anticipating accusations of gender essentialism, Marcuse then clarifies that the "feminine characteristics" are socially conditioned rather than naturally or biologically based—yet he qualifies this statement in suggesting that, due to the thousands of years of social conditioning under male supremacy, women at present do in fact represent a potent wellspring of anti-systemic resistance (2004: 165–168).

Marcuse proceeds to discuss a few fascinating historical examples of premodern European feminism, as in the emphasis on autonomy for women and eroticism found in the medieval concept of romantic love. Within the European context, Marcuse finds these developments to have constituted the "first great protests" against the established feudal hierarchies; he mentions Elinor d'Aquitaine's Courts of Love, which "practically always" ruled in favor of the autonomous right of love as against the hegemonically recognized rights of the feudal lord to maintain social control. Marcuse also notes that it "was a woman" who reportedly commanded the defense of the last Albigensian fortress "against the murderous armies of the northern barons" during the Crusade launched against the Cathar religious sect in the thirteenth century. Passing to the present, the critical theorist notes the importance of "Women and Capitalism," a paper Angela Davis had written while incarcerated in Palo

Alto, for it theorizes a revolutionary role for women as the definite negation of the capitalist performance principle. Marcuse then integrates such perspectives into a critique of the classical Marxian concept, which he notes here, as in "Re-Examination of the Concept of Revolution," to retain key aspects of the performance principle—the stress on the development of the productive forces, for example, in addition to the "progressive" exploitation of nature, and so on. He then counterposes the feminist-socialist concept as an alternative. Beyond the helpful role it would foreseeably play in yielding a blossoming of the myriad libertarian-socialist characteristics of the future society that Marcuse has previously delineated, this feminist socialism would expressly emphasize the attainment of full equality for women and the all-round development of their faculties, and as such, Marcuse argues that it would universalize the values which previously had been considered "specifically feminine," thus leading men and women to be synthesized into the "legendary" androgynous ideal (2004: 168–171).

Marcuse concludes his reflections on women's liberation in this intervention by reiterating his claim that the grounds for believing that feminism can become a disruptive and revolutionary force to be justified, though he cautions that future liberation will not result from merely formal changes to existing social institutions but must instead be produced through ongoing radical struggle at the individual and interpersonal levels. In this way, he clearly acknowledges that sexism could well continue under post-capitalist conditions. To prevent such a repressive outcome, the feminist movement must be *"aggressive,"* suggests Marcuse, and men will have to "pay for the sins of a patriarchal civilization and its tyranny of power." He closes by observing that the transition to feminist socialism will for heterosexual males constitute a process "permeated with bitter conflicts, torment and suffering," particularly in erotic terms—yet it will in the end represent a vitally important step for human liberation (166, 170–172).

International Relations: Vietnam and Israel/Palestine

As during all the previous decades of his adult life, Marcuse in his final years continued to study international affairs and intervene publicly toward the end of ameliorating suffering on the global stage. In this way, he continued the active resistance he had taken up against the Vietnam War in the previous decade by writing a disconcerting analysis of the popular reaction to the 1971 military conviction of Lt. William Calley, the u.s. commander who oversaw the horrendous My Lai massacre of 1968, and by integrating concern

for the ongoing war into other addresses, including the public comments
he made before the media in Frankfurt on the occasion of Angela Davis' acquittal in June 1972, as well as in his direct response to the war-wongering
presented by Secretary of State Henry Kissinger in the latter's December 1972
press-conference on the prospect of peace with the Vietnamese. In addition,
Marcuse visited historical Palestine with Inge in late 1971 to appraise the ongoing conflict between the Israelis and Palestinians and other Arabs. As shall be
demonstrated, though, Marcuse's take on Israel, while in part humanistic and
sympathetic to the plight of the Palestinians, is less consistently decolonial in
comparison with his view of the Vietnam War, in light of the critical theorist's
Zionist belief in the legitimacy of the Jewish State, its numerous crimes against
the Indigenous Palestinian population notwithstanding.

In "Reflections on Calley," written for the *New York Times* some weeks after
the lieutenant's conviction and sentencing to life imprisonment, Marcuse
announces his alarm at the "obscene haste" and "massive rush" with which
many U.S. officials and ordinary citizens alike expressed their outrage at the
military tribunal's decision, blindly defending the convicted war criminal.
The critical theorist finds this reactionary popular reaction especially disconcerting, given that it was not the result of any mobilization from above, but
"entirely spontaneous: an outburst of the unconscious" (Marcuse 2004: 51).
Starkly illustrating this phenomenon, historian Claude Cooke finds in a retrospective study published in 2007 that a full four-fifths of the U.S. populace
disagreed with the court's decision and found the sentence too harsh, and he
reveals moreover that, of the five thousand telegrams sent to the Nixon White
House in response to the conviction, the ratio calling for leniency was 100 to
1 (Cooke 2007: 154–162). It was this overwhelming response of repudiation
of responsibility for My Lai that led a disturbed Marcuse to declare Calley's
supporters to be "men and women madly in love with death, violence and
destruction."

> The silent majority has its hero: a convicted war criminal—convicted of
> killing at close range, smashing the head of a 2-year-old child; a killer in
> whose defense it was said that he did not feel that he was killing 'humans,'
> a killer who did not express regret for his deeds; he only obeyed orders
> and killed only 'dinks' or 'gooks' or 'V.C.'
>
> MARCUSE 2004: 51

In a parallel to his analysis of the "Inner Logic of American Policy in Vietnam,"
Marcuse here systematically examines the various rationalizations offered by
Calley's "worshippers" in defense of the actions of the murderous lieutenant,

observing these attempts at justification to contradict the very international rules governing warfare by which Calley was convicted—and indeed, to effectively legitimize the genocidal nature of the war against Vietnam. He even points out that other soldiers present at the massacre refused to go along with its prosecution, though he does not mention them by name—though the example of the helicopter pilot Hugh Thompson, Jr., who landed his vehicle between Calley's men and surviving Vietnamese and subsequently reported the atrocity through official channels, comes to mind. In addition, Marcuse dispatches the commonly employed argument that "society" rather than Calley was to blame for the My Lai massacre by arguing that, though Calley's superiors in the State and military hierarchy do bear responsibility for the crime, this reality in no way absolves Calley's individual responsibility for the hundreds of murders he committed and oversaw (2004: 51–52).

Broadly speaking, Marcuse in this article expresses his concern with the fascist potential which the reactionary popular mobilizations in Calley's defense represented to him. He raises the pressing question of whether the "sense of guilt turn[s] into its opposite: into the proud, sado-masochistic identification with the crime and the criminal?" In his concluding comments on the call made by some u.s. liberals for "compassion" for Calley, moreover, Marcuse essentially points out the reigning proto-fascism on hand in u.s. society: "Once again, we are confronted with that principle of *diseased justice* which was pronounced at Kent State and which expresses so neatly the perversion of the sense of guilt: 'not the murderer but the murdered one is guilty'" (2004: 53; emphasis added).

Marcuse also spoke out on Vietnam in the public statement he made to the press in Frankfurt following Angela Davis' acquittal in June 1972. Addressing a large crowd outside the Opera House, he links Davis' communist commitment to Black liberation to the general struggle against the Vietnam War, which evinces the "complete terrorism of late monopoly capitalism." Reiterating themes from before, particularly in "Repressive Tolerance," Marcuse argues that the extreme violence on hand in Vietnam is but the outer limit of the "normal" violence seen domestically in u.s. society, particularly as exercised in the interests of white supremacy. In this sense, brutality in the u.s. and in Southeast Asia are mutually reinforcing, just as the pollution of the environment at home mirrors the "total, systematic destruction" of the ecology of Vietnam. Optimistically, and presciently, Marcuse declares in his comments that the u.s. will fail in its war, and he sees the genocide as a stark illumination of the reactionary priorities of u.s. foreign policy, which are to suppress and terrorize all struggles for liberation, whether they be waged in Asia, Africa, Latin America, or at home (2014: 216–217).

In late 1972, Marcuse would write a short response to Henry Kissinger's December press-conference regarding peace negotiations with the North Vietnamese, which in fact broke down, yielding the infamous "Christmas bombing" of Hanoi—the single heaviest episode of aerial bombardments in the history of the war, involving 129 B-52 bombers—that had commenced the day before Marcuse penned this reaction. Describing Kissinger's presentation as an "Orwellian nightmare," Marcuse takes the criminal functionary and the Nixon administration as a whole to task for escalating the war, on the pretext that the North Vietnamese had been amassing troops in the country's south in the previous months. He frames the administration's line of thought as convenient and highly ideological, in light of the simultaneous intensification of bombing-campaigns and mass-transfers of matériel undertaken by the U.S. military. Marcuse upbraids the racism exhibited by Kissinger, who at a certain point in the press-conference ventures to suggest psychologically that the Vietnamese people would appear to prefer to continue the war than to face the "risks and perils of peace." In response, Marcuse notes acidly that the "eye witness reports on the burned villages of Vietnam and the mutilated remains of their inhabitants do not exactly support Kissinger's speculations." The critical theorist then takes media complicity in the war effort to task, juxtaposing the affirmative claims of a *Los Angeles Times* reporter that Nixon had been working to "wind down" the war effort, when in fact the president was executing the Christmas bombardment. Marcuse closes these reflections by referring to the U.S. populace, who either know or could *come to know* what is happening in Southeast Asia, yet would seemingly prefer to guard silence and continue with the normalcy of work, business, and the celebration of the holiday season. Marcuse thus argues that the people have "*abdicated*," and that their silence is louder than the propaganda of the State and mainstream media, for "it speaks the truth about this society" (2014: 332–334; emphasis added).

Turning to another contemporary conflict similarly characterized by militarism and neo-colonialism, Marcuse visited historical Palestine with Inge in late 1971 to assess the prevailing situation in the region first-hand and thus make recommendations in terms of a possible resolution of the antagonistic relations between Israel and the Palestinians, as between Israel and the surrounding Arab world. Once again, while Marcuse would develop a critique of Israeli policy toward the Palestinians and other Arabs in this visit to the region, his humanist perspective is certainly tempered by his sympathies with the Zionist project: as he had expressed briefly in a discussion on Vietnam held in Berlin in July 1967—that is to say, just a month after Israel had expanded its territory through the conquest of the West Bank, the Gaza Strip, the Sinai Peninsula, and the Golan Heights in the Six-Day War—Marcuse declared a strong "identification" and "solidarity" with the Jewish State. The philosopher cites Sartre's pro-Israeli position as equivalent to his own, and he moreover declares that the "State [of Israel] is a solid fact," thus betraying his lifelong opposition to positivism. Unfortunately, he would carry this perspective through to his visit to historical Palestine and even affirm it to the very end of his life—though it is true that his foundational enthusiasm for Israel would repeatedly be tempered by recognition of the atrocities committed against the Palestinians during the establishment of the Jewish State, as continuously thereafter (1980b: 141–142).

Marcuse's take on Israel is thus divided between two competing loyalties: chauvinist identification and revolutionary solidarity. As an illustration of this dynamic, the critical theorist claims the founding of the State of Israel to have represented a conscious effort to "prevent a recurrence of the concentration camps, the pogroms, and other forms of persecution and discrimination" targeting world Jewry. It is for this reason that Marcuse thinks Israel's founding formed "part of the struggle for liberty and equality for all persecuted racial and national minorities the world over" (Marcuse 2004: 54). Similarly in this sense, as a response to the Soviet State's increasing persecution and harassment of Jews, Marcuse in early 1971 signed an appeal to Premier Alexei Kosygin which called on him to allow Soviet Jews facing discrimination to be allowed to leave the USSR for resettlement in Israel or "the land of their choice" (Jewish Telegraphic Agency 1971). According to Richard Popkin, Marcuse's willingness to sign his name to this petition led to a flaring of tensions between the critical theorist and Inge, who Popkin describes as having adhered to a "very anti-Zionist" position (Sethness Castro 2013). In point of fact, as Inge likely recognized, it does not seem that Marcuse's call for emigration of Jews from the USSR to Israel was particularly sensitive to the repercussions such new migratory flows could have on the lives of Palestinians under occupation, in terms of the progressive dispossession of Indigenous land and the concomitant strengthening of the Israeli State.

Marcuse's thirteen-day visit with Inge to former Palestine at the end of 1971 and the beginning of 1972 was motivated largely by the couple's desire to examine the Arab-Israeli conflict with their own eyes, though it ultimately found its basis in Marcuse's acceptance of an invitation from the Van Leer Jerusalem Institute to present two addresses on aesthetics and politics at this time, the product of which was "The Jerusalem Lectures." During their time in Israel, Marcuse and Inge met with Knesset representative Moshe Sneh, a former member of the Zionist Haganah paramilitary grouping who by the 1950s had come to identify as a communist, as well as Amoz Oz, a member of the Hulda kibbutz and a peace activist, and Elizier Be'eri, who was affiliated with the

Socialist-Zionist United Workers' Party (Tauber 2012: 171–184). However, rather than limit themselves only to engaging with Israel and Israelis, the dyad also traveled to Nablus to discuss matters with Palestinian intellectuals under occupation, including the Nabulsi mayor, Hamdi Kanaan. Raymonda Hawa Tawil—a Palestinian militant journalist known as the "Lion of Nablus" whose daughter Souha would later marry Yassir Arafat—paraphrases Marcuse during these discussions as saying that, though he "had always felt sympathy toward Jews suffering persecution," he "could find no sympathy for Jews who persecute others" (Hawa Tawil 1979: 231–232). Given this statement which Marcuse shared with his Palestinian counterparts, it is rather perplexing to consider that he requested a meeting on this trip with Israeli Defense Minister Moshe Dayan. This request was granted and consummated a few days before the philosopher published his impressions of the political situation in Israel/Palestine in *The Jerusalem Post.* It is intriguing to reflect that contemplation of Marcuse's meeting with Dayan has been greatly neglected in most if not all Marcuse scholarship—perhaps thus echoing the philosopher's own self-consciousness about initiating a face-to-face discussion with the "hero" of the 1967 occupation war, a general who in 1966 also had paid a friendly visit to U.S. troops in Vietnam (Tauber 2012: 176).

With at least one glaring exception, however, the transcript of the conversation Marcuse had with Dayan does not suggest an overwhelming commonality of opinion between the two—for indeed, Marcuse would implicitly criticize the perspectives of the Zionist leadership in the *Jerusalem Post* essay that would come out a few days later. The major lapse in reason betrayed by Marcuse in this discussion comes near the outset, when Dayan asks, "what wrong did we [Israelis] commit in June '67?" Uncritically accepting the Zionist line, Marcuse responds by saying that he didn't think "you did any wrong," and he clarifies that he believes the Six-Day War to have been a "defensive" conflict for Israel—however vastly mistaken he is on both such points. Most of the rest of the conversation between Marcuse and Dayan has to do with the philosopher's inquiries regarding the possibilities of Israel withdrawing from the Sinai, accepting the demilitarization of the peninsula, and undertaking active peace negotiations with its Arab neighbors, particularly Egypt and Syria. In fact, Marcuse suggests to Dayan on three separate occasions that Israeli intransigence vis-à-vis its neighbors greatly increases the probability of another future war—a warning that would prove prescient, in light of the Yom Kippur War that would come less than two years after this discussion took place. Moreover, Marcuse expresses his surprise at Dayan's candor after the general explicitly acknowledges that the Zionist project effectively has "cut the two parts of the Arabic [*sic*] world off from one another"—this, by taking an

"Arabic land and ma[king] it Jewish." Marcuse declares that Dayan is the first Israeli he has met who has admitted as much. For Dayan's part, the Defense Minister shares a number of claims with Marcuse that roundly anticipate the mindlessly authoritarian "progression" of Zionism to date: he argues that it is "imperative" that the Palestinian educational system "stop preaching venom" in terms of Israel and its Jewish citizens; he rejects any proposed solution based on "small border corrections"; he rhetorically inquires why Jews should not be able to "settle in the whole area of what was once the Land of Israel"; he demands that the Palestinians accept Israel as a Jewish State and Jerusalem as a Jewish city, and that they give up on the right of the refugees to return; he declares his belief that the "key" to any solution is to "make a change of *motivation* among the Arabs" rather than to redistribute and return land and territory; and he paternalistically observes that negotiations with the Palestinians and other Arabs will come in due time, when the Jewish State is ready to do so (Dayan and Marcuse 2012: 186–190).

In "Israel is Strong Enough to Concede," published on January 2, 1972, in *The Jerusalem Post*, Marcuse details his various criticisms of mainstream Zionism. Considering the critical line he presents in this article, it is to be surmised that Inge's contributions to the argumentation of the essay were substantial. Reflecting on the very establishment of Israel, Marcuse openly acknowledges that a great "injustice" was done to the Indigenous Palestinians: born through the Palestinians' displacement, the power of Zionist settler-colonialism has "proceeded without the rights and interests of the native population" in mind. For Marcuse, then, Israel's genesis was "not essentially different form the origins of practically all states in history: establishment by conquest, occupation, discrimination." In light of the historically novel reality that the majority of the Palestinian population now lives under Israeli control—excluding the refugees who had fled, of course—Marcuse straightforwardly declares Israel an occupying power and the Palestinian liberation movement a "national liberation movement." He thus declares his solidarity with the latter, implicitly tying it to his established support for the Vietnamese resistance and all other Southern peoples fighting against imperialism. Delineating his practical recommendations for a reduction of tensions toward the goal of a Middle East free of war, Marcuse in this article calls for a peace treaty among Israel, Egypt, and Syria that would entail the latter's recognition of Israel, the demilitarization of the Sinai Peninsula and the Gaza Strip, as well as a "settlement" of Palestinian refugees, whether that would take place in pre-1948 Palestine or in a Palestinian State existing alongside Israel. Though the Jewish Marxist's terms for peace include full Western access to the Suez Canal, Marcuse's vision goes far beyond the standard liberal-colonialist tripe of his day and our own, for he argues that the shape and direction of a future Palestinian State must be decided through the self-determination of the Palestinian people—specifically, through a United Nations-supervised referendum on the question. With reference to Jerusalem, as with the Sinai, Marcuse calls for it to become a unified city under "international administration and protection"—presumably, again, under the guise of the UN. In sum, Marcuse considers his recommendations an "interim solutions" to the Arab-Israeli conflict, and he ultimately expresses hope for an "optimal solution" whereby Arabs and Jews would someday live together as "equal partners" in a Middle Eastern "socialist federation" (Marcuse 2004: 54–56). These utopian hopes aside, it bears mentioning that Marcuse's endorsement of a two-state solution was something of an unprecedented perspective at this time. The Soviet Union and the Israeli Communist Party would come to adopt such a position only years after Marcuse suggested it (Tauber 2012: 180–181; 2013: 131–132).

In a 1977 interview with the UCSD Jewish student publication *L'Chayim,* moreover, Marcuse reiterates many of the points he had made at the close of his trip to former Palestine, yet with a greater emphasis on the more Zionist aspects of his view. He clarifies that he disagrees with religiously based Zionism, considering the relation between Jewish dominion in Israel and the notion of the "Chosen People" to be a racist concept, but he incredulously tells the Jewish students that a secular Zionism would not be racist. He expressly asserts that the "solution to the Jewish Problem" would be a "Jewish state which can defend itself"—though he observes that Israel at present does not meet this criterion, given its ongoing difficulties with its Arab neighbors—and he entirely avoids the question of why the Jewish homeland could not be established somewhere other than in the pre-existing Arab land of Palestine. Responding to the question of whether Zionism and socialism are compatible, Marcuse claims that he can "easily imagine a socialist Israel," but he quickly clarifies that such a polity could in no way have a de facto military alliance with Apartheid South Africa, as Israel then did. Lastly, Marcuse stubbornly maintains that the first step to a solution to the Arab-Israeli conflict must be Arab recognition of Israel's right to exist: mirroring then-prevailing and now-current demands made by Zionists of all stripes, from the most reactionary to "progressive" ones, Marcuse insists that negotiations with the Palestinians cannot proceed as long as those occupied and dispossessed by Israel "feel that the destruction of Israel is a necessity" (Marcuse 2004: 180–182).

Continued Engagement with Aesthetics

In his final years of life, Marcuse continued developing his long-standing passion for aesthetics. Besides dedicating more than a third of the text of

Counterrevolution and Revolt to contemplation of art, as we have seen, Marcuse in his final decade presented two lectures on aesthetics and politics before Israeli audiences in West Jerusalem, engaged in a correspondence with a Surrealist grouping in Chicago, penned a poignant reflection on art after Auschwitz, and held a couple of significant interviews examining the place of art in the contemporary world.

In late December 1971, as part of his visit to historical Palestine with Inge, Marcuse gave two addresses at the Van Leer Jerusalem Foundation on art and philosophy. While many of the points the critical theorist made in these talks will be familiar to readers of this volume and as such need not be repeated, Marcuse does supply innovative ways of expressing himself in these lectures. For one, he notes the contributions made by Marx and the German Idealists in overturning the established hierarchical conception of the human mind in philosophy, which since Plato had privileged reason over imagination and sensibility. He also hails Kant's reconciliation of humanity and nature, as theorized in *The Critique of Judgment,* wherein the transcendental Idealist "discovers, or rather recaptures, the idea of nature as a subject in its own right" and indicates that natural beauty evinces "nature's capacity to form itself in its freedom also in an aesthetically purposeful way." Channelling Heidegger, Marcuse adds that the destruction of nature has "accompanie[d] the development of industrial society *from the beginning,*" and he argues that the liberation of nature from "repressive industrialization" constitutes an essential part of humanity's own emancipation. In the second lecture, Marcuse further observes that bourgeois literature has since the coming of the French Revolution expressed a "strong anti-bourgeois stance," as seen in its attacks on hypocritical morality, the concern for money, and the exploitation of women. In addition, he reiterates the call he has made previously for the abolition of the "elitist character of art" (Marcuse 2007: 152–154, 156, 162–164).

In a series of three letters written between October 1971 and March 1973, Marcuse carries out a correspondence with a Surrealist art collective based in Chicago. His introductory letter to the group is significant for the pleasure he expresses at the perceived convergence between the Surrealists' take on aesthetics and his own. In the first substantive letter he writes to his Chicago counterparts, he discusses a number of issues, including the role of the working classes and the relationship between art and revolution. Citing Marx's declaration that the workers are "revolutionary" or they are "nothing at all," Marcuse asserts that any possibility of placing art at the service of revolutionary social change presupposes an antagonistic subject that would pursue the true ends of art: that is, the overcoming of exploitation, the expansion of human freedom, and the reconciliation between humanity and nature. Marcuse leaves the question open as to whether the workers of the advanced-industrial societies will come to adopt such revolutionary ends; the analysis here is not closed, as in *One-Dimensional Man.* In this vein, indeed, Marcuse declares to the Surrealists that it is not "ideology" or "false interest" for workers to have humane living conditions, good food, and vacations (2007: 179–182).

Turning to consideration of aesthetics proper, Marcuse shares with his colleagues his view that art is "essentially tragic," that it should not be expected to serve affirmative ends—"and the proletariat is no Savior." Seemingly coming to moderate his views from *Eros and Civilization* and *An Essay on Liberation,* the critical theorist expresses skepticism regarding the idea that the id necessarily serves liberatory ends; perhaps with the mature Hegel's critique of anti-democratic popular movements in mind, he asserts unreservedly that the "cult of spontaneity has a long historical record of service to reactionary politics." Developing this thought, Marcuse suggests that, even under integral socialism, the associated individuals would have to engage in a modicum of the repression of desire—with the difference under such conditions being that this type of repression would be the result of autonomous deliberation rather than heteronomous imposition. As a contemporary model of reconstruction "from below," Marcuse expresses that he takes inspiration from the example of the "decentralized, largely autonomous industrialization of the Chinese Communes." He also reflects on his friend Benjamin's relatively optimistic view that a surrealist *shock character* ethic could help to undermine bourgeois culture and the society it upholds: Marcuse announces that the experience of Fascism has "dispelled this illusion," adding with a nod to the prevailing situation that "a society which easily absorbs genocide and geocide seems to be immune against shock in art" (2007: 185–187).

In his third letter to the Surrealists—the second one of substance, and the last—Marcuse continues sharing his ideas regarding aesthetics and revolution and the social position of the artist. Marcuse observes that authentic art is essentially autonomous and as such can have no well-defined or predetermined function vis-à-vis the cause of revolution—though all authentic art seeks social transformation. Explicitly endorsing Lenin's theory of the Party as an analogy, Marcuse declares that any contribution made by art to the end of revolutionary social change can be expected to come only *"from without"* the prevailing consciousness and existence of the masses." Returning to the concept of art as tragic, Marcuse reflects on the "grandeur" of Beethoven's symphonies, announcing that the "humanism which animated them" has been in essence refuted by the various brutalities of the twentieth century. In a similarly depressive-dialectical tone, Marcuse in this final letter acknowledges that, within the trajectory of the historical development of Western civilization, the production of art has largely been a privilege afforded to those freed from the need to toil—and he looks forward to such a time as when the social division of labor has been overturned, with the possibility for the "develop-ment of talent, genius, creativity among the people" thus broadened signifi-cantly (2007: 189–193).

Written in 1978, "Lyric Poetry after Auschwitz" presents Marcuse's emotive late reflections on Adorno's contentious claim that to compose poetry after Auschwitz would be a barbaric act (Adorno 1967: 19). Marcuse ultimately disagrees with his comrade's assertion, arguing instead that it is still possible to write poetry after the Holocaust, as long as poets somehow manage uncom-promisingly to give voice to the "horror that was—and still is." The critical theorist writes that the "cry," "despair," and "resistance" of the victims of the Nazi genocide can be preserved only in *memory*, and he observes that the pros-pect of literature's "legitimation" after Auschwitz is to be found in the chance of "preserv[ing] and develop[ing] the memory of those who did not have a chance," as well crucially as remembering "the many millions who [still] have no chance" at present. In this intervention, Marcuse readily rejects the obtuse idea that all of humanity is responsible for the fate of the European Jews, yet he claims that we all are responsible for remembering what happened to them, as for recognizing that genocide is "still happening in many areas of the globe," and that there exists no historical law which would prevent a recurrence of Auschwitz. Indeed, Marcuse grimly observes in this sense that the life-negating progression toward an "ever more efficient scientific-technological killing" apparatus points to the future likelihood of repeating rather than transcend-ing Auschwitz. With such considerations in mind, Marcuse closes by stress-ing that, just as the capitalist tendency toward genocide and destruction must not be excluded from aesthetic representation, neither must art succumb to despair in overlooking resistance to the imposed reality as an expression of the collective will to live. A legitimate synthesis is to be found, writes the critical theorist, in the possibility of an art that resists the providence of pleasure yet that appeals to the conscious and unconscious humanity of the work's audience (2007: 211–212, 215, 217).

In the 1978 interview with Larry Hartwick "On the Aesthetic Dimension," Marcuse discusses his major final work of the same name. As in the counter-part volume, wherein he writes that "[a]rt cannot change the world, but it can contribute to changing the consciousness and drives of the men and women who could change the world," Marcuse in this conversation argues that aes-thetics cannot itself directly contribute to the project of social change, but he claims that it can serve a preparatory function toward this end "via sev-eral negations and mediations," such as through the modulation of perception (Marcuse 1978b: 32–33; 2007: 220). Marcuse cites the Impressionist painters as a whole and Paul Cézanne in particular as illustrative examples of his claim.

Importantly, he raises the issue of Adorno's dialectical analysis of the alienation of aesthetics, whereby authentic art tends to take on an increasingly
alien and "estranged" character, the more authoritarian and repressive capitalism becomes, and he expresses the worry that art may on this account reach
such a point that it ceases to be able to communicate anything at all, thus
reducing itself to a mere "abstract negation." Recalling his recommendations
with regard to political language in "The Movement in a New Age of Repression," Marcuse here stresses that the Great Refusal in art must remain comprehensible. Speaking to the contradictions between the liberatory promise of art
and the highly unequal social conditions which inform aesthetic production,
Marcuse mentions the case of Mozart, who like many other artists produced
his works "for the nobility of his time." Despite this, Marcuse points out that
Mozart's music itself transcends and negates such a material and historical
relationship—Mozart wrote for all people, in essence. Very much like Adorno,
Marcuse concludes his conversation with Hartwick by noting that the "total
absence of all false hopes" seen in the literature of Samuel Beckett reflects the
profound need for thoroughgoing societal transformation to upend regnant
alienation and anomie (220, 223–224).

Lastly, in "The Philosophy of Art and Politics," an interview held with
Richard Kearney that was published posthumously in 1984, Marcuse presents
general comments on aesthetics as well as specific interpretations of prevailing musical art-forms. He opens by expressing a critique of Marx as positivist,
noting the German materialist's stress on exclusively economic considerations
to be reductive, and he instead emphasizes the importance of recovering Kant
and Schiller's analysis of aesthetics, the human imagination, and sensibility
for the advancement of revolution today. Transitioning to considerations of
aesthetics proper, Marcuse declares his view that authentic art is *negative,* or
critical of the established reality, and he identifies two means by which it can
express such negativity: by "giv[ing] asylum or refuge to defamed humanity"
and hence "preserv[ing] in another form an alternative to the 'affirmed' reality
of the establishment," or by *negating* this hegemonic reality by "denouncing
both it and the defamers of humanity who have affirmed it in the first place."
Authentic art, in this sense, serves activist purposes through its engagement
with society, its anticipation of the future, its criticism of the destruction
imposed by dominant relations, and its suggestion of non-alienating possibilities (2007: 226, 228).

Passing to a specific consideration of contemporary rock music, Marcuse
traces its origins as authentic protest in Black communities and notes its
regressive development into commercialized "'white' rock," a form that tends
toward an "orgiastic group therapy" which integrates the individual "into an

uninhibited mass where the power of a collective unconscious is mobilized but left without any radical or critical awareness." Rather than consider rock to have progressive potential, then, Marcuse warns that it may "at times" provide a "dangerous" means of expressing "irrationalism" *en masse*—much as he had written in *Counterrevolution and Revolt*. Returning to the relationship between art and social change with which he began his interview with Kearney, Marcuse notes that a contemporary aesthetic education of humanity toward liberation would have to begin with individuals and small affinity groups, the nuclei of a possible future emancipated society, though here he is reticent to sketch out how this approach might contribute to a more general vision of emancipation, for he acknowledges the risks of "ideological tyranny" which may be coterminous with such an approach. Marcuse does stress, though, that one cannot live a non-alienated life within a thoroughly alienated world (2007: 227, 229, 231). "Wrong life cannot be lived rightly," in Adorno's famous formulation (2005: 39).

1974 Paris Lectures at Vincennes University

In April and May 1974, Marcuse gave a series of seven lectures at the Vincennes University in Paris on global capitalism and the radical opposition. One of the philosopher's principal concerns in these lectures is to continue with a lifetime of investigation into the conditions underpinning the reproduction of the "bad totality" that is global capital, as juxtaposed with the possibilities of breaking free from this Iron Cage. As in his assessment of "The Movement in a New Era of Repression," he observes in these talks that the contemporary U.S. left lacks a "mass base" among the populace precisely because of the strength of integration, while on the other hand he laments the "sad phenomenon" whereby the oppressed racial and national minorities in the U.S. have been depoliticized and suppressed—thus blunting the revolutionary hopes he had identified as emanating from militant people of color at the conclusion of *One-Dimensional Man*. Marcuse moreover points out the blurring of distinctions between "legitimate" and "illegitimate" business and the associated penetration of the Mafia into the U.S. government, while on the international stage, the "arrangement" the U.S. ruling class has made with the Soviet Union contributes to the overall stabilization of world capitalism, on his account, and the philosopher presciently speculates that a similar "arrangement" would be made with the People's Republic of China. Defining the "objective conditions" as "the strength or weakness of the State or the ruling class [versus] the strength or weakness of the working class," Marcuse soberly acknowledges that the prevailing tendency is toward neo-fascism rather than any kind of socialism (Marcuse 2015: 2, 4, 7, 10, 13). In this sense, Marcuse observes knowingly that the problem of consciousness—the "subjective conditions"— does not have to do with any lack of knowledge regarding the factual situation, for the implicit and expressed political philosophy of the conformist majority in late-capitalist society would seem to be driven much more by *powerlessness:*

> Yes, there are the objective conditions which one knows well: It is repression; it is corruption; capitalism no longer works without inflation, unemployment, etc., etc. But what can one do? Nothing at all.
> MARCUSE 2015: 18

In idealistic terms, Marcuse counterposes against such widespread resignation the radical consciousness, which in Kantian terms mobilizes the "imagination as a cognitive faculty" to show "that the impossible is not impossible." It is in this sense that the radical consciousness is "way ahead" of the objective conditions, for it dialectically "projects potentiality in the objective conditions" and "anticipates possibilities not yet realized." Though Marcuse clearly sympathizes with this latter approach, he defines both the conformist and radical consciousness alike as manifestations of false consciousness—insofar as the latter refuses to apply a Marxist analysis to the changes in the capitalist system since the nineteenth century. Speaking to the disillusionment felt by many of those formerly in opposition when 'the Revolution' was not consummated at the end of the 1960s, Marcuse criticizes the disengagement into which many radicals fell: "Any absenteeism from political life, any absenteeism from links with political activity is escapist and is conformist." Taking an historical view, the critical theorist observes that social revolution is a process, and that it cannot be presumed to be without its regressions. This is particularly the case for the *world-historical revolution* that Marcuse anticipated as possible for the end of the twentieth century or the beginning of the twenty-first: being "more radical and more sweeping in scope than all preceding historical revolutions," this "would be a revolution not only in the political and economic institutions, not only a revolution in class structure, but also *a total transformation and subversion of values in all spheres and dimensions of the material and intellectual cultures*" (2015: 16, 18–19, 33, 59; emphasis added). The philosopher observes that

> we cannot possibly assume that the largest and most radical revolution in history [...] would come about in a straightly ascending curve and would come about in a relatively short time (2015: 34).

Though Marcuse remains faithful to the possibility of this world-historical revolutionary transformation, and agrees with Marx that it would have to centrally include the advanced-capitalist core of the world-system, he specifies in the Vincennes lectures that he expects this revolution to be the work of "75 to 150 years." He clarifies that, though he believes the prospects for this revolution to be long-term, it will never come if the radical opposition does not strive to incubate it now (2015: 34).

As in *Counterrevolution and Revolt,* Marcuse in these lectures also discusses the phenomenon of the vast extension of the U.S. working class. Citing statistics compiled by Stanley Aronowitz and the U.S. government, Marcuse shows that monopoly capital has largely suppressed the middle class and made 90 percent of the population into a dependent class. Citing Marx's famous letter to Engels stating that the proletariat is revolutionary or nothing at all, the critical theorist interprets Marx's declaration as suggesting that the laboring class is revolutionary insofar as its "needs and aspiration [...] are irreconcilable and incompatible with the capitalist system." Returning to the discussion on conformist consciousness, he then declares the contemporary U.S. working class not to be revolutionary as a whole, though he does endorse Marx's general point about the conflict between capital and labor, concluding that this antagonism is "bound to explode in the long run." As in a number of other contemporary addresses, the critical theorist points out the militancy of a radical minority among the U.S. working class, compelled as it is by the combination of workplace alienation and revolutionary consciousness to engage in spontaneous acts of subversion at the workplace. Marcuse sees in such acts, and in the parallel vague public awareness of the obsolescence of the capitalist mode of production, the decline of the performance principle and a growing threat to regnant obedience. Specifically, Marcuse observes the "gradual development of what we may call an *anti-capitalist consciousness* [...] and of an *anti-capitalist mental structure*" (2015: 40–42, 52, 56, 62–64; emphasis added).

The critical theorist concludes by suggesting that this militant minority among the workers could, like radical students and people of color in struggle, serve as the catalyst for the future disintegration of U.S. and thus global capitalism. Closing on an ecological and anarcho-syndicalist note, Marcuse foresees laborers challenging workplace hierarchy and humanity engaging in a "total redirection of production [...] towards the abolition of poverty and scarcity wherever it exists in the world today," together with a "total reconstruction of the environment and the creation of space and time for creative work." Anticipating the profound exacerbation of the environmental crisis which was already evident near the end of his life, Marcuse announces that the "abolition of waste, luxury, planned obsolescence, [and] unnecessary services and commodities of all kind" would imply a lower standard of living for the world's privileged minority, but he clarifies that such a "sacrifice" in capitalist terms would not be an excessively high price to pay for the possible "advent" of libertarian socialism (2015: 66–67, 69).

"It is Right to Revolt" and "Theory and Politics": Late Discussions with Sartre and Habermas

In May 1974, as reported by Hélène Lassithiotakis in *Libération,* Marcuse met with Sartre and colleagues in the existentialist's apartment in Paris to discuss the latter's new collectively authored book, *On a raison de se révolter* ("It is Right to Revolt"). Likely embellishing, Lassithiotakis describes Marcuse as holding this book to be a "new Bible," and she relates how he initiated the discussion among those present by expressing his general philosophical affinities with Sartre: he stressed the "decisive importance of the human will in all revolutionary movements to this day," particularly as regards the potentially "fatal contradiction" of capital, wherein it creates needs it cannot itself satisfy. He argues that this contradiction could indeed prove to be deadly for the system, "if humans so desire." In response to a question posed by one of Sartre's co-authors regarding the will of precisely *which* humans could advance the revolutionary goal of abolishing capitalism, Marcuse reiterates his late view that the vast majority of the "dependent population" have the potential of serving as an avant-garde in this sense. Marcuse's conversation with Sartre himself did not begin until over an hour into their meeting, according to Lassithiotakis, as the French intellectual would appear to have preferred to observe the unfolding of the discussion with his hands in his pockets, until deciding to break his silence and "provoke in Marcuse the greatest shock of the morning" (Lassithiotakis 1974).

Reflecting his marked shift in perspective toward actionism in the wake of May 1968—in interviews in the intervening period before his meeting with Marcuse, Sartre had argued that intellectuals must work directly in service of the oppressed and "smash" their privileges through direct action, if they are not to be considered counter-revolutionaries acting in bad faith—Sartre tells Marcuse that intellectuals should follow or accompany the youth and workers in rebellion rather than formulate demands and goals for them (Aronson 1980: 317–319, 322; Lassithiotakis 1974). Naturally, this perspective conflicts with that of Marcuse, who interpreted May 1968 as demonstrating the students leading the workers into revolt, such that, in his conversation with Sartre, he expresses skepticism with his counterpart's belief that laborers can themselves elaborate their goals better than if intellectuals were to assist them in this project in a relatively egalitarian manner. Both discussants admit that they are "classical intellectuals," with the difference between them being that Sartre expresses the need to contest such a role, while Marcuse confesses that he feels no guilt about adhering to the established conception of the public intellectual. However, for Sartre, it is precisely this "intellectual of the old type" which must disappear (Lassithiotakis 1974; Aronson 1980: 322–323).

Some years later, in 1978, Marcuse met with Habermas, Heinz Lubasz, and Telman Spengler to discuss "Theory and Politics." At the outset, this fascinating five-part interview examines biographical aspects of Marcuse's life and work, and then proceeds to explore a few of the misgivings Habermas and the two other interlocutors have vis-à-vis Marcuse's *oeuvre*. Regarding the idea of reason and the concept of the general will, Marcuse tells Habermas and company that it is mere ideology to suggest that the general interest is impossible to determine, that instead such interest is readily demonstrable, and even that "everyone knows" what this interest is, although precise certainty regarding its nature is muddled by the influence of the powers that be. Delineating his disagreement with the traditional political philosophy of Critical Theory, which held that an emancipatory consciousness could be expected to emerge only within "isolated individuals" rather than among the proletariat or society at large, Marcuse indeed argues that *everyone* is capable of fathoming the general interest. In this way, it would appear that Marcuse's account here is very reminiscent of the line of argumentation advanced by Chomsky in his 1971 debate with Foucault on justice, power, and human nature: as Habermas summarizes, Marcuse's concept of reason assumes that "it just takes healthy human intelligence to know what one really wants."[1] Though Habermas expresses the concern that his mentor is effectively grounding reason "naturalistically"—a

---

1   In contrast to Foucault, Chomsky presents a veritably Marxian or Marcusean argument as the basis of his advocacy of anarcho-syndicalism: "[I]f it is correct, as I believe it is, that a fundamental element of human nature is the need for creative work, for creative inquiry, for free creation without the arbitrary limiting effect of coercive institutions, then, of course, it will follow that a decent society should maximise the possibilities for this fundamental human characteristic to be realised. That means trying to overcome the elements of repression and oppression and destruction and coercion that exist in any existing society—ours for example—as a historical residue [...]. Now a federated, decentralised system of free associations, incorporating economic as well as other social institutions, would be what I refer to as anarcho-syndicalism; and it seems to me that this is the appropriate form of social organisation for an advanced technological society, in which human beings do *not* have to be forced into the position of tools, of cogs in the machine. There is no longer any social necessity for human beings to be treated as mechanical elements in the productive process; that can be overcome and we must overcome it by a society of freedom and free association, in which

charge which could justly be raised against anarchists like Peter Kropotkin and Ricardo Flores Magón, in addition to Marcuse—the critical theorist neverthe-less restates his view of the instinctual basis of rationality, as found "in the impulse of erotic energy to slow down destruction." Moreover, returning to the influence of Rousseau on his thought, he asserts that the idea of the *citoyen* assumes a type of human who can both distinguish between common and private interests and act radically against the domination of the latter—such that "*citoyens* are those human beings who have already become qualitatively different." In a similar vein, Marcuse speaks on the concept of solidarity, noting it "in itself" to be "of no value at all," given that among the Nazis and organized crime syndicates solidarity is clearly expressed. For it to be authentic and liberatory, insists Marcuse, solidarity must be based in Eros and the struggle for a classless society (Marcuse et al. 1978/9: 135–140).

During this conversation with Habermas, Lubasz, and Spengler, Marcuse clearly affirms the continued critical relevance of Freud's metapsychology. Responding to Habermas' provocative question of how Freud's late instinctual theory can be reconciled with the anthropological assumptions of histori-cal materialism, which hold human nature to be malleable, Marcuse clarifies that to claim human beings to have primary drives should not be taken as meaning that human nature is fixed; the instinctual drives are "fixed," argues Marcuse, only in the sense that Eros and Thanatos are perpetually in conflict with one another. It is entirely within the realm of possibility for Eros to have the upper hand in relation to Thanatos—though such an eventuality would both correspond to and presuppose decisive changes in human behavior and power relations within global society. Additionally, Marcuse hails the impor-tant contributions that Freudian metapsychology can have in terms of under-standing current events, given his view that the "intensification" of Thanatos remains a "political necessity for those in power": Marcuse suggests that, were the individual not to be acquainted with Freud's late theorizing on the instincts, she would be more vulnerable to resignation, considering the prevailing "rul[e] by madmen" to be natural rather than contingent (1978/9: 133, 147).

Proceeding toward the conclusion of the interview, Marcuse restates his view of the "expanded working class" as the potential agent of societal transfor-mation, highlighting especially the double exploitation of working women, the widespread international revolt led by students, and rising trends of absentee-ism and workplace sabotage as important aspects of the revolutionary struggle. The philosopher defines the potentially revolutionary subjects as those who

---

the creative urge that I consider intrinsic to human nature will in fact be able to realise itself in whatever way it will" (Chomsky and Foucault 2006: 37–39).

are oppressed. Exhibiting an admittedly prescient sense of pessimism for the future, though, Marcuse asks how long capitalism can be expected to remain stable, as he ruminates on the possibility that bourgeois power will simply "cemen[t] its position" on the basis of "an escalated economic and political imperialism," leading even China and the USSR to be opened once again to foreign exploitation. If such negative developments were to come to pass, Marcuse predicts, "then those in power will be able to sleep in peace for a few centuries yet," and "there will be no revolution." Yet dialectically, in response to Habermas' inquiry into what "realistically conceivable" revolutionary model Marcuse favors for the present day, the critical theorist outlines a positive, anarchical vision: "an upsurge of protest organized locally and regionally, [...] radicalization of self-administration—*a diffuse disintegration which becomes contagious,* so to speak" (1978/9: 150–152; emphasis added).

Marcuse's Final Interventions in Life: On Political Violence, the New Left, the U.S. Bicentennial, "The Reification of the Proletariat," Rudolf Bahro, Technology, and Ecology

Marcuse's very last essays, articles, and speeches address left-wing terrorism, forgiveness for crimes against humanity, the fate and legacy of the New Left, the means of transitioning beyond the twin nightmares of 'actually existing socialism' and monopoly capital, the increasingly apocalyptical environmental destruction for which capitalism is responsible, and the prospects for resistance and revolt against such negations. In these interventions, Marcuse expresses his criticisms of the Red Army Faction (RAF) in West Germany, condemning its approach on both practical and philosophical grounds, and in a separate piece he asserts that war crimes cannot and should not be forgiven. He presents a highly positive review of the legacy of the New Left, claiming the contributions made by its constituent members to have been decisive in bringing the prospect of thoroughgoing societal revolution that much closer—however potentially fatal the prevailing context of counterrevolution might prove for this prospect. Praising East German dissident Rudolf Bahro's critical account of the Soviet Union and the German Democratic Republic (GDR), as set forth in *The Alternative in Eastern Europe* (1977), Marcuse extends Bahro's analysis to the question of transcending late capitalist society. Whether the critical theorist ultimately shares Bahro's authoritarian prescriptions for achieving this end remains unclear. Marcuse's final addresses on the "Children of Prometheus" and "Ecology and the Critique of Modern Society" are truly poignant in their forthright recognition of the total assault launched by capital

against the basic life-systems of Earth, as in their affirmation of the continued urgent need for revolutionary transformation as a means of resolving this
world-historical threat.

To begin, Marcuse adds his voice to the colloquium of thinkers called on by
Holocaust survivor Simon Wiesenthal to debate the problem posed in the latter's 1976 volume *The Sunflower:* that is, whether he as a Jew interned in 1943 in
the Lemberg concentration camp should have complied with the dying wish
of an ss officer to grant him forgiveness for a grave crime he had committed
the previous year, when he oversaw the murder of an estimated three hundred
Jews who had taken refuge in a particular building in Nazi-occupied territory.
Marcuse agrees with Wiesenthal's response to refuse such a request; he claims
it to be "inhuman" and a "travesty of justice" for the executioner to request forgiveness from the victim. Passing to consider Vietnam, Marcuse asks whether
a member of the National Liberation Front should forgive a Marine who had
killed and tortured one's "friends, wife, children?" He even raises the question
of whether *anyone* is "justified" or "entitled" to forgive, observing that the "easy
forgiving of such crimes" sustains "the very evil it wants to alleviate" (Wiesenthal 1976: 169).

Continuing with the theme of political violence, "Murder is Not a Political
Weapon" (*Die Zeit,* September 1977) presents Marcuse's compelling critique of
the turn to urban terrorism taken contemporarily by the Red Army Faction
and associated groupings in the Federal Republic of Germany. The philosopher
asks in this article whether terrorism contributes to the weakening of capitalism, and relatedly whether such action is justified by revolutionary morality—
answering both questions in the negative. He observes that the "physical liquidation" of powerful individuals, "even the most prominent," hardly subverts
the normal operation of capitalism, amidst the "practically unlimited" supply
of willing substitutes who can readily be called upon to replace those eliminated by urban guerrilla warfare operations. This is not to say that Marcuse
absolutely opposes such tactics in principle, for he acknowledges that, within
certain contexts, the killing of those who "sponsor a policy of repression" may
in fact lead to a change in the system—he cites the possibility of assassinating
Hitler or the Franquist admiral Luis Carrero Blanco, whom the ETA had killed
in Spain four years prior—yet he observes that such a course of action becomes
revolutionary only if it coincides with the "disintegration" of the established
system. Self-evidently, this was not a condition that held in West Germany at
that time. Despite these qualifications, though, Marcuse actually comes quite
close to endorsing urban guerrilla warfare when he states that "[t]hose representatives of capital whom the terrorists have chosen as their victims are
themselves responsible for capitalism—just as Hitler and Himmler were

responsible for the concentration camps." However, while Marcuse recognizes that the targets of the RAF's assassination campaigns are far from innocent, he concludes that their "guilt" can be "expiated only through the abolition of capitalism itself." Additionally, in strictly practical terms, Marcuse argues that the considerable gap between the established strength of the West German State and the relative weakness of left-wing terrorist groups isolated from the people renders a resort to armed struggle inadvisable (Marcuse 1977: 7–8).

Reflecting on the question of whether terrorism can be justified morally, Marcuse asserts that the "laws of revolutionary morality" demand at least a relative congruence between means and ends: the "goal" of Marxist socialism, "the liberated individual," must "appear in the means to achieve this goal." Insofar as it is possible, then, revolutionary morality requires open struggle, which Marcuse clearly defines as *"class struggle"* (emphasis added). In closing, Marcuse asks whether the RAF can be considered an authentic outgrowth of the radical student movement of the previous decade, answering this question in the negative as well. As an alternative, he affirms the extra-parliamentary opposition (APO) as being an imperfect example of a "mass movement on an international scale" which in no way shied away from "open confrontation" but overwhelmingly did reject "conspiratorial terrorism." Marcuse ends this piece by tying urban terrorist groupings to the old capitalist society, claiming their efforts to be counter-productive for two reasons: firstly, because they consciously seek to provoke the overwhelming power of State forces, and secondly because they effectively split left forces at a time when they must unite against capitalism and authority (1977: 7–8).

"The Failure of the New Left?" is the name of an address Marcuse presented at the University of California Irvine in 1975; it was revised, expanded, and then reissued in *New German Critique* months after Marcuse's death, in an issue dedicated to contemplation of his life's work. Before coming to examine the question of whether the New Left has in fact failed, Marcuse begins this talk by defining this emergent movement: he describes it as being more left-wing than the established Communist parties; isolated from the workers; and strongly influenced by anti-authoritarianism, Romanticism, and aesthetics. Speaking to the question of the fate of the New Left, Marcuse argues that its activists confronted cooptation and open suppression by the Establishment—processes that were helped along by the New Left's alienation from the general populace, a reality that in turn can be partly explained by the dominance of pro-business trade unions among organized workers—in addition to internally destructive tendencies, such as factionalism, anti-intellectualism, an emphasis on private liberation, "contempt for theory," "narcissistic arrogance," and "a politically powerless anarchism." Yet despite the negative trends he observes, Marcuse applauds the New Left's astute political theorizing, for its adherents correctly assess the very "nature of integration in this society" in Gramscian terms: they know that advanced capitalism perpetuates itself through the conscious manipulation of human instinct and desire, and for this reason they also know that a non-conformist psychology holds great promise in terms of politicizing the unconscious and the ego toward the subversion of the dominant superego (2004: 183–187).

Passing to consideration of the very question suggested by the title of his intervention, Marcuse declares the New Left not to have failed. He observes that there is reason to believe that the New Left's "message" has resonated beyond its in-group members, as reflected in the militancy of workers engaged at that time in wildcat strikes, absenteeism, sabotage, and the undermining of established union bureaucracies, as well as in the opposition expressed by radical people of color and feminists. In stark contrast to a decade prior, when Marcuse was consumed by the argumentation of *One-Dimensional Man,* he now remarks that the very stability of the capitalist system has been upset, with worker morale declining and popular mistrust for the "basic values" of capitalism burgeoning rapidly. In short, "the overall breakdown of confidence in the priorities and hierarchies set by capitalism is apparent." Within this process, Marcuse argues that it was the New Left which intervened radically in the chaos of the 1960s to call for an "all-encompassing," *total* revolution against the existing order; it was the New Left activists who influenced and changed the consciousness of "broad sectors of the population" by personally embodying the very negation of the capitalist system and its various authoritarian exigencies (2004: 187–189). As he summarizes in libertarian-socialist terms,

> the New Left has made that which has long been abstract knowledge concrete with its assertion that "changing the world" does not mean replacing one system of domination with another, but rather a leap to a qualitatively new level of civilization where human beings can develop their own needs and potential in solidarity with one another (2004: 189).

Shifting to questions of strategy, Marcuse reiterates his emphasis on the need for popular recognition of the established power of reaction. As he writes, "[t]he transition to socialism is not now on the agenda; the counterrevolution is dominant." Within such a context, an oppositional movement should focus on developing regional and local bases of counter-power, claims Marcuse, and, as in "The Movement in a New Era of Repression," he argues that even reformist and liberal politics may help in the growth of a broad resistance movement—as follows from his new-found view that late capital "boasts a diminished tolerance threshold." Reaffirming his argumentation from "Marxism and Feminism," Marcuse here declares the women's liberation movement to represent a potential lever which could prove instrumental in overturning patriarchal civilization and capitalism in favor of a *feminine socialism* that would put an end to "destructive and self-accelerating productivity" and male aggression alike, thus opening the possibility of the emancipation of the senses and a generalized enjoyment of human life. In his conclusion, Marcuse repeats that the New Left has not failed; failure instead "characterizes those hangers-on who have fled from politics." He closes by warning of the worsening tendencies of capitalism to once again yield fascism, indicating the urgency of the socialist alternative (2004: 189–191).

Similar themes concern Marcuse in the text he submitted to *Le Monde Diplomatique* for its July 4, 1976, issue, which was specially dedicated to reflection on the bicentennial since the U.S. Declaration of Independence. Marcuse in this essay contemplates whether there can be considered to exist a system of repression specific to the U.S. Preliminarily, he observes that the U.S. political-economic system shares many of the same features with other Western monopoly-capitalist societies in terms of degrees of repressiveness, but he adds that U.S. society is unique as regards the extent to which the subordinated population is integrated. As before, he holds the "overwhelming productive power" of American capitalism largely responsible for this difference, but for the first time he now will add the "ruthless suppression" of militant labor in U.S. history as a second critical factor for understanding the conservatism of contemporary U.S. society. Echoing "The Failure of the New Left?" and other works from his final decade, Marcuse discusses the relative decomposition of capitalist values among the U.S. populace at large, noting the defiant legacy of the 1960s to have bequeathed a "heritage of refusal and renewal" that "continues to operate under the surface of integration." Still, he laments that this critical consciousness is effectively diffuse and fragmented rather than organized and revolutionary. Moreover, the theorist perceives a continued marked internalization of guilt among many U.S. laborers, and he hypothesizes that this dynamic aids in propping up the prevailing class hierarchy. Dialectically, though, Marcuse identifies trends toward *autogestion* at the workplace and declares that the subversive images evident within the cultural domain foreshadow "a revolution which, in depth and scope, would surpass all preceding revolutions": "the qualitative leap into freedom." Against such erotic, life-affirming trends nonetheless stands the organized power of monopoly-capital, which is preparing a counter-offensive in terms that clearly recall twenty-first century Mexico: Marcuse points to "the alliance of Mafia and legitimate business, the spread of violence, continued racism, the concentration of the weapons of annihilation in the hands of the powers that be, [and] the pervasive corruption of the democratic process." Amidst the threat of a newly incipient Fascism, the elder critical theorist continues to stress the need for the left to focus its efforts on the political education of the majority: that is, of convincing the people at large that the repressions which uphold the system are unnecessary, and that these can be overcome anarchically without having to institute yet another system of domination (2014: 358–361).

The last substantive essay written by Marcuse in life, "Protosocialism and Late Capitalism" (1978), presents the critical theorist's reflections on East German critic Rudolf Bahro's *The Alternative in Eastern Europe* (1977), a text he considers to have been an "authentic 'internal' advance of Marxist theory" and, indeed, "the most important contribution to Marxist theory and practice to appear in several decades." Marcuse's method in this work is to extend Bahro's critique of the "actually existing socialism" of the German Democratic Republic—that is to say, the "protosocialism" of East Germany—and to contemplate the problem of the transition to full communism from the late capitalism of Western society. It will be seen how similar the two theorists generally are in their perspectives, with the possible exception of their takes on the place of the centralization of power within the transition away from protosocialism and late capitalism, in light of Marcuse's ambivalence about this authoritarian strategy (Marcuse 1980a: 25, 40, 47).

At the outset of this final essay, Marcuse expresses his pleasure at having encountered Bahro's astute observation in *The Alternative* that any given polity cannot merit the term socialist merely for its having progressed beyond private ownership of the means of production—for, to be socialist, such a polity must crucially also include an emphasis on the self-emancipation of subjectivity and a radical-aesthetic change in consciousness. Indeed, Marcuse here hails Bahro's rejection of the well-established orthodox demarcation between socialism on the one hand and communism on the other, arguing that "[s]ocialism *is* communism from the very beginning—and vice versa." With reference to the Soviet bloc, Marcuse notes how bureaucratic-authoritarian domination rationalizes itself using the claim that the repressiveness it institutes is required to fend off the hostile Western-capitalist powers, as well as to reduce the gap in capabilities between the West and the "socialist" societies as quickly as possible—with the result that the "first stage" of socialism is perpetuated indefinitely, frustrating the liberatory arrival of full communism. Shifting from consideration of political science to social psychology, Marcuse affirms the distinction Bahro makes in his discussion of the "surplus consciousness," or the totality of free human capacities which are not confined to the struggle for existence, between the "compensatory interests" that tie the subjects of protosocialism and late capital alike into the dominant system and the "emancipatory interests" which oppose them. Observing compensatory interests to be hegemonic among the populace of both West and East, Marcuse comes to reflect on how such a vicious circle might be broken. Initially, he observes that revolutionary social change "cannot be carried through on the backs of the people" (1980a: 26–28).

In accordance with Bahro, Marcuse remarks that the *surplus consciousness* is most evidently found among the intelligentsia and the "catalyst" groups—students, feminists, dissident scientists, and company—but he specifies that it exists latently among the people at large, who possess at least a "dim awareness" of more affirming alternatives to the current system. This declaration notwithstanding, Marcuse elucidates Bahro's view of the need for an *elitism* of the "enlightened" intelligentsia, who are to *lead* the integrated working classes toward emancipation. In an echo of Marx, Bahro presupposes that such a hierarchical dynamic would be merely temporary, as the realization of integral socialism would overturn the privileges historically afforded to intellectuals, precisely by universalizing such privilege—much in the same way that the creation of art would be thoroughly democratized under liberated conditions. Expanding on this thought, Marcuse presents Bahro's theory of the political transition beyond protosocialism—though it is not immediately clear whether this exposition is a full endorsement. He relates Bahro's condemnation of such anti-statist approaches to the transition as "anarchism and adventurist left radicalism," and observes that the East German instead affirms a strong role for the State as the "*taskmaster*" that will coordinate emancipation from above. Whether Marcuse agrees with this line or not, he claims that the evident passivity of the masses and their domination by compensatory interests makes the immediate application of the Marxian call for the "withering away of the state" rather illusory—and in so doing, he contradicts the enthusiasm he had expressed for Bahro's interpretation of socialism as a single stage (1980a: 29–31).

Continuing, the critical theorist presents Bahro's paradoxical—if not expressly oxymoronic—theory of an *antistate State*, which is to undermine its own basis by encouraging the flowering of spontaneity, autonomy, and the development *en masse* of emancipatory interests. Specifically, Marcuse fleshes out Bahro's vision of the "requisite rational hierarchy" of a Communist League that, in contradistinction to the prevailing system of power in the Soviet bloc, is supposedly to be "democratically constituted and controlled," a "brain" whose membership is to be comprised of those "whose consciousness is most advanced." However, as a means of preventing the radical separation between pyramidal base and top seen contemporarily in West and East alike, councilism must be readily embraced and advanced by the people from below, argues Bahro. Yet whatever role the East German thinker sees for the grassroots in the transition to full communism, it is nonetheless clear that his strategy is generally dictatorial, reminiscent of the Committee for Public Safety from the French Revolution: as Marcuse points out, Bahro's idea is that the revolutionary directory must have the strength and clarity of purpose to "*stand up against*" the people's compensatory interests and to affirm the "necessity of repression" and the suppression of "subaltern consciousness" (conformism) and "unreflected spontaneity," in addition to "bourgeois and petit bourgeois egoism." Closing his presentation of Bahro's theory of a political transition beyond the established Communist Parties which entrap the GDR and the rest of the Soviet sphere within the confines of protosocialism, Marcuse explicitly acknowledges the proximity of this perspective to the authoritarian methods endorsed by Plato and Rousseau (1980a: 30–32).

After examining Bahro's theory of a political transition beyond protosocialism—and, by extension, late capitalism as well—Marcuse turns to exploring some of the material and existential means that could facilitate the coming of said transition. For one, he endorses Bahro's call for a mass "journey inwards" to combat alienation and yield a collective "mental upswing"; Marcuse happily recounts Bahro's dismissal of the contempt expressed by many mainstream Marxists for reportedly "bourgeois" concepts such as personality, subjectivity, and mind. Moreover, in material terms, Marcuse agrees with Bahro's call for a communist "equalization" in the distribution of consumer goods as a means of combating the reign of compensatory interests, and he affirms the project of radically reorganizing labor so as to abolish workplace hierarchy and minimize alienated labor as much as possible. In addition, the critical theorist suggests that the prevailing affirmation of the performance principle, as reflected for example in the fetishization of income and bank accounts, must be sublimated into interest in "nonalienated creative work" and "nonalienated enjoyment." Raising the question of how a transition incorporating such radical elements could be initiated, Marcuse states clearly that only social revolution opens that possibility: "now more than ever, it is true that a revolution is necessary to obtain reforms" (1980a: 34–36, 39–40).

Summarizing his development of Bahro's account in *The Alternative* thus far, then, Marcuse briefly provides a critique of Leninist strategy, claiming for one that armed rebellions and "seizures of power" by the workers or their representatives are out of the realm of possibility within most highly industrialized countries, ruled over as these are by oligarchical interests that in turn are protected by overwhelming military and paramilitary forces, and he furthermore challenges the very existence of revolutionary masses who are to readily institute socialism within said contexts. Distancing himself from his pronouncements in *One-Dimensional Man*, though—and clearly expressing his own disagreement with Bolshevism—Marcuse proceeds to qualify this latter challenge by remarking on the great ambivalence which surrounds the relationship between the *expanded* working classes and the established system, as it remains unclear that the former has "made its peace" with the latter (1980a: 36–37).

Marcuse concludes his reflections on Bahro and the prevailing situation by considering the interrelationship between revolution and the human instincts. As in *Counterrevolution and Revolt,* he declares that the dominant tendency of capitalism is toward self-destruction and a higher form of society, as through the progressive alienation of the working classes on the one hand and the stimulation of protective-defensive rebellious subjectivities on the other. Such radical subjectivity is in turn propelled by consciousness and embodied in activism, yet motivated as well as by an instinctual rejection of matters as they are and a Blochian anticipation of liberation to come. The prospect of social revolution depends upon the existence of a "vital, existential *need* for a revolution," and this need in turn finds its basis in the hope for a "*joyous* freedom"—one identified by Schiller as well as Beethoven, among others. Concluding ultimately optimistically, Marcuse explains that the drive toward revolution is buttressed by the very basic tendency of Eros to seek the satisfaction and "intensification" of the life instincts: thus, social revolution has its roots in the *erotic fundament* of the human organism, while the development and progression of Eros in turn demand the social transformations sought by revolution. Marcuse proceeds toward closing by associating the revolutionary upsurge of Eros with a *rebellious nature*, both human and external; asserting the latter to be the very "domain" in which happiness, fulfillment, and gratification are made possible—hence, the "environment of Eros"—Marcuse remarks that the "organized defense of nature threatens the profits of big industry and the interests of the military." Thus is the ecological struggle to protect nature a struggle against prevailing power relations and a direct challenge to the rule of capital. As a similar counter-image to hegemonic power, Marcuse invokes the women's liberation movement. In point of fact, he expresses in closing that the "anti-authoritarian movement, the ecology movement, and the women's movement have intrinsic links with one another"—in the sense that they all commonly seek to disrupt the destructiveness of the performance principle and in this way *put capitalism down* in the "late stage of its development." The critical theorist ends by applauding the "authentic forms of rebellion" seen at that time among militant workers, student protesters, and participants of communes: though these forces are not yet collectively strong enough to dispatch with the centralized power of domination, he observes—once again in terms reminiscent of Bloch—that they anticipate the final catastrophe for capitalism: its supersession through "economic and social units of autonomous control" (41–43, 46).

"The Reification of the Proletariat," an address Marcuse presented to the American Philosophical Association Convention in San Francisco in March 1978, summarizes many of the ideas Marcuse was contemplating at life's end. Mentioning Bahro by name, the critical theorist suggests dialectically that a surplus "counter-consciousness" is developing prominently among the dependent populations of Europe and the U.S. Though he acknowledges that the "overall capitalist policy is largely successful," in the sense that no revolutionary movements are evidently on hand in the advanced-industrial societies, he claims this surplus consciousness to have already achieved the preparatory work of tearing the veil of reification: "Can there still be any mystification of who is governing and in whose interests, of what is the base of their power?" He adds that the system now no longer conceals its "utter destructiveness," as reflected in the unchecked "proliferation of nuclear energy" and the "poisoning of the life environment." Marcuse closes by claiming the question of whether the observed destabilization of capital can be accelerated so as to prevent the rise of a new Fascism to be a "life-and-death" matter for the left—as for humanity and nature (2014: 393–395).

"The Children of Prometheus," a short collection of twenty-five theses on technology and society, is the very last lecture Marcuse gave in life; he presented it before the Frankfurt Römerberg-Gespräche debate club in May 1979. In this address, Marcuse's introspective concern for ecological matters is evident. His first thesis suggests that historical progress is defined by the relationship between human freedom and the domination of nature: on the one hand, the control of nature—human and non-human—has throughout recorded history been intimately tied up with social oppression and unfreedom, yet some degree of the domination of external nature seems necessary to secure the age-old promise of human liberation, as from the struggle for existence, argues the critical theorist. Developing this view, Marcuse frames the life-negating extremes of systemic pollution and nuclear energy within the generalized capitalist compulsion to develop the productive forces on the basis of the principle of "productive destruction"; furthermore, he sees this same principle at work in the alienation of labor, as in the aggressiveness manifested within popular culture—"sports, traffic, music, [and] pornography." Anticipating later advances in eco-socialist theory, reflecting contemporary claims made by anarchist social ecologists, and echoing his previously stated views regarding pollution and the profit motive, Marcuse in this final address emphasizes that the prospect of overcoming productive destruction is a project fundamentally at odds with the thanotic nature of capitalism.[2] Reasserting the affirming conclusions from his life-long study of the subversive possibilities of thought and art, Marcuse observes the great potential which exists in the cultural sphere for the negation of the destructiveness of capitalism—specifically, in the chance for cultural revolution, which is advanced by specifically anti-authoritarian groupings like student radicals and feminists, as well as by workers who spontaneously commit sabotage, demand a reduction in hours worked, and randomly engage in absenteeism (2011: 222–223).

Recalling his analyses from *Eros and Civilization* and *An Essay on Liberation*, Marcuse stresses the importance of the "subjective factor" in undermining the dominion of death that is capital; he calls for a reconstruction of the "psychosomatic structure" of individuals that would invert the prevailing "acceptance of destruction [and] alienated life as the routine" in favor of more erotic developments. Among those who resist the "children of Prometheus"— the name Marcuse here gives to the technocratic managers of the established system—and those who cannot continue to bear the "productive-destructive" type of progress advanced by dominant power-groups is born a "protest *from all classes of society,*" one that is "motivated by a *deep, visceral, and intellectual inability to comply,* by a *will to rescue whatever humanity, joy, and autonomy may still be rescued*" (emphasis added). Implicitly invoking Bloch and his analysis of the anticipatory "Novum," or *new*—true subverting forces in transition— Marcuse observes that progress toward this new is presently being propelled by the student and women's liberation movements, as well as by protests targeting "the nuclear power industry" and the destruction of nature taken as a whole—for the biosphere is an "ecological space [which] cut[s] across all fixed class boundaries." In closing, Marcuse dedicates his final thesis to reflection on Auschwitz. He condemns all modes of inwardness which do not "hold tightly" to the remembrance of the Nazi genocide or that disavow it as "inconsequential," and he claims any concept of historical advance to be false which does not consider a repetition of Auschwitz possible in the prevailing world (2014: 224–225).

Deploying a similar tone to that of the "Children of Prometheus"—at once catastrophic and authentic—Marcuse concerns himself centrally with Auschwitz and the destruction of nature in a public lecture he gave to a California youth wilderness society shortly before his death in West Germany, entitled "Ecology and the Critique of Modern Society." The arguments he makes in this

---

2   In a 1970 interview held with the *Street Journal & San Diego Free Press*, Marcuse had declared that "[i]t is precisely the profit interests in this society which make large-scale pollution inevitable" (2014: 350).

penultimate and characteristically critical intervention are to be presented in the following chapter, "Nature and Revolution."

The Aesthetic Dimension (1978)

The goal is not the dominated but the liberated world.
MARCUSE 1978b: 35

The release in 1978 of *The Aesthetic Dimension*—first published in German a year previously with the title *Die Permanenz der Kunst* ("The Permanence of Art")—demonstrates conclusively the ceaseless militancy of Marcuse's philosophical and political orientation. Being the last full-length volume Marcuse wrote before his death in July 1979, *The Aesthetic Dimension* is a testament to his deepest revolutionary hopes and dreams.

In this book, Marcuse develops a critique of orthodox Marxist analyses of aesthetics and presents his view of authentic art, which is to serve revolutionary purposes, as through the formalistic advancement of "radical change[s] in style and technique" or the representation of "the prevailing unfreedom" on the one hand and "the rebelling forces" on the other. True art for Marcuse subverts prevailing modes of "perception and understanding" and indicts the hegemonic reality through its form while holding out the prospect of "the image of liberation." Delineating his differences with other Marxist theorists, Marcuse argues that artworks are not revolutionary due to the mere fact that they are produced consciously *for* the workers or the cause of social transformation; instead, he claims that the relationship between revolutionary literature and a commensurate praxis is "inexorably indirect, mediated, and frustrating." Rather controversially, then, Marcuse finds more promise in the poetry of Charles Baudelaire than in the "didactic plays of Brecht" (1978b: x–xiii).

Permeating Marcuse's argumentation in *The Aesthetic Dimension* is a concern for the decidedly negative prevailing socio-political situation. At the outset of the text, Marcuse acknowledges that the *"miserable reality* can be changed only through radical political praxis," and just a few pages later he defines the contemporary world as being gripped by totalitarianism—thus linking the present state of affairs which he leaves to future generations with the historical horrors of Fascism (emphasis added). Recognizing the charge of idealism with which his final work could be accused—as it could be directed against Adorno's philosophy, specifically the dialectician's aesthetic theory, from which Marcuse borrows greatly in his final volume—the critical theorist observes that "the concern with aesthetics demands justification," for artistic explorations could well be said to reflect an "element of despair," as they signal a "retreat into a world of fiction where existing conditions are changed and overcome *only in the realm of the imagination*" (emphasis added). Yet Marcuse does not want to entirely concede this point, for he argues instead that authentic art contains characteristics which are "essential" for social revolution. In particular, Marcuse stresses the intimate relation between art and subjectivity. While orthodox Marxism notoriously dismisses the latter notion as inextricably tied to capitalist ideology, Marcuse claims that its affirmation and development through creativity in fact allow the individual to transcend prevailing bourgeois values and "ente[r] another dimension of existence," as through the eclipsing of the hegemony of the performance principle in favor of the internal resources of "passion, imagination, [and] conscience." In this way, rather than affirm the prevailing Marxist tendency undialectically to dismiss artistic traditions like Romanticism "as simply reactionary," Marcuse stresses that the experience of art-forms, whether Romantic or otherwise, can open psychical possibilities for alternatives to imperant one-dimensional society. Authentic art can help in the "rebirth of the rebellious subjectivity," the affirmation of a "counter-consciousness," and the resurrection of the "repressed potentialities of [humanity] and nature" (1978b: 1–9).

> Art breaks open a dimension inaccessible to other experience, a dimension in which human beings, nature, and things no longer stand under the law of the established reality principle. Subjects and objects encounter the appearance of that autonomy which is denied them in their society (1978b: 72).

True art, in this sense, serves an estranging and contradictory function with regard to the given reality, thus revealing its deep origins in Eros, as the affirmation of "the Life instincts [...] against instinctual and social oppression." Symbolizing the beautiful, art embodies the pleasure principle and hence opposes itself to the reality principle that impels domination. As such, authentic art effectively expresses a categorical imperative of its own, writes Marcuse, one that demands societal transformation. Crucially, however, Marcuse insists that revolutionary art does not always take on an affirmative character, but rather often betrays a pessimism that warns against the "happy consciousness" of established radical orthodoxies, such as the Marxist tendency to reduce the social question to class struggle. Implicitly recalling his friend Benjamin, Marcuse remarks that pessimism in no way necessarily contradicts advocacy of revolutionary transformation, citing George Büchner's play on the execution by Robespierre of the French militant Georges Danton as an example (1978b: 10–11, 14, 62).

Continuing with his critique of orthodox Marxist takes on aesthetics, Marcuse shares his heterodox view that authentic art envisions a universal humanity that cannot be reduced to any single class, even and especially the Marxian proletariat. Following from his previous revisions to established Marxist theory, Marcuse here claims that the precondition of the realization of a classless society is the subjective development of radical changes at the individual level that favor solidarity, community, and the subordination of Thanatos to Eros (1978b: 16–17). In this vein, Marcuse intriguingly advances a line of thought which could be taken as an attempt to resolve the tension between the radical politics he has favored throughout life and the various privileges he has enjoyed, from birth to old age:

> The fact that the artist belongs to a privileged group negates neither the truth nor the aesthetic quality of [her] work. What is true of 'the classics of socialism' is true also of the great artists: they break through the class limitations of their family, background, environment. Marxist theory is not family research. The progressive character of art, its contribution to the struggle for liberation cannot be measured by the artists' origins nor by the ideological horizon of their class. Neither can it be determined by the presence (or absence) of the oppressed class in their works. The criteria for the progressive character of art are given only in the work itself as a whole: in what it says and how it says it (1978b: 18–19).

With this comment, Marcuse controversially defends the contributions made by himself and many of his closest comrades, including Adorno, Horkheimer, and Benjamin, in addition to the work developed previously by Marx and Engels. Whether his argumentation here is sound is certainly a debatable point. Relatedly, though, Marcuse further claims that one's estrangement from the production process can represent "a refuge and a vantage point from which to denounce the reality established through domination"—a perspective covering the corpus developed by the Frankfurt School theorists, and one that reflects the hope Marcuse holds for non-integrated social groups, such as the *lumpenproletariat,* students, and racial minorities. The critical theorist continues by asserting that the obscure formulations of "esoteric literature" represent a "subterranean rebellion against the social order"; while such "elitist and decadent" art does little concretely to advance collective liberation, it opens "tabooed zones" for consideration, in his view. Expressing the apogee

of his heterodox approach in a manner that must have maddened other Marxists, Soviet observers, and working-class readers alike, Marcuse concludes that
art loses its "emancipatory impact" insofar as it allows itself to be popularized
(1978b: 18, 20–21).

Pressing forward, Marcuse claims authentic art to both impel liberation
and delimit the inescapable aspects of the human condition which revolution cannot overcome, no matter how total its scope may be. With regard to
the former question, Marcuse claims art to function anarchically as the cipher
of qualitative historical change, as reflected in "the protest against the definition of life as labor, in the struggle against the entire capitalist and state-
socialist organization of work (the assembly line, Taylor system, hierarchy), in
the struggle to end patriarchy, to reconstruct the destroyed life environment
[...]." Yet, even if the thoroughgoing social changes outlined here were to be
actualized, argues Marcuse, art itself would still persist, for while the conflict
between Eros and Thanatos occurs within the class struggle, it also transcends
it: bourgeois-feudal rule cannot necessarily be blamed for the fact that "the
lovers do not remain together," for example, just as "it is difficult to imagine a
society which has abolished what is called chance or fate, the encounter at the
crossroads, the encounter of the lovers, but also the encounter with hell." Even
a successful global libertarian-socialist revolution could never do away with
interpersonal conflict, tragedy, and the struggle between humanity and nature:
"Socialism does not and cannot liberate Eros from Thanatos." In essence, then,
art "bears witness to the inherent limits of freedom and fulfillment" and to
"human embeddedness in nature" (1978b: 24, 28–29, 72).

Marcuse stresses in *The Aesthetic Dimension* that the consciousness
advanced through the experience of art does not address itself exclusively
to the proletariat, as orthodox Marxists might claim, in light of Marcuse's
heterodox view that the workers are hardly freed from the hegemonic values
imposed by capitalism. Instead, artistic consciousness directs itself to all those
individuals and groups who are "united in their awareness of the universal
need for liberation—regardless of their class position." Expanding on this
line of thought, Marcuse reaches the conclusion that revolutionary art may
alienate and in turn be alienated from "the people" to an inversely propor-
tional degree to their integration within the dominant system: for this reason,
Marcuse recommends that art should in the first place address the militant
minority which consciously seeks liberation. If within this process it takes on
an "elitist" character vis-à-vis ordinary people—and even becomes "The Enemy
of the People"—then so be it, he says. Prior to the historical rupture which
transforms *the people* into allies against barbarism rather than upholders of
such, authentic artists cannot easily address their work to the exploited and

oppressed, argues Marcuse, and their attempts to radicalize consciousness may well lead them openly to oppose the people's expressed character. In the meantime, the aesthetic "flight into inwardness" has the potential to serve as a protective reservoir of subversive thought within which artists can anticipate and prepare the "emergence of another universe"—one to be born through the praxis of freely associated individuals in place of the presently reified masses (1978b: 30–35, 38–39).

As his argument progresses in this final work, Marcuse returns to consider the anarchical relationship between art and historical redemption in more detail. Following his observation that the "world was not made for the sake of the human being and it has not become more human," Marcuse declares that aesthetic beauty serves as a symbol of "the end of power" and the "appearance (*Schein*) of freedom." Marcuse identifies the concept of a "reversal of history" as one of art's regulative ideas: his answer, then, must be positive to the question of whether there are or can be "authentic works in which the Antigones finally destroy the Creons, in which the peasants defeat the princes, in which love is stronger than death." On Marcuse's account, authentic art remains true to the promise of the "vision of a better world," one that lives on "even in defeat." At the same time, though, he channels Benjamin once again in observing that art serves as a warning "against the notion of an iron progress" and "against blind confidence in a humanity which will eventually [and inevitably] assert itself" (1978b: 46–47, 69).

> If art were to promise that at the end good would triumph over evil, such a promise would be refuted by the historical truth. In reality it is evil which triumphs, and there are only islands of good where one can find refuge for a brief time. Authentic works of art are aware of this; they reject the promise made too easily; they refuse the unburdened happy end (1978b: 47).

Raising the specters of "Auschwitz and My Lai" as well as "torture, starvation, and dying," Marcuse explains that authentic art gives form to those realities and desires which survive the negating turns of historical fate and which may "one day make [such negations] impossible"; true art thus preserves the memory of human happiness despite and against Auschwitz. As consideration of the various atrocities of history attests to, the images of a freer, more joyous existence as projected by art hence are not promises, but "only chances." Then citing Bloch without mentioning him by name, Marcuse definitively grants to aesthetic works the ability to "create that other reality within the established one—the cosmos of hope." Such hope can be experienced within the human

consciousness, being a space wherein aesthetics can function to "keep alive
another image and another goal of praxis": "the reconstruction of society and
nature under the principle of increasing the human potential for happiness"
(1978b: 48, 52, 55–56).

Marcuse thus concludes his final work by considering the links that tie art
together with activism. Aesthetic works can protect the memory of the "goals
that failed" in history, and that hence are still to be realized—they can drive
forward the "conquest of suffering and the permanence of joy." For Marcuse,
art stands against all "fetishism of the productive forces" and the "continued
enslavement of individuals by the objective conditions" to affirm the ultimate
end sought by all revolution: "the freedom and happiness of the individual."
Claiming the "horizon of history" still to be "open," Marcuse speculates that,
were the "remembrance of things past" to be integrated into the struggle to
change the world, the revolutions of the future could well surpass the scope
and breadth of all previous historical attempts to change the world for the
better. As the critical theorist writes characteristically, "[t]he revolution is
[made] for the sake of life, not death" (1978b: 56, 69, 73).

PART 2

Reflections on Marcuse

∵

CHAPTER 7

Nature and Revolution

> Look up into the world! Is it not like an advancing triumphal procession
> by which Nature celebrates her eternal victory over all corruption?
>
> HÖLDERIN 1990 [1797–1799]: 164

> [T]he violation of the earth is a vital aspect of the counterrevolution.
>
> MARCUSE 2004: 173

Taking its title from the name of a chapter in *Counterrevolution and Revolt*
which is dedicated to consideration of "Nature and Revolution," this chapter
specifically examines Marcuse's thought on human and non-human nature,
evolution, and ecology. Juxtaposing the importance of the critical theorist's
progressively revolutionary stance on ecological questions and the self-
evidently profound environmental destruction being prosecuted in our own
day, this section proceeds through time much like previous chapters in chroni-
cling the efflorescent development of Marcuse's dialectical and revolutionary
views on nature—ones that are intimately tied to the thinker's affirmation
of Eros as a liberatory historical force. The argument then turns to reflect
on Marcuse's claim in the *Essay on Liberation* that there exists a biological
predisposition toward cooperation and socialism, and concludes by exploring
the relevance of "Repressive Tolerance" for animal and Earth liberation movements today.

Though Marcuse in his early writings focuses principally on art, politics, and
humanist-existentialist philosophy, it cannot be denied that nature is present
in his *oeuvre* from the beginning. Truly, it would have been difficult for Marcuse
not to have contemplated the non-human world while living and studying
within the Black Forest in Freiburg after the First World War. In his dissertation on *The German Artist-Novel*, Marcuse affirms the subversive existence and
practice of renegades and non-conformist artists in medieval Europe, noting
these artists' alienation from society as demanding fundamental changes in
that society—thus in a way signaling the introduction of the thinker's lifelong
commitment to "romantic revolutionary" perspectives, ones that he shared
with his comrades Benjamin and Adorno. Michael Löwy argues that Marcuse
from his youth expressed a *nostalgia for premodern Kultur* as a reflection of

his repudiation of reified industrial-capitalist technology and its destruction of nature (Löwy 1999: 211). This ecological tendency is later developed during Marcuse's period of study with Heidegger and subsequently thereafter, but it is evident from Marcuse's earliest postwar studies, especially within the context of Marcuse's first engagements with German Idealism, Charles Fourier, and Romanticism.

Critically, in his 1964 review of Benjamin's "Critique of Force" (*Kritik der Gewalt*, 1921), Marcuse acknowledges his indebtedness to the criticism Benjamin makes in this work of productivism and the exploitation of the non-human world, declaring an "emancipated and redeemed nature" to correspond to a "liberated people [who have been] redeemed from oppressive violence" (Marcuse 2014: 126). Continuing in this line, Marcuse in his *Habilitationsschrift* on historicity and ontology enthusiastically relays Hegel's declaration that humankind "is the whole of nature come to consciousness" (1987: 206). Though this type of Hegelian perspective could be taken as reflecting a tendency toward speciesism, whereby human beings regard themselves as superior to other terrestrial beings, the phrase itself is very close to a similarly shattering observation made by French anarchist Élisée Reclus—that humanity is "Nature becoming self-conscious" (Reclus 1905–1908: i). Reclus for his part was no Promethean, being known instead as the "Vegetarian Communard"; in this way, he shares much with the insurgent anarchist vegetarian Práxedis G. Guerrero and the anarcho-pacifist Lev Tolstoy, who also adopted a plant-based diet near life's end (Hochschartner 2014; Lomnitz 2014: 258). In parallel to these three thinkers and actors, Marcuse does not appear to take Hegel's interpretation of nature and reason in a speciesist direction, at least in his examination of *Hegel's Ontology*, where he announces in revolutionary fashion that the human subject or "I" must *"no longer seek and find satisfaction in an 'objectifying manner,' but as self-conscious being in another self-conscious being"* (Marcuse 1987: 245; emphasis added). Naturally, neither consciousness nor self-consciousness is limited to humanity, for both are evident in several other species that have evolved on Earth over time, including presently existing mammals, birds, and octopi, as the 2012 Cambridge Declaration on Consciousness acknowledges (Bekoff 2012). For this reason, Marcuse's statement on satisfaction and inter-relations reflects the profundity of his views on nature well.

Nonetheless, despite these promising beginnings to the development of a liberatory philosophy of nature, Marcuse succumbs to rather orthodox, retrograde views on the non-human world for a time in his early years, this largely under the influence of Marxist materialism and his colleagues at the Frankfurt School, who had by this time not yet outlined the radical-ecological analyses they would advance in the period after World War II. As an illustration of this unfortunate tendency, in his 1932 review for *Die Gesellschaft* of Marx's newly discovered *Economic and Philosophical Manuscripts* (1844), Marcuse writes that all of "'nature' (in the widest sense of extrahuman being) is the medium of human life, the life-means [or food] of [humans]," and accordingly that humanity must "appropriate" nature or "make it [its] own" rather than "come to terms with [it]" (Jay 1973: 74–75). Furthermore, in his contribution to the 1936 volume on *Studies on Authority and the Family*, Marcuse betrays the spirit of Benjamin's critical approach and instead affirms prevailing Marxian anthropocentrism by claiming the "general interest" to be "the reproduction of the whole society under the *best exploitation of the productive forces available*, for the greatest happiness of the individuals" (Marcuse 2008: 94; emphasis added). Even when writing on Heidegger and historical materialism in 1928, Marcuse would assert that the history of nature is none at all, thus reserving the category of history for human experience (*Dasein*) only (Marcuse 2005: 21).

Reiterating the point he makes in the *Study on Authority*, Marcuse in the *Negations* essays claims the future historical chance for reason and freedom to rest upon the domination of nature by production—thus reflecting the extent to which Marcuse and the rest of the Frankfurt School circle would seem to have been enthralled to Lenino-Stalinist notions of objectifying nature early on in their exile from Germany. In particular, Marcuse's treatment of the thought of René Descartes in "The Concept of Essence" (1936) is far from critical, especially considering the Renaissance thinker's association of autonomous thought and authentic being with the idea of controlling nature. This is an idea Marcuse does not explicitly call into question. Rather, the philosopher hails the arrival of Descartes' "practical philosophy" as a corrective to the merely "speculative philosophies" bequeathed by the Greeks of antiquity. Deeply contradicting his previous and future Romantic views of nature, Marcuse here would seem to uncritically accept Descartes' idea that humans "should be able to utilize [all bodies that surround them] in like manner for all the uses to which they are suited" (Marcuse 1968: 44–49; Descartes 1929: 49). If Marcuse does not affirm this attempt at rationalizing the domination of nature, he at the very least presents it neutrally. At best, Marcuse here is merely presenting Descartes' views for consideration—for after all, "The Concept of Essence" was written for the *Journal of Social Research*—just as he presents Engels' justification of "revolutionary" coercion in the *Study on Authority*.[1] Nonetheless, it is more likely that Marcuse here actually is

---

1 See Chapter 3 above.

contemplating the value and necessity of the Cartesian account of the domination of nature and so is continuing with the established anthropocentric tendencies of much of Western philosophy. Hegel for his part is known for having
famously distinguished between *zoe* ("biological life") and *phos* ("conceptual
life"), claiming the latter to be the exclusive realm of humans (Marcuse 1987:
205). While it is unknown to what degree Marcuse accepted this distinction,
he does mimic it in his claim that only *Dasein* is historical. Nevertheless it must
be acknowledged that it is one thing to acknowledge that humans are capable
of reason whereas other animals are not, and quite another to claim this difference to justify humanity's exploitation of the rest of nature. The problem is
that, in contrast to the critical theorist's initial period of study in Freiburg, it is
not entirely clear that Marcuse recognizes this distinction during the period of
his early exile.

   This chauvinist, nature-domineering phase in Marcuse's lifework must be
acknowledged; it cannot be overlooked—just as Sartre's Stalinist phase cannot
be. Yet it should also be emphasized that, in parallel to the case of Sartre, it was
only for a short time that Marcuse thoughtlessly accepted orthodox-Marxist
notions of subjugating nature. After parting ways with the Frankfurt School and
ending his governmental work, Marcuse would go on to develop a highly revolutionary philosophy of nature—this, by returning to his studies in Freiburg
and raising these to a higher level still. What is more, his changing perspectives
on nature echo those of his colleagues Horkheimer and Adorno, who present a fundamentally ecological-socialist critique beginning with *Dialectic of
Enlightenment* (1944). Hence, by the time of his meteoric rise to status as revolutionary prophet on the world stage in the 1960s, Marcuse would significantly
be calling for the supersession of Marxian prometheanism by utopian socialism, as in "The End of Utopia," *An Essay on Liberation,* and "Re-Examination
of the Concept of Revolution." Reflection on rural, agrarian, and pre-capitalist
settings and spaces, both historical and contemporary, would play a key role in
the development of Marcuse's libertarian eco-socialist alternative—regardless
of what André Nicolas has to say about Marcuse neglecting the role of the
peasantry (Nicolas 1970: 114). The most important source signaling the definitive shift in Marcuse's thought from ambivalence regarding the anthropocentric and positivist aspects of Marxist theory to a transcendental embrace of
revolutionary ecology is *Eros and Civilization.*

   In this philosophical inquiry into Freud, Marcuse deals most directly with
the question of the liberation of nature in the volume's second section, which
is dedicated to thinking beyond the hegemony of the reality or performance
principle—and, in truth, to surpassing it altogether in material terms. Here,
Marcuse invokes Kant, Schiller, and Fourier to postulate that non-human
nature, like humanity itself, must in a future revolutionary society be treated

as a partner endowed with autonomy and viewed as having rights to solidarity and liberation. Much in the way that Adorno and Horkheimer fiercely denounce the domination of nature in *Dialectic of Enlightenment*, Marcuse in *Eros and Civilization* claims there to exist an indelible instrumental link which ties humanity's domination of external nature into the domination exercised within human society; in particular, the depth of destruction of animal life undertaken by the historical course of repressive civilization does not go unmentioned in Marcuse's account (Marcuse 1966a: 87, 114). Though he does not here provide a sustained reflection on the relationship between human and non-human, as Adorno and Horkheimer do in the section on "Man and Animal" in *Dialectic of Enlightenment*, as elsewhere, it can be said that the sensual, Romantic vision Marcuse presents in the volume bears similarities with Schiller's letter on the concept of freedom among animals, as set forth in *The Aesthetic Education of Man*:

> When the lion is not gnawed by hunger and no beast of prey is challenging him to battle, his idle energy creates for itself an object; he fills the echoing desert with his high-spirited roaring, and his exuberant power enjoys itself in purposeless display. The insect swarms with joyous life in the sunbeam; and it is assuredly not the cry of desire which we hear in the melodious warbling of the song-bird. Undeniably there is freedom in these movements [...]. The animal *works* when deprivation is the mainspring of its activity, and it *plays* when the fullness of its strength is this mainspring, when superabundant life is its own stimulus to activity.
> SCHILLER 1954: 133

This excerpt demonstrates the ties Schiller sees among toil, play, freedom, and the animal kingdom—associations which Marcuse may well have internalized. In this vein, it is significant that the critical theorist opens this second half of *Eros and Civilization* by citing an intimately ecological vision, as penned by the Irish socialist dramatist Sean O'Casey:

> Oh, we have had enough of the abuse of this fair earth! It is no sad truth that this should be our home. Were it but to give us simple shelter, simple clothing, simple food, adding the lily and the rose, the apple and the pear, it would be a fit home for mortal or immortal [humanity].
> MARCUSE 1966a: 127

In discussing the contributions Kant and Schiller's aesthetic theories could make to the development of a new sensibility which could in time displace the performance principle in favor of a new reality principle that would enshrine

Eros in the life-world, Marcuse explains his advocacy of a non-instrumental relationship with nature. On this account, the external world is to lose "its mere utility" and be encountered and related to not "in terms of its usefulness" or "according to any purpose it may possibly serve" in a future emancipated society, but instead come to be considered as having intrinsic value (1966a: 164–166, 177–178). In other words, the non-human world must come to be considered "a subject with which to live," as the critical theorist writes later in *Counterrevolution and Revolt* (1972b: 65). Crucially, Marcuse employs the figure of Orpheus as an illustration of this libertarian, anti-promethean environmental vision, announcing the emancipatory mythological countercurrent symbolized by Orpheus as promising a non-repressive unification of humanity with nature, replete with beauty, tranquility, sensuousness, Eros, and order. In similar fashion, Marcuse argues that the figure of Narcissus serves to preserve memory of the very real interrelatedness of human life with nature and evolution as a whole: Narcissus, in reflecting on his own beauty, also contemplates the limitless beauty of the cosmos and in this way exhibits what Freud termed an "oceanic feeling" of oneness with the known universe (1966a: 161–168). While Marcuse's claim that non-human nature should be allowed "just to be what it is" may appear somewhat abstract, it reflects the theorist's Schillerian concern for the project of a reconciliation between humanity and nature and idealistically and anarchically points to the importance of the development of autonomous, ecological sensibilities within the revolutionary struggle against domination and hierarchy. In *Eros and Civilization*, the images of Orpheus and Narcissus represent anticipatory references for the development of the Great Refusal and the progression of the dialectics of history toward liberation for humanity and nature.

In comparison with the account Marcuse provides in *Eros and Civilization*, ecological reflection would seem to ebb in *One-Dimensional Man*. Still, Marcuse in this work does discuss the natural world at points, associating the reign of one-dimensionality with the conquest of nature that predates it and renders it possible. Marcuse suggests that the power of nature as a force of opposition and negation is degraded "when cities and highways and National Parks replace the villages, valleys, and forests [and] when motorboats race over the lakes and planes cut through the skies." Moreover, in a short series of provocative illustrations depicting the "happy marriage of the positive and the negative," Marcuse satirically takes on the persona of a car-owner experiencing pleasure in an automobile who then precipitously comes to realize the "unnecessary" power and "idiotic" size of the machine (1964: 56, 66, 70, 226). Beyond this, he dedicates a whole sketch to a hike in the woods:

I take a walk in the country. Everything is as it should be: Nature at its best. Birds, sun, soft grass, a view through the trees of the mountains, nobody around, no radio, no smell of gasoline. Then the path turns and ends on the highway. I am back among the billboards, service stations, motels, and roadhouses. I was in a National Park, and I now know that this was not reality. It was a 'reservation,' something that is being preserved like a species dying out. If it were not for the government, the billboards, hot dog stands, and motels would long since have invaded that piece of Nature (1964: 226).

Clearly, the reference here to government as guarantor of the protection of the environment is ideology, the expression not of Marcuse but of the persona he has donned—in an echo of the pleasure which the critical theorist has the automobile-owner take in his car. Marcuse's specific mention of gasoline here may be significant as a possible allusion to Heidegger's critique of the instrumental rationality which reduces nature to "a gigantic gasoline-station" (Adorno 2006: 45). In point of fact, the Heideggerian imprint on Marcuse's comments regarding nature generally in *One-Dimensional Man* is marked, and the social critic even quotes his former mentor in the text: "Modern man [*sic*] takes the entirety of Being as raw material for production and subjects the entirety of the object-world to the sweep and order of production." Significantly in this sense, Marcuse expressly identifies the denial of the human duty of respect for non-human animals as an oppressive vestige of philosophical idealism, and he counterposes a materialist vision that would recognize the "ill-treatment" of animals as part of the capitalist "Hell" to be abolished (1964: 153–154, 237).

Though brief and fragmentary, Marcuse's ecological account in *One-Dimensional Man* is radical and devastating, thus reflecting Heidegger's thought on the question. Nevertheless, the critical theorist does here express his disagreement with the author of *Being and Time*, arguing dialectically that the development of industry and technology can "proceed" in a fashion "different" to that imposed by the unreason of capital and State (1964: 222). In this way returning implicitly to the existentialist engagements of his youth, Marcuse criticizes what he perceives as Heidegger's conflation of technology, destruction, and domination. As a matter of fact, in "Socialist Humanism?", published in an eponymous volume edited by Fromm the year after the release of *One-Dimensional Man*, Marcuse provides an anarchistic definition of the technological rationality to be wielded by humanity after it has "do[ne] away with the masters who guide them to desist from this effort," postulating a new relationship with nature as being among the myriad examples of possible future manifestations of this new rationality (1965b: 103). In a 1971 interview, additionally, Marcuse calls for the "dissolution of the present cities," the abolition of the private automobile, and the elimination of "noise and massive togetherness," presenting the alternative of a "symbiosis" between humanity and nature at the architectural, political, economic, and instinctual levels of existence (2011: 197).

In 1972, at a French conference on the environment, Marcuse presented an address on "Ecology and Revolution." Beginning with reflections on the Vietnam War which was raging at the time, Marcuse identifies the imperial war as both genocidal and ecocidal, for besides indiscriminately and purposely targeting the Vietnamese civilian population, it also "attacks the sources and resources of life itself," as is reflected in the sordid use of napalm munitions, herbicides, and defoliants by the u.s. military. Marcuse frames the war as the "capitalist response to the attempt at revolutionary ecological liberation" taken by the Vietnamese people, who seek the "economic and social rehabilitation of the land." Passing to a social- or metapsychological discussion of nature as a symbol of liberation and tranquility, Marcuse remarks on the tendency toward the cooptation of environmentalism in the u.s., in light of the ubiquity of ads calling on spectators to "save the environment," and of the numerous governmental commissions which are set up to supposedly regulate environmental degradation. While the critical theorist is wary of such trends, he also acknowledges that environmental reforms can help advance the progression of deeper tendencies toward revolutionary thought and action, though he is clear to maintain that "the issue is not the purification of the existing society but its replacement." Declaring "the ecological logic" to be inherently at odds with capitalist unreason, and announcing that the "struggle for an expansion of the world of beauty, nonviolence and serenity" is a "political struggle," Marcuse concludes by insisting that authentic ecology must be militant and socialist: it must "attack the system at its roots, both in the process of production and in the mutilated consciousness of individuals" (2004: 173–176).

Next to this short intervention on "Ecology and Revolution," and with the exception of the *Essay on Liberation*, which is duly discussed below, it is undoubtedly in *Counterrevolution and Revolt* that Marcuse focuses most systematically on ecological politics, providing a vision that logically follows from the initial sketches provided in *Eros and Civilization*. Here, as has been mentioned, Marcuse dedicates an entire chapter to "Nature and Revolution" wherein he claims the non-human world to be an "ally" in the human struggle against the nexus of triple domination on hand in late capitalism: that over self, other humans, and external nature (1972b: 59). Marcuse identifies the "radical transformation of nature" as now of necessity becoming a central aspect of the project of revolutionary social change, for he quite rightly claims it to be "obvious" that "the violation of nature is inseparable from the economy of capitalism." Approvingly citing Murray Bookchin's 1971 essay "Ecology and Revolutionary Thought," Marcuse here extends the critique of the capitalist exploitation of nature to the traditional Marxist concept—and, it should be added, his former self—given that Marx and his more orthodox followers largely objectify nature, considering it to be little more than the "field" wherein the "rational" development of the productive forces will take place. Following from his argumentation in *Eros and Civilization*, Marcuse endorses the "liberation of nature" as against the Marxian "*hubris* of domination," noting that the libertarian alternative of "letting-be" promises the very negation of existing relations of nature-objectification (1972b: 59–62, 67–69). Marcuse here is expanding on the radical ecological vision he outlines in "Cultural Revolution" (1970), wherein he insists that the "heritage" of exploitation cannot be considered as having been "thrown off" until nature's autonomy is recognized and respected (2001: 131–132). In this vein, in his 1972 book, Marcuse expands on his prior comments regarding non-human animals from *One-Dimensional Man*, arguing that "no free society is imaginable which does not [...] make the concerted effort to reduce consistently the suffering which [humanity] imposes on the animal world." In light of such a statement, it is curious that Marcuse dismisses the chance for ending the "war" between humanity and nature as being a mere delusion related to the "Orphic myth" which he previously had endorsed so passionately; in this sense, he advances the puzzling claim that a movement for "universal vegetarianism" would be "premature" amidst the depth of suffering experienced contemporarily among humans themselves. Thus, it would seem that Marcuse contradicts himself to a degree in "Nature and Revolution" in holding out the future historical possibilities of a new "nonviolent, nondestructive" relationship between humanity and the rest of nature, criticizing Marx's materialism for denying the autonomy of non-human nature, and then dismissing vegetarianism as utopian (1972b: 67–69).

This significant lapse notwithstanding, Marcuse's subversive account of ecology in *Counterrevolution and Revolt* is provocative in its demand that future revolution overturn the normalization of pollution and repressive industrialization. As an illustrative example of the relationship among art, nature, and revolution, Marcuse cites William Blake's epic poem on the French Revolution, which concludes with the "mountains, valleys, and streams" themselves coming to join the historical meeting of the Estates-General, at which the Third Estate unites to commit itself to toppling the Bourbon monarchy, as announced during the Tennis Court Oath of 20 June 1789. Similarly, he raises the question of freedom and beauty by citing Brecht's stark lines delineating the conflict between Eros and Fascism: "Within me there is a struggle between/ The delight about the the blooming apple tree/And the horror about a Hitler speech./But only the latter/Forces me to my desk" (1972b: 17, 103–104, 117). The experience of taking pleasure in natural beauty, then, should not be considered an apolitical act, but rather much the opposite; as Adorno writes in *Aesthetic Theory*, when one encounters natural beauty, she is simultaneously led to become conscious of freedom and anxiety—for nature represents a cipher of the "not-yet," while reflection on possible freedom leads the subject into angst regarding the prevailing obstacles to liberation (Adorno 2002a: 65). Lastly in this sense, Marcuse cites a longer poem by Brecht, "The Lovers," which contemplates the aerial path of a pair of partnered cranes, "[o]ne life to fly into another." Marcuse observes that the poem invokes the image of a free nature: the cranes fly "through their beautiful sky, with the clouds which accompany them: sky and clouds belong[ing] to them—without mastery and domination" (1972b: 119–120).

Another critical aspect of Marcuse's philosophy of nature is his critique of science under capitalism. Marcuse dedicates a significant amount of attention within his life-work to elucidating and critiquing science and its various applications within bourgeois society, employing a utopian-socialist, quasi-Heideggerian perspective. From the early 1960s, and especially around the time of the publication of *One-Dimensional Man*, Marcuse focuses especially on the theory and practice of science, as in his 1964 essay "World Without Logos," his address on the "Science and Phenomenology" of Husserl the same year, and his 1969 lecture to the Scripps Oceanography Institute. These critical evaluations of established science follow from the distaste Marcuse had expressed since his youth for the legitimative philosophy of positivism, in contrast to the revolutionary potentialities of dialectical thought and action. Marcuse's critique of science mobilizes Hegelian negativity and a Heideggerian notion of the "fallenness" of historical development under capital to illuminate prevailing depravity and counterpose an emancipatory model based on a "new science" that would aid humanity in its struggle against domination, social and environmental. Marcuse formally introduces this "new science" in *One-Dimensional Man*, though it is anticipated to an extent in *Eros and Civilization*.

In *An Essay on Liberation*, Marcuse restates his dialectical sublation of Heidegger's take on technology, observing that science and technology have critical roles to serve within the struggle for emancipation—with these being potentialities that are presently blocked by the repressive demands of monopoly capital. In this volume, he raises the possibility of a *gaya scienza* freed from "service to destruction and exploitation" which could assist in the liberatory reconstruction of the life-world (1969a: 12, 30–31). Similarly, Marcuse argues in the "Re-Examination of the Concept of Revolution" that any theory of the radical transformation of society must reject the Marxian fetishism of production and industry and in its place advance the alternative of autonomous, decentralized disruption and overhaul of the productive apparatus from below (1969b: 32). Such heterodoxy was already on display in Marcuse's discussions with the German Socialist Students Union in West Berlin a year before the *Essay* and the "Re-Examination," as is particularly evidenced in the address on the "End of Utopia." Furthermore, in the "Reconsideration" on the "Realm of Freedom and the Realm of Necessity" that he presented in Yugoslavia in 1969, Marcuse depicts the possibility of reformulating industry by keeping it on the human scale (à *la mesure de l'homme*) and thus averting the "massive, noisy, ugly, joyless, competitive features of capitalist production and consumption" while concomitantly providing a suitable life-world for the life-enhancing development of humans and their sensibilities (1969c: 25). In "Nature and Revolution," Marcuse quotes Adorno's *Aesthetic Theory*:

> In schema borrowed from bourgeois sexual morality, technique is said to have ravished nature, yet under transformed relations of production it would just as easily be able to assist nature and *on this sad Earth help it attain what it perhaps wants.*
>
> ADORNO 2002a: 68; emphasis added

These later critical treatments of technology are latent within the lecture on "The Obsolescence of Psychoanalysis" from fifteen years prior, wherein Marcuse argues for a melding of technique with Eros that would accelerate the coming of a "less repressive yet higher stage of civilization" (1970a: 56). As with revolution in the political and economic spheres, Marcuse envisions scientific revolution playing a critical role in the confluence of anti-systemic countercurrents (1972b: 55).

Marcuse's critical analysis of science and technology reflects the thinker's Hegelian and Romantic wish to have anti-capitalist modes of thinking and acting displace hegemonic thought and established power, heralding the birth of *society as a work of art*. Indeed, Marcuse integrates his libertarian interpretation of science into the civilizational alternative he proposes beginning with *Eros and Civilization*; at the end of his life, he will declare that technology ideally should "be used creatively and imaginatively to reconstruct nature and the environment," and that its employment should be guided by the "criteria of beauty" (2007: 232). Both in and beyond *Eros and Civilization*, Marcuse stresses the call for the abolition of unnecessary labor and the transformation of socially necessary labor into "attractive labor" or *play*, and in so doing he again expresses disagreement with Marx, who in the *Grundrisse* famously denies the possibility of this Fourierist goal (Marcuse 1965b: 101; Marx 1953: 599). In insisting on the point, Marcuse foreshadows the call he would make in "The End of Utopia" for the superiority of Fourier over Marx (Marcuse 1970a: 78). Characteristically, Marcuse's revolutionary hopes for nature and scientific revolution are summarized well in "Cultural Revolution": the realization of *humanitas*, or a humanity in solidarity,

> implies the establishment of a new (sensuous) relationship between [humanity] and nature. Nature would become a Subject in its own right and *Telos:* as the environment and soil of freedom, which is incompatible with the enslavement and violation of nature, its treatment as a mere object. In other words, the object would be experienced as subject to the degree to which the subject, [humanity], makes the object world into a humane world. *Realization of nature through the realization of [humanity] as 'species being':* for nature too, has become an object of destructive exploitation—nature too calls for liberation.
>
> MARCUSE 2002: 132; emphasis added

Marcuse exhibits highly Romantic and optimistic hopes within the revolutionary philosophy of nature he develops in his writings on nature and ecology. Yet it should be noted that his Romanticism is tempered dialectically by negativity and marked concern, particularly as seen at the very close of the critical theorist's life. In his updated version on the question of the "Failure of the New Left?" (1979), Marcuse sounds the tocsin against the increasingly fatal state of the world as subjected to capitalist "progress," warning that "the system can now develop only if it destroys the means of production, even human life itself, on an international scale" (2004: 188). In point of fact, Marcuse's very final address in life on the "Children of Prometheus" emphasizes the worsening "productive destruction" demanded by capital of necessity, and "Proto-socialism and Late Capitalism" examines ties between Eros and the ecology movement, feminism, and anti-authoritarianism in general. Similarly, one of the last public lectures he gave in California, "Ecology and the Critique of Modern Society," deals centrally with the question of the tensions between environmental degradation and the chance for emancipation. Addressing himself to students of a local youth wilderness class—and thus returning at the end of life to his adolescent participation in the *Wandervogel*—Marcuse presents an especially moving analysis of the destruction of nature and resistance to such as embodied by radical ecology movements, associating the profundity of the former with the hegemonic strength of Thanatos and the prospects of the latter with the resurgence of Eros. In fact, Marcuse interprets the destruction of "other living beings [...] and nature" as an externalization of the strength of Thanatos—one that wards off a quick resolution by means of suicide in the individual case, thus prolonging the "long detour to death" (2011: 206–207, 212).

As a final statement of sorts from the critical theorist, this address to the wilderness hikers centrally examines the social psychology of destructiveness, with Marcuse distinguishing between the radical character structure, defined as "a preponderance in the individual of life instincts over the death instinct," and the affirmative character structure, which serves to uphold hegemonic depravity and unreason. Marcuse recognizes that, amidst the grip of dominant ideology and relative material comfort in U.S. society, resistance to the vast ruination of late capital will at least temporarily be reserved to numerical minorities of conscious individuals and groups. However, with implicit reference to Rudolf Bahro, he resolutely claims emancipatory needs—far from being bested by the compensatory needs that prop up the given state of affairs—to "permeate the lives of individuals." As evidence of such trends, he shares his observations regarding the accelerated breakdown of the Puritan work ethic and patriarchal morality (2011: 208–211).

In closing, Marcuse discusses the intimate relationship between Eros and militant environmentalism. He depicts ecological concern as a manifestation of the erotic goal of "protect[ing] and enhanc[ing] life itself," of expressing "protective care" for nature and life. The viewpoints and demands made by radical ecologists show such groupings to be "political and psychological movement[s] of liberation," in light of their clear antagonism to capital on the one hand and their emphasis on the restoration also of *human nature* on the other (2011: 212). Marcuse considers the increasingly prevalent fragmentation of contemporary radical movements to nearly be canceled out by the highly erotic standpoints taken by their constituents, whose rebellions—far from desiring to replace "one power structure for another"—instead represent

> *existential revolts* against an obsolete reality principle [...] carried by the mind and body of individuals themselves [...]. A revolt in which the *whole organism*, the *very soul of the human being*, becomes political. A revolt of the life instincts *against organized and socialized* destruction (2011: 212; emphasis added).

Recalling the libertarian rebels of medieval Europe he first examined in *The German Artist-Novel*, Marcuse speaks to the perceived weakness and powerlessness of existing radical political formations, observing that their marginality reflects their authenticity, and that their isolation points up the categorical necessity of breaking totally with the "realistic, profitable destruction" of capitalism. Much like Adorno in *Negative Dialectics*, Marcuse concludes by providing his definition of the "human goal" of radical social change: that is, the emergence of human beings who are "physically and mentally incapable" of allowing for the future recurrence of Auschwitz (2011: 213).

Nature, Evolution, and Morality

Within the context of the militant heights of the late 1960s, Marcuse presents one of his most imaginative and utopian claims on revolution and human nature: that political radicalism employs morality as a forerunner of liberation, and that the exercise of moral radicalism activates the "elementary, organic foundation of morality in the human being" (1969a: 10). Expanding on this latter point, Marcuse makes the following speculative claim:

> Prior to all ethical behavior in accordance with specific social standards, prior to all ideological expression, morality is a 'disposition' of the organism, perhaps rooted in the erotic drive to counter aggressiveness, to create and preserve 'ever greater unities' of life (1969a: 10).

The claim is surreal—shattering, Romantic. Marcuse raises the point metaphysically in the *Essay on Liberation*, and so does not directly develop or expand upon the idea. Neither does he present much of any evidence to support such a foundational claim from biological science. Yet in light of the stipulated radicalism which Marcuse claims for his conception of *bios*, the question arises to consider the merit of his erotic views on life. What sort of evidence can be contemplated to either support or reject Marcuse's argument regarding biology and Eros?

Admittedly, it is difficult to ascertain whether Marcuse's claim refers to nature in general or just to human nature; it is unclear which "organism" the critical theorist has in mind. Whether or not Marcuse means to distinguish between humanity and the rest of nature in his Romantic-metaphysical speculation, the reality is that the two cannot be so readily differentiated, considering the course of the evolution of life on Earth: humans, like all other terrestrial and marine species, have evolved from other animals and developed in co-evolution with numerous other beings. Intriguingly in this sense, recent discoveries have shown that all humans of Eurasian descent contain between 1 and 4 percent Neanderthal DNA—the result of a dialectical intermixing which in some ways allowed the non-human "rival" species to live on even after its extinction some forty thousand years ago (Kolbert 2014: 238–247; Green et al. 2010: 710–722; Vergano 2014). Considering the fate of Neanderthals, as well as the devastating paleolithic extinctions of various megafauna for which early hunter-gatherer human groups were at least partly responsible—to say nothing of the current situation, marked as it is by relentless destructiveness—*homo sapiens sapiens* should not consider itself to be the pinnacle of terrestrial evolution. As with the work of Copernicus and Galileo, which displaced the Earth from being located at the presumed center of the universe, the vast body of contemporary biology and ethology decenters humanity by demonstrating the great commonalities humans share with other animals—as is to be expected, of course, given their co-evolution together. The question of whether morality is manifest in nature in turn raises the question of whether morality is possible for non-human beings. It is unclear if Marcuse would mimic Hegel and Marx in reserving consciousness and morality for humanity and denying agency and the possibility of moral action to the rest of nature, though his explicit criticisms of Marxian hubris suggest that he might not parrot the giants of German dialectical thought in such a fashion, but rather follow the findings of science. If morality is not considered to be the exclusive preserve of humanity, it can certainly be said to be manifested in nature, in accordance with a wealth of scientific observations and investigations. In this way, there seems to be some basis for Marcuse's claim.

In his defense, Marcuse readily could have mentioned the revolutionary hypothesis proposed by biologist Lynn Margulis suggesting serial endosymbiosis—or "living-together within"—as the ancestral origin of both plants and animals, an argument she sets forth in a paper that was published two years before the *Essay on Liberation*. In her 1967 essay and her later book *Early Life* (1982), Margulis argues that the evolutionary birth of eukaryotic (or "truly nucleated") cellular life 1.5 billion years ago took place through a number of mutually beneficial associations among prokaryotes lacking nuclei, as among larger anaerobes which assimilated aerobic bacteria into serving as mitochondria—thus allowing for the later rise of animals through respiration—and free-floating cyanobacteria which became chloroplasts, leading subsequently to the emergence of multicellular photosynthetic organisms, or the plants. Margulis' endosymbiont theory surely exemplifies Marcuse's view of Eros, taken in turn from Freud, who viewed the life-drive as striving to "combine organic substances into ever larger unities," as through anabolism, to take another related biological concept (Freud 1950: 57). An additional consideration to support Marcuse's line is the presumed absence of predation during the early evolution of multicellular life in the Earth's oceans: the idea here is that the predator–prey relationship emerged only with the beginning of the

Cambrian explosion some 530 million years ago, coming a billion years after the rise of the eukaryotes (Reece et al. 2011: 518, 656–657). What is more, in his review of the evolutionary biology of the transition from marine to terrestrial life, Carl Zimmer hypothesizes in a similar vein that it was the innovation of herbivory 300 million years ago which allowed the amniotes—the precursors of reptiles, birds, and mammals—to radiate throughout the Earth's landmasses, thus "adapting" more successfully to the new environment than their rivals the amphibians, who lack the ability to lay shelled eggs on land (Zimmer 1998: 109–116).

In accordance with Zimmer's account, and as contemplation of the history of life shows, the course of cosmic time and the evolutionary process on Earth in no way suggest humans to be the *telos* of universal creation. In a reflective manner, Zimmer writes with wonder on the evolution of cetaceans (whales and dolphins), observing the process whereby ungulates not unlike hippopotami returned to the ocean from the land to become sea mammals as demonstrating "that in the history of life there are many stories worth knowing other than our own evolution" (Zimmer 1998: 134). With this in mind, it is important to consider the point made by Carl Sagan—who incidentally was partnered with Margulis for some years—that humans and all other life-forms are "children [...] of the stars," for we are all made from the stellar contents expelled by red giant stars in the deep past: hydrogen, carbon, oxygen, silicon, iron, calcium, magnesium, potassium, and so on (Sagan 1980b). Consciousness, human and animal, is a manifestation of universal order, and potentially a demonstration of historical progress. Still, it is not an emergent biological property that could justify disregard for or destructiveness toward life-forms lacking evident sentience or awareness. The strong sense of *biophilia*—"love for life"—felt by humans toward existence and nature provides further evidence for the claim about the morality of life; as Sagan declares, much like Marcuse would, "we are born to delight in the world" (Sagan 1980c).

Thinking of Sagan and the cosmos, perhaps at some time in the future, knowledge of the development of life elsewhere in the galaxy or universe will come to be known, and this could help to corroborate or reject Marcuse's fantastical claim regarding the erotic basis of evolution and existence. Certainly, much evidence exists regarding the centrality of cooperation, solidarity, and mutual aid in the Earth's evolutionary process, as has been observed among humans and the millions of other species of Earth. The classic text detailing these features remains Peter Kropotkin's *Mutual Aid: A Factor in Evolution* (1902), wherein the Russian anarcho-biologist demonstrates how sociability and association confer evolutionary advantages among animal species. He considers the behaviors of beetles, crabs, ants, bees, birds, and mammals,

finding among them all a marked stress on forms of collective action—
as in food-sharing, movement and migration in common, mutual protection and
defense, and even a simple Schillerian conviviality for the "enjoyment of life"—
which play key roles in the survival and propagation of the species. In a parallel
of sort to Zimmer's comments on the early amniotes, Kropotkin holds association and mutual support to be most evidently practiced among mammals by
the herbivorous ungulates and ruminants—deer, antelopes, gazelles, buffalo,
goats, sheep, horses, donkeys, zebras, cows, elephants, hippopotami, rhinoceri—as well as by the marine carnivores, including walruses, seals, whales, and
dolphins. He remarks that it is quite telling to see that the animals which "most
approach [humans] by their structure and intelligence" are "eminently sociable," and that consciousness advances hand-in-hand with life in the process
of natural selection. Reflecting particularly on the lives of apes, Kropotkin
concludes from his ethological data that compassion, which follows from
association, dialectically carries group welfare further; that the "fittest are thus
the most sociable animals"; and that "sociability appears as the chief factor of
evolution" (Kropotkin 1972: 33–65, 68–70). Half a century after the anarchist
prince published his theory of mutual aid, John Bowlby, the psychobiologist
who founded attachment theory, would argue in parallel to Kropotkin—as
well, in fact, as Fromm—that attachment relationships among humans origi-
nate from the affective parental bond with offspring which materially functions to protect infants and children and allow them to flourish (Bowlby 1958).
To revise the epigram by Ferdinand Kürnberger with which Adorno opens
Minima Moralia, life "wants" to live, in short, as the basic function of the animal immune system attests to, and as the myriad of the organism's physiological systems working together optimally in concert show (Adorno 2005: 19).

Expanding on Kropotkin's findings, one could look to species as distinct as
seahorses, elephants, moas, and bonobos to find matriarchal forms of social
organization—and in the unique case of the bonobo, one finds an animal that
regularly employs sex to address everything from greetings and farewells to
conflict resolution via the relief of anxiety, tension, and aggression (Quammen
2013).[2] Alongside chimpanzees, their neighbor species whose habitat is located
on the right side of the Congo River—with the bonobos living on the left—
these apes share the greatest genetic similarity to humans: 98.7% of the genes

---

2 Moas were large flightless birds that flourished in Aotearoa (later New Zealand) before Poly-
   nesian colonization in the thirteen century CE; they had been driven entirely to extinction
   by the time Europeans first arrived to the islands half a millennium later (Kolbert 2014b:
   225–226, 232).

of both species are identical to those of humans (Prüfer et al. 2012). Current scientific understanding hypothesizes the human genome as being a mosaic of the DNA that humans share with bonobos and chimpanzees—with such a claim suggesting the possibility that humans can live and act in more erotic, egalitarian ways like the bonobos, rather than hierarchically and violently, as chimpanzees have predominantly been observed to behave. As a matter of fact, in a presentation at Left Forum 2014 on "Developing a New Psychiatric Paradigm for Individual and Social Liberation," Dr. Carl Cohen explicitly criticized Marcuse's account of human nature for its supposed essentialism regarding the postulated fundamental predisposition toward Eros, yet he himself went on to elucidate the robust conclusions made in biological social research which emphasize basic human tendencies toward social justice, empathy, and cooperation—thus in fact providing evidence in favor of Marcuse's claim, as well as of Kropotkin's general argument. In point of fact, it is this highly subversive potential within Eros that forms the basis of the anti-authoritarian Freudian social psychology that was developed by Marcuse in concert with Fromm, yet also in conflict with him.

Though considerable evidence could indeed be marshaled in defense of Marcuse's erotic take on *bios*, the metaphysical hypothesis suffers from at least one major problem, for it presumes Eros to guide if not determine evolution. Empirically, the theory of natural selection—or *descent with modification*—shows the history of life on Earth to have developed highly randomly, far from reflecting any notion of purpose or outside influence, whether the work of "intelligent design" or Eros. The biological sciences make clear that evolution progresses on the basis of already existing species-variations in interaction with changing environments, and that it evidently does not tend necessarily toward improvement, as the various imperfections natural selection has yielded within species can attest to (Reece et al. 2011: 484–485, 529–531). Beyond consideration of the internal dynamics of evolution on Earth, a hypothesis presented by Professor Steven Benner raises the possibility that terrestrial life actually originated on Mars, with our red neighbor providing an environment which was more amenable to life than that of the early Earth, bombarded as the latter planet was *en masse* by asteroids, planetoids, and comets for the first billion years of its existence. Benner's claim is that life made it here to the oceans which formed after the cessation of bombardment by riding on meteorites, or having been dispersed via volcanic eruptions on Mars (Press Association 2013; Redfern 2013; Clark 2014). Assuming Benner's hypothesis to be true—with this being a conclusion that would require far more evidence than is now available to be considered robust—Marcuse might have seen the fact that life spread to Earth rather than remain on Mars as a reflection of the action of Eros, for evolution certainly would have been greatly constrained, had it been limited to developing within the Martian environment. It may have never progressed beyond the methanogens that were possibly discovered by the Curiosity rover in December 2014 (Sample 2014).

In a similarly fundamental way, NASA scientist Bernard Foing observes that the exceedingly random and catastrophic formation of the moon that resulted from Earth's collision with a small planet 4.5 billion years ago played a critical role in facilitating the emergence of marine and later terrestrial life, through Luna's stabilization of Earth's rotation axis and regulation of tides and oceans, as well as via its potential role in stimulating Earth's convection and thus plate tectonics and continental drift (Foing 2014). Besides the hypothesis on Martian origins and the unexpected emergence of the lunar satellite, a multitude of other events from the history of earthly life can be marshaled to challenge the idea of Eros as regulatory power over time, particularly if we consider the six mass extinction events experienced over the course of the past 4 billion years. Imagining for a moment that the basically erotic meaning of being could be said to persist within the process of evolution even after the worst of these catastrophes—for the Permian extinction event 252 million years ago destroyed well over 96% of marine animal species (Reece et al. 2011: 521–522)—Marcuse's theory still cannot be squared with the following realities: the observed randomness of mutation and natural selection; the influences geography has had on evolution in Earth, particularly as regards continental drift resulting from plate tectonics; or indeed the cosmological factors pertaining to the location and movement of Earth and the Solar System within the Milky Way galaxy, and those of that galaxy within the universe at large.

Marcuse hence would seem to be at least partly mistaken in his assumption that Eros guides evolution. To bracket this consideration for the moment, it is intriguing to note that it is not in fact in the *Essay on Liberation* where Marcuse first argues for instinctual morality and the erotic basis of life. For one, such points are implied in the discussion of aesthetics and pleasure in *Eros and Civilization*, though Marcuse identifies them explicitly much earlier in *Hegel's Ontology*. In this work, while discussing the *Science of Logic*, Marcuse quotes Hegel favorably as asserting that dialectical historical progress—realization of the Idea, concept, or "good"—"posits itself eternally as *purpose* and produces its actuality through its activity," and he observes positively that the good "is contained within the Being of beings"—this "as purpose, goal, and what ought to be" (Marcuse 1987: 170). In so holding that a natural predisposition to Eros exists in biological life, Marcuse expresses an implicit disagreement with Freud, who in his late instinct theory claimed neither Eros nor Thanatos to have any inherent or 'natural' advantage against the other. What remains clear—as Marcuse emphasizes, and as Fromm would concur—is that Thanatos dominates the 'factual' political world of existence. In this sense, Marcuse's interpretation of Eros and biology serves as a negative mirror-image of the 'bad totality' characterized by aggression and destruction toward nature and social unfreedom.

In sum, Marcuse's hypothesis regarding the basic erotic tendencies of life does not seem to be fully justified by the available evidence, though many data do exist to support it. Besides overlooking the nature of evolutionary change over time, as revealed to us through scientific investigation, Marcuse's account also runs the risk precisely of *naturalizing* social revolution and thus obfuscating the ethical, actively conscious, and autonomous dimensions of struggling for radical social change: "where there is no choice, there can be no liberation either," as Steven Vogel writes (1996: 140–141).

"Repressive Tolerance" and Radical Struggle for Animal and Earth Liberation Today

To conclude this chapter on Marcuse's revolutionary views on nature and ecology, let us consider an essay that has not yet been discussed: "Repressive Tolerance" (1965). The reader will recall that Marcuse in this essay—definitely one of his single-most insurrectional, dating from what is arguably his most militant period in life—distinguishes between liberal or hegemonic tolerance as a barrier to liberation and a subversive or discriminating notion of tolerance that would seek to invert prevailing trends toward total destruction. Critically, Marcuse writes in the third paragraph of this essay that "[t]he elimination of violence" is a "preconditio[n] for the creation of a humane society," and he specifically declares that, alongside humans, "*animals*" must be protected "from cruelty and aggression" (emphasis added). The philosopher also includes within his discussion of liberal tolerance the fatal acceptance of "entrenched and established attitudes and ideas *even if their damaging effect on* [*humans*] *and nature is evident*" (Marcuse 1965d: 82, 85; emphasis added). While these are the only two occasions on which Marcuse explicitly mentions nature and non-human animals in the essay, and though his conception of "true tolerance" as formulated here is mostly concerned with the promotion of human freedom, it is nevertheless significant that he does mention nature and the non-human in this intervention, echoing his earlier recognition that the progressive "advance" of civilization has destroyed not only human but also animal life (1966a: 87). The juxtaposition of the devastation of nature and animal life and the militant tactics endorsed by Marcuse in this essay shows "Repressive Tolerance" to be highly relevant to the projects of animal and Earth liberation a half-century later, in our own acute time. The latest biological studies show a loss of a full *half* of Earth's animal populations since 1970, with 41% of amphibians, 26% of mammals, 13% of birds, and a quarter of all marine species at immediate risk of extinction (Carrington 2014; McKie 2014; Bawden 2015). What is more, the Amazonia region has in recent years experienced an increasingly alarming severity, duration, and frequency of drought, due to a lethal combination of rising global temperatures and tropical deforestation (Watts 2015).

At the very close of his essay on tolerance, in the addendum which was added three years after its original publication, Marcuse suggests that the employment of discriminating tolerance as a means of progressing toward the birth of an emancipated society will most realistically be carried forward by "radical minorities" within society at large, at least initially; for Marcuse, these numerical minorities are to be "intolerant, militantly intolerant and disobedient to the rules of behavior which tolerate destruction and suppression" (Marcuse 1965d; 123). Thinking in terms of radical ecology and animal liberation, it becomes clear what this orientation means: uncompromising defiance, antagonism, and direct action. This is certainly not the approach favored by mainstream environmental groups—the "Gang Green" of the Sierra Club, the Natural Resource Defense Council (NRDC), the Worldwatch Institute, the Nature Conservancy, Greenpeace, and so on (St. Clair and Frank 2010)—but it would seem to approximate the theory and practice of groupings like Earth First!, the Earth Liberation Front (ELF), the Animal Liberation Front (ALF), the international Rising Tide movement, and the popular resistance movements arrayed against extractivism, as evinced by the radical opposition to the imposition of dams, mining operations, and deforestation schemes in Latin America and Asia, as elsewhere. The women of the Chipko movement of the Indian state of Uttar Pradesh, most active during the 1970s and 1980s, are legendary for their resistance to the State's facilitation of commercial logging in the region, following the example set previously by Amrita Devi, who in the eighteenth century organized hundreds of fellow female villagers to sacrifice their lives to prevent a sacred grove of trees from being felled, as ordered by the Maharaja of Jodhpur, who had wanted to have a palace constructed on the site (Guha 2000: 152–184; Kamat 2014). Similarly, forest-defense plays an important role in many of the self-defense movements that have arisen in Mexico's Michoacán, Morelos, and Guerrero states against the Narco-State in recent years—particularly in the Cherán community of Michoacán, as well as in San Francisco Xochicuautla, Mexico state (Sedillo 2013). Moreover, hundreds of thousands of "mass disturbances" rock the People's Repubic of China (PRC) every year to protest the increasingly fatal environmental degradation imposed by capital on the country since economic liberalization under Deng Xiaoping: mass-pollution of waterways and soils, entirely unprecedented levels of contamination in the major cities, astronomical cancer rates, and burgeoning carbon emissions (Katsiaficas 2013: 165; Pearl Delta Earth First! 2014: 101–113).

In parallel to the strategy of mass-political mobilization for radical-ecological purposes, a matter to which the present argument shall return, the social adoption of plant-based diets—that is to say, vegetarianism and especially veganism—can certainly be considered a form of radical intolerance to the prevailing destruction of nature: specifically, of the mass-murder of non-human animals for consumption. As a protest against animal cruelty, the practice of veganism accompanies Eros in seeking to "protect and enhance life itself." Like revolutionary ecology in general, then, veganism advances Marcuse's vision of a "drive for painlessness [and] for the pacification of existence" which is fulfilled *in protective care for living things,*" in opposition to their objectification and suffering (Marcuse 2011: 212). As has been demonstrated, Marcuse himself favors a thoroughgoing reduction in the destructiveness visited by humans onto nature and the animal world but outright dismisses vegetarianism in *Counterrevolution and Revolt,* such that the claim here associating veganism with Eros represents a creative extrapolation from Marcuse's own principles: it presents a perspective that contradicts the explicit claim Marcuse makes on the question in his penultimate book, yet one which stays true to his call to overthrow hellish conditions for both humans and nature—Marcuse against Marcuse, then. Incidentally, Marcuse's late rejection of vegetarianism contrasts with the perspectives of his erstwhile comrades Horkheimer and Adorno. In an early diary entry from the 1920s, the former uses the metaphor of a skyscraper to illustrate contemporary society, noting its very fundament to be the super-exploitation of colonized peoples who "perish by the millions" under capitalist rule together with the "indescribable [and] unimaginable suffering" of non-human animals—their "sweat, blood, [and] despair"—while in a later entry Horkheimer acknowledges non-vegetarians as bearing responsibility for the "unending fear of death and torture of millions of those animals" (Horkheimer 1978: 66, 97–98). For his part, in a 1963 lecture, Adorno declares the "eccentricity" of Arthur Schopenhauer's call for compassion toward other animals to be the "sign of great insight," and he accordingly endorses the legitimacy of resisting animal abuse (Adorno 2002b: 144–145).

In the same book in which he snubs vegetarianism, Marcuse paradoxically writes that "nature, too, awaits the revolution!" (Marcuse 1972b: 74). This claim immediately recalls the liberatory declaration made by the sixteenth-century German "mad monk" Thomas Müntzer—a line which is in fact cited favorably by the young Marx in his essay "On the Jewish Question" (1844)—that *"the creatures, too, must become free*" (Marx 1844; emphasis added). Both Marcuse and Müntzer's assertions on the necessity of the liberation of nature are in turn reminiscent of the observation made by Dr. Albert Schweitzer while contemplating hippopotami in equatorial Africa—the choice of animal in question being significant and symbolic, especially for Marcuse, who considered hippos his favorite animal—that "[t]he greatest evil is to destroy life, to injure life, *to repress life that is capable of development*" (Chelala 2014; emphasis added). All three of these German social critics would thus seem to share a commitment to Schweitzer's conception of "reverence for life," even if Marcuse did not share Schweitzer's vegetarianism and even consciously came out against the practice in *Counterrevolution and Revolt*. Nevertheless, to reiterate, one of the most logical-practical implications that would follow from Marcuse's advocacy of change toward a higher civilization in which nature is seen as a "subject with which to live" would be a generalized societal shift toward vegetarianism or veganism (Marcuse 1972b: 60). As Bob Torres writes in *Making a Killing: The Political Economy of Animal Rights*, veganism is a lived expression of one's repudiation of speciesism; in truth, it is a "great refusal" of the system that instrumentalizes animal life (Torres 2007: 131, 145). Beyond this, and critically, Torres is right to insist that veganism must be a *baseline* for the animal-rights movement, though it should also become a baseline for the radical-ecology and revolutionary movements as a whole, insofar as this is possible. This is in no way to claim that the struggle for animal liberation begins and ends with veganism, for direct action to free incarcerated non-human animals is also necessary, as would be the societal abolition of animal testing for research purposes, pharmacological and otherwise—an end to which a Marcusean "new science" could conceivably contribute. Naturally, of course, returning to the latest findings on biodiversity loss, animal life on Earth is profoundly imperiled as long as capitalism and productivism live on, such that the introduction, diffusion, and development of perspectives demanding the liberation of nature could, when paired with the radical praxis that follows from such ideas, significantly help in displacing these dominant material systems from the stage of history.

Beyond the question of animal liberation—though still indissolubly tied up with it—Marcuse's arguments in "Repressive Tolerance" hold great importance for the contemporary possibility of a generalized revolutionary struggle against capital-induced global ecocide, particularly as manifested in the ever-accelerating specters of climate change and species extinction. The present state of the Earth's natural systems, from the oceans to the tropical rainforests, freshwater supplies, the phosphorus and nitrogen biogeochemical cycles, and the state of stratospheric ozone, is in utter disarray, due principally to the devastation wrought by the capitalist mode of production during the past half-millennium—such that life itself is at risk, as two separate January 2015 studies have concluded independently (Milman 2015). Indeed, as Elizabeth Kolbert details in her eponymous 2014 volume, echoing the warnings that biologists have been making for years, the Earth is currently in the throes of the sixth great mass extinction event, with the present extinction rate of species being 1000 to 10,000 times the natural background rate (Kolbert 2014b; Chivian and Bernstein 2008). Within the various dimensions of ecological catastrophe, the most threatening environmental crisis is anthropogenic climate disruption, which is already responsible for massive droughts and famines on the one hand and severe storms and historically unprecedented flooding-events on the other. At its worst, climate catastrophe threatens to annihilate humanity and essentially all the rest of Earth's species by giving rise to positive feedback loops that would produce a self-perpetuating warming phenomenon which could lead the Earth into becoming another Venus, as Carl Sagan and James Hansen alike have warned (Sagan 1980a; Hansen 2009).

In point of fact, the prevailing tendencies on climate themselves leave little room for hope, considering that capitalist humanity has caused the Earth's average global temperature to increase by 1°C since the onset of industrialism, with an additional 6°C rise being possible and even likely this century, assuming the carbon-emissions trajectory to continue breaking all previous records with each passing year. For comparative purposes, an Earth that is on average warmer by 6°C corresponds in geological history to the state seen during the very worst of the mass-extinction events that have occurred since the emergence of life on this planet: the aforementioned Permian event, that is. Meanwhile, quite like Nero, the corporations and competing heads of state dither and indefinitely postpone the introduction of a binding international agreement that would radically reduce carbon emissions and so provide humanity and nature with a chance of survival—to say nothing of flourishing, happiness, or liberation. Alarmingly, the Intergovernmental Panel on Climate Change (IPCC) in its July 2014 report on mitigation announces that the global rate of carbon emissions has steadily increased during the past generation, whereas rationality would demand precisely the opposite: while emissions grew 1.3% annually from 1970 to 2000, they increased by 2.2% in the first decade of the new millennium, reaching a 3% increase in the first two years of the twenty-first century's second decade (Goldenberg 2014b).

Hence, as Marcuse's stepson Osha Neumann observes in a paper presented at the 2011 Marcuse Society Conference which has been published in *Radical Philosophy Review*, it would seem that Thanatos is besting Eros at present, this time perhaps for good—precisely because there is no Planet B (Neumann

2013). Though Marcuse himself did not foresee the profound threat posed by climate destruction—while his contemporary Bookchin did, in contrast—his thought certainly does engage with the exterminist tendencies of capital. For one, the critical theorist allows for the very real possibility in his 1967 lecture on "Aggressiveness in Advanced Industrial Society" that a truly "suicidal tendency" may exist in the national and international spheres, with the tendency toward annihilation having "found a firm basis in the instinctual structure of individuals" (Marcuse 1968: 268). Moreover, as has been illustrated, Marcuse in his last decade of life was increasingly wont to invoke Rosa Luxemburg's identification of the fateful choice faced by humanity between socialism and barbarism, and he referred evermore to Auschwitz in his final years, thus declaring the looming threat of genocide to hardly have been resolved by the military defeat of Nazism some thirty years prior. Indeed, Marcuse's final addresses on "Ecology and the Critique of Modern Society" and the "Children of Prometheus" consider capital's progressive destruction of nature alongside the continued threat of a recurrence of industrial genocide. Self-evidently, the critic's engagement with the "dark side of capital" represents a constant through the entirety of his adult life, yet the tireless investigations undertaken by Marcuse into the possibilities for resistance, revolt, and revolution signal a crucial difference between his critical theory and that of his more resigned and ultimately conservative colleagues Horkheimer and Adorno. With regard to Benjamin, one can only speculate how his social criticism would have developed had his life not been cut short on the Spanish border in 1940, though it seems fair to say that his perspectives would likely have been closer to those of Marcuse than those advanced late in life by Adorno and Horkheimer.

It is in this radical-dialectical sense that "Repressive Tolerance" holds great importance for the chance for inverting the prevailing trends toward eco-apocalypse—insofar as this project is admittedly even still possible. Marcuse argues in this essay for a fundamentally radical rejection of the oppression and destruction underpinning existing society, whether as manifested in colonial wars, prisons, mental institutions, police brutality, domestic violence, or the degradation of nature and the annihilation of non-human animals. Tactically, he calls for a *militant minority* to lead the way in illuminating the basic authoritarianism of prevailing society and showing the people as a whole that it can and must be resisted and overcome. In this way, Marcuse's practical suggestions recall those advocated by Bakunin before him—the praxis of the militant minority is to be taken as a transitional strategy that will encourage and eventually yield an autonomous majority that would opt to progress beyond capitalism, fascism, and mindlessness. Marcuse's favored approach here, in turn, has been reflected in the radical ecology movement for decades, from the work of Judi Bari and Earth First! to that of the ELF and ALF and the multitudinous popular socio-environmental struggles of the Global South. It was evidently on exhibit during the recent "People's Climate March" before the United Nations preparatory meeting in New York City for the Twentieth Conference of Parties (COP20) to the United Nations Framework Convention on Climate Change (UNFCCC) held in Lima, Peru. Though the official organizers of this action acted purposefully to prevent the march from resembling or even recalling the anti-World Trade Organization (WTO) protests in Seattle, 1999, the fact that hundreds of thousands took to the streets of New York to protest climate-destruction is significant (Gupta 2014). It remains to be seen what relationship the mobilization will have on the construction of a radical, popular climate movement within the core of the capitalist world-system: little concrete has been accomplished in the time since the action, though "Flood Wall Street" and "Flood the System" have emerged as more militant developments.

À la Paulo Freire, the idea is to develop the radical popular consciousness both through and alongside revolutionary direct action targeting those forces that are most responsible for the enormity of human suffering and ecological destruction in our day—that is to say, capital and the State. The chance for liberation will be helped along by simultaneous and mutually reinforcing transformations of the realms of the social imaginary (collective fantasy life), the social ethos (culture and habits), the social ideology (representations and misrepresentations of reality), and the social institutional structure (capital, State, technology, and governing rules), in John Clark's formulation (2013: 2).

Conclusion

In terms of building and intensifying anti-systemic ecological struggle, Marcuse's *oeuvre* taken as a whole has many critical contributions to make. For one, Marcuse's foundational claims on the purportedly erotic basis of existence provides hope that Thanatos does not in fact have the last word. In mirroring the optimistic conclusion made by Bloch at the close of the first volume of *The Principle of Hope*, where he declares that humanity should be considered as carrying within it enough potential for the "good end" of life-affirming revolutionary social change, these claims on Marcuse's part recall the theorist's earlier claims in "On Hedonism" (1938) that the happiness experienced by the individual allows her to "feel secure and protected from ultimate desperation" (Marcuse 1968: 191). Whether Marcuse's claims on biology are justified by the evidence is another matter, though it seems at the very least that enough potential exists for these arguments to have some merit. Moreover, the

heterodox and anarchistic revisions Marcuse made of established Marxist theory are critical today for confronting the complexities of the ecological crisis,
in light of his utopian-socialist critique of productivism and prometheanism
and his related aesthetic-erotic stress on tranquility and mindfulness as goals
to be achieved in individual and social life. Such perspectives evidently share
much in common with the "voluntary simplicity" or "Simpler Way" movements
which call on peoples in the overdeveloped societies to institute autonomous
lifestyles that break radically with the commodity fetishism and mass-objec-
tification inherent to capitalist consumerism (Trainer 2010). In point of fact,
Marcuse in *Eros and Civilization* argues that overdevelopment must be rejected
by a conscious humanity, achieving this end by concomitantly repudiating the
false needs imposed upon it (Marcuse 1966a: xviii). In particular, Marcuse's
advocacy of the abolition of alienated labor is part and parcel of his ecological vision: as his comrade Benjamin observed in his theses "On the Concept
of History" (1940), the fetishization of work is intimately tied into the dispossession of nature (Benjamin 2003: 393–394). In addition, Marcuse's Gramscian
stress on the necessity of developing a new liberatory sensibility as a precondition for successful anti-authoritarian social change bears much relevance
today for the struggle against eco-destruction. Finally, as has been discussed,
Marcuse's alternative socio-political vision in no way rejects science but rather
seeks to divorce its practice from the perpetuation of oppression and hierarchy, in favor of redirecting it toward the emancipation of humanity and nature.

   Above all, the continued importance of Marcuse's work vis-à-vis radical
ecology lies in the critical theorist's emphasis on the militant and erotic possibilities of collective action. In his final essay on Rudolf Bahro, Marcuse duly
writes that a partnership between "rebellious human and external nature"
could indeed come to *halt capital altogether* within the "late stage of its development." The critical theorist observes how radical ecological movements
threaten militaristic interests and capitalist profitability, in that they seek to
reconfigure nature and the world into the "domain of happiness, fulfillment,
and gratification," or Eros. In this sense, it is critical that he declares in the
essay on Bahro that "[t]he anti-authoritarian movement, the ecology movement, and the women's movement have intrinsic links with one another." As he
observes rightly, the health of Eros and of Earth depend in the first instance on
the chance for revolution, while the prospect of said revolution in turn depends
upon the erotic strength of the human instincts (Marcuse 1980: 42–43). And
yet, to invoke Marcuse's close to *One-Dimensional Man,* the possibilities for
a liberatory transformation of said instincts and of a future world-historical
revolution to overthrow capitalism, abolish social domination, and save nature
remain "nothing but a chance" (Marcuse 1964: 257). With all due respect to

Hegel and Marx, the course of world history cannot be said to be governed by a spirit that mechanistically assures reason and liberation; Marcuse thus was right to observe that history "is not an insurance agency" (Marcuse and Popper 1976: 75). The environmental crisis and looming climate catastrophe, juxtaposed with the at-times exuberant popular response to worsening ecocide, illustrate this point starkly. As Freud writes at the very close of *Civilization and its Discontents:*

> [Humans] have gained control over the forces of nature to such an extent that with their help they would have no difficulty in exterminating one another to the last [person]. They know this, and hence comes a large part of their current unrest, their unhappiness, and their mood of anxiety. And now it is to be expected that the other of the two 'Heavenly Powers,' eternal Eros, will make an effort to assert [it]self in the struggle with [its] equally immortal adversary. *But who can foresee with what success and with what result?*
>
> FREUD 1989: 112; emphasis added

CHAPTER 8

Critique of Marcuse

Critical theory is, last but not least, critical of itself and of the social forces that make up its own basis.

> MARCUSE 1968: 156

The mind thinks what would be beyond it.

> ADORNO 1973: 392

Continuing in the spirit of creatively interpreting and applying Marcuse's theses and arguments for the present, this chapter examines criticisms that have been leveled against the critical theorist, and considers some theoretical and practical issues related to Marcuse's lifework that remain unclear or potentially problematic. To be sure, this section will not consider reactionary "critique" raised against Marcuse, such as that entertained by the contemporary mainstream press and far-right groups, with both such currents converging in Eliseo Vivas' *Contra Marcuse* (1971). This chapter instead focuses on some of the most pressing and reasonable misgivings readers might have when encountering Marcuse's critical theory of society. Specifically, this chapter will examine seven areas of confusion, ambivalence, conflict, and criticism: the thesis of one-dimensionality, the problem of Marcuse's employment of reactionary sources and questionable empirics, the charge of aloofness and a bourgeois lifestyle, the question of Zionism and the Palestinians, Marcuse's views on gender and feminism, the conflicts between Marcusean materialism and poststructuralism and postmodernism, and the critical theorist's take on authority and the transition away from capital.

The Limits to Integration

One of the most lucid critiques raised against Marcuse—one that the critical theorist himself recognized as being among the best critiques made of his thought—comes in Paul Mattick's 1967 essay, "The Limits of Integration," wherein Mattick's concern is to assess the validity of Marcuse's thesis on one-dimensionality. As Mattick shares many of the claims Marcuse sets forth in *One-Dimensional Man,* particularly in terms of pessimism regarding class struggle in advanced-industrial settings, the result is not an especially shattering assault on Marcuse's thought. The difference between the two thinkers is seen in Mattick's relatively more optimistic view, which foresees the eventual destabilization of capitalist rule via mass-immiseration of core-industrial workers—a *denouément* that would finally prove Marx right, as it were. However, this divergence between the two is actually overcome in Marcuse's analysis of the progressive cultural delegitimization of capital, presented nearly a decade after the study on one-dimensionality.

In his account on the limits of integration, Mattick specifies the various commonalities he shares with Marcuse, declaring that he "agree[s] with all [Marcuse's] observations and [is] thankful for" the latter's "penetrating critical analysis" of dominant ideology. He remarks that the profound negativity of Marcuse's argument in *One-Dimensional Man* is "warranted in view of existing conditions," and he outlines his sympathy with Marcuse's point that "the world is in a bad and hopeless state just because there was not, and apparently will not be, a proletarian revolution." Expanding on this latter point, Mattick reflects grimly that "the age of revolutions may well be over and the one-dimensional, stationary, totalitarian society unavoidable" (Mattick 1967: 377, 396–397).

> One has only to think what in all probability is bound to happen without a socialist revolution in order to think of the possibility of a different kind of behavior on the part of the laboring classes. What is bound to happen is in some measure already happening [...]. The phrase "socialism or barbarism" states the only real alternatives.
>
> MATTICK 1967: 399

Reiterating Marx's witticism that the laborers are either revolutionary or they are nothing—a line which Marcuse too liked to quote, as we have seen—Mattick expresses that the labor movement presently is "nothing and may well [...] continue to be nothing. But there is no certainty." Delineating the limits to integration he anticipates asserting themselves, Mattick argues that ruling ideological conformity will begin to break down as the capitalist apparatus fails to provide tolerable living conditions for the working classes of industrialized societies, thus inverting the relative comforts it had provided them in the monopoly-capitalist phase, as through the construction of "small oases in a huge desert of human misery." Claiming anarchically that the "ruling class cannot act otherwise than it does; [...] it will do everything to perpetuate itself *as* a ruling class," Mattick warns that the contradictions of capital likely will evermore be "solved" through a resort to an intensification of violence from above—"internally, by more and more waste production; externally, by laying waste territories occupied by people unwilling to submit to the profit requirements of foreign capital." He predicts that one-dimensionality will break down just as affluence does, amidst an increasingly "slaughterous competition for the diminishing profits of world production" (Mattick 1967: 395, 399).

In a further two paragraphs he adds to a 1972 version of the essay—now renamed "Critique of Marcuse"—Mattick expresses his faith that, though the workers in the imperial core may not presently be revolutionary, they are naturally highly intelligent, such that they may at a certain point reach a "breaking-point where intelligence may come to include class-consciousness." In a manner reminiscent of Bloch, Mattick explains that the prevalence of apathy does not ensure its indefinite reproduction in the future: "an apathetic working class under certain conditions can become an aroused working class under different conditions." As the industrial proletariat will be the force Mattick foresees as being "most deeply affected" by the barbarous course taken by capital, he believes that the labor movement could very well be the "first" bloc in the industrialized societies "to break with the one-dimensional ideology of capitalistic rule." In this way, he effectively employs Marxian critique and logical reasoning against the pessimism of *One-Dimensional Man*—with this being a negative minor chord that would yield to the Marcusean major chord later in the 1960s, followed by a dual-chord structure in the 1970s—though Mattick closes by emphasizing the pressing relevance of negative perspectives à la Marcuse, amidst the very real possibility that "*capital may destroy the world before an opportunity arises to stay its hands*" (Mattick 1972: 106–107; Mattick 1967: 400; emphasis added). The final lines of Mattick's "Critique of Marcuse" express sentiments with which the critical theorist likely would not disagree:

> Capitalism, at the height of its powers, is also at its most vulnerable; it has nowhere to go but to its death. However small the chances are for revolt, this is not the time to throw in the towel.
>
>   MATTICK 1972: 107

Raya Dunayevskaya provides similar commentary in the mildly critical review of *One-Dimensional Man* she wrote for *The Activist* in fall 1964. In this article, the Marxist-humanist criticizes the critical theorist for using bourgeois and management sources for the construction of his argument regarding the hypothesized integration of the proletariat, and she chides him for collapsing the entirety of the u.s. working class into one conservative entity. In doing the latter, Dunayevskaya claims, Marcuse overlooks key divisions and disagreements between rank and file laborers and union leaders. Though her review of *One-Dimensional Man* is generally positive—rather like Mattick's, in this sense—Dunayevskaya stresses that the volume's argumentation shows Marcuse to have "fail[ed] to hear th[e] powerful oppositional voice[s] at the point of production itself" (Dunayevskaya 1964: 32–33).

The Problem of Sources: Political Philosophy and Empirics

Beyond the evaluation of Marcuse's line of argumentation in *One-Dimensional Man*—a question to which entire conferences have been dedicated, indeed—another evidently pressing issue in the Marcusean *oeuvre* is that of the critical theorist's dependence upon highly reactionary sources for some of his most important concepts. Beyond Marx, Fourier, Kant, and Schiller, Marcuse borrows heavily from Heidegger, Weber, Freud, and Hegel. All of the latter figures—save for the youthful Hegel—were conservative, authoritarian, or fascist in orientation! Nonetheless, having reactionary politics may not of necessity invalidate the scholarly contributions one can make to fields like philosophy, psychology, history, and sociology, such that concepts developed by conservatives can in theory be employed toward ends that totally contradict their conscious designs for political order. In Marcuse's defense, this is the approach on which *Eros and Civilization* is based—in turn itself much like Marx's exhaustive research of neoclassical economics, which served as the fundament of *Capital*.

As Marcuse writes at the beginning of his 1955 book, Freud's analysis in *Civilization and its Discontents* is at once a great defense of capitalism—at its most basic, in the Freudian equation of mental health with the acceptance of bourgeois cultural norms (Jay 1973: 97)—yet also an unconsciously and terribly subversive indictment of class society. In his 1964 lecture on Weber, moreover, Marcuse suggests that Weber was himself at least implicitly critical of prevailing notions of bourgeois "reason," even as he would expressly call for the execution, incarceration, or institutionalization of political radicals. With regard to Heidegger, Marcuse cannot justly be accused of exhibiting an uncritical attitude toward his mentor, in light of his adherence to revolutionary Marxism before, during, and beyond his Heideggerian period—a time when he creatively integrated materialism with existentialism and phenomenology. Such philosophical differences aside, and Heidegger's odious sympathy for Nazism notwithstanding, the Heideggerian imprint is readily on display in much of Marcuse's *oeuvre*, especially in *One-Dimensional Man*. Lastly, Marcuse's take on Hegel is deeply appreciative yet highly critical, as detailed in *Reason and Revolution*, particularly in terms of the legitimative role that Hegel took on late in life as the "dictator of philosophy" representing State and capital. As has been intimated above, Marcuse's take on Hegel bears much resemblance to that taken up by the young Marx, and it reflects Marcuse's interpretation of the founder of historical materialism as well.

One just criticism that can be made of Marcuse's approach to Critical Theory certainly revolves around the intellectual's distaste for empiricism and the presentation of evidence. Alasdair MacIntyre asserts that the radical swings between optimism and pessimism Marcuse underwent in the 1960s were "only very loosely supported by an appeal" to empirical reality, thus illustrating the theorist's systematic refusal "to use evidence in a rigorous way," on MacIntyre's account (MacIntyre 1970: 70–71). Leaving aside the question of whether the progression of Marcuse's view of the human condition in the 1960s can justifiably be said to have followed from the philosopher's misrepresentation of the empirical facts of the day, MacIntyre does have a point, in terms of Marcuse's eschewal of appeals to evidence, which the thinker indelibly associates with positivism and hence apologism. Admittedly, such an approach on Marcuse's part may be problematic.

Freud's formulation of the death instinct (Thanatos) is a concept that has been overwhelmingly rejected in clinical psychology. In point of fact, both Erich Fromm and Wilhelm Reich repudiated it, with the former pointing to the radically differing levels of destructiveness seen across cultures and in history as evidence disproving the putatively basic dimension of the death-drive (Rickert 1986: 364). In parallel terms, as we have seen, Marcuse claims biological life to be intrinsically oriented toward Eros, yet he provides exceedingly little supporting evidence for such a foundational claim—though certain aspects of evolutionary biology and the history of life on Earth may provide evidence for it, but not without problems, as the review in the previous chapter has shown. As regards political-economic analysis, Marcuse does invoke empirics in his original analysis of one-dimensionality—though one could, like Dunayevskaya, take issue with the *sources* for such empirical data—and does so as well in his subsequent revision of the theses of *One-Dimensional Man,* as in his attendant welcoming of the cultural and material breakdown of hegemonic capitalist ideology he witnessed in the 1970s.

It may well be true that most of the evidence does not support the idea of Thanatos, although some studies do. Dr. Otto Kernberg finds the death-drive useful for understanding the unconscious motivation toward self-destructiveness manifested in severe psychopathology, while Hanna Segal believes it both to exist, and to provoke pathology when the defenses established against it fail (Kernberg 2009; Segal 1993). In a fascinating "Reevaluation" of Thanatos, moreover, Dr. Edwin R. Wallace IV considers the emergence of the concept in juxtaposition with the biographical details of Freud's life: he concludes that the psychoanalyst's "discovery" of the death-drive had at least as much to do with the legacy of World War I and the personal deaths of his friend Anton von Freund and daughter Sophie as it did with intellectual investigation. Incidentally, in a Marcusean aside, Wallace expresses his curiosity that Freud's views on sex and aggression would be so well-accepted in mainstream clinical psychology, while Thanatos is not (Wallace 1976: 386–393).

Whatever the case may be, and even if the death-drive is an illusory concept, Marcuse's allegorical appropriation of the "eternal conflict" between Eros and Thanatos can prove highly illuminating in terms of comprehending politics under capitalism and advancing the ends sought by radical psychology, rebellious subjectivity, and the "journey inwards." The same is true of the rest of the concepts Marcuse borrows from conservatives other than Freud: rationalization and the Iron Cage (Weber); authenticity, care (*Sorge*), being-in-the-world (*Dasein*), the philosophy of nature, and the threat of nihilism (Heidegger); and negativity and the dialectical struggle for reason, freedom, and liberation (Hegel).

Marcuse the Edelkommunist

As was stated at the very outset of this biography of Marcuse, one would be remiss to overlook the various privileges the man was afforded in life before and after exile from Nazi Germany—despite the undeniable trauma which this process of displacement implied for Marcuse and the rest of the Frankfurt School intellectuals, not least due to survivors' guilt, with most of them being Jewish Germans who escaped Hitler. In these terms, in his conclusion to *Considerations on Western Marxism* (1976), British leftist Perry Anderson remarks on the striking fact that "[v]irtually all the major theorists of historical materialism,"

> from Marx or Engels themselves to the Bolsheviks, from the leading figures of Austro-Marxism to those of Western Marxism, have been intellectuals drawn from the possessing class: more often than not, of higher rather than lower bourgeois origin.
>
> ANDERSON 1976: 104

As Anderson observes, Marcuse hails from higher bourgeois origins, much as Luxemburg, Horkheimer, Adorno, Benjamin, Lukács, Lenin, Georgi Plekhanov, and Paul Sweezy did. Of course, several anarchists—namely Herzen, Bakunin, Kropotkin, Tolstoy, and Práxedis G. Guerrero—could be added to this list of privilege as well, if it is expanded to allow for the inclusion of radicals with feudal-noble origins. Like these anarchists, Marcuse can be considered an *Edelkommunist,* or "aristocratic communist." Nevertheless, in *The Aesthetic Dimension,* Marcuse downplays the point Anderson is trying to make, arguing instead that "Marxist theory is not family research" and that the degree to which an art-work or political intervention contributes to the revolutionary struggle should be measured neither by the class origins of the art-work's creator nor by the presence or absence of the oppressed classes in a given work (Marcuse 1978: 18–19). The critical theorist's claim here is sharp, almost defensive. Perhaps it reflects anxiety on the part of the elderly Marcuse, reflecting retrospectively on the various privileges he enjoyed in life. If we are to weigh Anderson's claim that the class origins of radical critics are relevant against Marcuse's insistence that they are not, it should be clear which position is more reasonable. To concur with Anderson on this point means to share his hope that the revolutions of the future will see mass-popular movements taking the place of privileged intellectuals propelling anti-systemic social transformation forward, but it is not necessarily to endorse the criticisms Anderson would make separately of his perception of the "bourgeois lifestyle" Marcuse enjoyed in La Jolla during his time at UCSD. In terms of this charge, the house in which Marcuse and Inge made their home in La Jolla is and certainly remains no mansion, and its location within that affluent neighborhood is explained at least partly by Marcuse's desire to be close to campus, so as to be able to walk to and from school and thus avoid having to use an automobile for transport (Katsiaficas 2004: 193).

Thus, while Anderson's latter charge against Marcuse may be less compelling, his point in *Considerations on Western Marxism* regarding the class background of most major Western Marxists should be considered germane to any assessment of the relevance of Marcuse's critical theory. The high-bourgeois origins of most if not all Western Marxists may lead one to express a degree of skepticism regarding the accuracy of their analyses and conclusions, particularly in terms of economics. Principally in the case of Marcuse, it may be that the very alienation and lack of familiarity he felt with regard to U.S. working-class life and culture influenced the reasoning behind his thesis regarding the putative integration of labor into the monopoly-capitalist monster. What is more, the views expressed by Marcuse and a number of the other Frankfurt School theorists—particularly Horkheimer and Adorno—as regards the "status" of the Western working classes may to a degree simply reflect the very privilege enjoyed by these social critics. At least in Adorno's case, cultural elitism widened the chasm between Critical Theory and everyday working people. This tendency was less of a problem for Marcuse, though, thanks in no small part to Inge's tireless efforts at making his arguments more accessible.

Undoubtedly, as Marcuse acknowledged, the thesis on one-dimensionality was not meant to be a universal diagnosis when it was first presented in 1964, and Marcuse even then believed minorities in U.S. society to represent important countercurrents to the established trends toward mobilization and total administration. Yet it is to some degree true, as MacIntyre writes, that the brutal negations of everyday life for working-class people—the "steady erosion of welfare institutions" and the "continuous re-creation of poverty," for example—mostly go unmentioned in Marcuse's writings (MacIntyre 1970: 78). This claim is particularly well-reflected in a comment the critical theorist makes in his 1968 preface to *Negations*: that the Marxian "image of the realm of necessity does not correspond to today's highly developed industrial nations" (Marcuse 1968: xvii). However, Marcuse contradicts this assertion in turn in an interview from May of that same year, when he remarks on the fact that one-third of the U.S. populace "still lives in hunger" (Marcuse 2014: 277). Marcuse specifies in his 1968 preface as well that the Critical Theory developed by the Institute in the 1930s and 1940s was then inspired by the possibilities of class struggle, yet neither Marx nor the workers make an appearance in *Eros and Civilization*, and Marcuse, like Adorno, has at times justly been accused of advancing a "Marxism without the proletariat." Such Marcusean ambivalence regarding class stands in stark contrast to the approach taken by Franz Neumann, who as a labor lawyer and a former SPD member focused his exilic critical theory much more on economics, workers' rights, and class struggle than philosophy, aesthetics, and the new sensibility.

In terms of considering the relevance of Marcuse's economic analyses today, it would seem that the trend toward the destabilization and delegitimization of capital identified by Marcuse in his final years has continued precipitously, though in a dialectically fatal symbiosis with a continuation and intensification of one-dimensionality alongside it, particularly as propagated by the neoliberal counterstrike. In 2016, there is much less indication from the world-stage that workers and people in general accept the rule of capital, as compared to a half-century ago. It remains to be seen whether further shattering waves of revolt and revolution will progress from the discontent which today prevails to surpass the historical opening provided by the global uprising of 1968.

Marcuse the Zionist?

Unfortunately for Marcuse's credentials as an anti-imperialist, there is clear evidence suggesting that the critical theorist was sympathetic to Zionism. Still, his version of Zionism should be distinguished from the fascist-aggressor type that has predominated since Israel's founding, and which reigns at present. As discussed above, Marcuse in July 1967 publicly expressed his solidarity with Sartre's uncritical call for the primacy of preventing "a new war of annihilation against Israel" in the wake of the Six-Day War—rather than forthrightly demand that the Jewish State withdraw from the territories it conquered from Egypt, Syria, and Jordan in that conflict (Marcuse 1980b: 141–142). In "Israel Is Strong Enough to Concede," published for *The Jerusalem Post* in January 1972 following Marcuse's visit with Inge to historical Palestine, the philosopher declares his full support for Israel's foundational mythological claim: that it was created following the Holocaust to prevent another genocide of Jews, and that hence the birth of the Jewish State represents the legitimate fruit of national-liberation struggle (Marcuse 2004: 54). Marcuse truly sounds like a neo-conservative at points in his 1977 interview with the UCSD Jewish student newspaper *L'Chayim* on Judaism and Israel, especially when he stresses that one of the principal preconditions of peace negotiations must be official recognition of Israel's sovereignty by the Palestinians and Arabs throughout the region. In Orientalist fashion, he expounds on this point by claiming that no basis for negotiations between Israel and the Palestinians can exist, as "long as the Palestinians feel that the destruction of Israel is a necessity" (Marcuse 2004: 54, 181–182). Marcuse even goes so far as to declare that a secular Zionism need not be a racist project, and he states his opposition to the U.N. General Assembly's equation of Zionism with racism. Additionally, in a 1970 interview with *Street Journal and San Diego Free Press,* the critical theorist admits that he had up to that time "always defended Israel," while in a subsequent interview from 1978, Marcuse continues to express his support for the "protection and integrity of Israel as a state" (Marcuse 2014: 353, 390).

Why it is that Marcuse insists that among the principal preconditions to any resolution between the Jewish State and the Palestinians and other Arabs must be included a recognition by the latter of the legitimacy of the settler-colonialism and military dictatorship exercised by Israel against the Palestinians is quite a puzzling question to ask, if one were to juxtapose this assertion with Marcuse's clear life-long commitment to reason and the collective liberation for humanity. The conundrum of Marcuse's Zionism rears its head in the theorist's request for a clandestine meeting with General Moshe Dayan during his visit to Israel/Palestine with Inge. Zvi Tauber is right to observe that Marcuse may well have meant to keep his meeting with Dayan a secret, considering how embarrassing and awkward it might be for the world-renown prophet of revolution to be seen as having a friendly chat with the supreme commander of the Israeli occupation of Palestine (Tauber 2012: 176). Nevertheless, upon examination of the text of the protocol of the conversation between these two, it becomes evident that Marcuse is interested in intervening here toward the end of convincing Dayan to accept the peace terms offered by Egypt in coordination with UN Special Envoy Gunnar Jarring in 1971—terms which would have demanded Israel's withdrawal from the Sinai Peninsula and all other lands occupied in June 1967, in accordance with UN Security Council Resolution 242—in order to prevent future wars between Israel and the Arabs. However humanistic the motivations underpinning the desire to hold this meeting with Dayan may thus have been, the famed anti-authoritarian scholar certainly makes a considerable *faux pas* in thoughtlessly reassuring the general that the Jewish armies did no wrong in the Six-Day War (Marcuse and Dayan 2012: 186).

These problematic tendencies notwithstanding, the support Marcuse grants Israel in principle is tempered by his clear recognition of the great "injustice done to the native Arab population" in the very founding of the Jewish State: *al-Nakba,* or "the catastrophe," the predictable and desired outcome of the ethnic cleansing engaged in by Zionist terrorist groups during Israel's so-called "War of Independence"—this being a campaign that resulted in the forcible displacement of some three-quarters of a million Palestinians (Marcuse 2004: 54; Pappé 2006). Like Chomsky, then, Marcuse breaks from mainstream Zionism in acknowledging the foundational violence that accompanied Israel's birth—even in July 1967, he notes its founding to have proceeded "without taking into consideration the problems of the local population and what happened to it"—and in insisting that the Palestinians be allowed their own state, the character of which they are to decide by means of popular referenda, in accordance with their right to self-determination (Marcuse 1980b: 142). While Marcuse's public call for two states in early 1972 cannot match the dignity and rationality of the Palestinian Liberation Organization's contemporary demand for a secular binational arrangement in historical Palestine, it is fairly novel all the same. Sympathetic to the Palestinians, this position certainly distinguishes Marcuse from Sartre and de Beauvoir, and recalls Hannah Arendt and Albert Einstein's warning nearly a quarter-century before of the very real specter of fascist power emanating from the Jewish-supremacist ideology and practice of Israeli State and society (Einstein et al. 1948). In fact, Marcuse's activism in favor of Palestinian rights should allow him at least a partial reprieve from the

charge Edward Said directs at Sartre, who authentically supported the Algerian Revolution at considerable risk to his life—for his apartment was bombed
twice by French reactionaries incensed by the philosopher's activism in favor
of Algerian independence—yet chauvinistically supported the Jewish settler-
colony established in Palestine (Aronson 1980: 157; Said 2000).

In point of fact, the historical alternative Marcuse strove for in historical
Palestine is symbolized well in the Nablus *salon* in which he and Inge participated together with Palestinian intellectuals and Israeli academics, as hosted
by the militant Palestinian journalist and organizer Raymonda Hawa Tawil.
Tawil movingly recalls that Marcuse at the *salon* shared his repudiation of
Jewish persecution and oppression of Palestinians (Tawil 1979: 231–232)—a
position which is clearly more consonant with the lifelong trajectory of his
critical theory, in contrast to the reflexive defense of Jewish supremacy that is
manifested by his support for Israel's right to exist. The conflict is particularly
illuminated when one contemplates Marcuse's Zionism alongside the theorist's world-famous interpretations of Hegel and historical reason, intimately
tied as they are to the public intellectual's practical affirmation and defense of
Third-World struggles against the violence of Euro-American imperialism and
settler-colonialism, as manifested at this time in Vietnam and Cuba *as well as
Palestine*. Characteristically, in the aforementioned interview from 1970 interview he held with countercultural youth in San Diego, Marcuse authentically
admits that, while he had usually stood with Israel up to that point, he could
no longer continue doing so as a Jew and a member of the New Left, in light
of Israel's indiscriminate bombardment of civilian populations and the Jewish
State's systematic use of torture against Palestinian prisoners. Having reflected
on such crimes, he asserts that he must "agree with those who are radically
critical of Israel." Still, he clarifies in a 1978 interview that his criticisms of Israel
would not lead him to support the perspectives taken by Yassir Arafat and the
PLO, presumably as regards their call for a single democratic and secular state
in historical Palestine—a proposal which Marcuse's Palestinian host Hawa
Tawil herself advocated (Marcuse 2014: 353–354, 365; Tawil 1979: 164).

Clearly, then, the Zionists of today who rally in support of Israeli Fascism
cannot justifiably claim Marcuse as one of their own, given the philosopher's
strong criticisms of the workings of Israel's military and the repressiveness
directed by the Jewish State against Palestinians. Perhaps a contemporary
approximation of Marcuse's position is that held by Norman G. Finkelstein,
who firmly opposes Israeli militarism, racism, and expansionism, but does not
favor a binational state that would subsume the Jewish State at this time. With
this parallel in mind, it is inconceivable that Marcuse's thought could justly be
marshaled in defense of Israel's ongoing occupation of historical Palestine in
the decades that have followed his death, as manifested most acutely in the

ever-worsening land-grabs for settlements in the West Bank, the serial massacres visited on the people trapped in Gaza, and the daily humiliations, arrests,
shootings, and murders generally visited by the Jewish State on the Palestinians. While it remains a long-term goal—one that may seem even more remote
now than before—Marcuse's explicit endorsement in his 1972 *Jerusalem Post*
essay of the possibility of coexistence among Jews and Arabs in a future socialist Middle Eastern federation speaks to the humanist basis of Marcuse's view
of the conflict between Israel and the Palestinians. The critical theorist's take
on the question of Palestine follows naturally from his established interest
in helping along the institution of the Kantian notion of perpetual peace in
history.

Feminism, Gender, Eros

One issue for which Marcuse has been roundly criticized is his take on gender.
First and foremost in this sense, Marcuse's views on gender run the serious
risk of betraying essentialism in their confused association of liberation, joy,
and tranquility—Eros—with females and the "female principle" and toil,
intrigue, and power-struggles with males and the ruling "masculine principle"
(Marcuse 1966a: 161; Marcuse 1972b: 74–75). In point of fact, this problematic
was identified and debated at a recent one-day conference on Marcuse held at
Cornell University in April 2014. Nonetheless, as against the clearly worrying
Marcusean tendency toward essentialism, it bears noting that the critical
theorist in *Counterrevolution and Revolt* speculates that those who adhere to
gender essentialism in fact overlook the degree to which their views have been
shaped by the historical power of patriarchy and capitalism, while in "Marxism
and Feminism" (1974) he outright declares his belief that the supposedly
"feminine characteristics" of Eros are socially conditioned rather than biologically determined—such that these erotic traits presumably could be expressed
by persons belonging to any gender. Additionally, in this address, Marcuse
presents the visionary ideal of a "synthesis" of the hegemonic gender binary
which would yield the "legendary idea of *androgynism*" (Marcuse 2004: 171).
    We have already seen that Marcuse was a pioneer in advancing the cause
of queer liberation within the socialist tradition, as his vision of an Orphic or
gay Marxism suggests (Mielo 1977). When juxtaposed with his comments on
androgyny, moreover, his vision of a "polymorphous-perverse" sexuality may
in fact reflect a favorable attitude toward the trans* dimension of the LGBTQ
world as well. The critical theorist likely shared the hope of Gad Horowitz, as
expressed in her reflections on psychoanalytical feminism after Marcuse, that

gender polarization results from maternal child-rearing customs practiced under particular circumstances "having to do with competition, war, the state, and class," such that contexts freed from such corrupting forces could allow for more gender-fluid forms of expression, being, and inter-relating (Horowitz 1994: 128).

With regard to feminism, it should be stressed that Miles has a point when he observes that, of all the thinkers affiliated with the Frankfurt School, it was only Bloch who "made a case for the historical role of women in revolutions"—this by citing the "red democrat" Louise Otto in volume two of *The Principle of Hope* (Miles 2012: 90–91). Compared with Bloch, Marcuse's late engagements with feminism could be considered rather tardy, first emerging as they do in the thinker's seventh decade of life, during his conversation in 1962 with Peter Furth of *Das Argument* on "The Emancipation of Women in a Repressive Society" (Marcuse 2014: 161–169). Nancy Chodorow makes a similar observation to that of Miles in her *Feminism and Psychoanalytic Theory,* a work in which she subjects Marcuse's *Eros and Civilization* and Norman O. Brown's *Life against Death* to critique. Chodorow correctly and importantly observes that, while Marcuse and Brown certainly express a "definite anti-masculinist stance" in these works, both authors "manifest a near-complete invisibility or denial of women as subjects." Indeed, Chodorow emphasizes that Marcuse mentions women on only two occasions in *Eros and Civilization*: firstly, when he considers Pandora, the first human woman in Greek mythology, as a possible archetypal alternative to Prometheus—only to immediately drop this line of thought and embrace Orpheus and Narcissus instead—and secondly, when he mentions the "crazed Thracian women" who Ovid claims to have killed Orpheus out of jealousy and resentment, following his sexual rejection of them in favor of relations with young males. She further criticizes Marcuse for uncritically accepting Freud's sexist "primal horde" theory, pointing out the philosopher's seeming obliviousness to the fact that the brothers who rebelled against the primal father on this account did so to assert "the[ir] equal right to dominate women, against the father's claim that only he had that right." Furthermore, Chodorow takes issue with what she sees as Marcuse's enthusiasm for primary narcissism, as she interprets this to be an implicit denigration of motherhood, for it is mothers who most commonly enforce the "primary restraints" that lead the infant or child to engage in separation and thus become social beings. Less legitimate, of course, is Chodorow's heteronormative view that Marcuse's repudiation of "normal Eros" amounts to a rejection of "relations with women" or even a "rejection of women" altogether (Chodorow 140–142, 144).

While Miles and Chodorow raise important points about Marcuse's stated commitments to feminist thought and practice, it bears mentioning, against both of these critics, that Marcuse does come around to affirm the role of women in social-revolutionary processes: one need only review the text of "Marxism and Feminism" or consider Marcuse's invocation of Delacroix's "Lady Liberty" in *Counterrevolution and Revolt* to be assured of that point. Furthermore, in an interview he gave just months before dying, the critical theorist asserts that feminists are "fighting for a free life" and carrying Eros forward toward the end of the creation of "happy human relations" for all (Marcuse 2014: 417). Prior to these interventions, one can look to "The Emancipation of Women in a Repressive Society" as well, for Marcuse there claims the observed trend of increased women's participation on the labor market to be an illusory sort of emancipation. With these three examples in mind, it is telling to contemplate that Chodorow focuses exclusively on *Eros and Civilization* in her critique of Marcuse. While it is undoubtedly lamentable that Marcuse affords women so marginal a role in that book, and though—to extend the argument—Marcuse's choice of title for *One-Dimensional Man* is unfortunate, Chodorow should not have excluded Marcuse's later public engagements with the women's liberation movement in her argument from *Feminism and Psychoanalytic Theory*.

Providing a rather different perspective than Chodorow in "Marcuse, the Women's Movement, and Women's Studies," an essay from 1994 which considers the theorist's views in the wake of the counterrevolution of the 1980s, Trudy Steuernagel sympathetically associates Marcuse's affirmation of women's liberation with the approach favored by the radical feminists, who had more influence on the movement in the early 1970s, before they were eclipsed by cultural or liberal feminism (Steuernagel 1994: 94–96). Hence, while Miles and Chodorow may well be right to stress that it took Marcuse quite some time—about forty years of theorizing, in fact—to express specifically feminist concerns, and though it is unclear that Marcuse's late theorizing on feminism entirely resolves the problems Chodorow identifies, any honest appraisal of Marcuse's relationship with feminism must not overlook the profound militancy of the theorist's recommendations for a *feminist* or *feminine socialism,* as first set forth in "Marxism and Feminism." These are critical theoretical-practical approaches that foresee women and feminists organizing radically to topple hetero-patriarchal domination, capitalism, and the State altogether—in consonance with Steuernagel's observation that Marcuse's take on feminism emphasizes collective action and struggle toward emancipation (Marcuse 2004: 170; Steuernagel 1994: 95–96).

Rather self-evidently, Marcuse's enthusiasm for the tremendous potential feminism has for bringing about thoroughgoing societal change is an orientation that holds great contemporary importance, in light of the enormity of suffering and negation experienced by women the world over in our day, as Teresa Ebert stresses in *Ludic Feminism and After: Postmodernism, Desire, and Labor in Late Capitalism* (1996). Generally, the situation would seem only to have gotten worse in the two decades since Ebert wrote this book, as follows from the thanotic retrenchment of patriarchal power under conditions of an increasingly authoritarian capitalist mode of production. The critical contributions to be made by feminist resistance in the twenty-first century will be examined specifically in the concluding chapter.

Conflicts with Poststructuralism and Postmodernism

One clear theoretical conflict is seen—albeit sharper and less involved than the case with feminism—between the thought of Marcuse and that of the poststructuralists and postmodernists who followed him and were to varying degrees influenced by him. In particular, as Joseph Winters writes in *Telos*, Michel Foucault's development of the "repressive hypothesis" and this French thinker's concomitant reconceptualization of power as generative can be taken as an indirect *or direct* response to Marcuse. As Winters writes, Foucauldians and other poststructuralists "cast a suspicious eye on any position that affirms the possibility of organizing human desires and relationships without some kind of coercion" (Winters 2013: 151–152). They are especially skeptical about claims made to nature, biology, and human essence—claims which Marcuse on the contrary proudly employs. In point of fact, the conflicts between Marcuse and poststructuralism are analogously well-illustrated in the debate held between Chomsky and Foucault himself in 1971, on "Human Nature: Justice versus Power." In this exchange, Foucault critiques Chomsky's advocacy of anarcho-syndicalism as justice using the charge of essentialism in terms of human nature: if he is not arguing in bad faith, Foucault expresses his concern that Chomsky and other anarchists are insufficiently cognizant of the repressiveness which supposedly pervades their own alternative philosophies (Chomsky and Foucault 2006). As Winters explains, poststructuralists like Foucault and Judith Butler claim "violence, coercion, and exclusion" to be inescapable facets of the human world. Articulating this type of attitude, they effectively deny the possibility of the erotic, liberated world which Marcuse desires and dialectically sees developing in history (Winter 2013: 155–156).

Undeniably, Marcuse's foundational claims regarding human nature and Eros represent a basic contradiction to poststructuralist and postmodernist thought. In his 1932 essay on "New Sources on the Foundations of Historical Materialism," Marcuse presents two of his most fundamental claims regarding human essence and social revolution—both of which would surely be rejected by poststructuralists. Asserting that it is "precisely the persistent focus on the essence of [humanity]" that drives the "inexorable impulse for the initiation of radical revolution," the critical theorist continues, declaring the "factual situation of capitalism [to be] characterized not merely by economic or political crisis but by a *catastrophe affecting the human essence*" (emphasis added). For this reason, "any mere economic or political *reform*" is consigned to fail "from the onset," such that what is needed would be the "*cataclysmic transcendence of the actual situation through total revolution*" (Marcuse 2005: 106; emphasis added).

As this bold blending of existentialism and revolutionism attests, and considering the central place which Eros would take in Marcuse's critical theory, especially in terms of existence and evolution, the philosopher can be viewed as effectively grounding reason *naturalistically*. Indeed, as was reviewed above, this is the very charge Habermas raises against his mentor during their 1978 conversation together (Marcuse et al. 1978/9: 133, 135). Such naturalistic claims to reason, biology, and Eros, of course, are indelibly related to Marcuse's militant appeals to natural law, by means of which he passionately defends the right of resistance in the question-and-answer period after "The Problem of Violence and the Radical Opposition" (1967), as elsewhere. In this case, poststructuralists and postmodernists would be the student who questions and presumably rejects the existence of the universal higher law that Marcuse believes to found the right of resistance and the associated human rights to enjoy peace and to "*abolish exploitation and oppression*" (Marcuse 1970a: 73; emphasis added). Classical natural law, as Bloch writes, has since its inception in antiquity been concerned with securing human dignity, much as the the various social utopias of history have been directed primarily toward promoting human happiness: "The wish of natural law was and is *uprightness as a right*, so that it might be respected in *persons* and *guaranteed* in their collective" (Bloch 1986b: 203–208). Such lines of reasoning are quite naturally anathema to poststructuralists and postmodernists, for Marcuse and Bloch—quite like Chomsky debating Foucault—cannot ultimately convince their audiences of the foundations of the natural right to resistance, unless said audience accepts "on faith" the legitimacy of concrete and abstract universals aiding along progress in history—with the right to social revolution being primary in this sense. As Marcuse observes in an interview given shortly before his passing, Bloch was right to insist that "hope is expressed by the negation of the givenness" (Marcuse 2014: 421).

The basic conflict separating Marcuse's theories from the perspectives adopted by poststructuralists and postmodernists is clear enough, yet it is unclear that Marcusean revolutionaries and libertarian Marxist-Hegelians should be terribly concerned about these lines of argumentation. That Foucault and postmodernism followed Marcuse and Critical Theory in time does not make them by necessity any superior or more insightful. Moreover, these two more recent schools of thought have in truth unfortunately served reactionary ends since their inception, their claim to sophistication, innovation, and pseudo-radical originality notwithstanding. As Pranar Jani and Kevin B. Anderson explained at Left Forum 2014, Edward Said was right to condemn the postmodernists inspired by poststructuralism as engaged in "fruitless cynicism and standing-aside"—however convenient this comment admittedly may be, in light of Said's own problematic employment of Foucauldian categories at times, particularly in *Orientalism,* his best-known work (Jani et al. 2014). Critically, Teresa Ebert provides a devastating left-wing critique of poststructuralism and postmodernism in *Ludic Feminism and After,* where she demonstrates how those taken by these approaches effectively legitimate bourgeois society in their dismissal of revolution, their erasure of class from social theory, their condemnations of "emancipation as an Enlightenment myth," and their calls for a focus on local spaces and reforms. Truly, Ebert captures the irrelevance of poststructuralist and postmodernist critique well in her characterization of these philosophies as amounting to little more than conformist apologism developed by core-imperial property-holders more interested in withdrawing from society and satisfying their "ludic desires" than promoting liberatory social transformation (Ebert 1996: 17, 26, 28, 69, 87). This type of criticism is shared by John Sanbonmatsu and Barbara Epstein, Anderson and Jani's co-panelists at Left Forum, who denounce poststructuralism for its repudiation of ethics, truth, rationality, and causality, its stress on spectacle and performance, and its giddy celebration of anything "in resistance" (Jani et al. 2014).

Using a similar analysis, Wolin in his work *The Seduction of Unreason* discusses the seemingly perplexing affinities between postmodernism and the reactionary Counter-Enlightenment movement of European history, as typified by Joseph de Maistre—whose hegemonic-traditionalist apologism was examined by Marcuse, if we recall, in *A Study on Authority.*[1] Since poststructuralist pseudo-radicals embarrassingly embrace the conservative repudiation of reason, ethics, and humanism in politics, the enthusiasm Foucault evinced over the Iranian Revolution of 1979 can be readily understood, as can his support for Israel (Wolin 2004: 1–7; Said 2000). In a sense like Fredric Jameson, author of the famous study *Postmodernism: The Cultural Logic of Late Capitalism,* Wolin

---

1   See Chapter 3 above.

holds postmodernist trends responsible for giving rise to "culturalist" and narcissistic political trends that stress identity, text, and theory in place of militant
struggle (Wolin 2004: 14–16). He writes:

> As commentators have often pointed out, during the 1980s, while Repub-
> licans were commandeering the nation's political apparatus, partisans of
> "theory" were storming the ramparts of the Modern Language Associa-
> tion and the local English Department.
> WOLIN 2004: 9

Beyond raising the questions of the compatibility of postmodernism and
capitalism and of the philosophical affinities between poststructuralism
and the Counter-Enlightenment, Wolin expresses concern about the reactionary sources to which poststructuralists and postmodernists consciously
have turned in their desire to distance themselves from Marx—sources like
Nietzsche and Heidegger, that is to say—in light of the well-established
authoritarianism of both such historical figures (Wolin 2004: 11–12, 15–16).

We have seen, then, how far-removed are the premises of poststructuralism from Marcuse's thought. Yet, when poststructuralists and postmodernists
dismiss Marcuse's radical notions of politics and existence as essentialist, they
may well be guilty of exaggeration, given the great stress placed by the critical
theorist on human malleability and creativity, particularly as regards the vicissitudes of the basic instinctual struggle between Eros and Thanatos (Winters
2013: 156–158). More fundamentally still, if we care for human well-being, it
would clearly seem preferable for people to have the right to appeal to natural law to justify revolution and insurrection than for them *not to have such a
right*, as the poststructuralist and postmodernist lines of thought would seem
to favor. While those enthralled to these approaches prominently declare their
opposition to all supposed "meta-narratives" which try to "explain the world
and give people a guide to action," as John A. Rapp writes, it is unclear how
their own critique is to be taken as something other than another meta-narra-
tive on its own terms (Rapp 2012: 102–103). Though often taken as cutting-edge
and critical, these ideologies are in fact quite pseudo-radical and affirmative.
Hence, whatever limited degree to which such perspectives could serve emancipatory theoretical and practical projects today may be found precisely in
their negativism, as in their stress on the inertial persistence of repression and
exclusion—a motif which Marcuse for his part sees expressly depicted in the
tragedies of art and literature, and Benjamin in the rubble piles of history.

As Winters writes, much in the spirit of Marcuse's comments on physical
demise in *Eros and Civilization,* the radical hope for a better future "cannot

escape the indelible human realities of death, suffering, and discord," such that "[p]ossibility and failure will forever be joined at the hip." Nevertheless, the recognition of finitude "should not discourage us from cultivating practices and habits that promise less destructive ways of relating to and being with one another," no matter the detached desperate critique advanced by poststructuralists and postmodernists (Winters 2013: 168). Beyond this contribution made by poststructuralism—one that is by no means unique to this philosophy—little of the theorizing done by poststructuralists and postmodernists would appear to serve the project of global social revolution, as follows from their favored nihilistic and "ironic" premises. Objectively speaking, libertarian Marxist-Hegelianism or class-struggle anarcha-feminism provide much better frameworks for a future emancipatory resolution than does any sort of ludic-nihilist individualism.

Marcuse on Authority and the Transition: Between Jacobinism and Anarchism

Among the most compelling as well as fascinating unresolved problematics in Marcuse's political philosophy is the question of the critical theorist's view of two interrelated issues: authority and the transition beyond capitalism. Regarding these two matters, it can be said that, over the nearly sixty years which spanned Marcuse's writing career, the thinker's political philosophy was seen to have been informed by and in turn advance two somewhat contradictory viewpoints: that of a libertarian socialism or social anarchism which follows left-Hegelianism and the original "Marxian concept" in tension with a more authoritarian tendency informed by Plato, Rousseau, Jacobinism, and Leninism. While Marcuse consistently rejects Stalinism—in contrast to Max Horkheimer, for example, who in 1930 still had illusions about the Soviet Union—he does present variable appraisals of Leninism, and the question of a transitional "intellectual" or "educational" dictatorship emerges as a recurring theme in his later works. Kellner, Martineau, and Christopher Holman all accuse Marcuse of desiring to change society *from above*, with Martineau paradoxically linking the critical theorist to Gracchus Babeuf, the Conspiracy of Equals, and the idea of a forceful imposition of direct democracy (Kellner 1984: 314; Martineau 1986: 38; Holman 2013: 80–81). It is arguably the Adornian and Heideggerian negativity that Marcuse expresses in *One-Dimensional Man* regarding the hypothesized monopoly-capitalist colonization of the life-world and the related integration of the U.S. proletariat that served as a turning-point for the ambivalence he would come to express in terms of this strategic option in his remaining years. Certainly, he was no Sartre, who late in life came to favor a far different approach, calling on left intellectuals to abolish their privileges in service of popular liberation (Aronson 1980: 321–323).

On the other hand, though, it is clear that Marcuse embraced the anarchical tactics of the 1960s counterculture and the New Left, as is reflected well in the stress he places on the centrality of a developing new sensibility in *An Essay on Liberation* and the explicit endorsements he would make of councilism and spontaneity late in life. Prior to that, in *Eros and Civilization,* Marcuse would declare outrightly that humanity "must come to associate the bad conscience not with the affirmation but with the denial of the life instincts, not with the rebellion but with the acceptance of the repressive ideals" (1966a: 124). Yet the problem of the transition to a non-repressive society remains: "how can the people who have been the object of effective and productive domination *by themselves create the conditions of freedom?*" Declaring the proposal to "impose Reason upon an entire society" to be "scandalous," Marcuse in *One-Dimensional Man* indicts the idea of any tribunal "arrogat[ing] to itself" precisely what constitutes false as against true consciousness (1964: 6–7; emphasis added). He will restate his opposition to vanguardism in "Protosocialism and Late Capitalism" (1979), his last essay, wherein he asserts that the revolution "cannot be carried through on the backs of the people," even if "the people" in general overwhelmingly express compensatory interests rather than emancipatory ones. According to Rudolf Bahro, social revolution itself demands an inversion of the prevailing hegemony of compensatory interests—an overturning which has its parallel in Eros gaining in its struggle against Thanatos—yet paradoxically, this very action of a flowering in favor of emancipation already presupposes revolutionary change! This is the "vicious cycle" Marcuse identifies, one he provocatively terms the very *"central historical problem of revolutionary theory of our time"* (1980a: 27–28; emphasis added).

To explore Marcuse's sustained engagement with questions regarding authority and the transition, we will examine the philosopher's views of the radical developments of his day alongside the intellectual contributions Marcuse made as a theorist of revolution to the practical problem of displacing and transcending capital and domination.

In biographical terms, it is known that the youthful Marcuse joined the Social Democrats (SPD) during the First World War and renounced his membership following the murder of Rosa Luxemburg and Karl Liebknecht during the Spartacist uprising of January 1919. In his evaluation of the young Marcuse's response to the 1917 Bolshevik seizure of power in Russia, Wolin may be correct to assume that the student-turned-soldier favored Luxemburg's more autonomous and collective approaches to the dictatorial ones imposed by Lenin and Trotsky (Marcuse 2005: xiv). In this way, Wolin's framing of this youthful period alongside the "existentialist Marxism" Marcuse will develop in his postwar studies and Heideggerian years (1928–1932) hypothesizes a clear continuity in the orientation and course taken by Marcuse's critical theory of society, which is close to libertarian communism, autonomous Marxism, and anarchism. Nevertheless, matters are more complicated than Wolin would have it in his comment about Luxemburg and Lenin. For one thing, Marcuse concedes in a 1977 interview that he related "[v]ery positively" to the Soviet Union as long as Lenin was alive, while his volume on *Soviet Marxism* from two decades earlier presents a somewhat contradictory account of the relations among Marxism, Leninism, and Stalinism (Marcuse 2014: 429). As reviewed previously, the philosopher identifies the continuum of Party domination first established by Lenin over workers and peasants that was subsequently intensified under Stalinism without illusions, and he claims that a "straight road" leads "from Lenin's 'consciousness from without' and his notion of the centralized authoritarian party to Stalin's personal dictatorship" (1958b: 145).[2] In contrast, though, elsewhere in *Soviet Marxism,* as in *One-Dimensional Man*, Marcuse writes in passing about the "brief 'heroic period'" of the Russian Revolution, implying this phase to have preceded the rise of Stalin—with the question then coming to be whether Marcuse refers here more to Lenin and Trotsky's administration before Stalin or to the profound struggles waged from below against the Leninist autocracy and the reactionary Whites alike (1958b: 248; 1964: 43). His response in *One-Dimensional Man,* though, is clear: Marcuse associates this heroic period with the transient experience of workers' control of production and popular self-management, as in the *soviet* system—in an implicit snub of Lenin and Trotsky, perhaps, who smashed the *soviets* in favor of centralized control (Marcuse 1964: 43; Figes 1996: 685–687). In a similar vein, if one looks to the analysis in *Soviet Marxism,* she will see Marcuse the libertarian clearly criticizing Lenin for having instituted dictatorial power *over the peoples of Russia and Central Asia.* Yet near the end of his life, in the letters to the Chicago Surrealists, Marcuse affirms Lenin's arguments about false consciousness to illustrate the relationship between aesthetics and revolution: "whatever art may contribute to the development of revolutionary consciousness will be *'from without' the prevailing consciousness and existence of the masses*" (2007: 190; emphasis added). Discussing a more explicitly political matter in correspondence with Rudi Dutschke in 1970, Marcuse moreover claims there to exist an inherent conflict between "spontaneity and radical discipline" and "anarchy and organization" (2014: 335).

---

2   See Chapter 4 above.

These latter statements—which at first glance could be considered quite stunning in their potential for left-wing authoritarianism—represent a clear manifestation of Marcuse's sustained tendency in life to consider the possibility of a Platonic intellectual dictatorship as a means of accelerating the transition away from monopoly-capitalist depravity. Marcuse's discussion of Engels and revolution in *A Study on Authority* (1936) presents a preliminary and ambiguous treatment of the question. Coming to his section on Marx in this philosophical investigation of modern Europe—having examined the question of authority in Luther, Calvin, Kant, Hegel, the counter-revolutionary Edmund Burke, and the proto-fascist F.J. Stahl—Marcuse contrasts Marx's critical account of bourgeois authority over the means of production and the family with the positive account of transitional authority identified by Engels. In a short essay from 1874, Engels presents a "dialectical" rationalization of putatively revolutionary authority: he argues for the presumed necessity of subordination, management, and party vanguardism in effecting revolutionary social change; as he writes, "A revolution is certainly the most authoritarian thing there is [...]." In his commentary in the *Study*, Marcuse does not clearly indicate whether he agrees with Engels' hierarchical approach to revolutionary change; perhaps tellingly, though, he presses on from examining the views of Marx's immediate successor to the similarly authoritarian perspectives later advanced by Lenin. Implicitly, Marcuse's perspective in *A Study on Authority* is presumably anti-Leninist, in light of the ties he sees among Georges Sorel's late vanguardism, Leninism, and Fascism. In Hegelian-Marxian terms, Marcuse's own view would appear to be that the "general community which makes freedom possible" is a "quite particular form of organization of the whole society *which can only be realized through the supersession of its bourgeois organization*" (Marcuse 2008: 84–92, 96, 104–105; emphasis added). From this early volume, then, it is unclear that Marcuse agrees with Engels and Lenin on the need for an authoritarian strategy, and there is reason to think he may disagree.

Nevertheless, in his next major examination of the question, the "33 Theses" written for consideration in the *Journal for Social Research* two years after the end of World War II, Marcuse weighs the anarcho-syndicalist strategy against Communist Party dictatorship and expresses his clear preference for the latter, despite the positive regard he affords to the possibilities of proletarian self-management. In the face of the observed *embourgeoisement* and presumed integration of Western workers, he states that Leninist parties must intervene to carry the chance for liberation forward (Marcuse 1998: 217–227). This essay, written while Marcuse was working at the State Department, where he personally observed the stabilization of authoritarian control in Germany and on the international stage following the military defeat of Nazism, may be considered something of an anomaly—analogous in a sense to the uncharacteristically deep pessimism of the "Affirmative Character of Culture" (1937). Still, it signals the beginning of an internal conflict that Marcuse will continuously confront in his life and thought.

Returning to his more consistently libertarian views, Marcuse will in *Eros and Civilization* reject the concept of an intellectual dictatorship, as based in his argument that "knowledge of the real Good" is not possessed exclusively by any elite, but is instead readily available to the people as a whole. Moreover, Marcuse even speculates that said knowledge readily would become universal, were the people's consciousness not mobilized and distracted by hegemonic interests. In an autonomist-Marxist sense, Marcuse thus expresses his confidence in the people's capacity to distinguish repression from surplus-repression and "rational" from "irrational" authority, noting the procession of such a popular "course of trial and error" to approximate a "rational course in freedom." It must not be overlooked, of course, that Marcuse in *Eros and Civilization* claims there to *exist* such a concept as "rational authority"—though he is characteristically unclear in this work regarding just what he thought the nature of such authority should be, were it rational rather than irrational, as under capitalism (1966a: 36, 225). The anti-authoritarianism expressed in the theorist's middle age can be seen as consistent with his late reflections on Rousseau's concept of the general will, as explored in "Theory and Politics" (1978), a conversation that took place on a special occasion with Habermas and company, when he would declare faithfully that "everyone knows what is necessary," and that the truth of a revolutionary *general will* and "the possibilities for its realization are demonstrable" to all, rather than reserved for some Heideggerian or Nietzschean association of supposedly superiorly enlightened individuals, or "aristocratic radicals" (Marcuse et al. 1978/9: 136–138). This late announcement should be taken as definitive proof of the fundamental political differences Marcuse had with his phenomenologist mentor, however many times Marcuse refers to certain Heideggerian concepts and categories in his *oeuvre*.

During the mid- to late-1960s, Marcuse would seem to have been less assured of the optimistic analyses he had presented in *Eros and Civilization*, which he would also revisit later. In *One-Dimensional Man*, Marcuse ruminates on what he admittedly considers an inadequate justification for resorting to a transitional educational dictatorship: that the risks involved "may not be more terrible than the risks which the great liberal as well as the authoritarian societies are taking now." Attempting to clarify such ambiguity, he quickly suggests that the dialectic of freedom demands the self-emancipation of the oppressed, in accordance with Marx's insistence that the liberation of the proletariat will

be the work of the workers themselves (1964: 40–41). Marcuse returns importantly to this precise question in "Repressive Tolerance," where he declares
his preference for the creation of real, participatory democratic polities, yet
laments their utter absence on the contemporary world stage. Within this context gripped by the reified "power of an alien will," the theorist considers the
possibility of an educated vanguard leading the people toward global revolution against militarism and capitalism (2008: 89). In this essay, in an echo of
Marx and Engels on authority, he expresses his agreement with the "weak"
justification of educational dictatorship presented in *One-Dimensional Man*—
that a society subjected to a dictatorship of intellectuals may fare better than
under the prevailing dictatorship of a "non-intellectual minority of politicians,
generals, and businessmen," assuming those two options to be the only ones
available (1965d: 121). Additionally, in "Thoughts on the Defense of Gracchus
Babeuf," he questionably associates the Babouvist theory and practice of the
Conspiracy of Equals with those of the Bolsheviks. Tellingly in this sense, in the
question-and-answer period following his summer 1967 lecture on "The End of
Utopia" before the socialist student union in West Berlin, Marcuse asserts that
he finds it quite improbable that hegemonic one-dimensionality will "turn into
its opposite in an evolutionary way," and for this reason he claims that "some
intervention must occur in some way." As in *Eros and Civilization* with the
discussion of "rational authority," though, he is neither here nor in any other
work from this time very detailed in his proposal for how this intervention
should proceed. He merely raises the possibility of a "counteradministration"
that would suppress the oppressor ruling class and put an end to "the horrors
spread by the established administration" (1970a: 76, 80).

In an illuminating discussion from *Soviet Marxism* on Leninism—and, by
historical extension, Jacobinism—Marcuse argues that "[n]either centralization nor coordination militate by themselves against progress in freedom and
humanity," remarking that these historically "have more than once been effective weapons in the struggle against oppression and reaction" (1958b: 196).
In this very vein, in point of fact, Marcuse expresses great enthusiasm for his
contemporaries Fidel Castro and Che Guevara, as for the accomplishments of
the Cuban and Chinese Revolutions. Yet strangely enough, it does not seem
that Marcuse made many public criticisms of the increasingly authoritarian-
bureaucratic States which took power in China and Cuba after 1949 and 1959
respectively—these being forces correctly denounced by MacIntyre as instituting "right-wing Communism" (MacIntyre 1970: 101). What is more, in his correspondence with the Chicago Surrealists from the early 1970s, Marcuse praises
what he sees as the autonomous development of the Chinese communes, and
he hails the Cultural Revolution in the *Essay on Liberation* as a promising

model for a non-repressive implementation of socialism (1969a: 85). However, neither in these comments nor anywhere else does he seem to directly critique the Chinese Communist Party (CCP), as he would be expected to do, in light of his established anti-Stalinism on the one hand, and considering the profound atrocities for which Mao Zedong and the CCP were responsible after acceding to power on the other (Yang 2012). Of course, Marcuse did not live to see Deng Xiaoping's liberalizing reforms after Mao's death, and he may have considered reports regarding state-terrorism and mass-famine during the Great Leap Forward (1958–1961) to have been exaggerations produced by Western disinformation campaigns—or perhaps Marcuse simply did not focus adequate attention to the course of events in the People's Republic of China (PRC), in contrast to goings-on in the Soviet Union. It may also be that Inge's Maoist sympathies colored his analysis of the PRC (Sethness Castro 2013).

On Cuba, Marcuse's enthusiasm is seen in his welcoming of the armed struggle and popular mobilizations which deposed Batista alongside the initial phase of governance by Castro and the Cuban Communists, which he saw as an attempt to "establish a form of society fundamentally different from our own." In his 1961 address to the Brandeis student protest denouncing U.S. aggression against Cuba, speaking to the charge of repressiveness imposed by Castro and the *barbudos* since their toppling of Batista, Marcuse remarks that social revolution may well demand the suspension of the civil rights and liberties of those opposed to it (2014: 153–154). While this comment could be considered as betraying a Lenino-Jacobin sensibility in Marcuse's mind, one in keeping with Engels' comments on authority, it is far from a definitive statement on the Cuban Revolution, having come only after the first two years of its existence. It is clear that the critical theorist shared a distinct passion for Cuba quite similar to that felt by Sartre, who visited the island-nation in 1960, there to bask in the "dawn-till-dawn energy of the revolution," which he saw as the coming-alive of his deepest hopes for a popular and humanist construction of socialism (Aronson 1980: 233–236). At the end of his life, nonetheless, Marcuse did come to accord his views on the PRC and Cuba with his libertarian views. For one, he entirely repudiates Maoism in a March 1979 interview, declaring there to be "nothing common between Mao and me." Beyond this, in an interview from a year prior, he explicitly considers the technocratic-authoritarian policies instituted by the Cuban and Chinese Communist Parties to have prioritized "repressive modernization over liberating socialization" (2014: 366, 416).

Marcuse's variable interpretations of developments in China and Cuba—at once affirming vanguardism but then coming to critique its logical outcomes—may be said to have reflected gnawing doubts in the philosopher's mind regarding the problem of the transition away from capital, especially during

his most militant period, from the publication of *One-Dimensional Man* to that
of *An Essay on Liberation*. The imprint left by this problem would lead Marcuse
continuously to grapple with and attempt to resolve it in his final decade of life.
While the critical theorist explicitly tells Habermas and his colleagues in 1978
that his previous discussions of the concept of intellectual dictatorship were
made only for purposes of provocation rather than for any serious contemplation, he does specify that he remains open to the idea of dictatorship "within
democracy," presumably under the guise of maintaining a relative articulation
between popular choice and the general will, or reason (Marcuse et al. 1978/9:
136–138). Not dissimilarly, in "Protosocialism and Late Capitalism," Marcuse
presents an assessment of East German dissident Rudolf Bahro's centralist
strategy for the transition that is not—to return to Engels—"undialectically"
anti-authoritarian at first glance. Exploring the data and perspectives Bahro
provides in *The Alternative in Eastern Europe,* Marcuse details Bahro's vision
of a transitional "antistate state" that substitutes for the anti-systemic action
of the proletariat: a communist league comprised of individuals possessing
the "most advanced" consciousness that would dialectically repress the compensatory interests expressed by the masses—those which uphold capitalism
and oppression, that is—while helping with the flowering of emancipatory
interests in their stead. Although spontaneity and councilism do play a role
in Bahro's account of the transition, they clearly occupy a secondary place to
the communist league, which is to be considered the very "brain" of the movement. In point of fact, Marcuse relates Bahro's affirmation of the need for the
league to suppress "unreflected spontaneity" in order to secure hierarchical
rule (1980a: 30–32).

It is clear enough that Marcuse remains opaque in these comments on the
transition made at the end of his life. To help illuminate the tensions within
Marcuse's account of authority and the transition, we will pursue three potentially fruitful historical comparisons, and one contemporary one: the anarchistic conflicts within Daoism as it developed in classical China, the possibility
of an "anarchist dictatorship" during the Spanish Revolution (1936–1939), the
revolutionary-anarchist *Junta Organizadora* (Organizational Council) of the
Mexican Liberal Party (PLM), as well as the dual-power structure instituted by
the Zapatista Army of National Liberation (EZLN) between military command
and parallel participatory democracy since its founding in 1983.

Marcuse's variable account of the role of intellectuals, or *sages,* in the
transition toward emancipation recalls some of the philosophical currents
expressed within classical Daoism and neo-Daoism, which, as John A. Rapp
has written, are fundamentally anarchist. In contrast to the Confucian affirmation of "benevolent rule" by sages, Daoist writers like Lao Zi and Zhuang

Zi (sixth and fourth centuries BCE), respective authors of the *Daodejing* and *Zhuangzi*, recommended those in power to engage in *wuwei* ("non-action") and so destabilize their hierarchical power so as to allow their subjects and humanity in general to reconnect with the *Dao,* or natural human social morality. On Joseph Needham's reading, Lao Zi in particular desired to have existing rulers in China transform themselves into—or *revert to*—the tribal elders and wise men who had coordinated the anarcho-communist societies which are supposed to have predated the rise of states and empires. Both the *Daodejing* and *Zhuangzhi* discuss the anarchical "Golden Age" wherein small, autonomous agricultural communities putatively lived "in harmony both with each other and with animals" (Rapp 2012: 21–24, 37–38, 82–83). Described by the neo-Daoist writer Ruan Ji as a time in which *"there was no ruler, and all beings were peaceful; no officials, and all affairs were well-ordered,"* the image of this original form of utopia—which for the time was hardly a remote abstraction, in light of the continued contemporary existence of stateless societies in East Asia, particularly southern China—would greatly influence later neo-Daoist artists and political philosophers such as Tao Qian and Bao Jingyan (third and fourth centuries CE), who would take negative views of State and elite rule and counterpose to them a naturally communitarian human nature, as informed by the *Dao* (Holzman 1976: 195). In a parallel to Bahro's concept of the "journey inwards"—to be discussed more at length shortly—these neo-Daoist thinkers believe the prospect of achieving the Daoist utopia to be made possible insofar as one mindfully connects to the human *radix,* or root: that is, original simplicity amidst communalist, anti-authoritarian social relations (Rapp 2012: 24–46, 57–60). Though Lao Zi and Zhuang Zi directly addressed themselves to existing sages in an effort arguably to convince them to effectively abdicate their rule, the later neo-Daoists would seem to present a more unambiguously anti-statist and anti-Confucian orientation. It is to be imagined that they would for this reason take a negative view of Marcuse's contemplation of an intellectual dictatorship—or what is the same, "temporary" rule by sages. Still, taking into consideration the considerable societal and technological differences between classical China and the late-capitalist West, they may have analogously shared Marcuse's concern that the *Dao* is not readily accessible to the majority of people, who are in theory colonized by capitalist ideology, or so allow themselves to be. Yet under prevailing conditions of mass-cultural mobilization within monopoly capitalism, the neo-Daoists could be expected to give the highest priority to the journey inwards.[3]

---

3   For a creative contemporary elucidation of the journey inwards for societal liberation, see Parton 2015.

Another potentially helpful historical and philosophical comparison to Marcuse's proposals regarding authority and the transition would involve consideration of one of the central dilemmas faced by the CNT/FAI anarchists during the Spanish Revolution and Civil War: that is, that instead of joining the Republican government and popular anti-fascist front as the union leadership did, the emancipated workers engaged in self-management should have taken the paradoxical step of instituting an anarchist dictatorship. The perplexing proposal for anarchy by force was advanced by the "Friends of Durruti" grouping as well as parts of the Marxist POUM within the context of the Stalinist repression targeting anarchist revolutionaries during the "May Day" events of 1937 (Goldman 2006: 229, 249n33). The option had been considered even previously, though, as when the CNT/FAI first joined the Spanish Republic against Franco's fascist insurgency in November 1936, the same month that Buenaventura Durruti died in the siege of Madrid. As should be expected, the idea of resorting to a dictatorial imposition of anarchy proved highly contentious, with Emma Goldman for her part holding collaboration with the Popular Front government to have been a less problematic compromise for the CNT/FAI anarchists to make than directly to impose dictatorship (Goldman 2006: 13, 109, 113, 121). Of course, the proposal was never implemented during the Spanish Revolution, and it is doubtful whether it ever has been, unless one considers the Paris Commune to have been an anarchist dictatorship—or sees in the concept of a temporary centralization of power in a military command hierarchy to defeat the class enemy another manifestation of the same.[4] It may be that Babeuf's insurrectional plans to depose the Directory and thereafter institute a worker-peasant dictatorship could be considered as approximating a dictatorial anarchism. This confusing paradox is highlighted especially in light of the Conspiracy's fundamental philosophical emphasis on human equality. Critically, though, according to Ian Birchall, Sylvain Maréchal's "Manifesto of the Equals" was rejected by the Conspiracy's central committee precisely because it threatened the justification for a transitional dictatorship (Birchall 1997: 65). It is to be imagined that Marcuse's general calls for social revolution, which became increasingly councilist with time—especially in *Counterrevolution and Revolt* and *Revolution or Reform?,* where the philosopher hails the council system as a transitional political form—inhabit the matrix of these types of images and possibilities.

---

4   For a treatment of the temporary centralization of power among non-state peoples for military purposes, see Pierre Clastres, *Society against the State: Essays in Political Anthropology,* trans. Robert Hurley (New York: Zone Books, 1987) and *Archeology of Violence,* trans. Jeanine Herman (New York: Semiotext(e), 1994).

A complicating matter is nonetheless seen in Marcuse's late clarification to Habermas and company that his opposition to intellectual dictatorship still allows for realms of dictatorial control in the presumably otherwise liberatory political landscape that is to develop in the interest of radical-humanist social transformation. Besides the example of the "Friends of Durruti" faction within the CNT/FAI in this sense, one thinks of the Zapatista Army of National Liberation (EZLN), which has a hierarchical military command but also a parallel political system that remains highly participatory and inclusive, allowing for democratic control by Zapatista support-bases (BAEZLN) through assemblies and councils—as in the concept of *mandar obedeciendo,* or to "command by obeying." In accordance with Holman's observation, Marcuse at the very least is contradictory on the question of authority and the transition, in this sense much like Marx himself, whose positions essentially converged with those of Bakunin and anarchism in the reflections on the Paris Commune presented in *The Civil War in France* (1871), yet also affirm Engels' point about the "revolutionary" necessity of centralization elsewhere (Holman 2013: 66). It is doubtful that Marcuse shares Bakunin's affinity for the invisible anarchist dictatorship that is supposed to ensure the progression and success of liberatory revolutionary changes on the Russian's account, but the critical theorist's political philosophy would not seem to forbid a place for the resurrection of a Committee for Public Safety, whether more in the spirit of the Jacobin example or in that of the one that was empowered during the 1871 Paris Commune, alongside the directly democratic Parisian sections and workers-assemblies, in the respective cases.

Perhaps one of the most faithful historical expressions of Marcuse's views of authority and the transition is seen in the struggle of the anarchist *Junta Organizadora* of the Mexican Liberal Party (PLM), which included Ricardo and Enrique Flores Magón, Práxedis G. Guerrero, and Librado Rivera at different times, starting with its founding as a revolutionary organization dedicated to the fall of Porfirio Díaz in 1900. The members of the PLM's *Junta* prioritized the strategy of "combative journalism" against the *Porfiriato,* capital, and authority, as is reflected in the work they did to publish the libertarian newspaper *Regeneración* (1900–1918) and the various prison-terms they served in their exilic homeland of the U.S. for violating established neutrality laws—with Ricardo himself succumbing in federal prison in Leavenworth, Kansas in 1922 (Lomnitz 2014: 19–65, 82–89, 194–285, 390–492). Yet the PLM leadership also initiated a number of armed revolts in the lead-up to the Mexican Revolution—the first and most ambitious coming in 1906, with the plan of assaulting three Mexican border-towns, the second in 1908, and the third involving an an attack on federal troops in Chihuahua in December 1910—as during the progression of the Revolution, particularly in Baja California, where Wobblies and Magonistas liberated Tijuana and Mexicali from State control for a few months in 1911 (Lomnitz 2014: 257–265, 319–381). The *Liberales* hoped these uprisings would catalyze a larger popular insurrection throughout Mexico against the reactionary forces they had identified. Though influenced by Indigenous struggle in Mexico—particularly the Liberal, anti-clerical legacy to which they adhered—and Eurasian anarchism alike, and while the PLM's inner circle clearly advanced an anarcho-communist analysis of politics and society, the *libertarios* of the PLM synthesized Jacobinism and anti-authoritarianism in their political philosophy, much like Marcuse (Lomnitz 2014: xxv, 66, 74). Indeed, one can imagine Magón welcoming the basic anarchism of Marcuse's position, as was expressed well in a response to Habermas' inquiry in "Theory and Politics" about the critical theorist's favored revolutionary model: that of *"a diffuse disintegration which becomes contagious"* and topples capitalist power (Marcuse et al 1978/9: 152; emphasis added).

A focused examination of "Protosocialism and Late Capitalism" should confirm the thesis that Marcuse is closer to libertarian than authoritarian socialism. In this essay, Marcuse evinces no special affirmation of the particulars of Bahro's centralist-vanguardist strategy for the transition: in another parallel with the inquiry into Engels in *A Study on Authority*, Marcuse is neutral if not critical in his presentation of Bahro's theory. He expresses more interest in Bahro's insight into the importance of the "journey inwards" as a critical means of developing the transition, particularly in terms of the East German's hope that this journey mindfully would help to activate surplus-consciousness and the imagination. In the discussion which follows his presentation of Bahro's method, Marcuse explores the contemporary resurgence of class consciousness alongside rebellious subjectivity around the globe. This late in life, Marcuse definitively has jettisoned the hypothesis of unchecked one-dimensionality once and for all, declaring that the expanded working class of the industrial-capitalist countries has not resigned itself to capitalism, and that there are indications from the economical and cultural spheres which in fact reveal capitalist stability to face considerable threat. Marcuse implicitly criticizes Bahro in himself arguing that a transitional socialist strategy must be anti-statist from the very beginning—thus avoiding the problem of the two-stage implementation of communism—yet he seemingly comes to agree with his East German counterpart in holding that power may well need to be centralized as a temporary measure to realize the self-determination of peoples, even if this means violating said self-determination as long as the revolutionary transitional strategy is waged (Marcuse 1980a: 34, 37, 39–41). In making such a statement, which could be considered consonant with the affirmation of the need either for an intellectual or anarchist dictatorship, Marcuse echoes Saint-Just's declaration announcing the founding of the Committee for Public Safety and the beginning of the Terror in October 1793: "The provisional government of France is revolutionary until the peace" (Walter 1967: 135; Palmer 1941: 74–75). Such a convergence with Jacobinism notwithstanding, "Protosocialism and Late Capitalism" should not be seen as a final statement from Marcuse that returns to the openly dictatorial affirmations of "33 Theses" (1947) or "Ethics and Revolution" (1966), for the critical theorist in this late piece affirms the role of the "anti-authoritarian movement, the ecology movement, and the women's movement" in disrupting both the ideology of the performance principle and the material functioning of the death-machine of capital, and he highlights the journey inwards as a means to emancipatory instinctual and characterological changes that will in turn help along the prospects of the struggle against domination. The last point in Marcuse's concluding summary of the essay— the very last paragraph he would write for the public, in which he affirms the council system and demands the fusing of the realms of freedom and necessity—shows the thinker's great affinity with Fourier and libertarian communism, rather than with any sort of "socialism from above." Besides feminism, radical ecology, and anti-authoritarianism, Marcuse lists student protest, communes, "worker opposition, [and] citizens' initiatives" as anticipating the fall of capital and the self-managed social relations that could follow (Marcuse 1980a: 45–47).

Keeping in mind all these data-points, one is led to conclude that Marcuse's views on authority and the transition represent a hybridization of anarchism and Marxian categories at once, with the former arguably being ultimately stronger. The Spanish libertarian Abraham Guillén, author of *Strategy of the Urban Guerrilla* (1966), thus was right to categorize Marcuse as an anarcho-Marxist (Hodges 1995: 108). In this sense, it is not insignificant that Marcuse publicly declares himself as feeling "no antipathy with Kropotkin and Bakunin" in the discussion provoked by his presentation of the "Re-Examination of the Concept of Revolution" at the UNESCO conference held in Paris in May 1968 (Bergeron 1968: 91–92). In a 1970 interview with a San Diego-based radical youth newspaper, Marcuse calls for "[n]ew forms of organization, *flexible and decentralized,*" to bring about social change in U.S. society (Marcuse 2014: 353; emphasis added). Furthermore, in his 1969 conversation with Harold Keen, Marcuse clarifies his view of the libertarian-socialist alternative he favors: that of a society which is "indeed developing in accordance with the needs and faculties of the people, and not under dictatorship from authority" (Marcuse 2004: 130). Yet in contradiction to his deeply held libertarian impulses, as we have seen, Marcuse in his *oeuvre* at times does affirm authoritarian historical figures like Rousseau, Robespierre and the Jacobins, and Lenin and the Bolshe-viks. We must not forget Marcuse's declaration in "Theory and Politics" that the prospect of *citoyens* who enact the general will itself presumes qualitative social and existential changes, or the reminder in "Thoughts on the Defense of Gracchus Babeuf" that the "expressed will" of the people is "not necessar-ily their autonomous will," and "their free choice is not necessarily freedom," or concordant with reason (Marcuse et al 1978/9: 140; Marcuse 1967b: 96). Moreover, Marcuse is wont to invoke Robespierre's concept of the Terror of Liberty, in contrast to the prevailing and normalized Terror of Despotism, as reflected in capitalism, patriarchy, and imperialism: the revolution likely will require counter-violence and *terror once again,* Marcuse is suggesting—though he admittedly questions whether this latter, "positive terror" should be considered terror at all. As he explains in a 1967 interview, he is "for any movement, any possibility, which could mitigate or maybe even suspend the existing terror and the existing repression" (Marcuse 2014: 268). Still, Marcuse cautions anti-systemic movements to be careful not to wield necessary force to the detriment of the revolutionary process of creating a free humanity, as Robespierre, Saint-Just, and the rest of the members of the Committee of Public Safety did, in anticipation of Lenino-Stalinist atrocities.[5] For Marcuse, the means must be relatively harmonious with the desired end of liberation: "the end must be operative in the means taken to attain it" (1964: 41).

Unfortunately, Marcuse provides no sustained public reflection on his inter-pretation of the course of the French Revolution. For this reason, it remains unclear precisely what it is that Marcuse finds so attractive about the Jacobins, whether it be more their practice during the Terror, the humanist ends sought by Robespierre and other leaders of the Revolution—including Danton, Desmoulins, and Hébert—or some combination of these two, if not some-thing else entirely. In the example of Gracchus Babeuf and the Conspiracy of

---

5   After all, shortly before himself succumbing to the Thermidorian reaction that put an end to the Jacobin Terror altogether, replacing it with the White Terror, Robespierre eliminated two significant rival left-wing factions by guillotine, these being the Hébertists and the Dan-tonists, together with their respective leaders (Palmer 1941). Camille Desmoulins, who led the assault on the Bastille in 1789, was also guillotined on Robespierre's orders (Herzen 109n6). Lenin and Trotsky engaged in similar repressiveness against movements and currents to their left, as seen in the fate of the Left-Socialist Revolutionaries, the *Makhnovshchina*, and the Kronstadt Commune, to say nothing of striking workers and rebellious peasants (Figes 1996: 615–620, 632–642; Skirda 2004: 236–245; Avrich 1970; Maximoff 1940). In light of such con-siderations, it is unfortunate to see Marcuse associating Babouvism with Leninism in his "Thoughts" on the matter—and not unrelatedly, failing to mention the influence of Hébertist ultra-leftism on the thought and practice of Babeuf and the Conspiracy of Equals.

Equals, Marcuse considers a different militant minority, this one more autono-mous and egalitarian in its theory and practice than those of the Committee for Public Safety during the Reign of Terror. In Babouvism is Rousseau's con-cept of the general will carried forward: radical direct action is taken by an enlightened "minority" on behalf of the oppressed masses, who are themselves "deceived, hostile, or apathetic" in terms of revolutionary consciousness and practice—and specifically, in the case of France in 1795–1796, enthralled to roy-alism, on Babeuf's account. In his reflections on Babeuf's defense before the Court of Vendôme, Marcuse considers the Babouvists' plans for a libertarian insurrection against the Directory: the Conspiracy of Equals would through the uprising live out its principle of protecting the people—the poor—by overthrowing the privileged and prosecuting a radical redistribution of both wealth and power in favor of the popular classes, thus instituting socialism (Marcuse 1967b: 102–103). In spite of the overwhelmingly middle-class origins of the members of the Conspiracy, consideration of their strong egalitarianism may be reason enough to speculate that, had they succeeded in their insurrec-tion against the Directory, they could well have opened the political panorama to the militant possibilities of people's power and federalism in France, the rest of Europe, and the world as a whole—as against the past "revolutionary" centralization engaged in by Robespierre and the Committee of Public Safety.

Controversially, of course, Marcuse's essay on "Repressive Tolerance" shares much in common with Jacobinism, as it does with the political philosophies of Plato and Rousseau. The idea of social revolution being impelled by neces-sity through access to transcendental truth opens the door to the type of van-guardist politics Marcuse usually rejects, as in the example of "the people" proving recalcitrant to their own liberation and thus having to be "forced to be free," as Rousseau writes in *The Social Contract*—even if the critical theo-rist periodically flirts with such ideas (Rousseau 1996: 472). As we know, Mar-cuse lauds the action of militant minorities as leading the way toward general societal transformation in the 1968 postscript he adds to "Repressive Toler-ance." This affirmation of minoritarian tactics by itself jibes with Babouvism, Jacobinism, and anarchism alike. However, amidst the Heideggerian depths of radical falsity identified by Marcuse as prevailing in one-dimensional soci-ety, it remains unspecified in this essay whether he believes that these radical minorities should merely prefigure the future possibility of liberation in their autonomous practice, or directly come to exercise power. Still, one can look to his "Reflections on the French Revolution" of May 1968 to see the philoso-pher clearly affirming the strategy of mass-revolutionary direct action over the traditional stress on the conquest of State power (Marcuse 2004: 45). What is more, a return to the dilemma faced by the CNT/FAI can help to illuminate

this problem: beyond the dichotomous identification of dictatorship and statist collaboration as the only possible options for a radical anti-authoritarian
project, an approach emphasizing decentralization of power and federalism
remains a viable third option—as in the prospect for a free federation of associated communes. It is Marcuse's greater affinity for this type of decentralized
and decentralizing struggle that comes to be clear from a review of the breadth
of the theorist's works, as compared to the option of resorting to a transitional
intellectual or educational dictatorship. Rather than Robespierre, Marcuse
bears more resemblance to Babeuf and Magón. The common interest Marcuse
and Babeuf had in wielding natural law for liberatory, revolutionary ends is
characteristic of their similitude.

For this reason, and while not overlooking the uncritical attitudes Marcuse expressed toward aspects of the repressive ideologies and practices of
Jacobinism and Leninism, it is justified to regard his views of authority and the
means of transitioning away from capitalism and domination as anarchistic—
in spite of the thinker's explicit protestations to the contrary, in point of fact.[6]
As he himself declares positively in response to the charge as raised in a 1978
interview, if by anarchism is meant a position of resistance to "a society geared
and governed by a vast bureaucracy which is in reality no longer responsible to
the people," then he accepts the label (2014: 373).

That Marcuse's political philosophy is generally quite close to social anarchism is expressed well in this characteristic line from *One-Dimensional Man*:
"Peace and power, freedom and power, Eros and power may well be contraries!"
(1964: 235; emphasis added). Overcoming the pessimism that pervades this

---

6   In a 1966 interview with the *L'Archibras* journal, Marcuse claims that the "anarchist thesis
    runs up against the fundamental condition of an evolved industrial society," because the
    observed integration of the mass of the population putatively obviates "all revolutionary
    spontaneity [and] all need for negation, for total emancipation." For this reason, he argues
    that the cause of emancipation requires a "force" that could effectively develop oppositional
    needs (Marcuse 2007: 198–199). Subsequently, Marcuse's first explicit repudiation of anar-
    chism came at the May 1968 UNESCO conference, when he was asked if he foresaw a "recur-
    rence of nihilism" and whether he subscribed to anarchism. He responded by denying the
    accusation while disclosing his commonalities with Kropotkin and Bakunin and expressly
    acknowledging Fourier as a figure he could consider as a possible "master" (Martineau 1986:
    43). Less positively, in the summer 1968 interview "Marcuse Defines his New Left Line," the
    philosopher presents a caricatured understanding of anarchism from which he distances
    himself: he maligns anarchism by equating it to revolutionary posturing which lacks any
    means of organization (Marcuse 2004: 102). Also symptomatic of this tendency is the con-
    tradiction the critical theorist sees between anarchy and organization, as expressed to Rudi
    Dutschke (see above).

book as a whole, Marcuse would embrace and affirm the various autonomous and anti-authoritarian tendencies that came into bloom in the late 1960s and 1970s, and he would see great promise in the multitudinous global revolt of students, youth, and workers—the New Left—that shook the world at the end of the 1960s, especially in 1968. Far from the intellectual dictatorship discussed in "Repressive Tolerance"—an essay, incidentally, in which Marcuse favorably cites Edgar Wind's 1964 book *Art and Anarchy*—Marcuse welcomes council-ism and the self-management of society as a whole as these come to be prac-ticed by radical movements the world over in the 1960s and '70s. As a matter of fact, it is quite telling that he ends the *Essay on Liberation* with an implicit reference to Kant, presenting an image of a "young black girl" who responds to the question of what she and her people would do, once the presently lacking revolutionary changes had finally been realized in history: "[W]e shall be free [then] to think about what we are going to do" (1969a: 88, 91).

In chronological terms, anarchist themes are expressed in Marcuse's work beginning with the dissertation on the *German Artist-Novel*—as in the work's contemplation of renegade nomadic bands of non-conformists, artists, musicians, dissidents—and revolutionary libertarian ideas are present during the theorist's Heideggerian period and in his collaborations with the Frankfurt School, with the ambivalent case of the exception of the 1936 *Study on Authority*. It is in *Reason and Revolution* that Marcuse presents his most comprehensive early anarchistic work. Much as the young Marx does in his *Contribution to a Critique of Hegel's Philosophy of Right* (1843), Marcuse in *Reason and Revolution* describes the liberatory Hegelian drive toward freedom and reason, details its betrayal in the philosophy of the mature Hegel, and presents libertarian communism as an authentic continuation of Hegelian dialectics. Rejecting Hegel's late Hobbesian apologism for international relations among states being governed by force, power, and instrumental reason, Marcuse crucially cites the German Idealist's transcendental concept of the "World Mind" (*Weltgeist*), an "unconditional absolute" that checks capital and State in "materializ[ing] itself in world history" (Marcuse 1999: 223). Though Marcuse does not explore this concept much further, he can be imagined to be refer-encing *the people* or *revolutionary humanity* in raising the idea of the World Mind—a "third force" which is to intervene and disrupt the reified everyday operation of capital, State, and patriarchy.[7] Furthermore, from the political philosophy of Kant, Hegel's predecessor and main influence, Marcuse takes great interest in the anarchical concept of "perpetual peace" among peoples,

---

7 See the following chapter for a contemporary elucidation of the "World Mind" in interna-tional relations.

and he dedicates his 1969 addresses on "Peace as Utopia" and "Freedom and the Historical Imperative" to these ideas. In his 1964 "Afterword" to Benjamin's "Critique of Force," moreover, Marcuse provides his radical definition of peace: "Genuine peace is the real, material 'redemption'; it is non-violence [or non-domination], the advent of the 'just person'" (Marcuse 2014: 124). Here is seen the profundity of Marcuse's critique of violence—*Gewalt,* which can also be translated as domination—that he shared with his comrade Benjamin. Similarly, Marcuse applies critique to one of reason's greatest advocates in Western philosophy: in *A Study on Authority*, he impugns Kant's monarchical apologism for being quite incompatible with the autonomy in thought proclaimed by the German Idealist in his response to the question, "What Is Enlightenment?" (Marcuse 2008: 45–46).

Transitioning beyond Marcuse's early period, anarchist themes can definitely be gleaned from the three books Marcuse produced during his years at Brandeis University: *Eros and Civilization, Soviet Marxism,* and *One-Dimensional Man.* In the first of these volumes, Marcuse links aesthetics, the imagination, and Eros with Orphic and libertarian notions of collective emancipation: lamenting the sordid established history of revolution, which nearly always has defeated itself—as in the image of Saturn devouring his children—or given rise to regimes that have been even more repressive than their predecessors, Marcuse considers Eros and the pleasure principle as counter-blows against the dominance of death. *Soviet Marxism* presents Marcuse's employment of autonomous-Marxist categories against the institutionalized "Marxism" practiced in the Soviet Union; in the call he makes in this book to uphold the original "Marxian concept" of workers' self-management against established bureaucratic authoritarianism, Marcuse comes quite close to affirming anarcho-syndicalism. Hence is his previous affirmation of the necessity of domination by Communist leaders of the supposedly misled workers—as expressed a decade prior in "33 Theses"—rejected in favor of a more autonomous alternative. In *One-Dimensional Man*, as in the *German Artist-Novel,* Marcuse identifies hope for the struggle against hegemonic mindlessness in the "outcasts and outsiders": "the poor, the unemployed and unemployable, the persecuted colored races, the inmates of prisons and mental institutions" (1964: 53, 256). These fragmentary comments on the possibility of a catalyzing revolutionary subject arising from within late-capitalist society—still not fully developed, with much to add after Marcuse would take in the experiences of the profound anti-systemic movements that would erupt on the world-stage just a few years after the release of *One-Dimensional Man*—share aspects with Bakunin's notion of the revolutionary subject, as based in the *lumpenproletariat* rather than the workers proper. Nonetheless, both

Marcuse and Bakunin doubt that far-reaching revolutionary change will be possible without the central participation of the working classes in the process of social transformation (Martineau 1986: 44–45). What is more, Marcuse will significantly revise the pessimism evinced in *One-Dimensional Man* in subsequent investigations, and toward the end of his life, he will credit the New Left of the 1960s and '70s with helping to contribute to the demystification of capitalism in society at large, thus serving the ends of a possible destabilization of bourgeois power (Marcuse 2004: 123).

Hence, in this sense, even amidst the depths of the desperate Heideggerian analyses of a seemingly ubiquitous one-dimensionality, Marcuse will not present a resounding affirmation of the resort to an intellectual dictatorship, and in "Repressive Tolerance," he will state that the question of the transition should not primarily center around the resort to an educational dictatorship but should instead focus on the construction of a "real democracy" as a revolutionary return of the repressed (1965d: 122). In *Counterrevolution and Revolt,* moreover, he will cite Luxemburg in emphasizing that the "old habits of obedience and servility" must be "extirpat[ed] to the last root" by the workers in their process of autonomous self-radicalization (1972b: 39). In addition, once again, the course taken by history will further undermine the hypothesis on one-dimensionality in Marcuse's mind, and in this way further call into question his perceived need to continue contemplating a dictatorial means of transitioning beyond the fallen present. In point of fact, the aesthetic dimension Marcuse develops from Kant and Schiller in *Eros and Civilization* strongly foreshadows the emphasis the critical theorist will place on the growth of a *new sensibility* in *An Essay on Liberation,* wherein he declares plainly that the "anarchic element" is "an essential factor in the struggle against domination" (1969a: 90). Both of these concepts of aesthetics and sensibility can in turn be seen reflected in Marcuse's late interest in Bahro's discussion of *the journey inwards.*

Emboldened and heartened by the world-historical revolutionary movements of 1968, particularly May 1968 in France, Marcuse increasingly distances himself from authoritarian proposals for anti-systemic strategy in his final decade of life, while evermore highlighting promising existing trends toward the delegitimization of capitalism and the autonomous construction of resistance against it from below. In an interview on his "New Left Line" from summer 1968, Marcuse hails the "anarchist element" in the New Left and student movements as a "very powerful and very progressive force" and calls for a new form of militant anarchist political organization: a "very flexible kind of organization" that does not "impose rigorous principles" but instead "allows for movement and initiative," being freed from control by the "'bosses' of the old parties or political groups" (2004: 102). In addition, Marcuse's philosophical

defense of extra-parliamentary opposition and revolutionary direct action
in the *Essay on Liberation* certainly shares much in common with anarchism
(1969a: 65–69). Prior to 1968, moreover, at the Hegel Conference in Prague
(1966), Marcuse will identify the Hegelian negation of capital and unreason
of the day as a "chaotic, anarchistic opposition" that "[p]olitically and morally,
rationally and instinctively" is driven by "the refusal to join and play a part,
the disgust at all prosperity, [and] the compulsion to protest." Here, then, is
more evidence associating anarchism with the Marcusean Great Refusal—the
stance of being "in irreconcilable contradiction to the existing whole" (2014:
131). What is more, the idealist stress Marcuse places on the development of
consciousness and subjectivity in preparation for and amidst the progression
of revolutionary struggle remains anarchical in its acknowledgment of the
place of will, thought, and desire in impelling societal transformation—in contrast to more mechanical orthodox-Marxist accounts. In his almost Sartrean
emphasis on the subjective factor vis-à-vis the chance for revolutionary social
transformation, Marcuse implicitly recalls the anti-systemic, autonomous
compulsion of the Hegelian World Mind. Much like Adorno and Benjamin, he
hopes for the day when humanity will broadly challenge the direction of capitalist "progress" by simultaneously considering the horrors and negations of
capital—the "centuries of misery and hecatombs of victims"—and deciding
that enough has been enough (1969a: 90). *¡Ya Basta!*

In parallel terms, in his 1968 address "On the New Left," the critical theorist remarks that the presently integrated proletariat of advanced-industrial
societies cannot be expected to be "integrated for ever," and just a few years
later, in *Counterrevolution and Revolt,* Marcuse will hail the striking prevalence of wildcat work-stoppages, absenteeism, and workplace sabotage among
u.s. laborers (2004: 123). In his 1968 address, Marcuse welcomes innovative
experiments in participatory democracy, people's power, and councilism, and
he recommends the deepening of such experimental political forms, as well
as their diffusion throughout society. Similarly, in "Failure of the New Left?"
(1975/1979), Marcuse praises the radical anti-authoritarianism of the international revolutionary movement, which he considers to have been crucial to
the emergence of encouraging trends toward the destabilization of capitalist
normality.

Though Marcuse's call in *Counterrevolution and Revolt* for an anti-capitalist
"United Front" made up of "all dependent classes" could be taken to signal an
anomalous affirmation of social-democratic reformism late in life by Marcuse,
the idea that the left-wing opposition should dilute its messaging, agitation,
and preparations to find common cause with less radical elements certainly
contradicts the militant thoughts the critical theorist presents throughout

the rest of the book in question (1972b: 39–43). Most critically, Marcuse's reflections on the transition in the final essay on Bahro present a consistent *libertarian socialism* to the end. Above all, Marcuse in this last work points out the importance of individual and collective self-discovery through the "journey inwards" and the anticipatory role played by anti-authoritarian efforts to disperse power and disrupt the operation of thanotic capitalism altogether. While it is true that Marcuse presents no explicit critique of the authoritarian strategy proposed by Bahro for the transition away from capital, it is clear from his final essay that he favors autonomous self-management as a means of bringing down the system, in an echo of his previous affirmations from the 1970s, including *Counterrevolution and Revolt, Revolution or Reform,* "On the New Left," and "Theory and Politics" (1972b: 42–43; 2004: 127).

In sum, we see the essential anarchism of Marcuse's libertarian, autonomist Marxism and his view of revolutionary transition. As was first stated in the introduction to this work, Martineau surely is right to point out the convergence of Marcuse's Marxian-Hegelian approach with Bakunin's insurrectional emphasis on the necessity of totally destroying bourgeois society: much like the Russian anarchist, Marcuse intuitively "felt we must first demolish our prison, even if we have no detailed blueprint for the house that will replace it" (Martineau 1986: 43–45). The critical theorist states this belief clearly in his "Afterword" to Benjamin's "Critique of Force" by declaring the negation of prevailing power to be the "first positive" step that must be taken for revolutionary change: "What humanity has done to humanity and to nature must be stopped, *radically stopped—only then can freedom and justice begin*" (2014: 126; emphasis added). This radical struggle is for Marcuse to be developed in good faith through autonomous and anti-authoritarian means. Though the specter of an authoritarian solution to the transition beyond capital—as in an intellectual dictatorship, or a return to Jacobinism—certainly appears and recurs in Marcuse's *oeuvre,* the anarchist element is stronger, much as Eros is, relative to Thanatos. Ultimately, Marcuse's last testament on "Protosocialism and Late Capitalism" speaks for itself as regards authority and the transition, representing the culmination of a life's creative work analyzing and interpreting Western philosophy for emancipatory ends.

PART 3

Conclusion

∵

CHAPTER 9

Marcusean Politics in the Twenty-First Century

World-history is the world's tribunal.
SCHILLER 1943 [1786]: 168

On this planet a great number of civilizations have perished in blood and horror. Naturally, one must wish for the planet that one day it will experience a civilization that has abandoned blood and horror.
BENJAMIN 1968: 37–38

One can only laugh at the narrowness of spirit of those who believe that the power of the present can extinguish the memory of future times.[1]
BLOCH 1986B: 316

∵

Though Herbert Marcuse the person died over three decades ago, his critical spirit lives on, in a parallel to the revolutionary persistence of *Geist* beyond the time of the corporeal deaths of Hegel and Marx. Marcuse's capacity simultaneously to present sobering and even seemingly desperate analyses of the deeply thanotic trajectory of late capitalism and yet to hold out the militant-dialectical hope that humanity could autonomously and radically decide to overthrow the negativity of prevailing society resonates deeply in terms of our own predicament in the twenty-first century. While important and significant networks of resistance against the neoliberal authoritarianism of our time exist throughout much of the world, particularly among Indigenous peoples, it would appear that Marcuse's diagnosis on one-dimensionality retains some degree of relevance in terms of the industrial-capitalist societies of the world's core, especially U.S. society. This is not to make any ahistorical claim that resistance is absent from U.S. society, but rather to suggest that it is either not organized or concentrated among numerical minorities of the population, however much the legacy of the social movements of the 1960s and 1970s may

---

1 Though this quote is cited by Bloch at the close of *Natural Law and Human Dignity*, the author is the Roman historian Tacitus (56–117 CE).

have propagated critical orientations to existing society among U.S. people at
large, and even inspired action against the system. As they always have, the
youth of today retain the potential to act as a catalyst for radical social change
in U.S. society, as they have demonstrated recently in many other contexts:
Mexico, Egypt, and Occupied Palestine, as elsewhere.

The argument to be presented in this concluding chapter on Marcuse is one
adapted from Robert Jensen's formulation in a *Truthout* essay from November
2013: that any legitimate claim to a left-wing politics in the twenty-first century
must be red, green, black, and female (Jensen 2013). If one were to essentialize
the "female," feminist, or gender component of this equation with the color
purple—assuming one could avoid advancing traditionalism in so doing—
then, to expand on Jensen's vision, a proposal for a Marcusean "banner" in our
present century would be for it to have red (anti-capitalist), green (ecological),
black (autonomy, self-determination, anti-racism), and purple (feminist and
queer/transgender) dimensions. This final section, then, will contemplate
Marcuse's contributions as regards present and future revolutionary struggle in
terms of ecology, feminism, queerness, anti-racism, anti-fascism, global anti-
authoritarianism, counter-violence, and Eros. Clearly, though the discussion
will be divided into discrete sections, there is a great deal of commonality and
overlap among these pending tasks of liberation to be achieved.

Radical Ecological Politics

We have seen how grave the present climatic and environmental crises are: the
profundity of the predicament is fortunately or unfortunately clear now for
everyone to see. Each month now brings additional catastrophes undeniably
related to the progression of anthropogenic climate disruption (ACD). Indeed,
even before coming to a close, 2014 was declared the hottest year ever recorded,
while the UK Met Office anticipates that 2015 and 2016 will be hotter still
(Goldenberg 2014a; Carrington 2015). The mass-bleaching event of the world's
coral reefs in 2015, exacerbated by that year's strong El Niño Southern Oscilla-
tion (ENSO), has been reported as the worst in recorded history (Mathiesen
2015). In addition, a December 2014 study by the Woods Hole Oceanographic
Institute has found California's present three-year drought to be the worst in
the past 1200 years (Griffin and Anchukaitis 2014). For its part, *National Geographic* reduced the size of the Arctic icecap by approximately 50 percent in
the 2014 edition of its World Atlas, with the previous image having been based
on the extent of multiyear sea-ice which prevailed in the Arctic twenty-five

years ago (Dell'Amore 2014). Investigative journalist Dahr Jamail's monthly reports on *Truthout* on the progression of ACD and other environmental catastrophes—oil spills, mass-deforestation, chemical and air pollution, and so on—illuminate the peril run by humanity and much of nature amidst the dominion of capital and Thanatos in an *especially direct way* (Jamail 2014/5). One cannot forget that life on Earth is currently experiencing a sixth mass-extinction event, due to the senselessness of the dominant forms of human society. As Elizabeth Kolbert describes in *The Sixth Extinction*, the event can be seen reflected in the sordid fate of amphibians, bats, pachyderms (elephants), rhinoceri, large cats, marine calcifiers (such as seastars or foramnifera), coral reefs, and tropical rainforests under prevailing conditions of capitalist hegemony (Kolbert 2014b).

Just as the present ecological crisis reveals itself to be multifaceted when considered comprehensively—such that, while climate catastrophe should likely be considered principal among present and future environmental threats, a myriad of other environmental problems exist alongside and beyond it—so is the ecological crisis part of the multi-dimensional crisis of capital and the State (Fotopoulos 2007).[2] However much one may claim to be an ecologist, it is due to this very multidimensionality of the crisis that a specialization or focus on exclusively ecological concerns is inadequate, insofar as one fails to incorporate considerations of political economy, class conflict, and social-psychological investigations of phenomena like alienation, anomie, denial, depression, suicide, death-anxiety, and existential distress. Radical ecology is necessarily an interdisciplinary matter which takes from different traditions and models in its struggle against global ecocide. For there to be a chance of protecting the rapidly degrading integrity of the biosphere from utter destruction, as many radical-ecological thinkers and actors have argued and shown, capitalism must be forthright jettisoned. As such, the revolutionary potential of a synthesis of class struggle and ecology becomes a radical historical imperative.

Several revolutionary-ecological proposals have been made in terms of addressing the established existential threat of generalized environmental degradation and destruction. One promising call has been made for *green syndicalism,* wherein participatory economics integrates ecological concern both as an alternative to capitalist production and as a means of disrupting

---

2 According to the analysis of Takis Fotopolous, the other dimensions are political, economic, social, and cultural.

its normal operation. Relatedly, the *ecological general strike* foresees workers and the subordinated together refusing their labor and collaboration with capital toward the end of toppling it and so alleviating the pain and suffering of nature, as well as opening the chance for human happiness and liberation. The various *radical direct actions, especially blockades*, that have targeted ecocidal megaprojects in the North—as against the Keystone XL pipeline and tar sands infrastructure in the U.S. Pacific Northwest—and in the South—as in the movements opposed to the extractivism of both neoliberal and "socialist" regimes—hold similar promise as anti-capitalist, anti-systemic practices. The Ecosocialist Horizons' advocacy of a *climate Satyagraha* to blockade the flow of capital at the bottlenecks of the global economy is a particularly compelling vision in this sense (Saul and Sethness Castro 2015), as is Rising Tide North America's parallel call to "Flood the System" against the twenty-first meeting of the Conference of Parties (COP21) to the United Nations Framework Convention on Climate Change (UNFCCC) in Paris. Beyond this, the effort to construct *communities of resistance* remains critical, both grounded in place and interconnected via technologies like the Internet, as they experiment in free living, promote sensible social alternatives grounded in ecological and anti-authoritarian reason, and press for thoroughgoing societal transformation.

An especially cogent socio-ecological outlook has been developed by Richard Smith in a series of essays on *Truthout*, one of which he presented at the Climate Convergence in New York the weekend of the People's Climate March in September 2014. In this address, Smith calls for radical degrowth through a massive contraction of economic activity and a vast deindustrialization of the North, coupled by a sustainable industrialization of the South, in accordance with the demands that have been made for contraction and convergence—that is, for Northern societies to radically contract their greenhouse emissions, and for Southern societies to expand their own—as follows from a sensibilization to historical and regional responsibility for climate change. In addition to taking a radical view of the justice imperative for contraction and convergence of emissions, one that would demand *the shuttering of entire economic and industrial sectors*, Smith calls for social planning of production, participatory democracy, and equality in global society and politics (Smith 2014). In a way recalling the utopian socialists—and Marcuse himself—Smith presents a counter-vision in which people lead free and relatively materially simple lives, having overcome capital's ecocidal treadmill of production. Kolbert for her part recently raised the goal of a "2000-watt lifestyle" as a global egalitarian maximum for all people to enjoy in a critical review of Naomi Klein's *This Changes Everything: Capitalism vs. the Climate* (2014). Being six times smaller than the average u.s. lifestyle, yet over six times larger than that of the average Bangladeshi, the 2000-watt standard is a radical proposal, however unconvincing Klein and climatologist Kevin Anderson would seem to find the 1998 Swiss study on which Kolbert bases her argument (Kolbert 2014a; Klein 2014). In her defense, though, Kolbert reaffirms the findings of the 2000-Watt Society as a thought experiment which could be used as a means of highlighting the "really significant—and politically unpopular—changes in [u.s.] life that meaningful climate action requires," while Klein stresses that the emphasis should be placed on transitioning to a thoroughly renewable energy-system, rather than on reducing consumption at the individual level. Likely both approaches are needed.

Another sensible alternative—one Smith raises at the conclusion of his comments at the Climate Convergence—would be the adoption of *veganism as a baseline*, in accordance with Bob Torres' recommendation, as discussed above in "Nature and Revolution." Besides the instrumental effects a significant shift to plant-based diets would have as regards greenhouse gases, other forms of pollution, and the potentially devastating future risks posed by widespread antimicrobial resistance, the institution of this social alternative would also follow the past example of Reclus, Guerrero, and Tolstoy, in a parallel to Schopenhauer against Kant; plant-based diets were for these anarchist luminaries and German metaphysicist a critical expression of the development of reason and morality in history, as opposed to resignation to custom and prevailing cruelty. Presumably, the anarchist vegetarian societies which arose in Spain before the Revolution felt similarly about the question, as did the Sarvodaya vegetarians, being disciples of Gandhi (Clark 2013: 145–146, 180, 229). In a thought experiment on universal vegetarianism written for *Slate* in May 2014, L.V. Anderson presents an erotic vision of a future vegetarian world, wherein bourgeois power would have been destabilized, large areas of land previously dedicated to grazing would be freed up, and the risk of antibiotic-resistant infections would have largely disappeared, leading "people [to] band together to form communes in order to escape capitalism's ruthlessness, squat on the former pasture land, and adopt a lifestyle of free love" (Anderson 2014).

Broadly speaking, the project of melding the direct-action, vegan, and green-syndicalist currents with the eco-socialist strategy outlined by Smith represents a proposal for action which, in prioritizing disruptive praxis alongside the substantive democratization of global society, has great potential for inverting existing tendencies toward oblivion.

While thinking of these terminal, thanatopolitical trends, the problem of the timeline for the transition beyond capital becomes especially acute. The combination of evermore disconcerting climatological events and the entirely mindless compulsion to carry on profligately emitting carbon dioxide—and even massively expanding said emissions—is certainly depressing and distressing. It may well induce despair. To some extent, this seemingly desperate dynamic can, with "Repressive Tolerance" in mind, be expected at some level to provoke compensatory Newtonian actions from the radical minorities in the form of riots, revolts, and insurrections—at their most open and antagonistic. Thinking of historical precedents, including Marcuse's analysis of the Red Army Faction in West Germany, it becomes clear that the "militant minority" must be careful not to become isolated from the people at large, insofar as this is possible—for "the people" may not support all the means these militants take toward the end of accelerating the transition away from ecocide and capital, even if they similarly regard this end as desirable. This does not mean that radicals should abstain from participating in actions that might alienate the masses, but it is to raise the question of the relationship between such tactics and the strategy of dual power and revolutionary-popular intervention.

A more ideal solution, as suggested by Smith's proposals for participatory-democratic planning, would be in some way to catalyze a radical consciousness within a mass-base constituency that would in turn favor and struggle for profound changes in world society—with this being a consciousness that perhaps could be helped along via the journey inwards that Marcuse takes from Bahro. Nevertheless, the strategy of the journey inwards conflicts to a degree with the demands of time, which is "always against us" (Morpheus). As Marcuse soberly acknowledges in *Counterrevolution and Revolt*, and as the looming specter of environmental destruction reminds us, the fall of capital may not come until it is too late, such that a cultural approach that would prioritize existential and psychological change as a precondition to revolutionary praxis may be seen as less desirable, however critical it may in fact prove to the construction of the very movement which could do away with class society and authoritarianism. Neither is it reasonable simply to resolve Marcuse's ambivalence over resorting to a transitional intellectual dictatorship amidst the depths of environmental destruction by outright affirming the necessity of a eco-Platonic vanguard, as James Lovelock and others have decided to do (Hickman 2010). The most that can be hoped is for the new liberatory ecological sensibility, surplus consciousness, and emancipatory interests to assert themselves radically precisely *within and in parallel to* the processes of direct action and praxis that hopefully will continue to intensify toward the end of destabilizing the Thanatos of capital in defense of Mother Earth—as in the image of the "League of All Peoples Agency for Harmony with Nature" envisioned by Kim Stanley Robinson in *The Years of Rice and Salt* (Robinson 2002: 726). Insofar as it comes, the future global revolution will contain elements of a "return of the repressed" that previously made itself known around the globe in 1968, as in 2011, more recently. Sylvain Maréchal writes in the "Manifesto" of the Babouvist Conspiracy of Equals that "the French Revolution was nothing but the forerunner of another, even greater revolution, one which will be more solemn, and which will be the last" (Maréchal 1967: 91). While there can be no "final" revolution, since, as Bloch writes, freedom is both the alpha and omega of revolution, the hope remains for progressively intensified waves of radical cascades to disrupt the rule of capital and ultimately dislodge it altogether, before the Blochian concept of the irrevocable In-Vain comes to reign through eco-apocalypse (Bloch 1986b: 164; 1986a: 446).

In the U.S., the People's Climate March (PCM) of September 2014 showed the humanistic and erotic concern of vast multitudes for the dangers posed by climate destruction and environmental devastation. Though clearly the action itself had great limitations—consciously, it would seem, its organizers worked to ensure that it would have nothing to do with the militancy of the 1999 anti-WTO protests in Seattle, while no discernable green-and-black bloc was to be found at the mobilization itself—the popular resonance it had in New York and throughout much of the U.S. is an encouraging sign. At the very least, it is a beginning, though one that admittedly may have come too late. In this sense, thinking once again of the matter of the timeline, it is to be imagined that a far more militant action involving blockades and occupations could have better illuminated the way forward. Still, the resonance of the PCM could reflect the specter of a possible popular counter-power to come, aligned against the ecocide overseen by State and capital. This question remains to be seen.

In Ecuador, the Correa government's detention and appropriation of the flagship of the Climate Caravan through Latin America en route to the December 2014 counter-mobilization against COP20 in Lima, Peru, provides yet more evidence of the depravity of the State working in the interests of capital to maintain ecocidal property relations—in this case, the investment interests of Chinese petro-companies which are slated to drill in 6500 acres of the highly biodiverse Yasuní National Park, beginning as soon as 2016 (Vaughan 2014; Hill 2014). The harassment and repression visited on the Caravan by Correa's police should rightfully be placed within the reactionary continuum of means to which the State and capitalists turn to suppress dissent—a sordid custom that has been most acutely expressed in the recent disappearance and presumed murder of 43 teacher-students in Iguala, Mexico. Poignantly, next to the millions of impoverished and displaced victims of climatologically exacerbated extreme-weather events, such as droughts and floods, environmental activists and land-defenders themselves face grave risks as individuals amidst the power of the propertied, both domestic and transnational: from 2002 to 2013, over 900 eco-activists were killed in 35 countries, with Brazil, Honduras, and Peru being the most dangerous countries for these champions of Eros (Lakhani 2014).

Feminist Socialism and Anarcha-Feminism

Marcuse's late call for a *feminist* or *feminine* socialism opens a previously unknown connection between the growing women's liberation movement and the Critical Theory advanced by first-generation members of the Frankfurt School, all of whom were male and—by the time Marcuse began engaging with feminism near the end of his life—elderly if not deceased. The radical nature of Marcuse's expressed feminist commitments form part of the multitudinous confluence of radical feminist currents which developed in materialist and international fashions in the nineteenth and twentieth centuries (Ebert 1996: 78). Yet in light of the great historical and contemporary plurality of feminisms and the marked variety of feminist thinkers over time, it would be unnecessary to claim the totality of Marcuse's account of feminism to be the final word, or beyond question: as we have seen, his gender essentialism, as well as the marked *invisibilization* of women and feminist issues within the bulk of his critical theory (1922–1962), remain problematic. Revolutionary feminism in the twenty-first century thus should take heavily from the militancy courageously developed and lived by other philosopher-activist giants from the past: Harriet Tubman, Emma Goldman, Louise Michel, Vera Zasulich, Rosa Luxemburg, Alexandra Kollontai, Simone Weil, Simone de Beauvoir, Lucy Parsons, Rigoberta Menchú, Comandanta Ramona, Angela Davis, Assata Shakur, bell hooks, and Octavia Butler, to name but a few luminous examples. These figures are joined by the Gulabi Gang of northern India, the Revolutionary Association of Afghan Women (RAWA), the female Zapatistas (both from the Mexican Revolution of 1910 and those affiliated with the EZLN), the *partisanas* of Nazi-occupied Europe last century and the Kurdish *guerrilleras* confronting Islamic State and Turkey today, in addition to militant female Palestinians like Leila Khaled and Raymonda Hawa Tawil, eco-feminists and eco-socialist feminists, the Parisian women who participated in the March on Versailles to forcibly arrest Louis XVI in the French Revolution, the *Mujeres Libres* ("Free Women") of the Spanish Revolution, the female fighters and commanders of the 1946–1951 Telangana People's Struggle against feudalism and empire in central India, as well as a vast number of other unnamed women who have been engaged in revolutionary social processes throughout history and thus shown the way forward for approaching and confronting the hegemony of patriarchal power.

As a philosophy and practice intimately associated with egalitarian concerns, feminism is true to itself when its practitioners and adherents seek the revolutionary destruction and transcendence of capital and State alongside patriarchy and all other forms of domination, whereas its potential is betrayed when it is reduced to liberal reformism in order to accommodate prevailing privilege and power (Ebert 1996: 61, 121,182). In this sense, Marcuse is right to observe that the "ultimate goals of the feminist movement cannot be achieved within the framework of this [existing] society" (Marcuse 2014: 378). In parallel to the Critical Theory of the Frankfurt School, then, "authentic" feminist theory must necessarily be complemented by *radical feminist praxis*. It is to be imagined that radical feminist praxis today would take the form of intransigent resistance to the profound physical and economic violence faced by women everywhere, as Teresa Ebert writes (1996: 248). It is further to be imagined that a materialist feminism—or a feminist socialism—could arise precipitously as a destabilizing and subversive force throughout the world in our time, principally as manifested in direct action taken to protect the lives and well-being of women who are imperiled by the hegemony of capitalist patriarchy, as expressed in war, labor exploitation, environmental destruction, material poverty, social exclusion, and intimate-partner and other forms of interpersonal violence. Indeed, an anarcha- or materialist feminism seeks to promote solidarity, association, and community among humans of all genders and sexualities within the struggle to tear down the reigning necropolitical system (Ebert 1996: 301–302; Arizmendi 2014).

Though disagreement, debate, and critique are critical—as Chodorow shows vis-à-vis Marcuse and Brown in *Feminism and Psychoanalytic Theory*—it would seem less important for militant-feminist movements to agree entirely among themselves than it would be to unite anti-patriarchal and anti-systemic efforts together into a non-hierarchical association that advances the world-historical task of toppling male supremacy and the capital-State system. With this said, it would not seem that a "popular front" feminist strategy is the political form that would prove most fruitful in terms of feminist struggle in our century, as this would subsume differences of opinion within the "big-tent" approach. Perhaps a "united front" is better, as this is arguably more conducive to autonomous coordination and a diversity of tactics. Revolutionary feminists must not overlook the questionable aspects of the social philosophies expressed even by pioneers in the movement: the example of de Beauvoir's support for Israel is a case in point (Said 2000).

A brief point here on transgenderism and queerness, which have also been examined above: the association Marcuse makes of heteronormativity with surplus-repression, his "precocious" defense of the rights of non-heterosexual people, and his affirmation of androgyny suggest his erotic take on "polymorphous-perverse sexuality" and gender is more inclusive than more traditional conceptualizations of feminism, even Marxist and otherwise putatively radical ones. It is important to contrast Marcuse's critique of heteronormativity—which Vincent Geoghegan likens to Edward Carpenter's positive interpretation of homosexuality, or "Uranism"—with the chauvinist views his colleagues Fromm and Adorno held of this "deviation," for the former saw its practice as reflecting a regression from "normal" genital libidinality to pregenital stages and a concurrent sado-masochistic identification with those in power, while the latter similarly claimed "[t]otalitarianism and homosexuality [to] belong together" (Jay 1973: 128; Adorno 2005: 46). The reactionary perspectives of Marcuse's comrades on the question notwithstanding, that the critical theorist's conception of feminist socialism crucially incorporates queer and potentially trans* dimensions should clearly demonstrate the importance of its contributions to the *purple* facet of radical political struggle in the twenty-first century.

In terms of feminism, it bears mentioning that Fromm's investigations of and enthusiasm over matriarchy were quite provocative for his time, and may to varying degrees continue to be so today. During his collaboration with the Frankfurt School and subsequently thereafter, Fromm employed the findings of anthropologists like Robert Briffault, author of the 1927 volume *The Mothers: A Study of the Origins of Sentiments and Institutions*, to challenge Freud's assumptions that the Oedipal complex was a universal phenomenon and that the feeling of interpersonal love arose only through sex; instead, Fromm, following Briffault's example, postulated that "all love and altruistic feelings [a]re ultimately derived from the maternal love necessitated by the extended period of human pregnancy and postnatal care." Moreover, in the concept of matriarchal or matrilineal societies, Fromm found a compelling alternative to Puritanism and capitalism, given the importance placed in such contexts on solidarity, happiness, love, and compassion, and in light of the theorized absence of private property and repressive sexuality in these settings (Jay 1973: 94–96). For his part, Bloch finds in radical natural law the persistence of maternal law (Bloch 1986b: 192, 202).

Of course, one must not simply accept such theories of matriarchal society uncritically, for to do so could perpetuate the very notion of gender essentialism for which Marcuse has rightly been critiqued. Surely in some settings, furthermore, it is not only the mother who provides care for the newborn child, but rather other family relations, friends, community members, and even some men. The question of the empirical veracity of the claims attributed by Briffault and Fromm to matriarchal societies is another matter: admittedly, the task of assessing this is greatly complicated by the very dominance of patriarchy in most societies on offer today. This is not to deny that matriarchal societies have existed, as for example in various regions of the world prior to the rise of the Abrahamic faiths, but rather to express a healthy degree of skepticism regarding the specific nature of such societies. Lastly, as Marcuse writes in *Counterrevolution and Revolt*, "the image of the woman as mother is itself repressive," such that the project of advancing a putatively emancipatory political vision on the basis of women as mothers may well be quite problematic—though the theory of matriarchy may be less so, if the term is taken as focusing more on the sexual egalitarianism that reportedly existed in such societies (Marcuse 1972b: 75). Perhaps Fromm's theory of matriarchy could best be revised if it were to incorporate a more fluid approach to Eros and gender: that is, as Nina Power formulates it, to envision liberation as entailing the "overturning of the attachment of these characteristics [whether erotic or aggressive] to specific genders as such" (Power 2013: 79). Besides, as advocates of anarchism and anarcha-feminism would be expected to suggest, it is questionable to hold that any form of *archia,* whether led by fathers *or* mothers, will lead humanity to tranquility and emancipation. On the other hand, though, it may be the case that a social formation instituting the life-affirming values attributed by Fromm to mothers—or what Marcuse terms the maternal "*superid*" that reconciles rationality, compassion, and pleasure—could serve as an important means of transitioning toward the realization of the anarchical goals of liberation (Horowitz 1994: 120; Marcuse 1966a: 228–229).

In this way, the integration of Marcuse's views on feminism with the vast contributions made in theory and practice by other militant feminists should be taken as another highly promising prospect for radical politics in the twenty-first century. Even besides the matter of essentialism—which, once again, Marcuse does not definitively subscribe to, though he admittedly does verge on doing so—the critical theorist's feminist socialism remains a powerful conceptual and organizational tool for our day. As Power writes, in fact, the critique of one-dimensionality continues to be quite relevant, amidst the unfortunate eclipsing in recent decades of militant feminism by bourgeois feminism, which mystifies exploitation by hailing the integration of women into the labor market and rampant consumerism as means of "empowerment" (Power 2013: 73). In opposition to the favored approaches of liberal-bourgeois forms of feminism, the global struggles of poor women and female people of color must especially be made visible by feminist-socialists and anarcha-feminists. Militant feminism, in the words of Jennifer Cotter, must be concerned with "the economic, social, and political emancipation of all oppressed and exploited women on the planet" (Cotter 1993/4: 121).

As Ebert summarizes, an authentic feminism—which she calls red, but which we may term red, black, and purple—struggles "to end the exploitative regime of profit and with it the unequal global division of labor and distribution of wealth," toward the end of freeing all peoples from necessity (Ebert 1996: 24, 302). Beyond this, it seeks to reorder social relations in an egalitarian fashion, toward the destruction of all oppression.

The "World Mind" in International Relations: Global Anti-Authoritarianism

Perhaps most critically, the lucid and far-reaching analyses Marcuse provided of the vicissitudes of reason and freedom within the dialectics of history, when coupled with his practical defense of insurrection and social revolution, remain important for the present and future development of a revolutionary international movement opposed to racism, militarism, imperialism, fascism, and all other forms of authoritarianism that are now expressed on the world-stage, in an echo of the past. According to the discussion here, the interpretations Marcuse made of Kant and Hegel converge intimately with anarchism, particularly with regard to the former's concept of "perpetual peace" among peoples and the latter's mature concession to the *Weltgeist*, or "World Mind," which is to stand as a sort of tribunal above competing states and regulate the conflict and rivalry engaged in by the ruling classes of the world's various power-blocs. In so doing, the "World Mind" is to help reason along in coming to illuminate humanity's forms of political organization. Though Marcuse does not explicitly specify the means of how the "World Mind" is to intervene against capitalist and statist barbarism in *Reason and Revolution*, where he first raises the point, it is more or less clear from the context what Marcuse has in mind: an anarchist or anti-authoritarian International that catalyzes the supersession of capital, empire, racism, and patriarchy by a "classless, stateless globality"—the red and black we take from Ebert (1996: 61). As guerrilla warfare raged against capitalism and colonialism in the 1960s and 1970s, Marcuse insisted that the fate of this global upheaval would rest upon the prospect of breaking the chain at its strongest link within core-imperial societies. In this way, he inverted Lenin's claim, which held that the capitalist slave-chain must instead be broken at the weakest link, as in feudal Russia.

Thinking retrospectively, Marcuse may well have been right on this point, in light of the perpetuation and intensification of atrocity and brutality on the world-stage since the onset of capital's neoliberal period, which Marcuse did not live to see—with neoliberalism being a novel approach taken by the transnational capitalist class to entrench its hegemony, as David Harvey has described (Harvey 2005). Though Marcuse had developed the notion of the preventive counterrevolution in 1972, he also seems to have had a foreboding of Reagan and the coming reaction in an interview from 1979, wherein he describes the "terrible years that seem imminent" (Marcuse and Marabini 1979: 3). And yet, however much horror has reigned since that time, the dialectic continues to develop, much as unseen ocean currents do. For the young Marcuse writing "On the Problem of the Dialectic" in Hegel for *Die Gesellschaft* (1930/1931), the "history of life that realizes itself and the world as Spirit ends with the existence of the 'free people'" (Marcuse 2005: 83).

Though Marcuse's work for the State Department for some six years after World War II may complicate the congruence of the theorist's philosophies with his own philosophical commitments, he did leave government service before the Korean War, and as a radical public intellectual he militated against US aggression in Cuba and Vietnam. In his comments to a student protest-action at Brandeis against Kennedy's attempt to overthrow Castro's regime in 1961 through the Bay of Pigs operation, Marcuse makes a "utopian" and eminently rational proposal for negotiations with Castro, an immediate cessation of U.S. support for all foreign dictatorial regimes, and "full support" for insurgent revolutionary movements the world over (Marcuse 2005: 156). Beyond this, the thinker's sustained public activism at UCSD and beyond to resist the Vietnam War, alongside his support for the embattled political prisoner Angela Davis, was a central reason for the death-threats he received in the late 1960s—in a parallel to the repeated bombings Sartre sustained of his Paris apartment in 1961–1962 due to his opposition to the Algerian War (Aronson 1980: 157). In contrast to orthodox Marxists who hold morality in contempt, Marcuse did not believe this concept could be reduced to bourgeois ideology; instead, in *The Essay on Liberation*, he argues that, "[i]n the face of an amoral society, it becomes a political weapon" (1969: 8). It was a strong attachment to a political sense of morality, as well as Marcuse's profound affirmation of radical natural law and the right to resist and overthrow oppression and exploitation, that drove the critical theorist's political activism—a veritable expression of Marcuse's *Dasein*.

A Hegelian-anarchist "World Mind" intervening in international history is evidently very far from the vision of the "realist"—that is, apologist—school of international relations that was developed during the Cold War, and which still is hegemonic within international-relations theory, where it serves to rationalize statecraft and the machinations of capital. Today, as stated at the outset of this concluding chapter, Marcuse's libertarian conception of the "World Mind" could be conceived of as a kaleidoscopic, multitudinous association of red, black, green, and purple currents, as comprised and advanced by cosmopolitans—true citizens of space (κοσμος). Recently, anti-authoritarian and anti-systemic manifestations of this sort within popular social movements have been seen in the democratic self-administration (DSA) or democratic confederalism implemented by Kurdish revolutionaries, the Zapatismo of the neo-Zapatistas, the *aarch* council system instituted by Kabyles (Berbers) in Algeria, and the Palestinian *intifada* ("shaking-off") (Porter 2012). Mass-popular mobilizations in North Kurdistan (Turkey) and in Ferguson, Missouri, against racism and ethnic cleansing represent particularly illuminating contemporary materializations of dialectical upheaval, as do the the various popular uprisings that have erupted around the world of late, particularly in Egypt and Syria. In Mexico, the popular outrage over the forcible disappearance of the 43 students from Ayotzinapa has been translated into sustained, massive protests for months on end, while the atrocity led ordinary people in Guerrero to take over nearly half of the state's local governments and form five autonomous municipalities, following the Zapatista example (Goche 2014). Present-day anti-systemic upheavals advance the cause of revolution by approximating the "Eros Effect" that George Katsiaficas has seen reflected in the 1871 Paris Commune, as in the Commune's Korean expression as the Gwanju Uprising of 1987, and in the various "People's Power" movements of Asia, from Tibet to the PRC, Philippines, Nepal, Bangladesh, Burma, Thailand, Taiwan, and Indonesia (Katsiaficas 2013). It is the argument made here that the colors of the "World Mind" would be manifested most brilliantly with the advent of a *global people's uprising* against militarism, capital, patriarchy, and State, as Katsiaficas has theorized (Katsiaficas 2009). This would be the global self-conscious subject developing and intervening to disrupt the hegemony of death.

The "World Mind" is not about states, but rather about humanity—the people as "a critical intellectual unit" (Marcuse 2014: 107). Such critical struggle takes on a great diversity of forms. The international movement to blockade Israeli Zim ships at various ports of entry constitutes an act of practical solidarity with the Palestinian people, one that recalls the precedent of international dockworkers refusing to offload goods produced in Apartheid South Africa—a tactic that has even been taken up by South African dockworkers themselves in resistance to Israel (ILWU 2014; COSATU 2009). Were a blockade movement to expand precipitously through and beyond labor to shut down key points in the global flows of capital, as in the proposal for climate *Satyagraha*, this could be as threatening to constituted power as a sustained general strike—with neither such outcome being an eventuality which the transnational oligarchy likes to contemplate. The prospect of autonomous-cooperative worker movements remains crucial for the cause of social revolution, particularly by means of *autogestion*, or self-management by producers. In terms of the material conditions of the working classes, there is a great need today for a new "Poor People's Movement" throughout the world, as Noam Chomsky and Alexander Reid Ross discuss in *Grabbing Back: Essays Against the Global Land Grab* (Chomsky 2014). Similarly, specifically Indigenous struggles for self-determination and decolonization are central and will continue so to be. In this sense, one key transitional political demand can quite simply be identified using the Zapatista-Magonista cry for *Tierra y Libertad* ("land and freedom"): concretely, this could be implemented through the expansion of *ejidal* common property regimes and participatory democratic polities instituted by the Indigenous peoples of Mexico, and the devolution of vast regions of the lands of settler-colonial societies— the U.S., Canada, Australia, Israel—to the Indigenous peoples whose extirpation and forced displacement has provided the very bases of these countries. It is to be hoped that DSA and democratic confederalism might play a similar role in the Middle East, leading to the collapse of colonially imposed divisions, the defeat of Wahhabite reaction as embodied in Islamic State and the Gulf monarchies, and a peaceful and just confederation of peoples of the region, particularly in historical Palestine. In parallel terms, the Global Land Grab— the New Scramble for Africa—must be reversed, with the mass-cultivation of agrofuels ("biofuels") and the deplorable deforestation schemes this implies halted. The lived experiences of undocumented migrants, the internally displaced, and refugees—to say nothing of the estimated 230 million children today caught in warzones—are testament to the utter unreason and absurdity of all borders, and the grip that necropolitics has on existence (Reuters 2014). But just imagine if an ecological general strike could be coordinated simultaneously among workers in China, Mexico, and the U.S.—Eros and the revolutionary *Geist* would be greatly strengthened then.

The "World Mind" is carried on today in the theory and praxis of feminists, anti-fascists, anarchists, and anti-authoritarians. These groupings are no longer isolated and unknown; instead, in many cases they drive and sustain radical struggle in our day. The liberatory philosophies and practical militancy associated with such standpoints of resistance illuminate the *other dimension*, or what is beyond bourgeois society—the promises of humanity, humanism, and history. Like the medieval renegade-artists and contemporary Black radicals analyzed by Marcuse in *The German Artist-Novel* and *One-Dimensional Man*, respectively, as elsewhere, the anti-authoritarians of today comprise the "militant minority" that can press for thoroughgoing and life-affirming societal transformation early in this century, as the New Left did fifty years ago. Within this struggle, the chance for revolution is assisted by the permeation of emancipatory interests among the populace—the infamous "democratic deficit" often raised by Chomsky as regards the considerable gap between popular opinion and established State policy—as well as by the ever-present work of the dialectic under conditions of capital and authoritarianism, as metaphorically represented in nature by the ocean-currents, or the movement of the Solar System and Milky Way through space. The matter is to coordinate, intensify, and organize the resistance provided by this dialectic well. For the militant minorities to unite with the people as a whole and jointly create a world-historical international mass-movement advancing a vision of a world without borders, inequality, gods, or masters would be a true expression of political Eros. In activating Marcuse's hypothesized elemental morality and weakening the dominance of Thanatos, erotic struggle improves the position of revolutionary social change and thus provides grounds for hope, even amidst the depth of ghastly atrocities to which hegemony readily turns to maintain its rule.[3]

Means and Ends: The Question of Counter-Violence

Inescapably, reflections on violence and counter-violence form part of any worthwhile discussion on radical politics in the twenty-first century. The deprivation, subjugation, and world-alienation overseen and upheld by the ruling classes must be recognized as fundamentally and irretrievably violent—such that the structural violence of capital, State, and patriarchy should be considered the primary violence. Amidst this context, the question arises as to whether all types of violence are to be conflated and equally rejected—whether the "long series of dynastic and imperial wars" and the "wars of conquest [prosecuted by] Caesar and Pompey" can be equated with the *counter-violence* employed in historical revolutions against tyrannical power (Marcuse 1965d; 2011: 170). Marcuse felt an important distinction existed between this counter-violence and the violence imposed from above; as he explains in a 1969 interview, "For me it is hypocritical to name the violence of defense in the same breath as the violence of aggression. The two are completely different" (Marcuse 2014: 289). Like George Orwell, then, Marcuse was not a pacifist, and he generally took a negative view of that approach, particularly in the mid- to late-1960s. In "Ethics

---

3 Some recent expressions of the sordid means taken by domination to maintain its rule can be seen in the Gaza Strip during Israel's "Operation Protective Edge" in summer 2014, the ongoing civil war in Syria (2011-present), the mass-disappearance and presumed murder of 43 student protestors in Iguala, Mexico (September 2014), and Islamic State's numerous atrocities, including genocidal attacks on Yezidi Christians and the July 2015 suicide attack against dozens of socialist and anarchist youth preparing to cross from Suruç, Turkey, into Rojava to assist with the reconstruction of Kobanê.

and Revolution" (1966), Marcuse argues that non-violent revolution poses no serious threat to State and capital, while in "Repressive Tolerance," he claims violence from below empirically to have served humanist ends:

> it seems that the violence emanating from the rebellion of the oppressed classes broke the historical continuum of injustice, cruelty, and silence for a brief moment, brief but explosive enough to achieve an increase in the scope of freedom and justice, and a better and more equitable distribution of misery and oppression in a new social system—in one word: progress in civilization. The English civil wars, the French Revolution, the Chinese and the Cuban Revolutions may illustrate the hypothesis.
>
> MARCUSE 1965D: 107–108

Going back earlier in world history, Marcuse contrasts these social-revolutionary processes to the barbarism of imperial collapse under conditions wherein a revolutionary movement is lacking, as occurred at the end of the Roman Empire. He observes that the Dark Ages of Europe which followed the fall of Rome persisted for nearly a millennium, until a "new, higher period of civilization was painfully born in the *violence of the heretic revolts* of the thirteenth century and in the *peasant and laborer revolts* of the fourteenth century" (Marcuse 1965d: 108; emphasis added).

For Marcuse, who was enthused by the anti-colonial guerrilla warfare being waged in the 1960s, counter-violence is defensible and natural—justifiable, indeed, with reference to the right of resistance and the right to freedom, as based in natural law, being "the element that resists, the insurgent element in all revolution" (Bloch 1986b: 275). Echoing his analysis from "Ethics and Revolution" in "Repressive Tolerance," he notes that "[n]on-violence is normally not only preached to but exacted from the weak—it is a necessity rather than a virtue, and normally it does not seriously harm the case of the strong." He declares there to be a "difference" in historical function "between revolutionary and reactionary violence, between violence practiced by the oppressed and by the oppressors." Though he recognizes ethically that both forms of violence are inhumane and ultimately wrong, he then poses the question: "since when is history made in accordance with ethical standards?" For onlookers to "start applying [these standards] at the point where the oppressed rebel against the oppressors, the have-nots against the haves" in fact *serves "the cause of actual violence by weakening the protest against it"* (1965d: 108; emphasis added). In light of this viewpoint, it is to be imagined that he would have agreed with Ricardo Flores Magón's declaration that "[p]reaching peace is a crime" (Lomnitz 2014: 159). As a matter of fact, in May 1968 Marcuse will announce that, while most people are familiar with the saying that "violence

breeds violence," it should also be "abundantly clear" in the public mind that
"non-violence also breeds violence"—that is, presumably, by allowing hegemonic violence to persist (Marcuse 2014: 272).

In these ways, we see Marcuse affirming revolutionary violence as serving progressive ends, in an echo of Bakunin, the Jacobins, and also Lenin.
Yet an interesting potential exception to Marcuse's evidently non-pacifist
theory of revolution is found in his passing reference in "Repressive Tolerance" to India and the Sarvodaya movement inspired and led by Mohandas K.
Gandhi. Though he does not use the precise term, the critical theorist observes
Satyagraha ("truth-force") being "carried through on a massive scale, which
disrupted, or threatened to disrupt, the economic life of the country," as gov-
erned then by the British. Marcuse notes Sarvodaya and *Satyagraha* as illustrating the famous transformation from quantity to quality; in his view, for this
reason, the movement can no longer be considered as passive *or non-violent*.
Very much like Gayatri Chakravorty Spivak writing in *Tidal: Occupy Theory,
Occupy Action* in December 2011, Marcuse associates the direct action of
Satyagraha with recourse to the general strike (Spivak 2011). Unfortunately,
Marcuse here cuts short his discussion of Indian politics in the essay, and
no evidence can be found of any further engagements on his part with the
history or current events of South Asia. Still, Marcuse's fleeting reference to
Gandhi is compelling. As is known, Gandhi greatly influenced Martin Luther
King, Jr., but was himself influenced in his approach by Tolstoy—with whom
the Indian dissident carried on a correspondence for a year before the Russian
anarcho-aristocrat's death in 1910. Though many Western anti-authoritarians
may be reluctant to acknowledge Gandhi as an anarchist, there is some evidence to claim him so to be, as John Clark reviews, particularly considering the
Mahatma's theory of decentralization and *swaraj* ("self-rule") to be instituted
by the *gram sabha* (village assembly) and the *panchayat* (village committee),
in addition to his opposition to private property, the military, male domination of women, and untouchability (Clark 2013: 217–236). For Maia Ramnath,
writing in *Decolonizing Anarchism*, Gandhi belongs to the anarchical "counter-
modernists" of twenty-century India, a category that also includes Rabindra-
nath Tagore (Ramnath 2011: 163–205). The link between Gandhi and Tolstoy
could be helpful to contemplate in the present discussion, for the Russian's
rural anarchism certainly left its imprint on Gandhi's thought, especially on
the questions of violence, non-violence, and means and ends.

It is in this tension between means and ends that Marcuse's theory of
counter-violence departs from certain currents within the anarchist tradition,
while remaining consonant with others—particularly Bakuninist and Mago-
nist tendencies—as well as with more authoritarian conceptions, like Leninism

and Jacobinism. Within anarchism and left-wing thought as a whole, hence, there can be said to be considerable debate on the question of violence and counter-violence—and indeed, on whether the latter category can even be said properly to exist. Tolstoy for his part, like Gandhi and MLK in his stead, insisted on the unity of means and ends—his view was that the process of liberating oneself and humanity from coercive relations must not itself promote and reproduce coercion (Rapp 2012: 6). His critique of militarism, feudalism, and capitalism as well as his advocacy of pacifist resistance and non-cooperation alike stemmed from a common source, itself influenced strongly by religious devotion, and much the same could be argued for his successors (Tolstoy 1960). Emma Goldman would adhere to a similar sort of consistently anarchist analysis regarding means and ends, expressing her concern that the institutionalization of violence could prove dehumanizing and so compromise the cause of human emancipation, as in the case of the Soviet Union, yet she would also defend the Spanish anarcho-revolutionaries' right to resist Fascism and Stalinism using arms, and similarly would welcome the prospect of a mass-collective uprising to overthrow the totality of instituted violence (Goldman 1923/4 12, 254–256; 2006: 215–262). In contrast, the Daoists and neo-Daoists of classical and early-modern China subscribed to a political theory of a peaceful transition from hierarchy to egalitarianism, rather than call for any insurrectionary action against existing empires and states (Rapp 2012: 6, 26–27).

Yet Marcuse is closer to Bakunin, and he subscribes to the traditional radical-left view that the ends justify the means in terms of violence and counter-violence: "Reason must arm itself," as Magón put it (Hodges 1995: 51). The critical theorist would also seem to agree with Benjamin, who in his "Critique of Force" condemns those who hold that life—even the life of the oppressor—is to be more highly valued than happiness and justice *in life* (Marcuse 2014: 123–127). The philosopher's view of counter-violence evolved over time, though, such that the militant enthusiasm he evinced in the 1960s regarding the chance that guerrilla warfare had to weaken or outright break the chain of capitalist domination receded to a more pessimistic view late in life, when he would continue to defend the natural right of suppressed minorities to rebel and engage in counter-violence as a last resort, yet hold that the prospect of overcoming imperial domination would be a long-term struggle (Marcuse 2011: 232–233). It is also somewhat curious that Marcuse would so unequivocally denounce the Red Army Faction in West Germany, given the view held by its members and sympathizers that it was waging a parallel armed struggle against empire from within the metropole, and also considering Marcuse's own acknowledgment that the RAF's assassination campaign targeted individual "representatives of capital" who "are themselves responsible for capitalism—just as Hitler and Himmler were responsible for the concentration camps" (Marcuse 1977: 8). In truth, the critical theorist's opposition to the RAF's actions has more to do with their real and perceived practical effects than their philosophical implications: in opposition to murder, *terror* can serve as an effective political weapon in Marcuse's view only to the degree to which it has popular support (Marcuse 2014: 388). In this sense, he differentiates between the terror wielded by the Jacobins and the counter-violence employed by Russian nihilists against Tsarism, much like the RAF arrayed against the German State; with reference to history, Marcuse remarks that terror has served its functions only when "terrorizing" groups have already deposed the old order, such that terror by itself should not be considered a realistic means of overthrowing the *ancien régime* (Marcuse 2011: 199).

Marcuse subscribed to the complex view that all violence, including counter-violence, is wrong, and that anyone who "loves violence for the sake of violence is a fatally sick human being" (Marcuse 2014: 275). Despite this standpoint, which speaks to the closeness between Marcuse and Tolstoy, the critical theorist long insisted—in opposition to Tolstoy and Gandhi—that the violence of hegemony cannot be conflated with self-defense and revolutionary counter-violence. Whether we reflect on the matter as mediated by Marcuse's thoughts or our own, it would seem that revolutionary struggle in our time should be as non-violent—that is, non-coercive—as possible, and that the means should accord with the ends as much as humanly possible. At the Hague Congress of 1872, after having organized the expulsion of Bakunin and James Guillaume from the International, Marx famously declared that socialism could within certain contexts be achieved peacefully through electoral politics (Marx 1872). However, at the current juncture, amidst the evident prioritization which the State has granted to maintaining the unfettered power of the transnational oligarchy over protecting even formal-democratic rights, the "parliamentary road to socialism" would seem a self-evidently misguided strategy—hence the critical importance of a Marcusean-anarchist embrace of extra-parliamentary tactics and strategy. In parallel, Lenin's opportunistic dismissal of Tolstoy's pacifist critique should not thoughtlessly be reproduced by new generations of revolutionaries, as Fromm and Rapp have stressed separately (Fromm 1955: 349; Rapp 2012: 44–45, 82, 170n1)—nor should Tolstoy's philosophy be misconstrued by being reduced to *mere passivity*, for the famed novelist instead advocates *active non-cooperation* against militarism, private property, and the State, as through the mass-refusal of obedience by functionaries, conscripts, peasants, and workers acting in concert, and as would be modeled after his death by Sarvodaya and the U.S. Civil Rights Movement (Tolstoy 1960). On the other hand, though, Marcuse, Bakunin, Magón, and others have a point in distinguishing among different historical functions of particular uses of violence and counter-violence. Like Práxedis Guerrero, who wrote shortly before his own death in insurrection that "[d]espotism can be annihilated without hatred," Marcuse is right to stress that one can "vanquish an opponent without cutting off his ears, without severing his limbs, without torturing him" (Lomnitz 2014: 258–259; Marcuse 1970a: 79).

To conclude this discussion, we will contemplate two recent historical examples. The first is a statement made by the EZLN's Subcomandante Marcos—now Galeano—during his May 2014 speech to commemorate the murder of EZLN base member José Luis Solís, "Galeano," by state-supported paramilitaries. Taking a retrospective perspective on Zapatismo, and a particularly critical view of his own role within it, Marcos/Galeano expresses the thought that

> Nothing of what we have achieved, whether for good or ill, could have been possible if the armed Zapatista forces for national liberation had not risen up against the bad government by exercising their right to legitimate violence: violence from below, as against violence from above.
>
> Subcomandante Insurgente MARCOS 2014

The second example is taken from a communiqué published by the Popular Front for the Liberation of Palestine (PFLP) in the wake of the November 2014 attack waged by two members of its armed wing on a synagogue in West Jerusalem—an act which clearly was not revolutionary, however much the group's leadership has tried to depict it as an act of vengeance for the 1948 Deir Yassin massacre (Masi 2014). The problematic context to the side for the moment, Khalil Maqdesi, speaking in the name of group, declares the following, with regard to the struggle to free Palestine from Israeli settler-colonialism:

> Resistance is our only path; there is no other way in which Palestinians can liberate their land and achieve their rights. Resistance includes many methods of struggle, including, centrally, armed resistance and armed struggle. Revolutionary violence is necessary in order to confront and overthrow the colonization of our land and the confiscation of our rights [...].

Asserting rightly that "[o]ccupiers and racists do not belong to the land of Palestine," Maqdesi goes on to argue that there "must be consequences and repercussions" for those involved in the "theft of our land and our rights" (Popular Front for the Liberation of Palestine 2014). This type of analysis is readily applied to the historical and contemporary struggles of Native Americans against encroachment, dispossession, ethnic cleansing, and genocide, as it is to the armed resistance taken up by Africans in the late twentieth

century against the white-supremacist power structures concentrated in Rho-
desia, South Africa, and the Portuguese colonies—which is in no way to affirm
the highly oppressive regimes that have come to power after the formal decolonization of these spaces, as follows from the Leninist ideologies to which most
such resistance movements adhered. While Maqdesi is justified in arguing that
Zionists, like all other imperialists and oppressors, must be judged by history,
the "World Mind," and humanity's tribunal, it is evidently untrue that attacks
on places of worship represent defensible or productive targets as regards the
cause of holding Israel accountable for its vast crimes.[4] Surely the roles played
by despair and outrage in motivating "operations" like this must not be overlooked, but neither should they be used as cover for unjustifiable expressions
of counter-violence.

    As the Zapatista and Palestinian struggles demonstrate, resistance adopted
toward the end of the creation of a new and better future—or a new dawn,
this being the very name of one of the Zapatistas' Good-Government Councils
(*Juntas de Buen Gobierno*, JBGS)—takes on a great multitude of forms. While
a Tolstoyan or Gandhian stress on non-cooperation and militant direct
action is critical, and arguably should lead the way forward to the liberation
of humanity and nature—as through a global ecological general strike or
climate *Satyagraha*, a Great Refusal of mindless destruction and oppression—
a Marcusean, Bakuninist, or even Babouvist defense of the right to counter-
violence in self-defense and revolution should complement it, with an eye
to the practical concern of suppressing domination. In this sense, Marcos/
Galeano is likely right in his assessment of the legacy of the 1 January 1994
insurrection, for the EZLN's counter-violence opened the historical panorama
to the Indigenous autonomy and participatory democracy the movement
has significantly developed since its armed uprising two decades ago—the
various travails and massacres the neo-Zapatistas and their sympathizers have
suffered since coming out then notwithstanding.

Close: Eros and Revolution

For this twenty-first century of the common era, Marcuse's philosophy and
politics have much to contribute, as specifically Marcusean social movements

---

4   Regarding the former matter, Bloch is worth citing here: "Without the impulse of justice from
    below, no human rights would be installed; without the revolutionary tribunal, and without
    the court of justice that sits over the Nazis who threw the concentration camps and ovens
    onto the scales of justice, [...] there is no release of humanity." (Bloch 1986b: 202).

do. Like Hegel and Bakunin, Marcuse understood the *generative power* of negativity, critique, revolt, and revolution. His emphasis on pessimism, "in its proper place," dialectically helps to illuminate the various negations that are fundamental to existence under capitalism, empire, and patriarchy—not least of which are catastrophic environmental destruction and vast human suffering. Beyond these and other insights the theorist provides into the development of consciousness, *Dasein* and *Mitsein* ("being" and "being-together," respectively), and social psychology, Marcuse's politics remain committed to militant anti-systemic movements and practices, both as expressed during his lifetime, as they would be afterward, and into the future. As a political philosopher and historical figure, Marcuse shares much in common with Gracchus Babeuf, as we have seen, as well as with Jean-Paul Marat, the "People's Tribune" (1743–1793). The continued acute relevance of Marcuse's thought, as well as that of the thought and practice of these two French revolutionaries, reflects the distressing retrenchment of capitalist power over time. Yet once again, the dialectic persists, no matter how dominant Thanatos may seem. Against the monarchy and the aristocracy, Marat called for terror, while Babeuf organized insurrection against the pre-Napoleonic bourgeois appropriators of the revolutionary process: the Directory. In a world wherein the number of billionaires has more than doubled since the 2008 recession, in which it would take the wealthiest of these billionaires—Carlos Slim and Bill Gates—more than two lifetimes to exhaust their savings at the rate of spending $1 million daily, and wherein nearly two-thirds of all greenhouse gases emitted since the beginning of the onset of industrial capitalism have been produced by a mere 90 corporations, the egalitarian militancy of thinkers and actors like Marcuse, Marat, and Babeuf demonstrates its self-evident rationality (Elliott 2014; Sedghi 2014; Goldenberg 2013; Conner 2012).

As the palette of colors mentioned at different moments in this closing section suggests, a Marcusean vision for politics in our century could most consistently be described as favoring an *erotic feminist eco-socialism*. Proponents of this sort of radical politics need not agree with everything Marcuse has to say—let alone what they think amongst themselves—about authority and the transition away from capital, for the *erotic* component, like its black analogue in the palette, itself already suggests a libertarian orientation. Militant feminism is another integral dimension of this politics—anti-authoritarianism is feminist, or it is nothing at all—as is radical ecology, for there would seem to be future little chance for Eros, happiness, and liberation if capital's clearly relentless destruction of the biosphere is not somehow interrupted and overthrown.

Within this struggle for radical liberation for humanity and Earth alike, Marcuse's final conclusions that, firstly, everyone can access the revolutionary *general will*, and secondly that emancipatory interests *in fact permeate the lives of individuals* provide a solidly militant affirmation of the chances for social revolution, which in such light come to be seen no longer as so remote (Marcuse 1980: 136–138). The mass-spontaneous expression of radical character structure always remains a possibility within the historical process—moreso especially when nurtured and catalyzed by erotic political movements, as in Spain before the Revolution of 1936. In essence, the fate of humanity and nature depends on the Hegelian-anarchist chance for the emergence of a mass-revolutionary global people's uprising—the *photi zomenos* illuminating the life-world. Much like Rosa Luxemburg identified a century ago, and as Marcuse was increasingly wont to recognize toward the end of his life, the choice really is between libertarian socialism or barbarism. Yet however menacing and increasingly thanotic the established trends toward global ecocide and fascist repression are, the socio-political and ecological situation does not seem entirely irremediable at this point, though the time when it will be is quickly approaching, amidst the utter mindlessness of the exigencies of the transnational capitalist class. The message relayed by anti-Zionist Auschwitz survivor Hajo Meyer to the Palestinians before his death—that they "should not give up their fight" but instead continue to resist steadfastly "with human means" (*sumoud*)—applies also to all of humanity in struggle (Nieuwhof 2014).

In spite of everything, the spirit of a hopeful radical resistance is metaphorically expressed well in the humor and *joie de vivre*—joy for life—communicated by Subcomandante Marcos/Galeano in his writings and speeches, even and especially those addressing grave matters and piercing negations, from mass-killings to civil war and forcible disappearances (Marcos 2014; Marcos 2002; Marcos 2007). Like Marcos/Galeano, Camus provides a similar existential affirmation of life and radical struggle in the face of absurdity, subjugation, terror, and death—just like his erstwhile comrade Sartre, though in different ways (Camus 1957; Sartre 1948; Sartre 1976). Naturally, Marcuse as philosopher of Eros and revolution plays a similar role within the historical—and potentially future-historical—dimensions of existentialist-humanist and libertarian-communist philosophy and action, echoing his comrade Benjamin's call for a material struggle that *"ruptures the continuum* 'through care, courage, humor, deception, [and] resoluteness'" (Marcuse 2014: 127; emphasis added).[5] Against constituted power, as Marcuse declares in "The Relevance of Reality" (2011: 182), our resistance ultimately must become *"increasingly serious*, and, I hope, [...] increasingly RISKY"!

---

5   Coincidentally or not, this last quality named by Benjamin and Marcuse, resoluteness, is another equivalent to the Arabic *sumoud*.

References

Abromeit, John. 2004. "Herbert Marcuse's Critical Encounter with Martin Heidegger, 1927–1933," in *Herbert Marcuse: A Critical Reader*, eds. John Abromeit and W. Mark Cobb. New York: Routledge.

Adorno, Theodor W. 1967. *Prisms*, trans. Samuel and Shierry Weber. Cambridge, Mass.: MIT Press.

———. 1973. *Negative Dialectics*, trans. E.B. Ashton. London: Routledge.

———. 1989 [1962]. "Progress," in *Benjamin: Philosophy, Aesthetics, History*, ed. Gary Smith. Chicago: University of Chicago Press.

———. 1992. *Mahler: A Musical Physiognomy*, trans. Edmund Jephcott. Chicago: University of Chicago Press.

———. 2002a [1970]. *Aesthetic Theory*, eds. Gretel Adorno and Rolf Tiedemann, trans. Robert Hullot-Kentor. London: Continuum.

———. 2002b [1963]. *Problems of Moral Philosophy*, trans. Rodney Livingstone (Stanford: Stanford University Press.

———. 2006 [1964–1965]. *History and Freedom*, trans. Rodney Livingstone. London: Polity Press.

———. 2005 [1951]. *Minima Moralia: Reflections on a Damaged Life*, trans. E.F.N. Jepchott. London: Verso.

Adorno, Theodor W. and Max Horkheimer. 2010 [1956]. "Towards a New Manifesto?" *New Left Review* 65.

Adorno, Theodor W. and Walter Benjamin. 1999. *The Complete Correspondence, 1928–1940*, ed. Henri Lonitz. Cambridge, Mass.: Harvard University Press.

Adorno, Theodor W. et al. 1950. *The Authoritarian Personality*. New York: Harper & Row.

Alford, C. Fred. 1985. *Science and the Revenge of Nature: Marcuse and Habermas*. Tampa, Florida: Univ. of South Florida Press.

Anders, Günther. 1982. "Die Toten: Rede über die drei Weltkriege," in *Hiroshima ist überall*. Munich: Verlag C.H. Beck.

Anderson, L.V. 2014. "What if Everyone in the World Became a Vegetarian?" *Slate*, May 1.

Anderson, Kevin B. 2010. *Marx at the Margins: On Nationalism, Ethnicity, and Non-Western Societies*. Chicago: University of Chicago Press.

Anderson, Perry. 1976. *Considerations on Western Marxism*. London: New Left Books.

Arizmendi, Luis. 2014. "Necropolitical Capitalism and Ayotzinapa," *Truthout*, Dec. 10.

Aronson, Ronald. 1971. "Dear Herbert," in *The Revival of American Socialism: Selected Papers of the Socialist Scholars Conference*, ed. George Fischer. New York: Oxford University Press.

———. 1980. *Jean-Paul Sartre: Philosophy in the World*. London: New Left Books.

Avrich, Paul. 1967. *The Russian Anarchists*. Princeton: Princeton University Press.

———. 1970. *Kronstadt 1921*. Princeton, NJ: Princeton University Press.

Babeuf, Gracchus. 1967. *The Defense of Gracchus Babeuf*, ed. John Anthony Scott. Boston: University of Mass. Press.

Bawden, Tom. 2015. "A quarter of the world's marine species in danger of extinction," *The Independent*, Jan. 30.

Bekoff, Marc. 2012. "Animals are conscious and should be treated as such." *Scientific American*, Sept. 22.

Benjamin, Walter. 1968. *Illuminations*, ed. Hannah Arendt. New York: Harcourt.

———. 1974. *Gesammelte Schriften* IV, vol. 2. Frankfurt am Main: Suhrkamp Verlag.

———. 1979. *One-Way Street and Other Writings*, trans. Edmund Jephcott and Kingsley Shorter. London: New Left Books.

———. 2003. *Selected Writings, Volume 4: 1938–1940*, trans. Edmund Jephcott and ed. Howard Eiland and Michael W. Jennings. Cambridge, Mass.: Harvard University Press.

Bergeron, Gérard. 1968. "Qui est Herbert Marcuse?" *Action pédagogique*, no. 12–13.

Bernstein, Richard J. 1988. "Negativity: Theme and Variations," in *Marcuse: Critical Theory and the Promise of Utopia*, eds. Robert Pippin et al. South Hadley, Mass.: Bergin and Garvey Publishers.

Birchall, Ian. 1997. *The Spectre of Babeuf*. London: Palgrave Macmillan.

Bloch, Ernst. 1961. *Philosophische Grundfragen I*. Frankfurt: Suhrkamp.

———. 1986a. *The Principle of Hope, Vol. 1*. Cambridge, Mass.: MIT Press.

———. 1986b. *Natural Law and Human Dignity*, trans. Dennis J. Schmidt. Cambridge, Mass: MIT Press.

Bowlby, John. 1958. "The Nature of the Child's Tie to his Mother." *International Journal of Psychoanalysis*, 39, pp. 350–371.

Brown, Norman O. 1985. *Life against Death*. Middletown, Connecticut: Wesleyan University Press.

Buck-Morss, Susan. 1977. *The Origin of Negative Dialectics: Theodor W. Adorno, Walter Benjamin, and the Frankfurt Institute*. New York: The Free Press.

Camus, Albert. 1957. *The Plague*, trans. Stuart Gilbert. New York: Knopf.

———. 1961. *The Rebel: An Essay in Man in Revolt*, trans. Anthony Bower. New York: Knopf.

Carrington, Damian. 2014. "Earth has lost half its wildlife in the past 40 years, says WWF," *The Guardian*, Sept. 29.

———. 2015. "2015 and 2016 set to break global heat records, says Met Office." *The Guardian*, Sept. 14.

Chelala, Cesar. 2014. "The Betrayal of Dr. Schweitzer," *Counterpunch*, July 18.

Chivian, E. and A. Bernstein, eds. 2008. *Sustaining Life: How Human Health Depends on Biodiversity*. New York: Oxford University Press.

Chomsky, Noam. 2010. *Hopes and Prospects*. Chicago: Haymarket Books.

———. 2013. "On Revolutionary Violence, Communism, and the American Left." *Pax Marxista*. Available online at http://paxmarxista.org/noam-chomsky-on-revolutionary-violence-communism-and-the-american-left/.

———. 2014. "Reconstructing the Poor People's Movement," in *Grabbing Back: Essays against the Global Land Grab*, ed. Alexander Reid Ross. Oakland: AK Press.

Chomsky, Noam and Michel Foucault. 2006. *The Chomsky-Foucault Debate: On Human Nature*. New York: New Press.

Clark, John P. 2013. *The Impossible Community: Realizing Communitarian Anarchism*. New York: Bloomsbury.

Clark, Stuart. 2014. "Mars volcano may have been site for life," *The Guardian*, May 28.

Cobb, W. Mark. 2004. "Diatribes and Distortions: Marcuse's Academic Reception," in *Herbert Marcuse: A Critical Reader*, eds. John Abromeit and W. Mark Cobb. New York: Routledge.

Conner, Clifford D. 2012. *Jean Paul Marat: Tribune of the French Revolution*. London: Pluto Press.

Cooke, Claude. 2007. "An American Atrocity: The My Lai Massacre Concretized in a Victim's Face," *Journal of American History*, pp. 154–162. Vol. 94: no. 1.

Congress of South African Trade Unions. 2009. "Free Palestine! Isolate Apartheid Israel! South African Dock Workers Refuse to Handle Israeli Goods," *MRZine*, Feb. 3. Available online at http://mrzine.monthlyreview.org/2009/sa030209.html.

Cotter, Jennifer. 1993/1994. "On Feminist Pedagogy," *Minnesota Review* 41/42.

Dahr Jamail. 2014–2015. "Planet or Profit?" in *Truthout*. Available online at http://truth-out.org/news/item/22419-planet-or-profit.

Davis, Angela. 1974. *An Autobiography*. New York: International Publishers.

Dell'Amore, Christine. 2014. "Shrinking Arctic Ice Prompts Drastic Change in National Geographic Atlas." *National Geographic News*, June 9.

Descartes, René. 1929. *A Discourse on Method*, trans. John Veitch. London: J.M. Dent & Sons.

Diaz, Joseph. 2013. "Schmitt and Marcuse: Friends, Force, and Quality," in *Telos* 165.

Dunayevskaya, Raya. 1964. "Reason and Revolution vs. Conformism and Technology," *The Activist* 11, pp. 32–33.

Ebert, Teresa. 1996. *Ludic Feminism and After: Postmodernism, Desire, and Labor in Late Capitalism*. Ann Arbor: Univ. of Michigan Press.

Einstein, Albert et al. 1948. "New Palestine Party. Visit of Menachen Begin and Aims of Political Movement Discussed," *The New York Times*, Dec. 4.

Elliot, Larry. 2014. "Explosion in wealth inequality needs urgent plan of action, says Oxfam." *The Guardian*, Oct. 29.

El País. 1979. "Marcuse sufre un ataque al corazón la víspera de su visita a España," *El País*, May 25.

Figes, Orlando. 1996. *A People's Tragedy: The Russian Revolution, 1891–1924*. New York: Penguin.

Fittko, Lisa. 1999. "The Story of Old Benjamin," in *The Arcades Project*, trans. Howard Eiland and Kevin McLaughlin. Cambridge, Mass.: Harvard University Press.

Foing, Bernard. 2014. "Earth's Moon—'Made the Emergence of Complex Multi-Cellular Life Possible,'" *Daily Galaxy*, June 12.

Fotopoulos, Takis. 2007. "The Ecological Crisis as Part of the Present Multi-Dimensional Crisis and Inclusive Democracy," in *The International Journal of Inclusive Democracy*, vol. 3, no. 3.

Fourier, Charles. 1971. *Design for Utopia*. New York: Schocken Books.

Franz Neumann Project. 2006. "Franz Neumann [1900–1954]," in *The Franz Neumann Project: Beyond the Behemoth*. Available online at http://www.wbenjamin.org/neumannproject.html.

Freud, Sigmund. 1950 [1923]. *Beyond the Pleasure Principle*, trans. James Strachey. New York: Liveright Publishing Corporation.

———. 1953–1966 [1937]. "Analysis Terminable and Interminable," in *Standard Edition Complete Psychological Works*, volume 23. Hogarth Press.

———. 1989 [1930]. *Civilization and its Discontents*, trans. and ed. James Strachey. New York: W.W. Norton.

Fromm, Erich. 1955. "The Human Implications of 'Instinctivistic Radicalism,'" *Dissent* 2:4.

Fromm, Erich and Michael Maccoby. 1970. *Social Character in a Mexican Village*. Englewood Cliffs, NJ: Prentice-Hall.

Galbraith, John K. Galbraith. 1956. *American Capitalism*. Boston: Houghton Mifflin.

Geoghegan, Vincent. 1981. *Reason and Eros: The Social Theory of Herbert Marcuse*. London: Pluto.

Goche, Flor. 2014. "Crean cinco gobiernos autónomos en Guerrero," *Contralinea*, December 16. Available online at http://contralinea.info/archivo-revista/index.php/2014/12/16/crean-cinco-gobiernos-autonomos-en-guerrero.

Goldenberg, Suzanne. 2013. "Just 90 companies caused two-thirds of man-made global warming emissions," *The Guardian*, Nov. 20.

———. 2014a. "2014 set to be the world's hottest year," *The Guardian*, Dec. 3.

———. 2014b. "UN: rate of emissions growth nearly doubled in first decade of 21st century," *The Guardian*, April 11.

Goldman, Emma. 1923–1924. *My Two Years in Russia*. St. Petersburg, Florida: Red and Black Publishers.

———. 2006. *Vision on Fire: Emma Goldman on the Spanish Revolution*, ed. David Porter. Oakland, California: AK Press.

Goldner, Loren. 2010. "Race and the Enlightenment Part I: From Anti-Semitism to White Supremacy, 1492–1676." *Libcom*. Available online at https://libcom.org/history/race-enlightenment-part-i-anti-semitism-white-supremacy-1492-1676.

Green, Richard E. et al. 2010. "A Draft Sequence of the Neandertal Genome." *Science* 328, pp. 710–722.

Griffin, Daniel and Kevin Anchukaitis. 2014. "How unusual is the 2012–2014 California drought?" *Geophysical Research Letters*.

Guerrero, Práxedis G. 1924. *Artículos literarios y de combate; pensamientos; crónicas revolucionarias, etc*. Mexico City: Placer Armada Ediciones.

Guha, Ramachandra. 2000. *The Unquiet Woods: Ecological Change and Peasant Resistance in the Himalaya*. Berkeley: University of California Press.

Gupta, Arun. 2014. "How the People's Climate March Became a Corporate PR Campaign," *Counterpunch*, Sept. 21.

Habermas, Jürgen. 2000. "Marcuse—Psychic Thermidor and the Rebirth of Rebellious Subjectivity," in *German 20th Century Philosophy: The Frankfurt School*, ed. Wolfgang Schirmacher. New York: Continuum.

Hansen, James. 2009. *Storms of My Grandchildren: The Truth About the Coming Climate Catastrophe and Our Last Chance to Save Humanity*. New York: Bloomsbury USA.

Harvey, David. 2005. *A Brief History of Neoliberalism*. Oxford: Oxford University Press.

Hegel, George Wilhelm Friedrich. 1900. *Philosophy of History*, trans. J. Sibbree. New York: Colonial Press.

———. 1936. *Dokumente zu Hegels Entwicklung*, ed. J. Hoffmeister. Stuttgart: Fr. Fromanns Verlag.

———. 1952 [1820]. *Philosophy of Right*, trans. T.M. Knox. Oxford: Oxford University Press.

———. 1977 [1807]. *Phenomenology of Spirit*, trans. A.V. Miller. Oxford: Oxford University Press.

Herzen, Alexander. 1968. *My Past and Thoughts*, trans. Constance Garnett. New York: Knopf.

Hickman, Leo. 2010. "James Lovelock: Humans are too stupid to prevent climate change," *The Guardian*, March 29.

Hill, David. 2014. "Ecuador pursued China oil deal while pledging to protect Yasuni, papers show," *The Guardian*, Feb. 19.

Hochschartner, Jon. 2014. "The Vegetarian Communard." *Counterpunch*, March 19.

Hodges, Donald C. 1995. *Mexican Anarchism After the Revolution*. Austin: University of Texas Press.

Hölderin, Friedrich. 1990 [1797–1799]. *Hyperion and Selected* Poems, ed. Frank L. Santner, trans. William R. Transk. New York: Continuum.

Holloway, John. 2010 [2002]. *Change the World Without Taking Power*. London: Pluto.

Holman, Christopher. 2013. *Politics as Radical Creation: Herbert Marcuse and Hannah Arendt on Political Performativity*. Toronto: University of Toronto Press.

Holzman, Donald. 1976. *Poetry and Politics: The Life and Times of Juan Chi (AD 210–263)*. Cambridge: Cambridge University Press.

Horkheimer, Max. 1978. *Dawn & Decline: Notes 1926–1931 and 1950–1969*, trans. Michael Shaw. New York: Continuum.

Horkheimer, Max and Theodor W. Adorno. 2002 [1944/1947]. *Dialectic of Enlightenment: Philosophical Fragments*, trans. Edmund Jephcott. Stanford, California: Stanford University Press.

Horowitz, Gad. 1994. "Psychoanalytic Feminism in the Wake of Marcuse," in *Marcuse: From the New Left to the Next Left*, eds. John Bokina and Timothy J. Lukes. Lawrence, Kansas: University Press of Kansas.

International Longshore and Warehouse Union. 2014. "Death of Nelson Mandela recalls decades of ILWU support for anti-apartheid struggle," *International Longshore and Warehouse Union*, Jan. 2. Available online at http://www.ilwu.org/death-of-nelson-mandela-recalls-decades-of-ilwu-support-for-anti-apartheid-struggle.

Jameson, Fredric. 2005. *Archaeologies of the Future: The Desire Called Utopia and Other Science Fictions*. London: Verso.

Jani, Pranar et al. 2014. "Poststructuralism and Post-Colonialism: Critique from the Left." Left Forum 2014, June 1.

Jay, Martin. 1971. "How Utopian Is Marcuse?" in *The Revival of American Socialism: Selected Papers of the Socialist Scholars Conference*, ed. George Fischer. New York: Oxford Univ. Press.

————. 1973. *The Dialectical Imagination: A History of the Frankfurt School and the Institute of Social Research, 1923–1950*. Boston: Little, Brown and Co.

Jensen, Robert. 2013. "The Future Must Be Green, Red, Black and Female," *Truthout*, Nov. 7.

Jewish Telegraphic Agency. 1971. "Marcuse Joins Appeal to Kosygin to Let Soviet Jews Emigrate to Israel." Available online at http://www.jta.org/1971/01/26/archive/marcuse-joins-appeal-to-kosygin-to-let-soviet-jews-emigrate-to-israel.

Juutilainen, Paul A. 1996. *Herbert's Hippopotamus: Marcuse and Revolution in Paradise*. Available online at http://www.youtube.com/watch?v=gbzhmMDFcFQ.

Kamat, Jyotsna. 2014. "The Bishnoi Community," *Geographica Indica*. Available online at http://www.kamat.com/indica/faiths/bishnois.htm.

Kant, Immanuel. 2000. *The Critique of Judgment*, trans. J.H. Bernard. Amherst, Mass.: Prometheus Books.

Katsiaficas, George. 2004. "Marcuse as Activist: Reminiscences on his Theory and Practice," in Herbert Marcuse, *The New Left and the 1960's: Collected Papers Volume 3*, ed. Douglas Kellner. London: Routledge.

————. 2009. "Toward a Global People's Uprising," *Occupied London*, July 28. Available online at http://www.occupiedlondon.org/globalpeoplesuprising.

————. 2013. *Asia's Unknown Uprisings Volume 2: People's Power in the Philippines, Burma, Tibet, China, Taiwan, Bangladesh, Nepal, Thailand, and Indonesia, 1947–2009*. Oakland, California: PM Press.

Kātz, Barry. 1982. *Herbert Marcuse and the Art of Liberation: An Intellectual Biography*. London: Verso.

Kellner, Douglas. 1984. *Herbert Marcuse and the Crisis of Marxism*. Berkeley: University of California Press.

Kernberg, Otto. 2009. "The concept of the death drive: A clinical perspective," *International Journal of Psychoanalysis* 90, pp. 1009–1023.

Klein, Naomi. 2014. "The Ethics of Climate Hope: A Response to Elizabeth Kolbert," *This Changes Everything*, Dec. 4. Available online at http://thischangeseverything.org/the-ethics-of-climate-hope-a-response-to-elizabeth-kolbert.

Kolbert, Elizabeth. 2014a. "Can Climate Change Cure Capitalism?" *New York Review of Books*, Dec. 4.

Kropotkin, Peter. 1972. Mutual Aid: A Factor of Evolution. New York: New York University Press.

———. 2014b. *The Sixth Extinction: An Unnatural History*. New York: Henry Holt.

Kreis, Steven. 2000. "The Utopian Socialists: Charles Fourier (1)," *The History Guide: Lectures on Modern European Intellectual History*. Available online at http://www.historyguide.org/intellect/lecture21a.html.

Lakhani, Nina. 2014. "Surge in deaths of environmental activists over past decade, report finds," *The Guardian*, April 15.

Lassithiotakis, Hèléne. 1974. "A propos du livre <<on a raison de se révolter>>," *Libération*, June 7.

Lauritsen, John and David Thorstad. 1974. *The Early Homosexual Rights Movement*. New York: Times Change Press.

Léger, Jean. 1949. "The Conspiracy of Equals and the Birth of Communism," *Socialisme ou Barbarie*, issue 2. Available online at http://thecommune.co.uk/2010/10/13/the-conspiracy-of-equals-and-the-birth-of-communism.

Leslie, Esther. 2000. *Walter Benjamin: Overpowering Conformism*. London: Pluto.

Lévinas, Emmanuel. 1994. *Nine Talmudic Readings*, trans. Annette Aronowicz. Bloomington, Indiana: Indiana University Press.

Lomnitz, Claudio. 2014. *The Return of Comrade Ricardo Flores Magón*. New York: Zone Books.

Löwy, Michael. 1999. "Under the Star of Romanticism: Walter Benjamin and Herbert Marcuse," in *Revolutionary Romanticism*, ed. Max Blechman. San Francisco: City Lights.

Lukács, György. 1969. "Marcuse is Objectively Our Ally." *Le Monde*, May 20.

MacIntyre, Alasdair. 1970. *Herbert Marcuse: An Exposition and a Polemic*. New York: Viking Press.

Mackey, Theresa. 2001. *Dictionary of Literary Biography Volume 242: Twentieth-Century European Cultural Theorists, First Series: A Bruccoli Clark Layman Book*, edited by Paul Hansom. University of Southern California: The Gale Group.

Marcos, Subcomandante Insurgente. 2002. *Our Word is Our Weapon*, ed. Juana Ponce de León. New York: Seven Stories Press.

————. 2007. *The Speed of Dreams: Selected Writings 2001–2007*. San Francisco: City Lights Books.

————. 2014. "Between Light and Shadow," *Enlace Zapatista*, May 27. Available online at http://enlacezapatista.ezln.org.mx/2014/05/27/between-light-and-shadow.

Marcuse, Harold. 2003. "Carl Marcuse." Available online at http://www.marcuse.org/others/carl/CarlMarcuse1864.htm.

————. 2004. "Herbert Marcuse's Death, Burial, and Gravestone." Available online at http://www.marcuse.org/herbert/newsevents/2003berlinburial/gravestone.htm.

Marcuse, Herbert. 1950a. "Review of Benjamin Farrington's *Francis Bacon: Philosopher of Industrial Science*," in *Annals of the American Academy of Political and Social Science* 271.

————. 1950b. "Review of 'Georg Lukács, Goethe und Seine Zeit,'" in *Philosophy and Phenomenological Research* 11:1.

————. 1951a. "Review of José Chapiro, *Erasmus and Our Struggle for Peace. Includes Peace Protests!* and *Erasmus of Rotterdam*," in *Annals of the American Academy of Political and Social Science*, 276.

————. 1951b. "Review of John U. Nef, *War and Human Progress: An Essay on the Rise of Industrial Civilization*," in *American Historical Review* 571.

————. 1953. "Review of *Russian Social Thought: Studies of Non-Marxian Formation in Nineteenth Century Russia and of Its Partial Revival in the Soviet Union*," in *American Slavic and East European Review*, 12:1.

————. 1954. "Recent Literature on Communism," *World Politics* 6:4.

————. 1958a. "Preface" in Raya Dunayevskaya, *Marxism and Freedom: From 1776 until Today*. New York: Bookman Associates.

————. 1958b. *Soviet Marxism*. New York: Columbia University Press.

————. 1964. *One-Dimensional Man*. Boston: Beacon Press.

————. 1965a. "Statement on Vietnam," in *Partisan Review* 32.

————. 1965b. "Socialist Humanism?" in *Socialist Humanism*, ed. Erich Fromm. New York: Doubleday & Company.

————. 1965c. "On Science and Phenomenology," in *Boston Studies in the Philosophy of Science*, eds. Robert S. Cohen and Marx W. Wartofsky, vol. 2. New York: Humanities Press.

————. 1965d. "Repressive Tolerance," in Robert Paul Wolff and Barrington Moore, Jr., *A Critique of Pure Tolerance*. Boston: Beacon Press.

————. 1966a [1955]. *Eros and Civilization: A Philosophical Inquiry into Freud*. Boston: Beacon Press.

————. 1966b. "Ethics and Revolution," in *Ethics and Society: Original Essays on Contemporary Moral Problems*, ed. Richard T. De George. Garden City, New York: Anchor Books.

————. 1967a. "The Question of Revolution," in *New Left Review* I/45.

————. 1967b. "Thoughts on the Defense of Gracchus Babeuf," in *The Defense of Gracchus Babeuf*, ed. John Anthony Scott. Boston: University of Mass. Press.

————. 1968. *Negations: Essays in Critical Theory*. Boston: Beacon Press.

————. 1969a. *An Essay on Liberation*. Boston: Beacon Press.

————. 1969b. "Re-Examination of the Concept of Revolution," *New Left Review* I/56.

————. 1969c. "The Realm of Freedom and the Realm of Necessity: A Reconsideration," *Praxis*, 5, no. 1.

————. 1969d. "Revolutionary Subject and Self-Government," *Praxis*, 5, no. 2.

————. 1970a. *Five Lectures: Psychoanalysis, Politics, and Utopia*. Boston: Beacon Press.

————. 1970b. "Only a Free Arab World Can Co-Exist with a Free Israel," *Israel Horizons*.

————. 1972a. *Studies in Critical Philosophy*, trans. Joris de Bres. Boston: Beacon Press.

————. 1972b. *Counterrevolution and Revolt*. Boston: Beacon Press.

————. 1977. "Murder Is Not a Political Weapon," trans. Jeffrey Herf. *New German Critique*.

————. 1978a. *Der Deutsche Künstlerroman*, in *Schriften*, vol. 1. Frankfurt: Suhrkamp.

————. 1978b. *The Aesthetic Dimension: Toward a Critique of Marxist Aesthetics*. Boston: Beacon.

————. 1980a. "Protosocialism and Late Capitalism: Toward a Theoretical Synthesis Based on Bahro's Analysis," trans. Michel Vale et al., in *International Journal of Politics* 10: 2/3.

————. 1980b. "Vietnam—Die Dritte Welt und Die Opposition in den Metropolen: Eine Podium-diskussion," in *Das Ende der Utopie*. Frankfurt am Main: Verlag Neue Kritik.

————. 1987. *Hegel's Ontology and the Theory of Historicity*, trans. Seyla Benhabib. Cambridge, Mass.: MIT Press.

————. 1998. *Technology, War, and Fascism: Collected Papers Volume 1*, ed. Douglas Kellner. London: Routledge.

————. 1999. *Reason and Revolution: Hegel and the Rise of Social Theory*. Amherst, New York: Humanity Books.

————. 2001. *Towards a Critical Theory of Society: Collected Papers Volume 2*, ed. Douglas Kellner. London: Routledge.

————. 2004. *The New Left and the 1960's: Collected Papers Volume 3*, ed. Douglas Kellner. London: Routledge.

————. 2005. *Heideggerian Marxism*, eds. Richard Wolin and John Abromeit. Lincoln, Nebraska: University of Kansas Press.

————. 2007. *Art and Liberation: Collected Papers Volume 4*, ed. Douglas Kellner. London: Routledge.

————. 2008. *A Study on Authority*, trans. Joris de Bres. London: Verso.

————. 2011. *Philosophy, Psychoanalysis, and Emancipation: Collected Papers Volume 5*, eds. Douglas Kellner and Clayton Pierce. London: Routledge.

————. 2014. *Marxism, Revolution, and Utopia: Collected Papers Volume 6*, eds. Douglas Kellner and Clayton Pierce. London: Routledge.

————. 2015 [1974]. *Paris Lectures at Vincennes University*, ed. Peter-Erwin Jansen and Charles Reitz. Charleston, South Carolina: CreateSpace Independent Publishing.

Marcuse, Herbert and Jean Marabini. 1979. "La Révolution du XXIe siècle sera poetique," *Les Nouvelles littéraires*, Aug. 2–9.

Marcuse, Herbert and Karl Popper. 1976 [1972]. *Revolution or Reform? A Confrontation*, ed. A.T. Ferguson. Chicago: New University Press.

Marcuse, Herbert and Moshe Dayan. 2012. "Protocol of the Conversation between the Philosopher Herbert Marcuse and Israel's Minister of Defense, Moshe Dayan, December 29, 1971," ed. and trans. Zvi Tauber, in *Telos* 158.

Marcuse, Herbert and Theodor W. Adorno. 1999. "Correspondence on the German Student Movement," *New Left Review* I/233.

Marcuse, Herbert et al. 1978/1979. "Theory & Politics," in *Telos* 38.

Marcuse, Peter and Erica Sherover. 1979. "To The Editors," *The New York Review of Books*, September 27.

Maréchal, Sylvain. 1967. "Manifeste des Egaux," in *The Defense of Gracchus Babeuf*. ed. John Anthony Scott. Boston: University of Mass. Press.

Martineau, Alain. 1986. *Herbert Marcuse's Utopia*, trans. Jane Brierley. Montréal: Harvest House.

Marx, Karl. 1844. "On the Jewish Question." Available online at http://www.marxists .org/archive/marx/works/1844/jewish-question.

————. 1865. "Marx to Engels in Manchester." Available online at https://marxists.anu .edu.au/archive/marx/works/1865/letters/65_02_18.htm.

————. 1872. "La Liberté Speech.' Available online at https://www.marxists.org/ archive/marx/works/1872/09/08.htm.

————. 1953. *Grundrisse der Kritik der Politischen Oekonomie*. Berlin: Dietz.

Marx, Karl and Friedrich Engels. 1975. *Collected Works*, vol. III. New York: International Publisher.

Masi, Alessandria. 2014. "Jerusalem Synagogue Attack: Motivation Was Not Religion But Revenge For 1948 Massacre, Says PFLP," *International Business Times*, Nov. 18.

Mathiesen, Karl. "World's oceans facing biggest coral die-off in history, scientists warn." *The Guardian*, Oct. 8.

Mattick, Paul. 1967. "The Limits of Integration," in *The Critical Spirit*, eds. Kurt H. Wolff and Barrington Moore. Boston: Beacon Press.

————. 1972. Critique of Marcuse. New York: Herder and Herder.

Maximoff, G.P. 1940. *The Guillotine at Work: Twenty Years of Terror in Russia*. Chicago: Globus Printing.

McKie, Robin. 2014. "Earth faces 'sixth extinction' with 41% of amphibians set to go the way of the dodo," *The Guardian*, Dec. 13.

Mieli, Mario. 1977. "Towards a Gay Communism." Available online at https://libcom .org/library/gay-communism-mario-mieli.

Miles, Malcolm. 2012. *Herbert Marcuse: An Aesthetics of Liberation*. London: Pluto Press.

Milman, Oliver. 2015. "Rate of environmental degradation puts life on Earth at risk, say scientists," *The Guardian*, Jan. 15.

Neumann, Franz. 1944. *Behemoth: The Structure and Practice of National Socialism, 1933–1944*. Oxford: Oxford University Press.

Neumann, Osha. 2013. "Who's Winning—Eros or Thanatos? *Eros and Civilization* and the Death of Nature," in *Radical Philosophy Review* vol. 16, no. 1, pp. 91–98.

Newton, Huey P. 2009. "A Letter from Huey Newton to the Revolutionary Brothers and Sisters about the Women's Liberation and Gay Liberation Movements," in *Smash the Church, Smash the State! The Early Years of Gay Liberation*, ed. Tommi Avicolli Mecca. 252–254. San Francisco: City Lights Books.

Nicolas, André. 1970. *Herbert Marcuse: ou la quête de un univers trans-prométhéen*. Paris: Editions Seghers.

Nieuwhof, Adri. 2014. "In last interview, Auschwitz survivor urged Palestinians 'not to give up their fight,'" *Electronic Intifada*, Aug. 25. Available online at http:// electronicintifada.net/blogs/adri-nieuwhof/last-interview-auschwitz-survivor -urged-palestinians-not-give-their-fight.

Occupation Committee of the People's Free Sorbonne University. 1968. "Telegrams," trans. Ken Knabb. Available online at http://www.cddc.vt.edu/sionline/si/ telegrams.html.

Palmer, R.R. 1941. *Twelve Who Ruled: The Year of the Terror in the French Revolution*. Princeton, NJ: Princeton University Press.

Pappé, Ilan. 2006. *Ethnic Cleansing of Palestine*. London: Oneworld Publications.

Parton, Glenn. 2015. "The Freudian Marcuse." Heathwood Press. Available online at http://www.heathwoodpress.com/the-freudian-marcuse-glenn-parton."

Pearl Delta Earth First! 2014. "Environmental Group Events in Contemporary China," in *Grabbing Back: Essays against the Global Land Grab*, ed. Alexander Reid Ross, pp. 101–113. Oakland: AK Press.

Popular Front for the Liberation of Palestine. 2014. "PFLP: Israelis will not be safe before Palestinians," *Ma'an News*, Nov. 12.

Porter, David. 2012. *Eyes to the South: French Anarchists and Algeria*. Oakland, California: AK Press.

Power, Nina. 2013. "Marcuse and Feminism Revisited," *Radical Philosophy Review* 16:1.

Press Association. 2013. "Life on earth 'began on Mars,'" *The Guardian*, Aug. 28.

Proxmire, William. 1962. "Spendthrifts for Defense," *The Nation*, Aug. 25.

Prüfer, Kay et al. 2012. "The bonobo genome compared with the chimpanzee and human genome," in *Nature* 486, pp. 527–531.

Quammen, David. 2013. "The Left Bank Ape: An exclusive look at bonobos," *National Geographic*. Available online at http://ngm.nationalgeographic.com/2013/03/125 -bonobos/quammen-text.

Ramnath, Maia. 2011. *Decolonizing Anarchism: An Anti-Authoritarian History of India's Liberation Struggle*. Oakland, California: AK Press.

Rapp, John A. 2012. *Daoism and Anarchism: Critiques of State Autonomy in Ancient and Modern China*. London: Continuum.

Reclus, Élisée. 1905–1908. *L'Homme et la Terre*, vol. 1. Paris: Librarie Universelle.

Redfern, Simon. 2013. "Earth life 'may have come from Mars,'" *BBC News*, Aug. 28.

Reece, Jane B. et al. 2011. *Campbell Biology Ninth Edition*. Boston: Benjamin Cummings.

Reuters. 2014. "UNICEF: 230 million children living in war-torn countries in 2014," *Al-Akhbar English*, Dec. 8.

Rickert, John. 1986. "The Fromm-Marcuse debate revisited," *Theory and Society* 15.

Robinson, Kim Stanley. 2002. *The Years of Rice and Salt*. New York: Bantam.

Rousseau, Jean-Jacques. 1996. "The Social Contract," in *Modern Political Thought: Readings from Machiavelli to Nietzsche*, ed. David Wootton. Indianapolis, IN: Hackett.

Rubel, Maximilien. 1973. "Marx, theoretician of anarchism." Available online at http://www.marxists.org/archive/rubel/1973/marx-anarchism.htm.

Said, Edward. 2000. "Diary: An Encounter with Jean-Paul Sartre." *London Review of Books*, vol. 11, no. 11.

Sagan, Carl. 1980a. "Heaven and Hell," *Cosmos: A Personal Voyage*.

———. 1980b. "The Lives of the Stars," *Cosmos: A Personal Voyage*.

———. 1980c. "Who Speaks for the Earth?" *Cosmos: A Personal Voyage*.

Sample, Ian. 2014. "Methane on Mars: does it mean the Curiosity rover has found life?" *The Guardian*, Dec. 17.

Sartre, Jean-Paul. 1943. *L'Être et le Néant*. Paris: Gallimard.

———. 1948. *Existentialism and Humanism*, trans. Philip Mairet. London: Methuen.

———. 1976. *Critique of Dialectical Reason: Theory of Practical Ensembles*, trans. Alan Sheridan-Smith, ed. Jonathan Rée. London: New Left Books.

Saul, Quincy and Javier Sethness Castro. 2015. "On Climate Satyagraha." *Counterpunch*, April 10.

Schiller, Friedrich. 1785. "Ode to Joy." *Raptus Association for Music Appreciation*. Available online at http://raptusassociation.org/ode1785.html.

———. 1882. *The Poems of Schiller*, trans. Edgar A. Bowring. London: G. Bell & Sons.

———. 1943 [1786]. *Werke: Nationalausgabe*, vol. 1, ed. Julius Petersen and Friedrich Beißner. Weimar: Böhlau.

———. 1954. *On the Aesthetic Education of Man: In a Series of Letters*, trans. Reginald Snell. London: Routledge.

Schoolman, Morton. 1980. *The Imaginary Witness: The Critical Theory of Herbert Marcuse*. New York: Free Press.

Scott, John Anthony. 1967. "Francois-Noel Babeuf and the Conspiration des Egaux," in *The Defense of Gracchus Babeuf.* Boston: University of Mass. Press.

Sedghi, Ami. 2014. "World's richest man would take 220 years to spend his wealth," *The Guardian*, Oct. 29.

Sedillo, Simon. 2013. "Self-Determination and Self-Defense in Cherán, Michoacán," *Earth First! UK*. Available online at http://earthfirst.org.uk/actionreports/content/self-determination-and-self-defense-cher%C3%A1n-michoac%C3%A1n.

Segal, Hanna. 1993. "On the Clinical Usefulness of the Concept of Death Instinct," *International Journal of Psychoanalysis* 74, pp. 55–61.

Sethness Castro, Javier. 2013. "Herbert Marcuse and Absolute Struggle in 2013." *Counterpunch*, Dec. 16.

Skirda, Alexandre. 2004. *Nestor Makhno: Anarchy's Cossack*, trans. Paul Sharkey. Oakland: AK Press.

Smith, Richard. 2014. "Climate Crisis, the Deindustrialization Imperative, and the Jobs vs. Environment Dilemma," *Truthout*, Nov. 12.

Spivak, Gayatri Chakravorty. 2011. "General Strike," in *Tidal* 1. Available online at http://tidalmag.org/issue-1-the-beginning-is-near/.

Steuernagel, Trudy. 1994. "Marcuse, the Women's Movement, and Women's Studies," in *Marcuse: From the New Left to the Next Left*, eds. John Bokina and Timothy J. Lukes. Lawrence, Kansas: University Press of Kansas.

St. Clair, Jeffrey and Joshua Frank. 2010. "Beyond Gang Green," *Counterpunch*, July 9.

Tauber, Zvi. 2012. "Herbert Marcuse on the Arab-Israeli Conflict: His Conversation with Moshe Dayan," in *Telos* 158.

———. 2013. "Herbert Marcuse on Jewish Identity, the Holocaust, and Israel," *Telos* 165.

Tawil, Raymonda Hawa. 1979. *My Home, My Prison*. New York: Holt, Rinehart and Winston.

Tolstoy, Lev. 1960 [1893]. *The Kingdom of God and Other Peace Essays*, trans. Aylmer Maude. London: Oxford Univ. Press.

Torres, Bob. 2007. *Making a Killing: The Political Economy of Animal Rights*. Oakland: AK Press.

Trainer, Ted. 2010. *The Transition to a Sustainable and Just World*. Sydney: Envirobook.

Vaughan, Adam. 2014. "Ecuador signs permits for oil drilling in Amazon's Yasuni national park," *The Guardian*, May 23.

Vergano, Dan. 2014. "Neanderthals Died Out 10,000 Years Earlier than Thought, With Help from Modern Humans." *National Geographic*, Aug. 20.

Vogel, Steven. 1996. *Against Nature: The Concept of Nature in Critical Theory*. Albany: State University of New York Press.

Wallace IV, Edwin R. 1976. "Thanatos—A Reevaluation," *Psychiatry* 39.

Walter, E.V. 1967. "Policies of Violence: From Montesquieu to the Terrorists," in *The Critical Spirit*, eds. Kurt H. Wolff and Barrington Moore. Boston: Beacon Press.

Watts, Jonathan. 2015. "Brazil's worst drought in history prompts protests and black-outs," *The Guardian*, Jan. 23.

Wiesenthal, Simon. 1976. *The Sunflower, with a Symposium*. New York: Schocken Books.

Williams, Robert. 1997. *Hegel's Ethics of Recognition*. Berkeley: University of California Press.

Winters, Joseph. 2013. "Towards an Embodied Utopia: Marcuse, The Re-Ordering of Desire, and the 'Broken' Promise of Post-Liberal Practices," *Telos* 165.

Wolin, Richard. 2001. *Heidegger's Children: Hannah Arendt, Karl Lowith, Hans Jonas, and Herbert Marcuse*. Princeton, New Jersey: Princeton University Press.

———. 2004. *The Seduction of Unreason*. Princeton: Princeton University Press.

Yang, Jisheng. 2012. *Tombstone: The Great Chinese Famine, 1958–1962*. New York: Farrar, Straus, and Giroux.

Zimmer, Carl. 1998. *At the Water's Edge: Fish with Fingers, Whales with Legs*. New York: Touchstone.

Zuidervaart, Lambert. 2011. "Theodor W. Adorno," in *The Stanford Encyclopedia of Philosophy*, ed. Edward N. Zalta. Available online at http://plato.stanford.edu/archives/win2011/entries/adorno/.

Index